W9-BPR-397

D0574018

THE LIFE OF
BENJAMIN DISRAELI
EARL OF BEACONSFIELD

THE MACMILLAN COMPANY
NEW YORK · BOSTON · CHICAGO · DALLAS
ATLANTA · SAN FRANCISCO

MACMILLAN & CO., Limited
LONDON · BOMBAY · CALCUTTA
MELBOURNE

THE MACMILLAN CO. OF CANADA, Ltd.
TORONTO

The Right Honourable B. Disraeli. 1867.
from a portrait in the possession of
Major Coningsby Disraeli.

Printed in England.

THE LIFE OF

BENJAMIN DISRAELI

EARL OF BEACONSFIELD

BY GEORGE EARLE BUCKLE
IN SUCCESSION TO W. F. MONYPENNY

VOLUME IV
1855—1868

WITH PORTRAITS AND ILLUSTRATIONS

*Read no history, nothing but
biography, for that is life without
theory.* — CONTARINI FLEMING.

New York
THE MACMILLAN COMPANY
1916

Norwood Press
J. S. Cushing Co. — Berwick & Smith Co.
Norwood, Mass., U.S.A.

LIST OF ILLUSTRATIONS TO VOL. IV

PREFACE

Since the publication of the third volume, the biography of Disraeli has sustained a heavy loss by the death of the principal Trustee of the Beaconsfield estate. The son of a personal friend, and a personal friend himself, sprung, moreover, from the same ancient race, Nathaniel Lord Rothschild, in addition to his other many-sided activities, carried on a great Disraelian tradition. Not only did he inherit a store of information about Disraeli's younger days, but he was directly conversant with some of the important transactions of the Beaconsfield Government; and so was able, of his own knowledge, to supply Mr. Monypenny and me with valuable material, and also to assist us in clearing up doubtful points in Disraeli's career. Throughout the work his time and his judgment have always been at our command; nor have his encouragement and confidence ever failed us. He has been, and will be, greatly missed; but happily there are others of his name and family to take his place, and to them, and to Sir Philip Rose, it is my pleasant duty to offer grateful acknowledgments.

Now that a time has been reached in Disraeli's life when his growing influence in the State brought him into ever nearer relation with his Sovereign, my obligations to His Majesty the King have largely increased. Halfway through this volume the period covered by *The Letters of Queen Victoria* comes to a close; and I tender my dutiful thanks to the King for graciously permitting me to publish Royal documents relating to affairs in the years between 1862 and 1868, similar to those whose publication King Edward sanctioned for the years from 1837 to 1861. The correspondence interchanged between the two chiefs

of the Conservative party is a main feature of this volume
as it was of the last; and I desire again to express my
sincere gratitude to Lord Derby for allowing me to make
free use of his grandfather's papers.   I thank, also, the
many others who have assisted me either by giving advice
or information, or by permitting the publication of letters.
I am once more indebted to Major Coningsby Disraeli for
most of the illustrations; to Mr. Murray for a critical
reading of the proof-sheets; and to my wife for the index
and much besides.

G. E. B.

CHRISTMAS, 1915.

THE LIFE OF
BENJAMIN DISRAELI
EARL OF BEACONSFIELD

CHAPTER I

WAR AND PEACE

1855–1856

Lord Derby's refusal to grasp the helm in 1855 gave Lord Palmerston his opportunity, and thereby determined for many years the course of Disraeli's career. It doomed him, now a man of fifty, to spend the maturity of his unique political talent, not, save for brief interludes, in translating his ideas directly into action as a Minister of the Crown, but in endeavouring to impress them upon a reluctant House of Commons as the leader of Her Majesty's Opposition. Except Sir William Wyndham, who gallantly but ineffectually strove to make head against Walpole, and Charles Fox, who waged an impetuous, if intermittent, war against Pitt, no politician ever had so prolonged and so continuous an experience of that post. For more than twenty years out of the five-and-twenty between 1849 and 1874 he sat facing the box on the Speaker's left hand, during long tenures of office by Russell, Palmerston, and Gladstone. The business of an Opposition is to oppose; consequently it is impossible for an Opposition leader to escape the reproach of being factious, and it is beyond human nature for him not, once and again, to deserve it. Disraeli certainly has no claim to exemption in this respect from human weakness. But that he incurred the reproach in comparative moderation, and that he deserved it but seldom, is one of his many titles to fame. His conduct is all the more striking when we remember how easily statesmen so worthy of honour as Russell and Palmerston fell, in their brief spells of

opposition, into obvious faction, both of them in 1858–59, and Russell also previously in 1852. But, though by general consent Disraeli's leadership of Opposition was in a high degree both patriotic and effective, these years of watching and waiting and criticising had their tragic aspect. His genius, abundant as it was on the critical side, was at least as much creative as critical; yet, when it was at its height, its creative side, so far as politics, his chosen sphere, was concerned, was starved, and the critical side abnormally developed. The marvel is that, when, in his declining years, he came tardily by his own, sufficient original faculty should have persisted, to enable him to leave an imperishable mark on the history of England and of the world.

Disraeli had hoped, early in 1855, to be a leading member of a Government formed vigorously to prosecute the Crimean War. Derby's timidity had deprived him of that prospect, and had left to him and to the Conservative party apparently only the humiliating function of supporting their opponents in carrying out a policy the burden of which they had shrunk from shouldering themselves. This was a function most uncongenial to Disraeli's temper; and it is no wonder that his mind soon turned towards the possibilities of an honourable peace. His first tentative movements in this direction, while Sebastopol was intact, were decidedly premature; but in the autumn after its fall he seized the propitious occasion, and began, in the teeth of a hostile public opinion, a peace propaganda which eventually culminated in the Conference and Treaty of Paris.

Palmerston had been placed in office, after the collapse of the Coalition, as a war Minister. But he inherited, as a legacy from the Aberdeen Government, an inchoate policy of peace. Before the close of the preceding year negotiations had been begun at Vienna between the Allies and Austria, and four points had been laid down to form the basis of *pourparlers* with Russia. Though the Emperor Nicholas had no intention of accepting the third and apparently most important point, the termination of

Russian preponderance in the Black Sea, he was anxious to humour Austria, and therefore agreed to be represented at a Conference to be held in Vienna in March. To safeguard British interests at the Conference, Palmerston appointed as plenipotentiary no less considerable a person than Lord John Russell, whose recent attitude in the Aberdeen Ministry had been that of a stiff opponent of Russian claims; while at the same time the Prime Minister applied all his own energies to remedy the grave deficiencies of the army in the Crimea, and to bring its numbers and equipment to a satisfactory level. He did not believe that, at the present stage of the war, Russia would agree to any terms with which the Allies could reasonably be content. But Cobden, Bright, and the peace party generally, were hopeful; and the consent of Nicholas to negotiate, the readiness of Russell to undertake a mission which a statesman of his eminence would hardly have accepted unless he thought there was a fair prospect of a favourable issue, and the unpopularity of the war among the French people, led even Disraeli to think that peace was impending. He said on February 24 that it was not a satisfactory prospect if Russell had gone to Vienna 'to be the promoter of peace with a foregone conclusion in favour of war'; but that, if the country believed that 'peace with honour' — a phrase he was to use with telling effect more than twenty years later — could be secured, the Ministry might count on the earnest support of the House. His conviction was strengthened by the sudden death, on March 2, of the Emperor Nicholas, whose overweening ambition had been so largely responsible for the war. The *Press*, at this time still under Disraeli's personal direction,[1] wrote, on the very next day, as if it anticipated a speedy arrangement;[2] and, a week later, attributed a pacific disposition to the new Emperor, Alexander, and recommended an immediate armistice in view of the opening of the Conference.[3] The first, second, and fourth of the Vienna points, which Russia was

---

[1] See Vol. III., ch. 14.   [2] *Press*, March 3.   [3] *Press*, March 10.

known to be ready to accept, involved very material concessions — the cessation of the Russian protectorate over the Principalities and over Serbia, the free navigation of the Danube, and the abandonment of the Russian claim to any rights over the Christian subjects of the Porte; and the *Press* evinced a disposition not to insist upon the apparently vital third point respecting the Black Sea.

Restrictions as to the amount of naval force to be maintained by a sovereign power are at the best but illusory guarantees, and it is difficult to believe that Europe will engage in war for the sake of obtaining a particular gradation of such an equivocal security. . . . The impending peace will be one mortifying for the Allies, but not humiliating. . . . Russia has escaped an immense retribution. She was in a vice; but the hands of the workmen were paralysed.[1]

How illusory such guarantees were was shown, it may be noted, in 1871, when Russia announced that she refused any longer to be bound by the Black Sea clauses of the Treaty of Paris.

To Lord Henry Lennox.[2]

March 27, 1855. — . . . The members of the Congress are sworn to secrecy, and the Emperor of the French confers only with Drouyn:[3] so nothing can be learnt at Vienna or Paris: but it oozes out a little from Berlin: and the general belief, among the cognoscenti, is that peace is imminent: the *Press* alone, among the journals, however, has taken this line: and some of its last Nos. have made much sensation. . . .

To Mrs. Brydges Willyams.[4]

GROSVENOR GATE, *May Day*, 1855. — But what a May Day! No maidens, no flowers, no songs, and no sun! The sky is like an Indian ink drawing, and the north-east blast withers everything. I hope you have escaped, tho', instead of being on the heights of Braddon, you ought to be on the warm

---

[1] *Press*, March 31.   [2] See Vol. III., p. 382.

[3] Drouyn de Lhuys was the French plenipotentiary at the Vienna Conference.

[4] See Vol. III., ch. 13.

borders of your bay. Everyone here is suffering, and everyone is gloomy, in body or in mind.

The imperial visit[1] was the exception. It was brilliant,
exciting, successful, and never flagged. We had the honor of
a royal invitation to some of the festivities, and, when I was
presented, Napoleon came forward, and shook hands with me
cordially, and spoke some gracious words. Our Queen was
on his right, the Empress next to her — Prince Albert on the
left of the Emperor, then Duchess of Kent, and Duchess of
Cambridge and Princess Mary — so one had to make seven
reverences !

Altho', years ago, I had seen the Emperor, and not unfre-
quently, I was very much struck by the smallness of his
stature. He did not seem taller than our Queen. I understand he enjoyed his visit very much, and greatly captivated
Her Majesty, once so much prejudiced against him. There
was immense embracing at the departure, and many tears.
When the carriage door was at length closed, and all seemed
over, the Emperor re-opened it himself, jumped out, pressed
Victoria to his heart, and kissed her, on each cheek, with
streaming eyes. What do you think of that?

I was greatly disappointed with the Empress. For me she
had not a charm. She has Chinese eyes, and a perpetual
smile or simper which I detest.[2] I understand she is very
natural — too natural for a sovereign, and that Napoleon looks
sometimes as if he would be pleased with more reserve and
dignity. She was always playing with the royal children,
who doted on her, and was sometimes found sitting on the
edge of a table ! What do you think of that? The courtiers
were horrified.

Lord John has come back. He made his appearance in the
House of C. last night. Everything looks very bad, but I do not
entirely despair of peace. I understand the siege is certainly
to be raised, but what are the new plans of campaign I know
not. Scarcely promising, I should think, or Napoleon would
not have given up his expedition to the Crimea, on which he
was quite bent. This makes me believe in peace, as nothing
but that would justify his relinquishment of his announced
project. He would otherwise be ridiculous, which he cannot
afford to be. . . .

Disraeli had been too sanguine. The Third Point had
proved an insuperable obstacle; Prince Gortchakoff, the
Russian plenipotentiary, entirely declined to give way.

---

[1] The Emperor and Empress of the French paid a state visit to England, April 16–21.

[2] For a more favorable impression of the Empress, see below, p. 56.

But, though the fact was not revealed for some months, not only Drouyn de Lhuys, but even Russell, approved a compromise suggested by Austria, under which Russia would limit her fleet in the Black Sea to its strength before the war, Austria engaging to join with the Allies in enforcing this covenant. As the Austrian proposal, instead of terminating, would perpetuate and legalise Russian preponderance in the Black Sea, it was rejected by both the British and the French Governments. Drouyn de Lhuys was recalled, and he thereupon resigned; but Russell, in spite of the repudiation of his advice, nevertheless consented to remain in Palmerston's Cabinet. Though Russell's action was not known at the time, the breakdown of the negotiations on the Third Point was palpable; and Disraeli persisted in maintaining in his newspaper the comparative unimportance of the difference. The *Press* wrote on May 19:

> To make European peace or war depend on the point of whether Russia is to maintain a few ships more or less in the Black Sea is a conception more worthy the statesmen of Laputa than of practical England. The negotiation should never have been opened on the basis adopted, or should never have been broken off on so trivial a difference.

Ministers had failed to make peace. Could they be trusted to make war with vigour and success? To the Opposition the Government appeared, after the Peelite defection,[1] to be merely the old feeble Whig combination of 1846–1852, with Palmerston and Russell transposed, and with no additional strength save Clarendon at the Foreign Office, Molesworth at the Board of Works, and Cornewall Lewis at the Exchequer. 'We have replaced a Cabinet of All the Talents by a Cabinet of All the Mediocrities,' wrote the *Press*.[2] Was this the strong Government, so superior to Derby and Disraeli and their friends, which the country needed at a critical time? Palmerston, indeed, septuagenarian as he was, was a host

---

[1] See Vol. III., pp. 568, 572.
[2] Aug. 11. By that time Russell had again left the Cabinet.

in himself, and the country, with a just instinct, put
its trust in him.   But the Opposition leaders believed
that he was quite past his work; 'totally unfit,' 'his day
had gone by,' Derby had told the Queen ;[1] 'utterly exhausted,' 'an old painted pantaloon,' Disraeli had written
to Lady Londonderry ; [2] 'you may see the breed, but the
action and power are gone,' was Disraeli's language to
Bright.[3]   The apparent vacillation between peace and
war was attributed to Palmerston's slackness in holding
the reins.   His language was somewhat ambiguous.   It
was not clear, from a speech which he made at a City
banquet on May 19, whether the Government were looking forward to 'peace with honour' or 'war with victory.'
Russell had been back from the Conference for some
weeks, but no explanations were given by Ministers ; there
had been a long delay in laying papers, and a great unwillingness to have a discussion.   The Whitsuntide recess
was approaching, and Disraeli determined to elicit something definite from the Government before the House
separated.   On May 24 he brought forward a motion
condemning their 'ambiguous language and uncertain
conduct,' and censuring them for slackness in carrying on
the war.   His position was a somewhat difficult one, as,
though he had made no announcement in his own name
to that effect, he would, we know, have been prepared,
however reluctantly, to make peace at Vienna on the
terms which Russia would concede — agreeing in this
with Russell and with the peace party ; and also, it
soon appeared, with Graham and Gladstone, who, having
as Ministers approved of the Four Points, were now, as
simple members of Parliament, ready to abandon what
was regarded as the most important point, the Third.
The two great parties and public opinion generally
would, however, have scouted such an arrangement ; and,
the Government having refused to entertain it, the
opportunity was now past.   That being so, the only pos-

[1] Vol. III., p. 560.   [2] Vol. III., p. 567.
[3] Trevelyan's *Bright*, Journal, Feb. 20, 1855.

sible course was a vigorous resumption of hostilities, as
Disraeli's journal pointed out. It was no longer any use
maintaining the 'farce of negotiation'; we must say,
'Our part is taken, our terms are known; we have confidence in the justice of our cause and the might of our
arms, and we dare the last dread issue . . . the appeal to
battle.' [1]

In his speech Disraeli called attention to Russell's dis-
qualifications as Special Envoy to a Peace Conference.
Russell had been one of the most bellicose of Ministers,
and his last exploit before going to make peace for his
country was to destroy a Cabinet because the Prime
Minister was not earnest enough in prosecuting the war.
'This was the dove sent out to the troubled waters of
Europe.' Was there to be peace, or was there to be
war? Had the Conference concluded, or was it still
sitting? Nobody knew, and Ministers differed in their
statements. Disraeli added that it was a mistake to
depart from the policy of protecting Turkey and adopt
that of invading Russia; but that was over and done.
An end should be put to the vicious double system, by
which they had so long carried on an aggressive war and
a protective diplomacy. The issue before the House
was a simple one: 'Will you put an end to this diplomatic
subterfuge and this Ministerial trifling?' The tone of
the debate was very hostile to the advocates of immediate peace, and Palmerston showed himself responsive.
He said that Russia had refused the fair conditions offered
her, and, since England was fully prepared, the war must
be carried on; the nation was in earnest and would support the Government. Disraeli exulted over what he
called Palmerston's change of front, as a justification of
the motion. His object had been to prevent war and
negotiations from proceeding simultaneously, and now
Palmerston had come out as a war Minister.

Neither those who were for war nor those who were for
peace desired to turn Ministers out for the benefit of a

[1] *Press*, May 26.

party which had acknowledged itself incompetent for office four months before; and therefore Disraeli's motion was lost by a large majority. After Whitsuntide the general debate was resumed, and eventually the Government received without a division [1] an assurance of the support of the House in the prosecution of the war. On the last night Disraeli, in an elaborate oration, impressed on Ministers the necessity of having a definite idea of the object for which they were struggling, and of the means by which they could accomplish it. A passage as to the responsibility of a majority in the House of Commons in matters of foreign policy is as applicable to-day as when it was spoken. In domestic policy the mistakes of a Parliamentary majority might be set right by another Parliamentary majority afterwards. But, in foreign affairs,

Every step that you take is an irretrievable one, and the consequences of your conduct are immediate and palpable. A false step in such a case cannot be retraced; you cannot, as you do on domestic questions, rescind your policy, calculate the loss you have sustained by the unwise system you have pursued, and console yourselves by thinking that for the future you will shun a policy proved to be injurious. If you make a mistake in your foreign affairs; if you enter into unwise treaties; if you conduct campaigns upon vicious principles; if the scope and tendency of your foreign system are founded upon want of information or false information, or are framed with no clear idea of what are your objects and your means of obtaining them, there is no majority in the House of Commons which can long uphold a Government under such circumstances. A majority under such circumstances will not make a Government strong, but will make this House weak.

The object of the Conservative party, said Disraeli, was to check the preponderance of Russia as against Turkey, and preserve Constantinople to the Porte. He

[1] June 8. Disraeli had expected a division, and wrote that morning to Lennox: ' We divide to-night. I think we shall cut down the majority half; and if our fellows were only steady, I have little doubt that before July was past a further parallel might be advanced into the enemy's camp: but I am vexed, every moment, with sad stories of crotchety idiots.'

did not himself attach special value to the Third Point ;
he thought the object might be secured by neutralising
the Principalities, and fortifying the Bosporus and the
eastern frontier of Turkey.

Russell, in these debates, had used very bellicose language, had treated the Russian proposals as futile, and,
in particular, had insisted that a limitation of Russian
naval power in the Black Sea was indispensable to the
security of Constantinople. This naturally provoked
Count Buol, the author of the Austrian compromise ; and
he published official papers which revealed to the world
Russell's readiness at Vienna to accept what he now
repudiated. Public indignation was deservedly roused
in England at such extraordinary inconsistency. Russell
defended himself lamely [1] by distinguishing between his
position as plenipotentiary and his position as Cabinet
Minister. As plenipotentiary he gave his advice ; as
Cabinet Minister he accepted the decision of his colleagues
overruling it. Disraeli took full advantage of so legitimate an opportunity for Opposition criticism. Russell,
he said, had in his own mind secured satisfactory terms
of peace, and then, when his colleagues in the Cabinet
refused to accept them, quietly pocketed his own opinions,
and remained 'in a Cabinet of war a Minister of peace.'
'Lax as have been the rules and regulations in recent
Cabinets with regard to open questions, I certainly cannot
conceal my surprise at learning to-night from high authority
that peace and war are open questions in the existing
Administration.' How could the Government prosecute
the war vigorously without losing Russell as a colleague ?
'Is this the end — that even peace and war have become
mere party considerations, that the interests of the country are sacrificed to the menace of a majority, and that
the turbulent assemblies of Downing Street are to baffle
all the sagacity of all the conferences of Vienna?' The
debate was especially gratifying to Disraeli by reason of
a candid confession made by Cobden. 'I look back,' he

[1] July 6.

said, 'with regret on the vote which I gave on the motion which changed Lord Derby's Government. I regret the result of that motion; for it has cost the country 100 millions of treasure, and between 20,000 and 30,000 good lives.'

The Opposition leaders determined to push their advantage. Bulwer Lytton, on their behalf, gave notice of a vote of censure on Russell's conduct; and they looked forward — Disraeli eagerly, Derby with reluctant acquiescence — to a vote of the House of Commons which should displace the Government.

To Lord Derby.

Confidential. HOUSE OF COMMONS, *Wednesday,* 6 o'clock [*July* 11, 1855].—Affairs very critical — the Cabinet sitting. Palmerston having put off supply for Friday, in order to prevent Bulwer coming on, I have given notice of a motion for to-morrow, which will secure Bulwer for Friday, if carried, and I think it will be.

Eighteen Irish members went up to Palmerston this morning and announced that, unless he proposed the restoration of the Retrospective clause to the Irish Tenant Bill, and agreed to support it with all the influence of Government, they should vote for Bulwer. Palmerston agreed to their demands immediately.

I have Seymour [1] in hand — who is bitter against the Government. He said to me to-day : 'Nothing can save them.' . . .

From Lord Derby.

KNOWSLEY, *Wednesday* [? *Thursday*].—. . . Matters seem critical indeed, and I am living almost in dread of a telegraphic message. I think the present state of things cannot go on. Palmerston may be able to save himself for a time by throwing Johnny overboard, but it will be only for a time. I expect to hear of his (Johnny's) retirement, which would put an end to Bulwer's motion; but the shifts of putting off Supply from day to day, merely to evade it, shows the extremity to which they are driven. . . .

[1] Lord Seymour, Whig M.P. for Totnes, but a personal friend of Disraeli. On January 6 of this year Disraeli had written to Malmesbury : 'I fear that Seymour will be going to the House of Lords, which I regret, as I always looked to the possibility of his taking a leading part in the reconstruction of parties.' Seymour succeeded as 12th Duke of Somerset in November, and was First Lord of the Admiralty in Palmerston's and Russell's Administrations, 1859–1866.

One thing only could save the Government — Russell's resignation; and that was forced upon him by pressure from his party, and by representations even, as Palmerston told the Queen, of 'those members of the Government who are not in the Cabinet.'[1] The announcement was made on July 16,[2] and Lytton's motion was withdrawn, but not until after a debate which gave Disraeli an opportunity for further sarcastic comment. Russell had spoken somewhat bitterly of his desertion by some of his friends; Bouverie, the Vice-President of the Board of Trade, had explained to a mocking House with what reluctance those friends had acted; and Palmerston had expressed his readiness to retain Russell and vindicate his proceedings, while at the same time protesting that there was no division of opinion in the Cabinet on the war. Disraeli dilated on the tempting theme of friends and friendships. Friendship was the gift of the gods, and the most precious boon to man. It had long occupied the thoughts and consideration of essayists and philosophers, who had analysed its various degrees. There was, for instance, 'the devoted friend who stands or falls by one,' like Palmerston, though, to be sure, Palmerston was neither standing nor falling, but sitting on the Treasury bench. But there was also another kind of friend, immortalised by an epithet unfit for ears polite. For a 'damned good-natured friend,' ready to tell one anything disagreeable — 'candid and not bad-natured friend' were the terms he actually used — commend him to Bouverie. Palmerston had accused Lytton of being either deliberately insincere or grossly ignorant, and talked of 'much ado about nothing.' Serious criticism, retorted Disraeli, should not be met by 'this patrician bullying of the Treasury bench.' It was not fitting that Palmerston should attempt to stop discussion by language not to be expected 'from one who is not only the leader of the House of Commons, which

---

[1] *Queen Victoria's Letters*, July 12, 1855.
[2] Russell was succeeded at the Colonial Office by Molesworth.

is an accident of life, but who is also a gentleman.'
Rather than meet debate, the foremost of their statesmen had mysteriously disappeared. Palmerston, who
did meet debate, had shown that night, ' by his language
and by the tone of his mind, that if the honour and interests of the country be any longer entrusted to his
care, the first will be degraded, and the last, I believe,
will be betrayed.'

Twice again during the session did Disraeli advance to
the attack on the question of the war, and in each case
the Government had some difficulty in avoiding defeat.
Roebuck moved, as the logical sequel of the damnatory
report of his Committee on the conduct of the war,[1] a
vote of censure on the Aberdeen Cabinet.   The Palmerston
Government, several of whose members were implicated,
feared that the House would not support them in meeting the motion with a direct negative, and so took shelter
under the Previous Question — a Parliamentary device
for avoiding the expression of an opinion either way.
An amendment of this kind was obligingly moved and
seconded by two of their opponents, Peel's brother,
General Jonathan Peel, and Lord Robert Cecil, who
probably represented public opinion in deprecating any
motion that might look like vindictive personality, or
might tend to weaken the Executive in time of war.
This evasive amendment was carried by a considerable
majority.[2]   Disraeli, however, contended that, though
from a party point of view the Conservatives might well
be content with the admission involved in the Government's acceptance of the Previous Question on a vote of
censure, the country had a right to call upon the House
to express an opinion one way or another on the Report
of the Committee.   This was no party motion ; Roebuck
had voted against the Conservative vote of censure in
May.   There was force in Disraeli's final sentence :

After two nights' discussion in this House, after the laborious
efforts for months of the Committee upon a most important

subject, with some of our most eminent statesmen appealing to the House for justness and frankness in our conduct, and with the whole country looking with interest to our decision to-night, we are coming to a vote which can confer honour and credit upon no body of men, and no individual member of this assembly.

The other attack was made on the following day, when the Government only succeeded in carrying by a majority of three a resolution for a joint guarantee with France of a Turkish loan of £5,000,000. Ministers did not come for authority to the House of Commons till the Convention with Turkey had been signed, and the French Chambers had signified their approval. Disraeli joined Gladstone and Cobden in resisting a policy which should have been submitted, he maintained, to Parliament at an earlier stage, and which should not have been entered upon at all without absolute necessity. The appointment of Anglo-French Commissioners to see to the appropriation of the loan was an arrangement pregnant with political difficulties and danger. We should give Turkey much more assistance if, instead of sending English capital to Turkey, we employed it ourselves in the vigorous prosecution of the war. The arguments against the guarantee were very strong, and the Government only just saved themselves by pleading that the honour of the country was at stake. It certainly appears to have been somewhat factious and unpatriotic of Disraeli to carry opposition to the loan to a division; and some of his friends, particularly Malmesbury, were shocked. Disraeli's own explanation of his vote to Count Vitzthum, the Minister of Saxony in London, was that he knew perfectly well what he was doing. It was of importance to him 'to give a hint to those in Paris, and let them know that Palmerston was standing on weaker legs than they supposed, and that the war party had lost ground in Parliament.'[1]

The violence of the Opposition during this summer, of

[1] Vitzthum's *St. Petersburg and London*, Vol. I., p. 190.

which this vote was a striking instance, was partly due
to resentment at Palmerston's refusal to join Derby
when Derby tried to form a Government early in the
year—a refusal dictated, they thought, rather by self-
interest than by public spirit.   When even so cold-blooded
a politician as Stanley could write that ' *vendetta* must be
our consolation,' [1] the feelings of warmer and more impetuous natures may be conjectured.   The events of
the session, at any rate, effectually cured Disraeli of
his illusions about Palmerston's being in his dotage.
With little help from any colleague, and supported, as
Disraeli scornfully said, by 'majorities collected God
knows how, voting God knows why,' that virile septuagenarian had successfully repelled a series of furious
attacks by the Opposition, and had shown himself,
as the *Press* confessed, 'a Triton among the minnows.'
He had laid himself open, however, to criticism of a
different kind by his levity on the most serious occasions.
' To be angry with such a farcical person would be absurd,'
wrote the *Press*.   It called him 'a sort of Parliamentary
grandpapa,' 'a great Parliamentary quiz.'   It talked of
'the jolly tone in which our Prime Minister laughs at the
public and both Houses of Parliament, and even himself';
and of 'the rollicking air with which he performs his
cajolery.'   He was a 'comic Premier,' with a 'wallet of
small pleasantries of an excruciating kind.'   Conservatives, it said, found it hard to take part against 'a gay
old Tory of the older school, disguising himself as a
Liberal, and hoaxing the Reform Club.' [2]

'A gay old Tory, disguising himself as a Liberal'—
there was the rub.   Disraeli had failed, in spite of all
his efforts and all his readiness to yield the first place,
to bring about that permanent junction between Derby
and Palmerston which the general similarity of their
opinions rendered natural; and he now had to face the
dreary prospect of an uphill fight in opposition against
a nominally Liberal Prime Minister whom many of the

[1] See Vol. III., p. 563.   [2] *Press*, Aug. 18.

Tory rank and file considered a better Conservative than himself, and who, far from showing signs of failing powers, appeared to grow younger every day. The situation frequently led Disraeli into common action with the Radicals, at which some of his colleagues looked askance.

From Lord Malmesbury.

HERON COURT, *July 22, 1855.* — . . . You have done two great deeds this year; for to you we owe the suffocation of the Peelites and the abasement of Johnny. Speaking to you openly, as I always shall, I think our error has been giving the lead in great questions to Radical personages. . . . If you permit or encourage Gibson, Roebuck, *et id genus*, to take a lead to which they are not entitled, we lose importance in the country and power in the House. This I am sure is the principal cause of the apparent want of unity in our ranks. . . .

An interesting specimen of Disraeli's table talk at this time — the end of July — is given us by Count Vitzthum, who sat next him at ' a luncheon party of friends of peace,' including Bright.

I have always thought Gladstone, Bright, and myself, the three most energetic men in the House. I have watched Gladstone very carefully, and am convinced that his strength of will is inflexible. Bright is sometimes blunt, but his eloquence is most powerful. He has not the subtleness of Cobden, but he has far more energy, and his talents are more practically applied. The session is at an end. Old Palmerston has taken the hint we gave him recently, and shook my hand yesterday so warmly that I am disarmed until November. When that time comes, the position will have become clearer, and public opinion shaped itself; and we shall then see what is to be done. Thus much I can say, that our Ministry is prepared : a strong Government, which will astonish the world. The men who are now at the helm cannot wield it any longer. It will not be necessary to upset them; they will fall by themselves. With the exception of old Palmerston, who for a man of seventy still displays astonishing energy, the present Cabinet has neither an orator nor a debater. But the old man is a desperado, who clings convulsively to power, because he feels that he would have no prospect of ever coming in again if he were now ousted.[1]

[1] Vitzthum, Vol. I., ch. 6.

Meanwhile the war in the Crimea, where the Allied forces had been augmented by an Italian contingent, was drawing towards its culmination.

To Lord Henry Lennox.

ROYAL HOTEL, TORQUAY, *Aug.* 21, 1855. — . . . I fear the news is not so good as it seems on the surface. With the exception of the move on the Tchernaya, which is still obscure, the affairs seem to have been got up for the royal visit;[1] at least, have that appearance. I doubt whether Sweaborg is more than another Odessa, and the revival of the bombardment of Sebastopol seems to contradict the prevalent idea, that the enemy was about to vacate the south side. The Allies would never incur the expense, to say nothing of any other consideration, of a bombardment, if there were a chance of the foe retiring. Every shell costs £2, and 25,000 may easily be fired in a short morning. No destruction of stores at Sweaborgs and Odessas can ever pay for the *cost* of destruction.

However, God is great — and much may happen in the next three months. I should think the French visit will end in renewed negotiations.

I trust an ignominious peace is not impending over our country!

To Mrs. Brydges Willyams.

HUGHENDEN, *Sept.* 2, 1855. — . . . There is a great pause in public events, and I see little prospect of anything happening. Lady Londonderry is in despair about her son, Lord Adolphus Vane, who is now in the trenches. The trenches are so near the enemy, that we lose forty *per diem* by casualties! *Casualties*, she says, and truly, what a horrible word to describe the loss of limb and life! Thank God, we are neither of us there, and that the only heights we have to scale are Mount Braddon and the Chiltern Hills.

Sebastopol fell on September 8, and the immediate objective of the Allied Expedition to the Crimea was thus at last attained. But Russia showed no disposition to conclude a peace; and public opinion in England supported Palmerston in a policy of energetic offensive till the enemy should be brought to his knees. Disraeli,

[1] The Queen and the Prince Consort, with the Prince of Wales and the Princess Royal, paid a visit to the Emperor and Empress of the French at Paris, Aug. 18–27.

however, saw that Great Britain had now secured all that
could be obtained without a struggle of indefinite duration and uncertain issue, and before the close of the
month he initiated in the *Press* a vigorous movement for
an early peace. To Vitzthum he described his policy
of this autumn as one of 'scaring the Ministers into
a more pacific line of conduct, by holding up the bugbear of an understanding with Gladstone and Bright.'
The articles seem to have been written by Coulton, the
editor, with perhaps occasional assistance from Stanley,
but unquestionably under Disraeli's direction and inspiration, though to people outside, such as Greville, he disclaimed responsibility.[1]

The present moment is critical. The aspect of the war is
changing. It is passing into a new phase, and the country
needs the guidance of its natural leaders. . . .
We can now say that every object for which the war was
originally undertaken has been conceded by negotiation or
won by arms. Russia no longer claims those exclusive privileges which placed her in perpetual antagonism with the
Turkish Government. She has resigned her claim to the
guardianship of the Greek subjects of the Porte, and to the
protectorate of the Principalities. She is willing to admit
Turkey into the European system — a point in itself of vital
importance — and to guarantee, in accord with the other con-
tracting Powers, the independence of its Government and the
integrity of its territory. She is also disposed to place the
free navigation of the Danube under the superintendence of
collective Europe. One obstacle only remained — the supremacy of Russia in the Black Sea. That supremacy is now
destroyed. The last Russian ship has been sunk or burnt, and
Sebastopol is in ruins. . . .
England and France have no longer an object in maintaining the war. They entered on it reluctantly, and for a specific
purpose — the defense of the Turkish Empire. That purpose
has been attained. Circumstances may render it absolutely
necessary for them to continue the contest; they cannot force
Russia to make peace, but their policy must be, if they
remain true to their original cause and professions, to prosecute war only till satisfactory terms of peace can be obtained.
The reduction of the Russian Empire was assuredly never
contemplated when their alliance was formed. . . .

[1] See Greville's *Journal* under date Nov. 12, 1856.

The statesmen of this country have never been favourable
to wars of extremity or wars of aggrandisement. Our policy
from the first was not to overthrow, but to maintain, the
balance of European power.[1]

The theme was pursued week after week; but there
was no attempt to disguise the hostility of public opinion,
within as well as without the Conservative party. Bright,
writing to Cobden on October 5, said of the *Press:* 'I
wish it represented the large party who sit opposite to us
in the House, or the Tory party in the constituencies.'
Not that Disraeli lacked influential support from the
outset of the movement; but the support came from
isolated individuals, and the rank and file clamoured for
war, along with many of the leaders. Lennox was
staying at Knowsley in October for Crimean festivities in Liverpool, and reported on the 15th: 'Derby's
speech of last night was the old roar of the British
Lion! . . . Young Morose [2] is for peace in the Crimea,
but certainly there is nothing in his manners to promote
it in his Lares. He is more morose than ever.' He had
seen Walpole: 'He is ultra-Peace.' One of the most
promising of the younger Conservatives, Sir Stafford
Northcote, who had been returned for Dudley at a by-
election in March, made a speech in this sense in the late
autumn. On the other hand, Bulwer Lytton sent to
Disraeli earnest and affectionate remonstrances against
peace propaganda 'in the present state of the struggle,
and the determined temper of the public.' 'Pause, pause,
pause, I entreat you again, my dearest fellow,' he wrote
on October 15, 'before you lend your name to any of
those argosies gone astray in the Pacific.' And in
November: 'The proper position for us to take seems
to me, not that of Fox in the French war, but that of Pitt
versus Addington. Treat Palmerston as Pitt treated
Addington — outwar him.'

On October 31 Lennox reported to Disraeli that there
was great indignation at the Carlton over the articles

[1] *Press*, Sept. 29.   [2] Lord Stanley.

in the *Press*. He added: 'Have you ordered the first
number of the new weekly journal, the Saturday's
Political Review?[1] Of course you know it is in the
hands of Layard and Public Morality Harcourt.'[2]

To Lord Henry Lennox.

HUGHENDEN, *Nov.* 1, 1855. — I am always delighted to hear
from you, and admire your courage in even alluding to politics.
'There is another and a better world!' for which it becomes
the numerous members of the Conservative party to prepare.
The Conservative party is entombed in the same sepulchre as
that Protectionist party at which it used to sneer.

It will not even conserve the map of Europe!

I had not heard of the Saturday Journal, or anything
else. . . .

There is not a more independent paper in existence than
the *Press*. . . .

Derby was as much disturbed as Lytton or the old
Tories of the Carlton, but he did not in the first place
remonstrate with Disraeli directly. He confided his dissatisfaction to Jolliffe, the Whip, who was to spend a
week-end at Hughenden.

Sir William Jolliffe to Lord Derby.

MERSTHAM, *Oct.* 23, 1855. — . . . Disraeli was in high health,
but, I think, I found him very dejected over the prospect of
our party, and left him less so; but I, at any rate, find it
difficult to contend against his arguments, that it is impossible for a party to exist without a policy, and still less possible for an Opposition to be of the same policy as the Government to which it is opposed.

At his request I read to him your letter, and, as far as I was
able to commit them to memory, he used words to this effect:
'That a party that had shrunk from the conduct of a war,
particularly under the circumstances which we did, were
bound to prepare the public mind for a statesmanlike peace;
that a war Opposition and a war Ministry could not coexist;
that stimulating the war, after we had shrunk from the responsibility of conducting it, degraded us to the level of the
mob who will huzza Lord P. through the City on the Lord
Mayor's day. Nothing can save the party but representing

---

[1] The *Saturday Review*.
[2] Afterwards Sir William Harcourt and Chancellor of the Exchequer.

a policy.' Such was the burden of his song, and though uttered in strict confidence, finding he did not propose to write to you himself, I told him I should reply to your letter, and endeavour to convey to you the substance of what he had said; and you will perceive that to a great extent he approves the writing of the *Press*, but he tells me it is not his own, that it has proved very beneficial to the paper. . . .

From Lord Derby.

KNOWSLEY, *Oct.* 25, 1855. — . . . I am not prepared to deny that our position as a party is one of extreme difficulty, and that it requires no little patience on all sides to keep any party together without some definite object to aim at; but I cannot admit that we shrunk from *conducting the war*. On the contrary, the existence of the war, and its general popularity with the country, would have given us our best chance of carrying on the Government. Whether we ought to have undertaken it, it is now too late to inquire; but having been, in common with the country at large, parties to entering into it, and having blamed previous Governments for want of vigour in carrying it on, we cannot with honour, or even with regard to party interests, constitute ourselves a peace Opposition, merely because we have a war Ministry, and I will never consent to weaken an Administration to which I am opposed, by increasing their difficulties in carrying the country through what has become an inevitable war. . . .

I am not insensible to the danger of a further extension of the range of war . . . but I always recur to the one overpowering consideration that, in the present temper of Russia, the greater the anxiety we show for peace, the less our chance of obtaining it. I am not desirous of saying or doing anything to 'stimulate' or embitter the war, but I hope that neither you nor any of our friends would desire that for party purposes we should seek to discourage the country, and increase the difficulties of those who are charged with bringing the war to a satisfactory conclusion. I wish I could think we were approaching such a conclusion, but I own I do not; and I must own further that, until we do, I think our position as a party — that is, our chance of office — is materially worsened. With me, indeed, the latter consideration does not weigh perhaps as much as it ought to do; but I hope I am led by higher motives in determining not at this moment to make a peace cry the means of attacking the Government, still less of making it the basis of any new political combination. If the Conservative party cannot be kept together on any other grounds, it is time that it should fall to pieces, or at least that

I should retire from the scene. I write to you most unreservedly, as I should be sorry that there should be any difference of opinion between us on a point of such vital interest; and I should be more distrustful than I now am of my own judgment, if I found it were opposed to yours. . . .

To Lord Derby.

HATCH BEAUCHAMP, TAUNTON, *Nov.* 7, 1855.—I learn from Jolliffe, this morning, that you expected to have heard from me. I should be sorry if you supposed for a moment that I ever neglected your wishes or your interests.

I understood your letter as an answer to the remarks on my part, reported by Jolliffe, and therefore anything further from me would not, according to my feeling, have been a reply, but a rejoinder, and I did not think that a controversy between us was desirable or could be agreeable.

I must candidly say that your letter has not convinced me that my reported remarks were unfounded. Granted that we are not a party who have shrunk from the responsibility of conducting the war : the world, unfortunately, thinks so, and it comes to the same thing. My own opinion is that, in the dilemma in which we find ourselves, silence and inertness are our wisest course, and for this reason I have refrained from saying, doing, or writing, anything which should bring my views, or even name, before the country.

I do not know what is taking place, tho' I have spared no means or exertions to obtain the knowledge. Had anything authentic reached me, I should have communicated it to you. Perhaps next week may somewhat unveil the mystery.

What Disraeli particularly dreaded was the opening of a fresh campaign which should commit the country to conquering the Crimea, and driving Russia back from the shores of the Black Sea. If any such attempt were made, a prolonged and obstinate struggle was inevitable. If peace were not practicable after the fall of Sebastopol, it would not be practicable, he thought, for years. He made, however, little progress in converting his chief and his party, and still less in 'scaring' Palmerston or impressing English public opinion. Fortunately for him, the logic of events had more effect in France than in England, and it was found in November that Napoleon III, was of entirely the same opinion as Disraeli. The

Emperor took the opportunity of the close of the Paris Exposition to express in public his desire for a prompt and durable peace; and he was already engaged in negotiations at Vienna with that object.

To Mrs. Brydges Willyams.

HUGHENDEN, *Nov.* 18, 1855. — . . . There has been a great stupor over affairs since we parted, or since I last wrote, but there are now indications of events. The Emperor of the French is wearied with the war, and is pressing our Government to accede to terms of peace which he considers satisfactory. Lord Palmerston will not listen to these overtures, and the consequences may be critical. If Lord Palmerston succeed, the war may last as long as the Peloponnesian, or the Thirty Years of Germany. The war expenditure of France is one million and a half sterling per week — that of England, one million and a quarter! This is a large sum for distant objects and somewhat equivocal success.

As you read the *Press* newspaper, I would recommend to your notice a very curious paper in the No. of yesterday, signed 'E. S.,' on war interests and passions. It is written by Lord Stanley, who, tho' not thirty, has recently refused the office of Secretary of State, as you know.[1]

On Friday we dined with Lady Londonderry, at Holdernesse House, which is quite dismantled, to meet her son, Lord Adolphus, who is on leave for a month from the Crimea. Her boudoir was the saloon, and an antechamber the *salle à manger*, but she contrived to collect and feed ten agreeable persons.

I am very well, and hope you are. The future is dark and anxious, but difficulty and care are what I thrive on. . . .

The Emperor's peaceful disposition was ascertained by Malmesbury at first hand in Paris, and reported by him to Derby and Disraeli. Malmesbury was anxious to exploit the situation in the interests of the Conservative party. To Derby he wrote on November 25: 'It is quite on the cards that Palmerston will be forced by France into a peace before February. If he is, and we

---

[1] On Sir William Molesworth's death, towards the end of October, Palmerston offered the Secretaryship of State for the Colonies to Stanley, who declined the offer. The article referred to, which evinces the abhorrence of war that distinguished Stanley throughout his career, sufficiently accounts for his reluctance to join Palmerston at such a time.

choose to condemn it, *we* can do so consistently and with
popularity; but then Disraeli must not prate peace before-
hand.   He will perhaps save Palmerston, as it is, by the
opinions already put forth in his cursed *Press*.'   To
Disraeli his language was naturally more moderate, but
to the same effect; he suggested specifically that Disraeli
and Stanley and their friends who were in favour of
ending the war at once should not open their lips till
the session.   Disraeli had no intention of speaking on
the subject; but he made use of the *Press* to explain his
position to the party, so that there should be no misunderstanding whatever about his opinions and intentions.[1] Taking advantage of an attack on Disraeli in a
French journal, the *Press* of December 1 wrote: 'Mr.
Disraeli is not an unqualified partisan, or a partisan at all,
of the Peace-at-any-price party.   He is as much opposed
to that party as to the War-at-any-price party — alike to
the dreams of Mr. Bright, and to the ensanguined prác-
tices of the Kossuths and Mazzinis.'

This country will recognise that throughout he [Disraeli]
principally of our public men has best understood the question at issue; and that in first counselling war, and then
recommending peace, on condition that the object of the
war should be accomplished, he has alike shown the energy
of a patriot and the sagacity of a statesman.

Urged by the French Emperor and by Austria, Palmerston and the British Government, sorely against their
will, agreed to an ultimatum which was despatched by
Austria to Russia on December 15.   It demanded the
acceptance, within five weeks, by Russia of the famous
Four Points, the third, which had before proved the
stumbling-block, now taking the form of the neutralisation
of the Black Sea; and, in addition, the cession to Moldavia
of a portion of Bessarabia.   Though Palmerston thought

---

[1] Disraeli told Malmesbury: 'We are off the rail of politics, and must
continue so as long as the war lasts' — a condition of things due to 'the
fatal refusal to take the reins last February, which lost us the heart and
respect of all classes.'

the terms much too favourable to Russia, yet he was apparently convinced that she would reject them; and both he and the British public hoped that the negotiations would break down. Disraeli's point of view was powerfully expounded in every issue of the *Press*.

The difference between the policy which the *Press* has advocated, and that proclaimed by some speakers and writers professing to represent Conservative sentiments, amounts to this—that we believe a solid and satisfactory peace may now be effected by treaty with Russia, while they believe it can only be effected by the annihilation of her power. Reason as we may, the difference returns to this. They have no faith in those principles of policy and those mutual guarantees and engagements upon which the division of European power and the integrity of the boundary lines of States depend. A treaty is with them but a bit of paper, a seal but a morsel of wax.[1] We believe, on the contrary, that it is those principles and guarantees which preserve the peace of the world; that without them there would be perpetual war; that the progress of civilisation is towards a more solemn recognition and sacred maintenance of treaties; and that as they extend wider and take in outlying nations (as, unhappily, Turkey has been until this day), and as they are joined in by a greater number of States, there is less probability that they will be invaded, and stronger assurance that the State which attempts to violate them will be promptly restrained in its aggressive course.[2]

At the beginning of the New Year the prospects of peace appeared to be gloomy. Russia's first answer was to accept the Four Points, but reject the cession of any part of Bessarabia, and the Allies replied by holding a Council of War in Paris. The *Press* still stood alone among the Metropolitan newspapers in its pacific line; the organs of the Government openly exulted in the belief that the proposals which Ministers had put forward would not be accepted. But at the last moment the Emperor Alexander yielded, and Lennox was able to write confidentially to Disraeli from Paris on January 16: 'Russia has within the last forty-eight hours intimated to the Allies her readiness to accept the whole ultimatum

[1] An anticipation of Bethmann-Hollweg's 'scrap of paper.'
[2] *Press*, Dec. 22.

without reserve, provided the Allies treat directly with her and not through the medium of Austria.' The *Press* of January 19 announced triumphantly that peace was resolved on.

Lord Aberdeen's Peace Government, against its will, drifted into war, and Lord Palmerston's War Government, equally against its will, has drifted into peace. . . . We forced Lord Aberdeen to engage in a war necessary to the honour of England and to the security of Europe; we have forced Lord Palmerston to agree to peace now that the objects of the war are accomplished.

To Lord Henry Lennox.

GROSVENOR GATE [*Jan.*, 1856] — The country is sulky: just come from the City, where I have seen all the great people. Even those favorable to the peace announce the above.

You have shown great energy and talent. It must have been an exciting scene.

The last Cabinet Council was on the Seebach [1] propositions: they were favored by France, and the majority of our Ministers supported them: Pam and Clar[endon] forced their rejection, and wished and believed that 'another campaign' would be the inevitable consequence. 'Another campaign' was Pam's *policy*. You may conceive his surprise! He told my informant, after the Cabinet, or at least somebody did as good, that 'another campaign' was now *inevitable*.

All this you may rely on.

I am too exhausted to write more, but would send one line to thank you. I am glad you have made Lytton's [2] acquaintance: study him, and tell me what you think of him. I saw little of him, but am in his favor from what I saw.

Palmerston and the war party were very restive; but now that Russia had, to their chagrin, accepted, the determination of the French Emperor to end the war left them no choice. Accordingly, when Parliament met,[3] 'the Government renounced all the designs which have been attributed to it in its own organs, and by its most eager supporters.' [4] With the Opposition, too, Disraeli's

---

[1] Count Seebach, Minister of Saxony in Paris, brother-in-law of the Russian Chancellor, Count Nesselrode, exerted himself behind the scenes to bring Russia and the Allies together.

[2] The 1st Earl of Lytton, afterwards Viceroy of India.

[3] Jan. 31.   [4] *Press*, Feb. 2.

policy prevailed; and the temptation to adopt Malmesbury's and Bulwer Lytton's advice, coalesce with Roebuck, Layard, and the war party, and 'outwar' Palmerston, was resisted, though in the existing temper of public
opinion the overthrow of the Government might possibly
have been thereby achieved.   Disraeli's speech was a
model of good feeling.   He welcomed the prospect, which
the Queen's Speech held out, of 'a safe and honourable
peace.'   He deprecated the continuance of the war for
the sake of adding lustre to our arms.   The abstract
principle that we should continue a war, after attaining
its objects, to gratify the vanity or support the reputation
of a community was exceedingly questionable.   But in
any case it did not apply, as the lustre of our arms had
not been dimmed.   It was monstrous to say that nations
should never engage in war unless they were certain to
achieve great victories that would figure among the
decisive battles of the world.   That would degrade us
from being the vindicators of public law into the gladia-
tors of history.   He ended with the patriotic assurance
that, if, unfortunately, the peace negotiations should fail,
which he did not anticipate, Her Majesty might appeal with
confidence to her Parliament to support her in a renewed
struggle.   Disraeli gave an amusing and instructive
account of this debate and of his own policy to Vitzthum :

The war party is dead. Roebuck has made a fiasco with
his declamations, and Layard, who came to the debate on the
Address with a whole library under his arm, never ventured
to deliver his carefully prepared speech.   All this because I
did not neglect to take in hand the conduct of the debate
from the outset, to calm down passions, and to deprive
Palmerston of any excuse for coming forward with a warlike rodomontade about the honour of England, and so forth.
The Premier had nothing left but to thank me for my moderation, and to declare as mildly as a lamb his entire concurrence
in my views.   Thus I forced him to separate himself at the
very commencement of the sitting from his own most bellicose
followers, and induced the Liberal party to believe that the
Ministry had gone over bodily to our camp.[1]

[1] Vitzthum, Vol. I., pp. 190, 191.

The Peace Conference met very shortly afterwards in Paris, and did not separate till the Treaty had been signed.

To Mrs. Brydges Willyams.

HUGHENDEN MANOR, *Easter Monday* [*March* 24], 1856. — I wrote my last letter to you from this place on the eve of my departure to London, and I write you the first on my return.

Two months we have had, and more, of great interest and excitement, tho' apparently calm and tranquil — with the question of peace or war always in the balance, and the first at length secured in the teeth of an unwilling Ministry.

What would have happened in France if peace had not been secured I tremble to think; a financial convulsion, worse than that of Chevalier Law, occurring with a pestilence in the French army in the Crimea, must have brought about political convulsions of which a general European struggle would probably have been the ultimate consequence. Even for the signal blessing of retaining the services of Lord Palmerston, it was scarcely worth this sacrifice.

The Emperor of the French has just pulled up in time, and, with his usual good fortune, the birth of a son seals the windup with public sympathy and approbation.

We dined at Ld. Jersey's on the Saturday of the expected imperial birth; the state of the Empress had been announced by telegraph in the morning. I sate next to the French Ambassador, who expected every servant who entered the room would bring him the anxiously expected bulletin. Lady Jersey counted on the event making her dinner an epoch. Hours flew on, Comte Persigny grew every moment more absent and disturbed. At length, at 12 o'clock, we all separated. I had ordered my servant to go to the Embassy on the following morning by 8 o'clock for news : but at half-past 6 o'clock in the morning (Sunday) a messenger arrived with a letter from the Ambassador, and an autograph letter, informing me of the great news; a child, and a man child ! I shall preserve this epistle in my family papers. I knew the Ambassador when he was the faithful friend and attendant of Louis Napoleon in adversity, and had been in prison with him seven years in Ham.

On this occasion, on his return from the Jerseys', he did not retire to rest. The birth of the Prince occurred at Paris at 3.15 in the morning of Sunday; it was known at the French Ambassador's in London by 4 o'clock.

It was telegraphed to the Queen of England, who had given directions that she should be roused at any hour, and replied immediately by telegraph to Paris.

Our Sovereign is very well. We had the honor of dining at the Palace a short time back, when she said that she never had been better, and that from the life she led, rising early, taking cold shower baths every day, and being frequently in the air, she had almost come to defy *catching cold*, which Prince Caraccioli called the English complaint. . . .

The Treaty of Paris was signed on March 30. Its terms, which were in accordance with the December ultimatum, corresponded sufficiently with those which Disraeli desired for him to regard it as on the whole satisfactory. Most of his political friends, however, considered it a decidedly inadequate return for our sacrifices, Derby even describing it in the Lords as the Capitulation of Paris. But Disraeli was able to restrain his party from taking any more serious Parliamentary action against it than the support of a very reasonable proposal (which was not even pressed) to substitute, in the Address to the Queen, ' satisfaction' for ' joy,' as the fitting word to express the emotion with which Parliament received the news. He did not speak himself on the treaty at all; but he encouraged a well-merited, though unsuccessful, attack on the Government for their desertion of the heroic General Williams, the defender of Kars; and on that occasion remarked incidentally that he would express no opinion ' except to say in general terms that peace is a great blessing where war has been carried on so inefficiently ; and that, for my part, after all I have seen, I should be disposed to welcome any peace which is not disgraceful.'

This peace was certainly not disgraceful, though it was not, and hardly professed to be, a permanent settlement. 'Nous avons fait une paix,' said Clarendon, ' mais pas la paix.' What it did was to stop the precipitate solution of the Eastern Question, which Russia had endeavoured to force, to give Turkey a respite and breathing time, and incidentally to afford the Christian races an opportunity of showing whether they possessed the vitality to win the independence of both their would-be protectors. Russia's ambitions were curbed,

but she was in no way humiliated ; there was no serious obstacle erected to friendly relations between her and her late foes. If, as Lord Salisbury said many years afterwards, we 'backed the wrong horse' in the war, we were wise enough to 'hedge' in the peace. One result, which should have been, but hardly was, anticipated, was that Russia's energies were largely diverted from Europe to Asia, and that her policy received an impulse which brought her eventually into collision with Japan and into critical relations with British India.

In promoting, and preparing the national mind for a reasonable peace, Disraeli undoubtedly rendered public service of a notable character. This movement was, it may be added, the last enterprise which the *Press* carried through under his immediate inspiration. Mrs. Disraeli wrote to Mrs. Willyams on March 18 : 'Dizzy says he always forgets to tell you that the *Press* newspaper has for some weeks past ceased to be under his control ; perhaps therefore you may prefer some other paper.' Hitherto he had been the managing director, and, so to speak, super-editor, and the paper had taken no step of importance without his sanction. Now he left the direction to Coulton, the editor, and Rose, his personal and political agent, though he remained a proprietor for two years more. He may have felt that the venture was now fairly launched, and that there was no need for him to add the burden of its management to his other heavy work. But it is quite likely also that this peace campaign, and the discord raised in the party and among the leaders by the articles in the *Press*, may have convinced him that it was very anomalous and inconvenient for the party leader in the Commons to be also the leading party journalist. Had he not been such an expert 'gentleman of the press' himself, it would probably never have occurred to him that the two positions were properly compatible. He seems to have been just as careful to conceal his relinquishment of control as he had

been to conceal his assumption of it. Malmesbury, with whom his relations, owing largely to the articles in the *Press*, were not so close as they had formerly been, was clearly unaware of the change, as, both in April of this year and in March of the next, when commenting in his diary on the growing tendency of the *Press* to exalt Disraeli at the expense of Derby, he treats Disraeli as responsible.

In truth, while Disraeli was in regular control, Derby was supported in the *Press* with steady loyalty, even when he made his great blunder of 1855. When, however, Disraeli's restraining hand was removed, it was natural that a body of writers whom he had himself collected, and who had sat at his feet for two years, should work for the substitution of their own chief, who had long done the drudgery of leadership, in place of one who had so bitterly disappointed his party at the crisis, and had shown so little activity since. Moreover, Derby's notorious indifference, amounting almost to dislike, to the political press — an indifference which Malmesbury deplored [1] — was not likely to conciliate the good opinion of political writers. Disraeli does not seem himself ever to have countenanced any movement of the kind, though often urged by enthusiastic followers in Parliament to put an end to what one of them called about this time 'the farce of a Derby leadership.' He was throughout loyal to Derby, after they had joined forces, as he had been in earlier days to Bentinck ; he acted up to his own sincere but theatrically expressed protestation: 'Come what will, we will stand or fall together.' [2] But he claimed and exercised a large liberty of initiative as leader of the party in the House of Commons. Uncongenial as were their temperaments, and clearly as each saw the other's deficiencies, neither Derby nor Disraeli at any period of their association lent himself to an intrigue against his colleague. Each was necessary to the other, and both knew it.

[1] *Memoirs*, under date June 29, 1857.   [2] See Vol. III., p. 527.

CHAPTER II

ADMINISTRATIVE REFORM

1852–1856

Among the qualities most desirable in a statesman are capacity for, and interest in, administration. These qualities the world in general has seldom credited Disraeli with possessing, and few even of his admirers have claimed them for him. Certainly, in the conduct of Treasury business — and the Treasury is the only public office over which he ever presided — he would as a rule content himself with laying down principles, and leave the general course of administration and the working out of detail almost entirely to subordinates. Yet there is no doubt that his first term of office infected him, at least temporarily, with administrative zeal; and he devoted considerable time and thought, both then and at the period of the breakdown of public departments during the Crimean War, to the question of administrative reform — a phrase which he claimed to have been the first to use in the House of Commons. He called Derby's attention to the subject when the Ministry of 1852 were preparing for the autumn session:

To Lord Derby.

Private. GROSVENOR GATE, *Oct.* 28, 1852. — I submit to you a confidential memorandum drawn up, at my request, by Mr. Anderson, of the Pay Office, a first-rate man of his kind, and who with Trevelyan,[1] and a man named Bromley, in the Audit Office, appear to me masters of administration,

---

[1] Sir Charles Trevelyan, permanent head of the Treasury.

and may be turned to great account.   The memorandum opens the great field of administrative reform in a practical method.   I wish you to consider whether I should advert to this specific subject in the statement of the 26th November, and announce our intention of bringing forward the question in exposition when the measures of financial reform are carried.

In my opinion, such a course would not only secure the session, but as many sessions as you wish, for we should then have taken possession of the only questions which really interest the country, which is progressive, but prosperous and therefore not favorable to political change. . . .

Derby expressed interest, but urged caution, so as 'not to sacrifice material and real advantage, either to the object of enabling departments to make a good show as to economy, or of giving our Government the means of evincing their readiness to allow all their accounts to be open and aboveboard.' Disraeli pressed the matter forward. He recognised that great changes were required in all the departments of the public service, and he was convinced that in promoting efficiency he would secure economy, and so be able to obtain that large surplus which his contemplated revision of taxation required. He appointed Lord Chandos, then a Lord of the Treasury, afterwards chairman of a great railway company, to overhaul and revise the Irish departments, with the result of an increase of efficiency and an immediate saving of 25 per cent. After the success of that experiment, the Government determined, if they survived the Budget, to bring the whole question before the House of Commons, with a view to the appointment of a Royal Commission. Two reforms Disraeli had matured and was prepared to introduce at once: one for the better administration of the Customs, and another securing for the first time the payment into the national Exchequer of the gross income of the country. The defeat on the Budget cut short this excellent work. The two detailed reforms had to be left to be carried through by the succeeding Government, and the comprehensive Royal Commission was never appointed.

Two years later the breakdown of the military departments in the Crimea forcibly directed public attention to a matter which had been regarded with indifference when Disraeli, in his speeches on the December Budget,[1] first broached it. An Association for Administrative Reform sprang up, and during the summer of 1855 there were several interesting, but somewhat confused, discussions in Parliament. The point most hotly debated was that of open competition by examination for the Civil Service, then a close preserve of patronage. Ministers resisted the introduction of the competitive system, which was pressed upon them by Gladstone, who had converted the Aberdeen Government to it in theory, and by Northcote, who had at Gladstone's instance drawn up, with Sir Charles Trevelyan, a report in its favour. Disraeli went a long way with these reformers. He expressed the opinion[2] that admission to the Civil Service should not be obtained by favouritism, but should be the result of substantial tests of fitness ; that the service should be better rewarded, and be made a distinct profession ; that the higher posts should be reserved as a rule for its members, who, having entered by merit, would naturally rise by merit ; but that the selection inside the office must be left to the Minister in charge, and not be decided by any fanciful system of competition. It was, however, with larger changes in the public departments that Disraeli was especially concerned. The *Press*[3] explained that his object was threefold : first, to secure more talent in the Civil Service ; secondly, to render the working of public departments more efficient ; and, thirdly, by a judicious classification of offices, to economise expense wasted on superfluous posts.

One of the eminent Civil Servants whose names Disraeli had mentioned in his letter to Derby, Mr. (afterwards Sir) Richard M. Bromley, was an enthusiast for administrative reform, and had communicated some of his enthusiasm to Disraeli. He kept up correspondence on the subject

---

[1] See Vol. III., pp. 433, 446.   [2] June 18.   [3] June 23.

with his late chief in opposition, and, now that public interest had been roused, urged him to take it seriously in hand. The Crimean War had led to one important administrative change — the separation of the War Department from that of the Colonies, and the creation of a Secretaryship of State for War, to whose office the Commissariat, hitherto under the Treasury, was also assigned. But even this change, necessary as it was, had not prevented the mismanagement which, by shocking the country in the preceding winter, had led to the replacement of Aberdeen by Palmerston. The new Ministry had taken the consequential step of amalgamating the offices of Secretary at War and Secretary of State for War, and had also, with very doubtful wisdom, suppressed the Ordnance Department, but appeared to contemplate no further substantial change; and so Bromley was encouraged by Disraeli to draw up a paper working out his plan in detail. It was of an ambitious character, and could be made, he assured Disraeli, 'in your hands . . . a popular reform and reorganisation far exceeding that brought about by Mr. Burke in 1780.' The scheme was completed in the middle of November, and for a month was discussed between its draftsman and Disraeli, who, when the draft had been settled to his satisfaction, forwarded it to Knowsley with a warm commendation.

To Lord Derby.

Private. HUGHENDEN, *Dec.* 18, 1855. — . . . These papers contain the cream of a great and practical measure of *Administrative and Departmental Reform.* — There is a third part, but it does not involve any principles, and is a consequence of the preceding portions, and therefore I have spared myself the vile pain of copying. What I have forwarded will convey a clear idea of my views; what remains refers to the analysis of offices in detail. Intimated occasionally on the MS. you have . . . the institution of an Audit Office as independent as the Queen's Judges, etc., etc.

If the principles are accepted by the Captain, I should propose that, when the details are well matured, the whole should be thrown into a *Bill for the more efficient Administra-*

tion of the Public Affairs of this Realm, or some similar title,
and that we make it the groundwork of our policy.

I have not been able to give any of the reasons which have
induced me to adopt any of these methods — it was totally
impossible to attempt that. I assume — I more than assume,
I know — that you are master of the subject in all its aspects
and bearings. It is the subject of the age, so far as English
politics are concerned, and we, fortunately, at present may
have it. It will be taken by the other party if we do not
appropriate it. There will be squatters on our common.
Perhaps John Russell means to ride into power on this matter.
He has settled so many things ; this only remains. A Government will never dare to act, except on their immediate accession to power for the purpose. If anything is done, it should
be bold and complete. You know, or should, that the Ad.
Reform Society has given notice, in its address issued since
the prorogation, of a Bill to be introduced, at the reassembly,
for the nomination of clerks by competition. I hear also that
Napier will immediately bring in a Bill to terminate Admiralty
Board. These are straws, but they show, etc.

I should like that we should take the lead of all. Everything, however, depends upon the Captain, and I shall await
with interest his decision.

I may be wrong, but I think there is an opportunity of
putting the party in a commanding position, and of doing
our country some real and lasting service. . . .

In the enclosure which Disraeli forwarded, the object
of the plan was described as 'to establish a thoroughly
efficient administration of public affairs in a manner consistent with our Monarchical and Parliamentary Government'; and its principle was explained at the outset.

It is founded on the principle of individual responsibility.
Therefore, in the first place, it abolishes all Commissions and
all Boards. It admits of no sinecure office. It arranges the
business of the country under particular departments, [so] that
each Minister is charged with a due amount of responsibility.
It makes every Minister a member of the Cabinet, and it
provides that the salaries as well as the duties of these Ministers shall, in amount, be [as] nearly as possible alike. In some
instances, it will be found that I propose to blend the administrative functions of one office with that of another, by placing
them in charge of one Cabinet Minister, but, in doing this, I
always propose to place a Parliamentary officer, subordinate
to the Minister, over every such department. The effect of
this will be, of course, to reduce the number of Ministers, and

to permit them all to have seats in the Cabinet, with salaries equivalent to their official labor and responsibility. It will also have the effect of training a number of subordinate Parliamentary officers for the higher charge of State, by allotting to them specific duties of such importance as will thoroughly test their qualifications for State business.

The Boards of Treasury, Admiralty, Trade, Control, Poor Law, and Public Health, and the Committee of Council on Education — all these, and others of the same kind, were to disappear, and the responsibility in each department was to be fixed on an individual Cabinet Minister. Disraeli proposed to limit the number of the Cabinet to ten, to be composed of the following Ministers:

    I. Lord President of the Council (Prime Minister).
    II. Lord Chancellor.
    III. Chancellor of the Exchequer.

And seven Secretaries of State,

    IV. Minister for Home Affairs.
    V. Minister for Foreign Affairs.
    VI. Minister for the Colonies.
    VII. Minister of War (Army, Navy, and Ordnance).
    VIII. Minister of Education.
    IX. Minister for Trade, Navigation, and Public Works.
    X. Minister for India.

Several of these Ministers were to assume duties hitherto assigned to separate departments, and effective administration was to be secured by the creation of a number of Parliamentary Secretaryships, subordinate to the Ministers. Thus, the Prime Minister was to be not only President of the Council, but also Chancellor of the Duchy and Privy Seal, with Parliamentary Secretaries under him for the two latter departments. The Postmaster-Generalship was to be abolished, and the duties transferred to the Chancellor of the Exchequer, who was to be assisted by a Secretary of the Post Office. Education was to be taken from the Lord President, and constituted a separate Ministry. The Education Minister was, however, to be responsible also for all public registrations, from those for designs to those for births, marriages,

and deaths, and was to be assisted by two Secretaries, one for Education, and the other for Registration. The most sweeping changes proposed were in the Home Office and the War Office. The Lord Lieutenancy of Ireland was to be abolished, and the Home Secretary was to have under him five Parliamentary Secretaries — for Ireland, Scotland, Justice and Police, Public Health, and the Poor. The War Minister was to have a still more comprehensive control, as he was to be responsible, not only for the regular army and the militia, and for the ordnance, commissariat, and transport services, but for the navy and its administration as well. In this gigantic task he was to be assisted by three Secretaries, one for the Navy, one for the Army, and one for Transport. The Board of Admiralty was to be replaced by a Council of Naval Officers. The Prime Minister was to have £6,000 a year, the Lord Chancellor's salary was to remain as before, all the other Ministers were to have £5,000, and the Secretaries £2,000, a year. 'The effect of these changes,' Disraeli wrote, ' will be no inconsiderable saving to the country, but I do not now dwell on that point. They have not been planned with reference to economy, solely to efficiency. But I have mentioned more than once in the House of Commons ; the true parent of economy is efficiency.'

The second part of Disraeli's scheme referred to the Permanent service of public affairs, as distinguished from the Parliamentary. It had two main features : the condemnation of the growing system of semi-independent Boards and Commissions ; and the introduction of competition, but in a very limited form, for the Civil Service.

The general feeling of public departments, as hitherto constituted, has been to disown work : that is, not to admit of any increase of business differing from their routine.

The result has been to create new departments at very considerable cost, but, still worse, without any immediate Minister to refer to, or permanent departmental officer to advise with. Hence the necessity to create Boards or Commissions, in order that three or more persons may be brought

together to do the work, which should be done by *one* permanent head officer, with the advice and assistance of a Minister of State and his Permanent Secretary.

Discussion and delay are the result of this ponderous and expensive system, as in most instances persons are appointed members of a Board without business habits, or any knowledge whatever of the details required to be controlled. . . .

All nominations of writers, clerks, and other functionaries, to a department to be made by the Minister of State, subject to the following conditions and restrictions :

When a vacancy occurs, the Minister shall either nominate an individual, who will be referred to a Board of Examiners, and be subject to a minimum test to be settled by the heads of departments, or he shall send in the names of not less than three candidates, who shall be subjected to competition based on the minimum test.

However appointed, the successful candidate shall be subject to a probation of not less than twelve months, and the confirmation of his post shall rest with the permanent head of the department.

Disraeli's scheme had some conspicuous merits — a smaller Cabinet, abolition of Cabinet sinecures, clearer allocation of responsibility. It was undoubtedly right to give greater precedence to the First Minister, and the Presidency of the Council was in many ways his natural office. ' The records of the Privy Council, being the acts of the Sovereign in Council, should,' Disraeli submitted with some force, ' be in the custody of the Prime Minister.' The Treasury should be nominally, he thought, as well as really, under the control of the Chancellor of the Exchequer. But the breach with history involved in discarding the famous title 'First Lord of the Treasury' seems unnecessary; and in 1905, by King Edward's command, proper precedence was at last accorded to the office of Prime Minister, though Mr. Balfour, then in power, provided that the change should only take effect on his successor's appointment. The equalisation of Ministerial salaries which Disraeli advocated was effected in 1915 by private arrangement in Mr. Asquith's Coalition Cabinet. In proposing to make Education a separate Cabinet department, Disraeli anticipated a reform which was delayed for nearly half

a century.   To bring the Poor Law into proper Ministerial subordination was obviously desirable, and has since
been done; and the Scottish department which Disraeli
suggested was established in an extended form thirty years
afterwards.   But his Home Office would have been hopelessly overloaded, and his plan for insuring the harmonious
co-operation of Navy and Army by putting them both
under one Minister was clumsy and impracticable.   The
same object has been promoted in recent years in a
happier way by the Committee of Imperial Defence.

Derby was on the whole favourably impressed by the
scheme, though he did not concur in the abolition of the
Lord Lieutenancy of Ireland, and took strong exception
to the proposal to amalgamate the Admiralty with the
War Office.   In the course of a memorandum which he
drew up on December 26, he wrote:

The scheme is bold and comprehensive, and capable of
being worked into a system, which, if honestly acted on, may
produce a great effect in the public service.   If he will take the
further trouble of embodying his propositions in a Bill, to be
confidentially printed, it will well deserve the serious consideration of our friends; and I should approach the subject
with a strong prepossession in its favour: but I should anxiously deprecate a hasty promulgation of a not fully matured
plan, more especially if it could be held to commit a party
who have a full right to be previously consulted.   No supposed risk of rival projects from other quarters can counter-
balance the evil, in every point of view, of such a hasty step.

As a result of Derby's conditional approval, Stanley
came to Hughenden to confer with Disraeli.

Lord Stanley to Lord Derby.

HUGHENDEN, *Jan.* 5 [1856]. — Disraeli and I had yesterday
a five-hours Cabinet on his scheme — the result, I think, satisfactory.   Removing all that you most strongly object to,
there would remain — (1) First Lord;   (2) Lord Chanc.;
(3) Chanc. of Ex.; (4) Home, (5) Foreign, (6) Colonial, Secretaries; (7) Minister of War; (8) Admiralty; (9) India; (10) Trade
and Works; leaving the Cabinet with ten members, and
leaving as offices of the second rank — (11) Education;

(12) Board of Health; (13) Poor Law; the two last cut off from his overgrown Home Office, which he seems to admit is beyond one man's control.

If it were important (I don't think it is so) to have all the heads of departments in Cabinet, and of equal rank, the inclusion of the three above-named would give only 13 Ministers. And two (Education and Health) are subjects of first-rate importance. There is no great harm in making one man, the Minister of Poor Laws, a rather more important personage than he need be.

I object quite as strongly as you to the union of Army and Navy. That must not be thought of. D. does not seem to have much to urge in its favour. . . .

We are both anxious to introduce the competitive system to the full extent into this plan, as regards the permanent Civil Service. I will not discuss it now — but my opinion, formed after long hesitation, is decided for it. We should, by adopting this principle, gain support out of doors, and within the H[ouse of] C[ommons] still more : and certainly double our chances of success, whatever they may be. D's fear was lest you should be hostile to competition as a principle : I don't believe you are so ! . . .

Sunday. — Further conferences—more agreement. D. concedes the two points most in dispute—the union of the services and the concentration of power in the H[ome] O[ffice].

London, *Jan.* 8. — . . . My feeling about D.'s plan, after full and careful examination of it, is that, as regards the Parliamentary service, his changes, as now modified, are desirable, but not important : what relates to the permanent service is more material, and will be valuable if, as is quite possible, you and he adopt competition as a basis. But that principle is the only one involved in the scheme : and there is nothing else about it that will excite the slightest degree of popular enthusiasm. . . .

It was certainly rather an emasculated plan which issued from these elaborate consultations. Though it still contained excellent features, and, indeed, had been stiffened in regard to the principle of competition, the mutilation it had undergone had probably damped Disraeli's ardour; or he may have become alive to the futility of assuming the initiative, when in opposition, in so essentially Governmental a question as administrative reform. At any rate, though he lived to see several of the improvements which he desired carried into effect,

he never took a prominent part in the work, save by the
establishment in 1858 of a Secretaryship of State for
India, and by the very practical step of confining his own
Cabinet of 1874 to twelve persons. Palmerston's Government made a beginning themselves in the session
of 1856 by creating an Education Minister, in the
characteristically English and clumsy guise of a Vice-
President of the Committee of Council on Education;
and, in spite of their resistance to the principle in the
previous year, announced their intention of introducing,
gradually and cautiously, open competition for the Civil
Service. But no comprehensive remodelling of British
administration, such as might well have been undertaken by Disraeli had he attained real power in the full
vigour of his energies, has ever been attempted.

Disraeli recommended Bromley for the K.C.B. in 1858,
and used him during the Government of 1858–59 for
much confidential work. But Bromley's enthusiasm for
administrative reform outran his discretion, and he
ended by wearying the statesman whom he had for long
impressed.

To Sir John Pakington.

GROSVENOR GATE, *Jan.* 18, 1864. — I should keep very shy
of B[romley].

Nothing can ever satisfy his ravenous egotism. He used
to send me, some years ago, many plans of administrative, and,
especially, Admiralty reform : but I found out that the object
of all his changes was to advance the permanent at the ex-
pence of the Parliamentary officials. Such reform is not our
'métier,' as the Emperor Joseph said to the first French
Republicans.

B. wants to turn clerks into Privy Councillors. He had
energy and organising ability, but he has been over-rewarded
and over-promoted, and, tho' still restless, is, I think, used
up. . . .

CHAPTER III

TORY DEMORALISATION AND DEFEAT

1856–1857

Disraeli had an exceptionally representative gathering at his Parliamentary dinner on the eve of the session of 1856, and he took it, somewhat prematurely, as evidence of the union of the party in general in his support. The *Press* drew special attention to the assemblage. 'Never before did the banquet of any Opposition leader in the Lower House at the opening of the session exhibit such an array of names, representative of rank and property, and associated with proud historical associations.' A list was paraded, somewhat similar to that given, in *Lord George Bentinck*, of the old guard who refused to follow Peel;[1] and the presence was specially noted of Lord Robert Cecil, 'on whom so many eyes are fixed as a future chief, and who bids fair to uphold his great English name.' The article[2] boasted that even Peel, at the head of "the gentlemen of England," had never met Parliament with a more united party in the Lower House.

The unity of the party under Disraeli's leadership was nothing like so complete as his buoyant optimism conceived it to be. We have the evidence of two new members who were eventually to be among Disraeli's most trusted colleagues. Gathorne Hardy, who entered the House at a by-election in February, found the party seething with intrigue against him; and Northcote wrote in April of 'indecisive manœuvring,' 'our people's imbecility,' and the 'hash' they were making, and reported a friend as having given in disgust

---

[1] See Vol. II., pp. 401, 402.   [2] *Press*, Feb. 2.

'formal notice that he would no longer attend meetings of the party or answer their circulars.'[1] Moreover, Robert Cecil, so flatteringly referred to in the *Press*, took a very independent line, and before long was a centre of disaffection to Disraeli's leadership. Another constant detractor was George Bentinck, member for Norfolk from 1852, a distant cousin of Lord George's, and known familiarly at Westminster as 'Big Ben.' Bentinck set, or popularised, the fashion, among the anti-Disraeli Tory clique, of always calling their leader 'the Jew.' A leading member of the clique, though he was not in the House during this Parliament, was Alexander Beresford Hope, Robert Cecil's brother-in-law; a man of artistic tastes and High Anglican opinions, founder and proprietor of the *Saturday Review;* who claimed in 1867 that he had jeopardised his political career by refusing to 'fall down and worship the golden image set up in the deserts of Arabia,' and whose journal was conducted in the spirit exemplified by this outburst.

The session of 1856 was rather a barren one, with much promised in the Queen's Speech, and but a poor harvest at the close. The Peace, its preliminaries and its consequences, absorbed attention. In July Disraeli repeated the experiment which had had such brilliant results in 1848[2] — a review of the session, exposing Ministerial shortcomings. This time he had no such striking success. It was rather a laboured performance. His main point was that Palmerston's Government was really a Conservative Government carrying out a Conservative policy, and so was in a false position. The truth is that it was a period of transition, and all parties were in false positions. Graham told Greville on April 2 that there was not one man in the House of Commons that had ten followers, 'neither Gladstone, nor Disraeli, nor Palmerston.' He added that Disraeli appeared to be endeavouring to approach Gladstone, and a confederacy between those two and Stanley was by no means an improbability.

[1] Lang's *Northcote*, pp. 88, 89. [2] See Vol. III., Ch. 4.

Disraeli's letters to Mrs. Willyams, which show that he had been taking his share of social and Court festivities in this bustling season after the Peace, show also that he was seriously occupied with negotiations to bring back to the fold that incalculable body, the Peelites, now merely a scattered group of leaders, with hardly any followers, and more distrustful of Palmerston than even of Disraeli. In this work Northcote, a reconciled Peelite himself, was the principal agent.   He wrote to his wife early in May : 'I have been acting as a sort of go-between to the Peelites and our own side, and I am sure there is an excellent feeling springing up between us.'   But in June he was less hopeful : 'The reconstruction of the conservative party goes on at about the pace of a Tertiary formation.'[1]

To Mrs. Brydges Willyams.

HUGHENDEN MANOR, *May* 15, 1856. — . . . We are returning to town to-day instead of next Monday, as we anticipate great disturbances in Hyde Park from the stoppage of the bands playing to-morrow (Sunday).   This Sabbatarian controversy is likely to become very serious.[2]   What a great man Moses must have been, to have invented a law which should agitate the 19th century, with all its boasted progress !

We had a very brisk and bustling season during the six weeks that elapsed between Easter and Whitsun, and there is a prospect of still greater gaiety, especially if the Prince of Prussia[3] comes to claim the hand of the Princess Royal. . . .

Negotiations have been going on for some time to effect a reconciliation between the two sections of the Conservative party, and a reconstruction on the former extensive basis. Tho' there are many difficulties to be overcome, my opinion is they will be successfully combated.   In this case, very great changes will, in due time, take place in the world of politics, and, between ourselves, it is not at all desirable that any change of Government should take place until this great reconstruction is arranged and *matured*.   However, these are State secrets — and it is possible that the effort may fail, but I think not, because it seems to me to be a necessity.   If it

[1] Lang's *Northcote*, pp. 89, 90.

[2] The First Commissioner of Works arranged that bands should play in the London parks on Sunday, but the Sabbatarians raised a great clamour and the Government stopped the bands.

[3] Afterwards the Emperor Frederick.

happen, Lord Derby will have a good chance of carrying on the administration of affairs as long as he could well desire. . . .

GROSVENOR GATE, *July* 7, 1856. — . . . The season is approaching its end; it will be a *coup de grâce*. The town is quite mad — fêtes and festivities night and morn. Never were there so many balls and banquets. No roof so hospitable this year as the Palace itself. Two young Princes reconnoitring young Princesses will account for this.

The Prince of Prussia, *fiancé* to our Princess Royal, is well informed, and appears able — but more like a German student than a Prince.

Prince Oscar of Sweden, tho' he is a Scandinavian Prince with a Scandinavian name, is a veritable grandson of Bernadotte; dark, with glowing cheeks, and sparkling eyes — a veritable Gascon. I have not conversed with him. He came over to make his bow to the Princess Mary of Cambridge,[1] but appears to be less absorbed in her society than is desirable; and, it is thought, he will quit us without making the most important speech which a man can in this world.

The new ball-room is opened at the Palace this year. It is a colossal chamber, but of fine proportions — much decorated in the German style, and much criticised — but all must agree that the English Court was never before assembled in so fine a chamber. We were there at a ball some weeks ago, with more than 1,500 guests; but the other night, last Wednesday, Her Majesty did us the honor of inviting us to a full-dress concert, held in the same ball-room, where there is a permanent organ. There were only 500 invited, and all in costume. It seemed to me that I had never seen before in England anything which realised my idea of a splendid Court.

The orchestra was very strong; there were 125 performers — among them Johanna Wagner. All the music was German, and the second act, entirely consisting of the 'Walpurgis Night' of Mendelssohn — Goethe's poetry wedded to such wild harmonies — made a whole of supernatural splendor.

I enjoyed myself very much, being fond of German music, but at the same time I can't help fancying that one cause of my satisfaction was that I had a seat. In the old concert-room the space was so limited that gentlemen were never seated. This was very wearisome. . . .

GROSVENOR GATE, *July* 31, 1856. — . . . This has been the gayest season, Mr. Gunter assures me, since 1851 — that of the great Exhibition. As for politics, altho' it is abused by

---

[1] Who married eventually the Duke of Teck, and became the mother of Queen Mary.

the million as an uneventful session, I do not think it so, but
hold rather that a broad and deep foundation is laid for future
action, so far as the Conservative party is concerned.

The Queen really talks of going to Lisbon; H. Majesty is
always in motion; and I suppose movement and air are the
great sources of health and happiness.

If ever you want a book to read, try Lyell's 'Principles of
Geology.' It is quite in your way: full of science and the
observation of nature, but most entertaining as well as instructive. I should like to know whether you think he makes
out his case, that the great changes which have taken place
in our globe are not the consequence of vast, sudden, and
spasmodic changes, but the result of that continual change,
thro' countless ages, which is now, as it always has been, going
on. This philosophy is entirely founded on Induction, the
only safe basis. . . .

The approximation of Peelites to Derbyites continued
during the autumn, being assisted by Palmerston's
vagaries in foreign policy, which particularly disgusted
Aberdeen. Lennox in October reported Aberdeen as
saying that never was there a pilot in whom he had so
little confidence as 'Pam,' and that the Conservative
party must at once be consolidated.

To Lord Henry Lennox.

HUGHENDEN, *Oct.* 26, 1856.—. . . I know nothing of public
affairs, tho' I can easily understand the feelings of the Peelites.
They and the Derbyites are like the two Bourbon factions
playing at fusion: they have delayed the process so long
that there is someone in possession who cries 'A plague on
both!' . . .

Foreign policy had given Disraeli some opportunity
during the session of escaping from Court festivities
and party manœuvring into those wider problems with
which he delighted to deal. The impetus given to change
in Europe by the Revolution of 1848 had been increased
by the Crimean War; and during the ten years of Palmerston's predominance foreign policy was, again and again,
more of a preoccupation than domestic affairs with
British parties and statesmen. Italy was in the making;

Germany was in the making; France had not yet found
a constitution to her mind, but was restlessly trying yet
another of her many experiments in government since
1789; Russia had been rudely awakened, and was stretch-
ing herself.   To difficulties in the Near East were succeeding mighty problems in the Far East.   Across the
Atlantic a young nation was beginning to feel its strength,
and, though torn by acute domestic conflict, to call somewhat loudly for external recognition.   All these movements touched either the interests or the sympathies of
Great Britain and her worldwide Empire; with all of
them Disraeli dealt, from time to time, in penetrating
and philosophic fashion.

In his review [1] of this session of 1856, he laid it down
that in foreign affairs there were three great questions
on which it behoved British statesmen and British parties
to have precise and clear ideas — the Russian Empire,
the Austrian Empire, and our relations with the United
States of America.   France he did not mention, because
at that time the French alliance was acknowledged by all
parties to be the basis of our foreign policy.   With regard
to Russia, Disraeli's views had been sufficiently shown
during the recent movement for peace.   He was opposed
to all idea of the dismemberment of Russia; it could not
be attained without a fatally prolonged and exhausting
war; and, when it was attained, we should find the balance
of power in Europe altered to our disadvantage.

Disraeli was opposed also to the dismemberment of
Austria, holding that the Austrian Empire was necessary
to the independence, the civilisation, and even the
liberties, of Europe.   Though the doctrine sounds strange
to us now, this had been hitherto the general opinion of
European statesmen, with the exception of the partisans
of revolution.   France and Russia were regarded as
explosive forces; and without the presence of a strong
central Power, such as Austria, with its lingering traditions of the old Holy Roman Empire, it was thought that

[1] July 25.

European peace could not be preserved. In the interests, however, of unemancipated Italy, a hostile feeling to Austria was growing up among the Liberal party, of which Russell, now in a position of independence, made himself the mouthpiece. Disraeli deprecated the encouragement that was given, in the protocols of the Treaty of Paris, to Sardinia to persist in her efforts for the liberation of Italy — encouragement which was strangely simultaneous with the signature of a tripartite treaty between England, France, and Austria. Had we played our cards so badly in the late game of diplomacy that we were at the same time pledged to support both Austrian authority and Sardinian regeneration? Russell seemed to think that the contest in Italy lay between worn-out dynasties and constitutional reformers, ignoring that danger from secret societies which Disraeli was one of the few statesmen of the day to appreciate at its proper value. These societies, which were spread like a network over Europe, did not desire votes or constitutions; they wanted to change the tenure of land, to drive out the present owners of the soil, and to put an end to ecclesiastical establishments.[1] Disraeli, therefore, deprecated very strongly any policy of active adventure in Italy, reminding Parliament of the unfortunate results of meddling in the forties; of 'those scenes of popular tumult which, excited by English influence, were deserted by English power — a desertion remembered to this day on the Continent with anguish and indignation.'

Disraeli's hopes were justified. Palmerston, strengthened by his support, resisted the movement of Russell and the Radicals for active intervention, if not in arms, at least by diplomacy, against Austria in Italy, and did not go beyond general expressions of friendship for Sardinia and sympathy with Italian aspirations. That sympathy Disraeli, who also had profited by experience, no longer withheld. But, while giving eloquent expression to it, he wisely reminded Parliament that a nation that would

[1] July 14.

be free must work out its own destinies, and not rely for emancipation upon the good offices of others.   This truth Italy was herself to recognise : ' Italia fara da se.'

I feel a deep interest in the future of Italy, and sure I am that there is no honest man in this Empire who does not look forward with delight to the day when that immemorial land to which we all owe so much shall take her proper place among the nations, and be again one of the leading communities of the world.   But I for one base my hope of that consummation on my faith in the genius of the people and the resources of the country.   Time, the great reformer, will save Italy ; but if there can be anything that will throw her back in her career, anything that will baffle her destinies, it will be the intrigues of politicians who are not Italians, and who, for the sake of getting an impulse and support which otherwise they might not command, trifle with the fate of a great people, pander to the lusts of secret societies, pretend to sympathy they do not feel, and, for the love of popular applause and a momentary success, compromise the destiny of a great and gifted nation.[1]

If Disraeli's treatment of the Italian question was at once sympathetic and conservative, so was his treatment of British relations with the United States.   These relations were at this time somewhat strained, owing to American expansion and to difficulties arising out of the ill-starred Foreign Enlistment Act.[2]   Disraeli did what he could to ease the situation.   England should recognise that the United States, like all the great countries of Europe, had a policy, and that they had a right to have a policy.

There are those who view with the utmost jealousy, and regard in a litigious spirit, the progress of the United States of America ; who think that any advance in their power, or any expansion of their territory, is opposed to the commercial interest, and perhaps also to the political influence, of England.   But I am not of that opinion.   I am of a contrary opinion. . . .   I cannot forget that the United States, though independent, are still in some sense colonies, and are influenced by colonial tendencies ; and when they come in contact

<hr>

[1] May 19, 1856.   [2] See Vol. III, pp. 554, 555.

with large portions of territory scarcely populated, or at the most sparsely occupied by an indolent and unintelligent race of men, it is impossible — and you yourselves find it impossible — to resist the tendency to expansion; and expansion in that sense is not injurious to England, for it contributes to the wealth of this country.[1]

Disraeli expressed himself confident that, when once the United States saw that England was no longer jealous of their legitimate development, all these disputes and angry discussions between the two countries would cease. It was, he maintained, the business of a statesman to recognise the necessity of an increase in American power.[2] Surely a thoroughly statesmanlike attitude! Disraeli was, indeed, one of the few public men of the day who displayed constant tact and good feeling in his treatment of the United States. If he never courted America, he never ruffled her susceptibilities.

At the beginning of August, directly the session was over, Disraeli, who had been suffering from nervous debility, started with his wife for a course of treatment at Spa. They told no one where they were going, and only took their friends into their confidence just before their return.

To Mrs. Brydges Willyams.

SPA, *August* 30, 1856. — When I crossed the Channel, I had been ordered to go to Vichy or Spa — and fortune or the humor of the moment brought me here. I have experienced the greatest benefit from the waters and mineral baths. Both are tonic in a high degree, and as, tho' suffering generally from nervous debility, I have never had recourse to such remedies, their beneficial effect upon me has been remarkable. I feel entirely renovated. Nevertheless, I am about to direct my steps homeward, *via* Amsterdam, which I have never seen. . . .

This place, Spa, is extremely pretty; a valley, tho' 1,000 feet above the ocean, very green, with brushwood of dwarf oak and spruce and silver firs; a picturesque village of hotels; walks of linden-trees; ponies and carriages of all forms, cantering and coursing about from spring to spring, and making

---

[1] July 25.   [2] June 16.

the tour of silver fountains shrouded in sunny woods. The ghost of the eighteenth century seems to haunt its favorite watering-place, where Sovereigns and Ministers of State settled once the affairs of Europe as they walked before breakfast to drink a sparkling glass of the renovating element, or hazarded some *louis d'ors* at the Redoute, still open, and much frequented.

Spa was nearly dead, having been eclipsed by its modern rivals, the German bathing-places, when a railroad of late years revealed it to the 19th century, and now it is fuller than in the days of the Prince de Ligne, when it was the resort of the whole European world. But tho' there are four or five thousand visitors here, and an unceasing round of balls, concerts, colossal riding-parties, and rural festivals, you may live, as we do, in profound solitude. And what is most agreeable, without entering into gaiety, you may command and enjoy that rarest of all things — society — the conversation of a few congenial spirits and cultivated minds.

I have not seen a newspaper, in any language, for more than a month, and I did not tell our own household where we were going, so that we have not received a single letter. This complete breaking of the perpetual chain of public circumstances and the cares and trouble of business has perhaps done me as much good as the waters of Pouhon. . . .

The only persons we know here are some Devonshire people (London friends), Lord and Lady Poltimore, and the Prince and Princess of Capua, whom we have met again after many years of their adventurous life of strange vicissitudes. . . .

A week later Disraeli wrote a very similar letter to Lady Londonderry. By this time the fashion of repeating phrases, and indeed whole passages, in letters to different persons written at the same time, had grown into a settled habit with him.

The Disraelis returned to England in the middle of September, and, after paying their annual visit to Mount Braddon,[1] spent a quiet six or seven weeks at Hughenden.

To Mrs. Brydges Willyams.

HUGHENDEN MANOR, *Nov.* 6, 1856. — . . . We have vegetated here since we left Torquay — planting and pruning, and almost in perfect solitude. Lord[2] and Lady Villiers came

---

[1] See Vol. III., p. 461.

[2] M.P. successively for Honiton, Weymouth, and Cirencester; 6th Earl of Jersey from Oct. 3 to 24, 1859.

here, and Lady de Rothschild, the only persons we have seen
and we have refused all invitations. I have myself been
much engaged with the new Rural Police, which is to be
established forthwith in this county. The magistrates at
Quarter Sessions appointed a Committee for this purpose,
who chose me as chairman, and I have been as busy this
autumn as if I were in the House of Commons. As I have
no railroad to Aylesbury, I am obliged very frequently to
travel by road between 30 and 40 miles a day, which in the
decline of the year is not agreeable; but I have always risen
not later than seven o'clock.

All this, however, is now going to change, for in a very few
days we shall proceed to Grosvenor Gate *en route* to Paris. I
am now sorry to depart; the weather is so beautiful, the
evergreens so bright, and planting so interesting and creative;
but go I must. Affairs are very perplexed, and, as I told
you at Torquay in confidence, there is someone who wants to
see me, and whom I have promised to pay my respects to. . . .

The mysterious friend in Paris was, of course,
Napoleon III., with whom, in his period of exile in
England, Disraeli had had considerable acquaintance,
and who owed his prompt recognition as Emperor to a
Government of which Disraeli was a leading member.
Disraeli was anxious about the relations between England and France, which, since the differences between the
two Governments about the Peace, had not been as
cordial as was desirable in the interests of both countries
and of the tranquillity of the world. He had laboured
in the forties to improve those relations in audiences of
Louis Philippe; he was ready to do the same now with
Louis Napoleon. He was also particularly anxious to
remind the Emperor that there were other statesmen
in England prepared to work in cordial unison with him,
besides Palmerston. He had intended, in any case, to
spend the winter in Paris, and a letter just received from
Lennox opened a direct channel of communication with
the Emperor.

From Lord Henry Lennox.

Most private. HAMILTON PALACE, *Oct.* 29, 1856.—. . . An
opportunity has arisen by which you can convey direct to

the French Emperor any views you have : direct and privately
to His Majesty. . . . The Dss. of Hamilton is Napoleon's
cousin [1] and in constant correspondence with him. Two days
ago she received a letter from him, complaining of *The Times*
and other papers, and saying that he was deeply annoyed,
and expressing his hope that at all events the Conservative
organs would rebuke licentiousness of Press, and support
him and the alliance. One phrase in the letter is remarkable.
He says : ' The moment that I feel called upon to refuse to go
full length with the English Govt. down come these slanders
of me and my Govt., as though England was to be all in all
and France as nothing to me.' . . .

The Dss. under a solemn promise of secrecy showed me the
letter, and asked if I could write to any Conservative Powerful ;
if so, she would be grateful, and would ask permission to forward the answer direct and privately to Nap. . . .

Disraeli availed himself of the suggested channel of
communication, and wrote Lennox a letter, which was
forwarded by the Duchess to the Emperor.

To Lord Henry Lennox.

HUGHENDEN, *Oct.* 31, 1856. — Your letter, from Hamilton,
arrived here this morning. I had previously written to you,
directed to Portland Place, informing you of my plans ; that
I should be in town early in November, *en route*, probably
after some little time, for Paris.

I have long watched, with great anxiety, the circumstances
to which you allude. They are symptoms of a deep disorder
in the relations between the two Governments, but are also,
in my opinion, the inevitable consequences of the narrow,
and narrow-minded, basis, on which Lord Palmerston has
rested the alliance. An alliance with England may be of
great importance to the Emperor, but an imperial policy is
not less so. It is indispensable, for the welfare of both
countries, that they should be combined ; but this Palmerston,
much from his temperament, and partly from ancient' preju-

---

[1] The Duchess of Hamilton, wife of the eleventh Duke, was the Princess
Mary of Baden, youngest daughter of Charles Louis Frederick, reigning
Grand-Duke of Baden. Her mother was Stéphanie de Beauharnais,
daughter of Claude de Beauharnais, whose youngest brother, Alexandre
de Beauharnais, was first husband of the Empress Josephine, and father,
by her, of Hortense, Queen of Holland, mother of Napoleon III. The
Duchess was therefore Napoleon's second cousin.

dices, will never understand. With all his rodomontade, his diplomacy is of the age of the *blocus continental*.

I think, if the present state of things becomes chronic, and it has a tendency that way, great disasters may occur. No effort should be omitted to prevent them. But partial and precipitate attempts will not be remedies. I will deeply consider — indeed, I have deeply considered — the subject, and I do not despair that, during the next session of Parliament, a healthy and decided feeling will animate the Conservative party on this all-important head.

Unfortunately, some persons of influence, who call themselves Conservatives, while they abuse Palmerston, and affect to sympathise with the Emperor, are carrying on Orleanist intrigues. I made some curious discoveries on this head, at Spa, this year.

With respect to our alliance with France generally, my opinions are upon record: in detail, even so late as 1853.[1] I inherited them from Lord Bolingbroke, and the changes in the world, subsequent to his time, only confirm his prescience. With regard to the Emperor personally, there are many private as well as public reasons why I should wish to serve him.

I shall hope to see you in London, but altho' I have received communications, this autumn, from all persons and all quarters, I am anxious in the present state of things to keep aloof. And this is one reason why I am going to Paris — to get rid of the *châteaux*.

The Disraelis were warmly welcomed by the Court and by society in Paris, but the political mission for long made little progress.

To Lord Henry Lennox.

PARIS, *Dec.* 26, 1856. — . . . Now to business: I should have written, but there has been nothing to say — anything would have misled you. It is not hopeless; it is not absolutely unfavorable; all that has occurred, or transpired, is good. I am supposed to be, and perhaps am, in high favor: banquets from Fould, Walewski, etc., etc. — all the diplomatists on their knees; all secrets told from all sides: and Cowley confidential: but nothing from the all-commanding mind definite: it is still brooding in its unfathomable recesses.

[1] See Vol. III., pp. 484-487.

To Mrs. Brydges Willyams.

PARIS, *Jan.* 1, 1857.— I wish you a happy New Year from the Imperial City. It is the first letter that I have written this year, and I will accept it as a good omen that it is addressed to Mount Braddon.

Ten years, as long as the siege of Troy, since I found myself last in this place : Troy could not be more changed in the time. Everything squalid has been pulled down, or driven out of sight — a city of palaces and glittering streets, and illimitable parks and pleasure-gardens, statues and gondolas, and beautiful birds and deer. The Tuileries and Louvre joined formed a kingly residence worthy of Babylon : the Rue de Rivoli, with its bright arcades, extends from the Place de la Concorde and the Elysian fields to the Hôtel de Ville and Notre Dame : the old Bois de Boulogne is converted into a Paradise, compared with which, in extent, all the Parks in London, together, would form an insignificant section.

Paris is a beautiful woman, and London an ugly man ; still, the masculine quality counts for something.

Our reception here has not turned our heads, but has tried the strength of our constitutions ; once we dined out eleven days running. The Ministers here live in palaces, with appointments and service, quite as gorgeous and stately as our own Court — very different from the position of English Ministers. Nevertheless, I don't think English gentlemen would ever feel easy under roofs which were not their own, however splendid. They would think they were too much like the Lord Mayor.

Our most interesting dinner was, however, certainly at the Tuileries, for my wife sate by the Emperor, and I sate by the side of the beautiful Empress. I have seen such faces, often, among the ladies at a bull-fight — and I dare say many a Mendez da Costa has worn such. Round her swanlike neck she wore a necklace of emeralds and diamonds such as might have been found in the cave of Aladdin ; and yet, tho' colossal gems, for her they were not too vast. After this I will tell you no more : the curtain should fall amid the brightest fire.

Send me, if only one line, a word to say you are well, to Grosvenor Gate, and it will reach me. Mrs. D. sends you more than a word — 1,000 kind thoughts and wishes.

Disraeli has left little in his papers to show exactly how his political mission fared. There is one short memorandum, which does not tell us much, except that

he entirely failed to persuade the Emperor that he would do wisely to transfer his confidence from Palmerston to the Conservatives.

In 1856–57 (Dec.–Jan.), at the Tuileries, the Emperor said to me : ‘ I have always thought that the principle of the Anglo-French Alliance was this : that France should assist England in her policy, and the converse ; but Lord P[almerston] seems always to think that the first condition of the alliance should alone prevail.’ When I left the T. that day — farewell audience, the Emperor having entered into every point, and I having reiterated my opinion previously expressed, that the then English Government would not stand (Lord P.’s first Government, which was placed in a minority a few weeks after, shortly after the meeting of Parliament, dissolved it, obtained a triumphant majority, and yet was turned out by their own Parliament the succeeding year) — I saw the Emperor was quite sceptical as to my opinion, and was entirely with Palmerston. His Majesty said to me : ‘ Lord Derby has no men.’

To Vitzthum, three years later, Disraeli gave the following account of these conversations:

The Emperor Napoleon will remember my having warned him some years ago against throwing himself into the arms of Palmerston. He declared then that we Tories were his hereditary enemies, and that he had, therefore, no choice in the matter. I denied it, and assured him we would go with any government in France which respected treaties, but not with any that did not. Palmerston would make many promises, but keep none of them, because he had not the power to do so. He had a few followers, but no party.[1]

Disraeli apparently did not impress the Emperor so much as he wished to do, and perhaps thought he had done. At any rate, Louis Napoleon, a couple of months later, told Malmesbury that his opinion of Disraeli was that he ‘ has not the head of a statesman, but that he is, like all literary men, as he has found them, from Chateaubriand to Guizot, ignorant of the world, talking well, but nervous when the moment of action arises.’[2]   A singu-

[1] Vitzthum, Vol. II, pp. 40, 41.
[2] *Memoirs of an Ex-Minister*, under date April 19, 1857.

larly inept judgment, which shows only the Emperor's
want of insight.

Before leaving for Paris, Disraeli had arranged with
Jolliffe that a serious attempt should be made to get the
magnificoes of the party, and particularly Derby, to bestir
themselves, and by personal exertion, organisation, and
subscriptions, to bring the chaotic and dispirited Conservative party together, and fit it for the possibility of office.
One of the difficulties was Disraeli's own unpopularity.
Malmesbury, discussing the 'destitute condition' of the
Tories in a letter to Derby on December 7, 1856, wrote
that their best men reported 'that you are supposed to be
tired of politics and no longer ambitious of office, and
that this impression and the unpopularity of Disraeli
are distracting our party.' Derby replied, on December 15, in an interesting letter printed in full in the
Memoirs of an Ex-Minister: 'As to Disraeli's unpopularity, I see it and regret it; and especially regret that
he does not see more of the party in private; but they
could not do without him, even if there were anyone
ready and able to take his place. For myself, I *never*
was *ambitious* of office, and am not likely to become
more so as I get older; but I am now, as I have been,
ready to accept the responsibility for it if I see a chance,
not only of taking, but of keeping it.' These confidences
of Derby and Malmesbury about Disraeli accord very ill
with Disraeli's own impression of his position, based on
the representative attendance at his Parliamentary dinner
in the spring. But it is apparent from his correspondence
that, beyond his personal friends, Disraeli — following, it
may be said, Derby's example — made little or no attempt
at this period to cultivate, and exchange ideas with, his
followers, or even his colleagues ; and, of course, his
recent policy with regard to the Peace had been resented
none the less because it had prevailed. He knew himself
to be necessary, and felt that popularity would come
with success. He, at any rate, was not open to some
of the reproaches cast upon Derby. Lennox spent a

week with Derby in a country-house this winter, and
reported to Disraeli his impressions of the 'Captain.'
'As a leader of a party, he is more hopeless than ever
— devoted to whist, billiards, racing, betting. . . .
Bulwer Lytton came to Bretby for three days, and was
in despair! Not one word could he extract from
Derby about public affairs; nothing but the odds and
tricks.'

In spite, however, of this appearance of frivolity, Derby
had proved more amenable than usual this winter to the
earnest representations of colleagues and Whips.

From Sir William Jolliffe.

HEATH HOUSE, PETERSFIELD, *Dec.* 27, 1856. — . . . My
letter to Malmesbury, written soon after I had last the pleasure
of seeing you, has appeared to have had all the effect that I
could desire, and far more than I expected; it has led to
consultation and conference in high quarters, and appears to
have set the wheels agoing. We shall attempt a subscription
with an offer of handsome contribution from the Chief; we
are to have more consultation in a small Cabinet formed from
both Houses; I believe Pakington and Walpole have been
asked to Knowsley; some much required encouragement has
been given by old Lyndhurst to his Lordship; he has heard
from me that you are *all right*, and will cordially second him,
so I think things are really looking up.

Of course, it is doubtful what can be done with the Peelites,
but I have heard that Gladstone has (of course in a round-
about way) conveyed his wishes to Lord D. . . .

Unfortunately, the two objects which Derby — in complete accord with Disraeli — was pursuing were incompatible. No hearty consolidation of the rank and file
was possible while the leaders were endeavouring to win
back the Peelites, and to make arrangements for harmonious working in opposition first, and eventually in
office, with politicians so thoroughly distrusted by the
party. Malmesbury wrote in his journal on February 3,
1857: 'The Duke of Beaufort, one of our staunchest adherents, told me at Longleat that, if we coalesced with
the Peelites, he would leave the party, and I remember

in 1855, when Lord Derby attempted to form a Government, and offered places to Gladstone and Herbert, that no less than eighty members of the House of Commons threatened to leave him.'   Jolliffe reported to Disraeli from Burghley on January 29 in the same sense : ' Chief and I are both taken sadly aback at having Burghley and R. Knightley [1] both saying that they will never submit to a junction with Gladstone ; and the latter told me to-day, out shooting, that he was not speaking only for himself when he said he would give a bitter opposition to any Government which included Gladstone.'

While these winter manœuvres were in full progress, Disraeli returned from Paris to make preparations for the session.   As if the internal difficulties of the Conservatives were not already sufficient, he found himself immediately threatened with a breach with the most intimate of his colleagues, his political pupil and personal friend, in conjunction with whom, in council, Parliament, and the *Press*, he had endeavoured to educate and liberalise his party.   He had sent out invitations to his principal colleagues and followers for a political dinner on the eve of the session.   Stanley declined, giving no reason except that ' it is probable I shall not be in London on that day.   I delayed my answer, hearing you were still at Paris.'

To Lord Stanley.

GROSVENOR GATE, *Friday morning* [*Jan.* 23, 1857]. — Your letter this instant received greatly afflicts me.

Certainly, if I had contemplated your refusal, I should not have ventured on soliciting the presence of the chief followers of your father ; for I am quite sure that your absence under such circumstances would injure him much more than the gathering, however numerous and influential, of others would bear him benefit.

I wrote to you and three more persons before I sent out the general invitations.   They answered me by return of post ; I still waited a week, and, as no reply came from you, I con-

---

[1] Sir Rainald Knightley, of Fawsley, M.P. for Northants 1852–1892, afterwards Lord Knightley.

Lord Stanley
from a portrait after Sir T. Grant. P.R.A.
at Hughenden.

strued your silence favorably, and consonant with your declaration to me last year, that so long as your father maintained the position, which he now occupies, your presence on such an occasion might be counted on.

With respect to requesting your reply to be sent to Grosvenor Gate, that was not because it was held unimportant, but because, my letters being opened by the French Post Office, it was necessary that they should be forwarded to me, which they were regularly by Rothschild's couriers.

These few words as to the political considerations which your letter calls forth. Grave as they are, they are slight compared with the sad impression that its tone involves a sentiment of personal estrangement. As I am not conscious that I have ever been wanting in that feeling of deep attachment and high appreciation which I have now for many years entertained for you, I cannot conceal that my feelings are deeply moved. My friendships, though I have to deal with many men, are rare, and notwithstanding the many circumstances, public and private, which might for the moment modify or diminish our intimacy, I had such confidence in the depths and stability of your character that I have ever contemplated that during the remaining years of my life you would form an important element of my existence.

Stanley replied in a lengthy letter which fully set out the difficulties of his political position. He first explained that his delay in replying was due solely to reluctance to make an unpleasant communication, and then continued:

From Lord Stanley.

Private. St. James's Square, *Jan.* 27, 1857.— . . . You will probably believe my earnest assurance that of personal estrangement between us there exists, and has existed, none, so far as I am concerned. From your conversation I have learnt more of practical politics than from that of any other person; and the recollection of pleasant days passed together at Hughenden long ago is one which will never leave me. An unreserved interchange of ideas on almost every subject; a general agreement in tastes, habits, and modes of thought; the ready recognition on my part of an intellectual superiority on yours founded at once on genius and experience; and the kindness which, as a young man, in the course of our earliest intercourse, I have always received from you, could not but leave behind them a very real, a lasting, and, I hope, a still subsisting, intimacy.

If within the last two years any semblance of alienation has arisen between us, it has been a semblance only, produced by causes which were intelligible enough to need no explanation, and which were and are consistent with the most friendly feeling.

The causes to which I allude are political, turning on the state of public affairs and the relations of parties.

I need not tell you that, both from personal feeling and from considerations of what a family owes to itself, I shall never, during my father's public life, connect myself with any party opposed to his. Had I entertained such a desire, the opportunity was offered 14 months ago. To withdraw from party politics is for me simply to retire into obscurity. So much for the possibility of being actuated by motives of self-interest.

Neither need I remind you of what since February, 1855, has been abundantly clear — the impossibility of your and my father's taking office, except in coalition with other leaders, and at the head of a larger following than your own. . . . That in such a coalition all moderate politicians might join, I see no reason to doubt. Permanent separation between us, therefore, there need be, and I hope there will be, none.

But in the meantime, between 1852 and now, many measures have been discussed in Parliament on which I have had the misfortune to differ from the great bulk of those whom you represent: I don't say from you individually, because it is impossible for me not to distinguish between what I must imagine to be your private convictions, and those in which your position compels you to acquiesce.

Church rates, religious tests in Parliament, religious tests for the Universities, the repeal of the newspaper stamp, the constitution of the army, the constitution of the Civil Service, Irish education, English education, are all topics which more or less call into play those deep-lying differences of temperament and opinion on which the more superficial differences of party are based. On all these questions I have been in a small minority, on some I have stood alone, among the members who sit by or behind you. . . .

The question I have now to ask myself is this : Can I with truth consider myself as a representative of agricultural Conservatism? If not, and if nevertheless I continue to hold the ostensible position of one, those who dissent from my views have just cause of complaint. . . . I came last year to the conclusion that a seat on the front Opposition bench was inconsistent with the political position into which I had gradually and half unconsciously passed : the same reason which made me leave that bench prevents my return thither.

I must be free to judge (though, of course, your opinion will carry no slight weight with it) as to the course to be taken about the Income Tax: Pakington's education scheme I am pledged to support: and if, as is likely, fresh debates on the purchase system arise out of the Report of the Commission on that subject, I fear I shall again find myself opposed to nearly all your supporters. It seemed to me that to receive as a *political* guest one thus circumstanced would embarrass more than it could either help or gratify you. Hence my refusal.

If, knowing these things, and understanding that they must be so, you renew your invitation, I need not say that I shall accept it with personal pleasure. . . .

Disraeli, who shared many of Stanley's opinions, was able to reassure him as to the amount of agreement implied in the acceptance of an invitation to a political dinner. Stanley consented to come, expressing his great satisfaction at being relieved 'from the most disagreeable of all sensations — that of a misunderstanding between friends.'

Disraeli was threatened with another secession from his political dinner-table. Pakington had an education policy of a liberal character which was supported by Disraeli and Stanley and Lytton, but bitterly opposed by a section of the 1852 Cabinet, headed by Henley. If National Education could not be treated as an open question among the Conservative leaders, Pakington wrote that he would have to retire from the front bench, and assert his opinions from another seat. Disraeli was able to placate him. 'I am opposed,' he wrote, 'to all secessions from the front bench of an Opposition. They never are happy in their results, and are always imputed to unworthy motives or looked on as a *coup de théâtre*.' The affair was not urgent, and even if it were the *cheval de bataille* of the party, he should deprecate giving any immediate notice. 'I shall count,' he concluded, 'on your presence on the 2nd, particularly as under my roof you will never meet the grim visage of our amiable colleague, Henley.'

To Derby, Disraeli was more outspoken about what he regarded as Pakington's inopportune persistence. Disraeli was full of his own schemes, and impatient of the alarums and excursions of others.

To Lord Derby.

GROSVENOR GATE, *Jan.* 28, 1857. — . . . I cannot bring my mind to Education at present. I am as sick of it as the country is. Nobody wanted it to be mooted till a new Parliament. The public wants to digest all the perplexities of recent debates, and John Russell's resolutions [1] were the climax of confusion, and there the curtain, for the present, ought to have fallen.

CARLTON CLUB, *Wednesday.* — I wrote this morning. I now return Pakingtoniana. I really have no head, at present, for this subject, so uncalled for and so inopportune.

Jolliffe, whom, I hope, you will see to-day, will give you, for your musing, my sketch of the campaign. If you adopt it, the Government will, probably, not be alive this day month; and even if we be defeated, we shall have got out of the mud of 1855, and, at least, be at the head of a powerful and popular Opposition. . . .

Disraeli's plan of campaign was in the main of a two-fold character, and calculated, in both its aspects, to attract Peelite support. He proposed, on the one hand, to attack the Government on their foreign policy, as turbulent and double-dealing; and, on the other, in concert with Gladstone, to insist on retrenchment, and especially on a reduction of income tax, on the principle that taxes granted for military purposes in time of war ought not to be levied in time of peace. He developed both lines of argument in the debate on the Address.[2] On foreign policy, he contrasted the expectations entertained when the Peace of Paris was signed with 'the wars and rumours of wars' which pervaded the Queen's Speech. There was a difficulty with Russia over the

---

[1] Russell had introduced, in the previous session, twelve resolutions as a basis for a system of National Education. They had rather a mixed reception, and in the course of the debates he surrendered the most characteristic portions of his scheme. He was advised by Disraeli to withdraw the remainder, but refused, and was beaten by a majority of over a hundred.   [2] Feb. 3.

treaty owing to a blunder of Clarendon's ; a difficulty between Prussia and Switzerland over Neufchatel, in which
a 'firebrand Minister' had nearly embroiled Europe in
war; Canton was blazing; Persia was invaded.   But his
main attack was on Ministerial policy towards Italy and
Austria.   Reverting to the raising of the Italian question
in a sympathetic fashion in the protocols of the Peace, he
startled Parliament by revealing the existence at the time
of a secret treaty with Austria.

Will it be believed that all this time, while Lord Clarendon
was listening to the passionate representations of Count
Cavour, in which he impeached the very existence of Austrian
rule in Italy — at the time when the noble lord, unable to
extricate himself from some fatal engagement into which he
had entered with Sardinia, found it necessary to commence
those protocols which have led to so much excitement, from
which so much was expected, and on which were wasted, I
may say, six months of the attention of the people of this
country — will it be believed that at this very time a secret
treaty was in existence guaranteeing to Austria the whole of
her Italian dominions ?

The guarantee, said Disraeli, was given by France, and
given not merely with the sanction and approval of
Palmerston and the British Government, but by their advice and at their special instance.   The Power that gave
the guarantee was the Power that was to aid Palmerston
in the great plan for the emancipation of Italy.   What
had happened in consequence of this ruinous imposture
on the credulity of the country ?   Ruthless assassinations,
unsuccessful insurrections, the death of many excellent
and of some brave and distinguished men, and an aggravation of the evils complained of.   The whole affair was
a great hoax — for the people of England. 'Generally
speaking, the noble lord extricates us from the embarrass-
ments he has himself created, and that is his great claim
to the public approbation.'
Palmerston, in his reply, twitted Disraeli with his powers
of imagination, and said that his statements about foreign

policy were mostly pure romance. He had been imposed upon by the *gobemouches* of Paris, and had discovered a treaty of which the Government had never heard till that moment.

So far are we from having advised the adoption of such a treaty that, if we had been consulted with reference to its conclusion, we should certainly have given advice in a precisely opposite direction. That treaty is entirely a romance — totally without the slightest foundation; except this, that I believe in the early part of the war with Russia, when the question was raised what line Austria should take in reference to the contest, communications did pass between the French Government and the Austrian Government with respect to the course which France might take if, after Austria should have joined the Allies, an insurrection were to break out in Italy; and the Government of France, I believe, then stated that they would in that case take no part against Austria, but would leave her in the complete possession of her Italian dominions. But there was no treaty entered into by France with respect to the Italian possessions of the Austrian Empire.

It is difficult to decide whether, in thus (as Disraeli said) treating a grave subject with 'ribald ridicule,' Palmerston was boldly bluffing, or whether his memory had failed him. Disraeli rejoined, a week later,[1] by giving the date on which the treaty was signed — December 22, 1854 — and by repeating that the British Government were privy to, and counselled, the whole of the negotiations, and were formally advised of the treaty. Palmerston, again, in Greville's words, 'flatly contradicted him, and with great insolence of manner,' but he had to make some substantial admissions. It was, he said, perfectly true that, about December, 1854, it was hoped that Austria would join offensively and defensively with England and France. The French Government did inform that of Austria that, as an honourable ally, it would not take advantage of any disturbance or insurrection in Italy; and, if such disturbance should break out, any French force in Italy at the time would act in concert with the Austrian forces there in putting down insurrec-

[1] Feb. 10.

tion.   This arrangement was known to the English Government, and the reply of France was fit and proper under
the circumstances.   The arrangement was embodied in
the shape of a convention, but it was doubtful if it was
ever signed at all.

Thus, as Lytton, with 'the affectionate and, if I may
say so, brotherly interest I take in all that concerns you,'
pointed out in a letter to Disraeli, Palmerston had already
admitted two facts he formerly denied : 'first, that there
was a treaty (or, to use Palmerston's expression, a convention — viz., a convention for a treaty) ; secondly, that
the Government knew it, and if not at their "instance,"
as you said, at least it had their approval.'

Palmerston had to make a still further retractation.
In Greville's words, 'two nights after,[1] Palmerston came
down to the House, and in a very jaunty way said he
must correct his former statement, and inform the House
he had just discovered that the convention *had been
signed*.   Great triumph, naturally, on the part of Disraeli,'
who insisted that the document was a treaty, and not,
as Palmerston described it, a mere military convention,
and that it had been extensively acted upon.   Thereupon Palmerston completely lost his temper — 'a rare
occurrence with him,' wrote Malmesbury, 'and which
makes me believe that he felt himself in a scrape' — and
talked absurdly about Disraeli's 'vapouring.'   This time
the Minister did not impose even upon his own party,
and Disraeli was seen to have sufficiently proved his contention.   Though, however, he obtained a personal success, it was felt at the time, and is clearly evident now,
that he greatly exaggerated the import of the treaty
which he had unearthed.   It was an arrangement — and
an unsuccessful one — to secure the desirable object of
Austria's aid to finish off the Crimean War ; and though
it placed Palmerston and Clarendon in rather an equivocal
position towards their Italian friends, Italian movements
against Austria could hardly expect active English sym-

[1] Feb. 12.

pathy while the war was in progress. The attitude of both France and England at the Conference of Paris showed that they did not consider the secret treaty to be in effective force after the war was over.

Disraeli's elation in penetrating a mystery must have affected his sense of proportion. His information was, of course, the result of his visit to Paris. But it was not, as Malmesbury imagined, derived from Walewski or from any French source. It will be remembered that the diplomatic world of Paris was specially warm in its welcome to Disraeli; 'all the diplomatists on their knees; all secrets told from all sides.' There was at that time in the British Embassy at Paris a very clever, attractive, well-informed, and ambitious young man, of Whig stock, but with Tory leanings, who proceeded at once to make himself useful and agreeable to the distinguished visitor. Ralph Earle attracted Disraeli in the same sort of way that Lennox had attracted him; but Earle was an abler man than Lennox. Confidential relations were soon established between the young diplomatist and the Opposition leader. Earle shared that taste for intrigue in high politics which was part of Disraeli's Oriental equipment; and he it was who furnished Disraeli with information about the treaty. Between the end of January and February 10, while the debates were in progress in the House of Commons, he wrote to Disraeli from Paris as many as half a dozen letters, several of them of considerable length, either unsigned or signed mysteriously 'X.,' supplying him with a constant series of facts and arguments on the subject. His conduct, as a member of the diplomatic service, in furnishing the Opposition leader with confidential material for a Parliamentary attack on the Government cannot be defended, though it may be excused on the ground of his youth; and Disraeli showed some lack of scruple and of delicacy in availing himself of such help. The political intimacy established in this way lasted for ten years, during which Disraeli forwarded Earle's political ambition, and Earle placed his abilities

and devotion at Disraeli's disposal, and was employed
by him in many services of a delicate and confidential
character.

Disraeli's absorption in the secret treaty and its Parliamentary fortunes somewhat annoyed Derby, who estimated more justly than its discoverer the true diplomatic
and political value of that instrument, and who was himself strongly bent on the second branch of Disraeli's
plan of campaign, the movement for retrenchment, which
was to bring Gladstone into line with his old party.
There had grown up a considerable agitation in the
country against what was called the 'War Ninepence,'
that being the amount which had been added to the rate
of income tax to pay for the war. It was feared that the
foreign difficulties, the Persian and Chinese wars, might
serve as an excuse for keeping the tax at a high figure.
Disraeli adopted, in his speech on the Address — and
maintained as the basis of his financial policy, in opposition and in office, for the next few years — the policy of
Gladstone's great Budget of 1853, which, it may be remembered, he had claimed at the time to be largely
founded on the same principles as his own Budget of
December, 1852.[1] A leading feature of Gladstone's
Budget was the reduction of the rate of income tax by
successive stages, with a view to its final extinction in
1860. During the war this scheme had perforce been
abandoned, and income tax had been raised, not lowered.
Now that the war was over, Disraeli proposed that the
settlement of 1853 should be resumed and adhered to.
He regarded that settlement as a 'compact' — though
Gladstone would not admit that it amounted to more
than a 'pledge' — under which, in return for the prospective abolition of income tax, Parliament consented to a
succession duty. He gave notice at once that he would
move resolutions against the continuance of war taxes in
time of peace, and in favour of adherence to the settlement of 1853. If his resolutions should be carried, 'I

[1] See Vol. III., p. 507.

think we shall give a great impetus to salutary economy, and shall in a most significant manner express our opinion that it is not advisable that England should become what is called "a great military nation." '

This policy was admirably calculated to attract, and succeeded in attracting, the support of Gladstone, whose communications with Derby culminated on February 7 in a four hours' conversation of a cordial character. It was also to some extent favoured by Russell, who maintained the soundness of the time-honoured system of Great Britain, to keep up low establishments during peace. But Cornewall Lewis's Budget, which proposed to reduce the income tax from sixteenpence to sevenpence, thus taking off the War Ninepence, rather spiked the Opposition guns. The joint wisdom of Tories and Peelites found some difficulty in drafting a satisfactory resolution; and the motion ultimately proposed by Disraeli, which demanded reduced expenditure in order to insure the abolition of income tax in 1860, was resisted by Russell and Francis Baring for the independent Whigs, by Bentinck and Tyrell for the independent Tories, and by Cardwell as an independent Peelite, and was lost on a division by eighty votes. Gladstone's attack in the debate was felt to be too passionate and undiscriminating to be effective; and there was sound sense in Lewis's argument that, as the arrangements of 1853 were based on the assumption of peace, they could hardly be regarded as holding good now that war, and all the consequences of war, in the shape of increased debt and increased annual charge, had intervened. Even Lewis's provision for the defence of the country was meagre, at a time when Continental nations were laying the foundations of the gigantic national armies which we see to-day; and there was a regrettable recklessness in the manner in which Disraeli and Gladstone, in order to restrain Palmerston from a 'turbulent and aggressive policy,' pressed for wholesale retrenchment. It was Palmerston's application of his doctrine that was at fault; the doctrine itself

was sound. Our army, as he said in the debate on the
Address, must be more than a domestic police. It must
be at least sufficient to protect us at the outset from
insult and attack. 'Depend upon it, for a country great
and rich to leave itself without the means of defence is
not a method to preserve peace in the long-run.' 'It
is the duty of a responsible Government, having determined the amount of army and navy which is essential
for the safety and interest of the country, to present to
Parliament the result of the conclusions at which they
have arrived;' and, he might well have added, to resign
office if Parliament refuses the supplies asked for. Disraeli would throughout his public life have subscribed
cordially to these sentiments; but in the course of his long
opposition to Palmerston he sometimes seemed in practice
to ignore them.

Neither of the branches of Disraeli's plan of attack
had proved particularly successful, save in strengthening
the relations between the Conservative leaders and Gladstone. Derby now took command of the strategy of the
party, and, in spite of Disraeli's hesitation, insisted on a
course of action which, while productive of apparent
initial success, reduced in the end still further the Conservative forces in Parliament.

There had been high-handed proceedings by British
representatives in China. At Canton — a port which, in
breach of the Treaty of Nankin, the Chinese refused to
open to commerce — a mandarin had arrested, on the
charge of piracy, the Chinese crew of the lorcha *Arrow*,
which was apparently flying the British flag, though its
right to do so was very doubtful. In reply to British
protests, the prisoners were released, but apologies were
refused, whereupon Canton was bombarded. By way of
reprisals the Chinese Governor offered rewards for the
heads of Englishmen. In return the British fleet inflicted
further punishment on the town and the forts, and a
local war with China began. Palmerston's Government
upheld the action of its servants in the East, but among

independent men there was widespread disapproval.
Peelites, especially Gladstone, and Radicals, were very
indignant; and there was an obvious opportunity, which
Derby, who shared their indignation, determined to seize,
of defeating the Government. Disraeli, though he agreed
that the proceedings were indefensible, advised caution.
He had not forgotten how a similar combination, seven
years before, against another high-handed proceeding, the
Pacifico affair, had only strengthened instead of weakening Palmerston's position. He must have feared that the
result would be the same now, and that, if Palmerston
were driven to the country, the popularity which he had
earned during the Crimean War would give him a triumph
at the polls. Of that popularity, Greville wrote on
February 27 that it was 'a fact beyond all doubt or
cavil,' while 'every one of the other public men who
have been, are, or might be, his rivals are absolutely unpopular. Nobody cares any longer for John Russell;
everybody detests Gladstone; Disraeli has no influence
in the country, and a very doubtful position with his own
party.'

Disraeli was overruled. Derby led the attack in the
Lords in one of his finest speeches, and subsequently
intimated to his reluctant party that he was prepared to
join with Gladstone or with anyone else with a view of
ousting the existing Government and forming a Conservative one. In the Commons Cobden was the pro-
tagonist, and he was supported by almost all the leading
men in the House—Russell, Gladstone, Graham, Sidney
Herbert, Milner Gibson, Lytton, and Roebuck—and by
such rising politicians as Robert Cecil and Roundell
Palmer. Disraeli was at first unwilling to speak, but,
when he had yielded to the persuasions of his friends, did
not let his disapproval of the party tactics affect the
vigour of his eloquence. Palmerston, who had, in his
half-century of political life, 'professed almost every
principle and connected himself with almost every party,'
had talked of an unprincipled combination against

him. But, said Disraeli, 'it will not do, the instant that the blundering of his Cabinet is detected, and every man accustomed to influence the opinion of the House unites in condemning him, to complain to the country that he is the victim of conspiracy.' Thus had he covered 'a weak and shambling case,' but he had laid down no principle on which our relations with China should rest. Disraeli, according to his wont, did consider those relations in a sober and philosophical spirit. He maintained that something more than energetic action was required of England in the Far East.

This country must dismiss from its mind the idea of dealing, as barbarous and uncivilized, with States with which Powers like ourselves [*e.g.*, Russia and the United States] have sympathies; and we must habituate ourselves to the idea of extending to countries like China the same diplomatic intercourse that we adopt with other nations. You cannot do that in a moment; it must be a work of time. . . . You are dealing with a country of immense antiquity. You have been reminded in the debate that China enjoys a civilisation of twenty-five centuries. In point of antiquity, the civilisation of Europe is nothing to that. But the result of those ancient habits and customs is an existence of profound ceremony and formal etiquette; and yet you expect that such a country will not be startled by the frank and occasionally, I am sorry to say, the brutal freedom of European manners. With a policy of combination with other powerful European States in attempting to influence the conduct of the Chinese by negotiations and treaties, it is my belief that ultimately, slowly but surely, we may attain our end.

When Disraeli spoke, on the last night of the debate, it was known that Government would be beaten, and it was anticipated that, if beaten, they would dissolve. However little he might like a prospect which others had rendered inevitable, at this stage boldness was the only possible course. Accordingly, he wound up his speech with a challenge to Palmerston to appeal to the country on a programme, as a Liberal leader, of 'No Reform! New Taxes! Canton Blazing! Persia Invaded!' Palmerston, who was defeated in the House by a majority of sixteen, took him at his word, with results

by no means satisfactory to the Conservative party.   To bully China was found to be as popular as to bully Greece had been.   Palmerston, in his address to the electors of Tiverton, described the provocation we had received in picturesque language : ' An insolent barbarian, wielding authority at Canton, had violated the British flag, broken the engagement of treaties, offered rewards for the heads of British subjects in that part of China, and planned their destruction by murder, assassinations, and poisons.'   That form of appeal proved more attractive than Disraeli's denunciation, in his election address, of a ' cruel and double-dealing policy,' or his not undeserved criticism of the Prime Minister :

Lord Palmerston is an eminent man, who has deserved well of his country ; but as Prime Minister he occupies a false position.   He is the Tory chief of a Radical Cabinet.   With no domestic policy, he is obliged to divert the attention of the people, from the consideration of their own affairs, to the distraction of foreign politics.   His external system is turbulent and aggressive, that his rule at home may be tranquil and unassailed.   Hence arise excessive expenditure, heavy taxation, and the stoppage of all social improvement.

His scheme of conduct is so devoid of all political principle that, when forced to appeal to the people, his only claim to their confidence is his name.

But it must fairly be said that Palmerston had other claims to confidence than his name.   His readiness to assume responsibility at a critical moment of the Crimean War, and his prosecution of the war to a successful close, were the real grounds of his political strength.   In the rough, but on the whole just, judgment of the country, Derby, Russell, and the Peelite chiefs—in fact, every possible leader except Palmerston, as Disraeli had loyally associated himself in public with Derby—had all failed in one way or another when put to the test.   The General Election of 1857, therefore, resolved itself into a *plébiscite* for Palmerston.   All his principal opponents of the peace party—Cobden, Bright, Milner Gibson, and W. J. Fox— were defeated at the polls.   So was Layard, who made

the mistake of being more warlike even than Palmerston, and so was a prominent Peelite, Cardwell. The one General Election since the Repeal of the Corn Laws in which the two wings of the old Conservative party worked in harmony, though not in coalition, resulted in a serious weakening of the Conservative forces. The mere fact of combination in any form with the distrusted Peelites diverted Conservative votes from Derby to Palmerston; and the Peelites themselves were dissolved as a party, only a few disconnected leaders reappearing in Parliament. Palmerston's popularity proved to be unbounded, and he returned with a personal following of 370 in a House of between 650 and 660.

Disraeli's own election was unopposed — 'a bloodless victory, but not less a triumph,' he told Mrs. Willyams. He was returned as the advocate of a policy concisely expressed in his address as one of 'honourable peace,' reduced taxation, and social improvement.'

To Mrs. Brydges Willyams.

GROSVENOR GATE, *March* 23, 1857. — . . . When all the hubbub is over, and men have settled down to their right position in the new Parliament, I suspect it will be found that there is a little difference in the relative strength and influence of parties, and that the same situation will be reproduced. Identical elements, in due time, will produce the same results. However, a man must be very prescient, who foresees the consequences of 650 popular elections. An election, a play, a race, a speech, to a certain degree, are always a chance.

Public appeals made in favor of a *name*, and not a *policy*, are convenient, but at the same time deceptive. A man returned pledged to support Palmerston really means nothing, for there is always the proper mental reservation, when Palmerston, in his, the pledger's opinion, is not wrong. It is not like a specific measure, the ballot, etc., which admits of no shuffling. . . .

Buoyant as ever, Disraeli refused to be cast down by the result of the elections. He had expressed the hope, in the House of Commons, that, inasmuch as party was the best guarantee for public and private honour, Parlia-

mentary parties would become more defined, and members would be returned with definite opinions. That he considered had, in fact, happened.

To Mrs. Brydges Willyams.

HUGHENDEN MANOR, *April* 13, 1857. — . . . I am by no means dissatisfied by the result of the General Election, strange and startling as they have been. They realise what I foretold : we shall now have a House of Commons with two parties and with definite opinions. All the sections, all the conceited individuals, who were what they styled themselves, 'independent,' have been swept away, erased, obliterated, expunged. The state of affairs will be much more wholesome, and more agreeable.

The Conservative party have got thro' the ordeal very well. Tho' numerically a little lessened, they are much more compact and united, and even as regards numbers, when a due occasion offers, will bring a larger force into the field than in the last Parliament. Altho' we had then 280 and more on the muster-roll, still, when the hour of battle arrived, we never could count on more that 220, the rest absent, or worse, against us. Now we have, I am assured by Sir William Jolliffe, the chief of my staff, 260 good men and true, fresh and not jaded by the mortifying traditions of the last Parliament.

Enough of all this. How are you, and your sweet and silent companions, roses and violets ? We were nearly paying you a visit, but must postpone it for a while, to go thro' a series of county visits which are the inevitable consequence of a General Election, and being returned Knight of the Shire.

To-morrow we go to Norman Court, Mr. Thomas Baring's, for two or three days, long promised, and then to the north of this county, to the Pauncefort Duncombes, of Brickhill Manor, who proposed me in 1847, and then to Colonel Hanmer of Stockgrove Park, who proposed me in 1857 ; then to the Chesters of Chicheley, and to the Lovetts of Liscombe, and the Dayrells of Lillingstone Dayrell, and a great many more, all of whom, by their ancestors, came in with the Conqueror, tho' Colonel Hanmer had an ancestor, or something like one, I find, much more interesting, for he married a Miss Ximenes, a descendant of Cardinal X., and yet a daughter of Israel notwithstanding, so I think he must have been quite gratified proposing me as member for Bucks. . . .

These visits to the territorial aristocracy who supported him in his own county gave Disraeli, the squire of Hughenden, immense satisfaction.

To Frances Anne Lady Londonderry.

HUGHENDEN MANOR, *April* 29, 1857. — . . . You won't be amused by the visits we have been paying to some of my principal supporters in the north of this county during the last few weeks : people you never heard of before, yet living with a refinement and splendor quite remarkable. Nothing more striking than some of your English gentry with châteaux, parks, and broad domains ; greater men by a good deal than many German Princes, and yet utterly unknown in London society : among these one of our greatest Bucks squires, a Mr. Pauncefort Duncombe, whose home was really radiant, and contrasted very much with Woburn Abbey, which he took me over to see, larger, but the most gloomy and squalid palace that you can conceive.[1]

One day we went to see Mentmore, which one of the Roths-childs is building, or rather has built, in the midst of the Vale of Aylesbury, a hunting palace, which will be to this county what Belvoir is to the vale of that name. But all that even *you* can recall or fancy of interior taste, splendor, and magnificence and curiosity of art, can give you only a faint idea of the reality of this gorgeous palace. I have been told, for more than fifteen years Rothschild has had agents in every part of Europe, regardless of cost, collecting its contents, but the taste of their distribution is as remarkable as their curiosity and costliness. The hall appears to one the masterpiece of modern art and decoration, glowing with colour, lit by gorgeous Venetian lamps of golden filagree that once were at the head of Bucentaurs. Such chairs — Titian alone could paint them, such clocks of lapis lazuli, such cabinets of all forms and colors, such marble busts of turbaned Moors, such a staircase of polished marble from this vast central saloon, for such it really is, glittering with its precious contents, and yet the most comfortable and livable-in apartment in the world. . . .

Since Palmerston had been at the head of affairs, Parliamentary Reform, which had been taken up by Russell as a Cabinet question after his defeat on Locke King's motion in 1851, had been again laid aside. This was natural enough during the war ; but its absence from the Government programme of legislation both in 1856 and in 1857 had been conspicuous, and was no doubt rightly attributed to the very tepid affection with which it was

[1] But see below, p. 421, for a more favourable verdict on Woburn.

regarded by the Prime Minister. Palmerston was faithful to what Disraeli at the end of the session of 1856 had called 'the Conservative principle which, without blind or bigoted adherence to the doctrine on all possible occasions, believes that tampering with the suffrage is a great evil to the State.' Disraeli, in these circumstances, conceived that the moment had now come when the Conservatives might take up, with advantage to the country and to themselves, a question which, at least ever since 1848, he had protested against regarding as the peculiar property of the Liberals. Accordingly, in his speech on March 31 on the hustings at Aylesbury — a speech which attracted special attention as a first attempt to substitute for the usual claptraps of hustings oratory such serious treatment of current politics as was usual in Parliament — he devoted considerable space to Reform, and offered his audience suggestions of which they might 'chew the cud.' He was opposed to 'bit-by-bit' reform, so dear to the Whigs, as he invariably found that it ended in a job; the Reform Act, for instance, put an end to the close boroughs of the Tories, but preserved those of the Whigs. If a large Reform Bill were brought forward by the Tories, the injustices of that Act might be remedied, and he should look at any great change in representation with no prejudice, though it was not advisable that the two parties should bid against each other. But he was opposed to two proposals of earnest reformers — electoral districts and the ballot. Disraeli followed up his speech by a letter to his chief, who had been laid up with a bad attack of gout during the election.

To Lord Derby.

Confidential. HUGHENDEN MANOR, *April* 21, 1857. — I hope you have quite recovered. . . . I wish you would think over this state of things very much. As Conservatives, it was not for us to disturb the settlement of 1832, but that settlement is disturbed, and, so far as 'true reformers' are concerned, is to be disturbed in a sense still more unjust than the existing arrangement.

I don't think the country, dinned to death with the unjust

representation of large towns compared with small ones, has the slightest idea of the real state of affairs: and nothing but discussion in Parliament in an authoritative manner can enlighten them. I suggest to you whether a juster apportionment of M.P.'s may not be the question on which a powerful and enduring party may be established: whether we should not at once originate such a discussion by a resolution something like the following (or by other means): 'That in the opinion of this House, in all measures for improving the representation of the Commons in Parliament, it is expedient that there should be a juster apportionment of members to counties and boroughs than at present exists': whether a notice of 'a resolution on the subject of Parliamentary Reform' should not be given the first night of the session: and that, whether the Queen's Speech refers to the subject or not. In either case it might convey to the Government the spirit in which we wish the reform should take place, and prove the strength of the Conservative view on the subject.

Also consider whether a reform, in such a spirit, would not be extremely beneficial to the Conservative party, as the present arrangement, which leaves the balance of power in small boroughs, which are ruled by cliques of Dissenters, seems fatal to the maintenance of the present aristocratic and ecclesiastical institutions.

I think it highly inexpedient that, if such a motion is made, we should at all meddle, at present, with the question of the suffrage; we should confine ourselves to the point expressed in the resolution.

But the question of the suffrage may be dealt with extensively, but in an eminently conservative manner.

If fifty members were added to the counties, by reducing the small boroughs to one member, and every ten-pound householder in the county population were annexed to a borough constituency, you would add much to the constituency of the boroughs, and greatly increase the Conservative power at the same time.

There are 10,000 other things to say, but I have roughly jotted down these materials for reflection. Our party is now a corpse, but it appears to me that, in the present perplexed state of affairs, *a Conservative public pledged to Parliamentary Reform*, a bold and decided course might not only put us on our legs, but greatly help the country and serve the State. But I am for beginning mildly — in a conciliatory spirit — giving the Government credit for justice and patriotism, and placing our case before them, that they and Parliament may not otherwise become pledged to a further development of the present unjust and injurious system. . . .

Remember the great effect produced by statements which I made in H. of C. in 1852 (on Hume's motion for Parliamentary Reform — *i. e.*, giving more members to great towns, and disfranchising small ones) as to the injustice of counties like N. Lincolnshire, etc., with 200,000 or 300,000 inhabitants, exclusive of separate town population, having only two members, when a lesser boro' with 20,000 or 30,000 inhabitants had the same number.

Lord J. R., when he introduced his R. Bill in 1853–54, referred to this view of the case, and acknowledged its justice. The more extensive view appears still more telling.

From Lord Derby.

Confidential.   KNOWSLEY, *April* 24, 1857. — . . .   The elections have undoubtedly given Palmerston a large majority, though rather of a heterogeneous character.   He has at present the game in his hand, and our object must be to make him play it in our sense.   The Peelite and Manchester parties are obliterated, but it would be a mistake to say that the House is divided into two parties only ; among the Liberals there are two divisions, the differences between whom must shortly become more marked than they are at present.   The old Whigs are far less numerous than the Radicals, and are proportionably afraid of them.   Pam has ousted Johnny from the command of the Whigs, and the necessities of the latter's position will make him bid for the support of the Radicals, with whom, however, he will never obtain a cordial acceptance.

Palmerston, on the other hand, would not be sorry to see him take this course, and, if he finds him committed to it, will take the line of great moderation, and lean upon Conservative support.   To encourage this tendency on his part, if it exists, and to foment divisions and jealousies between the discordant elements of the Government majority, must be our first object ; while we should carefully avoid multiplying occasions for their voting in concert, in opposition to motions brought forward by us.   Among our own friends there are many favourably disposed to Palmerston, and among the Palmerstonians proper there are as strong Conservatives at heart as any in our ranks ; and, looking to Palmerston's age and increasing infirmities, the oftener these can be brought into the same lobby, in opposition to Radical moves, the better for us and for the country.   This should be, I think, the leading principle of our policy during the present session ; to avoid attacks on the Government, and especially on Palmerston individually ; to profess a readiness

to consider candidly measures of internal improvement which
he may recommend; and to intimate, rather than profess,
our readiness to support him in resisting violent counsels
forced upon him by his colleagues or supporters.

This leads me to the particular question of Reform which
is discussed in your letter. My own opinion is that we shall
have *no* Reform Bill this session, but that Palmerston will
try to turn John Russell's flank by compelling him to show
his cards, and then promise to bring forward the subject of
Parliamentary Reform, after mature consideration by the
Government, in the session of 1858. If he takes this line, I
think we ought to support him in it. . . .

With the knowledge that there are two rival chiefs in the
field, and the probability that the question will be adversely
discussed between them, I think our obvious policy is to wait
till both of them have opened their budget, or at all events
committed themselves to some course; and on this account
I own I should deprecate the giving of any notice from our
side of the House, on the subject of Reform, on the first day
of the session, especially if it be not noticed in the Speech
from the Throne. We must, after all, look to our own adherents, and I do not think it would please them to see us
apparently anxious to take up the question, however they
may acquiesce in the prudence of meeting it with great forbearance, if brought forward by our opponents.

When we come to discuss the principles themselves which
we should lay down, I do not think there will be found much,
if any, difference between you and me. . . .

I think our two principles should be, adherence to the
present franchises for county and town respectively, and
approximation to a just proportion between the number of
representatives allotted to each. We ought to resist lowering the franchise, abolition of rate-paying clauses, and the
ballot. . . .

Derby thus damped down, as on so many previous and
so many subsequent occasions, his lieutenant's ardour
for a 'bold and decided course.' He was already showing a disposition towards that policy of keeping Palmerston in office as on the whole a Conservative Minister
which he erected after 1859 into a regular system, and
which incidentally obliged Disraeli to spend some of the
best years of his life in leading an Opposition which did
not seriously oppose. It is impossible to deny that there
was good sense in Derby's reasoning on this occasion;

and Palmerston adopted very much the course he anticipated, omitting Reform from the Queen's Speech, but
promising a Bill for 1858, and thus shelving, so far as he
could, debate for the present.   Disraeli, as Derby objected
to his taking the initiative, preserved a dignified silence
on the Address, but could not prevail on Malmesbury,
who was acting in the Lords for the gout-ridden Derby,
to do the same.   On this question of procedure Disraeli
displayed a characteristic contempt for the opinion of the
mediocrities among his late colleagues in Cabinet.

Lord Malmesbury to Lord Derby.

LONDON, *May* 4, 1857. — . . .   I saw Disraeli, and showed
him your letter, but I could not prevail upon him to call together our usual knot of Councillors to go over the Speech. . . .
   D. said it was sufficient for *him* and *me* to agree upon what
was to be done.   I would not, however, take that responsibility with his single backing, and I found that Eglinton and
Hardwicke were quite of my opinion.   We have, therefore,
made him ask Walpole, Pakington, and Lytton, to meet us
at Eglinton's house on Thursday morning to go over the
Speech. . . .
   I found Dizzy last night at the Carlton sitting at table with
the Duke of Buckingham, and in a very amusing mood.   It
seems he had come up on business for an hour, and went in
to speak to Taylor, who he was told was dining there.   To
give his own description: 'You find me poisoned and robbed.
God has made me blind.   I came in here expecting to find
Taylor.   I see a large man at dinner, and fall into the arms
of "Robert Macaire."   He forces me to drink a bottle of champagne with him, which always makes me ill, and then bor-
rowed £50 of me.'   It was worth £50 to see Dizzy's face. . . .

We were at the Duchess of Manchester's[1] on Friday night; a ball of very *haut ton*, and Mrs. Anson was there, very gay. I talked to her a good deal, and of the opportunity which was now offered to her husband, General Anson,[2] for showing those abilities which his friends always knew he possessed — a man of singular firmness and intrepidity. She was of the same opinion, and evidently saw, in the future, victories and a coronet. Alas! at that moment her husband had been six weeks dead. Hastening from the Hills to take command of the forces before Delhi, he was struck by cholera and carried off.[3]

Anson had been a *roué* in his youth, and of singular success. Then he took much to play, and, when he left England, had been long considered the finest whist-player in Europe. When the news first arrived, about ten days ago, and some were doubting whether Anson had sufficient experience for the occasion; the native army in revolt, the ancient capital of Hindostan in possession of the rebels, and the Great Mogul declared Sovereign; I said that for my part I had confidence in George Anson, because he had seen the Great Mogul so often on the ace of spades that he would know how to deal with him. All the world laughed very much, and Mrs. Anson sent off the joke to the General. Alas! alas! . . .

London is very gay: fêtes every night, and the Court itself at many, for the Prince of Prussia is here visiting his *fiancée*, the Princess Royal, and young Princes and Princesses require balls. There are also the Duke and Duchess of Montpensier, the King of the Belgians, his pretty daughter, the Princess Charlotte, and his son, the Comte of Flanders; also Princess of Hohenzollern-Sigmaringen and Schleswig-Holstein, etc., etc., so the Court is very brilliant. There is also a famous beauty here, the Comtesse Castiglione, who, having charmed the Emperor of the French, is now on a tour of conquest in foreign parts, and, as she is universally decried by all the grand ladies, I take it is of ravishing excellence.

The most remarkable fête of the season, and indeed of many seasons, was given by the Prussian Minister at Prussia House to the Queen and Court last Monday. We had the honor to be invited. It recalled old days of Carlton House splendor, fanciful illuminations, and golden fish in endless fountains. There was a pavilion two hundred feet long, lined with the most splendid trees and shrubs I ever saw — araucarias and Norfolk Island pines. . . .

---

[1] Wife of Disraeli's friend, Lord Mandeville, who had succeeded to the dukedom in 1855. See Vol. III., p. 117.

[2] Commander-in-Chief in India.

[3] On May 27.

The Opposition, as a whole, were content to throw the responsibility of dealing with the Mutiny on Ministers, though Ellenborough, as an old Governor-General, pressed in the Lords for more vigorous measures. But Disraeli, convinced that the troubles in India were deep-seated, and that, unless Parliament and the country came to realise them and insist on a change of policy, still more grave disasters might be apprehended, resolved to brave the reproach of faction, certain to be raised at this critical moment, and to expose the whole Indian situation, as he saw it, for the serious consideration of the House of Commons. Few speeches have ever been contributed to Indian debates in Parliament more worth study than that, three hours long, which he delivered on July 27.

It was essential, he said at the outset, to settle one point. Was this a mere military mutiny, or was it a national revolt? Did it spring from sudden impulse, or was it the result of organized conspiracy? Till these questions were answered, it was impossible to decide what measures the situation demanded. He was persuaded that the mutineers of the Bengal army were not so much the avengers of professional grievances as the exponents of general discontent. The old principle of our rule had been to respect nationality; but the Government of India of late years had alienated or alarmed almost every influential class. He deprecated talk of reconquering India. Glorious as the annals of our warfare in that country had been, what had been the nature of our 'conquest'?

I deny that, in a vulgar sense of the words, we have ever conquered India. . . . Our conquest of India in the main has been a conquest of India only in the same sense in which William of Orange conquered England. We have been called in — this happened very frequently in the earlier periods of our Indian history — by populations suffering under tyranny, and we have entered those kingdoms and principalities to protect their religion and their property. It will be found, in that wonderful progress of human events which the formation of our Indian Empire presents, that our occupation of

any country has been preceded by a solemn proclamation, and concluded by a sacred treaty, in which we undertook to respect and maintain inviolate the rights and privileges, the laws and customs, the property and religion, of the people whose affairs we were about to administer. Such was the principle upon which our Indian Empire was founded; and it is a proud as well as a politic passage in the history of Englishmen, that that principle has been until of late years religiously observed.

Our empire in India was, indeed, founded on the principle of *divide et impera*, in no Machiavellian spirit, but because of the number of independent states, of religions, and of languages, in the country. The Mohammedans and Mahrattas had failed in India because they had persecuted religion and confiscated land. England came in with a guarantee of the land and a pledge not to tamper with religion. But now everything in India had been changed, or attempted to be changed — law and manners, customs and usages, political organisations, tenure of property, and religion.

The causes which had produced discontent among all classes might be ranged under three heads: first, our forcible destruction of native princes; next, our disturbance of the settlement of property; third, our tampering with the religion of the people. These changes began about 1848, when it was necessary that the revenue of the Government should be increased. The doctrine of 'lapse' of the States of native rulers who died without natural heirs was invented, and the Hindu law of adoption set aside, first in the case of the Rajah of Sattara, and afterwards in some ten other cases, including the important state of Berar. The States were annexed and the riches of the rulers appropriated. This was done in the teeth of the remonstrances of some of the most experienced Anglo-Indians. Then, in regard to property, commissions had been issued to inquire into the titles of landed estates, and a great quantity of freehold land had been resumed by the Government. Here, too, the law of adoption had been abolished. Moreover, the hereditary

pensions of descendants of royal houses which we had dispossessed had been turned into annuities for life. As to tampering with religion, there was no objection among the Hindus to missionary enterprise, but to the union of missionary enterprise with the power of the Government. 'No taxation, however grievous, no injustice, however glaring, acts so dangerously upon the Hindu character as the persuasion that the authority of the Crown is exercised to induce him to abandon the religion he professes.' Now, the legislative Council of India, under the new system, had been constantly meddling with the Hindu religion. Under the national system of education recently established, the Scriptures had appeared in the schools, 'and you cannot persuade the Hindus that they have appeared there without the concurrence or the secret sanction of the Government.' Female education in India was also a dangerous measure to take in hand. There were two much more reprehensible acts: the first, the law that no man should lose his property on account of a change of religion; the second, the law permitting a Hindu widow to marry a second husband. These two laws, more than anything else, had disquieted the religious feelings of the Hindus, and a powerful society had been started to defend the religion of the country.

Then came the annexation of Oude. Whatever might be thought of the king's conduct, no right could be founded on that for dethroning him; for, by the treaty we had with him, the very matter of misconduct had been anticipated and provided for. Owing to that annexation the Mohammedan princes felt that they had an identity of interest with the Hindu Mahrattas. So the whole of the native princes, and also the proprietors, had a common interest against the English Government, and the peasant was alarmed about his religion. 'Never mind what were *your* intentions; the question is, what were *their* thoughts, what were *their* inferences?' The Bengal army was mainly recruited from Oude, and by the annexation the

sepoy lost a privileged position. The sending of mysterious symbols from village to village, and from regiment to regiment, showed there was a wide-spread combination. 'The people of India were only waiting for an occasion and a pretext. That occasion was furnished, and that pretext was soon devised.' The Russian war had disquieted the Indian mind. The English Government chose that time, not to tranquillise India, but to go to war with a great Mohammedan State, Persia, and to send troops to China and Pegu. Here was the occasion, and a pretext was found in the greased cartridges. 'The rise and fall of empires are not affairs of greased cartridges. Such results are occasioned by adequate causes and by an accumulation of adequate causes.'

As to the means to be adopted to meet the present emergency, in one sense there was no controversy, because all were agreed on the employment of force. But what amount of force? 'A merely military mutiny may be met by a merely military effort.' But this was a national revolt, and even for a military mutiny what Government proposed was hardly adequate. He recommended that there should not only be an advance from Calcutta through Bengal, but also an expedition advancing up the Indus, and that the militia should be called out and embodied. But force was not all that we should look to.

We may pour our legions and our fleets up the rivers and through the provinces of India; we may be successful; but to my mind we should add to that success and doubly strengthen our force — and I am prepared, for one, to give any support to Her Majesty's Government which they may require for that purpose — if at the same time we should say to India that supposes she is aggrieved and outraged, to India perhaps despairing of pardon: 'Although we will assert with the highest hand our authority, although we will not rest until our unquestioned supremacy and predominance are acknowl-edged from the Punjab to Cape Comorin, it is not merely as avengers that we appear.' I think that the great body of the population of that country ought to know that there is for them a future of hope. I think we ought to temper justice with mercy — justice the most severe with mercy the most indulgent.

India could not be governed by English regiments and European agency alone. The difficulty should be met boldly and completely.

The course which I recommend is this : You ought at once, whether you receive news of success or defeat, to tell the people of India that the relation between them and their real Ruler and Sovereign, Queen Victoria, shall be drawn nearer. You must act upon the opinion of India on that subject immediately ; and you can only act upon the opinion of Eastern nations through their imagination. You ought to have a Royal Commission sent by the Queen from this country to India immediately to inquire into the grievances of the various classes of that population. You ·ought to issue a royal proclamation to the people of India declaring that the Queen of England is not a Sovereign who will countenance the violation of treaties ; that the Queen of England is not a Sovereign who will disturb the settlement of property ; that the Queen of England is a Sovereign who will respect their laws, their usages, their customs, and, above all, their religion. Do this, and do it not in a corner, but in a mode and manner which will attract universal attention and excite the general hope of Hindostan, and you will do as much as all your fleets and armies can achieve.

Only a man of high imagination could, without ever visiting India, have grasped, so completely as Disraeli in this speech showed himself to have done, the native point of view; could have understood so clearly how Dalhousie's repeated annexations and well-intentioned reforms must have appeared to Hindus and Mohammedans, and by what means native opinion could best be conciliated and impressed. Subsequent Indian policy has largely followed the lines which Disraeli suggested. Dalhousie's policy of 'lapse,' then so much in vogue, was reversed when the Crown took over the Indian Government, with the result that there are no more loyal denizens of the Empire than the ruling princes of India. Moreover, that neglect of native feelings, customs, and religion, which Disraeli discerned and reprobated, has entirely disappeared. Careful attention to Indian susceptibilities is a special mark of the Supreme Government. In both these respects Disraeli has been vindicated, but in nothing

has he been more vindicated than in his recommendations affecting the Crown.

No more pregnant suggestion has ever been made about Indian government than his admonition to draw closer the relation between India and the person of the Sovereign. He knew that persons, not constitutional abstractions, Emperors, not Parliaments, impress the Oriental mind. To the following out of this policy, more, perhaps, even than to the increasing association of native Indians in the responsibilities of government, is to be ascribed the admirable harmony between Great Britain and India which we witness to-day[1]; and during his life all the principal steps were taken under Disraeli's auspices. The transference of the government from the Company to the Crown, and the issue of just such a royal proclamation as he recommended in his speech, were effected by the second Derby-Disraeli Ministry. When Disraeli became Prime Minister for the second time, he persuaded a reluctant Queen to sanction the visit of the Prince of Wales to India, thereby establishing a personal relation between the Indian princes and peoples and the heir to the throne; and in 1876 he carried through Parliament, in the teeth of much ill-informed scoffing, a Bill which added to the other glorious titles of an English King the dignity of Emperor of India. The great Durbar of 1911, in which the Emperor and his Consort appeared at Delhi in person to claim the fealty of the people, was the logical conclusion of Disraeli's policy. He knew that 'you can only act upon the opinion of Eastern nations through their imagination.'

Imagination was the last thing that the Whigs and Liberals of 1857 brought to bear on the crisis. Vernon Smith assured Disraeli that no native princes were engaged in the conspiracy, that the annexation of Oude had nothing to do with what had happened, that there was no national revolt, but a mere military mutiny. He ridiculed the idea of a Royal Commission, which would

[1] 1915.

necessarily supersede the Governor-General — and perhaps
this was not Disraeli's happiest suggestion; but of the
vital hint about the person of the Sovereign neither the
Minister nor any subsequent speaker took any notice.
Disraeli's motion was only for papers, and was in no sense
a motion of censure; but Russell, interpreting the general
feeling of a patriotic but unimaginative House, proposed
as an amendment, and carried unanimously, an address
to the Crown of support and confidence in the Government — 'one of those dry constitutional platitudes,' said
Disraeli, 'which, in a moment of difficulty, the noble
lord the member for the City of London mechanically
pulls out of the dusty pigeonholes of his mind, and shakes
in the perplexed face of a baffled House of Commons.'
The reproach of faction, which Disraeli had anticipated,
came not only from the Whigs, but from his own friend
and supporter, Thomas Baring, who had been chairman
of the Indian Committee, and had then and subsequently,
as was natural in a City magnate, upheld the cause of the
Company.

To Frances Anne Lady Londonderry.

CARLTON CLUB, *July* 31, 1857. — . . .   I have many things
I could say, if we were in your boudoir, but India is a whirl-
pool in which all merges — great or small.

The season is over, but Parliament will last a long time.
Everybody is alarmed and shocked at the private tone of the
Government, which is flippant.   Her Majesty sorely oppressed,
and believes, like her grandfather, she is destined to lose
provinces.

The Queen of Holland has been the heroine of the last
fortnight—indefatigably intelligent, and the *fête-champêtre* at
Orleans House the most considerable social incident since your
departure.   So much Royalty, that our friend, Lady Jersey,
seemed to me rushing about the gardens in perplexed ecstasy.

The Princesses, in fantastic hats, sat under the trees to
receive their guests; and never was a prettier Court circle.
The tables for the banquet — a variety of round tables — were
laid in a *bosquet*, surrounded with tall green trees; and, as
the day was burning, the site was delicious.   Everything was
well done, and the whole thing successful.

The Comte de Paris and the Duc d'Aumale came to me

after my Indian speech, which they heard on Monday, and
dined at Bellamy's! What do you think of that? Do you
know the young Ascanius? He is at present too slender,
being much above six feet; but his countenance is intelligent
and his manner simple but refined.

This is sad scribblement; but I must go down to the
House to fight about Sir Chas. Napier's despatches and Hindu
protests against Supreme Legislation about widows and converts.

The session was prolonged till August 28, but only a
small portion of the time was given to the question of
India. There was not, as Disraeli said, 'in the House
or in the country a due sense of the gravity of the
emergency.' The prolongation was mainly due to the
passionate opposition, led by Gladstone, to the Divorce
Bill; which, though of course it raised nice ecclesiastical
questions, was in its essence a Bill, not to legalise divorce
in England for the first time — that would have been a
matter of real principle — but to make it possible for the
ordinary man or woman to obtain a relief which was at
that time obtainable only by the rich. Disraeli's mind
was full of India, and he took no part in the discussion
of a Bill which he doubtless regarded as of comparatively
small moment, and in regard to which his own friends
were divided. Gladstone's mind was so full of the question of divorce that, to judge by the absolute silence of
Lord Morley's exhaustive *Life*, the thought of our
Indian Empire and its perilous situation hardly found
any lodgment there. Could there be a more illuminating
commentary on the differing genius of these eminent
rivals than their simultaneous absorption in subjects so
widely apart and of such different political consequence?

As the autumn advanced, the news from India grew
worse. It became evident that, in spite of Vernon
Smith's assurances, many dethroned princes, their heirs
and widows, had become tainted with the spirit of disaffection. The sinister figure of Nana Sahib, the adopted
son of the ex-Peishwa of Poona, appeared, massacred
the garrison of Cawnpore, and issued the most blood-

thirsty proclamations. Sarah Disraeli wrote on September 2: 'This sanguinary "Fakredeen"[1] who has issued out of his castle at Bithoor to regain "his rights," and this proclamation, begin to look something like a national revolt to the meanest capacity.' Happily the bulk of the civil population, whatever their grievances, remained quiet.

To Frances Anne Lady Londonderry.

HUGHENDEN, *Sept.* 16, 1857. — . . . I wish, like you, I could console myself with reading novels, or even writing them; but I have lost all zest for fiction, and have for many years. I have never read anything of Dickens except an extract in a newspaper, and therefore I cannot help to decide on the merits of *Little Dorrit.* . . .

One ought not to prophesy about India, when probably the new mail has by this time arrived, tho' it has not reached me; for altho' little more than 30 miles from town, I live in a forest, or what once was one — but I take a gloomy view of affairs. The Ministers underrated the business from the first. They are in a scrape, and trying to get out of it by the bullying of *The Times.*

I cannot altogether repress a suspicion, tho' it is only for your own ear, that many of the details of horrors, which have so outraged the sensibility of ʼ ̤ ̤ ̤ ̤ ̤ are manufactured.

The striking story of Skene at Jhansi, his deeds of heroic romance, worthy of a Paladin, then kissing his wife and shooting her, etc., etc. — all appear, now, to be complete invention. This story has produced a great effect in this neighborhood, and, I doubt not, in all others, and I dare say stimulated subscriptions, as it certainly has the warlike passions of the people. We must remember Captain Jenkins's ears. He appeared without them before the House of Commons, and the House declared war against Spain in consequence. It afterwards turned out that he had lost them in the pillory, and deserved to do so.

The details of all these stories is suspicious. Details are a feature of the Myth. The accounts are too graphic — I hate the word. Who can have seen these things? Who heard them? The rows of ladies standing with their babies in their arms to be massacred, with the elder children clutching to their robes — who that would tell these things could have escaped? One lady says to a miscreant: 'I do not ask you to spare my life, but give some water to my child.' The child is instantly tossed in the air and caught on a bayonet! Those

[1] See Vol. III., pp. 42–47.

hesitation declare my humble disapprobation of persons in
high authority announcing that upon the standard of England 'vengeance,' and not 'justice,' should be inscribed. . . .
I for one protest against taking Nana Sahib as a model for
the conduct of the British soldier. I protest against meeting
atrocities by atrocities. I have heard things said and seen
things written of late which would make me almost suppose
that the religious opinions of the people of England had
undergone some sudden change, and that, instead of bowing
before the name of Jesus, we were preparing to revive the
worship of Moloch. I cannot believe that it is our duty to
indulge in such a spirit.

In other respects the line of the speech was that all
the subsequent news from India had justified his original
appreciation of the gravity of the crisis; but, though he
foresaw evil, he did not counsel despondency or despair.
He believed that the country was now roused to the real
nature of the rebellion, and would therefore take steps
to vindicate our imperial power. Palmerston apparently,
however, according to Greville's gossip, reported to
Disraeli by Lennox on September 27, still laughed at
there being any real danger. Lennox continued: 'Pam
seems low in C. G.'s estimation, but he says nothing else
will or can go down. That everyone says he is the only
man possible; there is no one could take his place.
Derby he considers quite an impossibility. Were it not
for the general feeling that no one could follow him, he
thinks more disasters in India would rub Pam's prestige
off.'

To Lord Henry Lennox.

HUGHENDEN, *Oct.* 2, 1857.—. . . C[harles] G[reville]'s facts
are always more valuable than his opinions, or rather what
he chooses to circulate as his opinions, for he does not always
pronounce what he believes. I am not, however, surprised
that he should say what he does about Derby; nevertheless,
I recollect that in January, 1855, he used to several persons,
and among them, I think, to yourself, exactly the same
phrase. Nevertheless, we know what occurred in a couple
of months.

Returning from Ashridge, I contrived to pass a day at
Chicheley and dine with the farmers at Newport Pagnell, and,

tho' the assemblage was intensely bucolic, managed to say a few words in the right direction, tho' with great difficulty and caution.

Mill's opinion, or that of any E.I. Director, goes for nothing, and no £ s. d. view can now affect this question. What the fate of the Government may be I do not foresee: what it ought to be is not very difficult to pronounce. The act which brought about the rebellion is entirely attributable to them, and they ought to be held responsible for it. V[ernon] S[mith]'s words, in answer to me, remain: 'There is not the slightest reason to suppose that the annexation of Oude has anything to do with this outbreak.' Every paper now says that Oude is the centre of the rebellion. . . .

To Sir John Pakington.

HUGHENDEN, *Oct.* 6, 1857. — I read your speech to-day with great satisfaction. I am glad we are agreed. I am confident that, if the party will only act like sensible men, they may attain a far higher position than any that, for years past, they have held. What could be a more sure basis for public confidence, and a more glorious claim for a nation's gratitude, than to restore that Empire in India which the Whigs have all but lost?

I see old Henley is at his tricks again. It is really intolerable that, because his father was an E. Ind. shipbuilder, the party is to be broken up at such a crisis. He it was who mainly threw us in 1853 into that painful minority on Stanley's motion for the postponement of legislation until the inquiry was concluded — a motion which, if largely supported, would have been now a stepping-stone to power, and the defeat of which, I really believe, was the true cause that Stanley refused my proposal in 1856 to bring forward the Oude case. However, I am resolved that Henley shall not again play this game. The Government of India must be one of the main-springs on which any Ministry can now be formed, and I have myself not a doubt that, if the Tories go straight on this, and hold together, the defection from the commercial ranks of the Government will be large. . . .

It was with the utmost difficulty, and only by the forbearance and aid of Mr. Rose, that I prevented, before I left town, the *Press* being sold to that lot of mysterious capitalists who are buying up all the Tory papers, or in all probability by this time it would be writing up the E.I. Company and Lord P. As it is, I do not know whether this may not yet happen before Parliament meets. It will be a great blow to us.

To Lord Henry Lennox.

TORQUAY, *Nov.* 7, 1857. — . . . The Government, of course, wish to make the Company a scapegoat, and are feeling their way to that end. This must not be allowed. At the same time, it is not for us to vindicate the Company. If the motion of Lord Stanley, brought forward, at my request, in 1853, had been carried, the double Government would not have been in existence. This is a strong point in our position.

There are two questions as regards the government of India: one of administration, the other of policy. We have always opposed the administration of the Company, and what has occurred renders it still more expedient to reconstruct that administration; but the primary cause of the present disasters is policy, not administration, and Downing St. is responsible for policy. The question of administration will arise when that of policy is settled. The policy should be first censured, and, if Parliament sanctions such a course, the censurers will be responsible for the construction of a new administrative system. . . .

To Mrs. Brydges Willyams.

HATFIELD HOUSE, *Nov.* 23, 1857. — We came down here in the same carriage as Lady Stuart de Rothesay, the mother of Lady Canning. She was, as usual, very agreeable and chatty, and told us endless tales of Calcutta, and all the adventures of this perilous crisis.

One thing she said particularly amused me. She was very indignant at a statement made in Exeter Hall by Lord Shaftesbury, that mutilated Englishwomen were constantly arriving at Calcutta, and that he had read in a letter of Lady Canning that there were more than thirteen English ladies with their noses cut off at that moment at the Presidency. Lady Stuart said that there was not the slightest authority for this statement of Lord Shaftesbury, and that Lady Canning had never alluded to the subject in any letter.

In consequence of this statement of Lord Shaftesbury, a surgeon wrote to the Ladies Committee for the Relief of the Indian Sufferers, of which Lady Stuart de Rothesay is a member, stating that he had great experience in the formation of artificial noses, that he was ready to give all his skill, time, and devotion, to the cause, but as the machinery was rather expensive, he hoped, in accepting his services, the Committee would defray the prime cost of the springs! He then gave a tariff of prices, and offered to supply noses for English ladies by the dozen, and, I believe, even by the gross. . . .

Parliament was unexpectedly called together in the beginning of December, not in order to deal with the Mutiny in India, but because, as in the autumn of 1847, ten years before, the Government had found it necessary, in order to cope with a commercial crisis, originating in the present case with failures of banks in the United States, to authorise an issue of notes by the Bank of England in excess of the £14,000,000 prescribed by the Bank Charter Act. Derby wrote on November 15 to ask for Disraeli's opinion on the course which the party ought to pursue in Parliament. Attention could not be confined to the currency question. 'I own,' he continued, 'I think myself that we have arrived at a stage in Indian affairs in which we have a full right to inquiry both as to the past and the future, and when, without laying ourselves open to any imputation of faction, we may fairly challenge the Government to vindicate the measures they have adopted in the East, including the forgotten China!'

To Lord Derby.

TORQUAY, *Nov.* 18, 1857. — Our party is pledged against the Bank Charter Act by the course pursued by them in 1847, and also by the standing policy of the country gentlemen, which is adverse to a restricted currency. Nevertheless, in my opinion, the present Act has nothing to do with the existing state of affairs, and had it not been in force, a crisis equally disastrous would probably have occurred, and we should have been driven to £1 notes, as in 1825.

I doubt the expediency of fixing upon any particular rate of interest as the period of interposition, and, indeed, I question the propriety of the power of suspension in anybody being recognised. We should, I venture to think, support the policy advocated in 1847 — *i.e.*, a recurrence to the state of things existing before the Act of 1844, which we then held as aggravating evils at periods inevitable in a country of great commercial transactions.

The suspension of the Act by the present Government I look upon as rather pitiful, and I think, with their opinions, they ought to have been firm. The suspension by our friends, if they had been in office, would have been a consistent and, in their views, a beneficial course. The present state of

affairs is a triumph for the opinions advocated by Ld. G. Bentinck and Mr. Thomas Baring in 1848.

If by any chance you have a copy of G. B.'s biography at hand, you will find some curious details, which may be of use at this moment, regarding that similar period.[1]

I believe, if the Government had been firm, and that all the joint stock banks and the re-discounters of Lombard Street had suspended payment, which they would infallibly have done, that with the present produce of the mines you would have had money at 2 per ct. this time next year, and for an enduring period. This would have been much better for the country gentlemen than an inflated currency, but, without knowing it, they always play the game of the commercial gamblers.

I think the position taken up generally by our friends, that the currency of the country ought to expand with the commerce of the country, and that what might have been expedient in 1844 is not suited to 1857, is a fallacy. Currency always does expand with the commerce of the country. Bank notes are a very small portion of the currency of the country. That is represented mainly by bills of exchange, which always necessarily bear a due relation to the commercial transactions.

Peel's limit of 14 mill. was fixed, if I am not mistaken, upon returns, which proved that under no circumstances of pressure had the Bank circulation been reduced to that amount, which described also the amount of the Government debt to the Bank.

After all, what is wanted now is not currency, but capital.

There is, however, one subject of speculation the interest of which, at this moment, cannot be too highly imagined. What light does the present monetary condition of the country throw upon those vast returns of exports and imports which have been so ostentatiously paraded before us during the last seven years, accompanied by simultaneous assurances that trade was never in so healthy a state.

I agree with you entirely that we must not permit the impending session to be a merely monetary campaign. The whole policy of the Government must be opened — but tho' there are for the Cabinet, at the present moment, many points of difficulty, in Parliament all will be merged in that of India. . . .

I ventured in the H. of C. in the month of July to lay

---

[1] Derby, in his reply from Knowsley, Nov. 24, wrote : ' We have not here your biography of G. Bentinck, but it is in St. James's Square, and I have asked Stanley, who goes up to town to-morrow, to send it me down here ; and before we meet I will refer to the passages to which you allude.'

down that no measure would be efficacious unless we first ascertained the cause of the outbreak, and I staked my opinion that the paramount and proximate cause was to be found in the annexation of Oude. The Government expressed their astonishment at the bare suspicion of such a cause, and distinctly gave it as their opinion that Oude had nothing to do with the affair. At present it is generally held that my statement was justified.

But what has been the consequence of the Government attempting to quell a rebellion, of the cause of which they were not cognisant?

The insurrection in Oude cut off all their communications with the Upper Provinces. They have never been able to send a man to Delhi from the Metropolis. Had they recognised the annexation as the prime cause, acting, of course, on discontented materials long brooding, they might have sent troops early in the year overland, perhaps, to Bombay, forwarded them up the Indus, and through countries where camels abound; descended on Delhi, then on Oude, and prevented all the disasters that have occurred and the still existing dangers. At present, having assumed an erroneous basis for their operations, there seems a chance of the blunders of the Crimea being repeated on a larger scale — for the means of transport from Calcutta are very deficient, and we may find that we have a large army at the capital and none in the provinces.

I think on the first night the Indian case ought to be opened in both Houses.

You told me to write fully, and I have endeavored to do so without reserve, though very roughly. After all, a good talk together is better than all the letters in the world, but these are suggestions which you can, if you think them worthy of it, turn in your mind, and may lead, when we meet, to perhaps less crude conclusions. . . .

CARLTON CLUB, *Friday, Nov.* 27, 1857. — . . . I apprehend any unnecessary declaration against the Company, at this moment, would be extremely impolitic. Whatever the faults of the 'double government' the causes of the present calamities in India are attributable to the policy of the Cabinet. Who annexed Oude? Who sent the soldiers in sailing vessels? Who scornfully neglected the overland passage? . . .

When Parliament met on December 3, Disraeli criticised the Government both about the suspension of the Bank Charter Act and about their Indian policy on the

lines of his letter to Derby. He was especially severe on the feebleness of the course proposed with regard to the Bank Charter Act.

We shall be doing exactly what we did in 1847.[1] In 1847 the country was panic-struck and half ruined. Parliament was called together, and the country looked to it for the expression of some distinct opinion. A Committee was appointed. Ten years have elapsed. The same occurrence takes place. Parliament is again called together; and what is Parliament, and what are Ministers — the most influential members of Parliament — about to do in the difficulty? Again they are going to evade doing that which is the duty of every statesman in this country: to lay down in this House the opinion which they have formed on the subject, and to call on the House to maintain that opinion. Instead of that — and I deeply regret it — we are to have another Committee on the Bank Charter Act of 1844; and I suppose that in 1867, after a repetition of the same mischance and the same miseries, the same fruitless and bootless process will be adopted of appointing a Committee on that subject in this House.

There is much good sense in this criticism, and Disraeli followed it up by a motion that it was desirable to legislate at once without further inquiry. The motion was lost by a large majority, in spite of the exhaustive and ingenious manner in which he developed his abstruse subject. The course which the debate took made failure inevitable. The legislation which Disraeli desired was the repeal of the Act; but Gladstone rose and called for legislation to uphold it and increase its stringency; and between these two extreme views the Government had little difficulty in persuading the House that the safest course was to appoint a Committee. The apparently illogical plan of enforcing the Act in quiet times and issuing a licence, subject to a subsequent indemnity, to break it when matters are critical, has justified itself by its persistence; and after this unsuccessful protest in 1857 Disraeli ceased to tilt at it. He had been hampered throughout the discussions by an attack of his old enemy, influenza.

[1] See Vol. III., Ch. 1.

show, as indeed Disraeli had already recognised, the enormous practical inconvenience of the existing system of double government, the Board of Control on the part of the Cabinet, and the Court of Directors on that of the Company. The great majority of 318 to 173 by which Baring's amendment was defeated [1] sounded the Company's knell, even though the Bill itself, and the Premier who introduced it, disappeared almost immediately in an entirely unlooked-for Ministerial convulsion.

Before this happened, Prince Frederick William of Prussia and the Princess Royal, whose engagement had been announced just before the outbreak of the Mutiny, were duly married. It was a fateful alliance, charged, in spite of the admirable qualities of bride and bridegroom, with the seeds of evil for the countries of both; but there was no presentiment then of anything but good, and the Disraelis entered with zest into the accompanying festivities.

To Frances Anne Lady Londonderry.

Saturday, Jan. 23, 1858. — On Wednesday we were at the Bridal Ball at Court. It was more brilliant than numerous, being, as I thought, unbecomingly limited; for the new ball room was only half full, and all the other rooms were open and empty. However, I liked it, for I got a seat. There were as many Princes as at the Congress of Vienna. The royal party did nothing but dance with each other, and I thought, perhaps in consequence, looked bored. I saw the Princess of Prussia cram her pocket-handkerchief into her mouth to stifle a yawn. The Princess Royal, however, looked bright and gay, tho' I understand she is continually crying about leaving home; but then, they say, she is very childish and always cries.

The Queen rather expands too much in form, but she danced with the Prince of Prussia [2] and some others.

One of the Princes, the Duke of Brabant, a tall and otherwise good-looking young man, has so long a nose that it startles everyone who meets him, and makes the women almost scream. It is such a nose as a young Prince has in a fairy-tale, who has been banned by a malignant fairy, or as you see in the first scenes of a pantomime, or in the initial letter of a column of *Punch.*

---

[1] Feb. 18, 1858.   [2] Afterwards William I., German Emperor.

Lord Stratford de Redcliffe was there, and made a sensation. He came up to me and revived an old acquaintance. Still a very comely man, and had on the finest coat that was ever seen since Joseph's jacket.

A few days before we assisted at another royal party, tho' of a different character — a dinner at which we met all the illustrious exiles of France : the Duchess of Orleans, the Count of Paris, his brother the D. of Chartres, and the D. and Duchess of Aumale, and full suites.   The circle was, however, very agreeable, the guests to meet them choice, among them, by-the-by, Cardinal Wiseman, and the banquet not to be surpassed in splendour or *recherche* even at Windsor or B. Palace.   It was rather curious to dine with a Cardinal at Gunnersbury.[1]

Kielmansegge gave me, in confidence, a most interesting description of the audience at which, after so many years, the jewels were restored to Hanover.   The Queen herself was present, and the Prince; V[ice] Chancellor Page Wood,[2] and Garrard, the jeweller.   The jewels were all valued, and the aggregate £160,000; they were those which the Queen constantly wore in state, and of which she was most proud. When it was impossible longer to retain them, she behaved very well; thanked K. for the tact and regard for her feelings and convenience he had shown throughout, and said that from the first she had always been of opinion that she was not entitled to them.   I believe it was Melbourne who, in his off-hand way, advised her to keep them.   K. has got them all sealed up at Grosvenor Place, and is so nervous that he can't sleep o' nights.

Persigny[3] seized upon me at the Palace, and took me to a corner, where for half an hour he dilated on the theme that, if we would not introduce an Alien Bill, we must prepare for the worst, so far as France is concerned.

Heaven knows what will happen!   We have enough on our hands.

What was about to happen was in some respects a repetition of what happened in the winter of 1851–52. Palmerston's excessive complaisance to the Emperor Napoleon III. was once more to result in placing Disraeli in office.

[1] Baron Lionel de Rothschild's house.
[2] Afterwards Lord Chancellor Hatherley.
[3] French Ambassador.

CHAPTER V

CHANCELLOR A SECOND TIME

1858

Few things appeared more improbable, to judge by the events of 1857, than the return of the Conservatives to office early in 1858. Palmerston's personality and policy had received an emphatic endorsement from the electorate in the spring; and the stirring events of the subsequent months — the Indian Mutiny and the Chinese War — were apparently calculated to confirm the rally of people and Parliament to a patriotic Premier. But, to use one of Disraeli's favourite phrases, 'there is no gambling like politics.' On the night of February 18, 1858, the Government India Bill was read a first time, in spite of the strong protest of the Opposition, by the handsome majority of 145. As Palmerston walked home after the division, he was told by Bethell, his Attorney-General, that, like a Roman Consul at a triumph, he ought to be accompanied by a slave to remind him of his mortality. The reminder came the very next night, when, on the second reading of the Conspiracy Bill, he was defeated by a majority of 19, and driven to resignation.

Palmerston's position had not been really so strong as it seemed. His great personal success at the elections had made him careless and arrogant. A swaggering speech which he delivered at Guildhall on Lord Mayor's Day had offended the judicious; and judicious and injudicious alike were scandalised by his appointing to a seat in the Cabinet a man who, in the Prince Consort's words, was 'looked upon as a reprobate.'

To Frances Anne Lady Londonderry.

HUGHENDEN MANOR, *Jan.* 7, 1858. — . . . The succession of Lord Harrowby is, at present, the crisis of the Cabinet difficulties, but it is certain that a week ago Lord Lansdowne was on the point of retiring. The appointment of Lord Clanricarde has greatly injured the Government, but I hear that everything was tried, and everybody sounded, before it was decided on. Among others, the post was offered to Lord Overstone: when all failed, Lady Palmerston rallied, and made a successful charge, and carried her *protégé*. There is nothing like female friendship — the only thing worth having. . . .

Though the Clanricarde appointment and his own arbitrary behaviour had diminished Palmerston's popularity, these things would hardly by themselves have effected his overthrow. That was the result of a crime in France, for which the blame was largely thrown on England. On January 14 an unsuccessful attempt, resulting, however, in the death of several onlookers, was made in Paris to assassinate with bombs the Emperor and Empress of the French. The conspirators were Italians, members of the secret society of the Carbonari, to which Louis Napoleon had once himself belonged; but Orsini's plot had been concocted, and his bombs had been manufactured, in England. Very naturally, there was an outburst of anger in France against *perfide Albion*, who sheltered regicides. Colonels of the French army uttered violent threats, and their addresses were printed in the official *Moniteur*. Public feeling in England turned from sympathy with the Emperor to indignation against the French. Earle, from the Embassy in Paris, kept Disraeli informed of what was going on; that the British Ministry had promised the Emperor a measure directed against the refugees in England; that public opinion in France was strongly anti-English; that the Emperor's dread of assassination had redoubled.

When the session was resumed on February 4, Palmerston, mistaking, for once, the temper of the British people,

gave notice of his intention to bring in a Bill to amend the law of conspiracy. As the law then stood, conspiracy to murder was only a misdemeanour, and the Bill proposed to make it a felony, punishable by penal servitude for life. This was in itself a reasonable proposal; but John Bull never relishes making even reasonable concessions in response to menace, and on the introduction of the Bill, not merely free-lances like Roebuck and Kinglake, but even the old Whig leader, Russell, strongly opposed it. The threats of the French Colonels had been followed up by a despatch from Walewski, the Emperor's Foreign Minister, in which he pointedly asked whether the right of asylum ought to protect 'assassination reduced to a doctrine, preached openly, practised in repeated attempts, the most recent of which has struck Europe with stupefaction?' Was hospitality due to assassins? Should English law favour their designs? The Government had neglected to reply to this intemperate outburst, and the omission was strongly resented in England. Disraeli said in the debate that it should have been answered 'in some immortal State paper, breathing the fire and logical eloquence of a Canning.' He would vote for the first reading because he wished to maintain the Anglo-French Alliance, the key and corner-stone of modern civilization. But the Government had, in his opinion, acted in a clumsy and feeble manner; they had alarmed England without pleasing France; and he reserved his liberty of action on the subsequent stages of the Bill. The first reading was carried by a majority of 200,[1] as the bulk of the Conservatives voted with Ministers. The ten days that elapsed between the first and second reading produced a great hardening of public opinion against the Government. Palmerston, arrogantly relying on his majority and on his personal popularity, paid no heed; and his foes, of different parties, saw their opportunity. Milner Gibson, a Radical who had lost his seat in the previous year because of his opposition to the man of the hour,

[1] Feb. 9.

gave notice of an amendment which expressed no opinion
on the Bill, but censured Ministers for not answering
Walewski's despatch before bringing their Bill in.   Derby
realised at once what might happen, and was perturbed.
Gibson's motion, he wrote to Disraeli, was of the utmost
importance, and demanded the most wary walking on the
part of the Conservatives.   He was urgent that the debate
should be postponed, to give time for consideration before
the leaders or the party should be committed.   'C'est le
commencement de la fin,' he added.

Disraeli overbore Derby's hesitations.   The issue was
now changed.   Whether the Conspiracy Bill was reasonable or not was no longer in question.   Walewski's
despatch was still unanswered; the Government had
failed to interpret the feeling of the country.   It was a
matter of confidence.   If not on the India Bill, on which
debate was proceeding, then on Gibson's amendment
Palmerston's power must be broken.   'There must now
be no shilly-shallying, but heaven and earth, and all
below, moved for the issue,' Disraeli wrote to Lennox,
adding: 'There are great defalcations in the Ministerial
camp.'   He found no difficulty in reconciling his vote for
the first reading with his support of Gibson's amendment.   Ten days before, he said, it had been a question
between the Parliament of England and the Government
and people of France; and the way in which the House of
Commons agreed to the introduction of the Bill proved
their sincere sympathy for the people and their decorous
respect for the Emperor.   Now they were free to offer,
without the possibility of misinterpretation, their opinions
on the conduct of the British Minister.   There was no
valid excuse for the persistent omission to answer a
despatch which had been published to our detriment
everywhere in Europe.   It was now a question between
the House and the servants of the Crown.   Had they, or
had they not, done their duty ?

By 234 votes to 215 the House decided [1] that they had

[1] Feb. 19.

not done their duty; not only Graham and Gladstone, but as many as 84 Liberals, including Russell, voting against Ministers. Once again Palmerston had been defeated by a combination of all the most eminent men in the House of Commons. This time no dissolution was possible, and the Government resigned immediately.

To Mrs. Brydges Willyams.

GROSVENOR GATE, *Feb.* 20, 1858. — Ever since the meeting of Parliament, the 4th of this month, there has been an unceasing battle, and the struggle concluded last night in the signal defeat of the Ministers.

What will happen I know not, but it is a curious circumstance, and I hope it may be a coincidence, that on Sunday, the 21st Feb., 1852, Lord Derby was sent for by the Queen to form a Ministry, and on Saturday, the 20th Feb., 1852, I dined with the Speaker, a state banquet to the leaders of the Opposition ; and, strange to say, I am going thro' the same ceremony to-day — that is to say, if I can keep awake. I am very tired, not having got to bed till nearly four o'clock, and having had to rise from a troubled slumber very early. For the last fortnight there has been little opportunity for sleep or food — and I almost fear you will scarcely make out this scrawl — but I am very well, and hope you are.

On this occasion Disraeli was free from one anxiety. With or without extraneous help, with or without a majority in Parliament, Derby felt himself bound to accept office, if the Queen, after deliberation, thought fit to impose the task upon him. He was summoned to the Palace at once.

From Lord Derby.

Confidential. Saturday, 8 *p.m.* [*Feb.* 20]. — Matters are going on more rapidly than I expected. I am just come back from the Palace, where I was sent for at ½ past 6, to *consult.* I have laid fully before the Queen the existing situation, and have begged Her Majesty to take some time to consider her course ; adding that, if on full reflection she made up her mind to command my services, I should feel it my imperative duty to obey. I shall probably hear to-morrow. The Government were unanimous in resigning, but whether she will ultimately accept their resignation I cannot say. If she does, we accept

with some advantage in our favour. If not, we have not declined office.

Derby told the Queen that 'nobody was more surprised in his life than he had been at the result of the debate.' But Milner Gibson's amendment was 'so skilfully worded' that it was difficult for the Conservatives not to vote for it. 'He had to admit this, when they came to him to ask what they should do, merely warning them to save the measure itself, which the amendment did.' He explained his own position and that of his party thus :

After what had happened in 1851 and 1855, if the Queen made the offer, he *must* accept it, for if he refused the Conservative party would be broken up for ever. Yet he would find a majority of two to one against him in the House of Commons, would have difficulty in well filling the important offices, found the external and internal relations of the country in a most delicate and complicated position, war in India and in China, difficulties with France, the Indian Bill introduced, and a Reform Bill promised ; nothing but the forbearance and support of some of his opponents would make it possible for him to carry on any Government. The person who was asked first by the Sovereign had always a great disadvantage ; perhaps other combinations were possible, which, if found not to answer, would make him more readily accepted by the country.[1]

From Lord Derby.

St. James's Square, *Feb.* 21, 1858. — The Queen writes that further reflection has only confirmed her in her resolution to offer me the task of forming a Government, as being 'at the head of the only party which can secure a certain support, and which the country would accept as a substitute for that hitherto in power.' I have, of course, accepted the task ; and I think you will agree that I do so, *as regards the Court,* to more advantage than if I had at once, and without giving her time to weigh the difficulties, undertaken the responsibility. I shall be glad to see you as soon as you can come down.

Derby, after consulting Disraeli, went through the form of seeking outside assistance — an indispensable preliminary which he never omitted on these occasions ; but he

[1] *Queen Victoria's Letters*, memorandum by Prince Albert, Feb. 21, 1858.

did it this time without any illusions as to the probability of success. 'He fears that he can hardly hope,'
he wrote to the Queen, 'in the formation of a Government, for much extrinsic aid; as almost all the men of
eminence in either House of Parliament are more or less
associated with other parties, whose co-operation it would
be impossible to obtain.   Lord Derby will not, however,
hesitate to make the attempt in any quarters in which
he may think he has any chance of success.'[1]   According
to Prince Albert's information, the move which upset
Palmerston's Government had been dexterously planned
by Graham.   But Derby did not think it worth while
to appeal to him, or to Russell, who also had taken a
prominent part against Ministers.   The statesmen he
approached were two, Lord Grey and Gladstone, who,
in their respective Houses, had acted pretty steadily
with the Conservatives for the last three years.   Both
refused : Grey because all the political friends with whom
he had been connected would be opposed to the new
Government, Gladstone for a variety of reasons.   'Alone,
as I must be, I could not,' he wrote, 'render you service
worth your having.'   Further,

Those who lament the rupture of old traditions may well
desire the reconstitution of a party ; but the reconstitution of
a party can only be effected, if at all, by the return of the old
influences to their places, and not by the junction of an
isolated person.   The difficulty is even enhanced in my case
by the fact that in your party, reduced as it is at the present
moment in numbers, there is a small but active and not unimportant section who avowedly regard me as the representative of the most dangerous ideas.   I should thus, unfortunately, be to you a source of weakness in the heart of your
own adherents, while I should bring you no party or group
of friends to make up for their defection or discontent.[2]

This last was surely a point for Derby and Disraeli,
and not for Gladstone, to consider.   If they were prepared to disregard the prejudices of their party, it did
not become him to allege them as an excuse for refusal.

[1] *Queen Victoria's Letters.*   [2] Morley's *Gladstone*, Bk. IV., ch. 9.

Moreover, it is clear that, if Gladstone had cordially accepted the rôle of a Conservative statesman, his power and eloquence would have compelled the admiration and respect of the most reluctant partisans. Was the real reason of Gladstone's refusal, as Lord Grey believed, that he was not offered the leadership of the House of Commons?[1]

These were not the only refusals of importance which Derby experienced in his Cabinet-making, and his sanguine lieutenant thought it advisable at intervals to hearten him to continue his task.

From Lord Derby.

Private. Sunday night, Feb. 21, 1858. — Come and see me at 11 to-morrow. Things look bad. Grey and Gladstone decline[2] — with friendly letters, but you know what that is worth. *The* objection is to Ellenborough at the War Office. There is no difficulty as to Malmesbury. *Stanley* hesitates, and I think will refuse office. He 'had hoped we should not have accepted without a combination.' By the Queen's express command I have written to the Duke of Richmond to ask if he would take the War Office. I do not think he will, but if he does he saves us. St. Leonards thinks he is too old, and declines the Great Seal! If he persists, I have asked the Queen if I may *try* Pemberton Leigh. He would be an immense card, but he has refused it before. He is, however, a true friend, and may accept — the more so, if he thinks we are not likely to be long-lived, when he will have his peerage for nothing.[3]

I am to be with the Queen again at 3 to-morrow, to report progress, no progress, or retrograde. I dine at Bernstorff's to-morrow to meet the Duke of Cambridge — and the Aumales! How the unconscious foreigners will kotoo!

To Lord Derby.

GROSVENOR GATE, *Feb.* 22, 1858. — I have just heard that *The Times* has decided to support you. So much for public opinion.[4]

---

[1] See *Memoirs of an Ex-Minister*, under date March 2, 1858.

[2] Derby made an unsuccessful offer also to Newcastle.

[3] Pemberton Leigh declined, and Thesiger (Lord Chelmsford) was appointed.

[4] Greville noted on March 3 : 'There are symptoms of a disposition on the part of *The Times* to support the new Government.'

Delane says we 'shall do much better without Gladstone'
Assuming that General Peel does not join, I have drawn up
a complete scheme with the resources at our command. It
will obtain public respect.

There is really only one sorrow in all this: it draws tears
from my eyes, and from your heart, I am sure, drops of
blood. What mortifies me most is that I feel he [Stanley]
is making a great mistake.

From Lord Derby.

Confidential. St. James's Square, *Feb. 25, 1858.* — Another
hitch! Lytton informed Jolliffe, at 11 o'clock last night,
that he could not face his county election! The fact is, he
wants to be made a peer, which I will not do for him. *If*
he is to be of *any* use, it must be in the H. of Commons.
They parted on angry terms. I wish you would come down
here as soon as you conveniently can; unless you can, *en
route*, call on our refractory friend, and get him straight again.
I must have his answer *at once*, Aye or No; and I think it
would not be amiss to hint to him that we are not without
resources. I believe Sir J. Buller would accept, and would
fill the office better than Lytton. . . .

To Lord Derby.

Grosvenor Gate, *Thursday* [*Feb. 25*]. — Never mind — John
Manners must have the Colonies: he will do *very well*, better
than Labouchere. I wished him to have it, and, indeed, never
contemplated that Lytton should even have been in the
Cabinet had it not been for our Chief's too gracious notice of
him in 1855.[1] Sir John Y. Buller should have J. M.'s place.

All this, of course, humbly suggested to the Chief.

I shall be in St. James's Square in an hour. I think Lytton
too impudent.

At the last moment Stanley, 'on the urgent representation of his colleagues,' of whom Disraeli was certainly not the least pressing, though Malmesbury, in his
Memoirs, claims for himself the credit, consented to join
the Government and take the Colonial Office; and Manners, much to his own satisfaction, resumed his seat at
the Board of Works, instead of attaining an undesired
promotion to a Secretaryship of State.

[1] In Derby's speech in the Lords, explaining his failure to form a
Government in 1855.

Lord John Manners.
from the portrait by Sir F. Grant, P.R.A.
at Hughenden.

The Cabinet, as originally formed, was as follows :

First Lord of the Treasury	EARL OF DERBY.
Lord Chancellor	LORD CHELMSFORD.
Lord President	MARQUIS OF SALISBURY.
Lord Privy Seal	EARL OF HARDWICKE.
Home Secretary	S. H. WALPOLE.
Foreign Secretary	EARL OF MALMESBURY.
Colonial Secretary	LORD STANLEY.
War Secretary	GENERAL PEEL.
Chancellor of the Exchequer	B. DISRAELI.
First Lord of the Admiralty	SIR JOHN PAKINGTON.
President of the Board of Control	EARL OF ELLENBOROUGH.
President of the Board of Trade	J. W. HENLEY.
First Commissioner of Works	LORD JOHN MANNERS.

The Irish government was entrusted to Lord Eglinton and Lord Naas, as in 1852 ; Fitzroy Kelly was Attorney-General, and Cairns Solicitor-General. Adderley, Sotheron Estcourt, and J. R. Mowbray, filled important offices outside the Cabinet ; Gathorne Hardy and Lord Carnarvon became Under-Secretaries. 'I do not think at any time the secondary appointments were so strong,' Disraeli wrote to Delane.

'Lord Eglinton, who dined here,' wrote Disraeli to Lennox on February 28, 'said that the Court had expressed itself to a high personage (who told him) that it was very pleased with the new Cabinet.' 'Somewhat better' than the last Derby Cabinet was the unenthusiastic phrase used by the Prince Consort to Stockmar ; and public opinion was in agreement with the Prince in a temperate satisfaction. Greville wrote [1] that the Government 'presents a more decent-looking affair than anybody expected' ; and, after further consideration,[2] that Derby 'has brought forward some new men who have a good reputation, and may distinguish themselves in Parliament, and show us that we have something to look to beyond the old worn-out materials of which everybody is tired. The first class of this Government is not worse than that of the last, and the second class is a great deal better.' In *personnel*, except in one instance, the

[1] Feb. 27.   [2] March 2.

Cabinet of 1858 was decidedly stronger than that of 1852. If Chelmsford was a poor exchange for that eminent lawyer St. Leonards, Stanley, Ellenborough, and Jonathan Peel brought much more weight and capacity than Herries, Lonsdale, and Northumberland. Stanley, who was in his thirty-second year, was the most promising of the younger men in Parliament, and Palmerston had tried in vain to capture him, before he was thirty, for his own Cabinet. Ellenborough had been Governor-General of India, and there, and in the House of Lords, had displayed many brilliant gifts, but not discretion. Jonathan Peel, though not brilliant, had the family competence and integrity ; and it was felt to be a proof of Conservative reunion that Peel's younger brother, who had once challenged Disraeli to a duel in Sir Robert's interest,[1] should sit in Cabinet with the 'Peel-smasher.'[2]

It was well that the Ministry was stronger in *personnel* than that of 1852, for in Parliament it held a weaker position. Derby had indeed exaggerated when he told the Queen that the House of Commons was by two to one against the Conservatives ; the proportion was three to two — a proportion sufficiently unsatisfactory without exaggeration. Fortunately for them, the large majority of the House, though of a generally progressive tendency, had been held together only by the personal tie of allegiance to Palmerston. That allegiance it had repudiated by the recent vote, and it must be a matter of time to restore harmonious working between the fallen Minister on the one hand, and his jealous rival and recalcitrant followers on the other. The divisions among their opponents justified the Conservatives in taking office, but it was clear that they could not retain it unless they were prepared to govern in accordance with the dominant progressive sentiment of the House of Commons. With that sentiment Disraeli, and that section of the party which was represented by the *Press*, agreed ; and Derby himself, no reactionary, but a Reformer and a converted

Whig, recognised and accepted the necessity of acting in harmony with it. The adhesion, at the last moment, of Stanley, a Conservative who was so nearly a Liberal as to have been asked to sit in a Liberal Cabinet, must have been obtained by assurances of the progressive basis on which the new Administration was formed. He would certainly have persisted in his refusal if Reform, for instance, was to be shelved.

In truth, there was probably in these years less divergence in political opinion between the leading men of all parties, except on the extreme wings of Radicals and Reactionaries, than at any period of recent history. A good reception was therefore accorded to Derby's statement in the Lords, which, while announcing that Walewski's despatch would be answered and the Conspiracy Bill dropped, promised an India Bill for the present session, and a Reform Bill for the next. These two Bills, in a racing simile subsequently employed by Palmerston, were 'engagements' with which the Conservatives took the Government, and which 'they were bound to fulfil or else pay forfeit.' Apart from deficiency in Parliamentary support, the difficulties immediately facing the Ministry were serious. Clarendon wrote to Derby : 'We must not disguise from ourselves that the spirit in France is very bad against us, and that the Emperor may soon think it for his personal and dynastic interest to encourage that feeling'; and Earle reported to Disraeli from Paris : 'The Emperor thinks it so necessary to keep up the idea that all foreign Governments bow to his will that he is much annoyed at this check.' It would require no little skill to restore satisfactory relations with France while denying her request for penal legislation. Then the Indian Mutiny was still unsubdued, the Chinese War unfinished. The details of the India Bill in the present, and of the Reform Bill in the future, must be full of pitfalls. Finally there was the prospect of a large deficiency in the revenue, owing to the expense in India and China on the one hand, and to the severe

monetary crisis of the autumn on the other. In the actual situation in the House of Commons, the burden of almost all these difficulties must fall mainly on its Leader. Disraeli, however, was undaunted, and with the assistance of his clever young friend, Earle, who left the Paris Embassy to be his private secretary, got speedily into harness at the Treasury.

In his address to his constituents Disraeli had expressed a hope that ' by measures at once firm and conciliatory' the causes of misunderstanding with France might be speedily and entirely removed. In his speech on the hustings he emphasised once more his adhesion to the Anglo-French Alliance. Such an alliance was the essence, he maintained, not only of English, but of French policy. It was totally independent of forms of government, of dynasties, and even of the character of the rulers of France. It did, indeed, happen that the present ruler of France was a man eminently gifted, who exercised a great influence over events; who was not only a prince, but a statesman; who had not only a great knowledge of human nature generally, but of English human nature. It was to the ' sagacious and unimpassioned intelligence of the Emperor' that Disraeli mainly looked to settle the difference between the two countries. The Emperor would not send insulting messages — ' he would leave them to Counts and Colonels' — but he would appeal to the justice of the English people. The other main topic of Disraeli's speech was Reform. Was it decent, honest, politic, or honourable, that Reform should be made 'the stalking-horse of faction; that it should be hung up and taken down according to the exigencies of a distressed Minister; and that the highest principles of policy should be made part of the stock-in-trade by which a Government are to shuffle through a disgraceful and discreditable existence?' The question should no longer be trifled with.

Malmesbury's despatch to Walewski, though hardly breathing the fire and eloquence of Canning, achieved its

purpose; Walewski replied that the Emperor's intentions had been misunderstood, and that the French Government would 'place its reliance purely and simply on the loyalty of the English people.' Disraeli was naturally anxious to have this good news to tell the House of Commons on its reassembling on March 12 after adjournment. 'The Ides of March are approaching,' he had written to Rose, 'and I am getting rather nervous.' The despatch did not arrive till the very day, and, on receipt of a message from Derby, Disraeli, records Malmesbury, 'rushed up in such a desperàte hurry that he nearly knocked over the messenger, and entered the room in a great state of excitement. When the despatch was produced, his delight was indescribable and amazingly demonstrative, considering the usually phlegmatic manner in which he receives news of all kinds.' He went straight to the House, and announced in his most impressive fashion that the 'painful misconceptions' between the Governments of France and England had 'entirely terminated in a spirit friendly and honourable, and in a manner which will be as satisfactory to the feelings as it will be conducive to the interests and the happiness of both nations.' The Opposition, however, had come back in a very hostile frame of mind, and, instead of showing gratification at this happy ending of a critical situation, at once proceeded to attack Ministers for not having, immediately on entering office, procured the release of two English engineers who, eight months before, had been captured on the Sardinian steamer *Cagliari* and imprisoned by the Neapolitan Government. As it happened, the Derby-Disraeli Government did manage to obtain, in the course of this spring, ample satisfaction in a matter which Palmerston's Government had dallied with and neglected for more than half a year. Within a short time, too, the French Emperor showed his friendly disposition by sending Marshal Pélissier, the first soldier of France, to replace, as Ambassador in England, Count Persigny, who, though a friend to this country, had

inflamed the Anglo-French misunderstanding. Even the
acquittal by a London jury, amid popular applause, but
in the teeth of the clearest evidence, of one Simon Bernard,
who was tried for murder as an accomplice in Orsini's plot,
did not disturb the better relations that had been established with France; and the Emperor showed no umbrage
at the withdrawal of the indictment against Bernard for
conspiracy when the indictment for murder had failed.

To Lord Derby.

Confidential.   HOUSE OF COMMONS, *April* 21, 1858. — . . . If
there were the slightest chance of success for the 2nd indictment, or it could please or benefit in any degree our ally, I
should be prepared to make any sacrifice or forego any advantage.   But, on the contrary, persistence will aggravate
the anti-Gallic feeling and injure our ally; while it would
damage us.

Lord Cowley is very strong on this head, too, and mentioned
this morning to me that his conviction of the impossibility of
proceeding was so decided, that he would willingly take upon
himself the responsibility to the Emperor of having himself
personally urged on us the withdrawal. . . .

The country does not connect our Government with the
late trial : it will with the impending one.

The foreign policy of the new Government had got
successfully under way; and Disraeli's adroitness turned
the balance in the House of Commons, after an unpropi-
tious opening, in favour of Ministers.

To Queen Victoria.

HOUSE OF COMMONS, *March* 12, 1858 (*Friday*). — The Chancellor of the Exchequer, with his humble duty to your Majesty.

The Opposition benches very full; the temper not kind.

The French announcement, which was quite unexpected,
elicited cheers, but only from the Ministerial side, which, he
confesses, for a moment almost daunted him.

Then came a question about the *Cagliari* affair, on which
the Government had agreed to take a temperate course, in
deference to their predecessors — but it was not successful.
The ill-humour of the House, diverted for a moment by the
French news, vented itself on this head.

What struck the Chancellor of the Exchequer in the course

of the evening most was the absence of all those symptoms of 'fair trial,' etc., which have abounded of late in journals and in society.

Lord John said something; Mr. Gladstone said something; but it was not encouraging.

Nevertheless, in 1852 'fair trial' observations abounded, and the result was not satisfactory; now it may be the reverse.

The House is wild and capricious at this moment.

Your Majesty once deigned to say that your Majesty wished in these remarks to have the temper of the House placed before your Majesty, and to find what your Majesty could not meet in newspapers. This is the Chancellor of the Exchequer's excuse for these rough notes, written on the field of battle, which he humbly offers to your Majesty.

HOUSE OF COMMONS, *March* 15,[1] 1852 (*Monday, half-past eight o'clock*).— . . . This evening was a great contrast to Friday. House very full on both sides. . . .

Mr. B. Osborne commenced the general attack, of which he had given notice; but, after five years' silence, his weapons were not as bright as of yore. He was answered by the Government, and the House, which was very full, became much excited. The Ministerial benches were in high spirit.

The debate that ensued most interesting and sustained.

Mr. Horsman, with considerable effect, expressed the opinions of that portion of the Liberal party which does not wish to disturb the Government.

Lord John Russell vindicated the Reform Bill of 1832 from the attacks of the Chancellor of the Exchequer, and with great dignity and earnestness.

He was followed by Mr. Drummond on the same subject in a telling epigram. Then Lord Palmerston, in reply to the charges of Mr. Horsman, mild and graceful, with a sarcastic touch. The general impression of the House was very favourable to the Ministry; all seemed changed; the debate had cleared the political atmosphere, and, compared with our previous state, we felt as if the eclipse[2] was over.[3]

Disraeli's speech in this debate, modestly disguised in his letter to the Queen as an anonymous 'answer' by the Government, was a brilliant debating effort, which began by chaffing Bernal Osborne on his 'wild shriek of liberty' after five years of subordinate office.

[1] The date is wrongly given in *Queen Victoria's Letters* as March 22.

[2] Writing to Mrs. Willyams on the following day, Disraeli says: 'Nature seems to have been relieved by the eclipse, and to-day is quite spring.'

[3] *Queen Victoria's Letters.*

Disraeli stated the position of the Government in a few general words:

We represent the Conservative party. We wish to support and maintain the institutions of the country, but we also wish to improve them. We believe that the best way to maintain the institutions of the country is to improve them when improvement is necessary, and therefore we cannot permit the hon. gentleman to be such a monopolist of all plans for the amelioration of society as he and his friends, on all occasions, in a manner so greedy and covetous, aspire to be considered.

In the special instance of Reform, which occupied the final portion of the speech, 'nobody, it appears,' Disraeli said, 'may poach upon that manor except the Liberal party.' The Tory party had accepted the great Reform Act when it was the law of the land, and had supported Whig Ministers in resisting attempts to enlarge it. But when 'finality' was given up by the Whigs, the Conservatives considered themselves free in the matter. Russell's, Aberdeen's, and Palmerston's Governments had been nibbling in a half-hearted fashion at Parliamentary Reform for seven years, and had promised it in Queen's Speeches; a question of this vast importance could no longer remain unsettled.

If there is anything more likely than another to poison the feelings of the people and to alienate their best sentiments from the institutions of the country, it is the suspicion permitted to be engendered in the public mind that schemes for reconstructing those institutions are used by public men for party purposes. It is impossible that a question like that of Parliamentary Reform can be hung up and taken down at the convenience of any statesman, so that when in Opposition he is to brandish it in the face of those in office, and when a Minister to place it in a rusty scabbard. Under these circumstances we feel it our duty to consider that question, and we shall consider it with the earnest determination of endeavouring to make a settlement of it that will be satisfactory to the sober-minded people of this country.

Bernal Osborne had made use of the standing complaint of the Liberals, however split up they might be

among themselves, that the Conservatives had no business
to be in office, because they had not got a majority.
Disraeli entirely repudiated the assertion. Where was
the majority, he asked, and who had it? Had Palmerston got it? If so, why was he sitting on the Opposition
bench? Had Russell got it? Why, it was only a fortnight ago that Palmerston beat him by a majority of
200. In the absence of proof to the contrary, Disraeli
was prepared to maintain that the Government possessed the 'constitutional confidence' of the House of
Commons.

It was natural that those members of the Cabinet
who specially represented the interests of Churchmen
should be anxious to take advantage of the existence
of a Conservative Government to settle by some compromise the vexed question of Church rates.[1] Both
Walpole and Pakington had plans; but Stanley, who was
very unsympathetic, implored Disraeli to put a veto on
the introduction of any Bill of the kind. Disraeli agreed,
at least so far as regarded the present session.

To Sir John Pakington.

C. of E., *April* 3, 1858. — There are plenty of rocks ahead,
but I don't think we ought ourselves to sink ships to increase
the difficulties of our navigation. Depend upon it, if the
Angel Gabriel himself were to draw a Church Rate Bill for
us, it would never be accepted in this Parliament. The more
Liberal our measures, the less inclined they will be to accept
them. They will never permit us to poach on their manor,
and we must postpone our Liberal battue until we have a
Conservative majority.

India we could not avoid, and whatever form our legislation
had taken, the opposition would have been exactly the same.
If we pull through that we shall do wonders, but I am convinced our lawmaking this year should be confined as much as
possible to the Appropriation Act. . . .

'India we could not avoid.' By the welcome which
Parliament had accorded to the first India Bill in February, the authority of the East India Company had been
fatally undermined; and any Government which succeeded

---

[1] See below, Ch. 10.

Palmerston's must have given effect to the policy thus generally accepted. To Disraeli it was a matter of solid satisfaction to take a leading part in carrying out that transfer of authority from the Company to the Crown which, in advance both of his own party and of his Whig opponents, he had seen some years before to be necessary and desirable. But his first attempt at legislation in this direction, owing largely to the shortness of time available for preparation and to the over-cleverness of Ellenborough, the Minister in charge of the department, was unhappy and unsuccessful. It was on Friday, March 26, just a month after the completion of the Ministry, that Disraeli rose to introduce the Government Bill. Before explaining its terms, he paid an eloquent tribute of respect to the Company for the historic services which it had rendered to Great Britain and to India. It resembled Venice both in its greatness and in its fall, and like Venice had left 'a legacy of glory to mankind.'

That a Cabinet Minister of the rank, if not of the name, of Secretary of State, should be responsible to Parliament and the Crown for the government of India was inevitable, if the Company was to be superseded. That the Minister should be assisted by some form of Council, to take the place of the old Court of Directors, was also generally regarded as essential. Palmerston in his Bill had proposed a Council of eight, nominated by the Crown. That plan had been denounced as lending itself to party jobs. Ellenborough's Bill, which Disraeli introduced, provided for a Council of eighteen, half to be nominated by the Crown from among men holding special Indian qualifications. The other nine were to be chosen by popular election at home : four by a constituency of persons who had either seen service in India or possessed financial interests there ; and the remaining five by the Parliamentary electors of the cities of London, Manchester, Liverpool, Glasgow, and Belfast. It was claimed that this fantastic arrangement would give a democratic flavour to the Council, and secure its

independence of Ministers; but the Bill had a very unfavourable reception in Parliament. The democratic provisions were repudiated by the representatives of democracy: Bright denounced them as claptrap, and earnestly advised Ministers to reconsider them. Ellenborough was, no doubt, the author of these strange proposals; but to Disraeli, who always himself displayed a weakness for fancy franchises, their absurdity would not be so patent as to the ordinary member of Parliament.

The courtesy of a first reading was accorded to the Bill; but so general was the condemnation of its provisions, even among those independent members of the Liberal party who were friendly to Ministers, that Palmerston had great hopes of defeating it on second reading, and, if not of ejecting the Government from office, at least of restoring his own Bill, which had been laid aside. When Parliament separated for the Easter recess, Ministerial prospects were very gloomy. But the rivalry between the two Whig leaders, which had helped to place Derby and Disraeli in office, was still sufficiently active to keep them there. Russell was not disposed to aid Palmerston to return to power; and his patriotism was revolted by the idea of making a party matter of the exact form in which the government of India should be taken over and administered by the Crown. A hint of what was coming was conveyed, probably through Horsman, to Disraeli, who was spending a strenuous Easter in town preparing for his Budget, and superintending generally the tangled affairs of the Administration.

To Lord Derby.

Most confidential. GROSVENOR GATE, *Good Friday,* 1858 [*April 2*]. — Affairs are most critical, and everybody is out of town except myself; tho' I don't know that I should venture to speak to anyone except yourself, save Malmesbury and Jolliffe.

Ld. Palmerston is making every effort to defeat us on the 19th April. A condemnatory amendment, on the 2nd reading of the Indian Bill, is to be moved by Sir Erskine Perry.

The Independent Liberal Party, about ninety to a hundred,

are most anxious to prevent the triumph of P., but they will
not vote for the second reading of our Bill : and say that, so
great and various are the objections to it, that there are certainly no modifications of it which would influence any portion
of them to that course.

It has been suggested that, to prevent the defeat of the
Government, someone on their side should move that both
Bills be referred to a Select Committee, but then it is urged
that the theme is too vast for such a tribunal : then a Committee of the whole House has been discussed, but it is thought
that a very inefficient and unsatisfactory measure must be the
result of such a process : finally, it has been suggested that
some person of commanding position (I make no doubt that
Lord John Russell is meant, and is probably the author of
the suggestion) should move a series of resolutions as to the
opinion of the House of the principles on which a Bill for the
government of India should be framed.   This was done, they
say, by Lord Grenville.

It may be objected that, in the present instance, the Bills
are already introduced : but it is replied that in our case we
have acted in deference to the wish of the House of Commons,
and therefore the House of Commons can, without any slight to
us, counsel the Government in the course they should pursue.

All this has reached me from the most authentic quarter.
You may rely upon its accuracy, as if we had been present,
invisible, at the council.

I thought no time should be lost in your deeply meditating
over it.   There is a sincere and hearty desire, on the part of
the Independent Liberals, to hinder the restoration of P. ; but
he is very strong, and his opportunity, it is vain to conceal it
from ourselves, is a good one. . . .

To Mrs. Brydges Willyams.

Downing Street, *April* 3, 1858. — These are Easter holi-
days, but not to me, as the campaign is to be very brisk
when the House of Commons reassembles on the 12th.   I
think, however, we shall baffle the enemy.

I have got to dine with the Lord Mayor on Easter Monday —
a great effort.   It frightens me more than the Budget, which
comes on the 16th, or the Indian Bill, which is fixed for execu-
tion on the Monday following.

We have got the two poor English engineers out of the
jaws and cells of the King of Naples : but I fear that will not
satisfy John Bull.   He wants King Bomba to be bombarded.
How terrible to shell Parthenope !   One might as well think
of bombarding Torquay !

At the Easter Monday banquet at the Mansion House Derby spoke in such a way as to facilitate any friendly action which Russell might be disposed to take. He said that the Government courted the co-operation and advice of Parliament and the country; the one thing they deprecated was that a question of such overwhelming importance for both Great Britain and India 'should be made the sport of political parties or the battlefield of rival disputants.' With Disraeli's concurrence, but in his absence owing to some temporary indisposition, the Cabinet determined themselves to hang up the India Bill and proceed by resolution, on the ground that the objections which had been made were so various and conflicting that it was the better course to submit the principles separately and in detail to Parliament, rather than to take a vote on the whole. This decision was to be announced on the following Monday to the House at its reassembling; and Disraeli, who was convalescent, spent the intervening week-end as Her Majesty's guest at Windsor.

To Mrs. Disraeli.

WINDSOR CASTLE, *April* 11, 1858. — A pretty good night, and, generally speaking, rather better.

I sat between Lady Hardwicke and Lady Elizabeth at dinner, taking in Lady Hardwicke. The D'Aumales also here, and Lord Sandwich; I think that is all staying. The neighbours, however, dined, in the shape of the Duchess of Kent, the Van de Weyers, Sir W. Codrington.

The Queen very gracious, and seemed very much pleased that I had brought the Budget down for the Prince. H. R. H. himself talked to me a great deal, and said he was sorry to hear that I had been unwell, and had not been able to attend the Cabinet. Lady Churchill in waiting. The Duc d'Aumale asked very much after you.[1]

I am now going to Chapel.

Disraeli described with great humour, in his report to the Queen, the scene in the House on the following

---

[1] Writing next day to Mrs. Willyams, Disraeli said: 'Perhaps better conversation cannot be had than that afforded by the two Princes, the Prince Consort and the Duc d'Aumale — the two most richly cultivated minds I ever met, and men, too, of great abilities.'

day when Russell's intervention enabled the Government to pose as following, in deference to the advice of so respected a statesman and to the general opinion of Parliament, a course which they had already resolved to take, on their own motion, to avoid certain defeat.

To Queen Victoria.

HOUSE OF COMMONS, *April* 12, 1858 (*Monday night*). — The Chancellor of the Exchequer with his humble duty to your Majesty.

House reassembled — full. Chancellor of Exchequer much embarrassed with impending statement, on the part of your Majesty's servants, that they intended to propose Resolutions on the Government of India, instead of at once proceeding with their Bill.

Received, five minutes before he took his seat, confidential information that Lord John Russell, wishing to defeat the prospects of Lord Palmerston, and himself to occupy a great mediatory position, intended himself to propose the *mezzotermine* of Resolutions!

Chancellor of Exchequer felt it was impossible, after having himself introduced a Bill, to interfere with the Resolutions of an independent member, and one so weighty and distinguished: therefore confined his announcement to the Budget on Monday week, and consequent postponement of India Bill.

Soon after Lord John rose and opened the case, in a spirit most calm and conciliatory to the House and to your Majesty's Government.

The Chancellor of Exchequer responded, but with delicacy, not wishing rudely to deprive Lord John of his position in the matter, deeming it arrogant; but the real Opposition, extremely annoyed at all that was occurring, wishing, at the same time, to deprive Lord John of the mediatory position, and to embarrass your Majesty's Government with the task and responsibility of preparing and introducing the resolutions, *insisted* upon Government undertaking the task. As the Chancellor of Exchequer had the sketch of the Resolutions in his box, this was amusing; he undertook the responsibility, thus urged, and almost menaced; Lord John, though greatly mortified at not bringing in the Resolutions himself, for it is since known they were prepared, entirely and justly acquits Chancellor of Exchequer of any arrogance and intrusion, and the affair concludes in a manner dignified and more than promising. It is now generally supposed that, after the

various Resolutions have been discussed and passed, the Bill of your Majesty's servants, modified and reconstructed, will pass into a law.

The Chancellor of Exchequer will have a copy of the Resolutions, though at present in a crude form, made and forwarded to your Majesty, that they may be considered by your Majesty and His Royal Highness. Chancellor of Exchequer will mention this to Lord Derby, through whom they ought to reach your Majesty.

After this unexpected and interesting scene, because it showed, in its progress, a marked discordance between Lord John and Lord Palmerston, not concealed by the latter chief, and strongly evinced by some of his principal followers — for example, Sir C. Wood, Mr. Hall, Mr. Bouverie — the House went into Committee on the Navy Estimates, which Sir J. Pakington introduced in a speech, lucid, spirited, and comprehensive. The feeling of the House as to the maintenance of the navy was good.[1]

If Disraeli was indebted to Russell for extricating him without serious damage from his troubles over Ellenborough's Bill, he surmounted his financial difficulties by his native genius. He was faced, as the figures of his Budget, opened on April 19, showed, by a deficit of four millions, due partly to additional naval and military expenditure, and partly to the obligation to pay off during the year three and a half millions of war debt. The deficit was calculated on the assumption that the rate of income tax was to fall, as arranged in 1853, to 5d. Disraeli had adopted in the previous year, as the basis of his financial policy, the carrying into effect of Gladstone's original proposals, which involved the extinction of the income tax in 1860. From that standpoint he had criticized, side by side with Gladstone, Cornewall Lewis's Budget of 1857. That standpoint he maintained now, and thereby secured Gladstone's powerful support. He would not say that 'a solemn compact,' independent of all circumstances and events, was concluded with Parliament in 1853. But there were 'arrangements cordially entered into, and in the same spirit understood, and which the country

[1] *Queen Victoria's Letters.*

expected would be religiously fulfilled if the interposition of extraordinary circumstances did not render their fulfilment impossible.' The Crimean War had suspended the arrangements, but they ought to be resumed now. In Northcote's words, 'it was not merely a question whether a certain amount of taxation should be levied, but whether a certain tax, which the public wished to put an end to, should be continued or not. It was the critical moment for deciding whether the scheme of 1853 should or should not be carried into effect.'[1] Disraeli maintained that the income tax should not form a permanent feature of our finance.

The feeling of the community generally of the inequality, of the injustice, and of the odious nature of this tax, has unfortunately been sanctioned and concurred in by all those statesmen who have felt the necessity of levying it; and it has been impossible to maintain it for any considerable time, or to adopt it as a permanent feature of our financial system, without great acerbity of feeling and much violent controversy being excited as to its character and its incidence.

But, if the arrangement providing for the eventual abolition of the income tax was to be carried into effect, there was no way of meeting the deficit save by postponing the redemption of debt. 'The choice lay between the extinction of the debt,' as Northcote says, 'and the extinction of the income tax.' Disraeli accordingly, on the plea that the expensive warlike operations in progress in China precluded the year from being treated as one of peace, postponed the obligation to pay off £3,500,000 of debt, and thus reduced his deficit to half a million. For this he provided by raising the duty on Irish spirits to the English and Scottish level. He playfully deprecated Irish opposition to this increase of taxation.

At this moment, the only differential duty that remains between Ireland and Great Britain is the differential duty on spirits. I am sure that my Irish friends, who are always demanding justice for Ireland, and who define that justice to consist in an identity of institutions, of rights, and of duties,

[1] *Twenty Years of Financial Policy*, p. 339.

cannot, on reflection consider the position in which they are placed by this differential duty on spirits with any other but feelings of indignant humiliation. I remember once, when I was at Bristol, a ship came in from Ireland, and, to my great surprise, I saw it boarded instantly by Custom-house officers, and the crew treated just the same as a parcel of foreigners. All this was to see if there were any Irish spirits in the hold, which, if they had come in undetected, would have paid a duty of 6s. 2d. instead of 8s. Was that a position for high-spirited Irishmen to be placed in? How much better will it be for the Irish to have a command of the English market, and not only of the English, but of the British market; how much better for them to enter into active competition with English and with Scotch spirits, and, instead of confining themselves to the supply of a mere provincial demand, to be entitled to pour in their admirable products, which I am told the French now prefer even to their own brandy; how much better for them to pour their spirits into this country, and through this country into the Continent, and thus give a great stimulus to trade!

Finally, to obtain a small surplus, Disraeli imposed a penny stamp on bankers' cheques, and thereby secured for the public purse a steadily expanding revenue, which, however, for the coming year he only estimated at £300,000.

'The Budget has had a complete success,' Disraeli wrote that evening to the Queen; 'indeed, he may say it has met with universal approbation.' The verdict of the first night was confirmed on reflection; it was felt that Ministers were keeping faith with the nation about the income tax; and Cornewall Lewis's criticisms in a subsequent debate were answered by Gladstone, who protested strongly against the idea of treating the income tax as part of the permanent revenue of the country. It did 'more than any other tax to demoralise and corrupt the people,' and it hindered 'effective and extensive economy.' But though this Budget was successful, while the December Budget of 1852 failed, Disraeli was better advised when accepting in 1852 the income tax as a necessary part of a Free Trade Budget and endeavouring to mitigate its anomalies and injustices, than when vainly striving in

1858 to secure its ultimate extinction at a time of rising public expenditure,[1] and while the nations of Europe were steadily arming. Bright said truly in one of the debates that, with Parliamentary Reform imminent, 'your property tax, which you are assisting the Chancellor of the Exchequer to throw over, will come back to you, and come back in increased proportion.' Disraeli secured the support of Gladstone for the moment; but Gladstone nevertheless joined the Liberal Government formed on Disraeli's fall, and as Chancellor of the Exchequer disregarded altogether in 1860 his own arrangement by which the income tax was to come that year to an end. Disraeli had shrewdly prophesied in 1853 that the income tax would never be abolished;[2] all his strenuous efforts in 1857 and 1858 were of no avail to avert the fulfilment of his prophecy. The Budget of 1858 was adroitly composed to pass a House of Commons resting on the middle class, and containing a large majority against Ministers, but it has little claim to remembrance save for the admirably devised plan of taxing cheques. The Budget of December, 1852, had the higher merit of laying down principles which subsequent Chancellors have been compelled to follow.[3]

Disraeli was apparently contented. He wrote to Mrs. Willyams on April 24: 'The Budget is said to be the most successful for a quarter of a century. There is to be some warm fighting about India, but no one thinks now there is any chance of disturbing the Government. I never went through two such months.' But neither his friends nor his foes were content. The accommodations inevitable for a Government in a minority irritated both sides. Malmesbury noted in his diary on April 28: 'Our party, I am sorry to say, are, or pretend to be, offended with Disraeli. They, of course, ought to know that we are in a minority, and can neither help it nor disguise the fact.' Greville gives us the Opposition view.

---

[1] Over £10,000,000 more than in 1852.
[2] See Vol. III., p. 507.   [3] See Vol. III., Ch. 12.

On April 24 he wrote: 'There is no example of any Government consenting to hold office on terms so humiliating, and to such a powerless existence. They dare not originate anything, and they submit to everything that anybody proposes or suggests, having seemingly no object but that of currying favour and avoiding to give offence.'

The Indian Resolutions drafted by the Government were general in terms, but so far agreed with the principles of Ellenborough's Bill that they provided that the Council should be partly nominated and partly elected; and Disraeli, in debate, dwelt on the importance, if this was to be a real Council with real power, of introducing the elective principle. On going into Committee an obstructive motion was made from the Liberal benches to postpone legislation till the next year; but it was ill received, Palmerston hastened to disclaim it, and it was negatived by an enormous majority. The principal speaker for the Government in the debate was Stanley, and his success was a source of special gratification to his political tutor.

To Lord Derby.

HOUSE OF COMMONS, *April* 30, 1858. — It will make you happy to hear that Stanley has *greatly* distinguished himself: indeed, I hardly know a Parliamentary effort that, both on the House and his own party, ever produced a better effect. And quite unstudied; it occurred to me that it would be wise that he should rise after Palmn. instead of myself. I thought it was a great occasion, and that he *might* be equal to it. He WAS.

I never was so nervous in my life, and I never was so pleased. Except yourself, I don't know anyone who is so content.

It is difficult to convey to you the feeling of the party; it is really enthusiastic.

From Lord Derby.

Secret. ST. JAMES'S SQUARE, *Friday night* [*April* 30]. — You cannot doubt but that the report which you were kind enough to send me to-night of Stanley's success was in every sense, private and political, most gratifying to my feelings; and if the fact itself, which it announces, created such feelings,

they were not diminished by the very kind and sympathising feeling with which you conveyed to me your impression of the effect which he had produced.

But as it occurs everywhere, and has done in all times, that one agreeable intimation is generally balanced by something quite the reverse — 'medioque in fonte leporum Surgit amari aliquid' — I am compelled, at a moment when I should least wish to say anything unpleasant to you, to call your attention to a notice which I see to-day in the Votes of the House of Commons. Lord Ellenborough, in the House of Lords, first pointed out to me, *from a newspaper,* a very material alteration, of which public notice had been given by yourself as Chancellor of the Exchequer, in the Resolutions intended to be proposed by the Government on the India question. I doubted at first the accuracy of Lord Ellenborough's information; and even when I returned home, and saw in the evening papers the proposed amendments, I concluded that they proceeded from Ld. J. Russell or an opponent, or an independent member of the House. But, on looking to the Votes, I am compelled to come to the conclusion that the amendments are your own, and being your own, are presented to the House as the more mature result of the reflections of the Cabinet of which you are a (and in the House of Commons *the*) leading member. In that position you have a great latitude allowed to you, in which all your colleagues would acquiesce, and which no one would be more decided than myself in supporting.

But the Indian Resolutions, as you must be aware, are no ordinary question. Their substance, and their very phraseology, were carefully considered, and decided on, by the Cabinet. This being the case, I cannot but think that not the slightest deviation from those Resolutions ought to have been adopted, even verbally, without the consent of the Cabinet. That which I laboured to-day to impress upon the minds of the party, and that without which we cannot go on, is perseverance in our intentions once announced; and though, on matters immediately in discussion, it may be justifiable in the Leader of the House of Commons to act upon his own discretion, and recede from a position intended to have been maintained, in face of a formidable opposition, these considerations do not apply to an alteration, made without any external pressure, of a measure which had previously received the fullest consideration of the Cabinet.

Such, I deeply regret to say, appears to me to have been the effect of the amendments placed by you on the papers of the House of Commons, on the Cabinet Resolutions previously announced. The amendments are not verbal, nor technical.

They affect vitally the constitution of the Council, and the position of the Minister of the Crown — so vitally that Lord Ellenborough declares, and in my opinion justly, that no man who had ever had experience of the working of the India Board would consent to serve under such restrictions. The question whether the Minister should or should not be Secretary of State was discussed in Cabinet, submitted to, and approved by, the Queen. The Amendment, by being an amendment brought forward by the Government, virtually abandons this position; but it does more. Whereas our main principle was that the Secretary of State (whether so called or not) should exercise an absolute authority, his Council being only advisors, your amendment alters the whole form of the arrangement, and subjects him to the acquiescence, certified by signature, of three members of the Council. Lord Ellenborough plainly declares that, under such conditions, neither he, nor any man who knows anything of the affairs of India, would hold office for a moment. I name this, to show the *practical* effect of such a notice of amendment as you have apparently given. That I should have to say only *apparently* is the strongest opinion I could pass upon it. We have a Cabinet at 2 to-morrow, at which this question must be raised. Will you call on me in Downing Street at 1.30? This subject cannot be avoided; and I should be glad, by previous communication with you, to make as easy as possible the explanations which must follow, and the determination which must be taken as to ulterior proceedings in Parliament. I own I do not see how your proposed amendments can be justified to Parliament, and still less how their announcement to Parliament can be justified to your colleagues.

I need hardly say how sincerely I regret the first important difference between us as to the conduct of public business; and more especially on an occasion when every feeling on my part would have led me to wish that nothing should interfere with an entire and perfect sympathy between us, personally and politically, in reference to public affairs.

This letter illustrates the difficulties under which business is carried on in the House of Commons when its leader has not the authority of Prime Minister, and it says much for the good feeling of both Derby and Disraeli that this is the only serious remonstrance of the kind in their whole correspondence. No judgment can fairly be passed on the actual points in dispute without knowing Disraeli's explanation, which was no doubt

given verbally; but it may be said that Derby perhaps hardly makes sufficient allowance for a leader of the House of Commons in a permanent minority, with a constant necessity of humouring the majority on the details of legislation.

The Whigs by the end of April had become, as Greville has told us, very impatient of the existence of a Tory Government; and what they thought a favourable occasion for a combined onslaught was afforded by a glaring indiscretion committed by Ellenborough. Early in May there was published in England a draft proclamation issued by Canning, the Governor-General, after the fall of Lucknow, to the chiefs and inhabitants of Oude. It stated that those of the inhabitants who remained stedfast during the Mutiny would be rewarded, and accordingly that six landowners of Oude, who were named, would be regarded henceforward as the sole hereditary proprietors of the land which they held when the province became British; but that, with these exceptions, the proprietary right in the soil was confiscated to the British Government, which would dispose of that right as might seem fitting. To those who immediately surrendered, their lives and houses were guaranteed, provided their hands were unstained by British blood; but as to any further indulgence, they must throw themselves upon the justice and mercy of the British Government. This read like a harsh policy of general confiscation, though Canning's intention, it afterwards appeared, was to strike only at the chiefs and secure the farmers in the permanent tenure of the land. Ellenborough and the Government, taking the words in their natural meaning, thought that Canning had been won over to the vindictive policy which was widely advocated both in India and in England, and which had been expressly disavowed and disapproved by Disraeli in the previous autumn. Ellenborough at once forwarded a despatch to the Governor-General, condemning in strong terms the Oude proclamation. This was the most important passage:

Other conquerors, when they have succeeded in overcoming resistance, have excepted a few persons as still deserving of punishment, but have, with a generous policy, extended their clemency to the great body of the people. You have acted upon a different principle: you have reserved a few as deserving of special favour, and you have struck, with what they feel as the severest of punishments, the mass of the inhabitants of the country. We cannot but think that the precedents from which you have departed will appear to have been conceived in a spirit of wisdom superior to that which appears in the precedent you have made. We desire that you will mitigate, in practice, the stringent severity of the decree of confiscation you have issued against the landowners of Oude. We desire to see British authority in India rest upon the willing obedience of a contented people. There cannot be contentment where there is general confiscation.

The despatch was never submitted for approval either to the Queen or to the Cabinet, though it was read and approved informally by leading Ministers—among them by Disraeli.

Lord Ellenborough to Lord Derby.

Eaton Square, *May* 13, 1858. —. . . I took to the Cabinet on the 17th [April] the abstract of secret letters containing the proclamation and the letter which accompanied it. I showed the passage containing the confiscation to you, Disraeli, and others, by the fire. I wrote the letter early on the 18th, and you saw it and approved of it, saying 'it was very proper, and not too strong for the occasion.' Either on that evening or on the following morning Disraeli read it, Sir John Pakington, and Lord John Manners — no others.

I took it to the Cabinet on the 24th, but other business occupied all the time, and prevented my having the opinion of the Cabinet about it. . . .

The sentiments of Ellenborough's despatch were admirable, but the tone in which it was written was hardly one in which it became the responsible Minister at home to address a great Imperial officer upholding the honour of his country in circumstances of the utmost difficulty and danger. So long, however, as the terms were not published, the rebuke would not be known, either in England or — what was of more importance — in India. But Ellenborough's vanity would not be satisfied

without publication; he sent copies immediately, on his
own account, to Granville, the leader of the Opposition
in the Lords, and to Bright, the principal Radical critic
of Indian Government.   Publication was now inevitable,
and, when the papers were presented, Disraeli, acting
with loyalty to a colleague and in harmony with his
autumn deprecations of vindictiveness, declared that the
Government condemned the Oude proclamation 'in every
sense.'

Ellenborough's inconsiderate treatment of Canning
was deeply resented by public opinion. Notices of
censure were given in both Houses, and the fall of the
Government appeared to be imminent. Ellenborough,
however, who was solely responsible for the publication, sacrificed himself, as Russell had in the summer
of 1855,[1] to save his colleagues. But the Liberal Opposition in 1858 did not imitate the prudence and mag-
nanimity of the Conservative Opposition in 1855, and
abandon their attack when the offending Minister had
resigned. The opportunity appeared to be too good;
Palmerston and Russell were temporarily agreed; many,
if not all, of Canning's fellow-Peelites were expected to
vote for a resolution of censure to be proposed by
one of themselves, Cardwell. 'The line of attack,'
wrote Lennox to Disraeli, 'is . . . to give no opinion
upon proclamation, but to assert that, be that ever so
bad, the despatch should not have been written.' On
this line Lord Shaftesbury moved a vote of censure
in the Lords on May 14. The eminent philanthropist
disclaimed party feeling, from which indeed he was
conspicuously free. But he was intimately associated
with Palmerston, who was the moving spirit of this
attack, a fact of which Derby reminded him. The
Government were saved in the Lords by a majority of
nine; but, of course, the critical debate was that in the
Commons, begun on the same night, and continued, with
intervals, for a week.[2] Cardwell, the mover, was answered

[1] See above, p. 12.   [2] May 14, 17, 20, and 21.

by Cairns, the Solicitor-General, who laid that night the foundation of his great Parliamentary reputation. Russell severely censured Ministers for having written to Canning in a manner totally unbecoming the Government of a great Empire. But that, after all, was only one of the questions at issue, and was largely disposed of by Ellenborough's resignation. The Opposition were naturally shy of identifying themselves with a policy of confiscation as opposed to clemency, and it became more and more evident, as the debate proceeded, that the real issue was whether the House of Commons was disposed to eject the Conservatives and restore Palmerston to office.

The peril of the occasion stimulated all Disraeli's remarkable powers of political and Parliamentary management.

To Lord Derby.

[*May* 14, 1858.] — Cairns has made one of the greatest speeches since I have been in Parliament: perhaps, all things considered, the occasion, character of the man, etc., the greatest. He has completely destroyed the whole case. Cardwell a failure.

No news as to numbers.

GROSVENOR GATE, *May* 16, 1858. — I have quite made up my mind to continue the debate till Friday, and have ample resources for that end. I do not see how the Opposition can press for the close of the debate, or shrink from maintaining the indictment which they have preferred against us. When the fate of a Government, or perhaps a Parliament, is in the balance, a week's debate is not unreasonable — especially as we shall not be under the necessity of spinning out, having sufficient of first-rate men on the subject from the Government, Gladstonians, and Gibsonites.

Hamilton has ascertained about the financial portion of the dissolution question. One vote in supply is necessary. I regret this, but it could not be refused. On Friday next, I would at the commencement adjourn the House until Friday, the 28th, as a matter of course,[1] so that if we be in a minority the necessary time for deliberation will have been already prepared. But I am assured that we ought not to lose, and the only thing that makes the result doubtful is the general

---

[1] Sunday, May 23, was Whitsunday.

incredulity as to dissolution. Palmerston, I am informed, did all but pledge himself at his meeting that he knew from high authority that dissolution would not be permitted. This has worked greatly.

I hear the Peelites, with the exception of Gladstone, are all wrong. Sir J. Johnstone consulted Graham yesterday as to his course, and G. said, for his part, he thought he should not vote ; Sidney Herbert, it is now credibly said, against us, after much doubt. Robert Clinton, on whom we counted, to-day against us — and so on. Elcho against, etc.

Depend upon it, if you open the *pourparlers* with Aberdeen, as we arranged yesterday, all these materials now hesitating and hostile might be fused and appropriated. They want the word of command from their Director-General. Pray think of this : I even hope you have already done something in this respect.

Nothing must be spared. Active as are the exertions of the enemy, I hope our efforts are not less energetic. But 'tis a great stake ; for if they are beaten, it will really be the greatest Parliamentary discomfiture since the rout of Lord North and Fox, and perhaps in the present temper of the country might lay the foundation of as permanent results.

The prospect of dissolution was likely to have a very potent effect on the division. Palmerston was well informed. On May 11 the Queen had refused to allow Derby to make use of any threat of that kind. But Her Majesty, in view of the certainty that Derby would broach the question again, took the opinion of an elder statesman, Aberdeen, who, while approving her refusal to allow dissolution to be threatened, at the same time counselled her that it would be constitutional, if her Minister advised her to dissolve, to accept his advice. Accordingly, on Sunday, May 16, the day of Disraeli's letter quoted above, the Queen, in the Prince Consort's words, 'allowed him [Lord Derby] to know that a dissolution would not be refused to him, and trusted that her honour would be safe in his hands as to the use he made of that knowledge.'[1] The use made of the knowledge is shown in two notes which Disraeli sent in the next couple of days to Graham, who, influenced perhaps

---

[1] *Queen Victoria's Letters*, under dates May 11, 15, and 16.

by Aberdeen, had now definitely made up his mind to support Ministers, and a speech by whom in that sense would determine many votes.

To Sir James Graham.

Confidential.   May 17, 1858. — What might be said is that Lord Derby has not the slightest doubt of his power of dissolving.

May 18. — The division, I apprehend, will be close, and I am assured is still doubtful. The question of dissolution would decide the result. It is impossible for any of us to intimate it, but — if indeed I might presume to make such a suggestion — were a personage of your great authority, in the course of the debate, to announce that it would be scarcely possible, if the Government were defeated, not to appeal to the country, the effect might be conclusive.[1]

It was a memorable debate, and Sir William Fraser has given a spirited account of it, and of the passions generated both in society and in the House.

Ross, who for fifty years was the sagacious and excellent head-reporter of *The Times,* told me that, from beginning to end, there was not, in his judgment, one bad speech delivered. I was astonished to find what brilliant powers of argument and of elocution the House then held. The brain of every man of capacity was, of course, stimulated to the highest degree: and the result was a series of scenes that no one who took part in them, or witnessed them, will ever forget. . . .

I have never seen anything approaching the personal feeling and resentment which was shown during this debate, not only in the House, but in society. Wherever you went, nothing else was spoken of. Language almost transgressing the borders of decency was used, and it seemed at one time as if men would have come to blows. The Derby[2] intervened: this breathing-space gave a little time to cool: but the fury was renewed afterwards: nothing like it has occurred since.[3] . . . No one can form the least idea, from looking at Hansard, of what took place. The cheering, groaning, laughing, were beyond belief. We considered ourselves justified in

---

[1] Parker's *Graham,* Vol. II., p. 343.

[2] Wednesday, May 19. Lord Derby's Toxophilite was first favourite, but was beaten by Beadsman. Derby therefore missed the good fortune, which attended Lord Rosebery in 1894 and 1895, of winning the great race when Prime Minister.

[3] Published in 1891.

using inarticulate means of rendering the eloquence of the other side nugatory. . . . When I say that we absolutely demolished a man of such consummate effrontery as Bethell, ex-Attorney-General, and later Lord Chancellor, any reader who remembers him will wonder at our prowess.[1]

We can picture the sphinx-like figure of the leader of the House, watching with impassive face the battle surging round him day by day, never missing any indication of the movement of opinion and the disposition of parties, and waiting for the exact moment to intervene with success in person. In the early part of the week, in spite of a speech by Roebuck in their favour, the tide was still running strongly against Ministers; and Disraeli thought it wise to intimate his readiness to accept an amendment suggested by the Radical, Dillwyn, expressing approbation of Canning's conduct down to the proclamation, and declining to express any opinion on the proclamation itself without further information. 'It seems to me,' wrote his colleague Pakington to the Prime Minister, 'to be a descent, *per saltum*, from the highest ground on which a Government could stand to the lowest that a Government could condescend to occupy.' On the Thursday the tide began to turn in favour of Ministers. Palmerston was driven to read out in the House of Commons letters on Indian business sent by Canning to Vernon Smith, Ellenborough's predecessor at the Board of Control, and received after the change of Government; letters which, by all the rules of courtesy and frankness governing the relation of outgoing and incoming Ministers, should have been, but were not, passed on to Ellenborough, and which would have put a rather different complexion on Canning's policy, and would probably have prevented the Minister from expressing a hasty opinion. Then the news came by mail that Sir James Outram, the distinguished Commissioner of Oude, had protested against the draft proclamation as too severe, and had prevailed on Canning to modify it.

[1] Sir W. Fraser's *Disraeli and his Day*, pp. 252–254.

It began, moreover, to be generally understood that, if Ministers were defeated, the Queen would allow Derby to dissolve — a prospect very displeasing, as Parliament had been elected only twelve months before. The effect of all these considerations was heightened by two speeches in that night's debate. Bright treated the motion as a desperate party effort, and said that, if the question was between hurting Canning's feelings and sanctioning this proclamation, he could not hesitate. Graham announced the refusal of Aberdeen, now that the honour of his friend Canning was vindicated by Ellenborough's withdrawal, to take part in a faction fight. Graham's own conclusion was that the proclamation was wrong, and Ellenborough's despatch substantially right; that the error of the proclamation was in its essence, the error of the despatch in its form. A vehement party attack on Ministers by Bethell did not rehabilitate the case of the Opposition.

Fraser gives us a pleasant anecdote about Disraeli after this night's debate.

I was returning at a little past midnight from a party at the west end of Piccadilly. By the dead wall[1] between the gates of Devonshire House I met Disraeli, arm-in-arm with Sir William Jolliffe, then Secretary of the Treasury, and manager for the party. Disraeli said: 'Where have you been?' I replied: 'To Baron Rothschild's.' The street was empty, and a bright moon was shining. Disraeli said: 'What does the Baron say about it? He knows most things!' I replied: 'There was a great crowd, and I did not see him. You need have no anxiety; the motion will not be put from the Chair.' I shall never forget Disraeli's look of blank astonishment: his face was quite clear in the moonlight. He was silent: after half a minute had passed, he said: 'Good-night!' I answered: 'Good-night; *dormez bien!*'

'I shall never forget that night,' said Disraeli many years afterwards to Fraser. 'I believed that we were smashed. At the moment you met us I was arranging with Jolliffe the details of our going out. I had no more doubt that the Government would be defeated the next

[1] Before the fine central gates were brought from Chiswick and erected in the middle of the wall.

day than I had of my own existence.'[1] Fraser's pre-
diction was correct; but, in spite of the circumstantial
character of his story, it is difficult to believe that Disraeli,
after the cheering symptoms of Thursday's debate, was
so convinced of defeat as his reported attitude and
words suggested. The collapse of the Opposition was
admitted the next morning, when, according to Henry
Lennox's statement to Greville, Disraeli received a letter
from Cardwell asking if he might be allowed to withdraw his motion, and subsequently a similar request from
Palmerston himself. Disraeli, Lennox said, 'replied, in
a very lofty tone, that he would hear of nothing which
could possibly be construed into any admission, on their
part, of their meriting any part of the censure which the
Opposition had been labouring to cast upon them.'

The scene which followed in the House of Commons,
so mortifying for Palmerston and the Opposition, so
signally triumphant for Disraeli and the Government,
was described by Disraeli with great gusto, both in letters
to the Queen and to Mrs. Willyams, and within a week
in a public speech in his constituency.

To Queen Victoria.

HOUSE OF COMMONS, *May* 21, 1858. — The Chancellor of the
Exchequer, with his humble duty to your Majesty.

The fullest House; it is said 620 members present; it was
supposed we should have divided at three o'clock in the morning; Mr. Gladstone was to have spoken for the Government at
half-past ten — very great excitement — when there occurred a
scene perhaps unprecedented in Parliament.

One after another, perhaps twenty members, on the Opposition benches, rising and entreating Mr. Cardwell to withdraw
his resolution. After some time, silence on the Government
benches, Mr. Cardwell went to Lord John Russell, then to Lord
Palmerston, then to Lord John Russell again, then returned to
Lord Palmerston, and retired with him.

What are called the interpellations continued, when suddenly Lord Palmerston reappeared; embarrassed, with a faint
smile; addressed the House; and, after various preluding,
announced the withdrawal of the motion of censure.

A various debate followed; the Chancellor of the Exchequer

---

[1] Fraser, pp. 255, 256, 260.

endeavouring, as far as regards Lord Canning, to fulfil your Majesty's wishes. It is impossible to estimate the importance of this unforeseen event to your Majesty's servants. It has strengthened them more than the most decided division in their favour, for it has revealed complete anarchy in the ranks of their opponents. With prudence and vigilance all must now go right.

The speech of Sir James Graham last night produced a very great effect. No report gives a fair idea of it. The great country gentleman, the broad views, the fine classical allusions, the happiest all omitted, the massy style, contrasted remarkably with Sir Richard Bethell.[1]

To Mrs. Brydges Willyams.

DOWNING STREET, May 22, 1858. — . . . The great struggle, which has agitated the country the last fortnight, came to a sudden and untimely end last night; when it was thought that the very heat of the fight was to rage, the enemy suddenly fled in a manner the most ignominious! Never was such a rout! And never was a party in such a humiliating plight as was the great Whig Coalition that was to have devoured Her Majesty's Government, as an ogre does a child. I don't know I ever passed thro' a period of so much excitement, labor, and anxiety, encouraging the desponding and animating the timid. On the whole, however, our friends mustered gallantly, and the result of the attack has been greatly to strengthen our position. The country is with us, and had we dissolved Parliament, which we were prepared to do if the cabal had succeeded, I am convinced we should have crushed them. . . .

Montalembert, the eloquent Liberal Catholic, was present at this famous debate, and concludes his description thus: 'Ministers were victorious without one of them having risen to speak. Nothing remained for the Cabinet save to register its victory and determine its moral effect. This was done by Mr. Disraeli with infinite address and a triumphant modesty.' The motion, Disraeli said, was a vote of censure; but the Government had looked without apprehension to the result, and were ready to encounter the consequences of a division. Still, it was in the public interest that the debate should be terminated by a withdrawal of the motion. With the exception of

[1] *Queen Victoria's Letters.*

Ellenborough's despatch, intended only for Canning's eye, the Government had given and would give the Governor-General their cordial support, and they had telegraphed to him to that effect.

But permit me to say that if the relations between Her Majesty's Government and the Governor-General of India should be cordial, they should also be sincere; and if it is supposed that I or those with whom I act are prepared in any way to retract the opinions which we have expressed with regard to the policy of confiscation which Lord Canning, under evil influence, unhappily adopted, but which I hope, and have some reason to believe, he has by this time relinquished, the House will indeed have misinterpreted what I have said, and the country will be indeed be deceived as to the policy which we intend to pursue. I trust that Lord Canning will be influenced by those sentiments and that policy which distinguished his career at the commencement of these sad disturbances and disasters.

Disraeli's gallant fight and surprising victory brought him one of his first tastes of popular applause. Mrs. Disraeli wrote to Mrs. Willyams of the 'glorious news. Dizzy was cheered again and again by the multitude to and from Downing Street to the House of Commons.' The Whitsuntide recess immediately followed, and Disraeli went down into Bucks on the next Wednesday, and obtained from his constituents the same cordial greeting that the House of Commons and the people of London had already given him. The occasion was a public dinner at Slough to the members for the county. Disraeli claimed that Ministers had successfully surmounted three great sets of difficulties in their three months of office. In foreign affairs, where 'the question of peace or war when we acceded to office was not a question of weeks or days, but of hours,' they had preserved peace, vindicated the honour of England, and freed their imprisoned countrymen at Naples. In finance they had met an immense deficiency and reduced taxation. At the turning-point of our Indian Empire they had successfully laid down the principles on which it should be reconstructed.

Was it always to be massacre and confiscation? Or was it, on the other hand, to be a discriminating amnesty? Was it to be respect for private property, toleration for religious convictions, a due and decent regard for the manners and customs of the people? Were we, or were we not, to distinguish the great body of the inhabitants of India, who, after all, are Her Majesty's subjects, from those military and treacherous rebels who have received, or will receive, their merited punishment?

Though the House of Commons, as a body, had treated Ministers with a 'generous courtesy,' there existed a 'cabal,' consisting of some scheming English politicians and some foreign intriguers, working in a most reckless and unprincipled but determined manner to upset the Government. The cabal had corrupted the Press. 'Leading organs now are place-hunters of the cabal, and the once stern guardians of popular rights simper in the enervating atmosphere of gilded saloons'—a not very worthy sneer at Delane, who was a frequent guest at Palmerston's house, and who, in spite of his initial friendliness to the new Government, had encouraged in *The Times* the recent attack upon them.[1] To that attack Disraeli now turned. The cabal thought the occasion was favourable. 'Among all the shortsighted hangers-on of politics, our doom was supposed as certain as that of a man convicted and sentenced, who awaits only the arrival of Mr. Calcraft.' The cabal were resolved to 'loot' the Treasury, but they employed 'solemn and pious tools.'

The motion was brought forward in the House of Commons by a gentleman of unimpeachable reputation. The cabal, which has rather a tainted character, chose its instrument with pharisaical accuracy; and I assure you that, when Mr. Cardwell rose to impeach me, I was terrified at my own short-

---

[1] The quarrel with Delane was made up in the autumn. Samuel Lucas, the first editor of the *Press*, wrote to Disraeli on Oct. 11: 'I have just established regular communication between Earle and Printing House Square. . . . I had a long chat with Dasent to-day, and he assures me that in his opinion Delane bears no malice, but, on the contrary, like himself, he prefers you personally to most of the Whigs. As regards himself he says unquestionably, and as regards Delane he believes, that the effect of the Slough speech has entirely passed away.'

comings, as I listened to a *nisi prius* narrative ending with a resolution which I think must have been drawn up by a conveyancer. In the other House of Parliament a still greater reputation condescended to appear upon the human stage. Gamaliel himself [Shaftesbury], with the broad phylacteries of faction on his forehead, called God to witness that he was 'not like other men,' and was never influenced by party motives.

But independent members of Parliament, unconnected with the Ministry, 'saw through the flimsy web, and despised the authors of the perfidious and pernicious manœuvre.' The 'enlightened and indignant mind of England' declared itself in an unmistakable manner against the cabal, with the result which Disraeli once more described in an inimitable passage:

There is nothing like that last Friday evening in the history of the House of Commons. We came down expecting to divide at 4 o'clock in the morning, and I myself, with my armour buckled on, prepared to address them, perhaps, for two hours after midnight; and believe me, gentlemen, even with the consciousness of a good cause, that is no vain effort. We were all assembled. Our benches, with their serried ranks, seemed to rival those of our proud opponents, when there arose a wail of distress, but not from us. What ensued I can only liken to that mutiny of the Bengal army with which we are all so familiar. Regiment after regiment, corps after corps, general after general, all acknowledged that they could not 'march through Coventry' with Her Majesty's Opposition. Gentlemen, it was, I may say, rather like a convulsion of nature than one of the ordinary transactions of human life. I can liken it only to one of those earthquakes in Calabria or Peru, of which we sometimes read. There was a rumbling murmur, a groan, a shriek, distant thunder; and nobody knew whether it came from the top or the bottom of the House. There was a rent, a fissure in the ground. Then a village disappeared. Then a tall tower toppled down. And then the whole of the Opposition benches became one great dissolving view of anarchy!

Derby, who was present in the House of Commons on that Friday, testified a few days later to the perfect truth of this 'humorous and graphic description.' 'There was no exaggeration in the colouring, for no exaggeration could be applied to that extraordinary scene.' The

country in general joined in the laugh at the discomfiture
of the cabal; and the leaders of the Opposition were unwise enough to show their soreness, and to give Disraeli
a further opportunity of rubbing his criticism in. Russell,[1]
supported by Cornewall Lewis, rose to reply to the Slough
speech directly the House reassembled on Friday, May 28;
he was followed on the Monday by Palmerston, with Sir
George Grey for his supporter; and on the Tuesday
Clarendon, with Granville at his back, took up the tale in
the Lords, and gave Derby an opportunity to defend his
lieutenant. But Disraeli required no champion but his
own wit. No serious point was made against him, except
that he had exaggerated the danger of war at the time of
the change of Government. When, after Russell's re-
pulse, Palmerston advanced to the attack, Disraeli said he
was reminded of 'a very unfortunate circumstance' of
recent occurrence.

A gentleman of letters, having done, or said, or written
something that offended a very powerful army, was called to
account by a member of it. He met his opponent without
any hesitation, and in the first instance conducted himself
with fair repute and success. But no sooner was this first
affair over than another gentleman was sent for, one whose
fierce mien and formidable reputation were such that his
friends thought he would put the matter right. He, too,
demands satisfaction, and he is accompanied by a considerable
body of other gentlemen who seem by their appearance to
signify that, if the second assailant is not more successful
than the first, then they will find others to succeed him. In
short, having somehow or other got into a scrape, they mean
to bully him by numbers.

Disraeli reproached the Opposition leaders with wasting
precious time, when public business was backward, by
these unavailing expressions of discontent with the position
they now occupied. As to the cabal,

What I call a cabal is a body of men, whether it be in this
House or in another house — either a private house or a house

---

[1] Russell told Motley at the time that Disraeli's Slough speech was 'one
of the cleverest, wittiest, most mendacious, audacious, and besotted
speeches that were ever made' (Motley's *Letters*, Vol. I., p. 249).

devoted to affairs of State — banded together, not to carry out
a policy, not to recommend by their wisdom and their eloquence great measures to the approving sympathy of the community, but uniting all their resources, their abilities, and
their varied influence, for what? — to upset the Queen's Government, without even in so doing declaring any policy of their
own, or giving any further clue to their opinions than this —
that the first article of their creed is place.

Neither Liberals nor Conservatives, added Disraeli,
whatever their differences, would any longer allow themselves to be made 'the tools or the victims of an obsolete
oligarchy.' The Whigs had indeed exposed themselves
to derision and contempt. Bright's organ, the *Morning
Star*,[1] gave a description, at once truthful and humorous,
of the situation. It likened the consternation which the
Slough speech had produced in the ranks of Whiggery to
the clamour set up by the discharge of a fowling-piece
among a flock of wild-geese. Their fury was ludicrous
and uncontrollable. They could not conceal the intense
bitterness of their chagrin; their daily and weekly organs
harped upon it with 'damnable iteration'; their leaders
in Parliament 'nightly to the moon complained' of their
wrongs.

And the worst of it is that they come off second-best each
time they renew the assault. Beyond all question, their adver-
sary, whatever may be thought of his prudence as a statesman, is perfect master of the sort of fence to which they
are constantly challenging him. He evidently revels and
luxuriates in the sport, and no impartial observer, we believe,
will deny that his opponents have been obliged to retire from
the lists worsted in the encounter.

The principles underlying Ellenborough's despatch had
been vindicated; it remained to fill the place which his
resignation had left vacant. Disraeli, no less than Derby,
was anxious to utilise the vacancy to promote an object
which they had pursued at intervals for some years, and
which they kept constantly before them throughout the
course of the 1858–59 Ministry — namely, the recapture
of Gladstone for his old party connection, with or without

[1] June 2.

the other *disjecta membra* of the Peelite party, Aberdeen,
Graham, and Sidney Herbert. Aberdeen and Graham
were now veterans, no longer desiring office — the one
seventy-four, the other, though not more than sixty-six,
yet in failing health; Sidney Herbert was attractive and
accomplished rather than powerful. But Gladstone was
in his prime, still under fifty; and, though it was not yet
realised how volcanic was his pent-up energy, he was
already a political force of the first magnitude, condemned,
however, to temporary ineffectiveness through isolation.
Moreover, to a greater degree than his Peelite colleagues,
he had been for three years steadily associated in
political action, though not allied, with his old party;
and to the world in general, though some, like Bright,
saw more clearly the drift of his mind, he appeared to have
taken up a definitely Conservative position. That was
certainly the opinion of his own Conservative University,
which at the General Elections of 1857 and 1859 — and
at them alone of seven occasions on which he was a candidate — returned him unopposed. Now there was to be
a test whether the recent political course of this 'half-
regained Eurydice,' as Derby called him, had any serious
intention behind it. In 1855, according to his own
account, he was prepared to join Derby if Palmerston
would join also, in spite of having just resigned as a
member of that Coalition which Disraeli had done so
much to destroy.[1] Since then he had, like Disraeli,
supported a reasonable peace with Russia, and had, in
common with him, advocated a policy of retrenchment
and economy after the war, and vehemently opposed
Palmerston's aggressive adventures. He shared with the
Conservatives the responsibility for defeating Palmerston
both over the China War and over the Conspiracy Bill.
He told both Derby and his Peelite friends that his
principal object during this period was to overthrow
Palmerston's supremacy, in which he saw nothing but
evil. If he perceived no fatal objection to a junction

[1] See Vol. III., p. 563.

with Derby in 1855, surely *a fortiori* he must gladly come in now, when he had proved the possibility of common action, and when the consolidation in office of a strong Conservative Government was the only possible means of preventing Palmerston's return to power.

Derby, with Disraeli's complete approval, had applied to Gladstone, without success, immediately he received the Queen's commission to form a Government. Gladstone's reasons for refusal did not seem of a final or conclusive character; and his relations to the Government had been drawn closer by a Budget based on his own proposals of 1853, and defended by him against Liberal criticism. It was to Gladstone, therefore, that the thoughts of the Government chiefs mainly turned when Ellenborough's resignation placed a high office at their disposal. Rose, as the party agent, pressed on Disraeli the necessity of not being content with 'a mere patch-up' among the members of their own party, but of making every effort to strengthen the Cabinet from outside; Earle reminded him that what the Cabinet wanted was 'strength in the House of Commons.' Accordingly, after some preliminary soundings — in the course of which Disraeli vainly offered, in order to facilitate Gladstone's adhesion, to resign the lead to Graham — Walpole, on May 22, the morrow of the collapse of Cardwell's motion, formally on Derby's behalf asked for Gladstone's co-operation, placing either the Board of Control or the Colonial Office at his disposal, and stating that the spirit in which the offer was made was 'a desire that it should be taken to signify the wish of the Government progressively to extend its basis.' Gladstone still demurred, stating his objections in much the same terms as in the previous February, but consented to consult Graham and Aberdeen before finally refusing. Disraeli, however airily he might talk of Gladstone as a 'deserter' whose submission must be unconditional,[1] was determined to do

---

[1] Vitzthum, Vol. I., p. 269.

everything in his power to make the negotiation a success. Accordingly he seconded Derby's offer by a personal appeal, as magnanimous as it was impressive.

To William Ewart Gladstone.

Confidential. Grosvenor Gate, *May* 25, 1858. — I think it of such paramount importance to the public interests that you should assume at this time a commanding position in the administration of affairs that I feel it a solemn duty to lay before you some facts, that you may not decide under a misapprehension.

Our mutual relations have formed the great difficulty in accomplishing a result which I have always anxiously desired.

Listen, without prejudice, to this brief narrative.

In 1850, when the balanced state of parties in the House of Commons indicated the future, I endeavored, through the medium of the late Lord Londonderry, and for some time not without hope, to induce Sir James Graham to accept the post of leader of the Conservative party, which I thought would remove all difficulties.

When he finally declined this office, I endeavored to throw the game into your hands, and your conduct then, however unintentional, assisted me in my views.

The precipitate Ministry of 1852 baffled all this. Could we have postponed it another year, all might have been right.

Nevertheless, notwithstanding my having been forced publicly into the chief place in the Commons, and all that occurred in consequence, I was still constant to my purpose, and in 1855 suggested that the leadership of the House should be offered to Lord Palmerston, entirely with the view of consulting your feelings and facilitating your position.

Some short time back, when the power of dissolution was certain, and the consequences of it such as, in my opinion, would be highly favorable to the Conservative party, I again confidentially sought Sir James Graham, and implored him to avail himself of the favorable conjuncture, accept the post of leader in the H. of C., and allow both of us to serve under him.

He was more than kind to me, and fully entered into the state of affairs, but he told me his course was run, and that he had not strength or spirit for such an enterprise.

Thus you see, for more than eight years, instead of thrusting myself into the foremost place, I have been, at all times, actively prepared to make every sacrifice of self for the public good, which I have ever thought identical with your accepting office in a Conservative Government.

Don't you think the time has come when you might deign to be magnanimous?

Mr. Canning was superior to Lord Castlereagh in capacity, in acquirements, in eloquence, but he joined Lord C. when Lord C. was Lord Liverpool's lieutenant, when the state of the Tory party rendered it necessary. That was an enduring and, on the whole, not an unsatisfactory connection, and it certainly terminated very gloriously for Mr. Canning.

I may be removed from the scene, or I may wish to be removed from the scene.

Every man performs his office, and there is a Power, greater than ourselves, that disposes of all this.

The conjuncture is very critical, and, if prudently yet boldly managed, may rally this country. To be inactive now is, on your part, a great responsibility. If you join Lord Derby's Cabinet, you will meet there some warm personal friends; all its members are your admirers. You may place me in neither category, but in that, I assure you, you have ever been sadly mistaken. The vacant post is, at this season, the most commanding in the Commonwealth; if it were not, whatever office you filled, your shining qualities would always render you supreme; and if party necessities retain me formally in the chief post, the sincere and delicate respect which I should always offer you, and the unbounded confidence which on my part, if you choose, you could command, would prevent your feeling my position as anything but a form.

Think of all this in a kindly spirit. These are hurried lines, but they are heartfelt. I was in the country yesterday, and must return there to-day for a county dinner. My direction is Langley Park, Slough. But on Wednesday evening I shall be in town.— B. DISRAELI.

It was a generous and manly letter,[1] and deserved a worthier response than the stiff and frigid reply in which even Gladstone's biographer seems to hear the 'accents of guarded reprobation.'

From William Ewart Gladstone.

11, CARLTON HOUSE TERRACE, *May* 25, 1858.

MY DEAR SIR,— The letter you have been so kind as to address to me will enable me, I trust, to remove from your mind some impressions with which you will not be sorry to part.

---

[1] That Gladstone did not join, Disraeli told Bishop Wilberforce in 1862, 'was not my fault . . . I almost went on my knees to him.'

You have given me a narrative of your conduct since 1850 with reference to your position as leader of your party. But I have never thought your retention of that office matter of reproach to you, and on Saturday last I acknowledged to Mr. Walpole the handsomeness of your conduct in offering to resign it to Sir James Graham.

You consider that the relations between yourself and me have proved the main difficulty in the way of certain political arrangements. Will you allow me to assure you that I have never in my life taken a decision which turned upon them?

You assure me that I have ever been mistaken in failing to place you among my friends or admirers. Again I pray you to let me say that I have never known you penurious in admiration towards anyone who had the slightest claim to it, and that at no period of my life, not even during the limited one when we were in sharp political conflict, have I either felt any enmity towards you, or believed that you felt any towards me.

At the present moment I am awaiting counsel which at Lord Derby's wish I have sought. But the difficulties which he wishes me to find means of overcoming are broader than you may have supposed. Were I at this time to join any Government, I could not do it in virtue of party connection. I must consider, then, what are the conditions which make harmonious and effective co-operation in Cabinet possible; how largely old habits enter into them; what connections can be formed with public approval; and what change would be requisite in the constitution of the present Government in order to make any change worth a trial.

I state these points fearlessly and without reserve, for you have yourself well reminded me that there is a Power beyond us that disposes of what we are and do, and I find the limits of choice in public life to be very narrow. — I remain, my dear sir, very faithfully yours, W. E. GLADSTONE.[1]

Aberdeen, on the whole, advised Gladstone to decline; Graham, on the whole, to accept. Graham no longer thought it would be humiliation for Gladstone to sit on the Treasury bench with Disraeli as his leader, and believed that, if he accepted, he would eventually supersede him. The historian may well regret that so intensely interesting an experiment was never made. It would

---

[1] Both of these letters are printed (Gladstone's from a draft, which explains some slight inaccuracies) in Lord Morley's *Gladstone*, Bk. IV., ch. 9; but it seems material to the proper understanding of Disraeli's character and conduct to reprint them here.

have reproduced on the Conservative front bench the spectacle presented for some twenty years by Russell and Palmerston on the Liberal front bench. Disraeli, with a fine confidence in himself and with the spirit of adventure still strong within him, openly invited this friendly rivalry, and was prepared to carry it on in a chivalrous manner. Not every student of politics will agree with Graham that Gladstone would have superseded Disraeli, as Palmerston superseded Russell, as leader. It is at least possible that, subjected to the same intimate influence, Gladstone would eventually have yielded to the fascination which in the long run brought people so diverse as Queen Victoria, Derby, Salisbury, Metternich, Lyndhurst, Northcote, Gathorne Hardy, and many more, to repose their confidence in one whom most of them were originally disposed to dislike and contemn.

Gladstone was not willing to make the trial. 'If he supports him [Disraeli],' wrote, with robust common-sense, Gladstone's friend the Duke of Argyll, 'I cannot see why he should not serve with him.' [1] The Duke forgot that to Gladstone a fine distinction of this kind would make a special appeal. Gladstone wrote next day to Derby that he must adhere to his reply to Walpole, as he did not see 'a prospect of public advantage or of material accession to your strength, from my entering your Government single-handed.' He added that to a scheme which would embrace the Peelite leaders as a body he should be individually favourable; but even of such a scheme he should not be sanguine. 'Lord Aberdeen is the person who could best give a dispassionate and weighty opinion on this subject.' The Conservative leaders differed as to what this oracular letter meant.

From Lord Derby.

Private. ST. JAMES'S SQUARE, *May* 27, 1858. — I could not get away from Osborne. . . . We have much and important

[1] Letter to Lord Aberdeen, May 25, 1858. See the Duke's *Autobiography*, Vol. II., p. 120.

matters to talk on, in reference to personal arrangements. Stanley seems to think, and he says that you agree with him, that Gladstone's letter, like that of the K. of Naples, is not a 'refus catégorique,' but a 'réponse argumentative.' I am rather of the Queen's opinion, who wished to know whom he expected to take the responsibility of his accepting office. . . . I really hardly see how we can approach Aberdeen (which is Stanley's notion, and he thinks is Gladstone's) with any proposition which should not be either an insult to him or a degradation to us; but I will talk this over with you to-morrow. . . .

To Lord Stanley.

May 28, 1858] Friday, 11 *o'clock.* — Your father has just left me. He wishes that you should see Ld. A[berdeen] immediately, and sound him on the situation. What we want is that G[ladstone] should take India under the shield and cover of Lord Ab. joining the Cabinet, like Lord Lansdowne, without office — in short, as we settled together yesterday. . . . Time is very precious, which I need not press upon you. I give you no precise instructions, for all must depend upon the occasion, the humor of Ab., and your own tact.

The mission to Aberdeen was unsuccessful, and Derby and Disraeli had once more to fall back on the resources of their own party. It was decided to transfer Stanley, the man of the future in the Cabinet, to the India Board — an arrangement equally agreeable to his father and to his political mentor. For the Colonial Office Disraeli suggested his friend Chandos, who 'is a little Lord Grenville'; but eventually it was offered to, and accepted by, Bulwer Lytton, who had made difficulties in February, but was now ready to face his re-election. As Earle wrote, it was 'something to have a name of European celebrity added to the Cabinet.' The new Minister assured Disraeli that 'on accepting office I have no sensation so pleasurable as that of sharing in any difficulties that may beset you; and in the easier opportunities, so afforded, of removing any misconceptions which may yet leave a shadow on that affectionate friendship which I trust to carry with me to my grave.'

Lytton's tenure of the Colonial Office was shortly to

subserve Disraeli's determination, still persistent in spite of repeated rebuffs, to secure, if possible, Gladstone's co-operation in Government. The Ionian Islands, which had been a British protectorate since 1815, had been for years in a disturbed state, with a strong party agitating for union with Greece. Lytton considered it advisable to send a special mission, and fixed on Gladstone as an ideal High Commissioner. Gladstone's disposition was supposed, in spite of his refusal to take office, to be still friendly to Ministers. Rose wrote to Disraeli in August that a friend of his who had been visiting Gladstone reported: 'G. expressed himself warmly in favour of the Government, and in very friendly terms towards you, describing your conduct of the business in Parliament in most complimentary terms.'

From Sir Edward Bulwer Lytton.

COLONIAL OFFICE, *Sept.* 23, 1858.— . . . I have received some information privately which makes me believe that he [Gladstone] would listen more favourably to such a proposal than you might imagine at the first blush. The peculiar position of the man at present, his scholarly tastes and associations, the prospective fame of saving the freedom and reforming the constitution of a Greek people, might be so placed before him as to influence his choice; and at all events I think I could so put the proposal as to please and propitiate him.

As a party move for the Government, I think success here would be a masterstroke in negotiation; and, besides, if he would consent to be less crotchety, I believe he would suit the occasion better than any other man we could send. . . .

Disraeli cordially approved the suggestion. 'I was privy to the plot,' he wrote to Stanley on October 24, 'but never supposed it would result in anything but endless correspondence.' The idea, however, fired Gladstone's imagination, and on October 30 Lytton was able to tell Disraeli: 'All is settled, and Gladstone is to have a war steamer to meet him at Trieste.' Gladstone, undeterred by several untoward incidents, went to work with a will, drew up a series of constitutional reforms, and

Edward Bulwer Lytton, 1ˢᵗ Lord Lytton.
from the portrait after D. Maclise, R.A. at Hughenden.
presented by the 2ⁿᵈ Lord Lytton.

offered, on December 27, to remain for a time in the islands himself, as Lord High Commissioner, to introduce them. Lytton advised acceptance of the offer. 'His proposed constitution,' he wrote to Disraeli, 'is in reality a responsible Government approaching to that of a colony; and though it may need alterations to which he would agree, it is our safest choice to take it and leave it under his care.' Derby hesitated, foreseeing, it may be, the difficulty of maintaining the protectorate if a free constitution were granted; but Disraeli took prompt command of the situation.

To Lord Derby.

Confidential. DOWNING STREET, *Jan.* 6, 1859. — Lytton sent me last midnight the Ionian box from Knowsley. It is impossible to impugn the sound sense of your observations. Pardon me, therefore, if an overwhelming conviction of the inexpediency of exactly following the course which you recommend emboldens me to trouble you with one remark.

I view the strange circumstances solely with reference to the assembly for the management of which I am, through your confidence, mainly responsible.

If we decline Gladstone's proposal, it is clear to me that he will lose no time in bringing it forward in the House of Commons. There I am persuaded it will be carried, and Gladstone will be master of the situation.

If we accept his present offer, and he fails, the failure will be his: if he succeed, the credit will redound to the Government which selected him. When once he has embarked in the undertaking he must see it to its end. Every thought and feeling that govern man will bring this about.

I will not dwell on the question who, but he, in the present state of affairs, can be L. H. C. . . . Young[1] must be recalled instanter.

I confine myself solely, in these rapid but deeply considered lines, to the expression of one of the strongest and clearest opinions that I ever entertained, that the general refusal of Gladstone's proposal would be to extricate him from a most difficult position, and to place him in a commanding one. . . .

Disraeli prevailed, and Gladstone's offer was accepted. Unfortunately, the islanders could not be persuaded to

---

[1] Sir J. Young, the Lord High Commissioner.

take constitutional reform as a substitute for union with Greece. They rejected Gladstone's proposals; and the union with Greece, of which he would not hear at the time, was ultimately, in 1863, acquiesced in by a Government of which he was a leading member. Disraeli does not appear, on the present occasion, to have regarded the Ionian question, which was outside his departmental purview, in any other aspect than as a means of either attaching Gladstone more closely to the Government, or, in the alternative, discrediting him. The value of the islands from a naval and military point of view to a Mediterranean Power is not discussed in his correspondence of 1858–59.

Gladstone returned to England in March, 1859. He refused to join in the Liberal attack on the Government Reform Bill, and he supported Ministers on the vote of confidence.[1] But he declined renewed overtures from Derby in May, and in June unhesitatingly accepted an offer to be Chancellor of the Exchequer in a Liberal Government, under a Prime Minister of whose policy, save in his support of Italian unity, he had totally disapproved, and whom he distrusted, his friends thought, even more than he distrusted Disraeli. He thereby secured for himself a fairly certain succession to the veterans Palmerston and Russell, in preference to a dubious rivalry with Disraeli, who was almost his contemporary.

The appointment of Stanley to the Board of Control took the burden of conducting through the House of Commons the India Resolutions, and the subsequent India Bill, off Disraeli's shoulders; but his constant attention to the subject was insured both by his deep interest in the country and by his solicitude for the success of his political pupil. The collapse of the Opposition over the Cardwell motion had left them with little heart for further fighting; and the Government repelled, by considerable majorities, amendments to the Resolutions calculated to

[1] See below, Chs. 6 and 7.

substitute Palmerston's original provisions for their own.
Such being the temper of the House, Ministers introduced
their Bill without taking the trouble to carry all their
Resolutions, Stanley drily remarking, to the general
amusement, that those already passed had answered their
purpose.

To Mrs. Brydges Willyams.

DOWNING STREET, *June* 16, 1858. — It is a long time since
I said to you, ' How d'ye do ? '

My life has been passed in constant combat, but I am glad
to add, with respect to all important matters, constant victory.
The enemy, however, like the Sepoys, still keep the field, and,
like Sir Colin, I really have to carry on the campaign under a
scorching sky. Morning sittings and evening sittings, with
the duties of my department, Cabinet Councils, and the general
conduct of affairs, engross and absorb my life from the moment
I wake until the hour of rest, which is generally three hours
after midnight.

But I never was better. I am sorry to say I cannot aver
as much of my chief and colleague. Lord Derby has a raging
fit of the gout which terribly disconcerts me. Fortunately,
we are now, generally speaking, on velvet; but, unhappily,
all the measures which I have carried thro' the House of
Commons will soon be going to the Upper House, and he will
be required to advocate and conduct them.

Our settlement of the Neapolitan difficulties has gained us
great credit, and I hear from all parts of the country that the
Government is not only popular, but daily increasing in public
favor. Lord Stanley is of great use to me, and much distinguishes himself. . . .

I have never been in the country for five months, except
a little visit to Windsor. Even when I went to Slough — the
famous Slough — it was with a return ticket. But with
success one can bear anything.

To Queen Victoria.

HOUSE OF COMMONS, *June* 24, 1858. — The Chancellor of the
Exchequer, with his humble duty to your Majesty.

The India Bill was read a second time without a division.
Lord Stanley made a clear and vigorous exposition of its spirit
and provisions; Mr. Bright delivered a powerful oration on the
condition of India — its past government and future prospects;
the rest of the discussion weak and desultory.

No serious opposition apprehended in Committee, which

the Chancellor of the Exchequer has fixed for this day (Friday), and almost hopes that he may conclude the Committee on Monday. He proposes to proceed with no other business until it is concluded.

When the Bill has passed, the temper of the House, and its sanitary state, will assist him in passing the remaining estimates with rapidity; and he contemplates an early conclusion of the Session.

It will be a great thing to have carried the India Bill, which Mr. Thomas Baring to-night spoke of in terms of eulogy, and as a great improvement on the project of the late Government. It is, the Chancellor of the Exchequer really thinks, a wise and well-digested measure, ripe with the experience of the last five months of discussion; but it is only the antechamber of an imperial palace, and your Majesty would do well to deign to consider the steps which are now necessary to influence the opinions and affect the imagination of the Indian populations. The name of your Majesty ought to be impressed upon their native life. Royal proclamations, Courts of Appeal, in their own land, and other institutions, forms, and ceremonies, will tend to this great result.[1]

The constitution provided by this Bill is that under which, with slight modifications, the Government of India has ever since been carried on. The authority of the East India Company and of the Board of Control was transferred to the Secretary of State for India in Council. In regard to the Council, in deference to the general opinion of the House of Commons, the Government abandoned the elective principle, which had been a pet device of Ellenborough's and was favoured by Disraeli, but which was abhorrent to Stanley's plain common-sense. The number of the Council was fixed at fifteen, seven to be chosen by the Directors of the Company, and eight to be nominated by the Secretary of State, the majority of the Councillors to have the qualification of ten years' residence in India. As the result of later legislation, the Council is now twelve instead of fifteen, and they are all nominated by the Secretary of State. They were to be paid, might not sit in Parliament, and had a tenure of office as secure as that of the Judges. The decision of

[1] *Queen Victoria's Letters.*

the Secretary of State was to be final, save in financial
questions, and he had authority to decide, without consulting the Council, all matters which came within the
purview of the old Secret Committee.   Comparatively
slight changes were made in the Bill during its Parliamentary course, save that Gladstone procured by general
consent the insertion of a clause which, as modified in the
Lords, provided that, except for repelling actual invasion
or under other sudden or urgent necessity, the Indian
revenues should not be applied, without the consent of
Parliament, to defray the expense of military operations
beyond the Indian frontiers

It is a constitution which has upon the whole worked
well; but it required for its cordial acceptance in India,
as Disraeli wrote to the Queen, personal association with
the Sovereign in such a way as 'to influence the opinions
and affect the imagination of the Indian populations.
The name of your Majesty ought to be impressed upon
their native life.'   In after-years Disraeli was to effect
this in several striking ways.[1]   For the moment he was
anxious that the royal proclamation, announcing to
the people of India the assumption of direct authority
by the Crown, should be a document worthy of the
Sovereign and of the occasion.   Stanley, with great
business merits, was lacking in imagination,[2] and his
draft satisfied neither the Queen nor Disraeli.   He was
laudably anxious that the religious neutrality of the
Indian Government should be emphasised, but did not
seem to realise the importance, both in England and in
India, of emphasising also the religious character of the
Sovereign.

To Lord Stanley.

HUGHENDEN MANOR, *Aug.* 13, 1858. — I fear a storm is
brewing respecting the religious portion of the Ind. question.

[1] See above, p. 93.

[2] In a note, dated 1863, Disraeli writes that when he and Stanley 'were
discussing any grave point, and Stanley saw nothing but difficulties, and I
evinced my impatience, he used to say, " I know what you are going to
say." He meant, that he had no imagination.'

You appear at Lynn, and also to the deputation the other day, to have spoken of Christianity as 'the religion of Europe.' The dissatisfaction is not confined to the ultra-religious circles merely.   No Government can stand that is supposed to slight the religious feelings of the country. It is as important to touch the feelings and sympathy of the religious classes in England as to conciliate the natives of India; and I think both objects may be accomplished if the neutrality, on which all agree, is laid down in the right way and on the right basis. . . .

To Derby Disraeli had written to the same effect, adding: 'I shall write to [Stanley] by this post ; he will not like it, but it must be done.'   Stanley did not like it, and forwarded the letter to his father with a caustic comment.   The Queen interposed, and asked the Prime Minister to draft the proclamation himself 'in his excellent language,' 'bearing in mind that it is a female Sovereign who speaks to more than 100,000,000 of Eastern people on assuming the direct government of them after a bloody civil war, giving them pledges which her future reign is to redeem, and explaining the principles of her government.'   Derby justified Her Majesty's confidence. 'Firmly relying on the truth of Christianity,' ran the proclamation, 'and acknowledging with gratitude the solace of religion, we disclaim alike the right and the desire to impose our convictions on any of our subjects.   It is our royal will and pleasure that no one shall in any wise suffer for his opinions, or be disquieted by reason of his religious faith or observance.   We will show to all alike the equal and impartial protection of the law.'   The policy of clemency which Disraeli had throughout advocated was carried out in the proclamation by the promise of a general amnesty to all not guilty of murder.

To Mrs. Brydges Willyams.

Downing Street, *July* 26, 1858. — It is a long time since I wrote to you, but the last month has been one of almost supernatural labor. It has, however, been successful. Notwithstanding all the disturbance and hostility of the early

part of the session, there has seldom been one in which a
greater number of excellent measures have been passed than
the present.

The day before yesterday, altho' Saturday, the House sate
in the morning and worked well; then at three o'clock we
had a Cabinet, and at 6 o'clock we went to Greenwich for the
Fish Dinner. We ate it with a good relish. It is the carnival
of politics, and a great deal of nonsense is talked, which is not
difficult when you have won the day. Our chairman was the
Attorney-General for Ireland, Whiteside, who is witty and
eloquent and full of resource.

Lord Derby gave his health with a sentiment: 'Whiteside
and whitebait!'

On Saturday we go to Osborne to hold a Council and settle
the Queen's Speech. It will be a flourishing one, and on Monday we shall prorogue Parliament and give it a holiday — I
hope of at least six months.

We shall try to get to Hughenden immediately, that we
may see our trees with something of the bowery refulgence
of summer; and as the summer wanes, I shall not be surprised
if we find ourselves for a day or two at Torquay.

I don't count on much holiday for the rest of the year, as
public affairs are very urgent, and my labors of preparation
for the next campaign will not be light. I have declined to
go to Ireland [1] and to Scotland, and shall content myself with
the sylvan beauties of Bucks and the soft breezes of delicious
Devon. I hope to see you quite flourishing.

Disraeli was justified in his boast of the fruitfulness of
the session. The passing of the India Act alone would
have given it distinction; but several other beneficial
laws were enacted and thorny questions settled. Local
government in towns was improved; Scottish Universities were regulated; an Encumbered Estates Act was
passed for Ireland. These were useful but not showy
measures. More interest attached to the passage, after
a more than ten years' wrangle, of an Act admitting
Jews to Parliament. This measure of liberality and
justice, for which Disraeli had so long pleaded in vain,[2]
was at last granted under his official auspices, and a

---

[1] Lady Londonderry had pressed the Disraelis to come and stay with
her in the North of Ireland, and had promised him an enthusiastic reception at Belfast.

[2] See Vol. III., ch. 3.

constant source of dissension between leader and party
done away with. Then Bulwer Lytton carried a Bill
establishing the colony of British Columbia; and, in the
Queen's Speech, Her Majesty was happily advised to
express a hope 'that this new colony on the Pacific may
be but one step in the career of steady progress by which
Her Majesty's dominions in North America may ultimately be peopled, in an unbroken chain, from the
Atlantic to the Pacific, by a loyal and industrious population of subjects of the British Crown.' That hope has
been abundantly fulfilled; but Disraeli, as the guardian
of a not overfull Exchequer, did not feel justified in
offering more than a sympathetic hearing to a deputation
which came in the autumn from the Governments of
Canada, New Brunswick, and Nova Scotia, with a scheme
under which that 'unbroken chain' might be promoted
by means of an intercolonial railway. Finally, Disraeli
himself introduced and carried into law a Bill for the
purification of the Thames by a great scheme of main
drainage. The health of the people was always one of
the preoccupations of his statesmanship; some years later
he promulgated, as a Conservative watchword, *Sanitas
sanitatum, omnia sanitas.* An unusually hot season had
revealed the Thames in London for what it then was,
a common sewer; and its offensiveness to members who
met to legislate on its bank disposed them to facilitate
the rapid passing of the Government Bill. The Metropolitan Board of Works was chosen as the authority, the
expense was to be met by a sewage rate, and the Treasury
started the scheme with a handsome guarantee. The
success of the measure showed that practical efficiency
could be happily combined with a statesmanship of
ideas.

The India Act, both in its progress through Parliament
and in its subsequent administration, raised a number
of questions in which the prerogative was, or seemed to
be, involved, and in which the Court was particularly
interested. Stanley, the last President of the Board of

Control and first Secretary of State for India, was no courtier, and was somewhat impatient of the claims of prerogative; and not only Derby, but Disraeli, as Stanley's intimate friend and immediate leader, had to smooth away many difficulties. Stanley's prompt acceptance of Gladstone's amendment making the use of the Indian Army outside India dependent upon the consent of Parliament; his insistence on unrestricted competition and a Parliamentary title for Indian appointments; his delay in assimilating, to meet the Queen's wishes, the practice of the new India Office, in regard to submissions to Her Majesty, to that of the Foreign Office; his reluctance to allow the Commander-in-Chief, the Duke of Cambridge, to have any control over the Indian Army — were all causes of offence.

On the first two points Derby placated the Court by moving amendments in the Lords, which saved constitutional form without seriously modifying the meaning of the Act. In regard to the last two the Prince Consort sought Disraeli's aid; and an interesting letter to the Prince, dated November 18, printed in full in *Queen Victoria's Letters*, gives Disraeli's account of the tactful manner in which he carried out, in conversation with Stanley, the delicate mission. Stanley 'without reserve and cordially' accepted the position that he must act always as the Minister of the Queen, and not of the Council of India; and he agreed on all military matters, while reserving the authority of the Secretary of State, to communicate habitually with the Commander-in-Chief and take his advice. 'Throughout this interview,' Disraeli wrote, 'Lord Stanley's manner was candid, very conciliatory, and, for him, even soft. He was pleased to say that it was a source of great satisfaction to him that your Royal Highness had deigned to confer confidentially with me on the subject, and make me, as it were, a "mediator" on matters which, he assured me with great emphasis, had occasioned him an amount of anxiety almost intolerable. . . . He parted from me with an

earnest expression of his hope that the painful misconceptions which had prevailed might at once, or at least in due course, entirely disappear.' The Prince expressed in reply his satisfaction and gratitude.

As this correspondence shows, Disraeli's relations with the Court were decidedly better and closer during this Ministry than in 1852. Then he only received one invitation to Windsor in the whole ten months; in 1858–59 he was several times Her Majesty's guest. We may accept with confidence the first part of Mrs. Disraeli's statement to Mrs. Willyams after the fall of this Ministry : ' The Queen is all kindness to Dis, and would give him anything ' — that is, of course, in the way of honour or decoration. The Prince Consort was obviously beginning to shake off the strong distrust which he had originally entertained of Disraeli, and had many friendly conversations and much friendly correspondence with him on public affairs, recommending, for instance, ' to your paternal care the infant establishment at South Kensington.' Disraeli gratified the Court by his refusal to act on a private member's motion, carried by a majority of two in a thin House, in favour of placing the War Office and the Horse Guards under a single Minister, and thus ousting the then quasi-independent authority of the Commander-in-Chief — a reform for which the time was perhaps not ripe. He recommended to the House of Commons[1] the Lords' amendment about open competition for Indian appointments, in language which showed a due regard both for the prerogative of the Crown and for the privilege of Parliament. He said that he was a firm, but not an extravagant or headstrong, supporter of the competitive principle in public appointments. In this great work of a new Indian Government they had added much to Her Majesty's regality, invested Her Majesty with new prerogatives, new privileges, and new powers. But in doing so they had felt it their duty to insert conditions and regulations which they would not have

[1] July 30.

thought of inserting had they been dealing with ancient prerogatives of a different character. India was gained by the energy of the middle classes, who had long possessed all the patronage of that great empire. It had always been considered that the transfer from the Company to a more direct and satisfactory polity could not take place without great injury to the middle classes and a dangerous increase of the power of the Crown. Disraeli claimed that the Government measure had avoided both these dangers, and that by the Lords' amendment the constitutional form and spirit were more completely observed.

During the whole of this Ministry the intimacy between Disraeli and Stanley was particularly close, and Disraeli watched over Stanley almost as a father over a son. The correspondence between 'Dear S.' and 'Dear D.' was constant, and Stanley repaired to Disraeli whenever he was in a difficulty. There was withal a frequent difference of opinion; Stanley by no means always accepted his mentor's view.

To Lord Stanley.

[*July*, 1858.] — Ross of *The Times* earnestly begged me to impress on you always to speak to the *clock*.[1] I always do myself, and call it Mr. Speaker.

If you address the gallery or the Opposition front bench, people below your own gangway and behind you hear so imperfectly that they begin to talk among themselves; and it looks as if you were losing the ear of the House, when, in fact, their inattention rises from their not hearing you.

By addressing the clock, your face is half turned to your own side, instead of your back.

HUGHENDEN MANOR, *Aug.* 9, 1858. — . . . Read the enclosed,[2] and help me in due season, I pray you! For the Tyrwhitt Drakes to ask a service from me is the Hapsburgs soliciting something from a parvenu Napoleon. After thirty

---

[1] Charles Ross, in his advice, seems to have ignored the interest of the Reporters' Gallery, of which he was the head. A speaker in the House of Commons who addresses the clock turns his back upon the reporters.

[2] Letter from Squire Drake, of Shardeloes, near Amersham, asking for a cadetship. Stanley gave the appointment.

years of scorn and sullenness they have melted before time
and events. Their formal adhesion to me would add immensely to my power in this part of the world.

Aug. 10, 1858. — The more I think over your Indian Council, the more I feel convinced it will mortify your party and
the House of Commons. No Ministry ever slighted either
with impunity. The House of Commons is not in the least
considered in the matter. . . .

When a great measure like the India Bill is carried, and
a body like the Indian Council established, Parliament is
entitled to some portion of the spoil. It is often the only
means by which the labors and services of individuals who
have been a quarter of a century in Parliament can be publicly recognised by a Minister.

If the first appointments in the Civil Service are to be
regulated by statute, and the subsequent patronage is to
be withheld from M.P.'s, the House of Commons will soon
lose all authority, and be looked upon by the country as
a mere debating club. Patronage is the outward and visible
sign of an inward and spiritual grace, and that is Power.
The feeling of the House of Commons was that the lay
appointments should be reserved for public men in our
political life. You have crammed the Council with Indians.
Take a man like ——; he has been four and twenty years
in Parliament; able, cultured, a man of business, as all who
have seen him act as Chairman of a Committee well know;
he would make a very good Indian Councillor. . . . There
are several men of this class, who have given their lives to
public affairs and their party, and who would be made perfectly happy in their lot by such a post, for which they are
perfectly competent, bringing in the feelings of men of the
world and Parliament, in a circle of somewhat restricted
sentiments. . . .

I entreat you to think well of this matter. An over-scrupu-
losity in public life often leads to arrangements which are less
justifiable than a course of conduct which, at the first blush,
might seem more coarse and obvious.

From Lord Stanley.

Confidential. INDIA BOARD, *Aug.* 12, 1858. — I am never
insensible to arguments used by you, though in this case I
must fairly own that my opinion is adverse. Remember that
the interests to be consulted are various. Ellenborough is
quite ripe for opposition already, and some of his men I must
take, under penalty of offending him altogether: then each
Presidency must be represented, for they differ as widely as

Spain from France: again, all the nominees of 1853 are excluded by the Directors, and some have an absolute claim, by virtue of service and recognised talent: lastly, bear in mind that the H. of C., great as its power may be, is not what it was before the Press reached its present influence, and a suspicion of jobbery, from which we at this moment stand clear, and the Whigs as a body do not, would hurt us far more than we should be helped by gratifying one or two individuals. I know you will weigh these reasons fairly, and that is all I ask you to do. . . .

On this question of the appointments to the India Council, there is force in the arguments on both sides. Stanley at any rate maintained his position, and none of the members of Parliament whom Disraeli recommended were appointed members of the first Council.

Disraeli's letters to Mrs. Willyams this autumn contain several allusions to his intimacy with Stanley and his high regard for him.

To Mrs. Brydges Willyams.

HUGHENDEN, *Aug.* 28, 1858. — . . . Lord Stanley is coming down here to-day to stay with us until Monday. He is a source of great strength and popularity to the Ministry, and is a man of first-rate abilities and acquirements — a vast satisfaction to me to have such a colleague, and one with whom I have for many years, and ever since, indeed, that he entered public life, been on terms of intimacy and confidence. . . .

HUGHENDEN MANOR, *Sept.* 19, 1858. — . . . I am more fortunate than Lord Stanley, who never leaves town, and is at the E. India House in Leadenhall Street every morning at 10 o'clock. He is of inestimable service to me in all things, and I think the country greatly admires and respects him. It is fortunate for England that, at such a crisis, so powerful and devoted an intellect is working the question of Indian government. . . .

This autumn there was a by-election for Manchester, and the suggestion was mooted that Stanley, strong in the influential Lancashire position of his family and in his own progressive opinions, might be able, now that Protection had been abandoned, to obtain a seat for Conservatism in the home of the Free Trade movement.

The idea immensely attracted Disraeli; but Derby protested, and Stanley was too prudent to make the experiment.

To Lord Stanley.

HUGHENDEN MANOR, *Oct.* 24, 1858. — What do you think of Sir Chas. Trevelyan for Madras? It strikes me that it would be an efficient and popular appointment.

I hope you have deeply considered the Manchester proposition, and will accept it. It will be the inauguration of our new, and still infant, school; a public and national announcement that the *old* Whig monopoly of liberalism is *obsolete*. No doubt what you have to say will require equal tact and wisdom, if, indeed, there be any difference in those qualities. But our position is this: we represent progress, which is essentially practical, against mere Liberal opinions, which are fruitless. We are prepared to do all which the requirements of the State and the thought and feeling of the country will sanction: anything beyond that is mere doctrinaire gossip, which we should studiously avoid.

You will find some of the greatest persons at Manchester, for example, and — as I believe — the preponderant opinion there at present against the Ballot. It will not, therefore, be necessary to support, or, on the other hand, to repudiate it. And so on.

There is no doubt the country at this moment is eminently Conservative, but in the healthy sense of the word; and to a certain and even considerable degree because they have faith in our effecting prudently all changes which are necessary. We should carry into effect our policy by elevating and enlightening Conservative sentiment, not outraging it, or mimicking mere Liberalism.

I think you have hit this happy tone very successfully during the last year, and that it is one of the causes of your success and position.

There were times during the year when it was thought that not merely the Governorship of Madras, but the Governor-Generalship of India, would be at the disposal of the Derby Government; that Canning, disgusted with his treatment by Ellenborough and Ellenborough's colleagues, would resign. Rumour in that case suggested that the first ruler of India who was also Viceroy and direct representative of the Queen would be — Disraeli.

Delane, no *gobemouche*, mentioned the report in a letter in the autumn to W. H. Russell, the famous war correspondent, who was in India at the time. 'It would be a very bold step,' he wrote, 'but it is quite on the cards. He wants the money and the high station, and they want to get rid of him here. He has done so well during the last session as to have conciliated much opposition.' [1] The author of *Tancred* may perhaps have been attracted by the dazzling vision, and the discontented of the party may have hoped for his banishment and for the substitution of Gladstone as leader. But Canning very properly remained at his post; and Disraeli, instead of gratifying his tastes for splendour and the East by holding court in Asia, bent all his energies to grapple at home with the intractable question of Parliamentary Reform.

[1] Atkins's *Life of Sir W. H. Russell*, Vol. I., p. 342.

CHAPTER VI

A Conservative Reform Bill

1858–1859

The adoption of a policy of Parliamentary Reform by the Conservative Government of 1858 was attacked at the time, but rather by opponents than by friends, and has frequently been condemned since, by Conservatives hardly less than by Liberals, as a betrayal of Conservative principles. If the duty of Conservatives is merely, in Disraeli's words when satirising the party as reconstructed by Peel, 'to keep things as they find them as long as they can,' the case must go by default. But if the preservation of the fundamental institutions of the country be held to include their gradual modification to suit the needs of the time, there is a good defence. At any rate, so far as leaders can bind a party, Derby and Disraeli, and particularly Disraeli, had proclaimed openly that they did not consider Reform a Whig monopoly, but at the proper time and in the fitting way would be prepared to deal with it themselves. They had realised, and Disraeli had expounded in his writings, the mistake which the Duke of Wellington had made in committing the party in 1830 to absolute opposition to a policy advocated by the younger Pitt, the founder of modern Conservatism, and only postponed by him owing to the protracted war with France. Peel had done his best to retrieve the mistake by a public acceptance in 1834 of the Reform settlement; and for some fifteen years after that date the maintenance inviolate of the Act of 1832 was the policy of both front benches, Whig as well as Tory. No one was more identified for many years with

this position than Russell, the statesman who carried the great Reform Bill through the House of Commons; he earned, in consequence, the nickname of 'Finality Jack.' But a small but increasing band of Radicals and independent Whigs, led by Hume and Locke King, and eventually by Bright, kept up an agitation, which was more successful in the House of Commons than in the country, for a reopening of the question and an enlargement of the Parliamentary constituency.

Disraeli was one of the first of the Parliamentary leaders of either Whigs or Tories to disclaim absolute finality, and to express a readiness in due course 'to reconstruct,' as he phrased it, 'the estate of the Commons,' by providing, among other things, for a larger representation of the industrial class. This was on Hume's motion for household suffrage in 1848.[1] Though Disraeli was not at that time the acknowledged leader of the party, yet, in consequence of Bentinck's withdrawal, he was leading it *de facto* from the front bench; and after his accession to the leadership, whether in or out of office, he on his party's behalf maintained the same attitude.[2] The *Press*, too, advocated Reform in 1853 as part of the Conservative programme, and pointed to Derby, an old Reformer, as the natural leader to carry it into effect.[3] The increasing Parliamentary support obtained for Locke King's annual motion for assimilating the county with the borough suffrage, culminating early in 1851 in the actual defeat of Russell's Government on this very question, drove Russell from his old position of finality. Henceforward the Whig leaders, however reluctantly, accepted the principle of further Reform, and Russell assumed the conduct of the campaign, introducing a Bill on behalf of his own Government in 1852, and on behalf of Aberdeen's Government in 1854. The Bill of 1852 was lost through the fall of the Government; that of 1854 was withdrawn owing to the Crimean War. Palmer-

[1] See Vol. III., pp. 99–103.   [2] See Vol. III., pp. 285, 331, 337,
[3] See Vol. III., p. 500.   359, 368, 534.

ston's indifference had kept Reform out of the programme of his Government till after the General Election
of 1857; and Disraeli, as we have seen,[1] had then expressed his readiness for Reform on the hustings, and had
only been prevented by Derby's reluctance from formu-
lating practical proposals on behalf of the party in Parliament. Owing to the defeat of the Conspiracy Bill,
Palmerston's Reform proposals had never seen the light;
but that the question which had been talked about so
long should be taken up in earnest and pushed to a
conclusion was the general view in political circles, and the
Conservative Government saw no reason why they should
disappoint expectation. Disraeli and Stanley were no
doubt the most decided Reformers among them, but the
whole Cabinet accepted Reform as an essential element
of their policy. Disraeli told Mr. Kebbel at the time
that he and Derby thought it highly impolitic, if not impossible, for the Conservative party to take up a *non
possumus* attitude on a great popular question. Had
they done so, he said, they must have dwindled away in
time like the Jacobites or the Non-jurors. Parliamentary
Reform being a constitutional question, the Conservatives
had as much right to deal with it as the Liberals. 'I
was determined,' he added, 'to vindicate the right of
the party to a free hand, and not to allow them to be
shut up in a cage formed by the Whigs and Radicals,
confined within a certain magic circle which they were
not to step out of at the peril of their lives.'[2]

The Reform Act of 1832, by abolishing the majority
of the pocket boroughs and transferring the seats thus
gained to populous towns, and by establishing a £10
occupation franchise for boroughs, had transferred power
in the main from the aristocracy to the middle classes;
but the territorial interest retained a strong hold both on
the counties, where the freeholders were the main voters
and where the occupation franchise was fixed at £50, and

---

[1] See above, Ch. 3.
[2] *Lord Beaconsfield and Other Tory Memories*, pp. 16, 17.

on the remaining small boroughs, still considerable in number. Not only was the power of the aristocracy, but also that of the artisans, diminished by the Act. The establishment of a property qualification, and the extinction of ancient electoral rights enjoyed by the poor, resulted in the exclusion of the bulk of the working class ; and it was recognized that to bring any considerable portion of them within the constituency the borough franchise must be lowered. A lowering of the county franchise, unless it was carried beneath the level of the existing borough franchise, would only increase the same kind of electors as then returned the borough members. Hume's proposal, which included the whole Radical programme of household suffrage, equal electoral districts, and ballot, meant a transfer of the power of the State to the working men. Locke King's Bill, which assimilated the county to the borough franchise, would establish the middle classes still more firmly in their seat. Disraeli's general view was that all national interests of importance should find adequate representation in the House, and that no one class should be placed in a predominant position. Not only, therefore, was he in favour of new franchises of a varied character, educational and other, but he had constantly shown himself ready to redress the shortcomings of the Act of 1832 by an extension of industrial franchise. His latest proposals, at the time of the 1857 election, had dealt rather with redistribution than with franchise, and were calculated to give a larger proportion of members to the underrepresented counties, which were mainly Conservative, and so diminish the political power of the Radical boroughs. He had shown throughout a strong aversion to equal electoral districts, as being bound up with what he considered the mistaken theory that the franchise is a right, instead of a privilege. But he was sensible of the scandal caused by the excessive inequalities still retained, and was prepared to deal summarily with all the more glaring instances.

No sooner was the distracting session of 1858 over than the minds of Ministers were turned towards the great task before them in the coming year. It was desirable that as mature a consideration as possible should be given to a measure presenting difficulties to any Government, but very special hazards for a Government calling itself Conservative. For, though the party recognised that their leaders, in consequence both of their professions and of the Parliamentary situation, were bound to produce a Reform Bill, most viewed the necessity with regret, and some with suspicion. The Prime Minister himself took charge of the early stages, and in the second week of August had a long conversation on the subject with Rose, the party agent. Rose wrote to Disraeli on August 12: 'I had my first Reform interview with Lord Derby yesterday. It lasted for nearly *three* hours, and I came away quite convinced that no one ought to venture to talk to Lord Derby who does not thoroughly understand his subject.'

The preliminary discussion of Reform between Derby and Disraeli was mixed up with a matter of patronage. A Commissionership of Excise was vacant. The position was one that Disraeli thought would be competently filled by his brother James, who had been an efficient County Court Treasurer since his appointment by Derby in 1852, and whose promotion would make it possible to recognise suitably Rose's great services to the Conservative party by giving him the vacated Treasurership. But Disraeli was laudably anxious not to put personal and family claims above the public service, and the correspondence on the point between Derby and himself is creditable to both men.

From Lord Derby.

Confidential. St. James's Square, *Aug.* 12, 1858.— ... You are as much interested as I am in having a thoroughly competent man in a situation which, from the composition of the Board, must in all probability lead to the Chairmanship; and you are even more interested in not having

your name brought into question in connection with an unfit appointment. I therefore appeal to you confidently, but also most confidentially, for your candid opinion whether your brother is fully equal to the duties of such an office. Should you answer in the affirmative, I will with pleasure submit his name to the Queen, and his appointment will make an opening for Rose. Should you not be able conscientiously to recommend him, I am sure you will not do so; and in that case I must look elsewhere. . . .

To Lord Derby.

HUGHENDEN MANOR, *Aug.* 13, 1858. — I have no doubt that the individual in question is thoroughly competent, and that his appointment would ultimately reflect credit on your choice; but I nevertheless think at this moment the appointment would be injudicious.

We are now endeavoring to reconstruct the party on a wider basis, and trying to lay the foundation of a permanent system. In this transitionary state we depend entirely on opinion, and any appointment which has the appearance even of preferring private interests and feelings to the efficiency of the public service must be avoided.

I am sorry for the individual immediately concerned, still more for Rose; but if we succeed in our great enterprise you will, I doubt not, have opportunities of rewarding the services of the one, and perhaps of not altogether forgetting the sacrifice of the other. . . .

From Lord Derby.

Private. ST. JAMES'S SQUARE, *Aug.* 15, 1858. — This Commissionership of Excise is really a considerable embarrassment. I enclose you the list of candidates, among whom there is hardly a good name. . . . Would Newdegate take it? and, if so, could we keep his seat? . . . You would, I suppose, prefer keeping Lord R. Cecil in the House;[1] besides which I do not think we should have a 'Lord,' and it would hardly be fair to make another vacancy for Stamford. . . . I shall be very glad if you can assist me in this matter, for I really know not where to turn. After your last note, I cannot think again of the arrangement I proposed to you. . . .

[1] This was not the only suggestion made during this Ministry for providing Lord R. Cecil with a permanent post which would have taken him out of politics. His father, then Lord President, contemplated at one time making him Clerk of the Council in succession to Greville, who resigned while the Derby Government was in office; and he was one of the Members of Parliament suggested by Disraeli to Stanley for original membership of the new Indian Council. See above, Ch. 5.

Derby's difficulties in filling up the post ultimately brought him back to the arrangement which Disraeli desired, but had refrained from pressing.

From Lord Derby.

Private. 10, DOWNING STREET, *Aug.* 25, 1858.—I have a letter from the Queen this morning, approving of your brother's appointment as Commissioner of Excise, and of Rose to succeed him in his Treasurership. . . .

I am to have another conversation with the latter on Friday on the subject of the Reform Bill, at which I have been working, and of which I have good hopes. Let me know your opinion as to the lowering of the franchise in the boroughs. Rose is in favour of a £6 rating. I confess I am afraid of going lower than the present rate, or its equivalent, an £8 rating. The houses between £6 and £10 will add 50 per cent. to the present constituencies. The keystone of the whole must be making freeholders in boroughs voters for the boroughs, and not for the counties, as at present. . . .

To Lord Derby.

HUGHENDEN, *Aug.* 26, 1858.—. . . The line we should take about the borough franchise, I think, must depend upon the general character of our measure. Is it to be moderate, or is it to be large?

That again, I apprehend, depends upon the temper of the country. It may change by next year, but at present its inclinations in this matter appear temperate.

If you retain the £10 franchise in the boroughs, and extend the franchise in the counties, you will have a strong case in favor of the arrangement you mention of confining borough freeholders to borough voting. Indeed, this is the only mode by which even a colorable balance could be maintained between the county and borough constituencies.

I call a £6 rating a large measure, tho' it may be a safe one; but if you did not advance to that point, I think the wisest in every way would be to retain the £10 because in that case you would have the £10 interest on your side, while an £8 rating would not enlist many supporters, or any fervent support, while the 10 pounders would join the 5 and 6 pounders in opposition to your project.

But I make these remarks with great deference. I would like to have talked over the subject with you. It is hardly sufficiently cleared for correspondence. Indeed, if I had been aware you were so advanced in its consideration, and medi-

tated going to Knowsley before the Council on the 2nd, I should have proposed paying you a morning visit at Osterley, or even presumed so far as to intimate that it might be some distraction to you to discuss the matter in the woods of Hughenden.

I will apprise my brother of the great honor which you have conferred on him, and which I trust you may never regret. It is very satisfactory that you have rewarded Rose. . . .

The policy advocated in Disraeli's letter — the retention of the £10 franchise in the boroughs, the extension of the franchise in the counties, and the confinement of the borough freeholders to borough voting — was in large measure the policy of the Bill eventually produced to the House of Commons. But before that stage was reached Reform passed through many troubled moments in the Cabinet. In August and September, Stanley, who was detained in London or the immediate neighbourhood by the labour involved in bringing the India Act into effect, was frequently a guest at Hughenden; and he and Disraeli, as the representatives of the progressive party in the Government, worked out their own plan, which embraced (1) identity of franchise for counties as well as boroughs at £10; (2) new franchises, based on personal property, etc.; (3) optional ballot; and (4) disfranchisement ranging from sixty to ninety seats — the first and last points being those to which they attached most importance. They were led, no doubt, to put identity of franchise in the forefront by the fact that Parliament had accepted the principle of Locke King's Bill in the past session, as on several previous occasions, by a considerable majority, in spite of a deprecatory speech from Disraeli, who had objected to dealing piecemeal with a great question which the Government had determined to take in hand. If there were any principle of further Reform to which Parliament might be considered to be pledged, it was an identic suffrage for boroughs and counties. At the same time, for Disraeli to accept it, and make it, as he did, the outstanding

feature of the Government Bill, argues a great change of attitude towards the middle classes, whose power it was calculated so largely to increase, and may perhaps be attributed, at least in part, to Stanley's influence over him. For Stanley was pre-eminently a·statesman who trusted, and was trusted by, the middle classes. His plain common-sense and love of peace appealed to them almost as much as did Palmerston's good-humour and bounce, and on Palmerston's death he largely succeeded to his place in their favour.

For a time, though Derby and Rose were also pursuing their labours, no further communications passed between Derby and Disraeli. 'I thought it better,' wrote Disraeli to Stanley on September 19, 'that an interval of silence should take place. He [Derby] must be sick of me after six months — and such months — of constant deliberation. Now he will be fresh again, and I shall be less stale.' Unfortunately, Derby was not fresh again at the end of September, but had a severe attack of the gout.

To Mrs. Brydges Willyams.

GROSVENOR GATE, *Monday, Oct. 11, 1858.* — Lord Derby's second attack of the gout, which came on the day after he left Balmoral, has deranged all my plans, and occasioned me a great deal of trouble and anxiety. It has been very severe, but we kept it secret for a long time, so that when it got known, and we were found out, he had recovered, which, considering the severity of the attack, was as satisfactory as unexpected. Nothing disheartens a party so much as an invalid chief, and they are always afraid he is going to die and break up the Ministry.

One, however, may be compensated for a little extra toil or care by the state of the country, which, I believe, is as generally prosperous as it ever was at any period of its history. Everything succeeds, foreign and domestic, and the Ex[cheque]r is overflowing.

These gold discoveries must exercise an immense influence on mankind; nuggets and the comet open everybody's mind.

We have had a great many visitors at Hughenden of late; Lord Stanley, Sir Edward Lytton, the Rothschilds,

Sir W. Jolliffe, Mr. Baring; the greater part of them combined business with pleasure, for they settled State affairs as well as occasionally killing a bird for you.

We have been here these six days or so, incog. except to my private secretary, and have done a deal of work. The paint is not very bad, and we have preferred its inconvenience to Downing Street and the Thames, so we did not send for your great analyser, Sir Brodie!

I hope to be able to get back to Hughenden on Friday, and appear at Aylesbury at Q. Sessions on the following Monday. . . .

HUGHENDEN MANOR, *Oct.* 20, 1858. — Our visit to London incog. has come to an end, but to-morrow I must return, but not incog., to receive the Canadian Ministers, who have come over here, and who want, like all of us and all the world, some money. . . .

The Queen arrives on Wednesday (this very day), and a great deal is going on. Lord Derby's illness has very much put me out and deranged my plans.

The great thing now will be the new French Ambassadress [1] — a Spanish lady of high degree, and very haughty, they say, scornful, and all that. We have had nothing in that style for a great many years, and I think it will be amusing. The Emperor has given her a tiara of diamonds, and large pearls fit for the Empress. The Empress herself has given her a stomacher entirely of brilliants; the Queen of Spain a fan of diamonds and emeralds; the Duke of Malakhoff himself a corbeille, according to custom, full of all sorts of dainty devices — Cashmere shawls, brilliant trinkets, lace, pocket-handkerchiefs like the petticoats of the Madonna of Loretto, and no end of fancy splendor. But what we await with the greatest interest are — her favors.

HUGHENDEN MANOR, *Oct.* 30, 1858. — We have been here nearly a fortnight, enjoying the autumn, but business has been very active — couriers and despatch-boxes every day, and all the symptoms that graver days are at hand. The world gets serious in November.

To-day we go to Gunnersbury, Baron Rothschild's, to meet the French Ambassador and his bride, and stay there till Monday, on which morning I shall appear in Downing Street. All the Ministers will have arrived by that time — Lord Derby on Monday evening — and at 12 o'clock on Tuesday we two have our first confidential conference for three months. There will be no lack of matter to talk about.

The Cabinet will meet the next day, Wednesday. Their meetings will no doubt for some time be frequent. . . .

---

[1] Madame Pélissier, Duchess of Malakhoff.

One of the first acts of the November Cabinets was to appoint a Cabinet Committee to consider the details of the Reform Bill. Disraeli and Stanley, as the advocates of a comprehensive measure, resumed their special consultations, and determined, as far as possible, to mould in concert the decisions to be taken on the subject.

To Lord Stanley.

HUGHENDEN, *Nov.* 5, 1858. — You or I ought to be Chairman of the Reform Committee, in order to direct the course in a salutary stream.

I shall be at D. S. to-morrow at 12 o'clock, and propose you: but if, on the ground of E[ast] I[ndia] H[ouse], you demur, you can perform the office for yours ever, D.

The Committee reported on November 26, explaining that, though there had been individual differences of opinion, every proposition adopted had the sanction of a large majority. Their recommendations, with regard to franchise, were to retain the £10 franchise in the boroughs, to establish a £10 rating franchise in the counties, and a £20 lodger franchise for both town and country, while transferring the freehold franchise, where the property was situated within borough limits, from the county to the borough. With regard to redistribution, while repudiating any attempt at absolute equality, they recommended mitigating the more glaring anomalies. They would disfranchise totally boroughs with a population under 5000, thus gaining sixteen seats, and partially disfranchise those between 5000 and 15,000, gaining fifty-seven seats more. No new constituencies were to be created, except by the division of the West Riding and of South Lancashire; but every county constituency with a population above 100,000 was to have three members, and where it exceeded 50,000 two, thus giving fifty-two additional county seats. The same principle applied to towns disposed of eighteen seats. The small margin left might perhaps be used for the University of London or the Inns of Court. It was

proposed to disfranchise dockyard men, to allow polling papers, and to resist the ballot.

To Mrs. Disraeli.

WINDSOR CASTLE,[1] *Nov.* 15, 1858. — All well: *very* well. Coming up for a Cabinet, and just time to write this line. My visit has been an *endless conversation* with the Prince.

To Frances Anne Lady Londonderry.

DOWNING STREET, *Nov.* 27, 1858. — We have had as hard work this month as I ever recollect in public life, and a prospect of its continuance yet for some weeks. Cabinets, or Committees of Cabinets, every day — from 12 to 5 or 6 o'clock — and plenty of work afterwards. We are really working night and day.

On the whole, affairs are very satisfactory, and altho' I hear rumors of our career being cut short in February next, they don't give me sleepless nights. . . .

I sate next the Prince of Wales at dinner the other day, and was very much pleased with him — intelligent, informed, and with a singularly sweet manner. He was going off the next day to Berlin, on a visit to his sister, and seemed full of delight at the prospect. . . .

The last days of November and the early days of December were mainly occupied with Cabinet Councils on the details of the Reform Bill. The report of the Committee was by no means universally accepted. Malmesbury wrote on December 3: 'I have little expectation of the Government producing a measure that will satisfy either themselves or the public'; and he tells us of an important division in which Derby was only supported by Malmesbury himself and Manners. Disraeli, Stanley, Pakington, Salisbury, and Lytton, voted for a more liberal proposal; Chelmsford, Walpole, Henley, Hardwicke, and Peel, for a more conservative one. 'So nothing was done.' This division shows generally the parties into which the Cabinet was divided. The attitude of both Walpole and Henley was beginning to cause special uneasiness, when the leaders had an unexpected blow in letters from Lytton announcing his immediate resignation on grounds

---

[1] Disraeli was staying at the Castle from Monday to Wednesday.

the other are not to have it, although you may have
no trouble for a few years, yet as sure as the sun is in
heaven you will have all the people upon the outside of
the line, at some time or other, making a very ugly rush
to break over it. . . .   To draw a hard line and to leave
the working people behind it is to lay the foundation of
revolution.'   He thought the borough franchise should
be reduced, and Walpole also was prepared for such a
reduction ; but neither would consent to a reduction of
the county franchise to an identity with the borough
franchise.

In spite of this impeachment of the Conservative
character of the Bill, the party generally were prepared
to follow their chiefs, and an attempt to organise Conservative resistance had little success.   Though there
was no enthusiasm, Fraser was not justified in declaring
that the party 'loathed' the measure.   To the few dissentients Derby took a high line.   He wrote to Disraeli
on March 16: 'There shall be no mistake.   We must
command this Parliament, or throw the die for the next,
and let our friends know that it is the last cast.'   The
Opposition was at first in some doubt as to how the Bill
should be treated.   But Russell's obstinate determination
to destroy it prevailed, and Palmerston agreed to support
a wrecking resolution which his rival was to draft.   Interference with the freehold franchise in counties and failure
to reduce the borough franchise were the blots in the Bill
singled out for condemnation.   For a resolution of this
kind, both those who, like Palmerston, wished for either
no Reform or as little as possible, and those who, like
Bright, wanted much more Radical change, were prepared
to vote.   Palmerston's opposition was a disappointment
to the Government.   Anxious as he was to keep Reform
within moderate limits, he might have been expected to
welcome a Bill which bade fair to increase the power of
the middle classes upon whom he rested, while hardly
benefiting at all the Radicals, whom he wished to keep
down.   But the temptation to join hands with Russell

THE REAL UGLY RUSH

"HE FEARED THERE WOULD BE AN UGLY RUSH SOME OF THESE DAYS."

Mr. Henley on the Reform Bill. Reproduced, by kind permission of the Proprietors, from 'Punch,' April 30, 1859.

to regain power was irresistible, and he trusted to the
chapter of accidents to prevent Russell's more thorough-
going policy from being carried into effect—at any
rate during his lifetime.   In private, to a diplomat,
he condemned the Bill as too liberal, and continued :
'M. Disraeli, coûte que coûte, recherche la popularité
"out of doors."   C'est un démocrate recouvert de la peau
d'un conservateur.'

   The debate on the second reading was begun on Monday,
March 21, and occupied nearly a couple of weeks.   It was
conducted under curious conditions, for the interest it
excited was due almost wholly to its effect on party
fortunes, and extremely little to the question nominally
at issue.   In truth, for the present, Reform was merely
a Parliamentary, and not a popular, question.   Public
opinion, as Lytton pointed out in the House, was extremely apathetic.   'Doubtless, nine out of ten said
loudly, "We must have a Reform Bill"; but eight out
of every nine whispered to each other, "Does anybody
want one?"'   Bright had undertaken a campaign in
the country during the autumn, but had succeeded rather
in disgusting people by his extreme views than in evoking
public support for reform.   The situation was caustically
described by the Prince Consort in a letter to Stockmar.
'A Radical Reform Bill of a Conservative Ministry is
denounced as not Radical enough by the Liberal party
(who want no Reform, and are especially afraid of a
Radical one), headed by Lord John, whom they will not
have as leader.'   Though the Opposition had numbers on
their side, the better speeches were made, as the Whigs'
friend Greville insists, by Ministers and their supporters.
Conspicuous among these speeches was what Sidney
Herbert called 'a splendid declamation' by Bulwer
Lytton.   Following Stanley's line, he advocated the
measure as one to confirm and extend the political power
of the middle class, and to lift into the franchise of that
class the artisan who had risen by the exercise of economy
and forethought.   Russell's amendment, Lytton main-

tained in his peroration, would commit the House to a
pledge to the working class — 'a pledge which you can
never redeem to their satisfaction until you have placed
capital and knowledge at the command of impatient
poverty and uninstructed numbers.'

To Queen Victoria.

HOUSE OF COMMONS, *March* 22, 1859.— . . . A night of
immense power and excitement.   Two of the greatest speeches
ever delivered in Parliament — by Sir Edward Lytton and the
Solicitor-General. . . .   Both spoke in a crowded House : one
before dinner, the other concluding, just down.   Never was
a greater contrast between two orators, resembling each other
in nothing but their excellence.

Deaf, fantastic, modulating his voice with difficulty, sometimes painful — at first almost an object of ridicule to the
superficial — Lytton occasionally reached almost the sublime,
and perfectly enchained his audience.   His description of the
English Constitution, his analysis of democracy — as rich and
more powerful than Burke.

Sir Hugh Cairns devoted an hour to a Reply to Lord John's
resolution, and to a vindication of the Government Bill,
which charmed everyone by its lucidity and controlled everyone by its logic.   When he had in the most masterly manner,
and with a concinnity which none can equal, closed the business
part of his address, he directed himself to the political portion
of the theme, and, having literally demolished the mover of
the amendment, sat down amid universal cheers.[1]

Russell's speech was very hostile in tone.   Bright said
this was not the sort of Bill which Disraeli thought best
for the country, but was framed to meet the prejudices
of the territorial interest.   Palmerston, in Greville's
judgment, was 'very jaunty, but very insincere.'   He
was also 'infinitely audacious,' as Disraeli told the Queen,
even threatening a stoppage of supplies in the event of
dissolution.   Gladstone, however, though he disagreed
with many of the provisions of the Bill, opposed Russell's
resolution, as this was a golden opportunity for settling
the question, and should not be let slip.

Disraeli, though he had to endure the inconvenience
of being a Minister in a minority, was never, as he re-

---

[1] Martin's *Prince Consort*, Vol. IV, pp. 411, 412.

peatedly insisted, prepared to be a Minister on sufferance. Accordingly, he and the Government recognised in advance that a defeat on Russell's motion would entail either resignation or dissolution, though, as the Queen said in writing to Derby on March 21, 'a change of Government or a dissolution would be both very injurious to the best interests of the country.' Dissolution was clearly the preferable alternative, and Disraeli told Mrs. Willyams confidentially, as early as March 5, that it would be adopted.[1] A Parliament elected on a personal issue, which signally defeated two Ministries in two years, was a very unsatisfactory instrument of Government. In their present struggle Ministers received much more sympathetic treatment from the Court than in 1852.

From Lord Derby.

Friday morning [*March 25, 1859*]. — I have a long and very friendly letter from H.M. 'Anxious to give Lord D. every support he may require.' She sanctions the whole batch of peers and baronets. She wishes, before promising dissolution, to have a clearer view of our prospects of gain, as she says truly that our 'retirement after a defeat in a General Election would place her in increased difficulties.' She suggests doubts as to the prudence of our proposed course in making Johnny's the substantive motion, as in that case M.P.'s might vote for it who would oppose it as 'a factious move to displace a Government.' I hope you will not close even the first debate to-night. . . .

Wednesday [*March 30, 1859*]. — Rose is to be here at 11, and I am going through his list with him. I am to see the Queen at 3. I shall not commit myself on the subject of *immediate* dissolution, but I shall not conceal my opinion that an *early* dissolution of the present Parliament is indispensable, and would be so whoever might be the Ministers. What may I say as to the prospects of the division? The Queen will be very anxious to know. I shall tell H.M. that in the event of our being beaten we shall immediately withdraw the Bill. I think you must, on the numbers being declared, if against us, move the adjournment of the House till Monday. We must have that interval to consider our course, and submit it to the Queen.

---

[1] In the same letter Disraeli wrote: 'Labor, anxiety and responsibility seem to act on me as tonics.'

Disraeli was sanguine, though it is difficult to see on what grounds, and reported to Derby: 'The division is necessarily dark, but I am inclined to believe we shall win.'

Disraeli replied to his critics at the close of the last night's debate.[1] He claimed that there were three principles in the measure : First, the addition to the constituent body of large numbers and a great variety of persons — not less than the 400,000 added by the Act of 1832; secondly, the extension of representation to large communities which had developed since 1832; thirdly, the maintenance of the existing borough system as the only means of obtaining adequate representation of the various interests of the country.   All the rest was detail, open to revision in Committee.   He maintained once more that the working classes, who already constituted, as occupants of £10 houses and as freemen, about a ninth of the constituency, would obtain a material augmentation by the provisions of the Bill.   But he uttered a solemn warning against any large reduction of the borough franchise — a warning which his critics quoted against him in 1867.

I have no apprehension myself that, if you had manhood suffrage to-morrow, the honest, brave, and good-natured people of England would resort to pillage, incendiarism, and massacre.   Who expects that?   But though I would do as much justice to the qualities of our countrymen as any gentleman in this House, though I may not indulge in high-flown and far-fetched expressions with respect to them like those we have listened to — for the people may have their parasites as well as monarchs and aristocracies — yet I have no doubt that, whatever may be their high qualities, our countrymen are subject to the same political laws that affect the condition of all other communities and nations.   If you establish a democracy, you must in due season reap the fruits of a democracy. You will in due season have great impatience of the public burdens combined in due season with great increase of the public expenditure.   You will in due season reap the fruits of such united influence.   You will in due season have wars entered into from passion, and not from reason; and you will in due season submit to peace ignominiously sought and

[1] March 31.

ignominiously obtained, which will diminish your authority and perhaps endanger your independence. You will, in due season, with a democracy find that your property is less valuable and that your freedom is less complete. I doubt not, when there has been realised a sufficient quantity of disaffection and dismay, the good sense of this country will come to the rally, and that you will obtain some remedy for your grievances, and some redress for your wrongs, by the process through which alone it can be obtained — by that process which may render your property more secure, but which will not render your liberty more eminent. . . . That being my opinion, I cannot look upon what is called reduction of the franchise in boroughs but with alarm; and I have never yet met any argument which fairly encounters the objections that are urged to it. You cannot encounter it by sentimental assertions of the good qualities of the working classes. The greater their good qualities, the greater the danger. If you lay down as a principle that they are to enter the constituent body, not as individuals, but as a multitude, they must be the predominant class from their number; and if you dwell on their intelligence, you only increase the power they will exercise.

Disraeli's retorts on the great twin brethren of the Whigs were very effective. Palmerston and the moderate Whigs, who objected to reducing the county franchise below £20, had regularly voted for Locke King's motion for identity of suffrage; and Palmerston and his Whig and Peelite colleagues had agreed to propose a £10 county franchise in the Coalition Government's Bill of 1854. Russell, who was so shocked at what he called the disfranchisement of freeholders, had himself disfranchised freemen wholesale in 1832. Russell's constant recurrence, when in opposition, to faction afforded legitimate ground for severe criticism, and Disraeli did not spare him. It was 'a very effective philippic,' wrote Greville, 'and delivered with much dignity and in very good taste.'

I am sure the noble lord will not feel offended with me if I tell him that I think there is one quality in his character which has rather marred than made his fortunes. It is a restlessness which will not brook that delay and that patience needed in our constitutional government for the conduct of

public affairs. The moment that the noble lord is not in power he appears to me to live in an atmosphere of coalitions, combinations, *coups d'état*, and cunning resolutions. An Appropriation Clause[1] may happen to every man once in his life. But there is only one man living of whom it can be said that in 1835 he overthrew the Government of Sir Robert Peel upon an impracticable pretext; that in 1852 he overthrew the Government of Lord Derby with an objectless coalition; that in 1855 he overthrew the Government of Lord Aberdeen by a personal *coup d'état;* and that in 1858 he overthrew the Government of the noble lord the member for Tiverton by a Parliamentary manœuvre. Now, sir, I beg the noble lord at this moment to throw the vision of his memory for an instant back to the year 1852. He sat before me then, the head of a mighty host. He drew the fatal arrow that was to destroy our Government. He succeeded. He destroyed in breathless haste the Government of Lord Derby; but did he destroy nothing else? Did he not destroy also the position of a great statesman? Did he not destroy almost the great historic party of which he was once the proud and honoured chief? The noble lord does not sit opposite me now; but had he not hurried the catastrophe of 1852, and had he bided his time, according to the periodic habit of our Constitution, he would have returned to these benches the head of that great party of which he was once the chief and greatest ornament.

Disraeli at the close of his speech clearly anticipated defeat, and in dignified language recalled what the Derby Government had accomplished for the defence of the State and the welfare of the people, in spite of 'all the manœuvres of Parliamentary intrigue and all the machinations of party warfare.' The Government received in the lobby the unbroken support of their party, including the Ministers who had seceded, and all the reactionaries, such as Beresford, Newdegate, and Spooner, who had threatened at one time to be recalcitrant. By the aid of several independent members, such as Gladstone, Horsman, Elcho, and some Roman Catholic Irish, they reached the respectable total of 291, about thirty above the strict party strength. But the Liberal factions

---

[1] Peel was upset in 1835 on a motion by Russell insisting that the surplus revenues of the Irish Church should be appropriated to secular purposes; but three years afterwards in office Russell abandoned the principle, and accepted Peel's original arrangement. See Vol. I., p. 300.

had temporarily come together, and obtained a decisive majority of thirty-nine for the Resolution, more than half the whole House, 330 out of 650 odd, voting for it.

The Whig leaders destroyed the Reform Bill of 1859, and thereby made themselves responsible for the loss of a real opportunity of passing into law a moderate measure which would have been generally acceptable to Whig opinion. The Bill itself has sometimes been treated as if it were as purely a piece of tactics as undoubtedly much of the opposition to it was; and Disraeli, after his frequent fashion, at times used language in conformity with this view. 'We pricked the imposture,' he once said to Mr. Kebbel, contrasting the assumed eagerness of the Whigs for Reform in opposition in 1858–59 with their readiness to let it slumber during the subsequent six years of Palmerston's Administration. But both his letters and his labours, while the Bill was under consideration, are incompatible with any theory of the kind. He seriously meant to pass a measure which should content public opinion for the time, and he spared no effort to that end. The Bill contained one really bold feature — the sweeping reduction of the county franchise. But, of course, it was not his ideal, and was opportunist in its details. He would have preferred a larger working-class infusion and a less complete dominance of the middle class, and disfranchisement and redistribution on a bigger scale. But, after all, opportunism is hardly a serious reproach in a matter so essentially one 'of nicely calculated less or more' as Parliamentary Reform. Disraeli had to carry with him his party, containing a strong reactionary contingent; and his instinct for the movements of public opinion showed him that, while improvement of the representative system was desired, there was no demand for heroic or revolutionary remedies. It does not seem fanciful, in view of Disraeli's capacity for Parliamentary management, to suppose that, if the Bill of 1859 had been allowed to go into Committee,

it might have passed into law in a moderate and Conservative shape. Palmerston explicitly promised support to the general maintenance of the borough system, to the fancy franchises, and to the limited measure of redistribution. With the help of Russell and of the general sense of the House, the Government would easily have prevailed over the doubts of Palmerston and the Peelites, and of Walpole and Henley and the stiffer Tories, to carry the reduction of the county franchise to £10. They would probably have been forced into a slight reduction of the borough franchise, for which Disraeli was quite prepared, and into a compromise over the question of the freeholders. An Act of this character might well have lasted sufficiently long to enable us to 'educate our masters' before, instead of after, giving them the mastery.

The decision of the Government to dissolve Parliament was announced in both Houses on Monday, April 4. Derby consulted Disraeli as to the nature of the statement which he should make.

To Lord Derby.

Downing Street, *Sunday, April 3, 1859.* — . . . It is an address not merely or principally for Parliament, but for the country, to guide and to animate them, *and which should be read by every man.* The real issue, the broad great issue, is whether Parliamentary government is compatible with our existing institutions.

The House of Commons is broken into sections which, although they have no unity of purpose or policy, can always combine to overthrow the Queen's Government, however formed. Under present circumstances there is no reason why there should not be a dissolution, or a Ministerial crisis, every February. One is certain next February, if Lord Palmerston form a Government, such as he contemplates, and the Radicals are excluded.

This is the state of affairs which the country ought to be called upon to comprehend, and to remedy. Nothing more completely proves the total want of cohesion on the opposite benches than the fact that this flimsy resolution was the only means by which they could be brought together for the moment, and that, when carried, had we proceeded with the

Bill, the two leaders of the coalition were pledged to an exactly contrary policy: Lord John to defeat the Government measure, Lord Palmerston to support and, with amendments, carry it.

From Lord Derby.

Confidential.   ST. JAMES'S SQUARE, *Sunday.* — I quite concur in the spirit of your memorandum. Whether I shall be able to execute the task it indicates is another matter. I have this moment received a *most* cordial letter from the Queen, anxious to know what are the feelings of our party, and 'what is going on in the *enemy's* camp. Can you give me any information on the latter point for H.M.?

Derby was not well, and did not do himself justice in the House of Lords. 'I am better than I was yesterday,' he wrote next day, 'but not satisfied with my speech last night. I was not up to the mark, and was too long. *You* seem to have done very well, and to have been well received.' Disraeli spoke in the general sense of his letter to Derby, but with due acknowledgment of the courtesy he had received throughout from the House. On the same day he issued his address to his constituents. 'A Parliamentary majority,' he wrote, 'composed of discordant sections, has availed itself of its numerical strength to embarrass Her Majesty's Government, and, by a disingenuous manœuvre, to intercept the discussion of their measures.' This blow had deprived Government of authority; but there was no unity of sentiment in the Opposition.

It is for the country to comprehend and to remedy these evils. The moment is critical. England has engaged to mediate between two great monarchs, and, if possible, preserve for Europe the blessings of peace. It is necessary that the Queen's Government should be supported by a patriotic Parliament.

Disraeli or his wife kept Mrs. Willyams constantly informed of all the phases of this critical time.

Mrs. Disraeli to Mrs Brydges Willyams.

GROSVENOR GATE, *April 4, 1859.* — You will see, my dearest Mrs. Willyams, by all the papers early to-morrow that Ministers *do not resign.* Dizzy is just gone to the House, which we are

told is crowded inside and out — all the streets, etc., etc., — to
see and hear the Chancellor of the Exchequer's speech on the
intentions of Government. It is a great comfort to me to
write to you and to say that dear Dizzy is *quite well*, to everyone's great astonishment; for how much he has constantly on
his mind, and not a moment to himself! All the papers on
every side mention his last speech as fine, wonderful, etc., etc.

We are very popular in the country, the first time for 16
years. . . .

To Mrs. Brydges Willyams.

Downing Street, *April* 9, 1859. — . . . Here all is convulsion. What did you think of our *coup d'état?* I hope and
believe the country will rally round us, *as war seems at hand.*

Downing Street, *April* 19, 1859. — I wound up the affairs
to-day, and prorogued Parliament. Tho' not of a very vindictive nature, I must confess some satisfaction in paying off
the gentlemen who thought themselves so very clever in
placing Her Majesty's Government in a minority. I should
think at least two hundred of them will never see the inside
of a senate again, where they might have remained for three
or four years had they been a little less factious. . . .

We shall preserve peace. The news of this morning is very
favorable.

'War seems at hand'; 'we shall preserve peace.'
War and peace were indeed trembling in the balance in
Europe this spring. In their factious eagerness for place
the Opposition had disregarded the claims of patriotism.
What was the moment, Disraeli pointedly asked in his
reply in the debate, which the Liberals had chosen to
precipitate this party attack? A moment the most
critical in the affairs of England and of Europe for many
years past. Ministers were straining every nerve to keep
the peace between France and Austria, who were rapidly
drifting into hostilities owing to the patriotic intrigues of
the great Italian statesman, Cavour. It was of vital importance that the authority of the Government should not
be interfered with or embarrassed; and yet the Opposition deliberately paralysed it. The business community
required nothing but peace. 'But for this untoward,
this unhappy motion,' said Disraeli, it might have been
preserved. While England was distracted by a general

Election, which was the direct result of Palmerston's and Russell's action, the war she desired to prevent broke out.

Perhaps no Ministry, however patriotically supported, could have averted it.   Moved partly by the fears engendered by Orsini's plot, and partly by a dreamy idealism, Napoleon III., at Plombières in the previous summer, entered into engagements with Cavour which bound him to forward Italian unity in arms.   The meeting was a secret one.   It was followed by two public visits of the British Court abroad, which the Queen and Ministers hoped would improve international relations. On August 4, 1858, the Queen and the Prince attended the opening, by the Emperor of the French, of new docks at Cherbourg.   The result was, perhaps, rather to make the Court and the people realize the naval menace to England than to draw closer the Anglo-French Alliance. Disraeli, however, was optimistic.   He told Mrs. Willyams on August 28: "The visit to Cherbourg has dissipated the vain fears and idle panic which were afloat.'   Later in the autumn the Queen and the Prince paid a successful visit to Germany.

To Frances Anne Lady Londonderry.

HUGHENDEN, *Sept.* 14, 1858. — . . .   I went once to Osborne to attend a Council, and was unexpectedly commanded to an audience.   I found them both much pleased, and more excited, with their German visit, which was 'not sufficiently understood or rightly appreciated in our papers.'   'It was a homage of the German people — a demonstration that they were English, anti-Russian, anti-Absolutist.'   They found out the Prince's birthday, and would celebrate it.   Altho' incog., at Düsseldorf, where there was not even a guard of honour, ' and by our particular desire,' the people gave them a royal reception.

Still great alarm about Cherbourg, etc.   'The Emperor means all right,' but, etc. . . .

A cordial understanding with France was Disraeli's root-idea of foreign policy.   But he, like other well-wishers of the alliance, had increasing difficulties to contend with.   Her naval and military preparations,

following on the recent threats of her Colonels, disquieted both Ministers and the public; but a more certain danger was the steadily increasing divergence between her policy and that of Austria.   On friendly relations with Austria Disraeli, along with Conservatives in general, placed a high value; but, if he had to choose, all his regard for Metternich would not prevent him from sympathising with France.   Metternich, surveying politics from a detached and philosophic standpoint, foresaw what was coming, and endeavoured in vain to convince Disraeli that England and Austria were bound to act together.

From Prince Metternich.

DRESDE, *le* 28 *Octobre,* 1858. — . . .   Le grand Empire maritime qui en Europe n'est pas continental, et la puissance continentale qui n'est point maritime, finiront toujours par se rencontrer quand il s'agira, soit de questions véritablement générales, soit de questions pouvant toucher à leur intérêt direct.   Une grande confusion dans les situations et les relations les plus diverses pèse aujourd'hui sur le monde.   Elle arrivera à son terme ; ne me demandez pas ma prévision sur le *quand* et le *comment* — je l'ignore autant que vous — mais ce en quoi j'ai pleine confiance c'est dans l'heureuse influence que vous exercerez sur les dénoûments d'une mauvaise situation des choses.[1]

During his visit to Paris in the winter of 1856–57 Disraeli had come to the conclusion that Cowley, the British Ambassador, was not always sufficiently in touch with the real views and sentiments of the Emperor.   As the year 1858 drew to a close, it appeared to him of great importance that the Derby Government should penetrate more completely into Napoleon's counsels.   Not only had Palmerston, the British Minister with whom the Emperor had maintained the closest relations, been along with Clarendon, an Imperial guest at Compiègne in the autumn; but also it was evident that France and Sardinia had been drawing together, and it looked as if the Emperor might be seriously con-

---

[1] Metternich, *Mémoires,* Vol. III., p. 435.

templating active interference in Italy.   Cowley sent reassuring despatches, but Disraeli was not convinced. Moreover, public feeling in both countries was steadily getting more hostile.   As Earle wrote to Disraeli on November 6: 'Ever since the Queen's visit in 1855 our sympathy with France has been diminishing.   Our Court, Parliament, and people, look upon her with increasing distrust. . . .   The Emperor, irritated by our invectives and hampered by the restlessness of his own subjects, will be more than ever disposed, perhaps driven, to adopt an arrogant demeanour abroad.'   Disraeli considered, as he had shown in 1852, that nothing would do more to improve the relations between the two countries than a commercial treaty.

With these ideas in his head, Disraeli in December sent Earle, who had previously been attached to the Paris Embassy, on a confidential mission to the Emperor.   Earle found that Louis Napoleon was in no humour for the discussion of commercial arrangements, as his whole mind was absorbed by Italy.   He suggested that Disraeli should write him a letter of a reassuring character.

To Ralph A. Earle.

Confidential. Downing Street, *Dec.* 20, 1858.— I write to you passing through town from Knowsley, hurriedly, but what I really feel.

'War with all the world, but peace with England,' was the dictum of the proud Spanish monarchy.   I do not want His Majesty to adopt the letter of this principle, but its spirit is not beneath his notice.

I want to see His Majesty fairly reconciled with the people of this country.   The great majority is not now even against him.   The nation and the newspapers are different.   The Press is against the Emperor, because he is against their trade; and the Orleanist party, taking advantage of this mistrust, are using the journals in order to poison the minds of the English people.

What I want the Emperor to do is to take an early opportunity of showing to the people of England that for them 'the Empire is peace.'   The newspapers, under the influence

of the Orleanist, have persuaded them, or would persuade them, that for them 'the Empire is invasion.'

I have no jealousy of the external movement of France. I look upon the old political maxims about Spain and Italy as rococo in an age which has witnessed the development of America and the discovery of Australia. I have said this often to you: I have even expressed it, and in detail, to the Emperor himself.

I contemplate the possibility of the eventual increase of his dominions. He is an Emperor, and he must have an empire; but all this should be attempted with the sanction, or at least with the sufferance, of England, not in spite of her.

Let the Emperor take an early opportunity of referring to the state of the French Navy; let him allude with just pride to his efforts to restore the marine of France to its ancient and proper force; let him express his surprise that it should be looked upon with jealousy by the Power which he trusts will always prove the ally of France; that France seeks no undue supremacy on the sea; that she wishes to enter into no rivalry with England; that the careers of the two nations are different and distinct; that there would be no jealousy in France if the English fleet were twice the strength of that of France; and that France would then as little fear or believe in invasion from England as England does or ought to do from France.

Let him say something like this, and no one can say something so well, and the effect would be so great that, if in the spring there was any movement towards Italy, the public opinion of England would prevent interference in the quarrel, and no one would be persuaded, which otherwise, as in old days, would be the case, that an Austrian war was a good distraction from a French invasion from Cherbourg, and therefore that Austria should be encouraged and supported by England.

This is a policy which illustrates the Spanish maxim of State which I quoted.

From Ralph A. Earle.

[PARIS] *Dec.* 24, 1858.—I have a satisfactory report to make. Our efforts have proved successful.

The Emperor received me, a second time, to-day.

I began by explaining that, when you sent me here, you were under the impression that H.M. had abandoned his Italian views, otherwise you would have given to your communication another form. I referred, of course, in detail to Ld. Cowley's letter and to Ld. Malmesbury's reply,[1] which

---

[1] See Malmesbury's letter to the Queen, Dec. 10, 1858, in *Queen Victoria's Letters*. Malmesbury advised the Emperor to make an attempt, in conjunction with Austria, to improve the Government of the Papal States.

you were led to believe had convinced the Emperor to maintain the existing system in Italy.

The Emperor at once said, recapitulating what had occurred,
that Ld. Malmesbury's letter had not produced any effect
upon his opinions, that he thought that its arguments were
unsound and would never be accepted by the English, but
that, as no event had occurred to render an immediate decision
necessary, he had declined to continue a discussion which
offered no prospect of leading to any conclusion which could
prove satisfactory to both parties.

I then said that I had reported faithfully to you all that
had passed at the former audience, and that I had naturally
not omitted to notice H.M.'s observations with respect to
Italy. I was now, I continued, in possession of your views
upon this question, and altho' it was evident from the form
in which they were stated that they were not intended for
direct communication to H.M., yet, as it was desirable that
he should be made thoroughly acquainted with them, I had
no hesitation in placing your letter in H.M.'s hands.

The Emperor read it with great attention. When he came
to that part in which it is said that you desire H.M. to be
reconciled with the public opinion of England, he stopped
and exclaimed that that was the object he had most at heart.
What new sacrifices could he make for it? He had done all
in his power to strengthen the English alliance.

When he came to the end, he said that he had read it with
great pleasure, and he used various phrases to express the
satisfaction which he had derived from the statement of your
views. He contrasted your opinions with the declarations of
Ld. Malmesbury in a spirit decidedly unfriendly to his lordship.

I then observed that, if a new proof were required to convince H.M. that it was for the interest of his Government to
follow your advice, I would point to the efforts which were
pertinaciously made by H.M.'s enemies to attribute to him
the intentions which you asked him to repudiate. Only the
other day M. de Montalembert had recourse to this artifice,
and it was one which members of the exiled family had frequently employed to influence the English Court.

I continued for some time to urge all the arguments which
I thought would be likely to have weight with the Emperor,
who listened to me with kind attention.

At last he said: 'Well, you may tell Mr. Disraeli that I
will make the declaration for which he asks, in my speech at
the opening of the Chambers.'

I thanked the Emperor for this assurance, which he subsequently repeated.

He then asked me to leave your letter with him, and, as

there can be no reason for treating him with half-confidence, I complied with his request.

You had better write him a letter of thanks for the kindness with which he has received your emissary. Assure him of the pleasure with which you have seized the opportunity of proving to H.M. that the sentiments which you expressed in opposition are still yours. Express your satisfaction at hearing that he intends to take a measure which you are sure will be attended with the happiest results, and offer the same confidential co-operation in future should H.M. desire or circumstances appear to require it.

To the Emperor of the French.

TORQUAY, *Dec.* 27, 1858.

SIRE, — I request your Majesty's permission to acknowledge the kind condescension with which your Majesty has received my first secretary, Mr. Earle.

It has afforded me satisfaction to prove to your Majesty that the views which I had the honor to express to your Majesty when I was the leader of Opposition are influencing my conduct as a Minister of the Queen.

The declaration which your Majesty has graciously intimated to Mr. Earle it is your Majesty's intention to make at the opening of the Chambers will have, I doubt not, the happiest results, and will revive and strengthen that complete alliance between France and England which, in spite of a thousand superficial difficulties, is the keystone of the only policy which can secure the greatness of both countries. I have the honor to remain, Sire, with profound respect, your Majesty's obliged servant, B. DISRAELI.

Earle came back to Disraeli with his full report, and the Emperor intimated to the whole world what he had avowed to Earle, by saying in a marked manner, at his New Year reception, to Baron Hübner, the Austrian Ambassador, that he regretted that the relations between the Governments of France and Austria were not more satisfactory. Malmesbury, however, was still unconvinced, and treated Disraeli's information as of small importance. He wrote to Derby on January 14: 'I do not believe the crisis so near as most people, who are frightened by foolish speeches of Napoleon's, whose hatred of Buol and his envoy Hübner is unbounded.'

To Lord Derby.

Confidential. DOWNING STREET, *Jan.* 4, 1859. — Affairs here are, as you no doubt well know, very critical, and I regret that we are again all scattered, as we were in the Portuguese affair,[1] when decision and energy are absolutely requisite.

I did not go to Aylesbury on Monday, because I received from Paris a letter by messenger on Sunday which rendered it absolutely necessary that I should see Malmesbury, whom I could only catch on his way to Heron Court, where he has gone for a week. I have no hesitation in saying to you that he ought to be at the F.O., and nowhere else. Any appearances of negligence and any vagueness of language under these circumstances will have the very worst effect, whereas I have reason to believe that a calm and decisive carriage would oblige Austria to consent to the evacuation of the Roman States, and that would conclude the business.

It is not the army that is pressing the Emperor, but his own personal anxiety to do *something* for Italy, and a diplomatic triumph would satisfy him. In the meantime you may rest assured that the great diplomats want to see the Prime Minister and the Foreign Secretary. Personal interview is the main element of success in negotiation; writing does not do much good, and Cowley's letters are deceptive, even if they are unintentionally so.

The Emperor is anxious to put himself quite right with England again, but of this nettle danger we might extract a good result, menacing as it seems, if we are prompt and firm. But the Cabinet ought to be assembled. One false step at the commencement may ruin all.

Derby showed in his reply that he was disposed to agree with Malmesbury in thinking the danger not so imminent as it appeared to Disraeli; but he expressed his readiness to hasten his return to town if Disraeli held his presence to be necessary.

To Lord Derby.

Confidential. DOWNING STREET, *Jan.* 7, 1859. — I could not bear your coming up to town on Saturday, so I telegraphed that it was not necessary, and shall endeavour in this mode, though very imperfectly, to convey to you some of my views of what is going on, that you may digest them on your journey,

---

[1] The case of a French ship, the *Charles et Georges*, seized by the Portuguese as a slaver. The British Government arranged the dispute.

and so, when we còme to confer, shall not have lost much time.

I feel a difficulty in conversing with Malmesbury on these matters. I observe when I touch on them, which I do always with reluctance, an incipient reserve and jealousy, as if I were trenching on his manor: unwise, I think, and unfortunate, but perhaps natural, and a feeling, if it exist, against which it is useless to contend.

Malmesbury did not reassure me, and it was impossible that he could, because I perceived that he was himself very imperfectly acquainted with the state of affairs. Nor is this wonderful, since he relies solely upon Cowley, and Cowley, who has not yet recovered his surprise at what has happened, explains everything by the ingenious assumption that a personal feeling on the part of the Emperor against Hübner is at the bottom of all that has happened or may happen. Throughout all this Italian pother Cowley has been off the rails.

Ever since we have been in office the Emperor has been estranged from us : this is the reason of the Lisbon business, which might have been prevented, and which was persisted in to injure us. The Emperor has got Malmesbury's letter to Cowley upon Austrian affairs, and expresses himself as entirely dissatisfied with its reasoning and its illustrations. He says that he is surprised that an English Minister should admit that there is any analogy between the instance of Lombardy and those of Ireland and India.

With regard to Lord Cowley and his conversation with the Emperor on Austria, the Emperor found his views not only those of the time of the *blocus continental*, but Lord Cowley was so unfortunate as to impress on His Majesty that if he stirred in Italy he would probably revive the Northern Confederacy against France. Not very pleasing under any circumstances, but, with the existing relations between France and Russia, absurd. From that time the Emperor has never recurred to the subject with Lord Cowley, not because he was convinced, as Lord Cowley supposes, but because H.M. felt agreement was hopeless.

I will now attempt to convey to you some idea of the real state of affairs — *i.e.*, the real state of the Emperor's mind — for in this business he is Alpha and Omega.

Ever since the Orsini business he has been, more or less, fitful and moody, and brooding over Italy. The letter of Orsini produced a great effect on him. He is alarmed for his life. Having himself belonged to the Carbonaro Society, he knows that he is never safe while they continue to look upon him as a renegade. He is resolved, therefore, 'to do something for Italy.' It is purely a personal impulse in its origin,

but, indulged in, it necessarily mingles with political ideas.
Some reconstruction of Italy has been developed by personal
apprehension. Cavour, too, is always on the watch. But
nothing is yet definite, though it may be resolved on in an
instant. Sometimes he talks of placing himself at the head
of the army of invasion, as he once talked of going to the
Crimea. And he would do it, for in dealing with this personage we must remember we are dealing with a mind as
romantic as it is subtle.

But the French army is not in a condition to move with
effect. Its artillery is in a transition state. All its improvements have become obsolete — before they were completed —
and they must work day and night in founding rifle cannon
before they could venture on great campaigns. Next to, or
perhaps equal with, his desire ' to do something for Italy ' is
the Emperor's wish — I might say passion — to restore the
good opinion of the English people in his favor. For this he
is prepared to make great sacrifices, to force free trade in
France, perhaps even to reduce his marine.

At this moment he is meditating a great rhetorical *coup.*
This is a profound secret. His Chambers, or whatever they
are called, meet early in February. He will seize that opportunity, in a manner in which he excels, of taking a view of
the state of public affairs, and he will make a great effort
to put himself right with England. *Mind, England,* not the
English Ministry, though we shall be blunderers if we permit
the present estrangement to continue.

Now observe : there are two things at this conjuncture most
urgent. First, to impress upon Austria that, in the event of
war between her and France, England will not interfere.
Malmesbury has, I believe, urged this upon Apponyi, who is
a just and sensible man, and who, I doubt not, conveys
accurate impressions to his Court. But Austria is unwilling
to believe this : the relations between the Prince Consort and
Germany tend to convey a different impression. On this you
may rely. Messages have been conveyed (I will not say from
H.R.H.) which neutralise the declarations of our Ministry.
But if Austria is convinced that we shall be neutral, then she
will be conciliatory, and she would agree to a revival of the
Conferences at Paris to consider the condition of Central and
Southern Italy. This overture on her part would enlist English opinion on her side, and on English opinion at this moment
everything depends.

The Emperor is watching it with intenseness, down to an
article in the *Daily News.* He will never risk a war which
England disapproves. If opinion here sanction the conciliatory movement of Austria, he will agree to the revival of the

Conferences, and content himself with a diplomatic triumph. All immediate danger of war will certainly then be averted, and Malmesbury would meet Parliament with a feather in his cap.

But, to bring all this about in less than a month, every day, every hour, is precious, and a week is already lost — a week, too, of opportunities which may never occur again, for we should have had the advantage of counselling those who were in a panic.

You misunderstood my former letter on these matters, and I am not surprised. I was embarrassed, and I felt what I wrote was feeble and ambiguous. What I have said now I hope is clear, but I have been constantly interrupted, and have expressed only a tithe of what I wish to convey.

From Lord Derby.

Confidential. KNOWSLEY, *Jan.* 8, 1859. — . . . I think you are mistaken as to there being any feeling of jealousy in Malmesbury's mind as to your discussing foreign affairs with him, as being within his exclusive province. I have never heard him express any feeling of the kind, but I think, not knowing from what sources you derive your information, he is inclined, when accounts differ, to place greater reliance, which is not unnatural, on his recognised official channels of information than on private, and, so far as he is concerned, anonymous intelligence which reaches you. I do not know how far your obligations to your correspondents would allow of your removing this ground of partial mistrust.[1]

I believe you correctly estimate what is passing in the mind of the Emperor. . . .

Malmesbury has, as you are aware, spoken very strongly to Apponyi of the hopelessness of any assistance on the part of England to put down any insurrection, however fomented, in her Italian provinces, and from what he told me Apponyi seemed quite aware of the fact. I do not know that we can urge the conviction on him more strongly than we have done, but the tone which France habitually takes is such that resentment blinds Buol to the consequences, and leads him rather to provoke than to deprecate them. I cannot think that anyone in high places can have been so indiscreet as to hold out hopes to Austria in contradiction to the explicit declarations of the Government. . . .

---

[1] In a letter dated Jan. 7, which Derby had probably received when he wrote, Malmesbury had complained: 'Disraeli *never reads a word of my papers* which go round, and knows nothing but what the Jews at Paris and London tell him.' Malmesbury evidently thought that Disraeli's information came from the Rothschilds !

Malmesbury was soon driven from his optimism by the march of events, and forced to realise that Disraeli's information was correct. The entry in his diary on January 12 runs : 'The King of Sardinia has made a speech which can only mean war. Things look bad all over Europe'; and on January 16: 'I fear war cannot be avoided. The Emperor of the French seems determined, though his country is strongly against it.'

To Lord Derby.

DOWNING STREET, *Jan.* 14, 1859.—. . . The alarm in the City is very great: 'the whole of the Mediterranean trade is stopped.'

The reduced value in securities is not less than 60 millions sterling, the greater part in France. Another such a week will break the Paris Bourse.

'And all because one man chooses to disturb everything.' Only one feeling in the City — that the Government will have nothing to do with the affair. 'Though the thing were settled in a few days, months will pass before confidence is again restored, and we were on the eve of immense prosperity.'

The panic on the Bourse and the reluctance of the French people restrained Napoleon for the time from any forward movement. But it was generally felt that war was only postponed, not averted; and the desire of this country was so strong for peace if possible, and if not for neutrality, that, when Parliament opened on February 3, no attempt was made by Palmerston or Russell to attack the Government on Foreign Affairs, and Derby's and Disraeli's statements as to their efforts for peace were well received. The Government, said Disraeli, had given to all the Powers concerned the same frank, friendly, and cordial counsel. In particular they had impressed upon France and Austria 'the duty that devolves upon them of entering, not into hostile rivalry for the military command of Italy, but into that more generous emulation of seeking to advance its interests and improve its condition.' He recognised the popular sympathy in England for Sardinia.

The position of Sardinia is one which necessarily and naturally commands sympathy in a free Parliament, and there is no State in Italy which the English feelings have more clustered round than the kingdom of Sardinia, especially during the last few years. We have all hoped that Sardinia may be the means by which the improvement of Italy, morally and materially, in public liberty as well as in other respects, may be effected; and I do not relinquish — I will not readily relinquish — hopes which seemed so well founded, and which were so encouraging to every generous spirit.

' The high policy of an alliance with France ' was once again the theme of Disraeli's peroration. Napoleon had proved a faithful ally, and he relied on his sagacity not wantonly to disturb the peace of the world. These sentiments earned for Disraeli the condemnation of the Liberal press for servility and sycophancy, and at the same time obtained no return from the Emperor, who, in spite of Earle's mission and his own promise, made a very ambiguous speech at the opening of the Chambers, and, believing that his projects would be furthered by the return of the Italophil Palmerston to office, sent Persigny back to London as Ambassador to intrigue for that result.

Disraeli has left a short memorandum, written in the sixties, about the origin of the Italian War of 1859:

The Emperor of the French was a very romantic man. The Queen of England had a great personal influence over him. Unfortunately, the Prince Consort hated him. He said to me once : ' He is always a conspirator : it is the key-note of everything.' When the Italian War seemed to be inevitable, brought about by the intrigues of Cavour with the Emperor, and when there were secret understandings, it was supposed, between the parties, etc., as a last resource to maintain the peace of Europe, the Queen was advised to avail herself of her presumed personal influence with the Emperor, and write to him a private letter.[1] I did not see this letter, though I have no doubt it was well conceived and well expressed, with the advantage of Lord Derby's advice and criticism ; but I was permitted to see the Emperor's reply,[2] which was only shown to Lord Derby, Lord Malmesbury, and

---

[1] Dated Feb. 4.   [2] Dated Feb. 14.

myself.   To me it was one of the most interesting and most
satisfactory communications under the circumstances possible.   Full and frank, it told everything: how Cavour came,
what he said, what was said to him, what was contemplated.
It assumed that all must agree, that the position of Italy was
most unsatisfactory to all, and reminded the Queen that at
the Conferences of Paris the Emperor had wished to anticipate
what seemed to him inevitable by joint action.   But whatever the state of Italy, whatever the necessity of acting on
the part of France, whatever the conversations and contemplated conduct with Sardinia, etc., etc., such was his value
for the friendship and esteem of *ma très chère sœur* that he
pledged himself, and in the language the most solemn, affectionate, and precise, that, notwithstanding all that had
passed, he would never attack Austria unless she previously
attacked Piedmont.

These letters between the Queen and the Emperor were
printed in the fourth volume of Sir Theodore Martin's
Life of the Prince Consort, published in 1879.   The
Emperor's reply was not quite so full and frank as
Disraeli in retrospect thought it.   Napoleon did not
mention Cavour by name, though he wrote about the
confidential communications which he had received from
Sardinia; nor did he refer to the Conferences of Paris.
But he stated his policy to be in general such as Disraeli
has recorded.   He said he had told the Sardinian Government that his Government 'could not encourage an
aggressive line of conduct on the part of Piedmont, nor
support her in a struggle in which right would not be upon
her side, but that, on the other hand, she might rely upon
being vigorously backed, either if attacked by Austria
or if she became involved with this Power in a just and
lawful war.'   He declared — it was an audacious declaration — that he was under no engagements to Sardinia,
and denied that he was preparing for war.

The memorandum proceeds:

With this card in our hand, peace seemed secure, and with
this Lord Cowley went to Vienna.   Who could believe that
after this Austria should have attacked Piedmont without
any intimation to England, and, having attacked her and
released the Emperor of the French from his personal pledge,

should have behaved with such military imbecility that for a long time nobody actually knew where the Austrian army were. They crossed and recrossed the frontier, ravaged some of the enemy's land and then retired, and then wandered about like idiots. Nothing could have justified their conduct but a direct march to Turin. . . .

The young Emperor of Austria[1] was very conceited. He was literally sick of hearing the praises of the Emperor of the French. He had a fine army, and longed to command it, for which he had no quality. He said to Lord Cowley : 'I know that the French artillery may be superior to mine, but in no other branch have they any pre-eminence.'

In one of the long, frequent, and troubled interviews which took place between the Emperor[2] and the English Ambassador before the war broke out, the Emperor suddenly turned round and said, 'Cannot France and England understand each other?' and hinted at partition. But Lord Cowley would not listen to it. . . .

My opinion is that, even if Lord Cowley had been our Ambassador at Vienna, certainly if Lord Stratford or Sir Henry Bulwer had been there, there would have been no war. There wanted the unceasing vigilance of a commanding character to baffle the intrigues of a miserable camarilla. Our Ambassador, Lord (*sic*) Loftus, was not fit to be resident at a third-rate German Court, and was quite despised and disregarded by that of Vienna. He was a pompous nincompoop, and of all Lord Malmesbury's appointments the worst ; and that is saying a good deal.

In defence of Malmesbury, it should be said Lord Stanhope had refused the post, and Malmesbury always said he was driven in that and other instances to the office list ; but the first quality of a Minister is to select competent instruments.

An interesting note from Malmesbury to Disraeli shows his policy of neutrality — a right one in itself, but perhaps hardly maintained with sufficient adroitness and firmness.

From Lord Malmesbury.

[*Undated.*] The policy of insisting and threatening is Palmerstonian, and would commit us to one side or the other. From the moment we show a bias to one side our influence is gone, because they are now *bidding* for our friendship. We never can, I hope, be induced to join a protectorate of Italy. We have enough of the protectorate of Belgium, who will

---

[1] The Emperor Francis Joseph.   [2] Of the French.

probably be invaded by one of its protectors, and now of the Principalities, whose protectors are all pulling different ways. England always acts *de bonne foi* in these cases, and therefore has the disadvantage of being like a respectable clergyman cotrustee with 5 horsedealers.

That Malmesbury, with the most admirable intentions, was not strong enough for the post of Foreign Secretary at a time of European unrest is the view that emerges very clearly from Disraeli's correspondence and memoranda relating to this crisis. Palmerston's opinion of Malmesbury was the same. To a foreign diplomat he said: 'Il ne manque pas d'un certain aplomb et d'un certain don de parole, mais il est paresseux, insouciant, et ignorant au suprême degré dans tout ce qui regarde les affaires de son département.' On another occasion he called him 'our Magdalen in politics,' adding: 'Dans tout ce ministère un seul homme, M. Disraeli, entend quelque chose à la politique extérieure, et encore ne s'y entend-il guère.' Whether, however, Disraeli's amateur diplomacy and spasmodic interventions were calculated to benefit our foreign policy during this period may perhaps be doubted. His insight, as in the case of Napoleon's character and intentions, was far quicker and more penetrating than Malmesbury's; and, had he been at the Foreign Office, his despatches would have carried the weight of a statesman of the first class. But, not being either Foreign Minister or Prime Minister, he could not exercise regular control; and Malmesbury's irritation at his interference was not unnatural.

None of the various expedients which were tried, neither the appeals of England to France, Austria, and Sardinia, nor Cowley's mission to Vienna, nor a European Congress proposed by Russia, succeeded in averting the war. After the defeat on the Reform Bill, the British Government was felt to be in suspension till the election was decided, and Malmesbury's advice necessarily lost half its weight abroad. But it was not the wavering Napoleon after all, but Austria, who, losing patience, precipitated

hostilities by peremptorily demanding, on the very day[1] on which the British Parliament was prorogued, the disarmament of Sardinia. Disraeli remained hopeful to the last, and said in debate on the previous day that the elements of a settlement were in existence. But he did not disguise the seriousness of the prospect if peace were broken.

A war in Italy is not a war in a corner. An Italian war may be, and probably will be, an European war. The waters of the Adriatic cannot be disturbed without agitating the waters of the Rhine. The port of Trieste is not merely an Italian port; it is a port which belongs to the Germanic Confederation, and an attack on the port of Trieste is not an attack on Austria merely, but on Germany. If, then, a war spread beyond the precincts of Italy, England is interested, not only from those enlightened principles of civilisation which make her look with an adverse eye on any attempt to disturb the peace of the world, but England may be interested from material considerations of the most urgent and momentous character.

Simultaneously Derby said in the House of Lords:

If war break out, whatever may be the consequences, it is indispensable and necessary that, as long as our neutrality shall last, it must be to a certain extent an armed neutrality, enabling us in any case to take our part, on which side soever it may be, that honour and justice and dignity require us to take.

These apparently harmless words of Derby's were perverted by party spirit, during the elections and afterwards, into a hint that Government were contemplating a breach of neutrality on the unpopular Austrian side; a slander which was not even abandoned when Derby promptly denounced Austria's action in launching her ultimatum as hasty, precipitate, and criminal.

While the immediate issue absorbed the attention of the ordinary man and the ordinary politician, Disraeli, as was his wont, took a far wider view, and in his speech on the hustings at Aylesbury contrasted the imperial position of England with the local strifes of Europe.

[1] April 19.

The day is coming, if it has not already come, when the question of the balance of power cannot be confined to Europe alone. . . . You have on the other side of the Atlantic vigorous and powerful communities, who will no longer submit to your circumscribed theory of authority. The Australian colonies, though now in their youth, but in the youth of giants, have already, as it were, thrown their colossal shadow over Europe. And it is for old Europe I lament, that she is exhausting her energies and her resources in these wars. I could wish that she would rather prepare for that awful competition which in coming times she must encounter. I would rather see France and Germany and Russia develop their resources, improve their agriculture, increase their population, and cultivate the arts of life, social and scientific, instead of wasting their strength, risking their stability, and sinking, when the era to which I have referred arrives, by their own mismanagement and want of prescience, into an inferior and exhausted position. Remember always that England, though she is bound to Europe by tradition, by affection, by great similarity of habits, and all those ties which time alone can create and consecrate, is not a mere Power of the Old World. Her geographical position, her laws, her language and religion, connect her as much with the New World as with the Old. And although she has occupied not only an eminent, but, I am bold to say, the most eminent, position among European nations for ages, still, if ever Europe by her shortsightedness falls into an inferior and exhausted state, for England there will remain an illustrious future. We are bound to the communities of the New World, and those great States which our own planting and colonising energies have created, by ties and interests which will sustain our power and enable us to play as great a part in the times yet to come as we do in these days, and as we have done in the past. And therefore, now that Europe is on the eve of war, I say it is for Europe, not for England, that my heart sinks.

A noteworthy utterance indeed, whose full meaning can be much better appreciated in 1915 than in the far-off heyday of *laisser faire* in 1859; a year, it may be added, in which there were rejoicings in England as well as in Prussia over the birth of Queen Victoria's eldest grandson, now William the Second, German Emperor and King of Prussia.

CHAPTER VII

From Government to Opposition

1859

In the General Election of 1859, Disraeli, as he always felt, had no luck. The conditions were favourable to Conservative success. The Indian Mutiny had been suppressed; affairs in China were improved. There were no burning questions between parties, for the country was comparatively indifferent to the Reform which had agitated its representatives. Men's minds were largely occupied with the European situation; and the policy of neutrality pursued by the Government was universally accepted, though eager friends of Italy suspected them of a partiality for Austria. The daring, skill, and good-humour, with which Disraeli had conducted affairs for more than a year in a House of which three-fifths were against him, had won him both sympathy and admiration. The Opposition were still divided, and neither Palmerston nor Russell enjoyed his former measure of public esteem.

That the Conservatives would increase their numbers was certain. Would they gain only twenty or thirty seats, and so be liable to ejection on the Address; or as many as forty or fifty, and so be able to maintain themselves in power? Either result seemed equally possible. Luck would decide. Disraeli was very hopeful, and made an elaborate calculation, in which the element of luck received generous recognition. He considered that thirty-five seats were certain to be gained, and

232

thirteen to be lost — net gain, twenty-two. In addition, twenty-three other Liberal seats would fall to the Conservatives, if they had moderate luck ; while, if they had great luck, they would win twenty-five more. By assuming the capture of two-thirds of those which moderate luck would give them, fifteen seats, and one-third of those which only great luck could secure, eight seats, and adding these to the certain net gain of twenty-two, he obtained a final estimate of forty-five seats, not counting Ireland. He told the Queen on April 14: 'The general accounts from the country respecting the impending elections far exceed the most sanguine estimates of the Government.' His hopes were disappointed. The movement in favour of the Conservatives was not sufficient ; they only gained about thirty seats. The luck ran against them. There was less change in *personnel* than at any of the preceding elections in which Disraeli was concerned. Instead of 200 unreturning members, as he predicted, there were but little over 100. He took the result with his wonted fortitude and good-humour.

To Mrs. Brydges Willyams.

Downing Street, *April* 29, 1859. — The great battle commences to-day, and in eight-and-forty hours we shall know whether we are mice or men. . . . It is nervous work. . . .

Downing Street, *May* 20, 1859. — The elections are over, and altho' of late, and especially in Ireland, they have been extremely favorable to the Government, I was much disappointed with the early returns from the English boro's. We had no *luck*, and ought to have gained ten more seats, which we lost by units ! — in one case, my own county town, a tie ! These additional ten would have given us an absolute majority of the House, and we should have been on a rock of adamant : as it is, our position is critical, and nothing can describe to you the constant anxiety, vigilance, and labor, which it requires to manage this vast, however inadequate, host, and to cope with the perpetual menaces and stratagems of the enemy. . . .

I have written to you very little, but no language can convey to you the absorbing character of my life. It is that of a general in the field, and the sense of responsibility pre-

vents one from doing anything but what is a fulfilment of pressing and immediate duty.   I have two [1] excellent private secretaries, both young men, and very good-looking and clever. The first secretary, Mr. Earle, has been returned to Parliament, tho' he is only 23, but a man in matured thought and power of observation.   Without his assistance I could not get thro' my work.   I can trust him with interviews.   He can see men and manage them.

Earle's election for Berwick was a mere flash in the pan, as, under an arrangement with his opponent, he resigned the seat in August, and did not reappear in the House of Commons until he was returned in 1865 for Maldon. Disraeli's own return was unopposed, and he was able to devote the more attention to the general management of the elections.   There are some indications in his correspondence that he instigated the Conservative Central Office to support Radical candidatures against Whigs in cases where no Conservative was standing — a defensible policy, as the Radicals had often been willing to give the Government fair-play, while the factious opposition of the Whigs had been almost unremitting.   Derby thought this policy shortsighted.   'The Whigs,' he wrote, 'are disgusted with Johnny, and are hanging back.   We must avoid irritating them by supporting Radicals against them — at least in England.'   One electoral move which Disraeli earnestly pressed, for the benefit both of his friend Stanley and of the party, was brought to naught by Stanley's obstinacy.

To Lord Stanley.

April 8, 1859. — From some information which has reached me, I believe that you will be returned for London at the head of the poll.   It is the opinion of your opponents.   All I want now from you is *to hold your tongue*, and to throw no cold water on the movement, which is hourly assuming gigantic proportions.   If you are returned, it would do us more good than ten small borough seats, and give a tone to the whole election.   I have much to say to you on this head, but all

---

[1] The other Secretary was C. L. Ryan, then a clerk in the Treasury, now Sir Charles Ryan, late Comptroller and Auditor-General.

I wish for now is reserve on your part — a grand talent for silence.

Stanley had gained golden opinions in the City by his management of the transfer of India from the Company to the Crown, and by the business-like qualities which his administration of the new India Office had displayed. But he declined to respond to the enthusiasm of the City Conservatives, hesitating now, as throughout his career, to take risks.

While the election was still in progress, but when it had become clear that Ministers, though their following would be considerably increased, would fail to command an independent majority in the House of Commons, Disraeli made a final attempt to bring about that union in office of Palmerston and Derby which general similarity of political views and a certain correspondence in personal tastes and position rendered natural, and which would have been popular in the country. The elections showed that the conservative forces, in the non-party sense, were the strongest in the constituencies; a conservative Administration, consisting of Tories and Palmerstonian Whigs, would be the logical outcome. It was yet another favourable opportunity to form that 'manly alliance' which 'Manilius' had advocated in the *Press*.[1]

To Lord Palmerston.

[? *May* 3, 1859]. — I address you in our ancient confidence. Consider well the views I am taking the liberty of placing before you.

Lord Derby will count at the meeting of Parliament not less than 300 followers, probably a little in excess of that number. He has the offer of some irregular assistance which may be relied on at an emergency.

If you were to unite with him in forming a Government, and bring with you a following of about 20 or 30 gentlemen, you would have more than an absolute majority of the House, which would constantly be increasing.

Considering the state of affairs on the Continent, the extreme

[1] See Vol. III., pp. 495–498.

opinions professed on domestic politics by leading members
of the Opposition, and the ample means of official promotion
which could be placed at your disposal, it may be not an unreasonable assumption that such a number at least would
follow your advice.

You would then be entire master of the situation. The
foreign policy of every Government of which you are a member must be yours, even if you might not think it expedient to
undertake the Foreign Office.

As for domestic policy, when the occasion serves, you could
bring in your own Reform Bill, which, with our increased
force, may be as conservative as you please. You could dictate
your terms.

There is yet one point on which I speak with delicacy, but
without reserve. I have worked with Lord Derby for ten
years, and a shade of disagreement or estrangement has never
risen between us, and for the seven last years I have possessed
his unlimited confidence. A point of honor alone attaches him
to the party post which he fills. He feels that he can never
desert the Conservative party while it is in a minority, and
while there is no member of it to succeed him.

I have not written this with his knowledge. When I called
on him this morning he was at Roehampton. I have, however,
frequently and amply brought the general views of this letter
before him, and he has received them always with approbation.
Indeed, one of our reasons for the dissolution was that it must
so much increase our strength, that it would facilitate the reconstruction desirable.

I say nothing on this occasion about individual arrangements. When I cheerfully set the example of personal sacrifice
for a public purpose, I feel there is no one of my colleagues
who can demur at any change deemed necessary for the public
interest.

For myself, I can truly say that my principal object has
ever been the consolidation of the Conservative party, and
that what I am now proposing is only an arrangement that
I have long meditated, and more than once endeavoured to
accomplish. You would receive from me, not merely cordial
co-operation, but a devoted fidelity.

Let us consider for a moment, if you do not embrace these
views, what is probable to occur.

It is possible that Lord J. Russell, by some resolution or
amendment on the subject of Parliamentary Reform, with no
definite pledge, but with a radical bias, may place the Government in a minority. Whatever may be the disposition of
the Court, and whatever may be our desire to support your
nomination, I think it would be impossible for the Queen to

send for anyone but Lord J. Russell. It is possible that under
those circumstances you might become a member of his
Government, but you would sit with men who do not sympathise with you, and probably in the natural course of events
would quit his Administration. But even if Her Majesty were
to send for your lordship, what would be your position? The
extreme party would watch their opportunity to destroy you,
and no Government can permanently depend on the forbearance of an Opposition.

You must be aware that, if the union between Lord Derby
and yourself were now to take place, it would be one gratifying to an anxious Court and to the country.

From Lord Palmerston.

Brocket, *May* 3, 1859.

MY DEAR MR. DISRAELI, — I am sorry I was out when your
messenger arrived, and that I have thereby caused him to be
detained here longer than he ought to have been.

I am much obliged to you for the kind and friendly terms
of your letter, and if I say in answer that many reasons which
it is unnecessary to go into would prevent me from entering
into such an arrangement as that which you suggest might
be possible, I trust it is needless for me to assure you that no
want of personal good feeling towards Lord Derby or yourself, or towards any other members of your Government,
could form part of those reasons. — My dear Mr. Disraeli,
yours sincerely, PALMERSTON.

Palmerston, it may be assumed, was confident that
the outcome of the elections would be a Palmerston
Administration. But to other competent observers that
did not appear certain. His position was nothing like so
strong as after the 1857 election, when a large majority
was returned with no other mandate than to support
him. The prospective Liberal majority of 1859 would
contain many who followed Cobden and Bright, many
who followed Russell, some who followed Gladstone,
besides Irish members who looked to their own leaders.
Without Conservative support Palmerston's power would
be very insecure. That support he no doubt hoped to
obtain; but he meant to do so, if possible, without paying
for it with office.

Disraeli already foresaw this, for himself, uninviting

future, and, after receiving Palmerston's refusal, did all
he could to prevent its realisation.   He 'reconnoitred'
for support both among Roman Catholic Irish and among
independent Liberals;   and in particular applied to
Horsman, an independent Liberal who had played a
considerable part, generally friendly to the Government,
in the debates of 1858 and 1859.   In the draft of Disraeli's
letter to him, which has been preserved among the
Beaconsfield papers, there is the following illuminating
passage, which, however, was apparently struck out before the letter was despatched:

If the usual combination throws us out, Ld. Palmerston
is to be the next man, and will form a Government with his
friends, and is to be supported, not generally, but unvary-
ingly, by mine, sitting opposite to him.   I have no doubt he
will govern the country well, but I do not see why he should
do it better than us, nor do I see why this hocus-pocus should
be perpetually repeated.

Disraeli perfectly understood that Derby, as well as
Palmerston, was prepared to regard a prospect of this
kind with complacency.   In order to avoid it, he offered
Horsman one of the highest posts in the Cabinet, with
provision also for his friends and followers, adding:

The occasion is a great one, and not for ordinary men.
But you have energy, courage, and resource, equal to it.   A
following of fifteen would do the business.   It would be a
coup d'état, a great triumph, and the final blow to those personal traditions whose pompous mediocrity for a quarter of
a century has oppressed the House of Commons.

It looks at first sight as if Disraeli, in making offers of
this dazzling kind to that 'superior person' but second-
rate politician, Horsman — who refused because he was
himself conscious of his inadequacy — had lost for the
moment his usual shrewd appreciation of Parliamentary
values;   but his report to Derby suggests a different
explanation.

To Lord Derby.

Confidential.   GROSVENOR GATE, *May* 8, 1859. — I called on
you yesterday, after the Court, to give you the result of my

reconnoitring and consult over affairs. Time is so precious, and so much depends on the manner in which the next three weeks are employed, that I forward this to you at once.

I estimate our pure gains, for they must still be an estimate, at 26. There are six borough seats, in addition, which really have been won from the enemy. The 'independent' Irish party will, I hear, probably be increased to 15. This would make a force on which we could now depend, on a trial of strength, to the amount of 322, out of a House of 652, deducting the Speaker and Aylesbury.

Horsman has been confidentially sounded. He recognises the critical state of affairs, foreign and domestic, believes that the strongest man cannot change his political connection without sacrifices which pursue him through life, but would not hesitate to do his duty, though it might embitter his future existence. Fortunately, however, he is spared the cruel dilemma, as he feels he is not important enough for such an occasion, and that his adhesion would only destroy himself, without aiding us. I expected this sort of response to the appeal; it will, however, prevent him from precipitating himself into any combination against the Government.

Mr. Lindsay,[1] who is supposed to be the type of some dozen men of doubtful Liberal allegiance, has also been sounded: replied very favorably, but expressed a wish for an interview with myself, which he will have.

What effect the growing impression, that Palmerston is to be the new Minister, will have on the Manchester party I have not yet ascertained, though I have made arrangements which will probably obtain us that information ere long.

P. will serve under no one, and considers himself already installed. J. R., it is said, is starved out, and would serve under P. if he could manage to get rid of his new allies with decency and the appearance of honor.

The Whigs wish to precipitate the attack, that Liberal claims and Liberal dissensions should not have time to develop. They want a vague vote on which all would be obliged to unite, and then a Whig Administration under Palmerston. I suppose you observed the Marquis of Stafford's speech.

My own opinion is that a permanent working majority may be obtained from the present House of Commons on two conditions:

1. That we gain time.

2. That the Cabinet should obtain some additional weight and character.

I will reserve for conversation the tactics by which I think

[1] M.P. (L.), Tynemouth, 1854–1859; Sunderland, 1859–1865.

time may be obtained, and the scheme for an immediate vote be baffled.

I will consider now the second point, for it is urgent.

There is no doubt a very general wish, not confined to the unattached Liberals, that the Cabinet should be strengthened. Any scheme by which numerical force could be secured through a process of reconstruction I think must be abandoned. We must confine ourselves to an addition which will increase its intellectual authority. The following are the only persons by which, it appears to me, this result could be obtained: Lord Elgin,[1] Mr. Gladstone, Stuart Wortley,[2] Frederick Peel.[3] The latter is not popular : I think highly of him.

If Lord Elgin in one House, and Mr. Gladstone in the other, joined the Administration, I think it would rise in public estimation, and would permanently be established. When Gladstone was reconnoitred two months ago, it resulted that no personal feeling any longer existed which prevented him joining the Administration ; that he could not join alone ; and, thirdly, that he wished all invitations should be direct from yourself. This latter point was also much insisted upon by Mr. Gladstone in private conversation with Sir Stafford Northcote. You would, of course, be careful that this direct communication, if you decide upon it, should not take place by letter ; you would send for him, confer on the state of public affairs, and ask him really what he wanted. The application to Lord Elgin would probably greatly influence him.

With regard to Lord Elgin, who is at Paris, any mere offer forwarded to him would probably be fruitless. The Court, our own Ambassador there, and *The Times* newspaper, form Lord Elgin's opinion as to the political position ; and, of course, he thinks we are in an overwhelming minority, as the Emperor does himself, and Lord E. would decline. He must be informed, if you resolve on the step, that you are about to reconstruct the Government, and that you wish, consequently, to confer with him in London. Mr. Gladstone's knowledge of the House of Commons would permit him to form a juster estimate of our Parliamentary position than Lord Elgin, and you would have a natural and easy opportunity of enlightening him on the subject.

But what is Lord Elgin to be ? He must have a post of high administration, and it is difficult to place any other than that of the Foreign Office in the House of Lords. Lord

[1] The eighth Earl, who had just distinguished himself in China, and was afterwards Viceroy of India.

[2] Son of first Lord Wharncliffe ; Solicitor-General, 1856–57.

[3] Sir Robert Peel's second son ; afterwards Chief Railway Commissioner.

Malmesbury once told me, but in absolute confidence, that, if we succeeded in obtaining a majority at the General Election, he intended to retire from his post, and recommend you to take Lord Elgin in his stead. I cannot presume to give an opinion on such a subject. I think it would be a great misfortune to lose Malmesbury from the Cabinet, and that he should under any circumstances remain there, in as high a post as is practicable.

If Mr. Gladstone joins, I think that India should be his office. It is the only post which would absorb his superfluous energies. This arrangement would not be disagreeable to Stanley, who wishes to return to the Colonial Office.

Assuming that it may be desirable to provide for others, Stuart Wortley might be Chancellor of Lancaster, and Frederick Peel might be Secretary of the Admiralty, Henry Corry succeeding to the Chairmanship of the Inland Revenue. My dear Lord, I have now placed before you my general views, which it would have been much more agreeable and more easy to have discussed in conversation, but I feel that no time can be lost in their consideration. There is a great deal at stake: I think, really, the welfare of the country: certainly your honor in history. For myself, I will merely observe that I am prepared to take any step and make any sacrifice, provided you remain at the head of the Administration. If, therefore, any other arrangements more feasible than I have submitted for your consideration occur to you, you can have no delicacy in intimating your opinions to me, which I shall in that, as I hope I have done in every other instance, loyally endeavor to assist you in carrying into operation.

Derby deprecated any change at the Foreign Office, where it was, he wrote, of great importance to have a man 'who has at his fingers' ends the whole thread of the complicated negotiations in which we have been engaged.' But he made overtures to Gladstone, which, however, in spite of Disraeli's hopes, met with a more unfavourable reception than in the previous year. ' It is fair I should say,' Gladstone wrote, ' that I am not an approver of the dissolution, and that I am not able to flatter myself that in the present position of affairs I can make any useful suggestion.' This was, as Gladstone himself admitted, an 'uninviting preface,' and Derby went no farther.

Disraeli's attempts to procure support among the Irish brigade were the natural corollary of the good political relations which he had by now established with English Catholicism ;[1] but they brought him up against the Irish Government. He wrote to Eglinton, Naas, and White-side, urging, in accordance with his habitual policy of toleration, that appointments must cease to be purely Orange, and that places must be given to Roman Cath-olics, even though they were opponents. All three replied more or less indignantly and convincingly. Naas, indeed, turned the tables rather neatly.

From Lord Naas.

Private. DUBLIN CASTLE, *May* 17, 1859. — I agree with you this is a great emergency, and we are bound to do all we can to get every vote. We have made no Orange appoint-ments. That is only the hustings cant of the Whigs, infuriated at our success. We all feel that it would be most advisable to make a few Catholic appointments, but the difficulty is how to do it. . . . Our policy has been to appoint com-petent men to every office. Ten years of Whig rule has crammed every department with Catholic incapables, ap-pointed solely on account of their religion. We cannot follow that example. It is both dishonest and impolitic. Our friends would never support us if they saw political opponents of inferior merit put over their heads.

Whatever our policy has been, it has been successful, for we have won 8 seats in Ireland, and will bring 58 men of our own and 6 or 7 Independents into the field, making 64 on the first division. . . .

There is one way in which you can promote Catholics with-out offence : give them a fair share of the Colonial and Indian legal appointments. We have been very badly treated on this head. We give you a larger support than any other portion of the United Kingdom, and you have not given either to the Irish Bar or Church a single Indian or Colonial office. We can give you competent men for both. Pray, therefore, insist on this. . . .

---

[1] On June 25 Disraeli asked a Roman Catholic M.P. to ' convey to Car-dinal Wiseman my sense of the generous and courageous manner in which His Eminence accorded us his assistance. It was given ungrudgingly, without solicitation, and without condition, and with that true feeling which can only be prompted by a sense of duty ' (Wilfrid Ward's *Wiseman*, Vol. II, p. 449).

With Lindsay and the independent Liberals, who included a person of the considerable Parliamentary importance of Roebuck, Disraeli had more success. What they mainly wanted was a more comprehensive measure of Reform. Disraeli, as we know, was himself in favour of a more generous Bill than the timidity of some of his colleagues had allowed him to propose. He had, therefore, no difficulty in giving a general assent to the programme outlined by Roebuck in a letter which he wrote to Lindsay.

J. A. Roebuck to W. S. Lindsay.

May 22, 1859. — A Reform Bill which proposed a six pound value franchise for boroughs, a ten pound franchise for counties, and also the disfranchisement of a large number of the smaller boroughs, would, I think, command the confidence of the country. At this time, however, men's minds are very intently fixed upon foreign affairs; and what is required of our rulers by the people on this matter is that every means should be adopted to maintain an honest neutrality, and at the same time that every precaution should be taken to render England secure against foreign attack. I feel sure that if this course were pursued, respecting home and foreign politics, the country would support an Administration that thus showed itself truly patriotic. We are not at the present moment possessed of much confidence in the so-called leaders of the Liberal party, but the people have made up their minds that there shall be no return to the old Tory practices or principles, but they are not determined to have their ends sought by particular men only. They were content to see Catholic Emancipation and Free Trade carried by Sir R. Peel, and they would be quite ready now to receive Reform, and a wise foreign policy, from the present possessors of power. . . .

Lindsay explained that by 'large disfranchisement' Roebuck did not contemplate disfranchisement to anything like the extent proposed by Bright; and he proceeded to draw up a paper which he submitted to Disraeli, on behalf of Roebuck and himself, embodying the views agreed upon. Disraeli was asked, and consented, to rise at the beginning of the debate on the Address and make a statement on behalf of the Government in harmony with these views; and Lindsay undertook, if that were

done, that Roebuck and his other friends—in sufficient
number, he believed, to secure a clear majority — would
support the Government in a confidence division.   In
consequence of these arrangements, Disraeli contemplated the approach of the session with serenity.

To Lord Derby.

Confidential. DOWNING STREET, *May* 26, 1859. — Everything looks well. Be careful to keep all your places open.
Also a bold mien and confident tone. Any despondency
under your roof is noticed and repeated, and then people will
not believe we are going to win. If Stanley is with you, just
give him a hint in this direction. I have my reasons for all
this.

Up to yesterday, Palmerston and J. R. had agreed on all
points of foreign policy; on Reform; and on their Cabinet;
but not as to mode of attack. This you may rely on. J. R.
was strong for an amendment on Reform, but it was urged
that we should be great fools if we did not cut the ground
from under them in that respect; and then also, I am assured,
the real Whigs don't want to come in on Reform. There is a
small section for censure on dissolution, and they urge that
Gladstone has promised to vote for that, and also speak.
But this proposition is not favorably received. Lord Palmerston is for want of confidence, but whether on Address or on
a subsequent and substantive motion hesitates; but the
chances are it will be on the Address, the precedent of 1841,
which is in the mouths of Charles Wood and Ben Stanley.
These, I am assured, are the most violent. There are several
opponents, however, to want of confidence on the Address.
The hitch is that 'many Radicals hold aloof.' I believe
Bright and Gibson are secured by the Palmerston-Russell
coalition. A long time was wasted by a mutual desire of
each of these chiefs that the other should go to the Upper
House; ultimately they both declined. They therefore
remain in the Lower House. The form of settlement is — the
one sent for is to be acknowledged Premier, and the rest serve
under him; but J. R. said he knew the Queen would send for
Lord Palmerston.

Sir John Ramsden is to move the amendment.

Gladstone will vote against want of confidence. I wish,
now, you had seen him, and then we should have had all his
reasons against dissolution, and been able to discount his
objections before he spoke.

My plan of the battle would be this: to rise myself immedi-

ately after Ramsden, and state our case, and divide the same night if possible. But my reasons for this unusual course I will reserve till we meet. Peel, however, if I remember right, did it once. . . .

Disraeli's information that the Opposition were coming together was quite correct. They had fought in the elections a common enemy, and therefore were less disposed for the moment to fight one another. Moreover, the Whig leaders wanted office. All sections, represented by Palmerston and Russell, Sidney Herbert and Milner Gibson, joined in a requisition for a meeting at Willis's Rooms to settle the plan of attack. The meeting was held the day before the Queen's Speech, and was entirely successful. 'The two leaders,' says Greville, 'gave the required assurances that each would serve under the other in the event of either being sent for. There was a general concurrence in the plan of attacking the Government at once, in which even Bright and Ellice joined.' It was determined, in order to insure harmony, to avoid naming any special subject of censure, and simply to move as an amendment to the Address that the Government did not possess the confidence of the House. The motion was entrusted to a promising young member, the representative of a great Whig house, who was eventually to become one of his country's most trusted and respected leaders — Lord Hartington.

An accusation of bias in favour of the unpopular Austria seemed to be the most plausible form that the attack on the Government could take. Accordingly, Disraeli had supported his chief very strongly, as against the Court, in insisting that the terms of the paragraph in the Queen's Speech indicating the intention of the Government to preserve neutrality should be of the most unmistakable character; and the Queen gave way before their united representations.

To Lord Derby.

GROSVENOR GATE, *June 2*, 1859. — I humbly think the 'neutrality' paragraph, as amended, will endanger the

Government, and retard and embarrass the very policy which Her Majesty would wish to favor. At this moment there is great jealousy and suspicion of France in this country, but its open expression is modified, and even prevented,

1. By some genuine sympathy for Italian freedom.

2. By a general impression, industriously circulated by the Opposition, that the Court and the Ministry are favoring Austria.

It is of the utmost importance to discredit and discourage this general impression. The notice of neutrality in the Speech will be the test.

All distrust in the public mind on this head averted, the more unsuccessful Austria may be, the more public feeling will develop itself against France, and the interference of England will, at the ripe moment, be called for by the general voice.

All this will be postponed, and with a change of Ministry possibly definitively prevented, if there be a predominant feeling in the public mind that we have now an Austrian Government. . . .

With prudence, we have a majority on any amendment; but if they can raise a colorable point on Austrian bias, or imminence of war from our policy, the Opposition would at this moment succeed, though in a month hence it might be different. . . .[1]

The Opposition amendment was moved, and issue joined, directly the Address had been moved and seconded. The debate, which lasted three nights — June 7, 9, and 10 — gained much in interest owing to the uncertainty of the result. Though Palmerston and Russell, Sidney Herbert and Bright, had met together and kissed one another, there were known to be still Liberal, Irish, and Peelite dissentients ; and the Liberal majority was not sufficient to admit of much wastage. The Beaconsfield papers contain a sample of the bets that were made: 'Lord Lyndhurst has paid Mr. Charles Greville 20 sovereigns to receive one every week while the present Government continue in: Mr. G. stopping at 100.'

To Queen Victoria.

HOUSE OF COMMONS, *Tuesday, quarter past eight o'clock* [*June 7*]. — The Chancellor of the Exchequer, with his humble

[1] For the correspondence between the Queen and Lord Derby, see *Queen Victoria's Letters*, under this date.

duty to your Majesty. Lord Hartington spoke like a gentleman; was badly seconded. Chancellor of Exchequer rose
immediately at six o'clock, and is just down. The House
very full and very enthusiastic. The Chancellor of Exchequer
presumes to say he thinks he satisfied his friends.[1]

In rising at the beginning of the debate, Disraeli was
acting in accordance with his understanding with Roebuck
and Lindsay ; and in the course of his speech he made,
in no ambiguous terms, that advance on the Bill of the
previous session, in regard to the borough franchise and
redistribution, which, in accordance both with their
wishes and with his own conviction, he had promised.
He ridiculed the claim of Russell to a monopoly of the
question which he had been ' handling and fumbling ' for so
long. The Conservatives, forsooth, were not to be allowed
to have an opinion on the subject, but Palmerston, who did
not conceal his disinclination for any Reform, was yet the
popular candidate for the command of ' the united sections
of the Liberal party,' with the consent of Bright, who
had abdicated his ' portentous opinions ' in a ' lamb-like
manner.' Disraeli himself maintained — surely with good
sense — that no measure of Parliamentary Reform could
be, or ought to be, passed which was not a compromise
between Conservative and Liberal opinions. ' The happier
the compromise, the more successful will be the measure ;
and the great aim of whoever is to carry it must be to
bring forward a large, enduring, and satisfactory measure,
which, on the whole, the great parties in the State will
agree ought to pass.' The Government had dealt boldly,
he claimed, with the county suffrage in their Bill, and
they had been able to do so because that franchise had
been frequently and maturely discussed in the House.
The borough franchise was not in that condition of
maturity, and so there they proceeded cautiously. Their
plan of a variety of franchises had not found favour ; but
the question must be dealt with, so as to promote the
introduction of the working classes. That was the
opinion of Parliament and of the country.

[1] *Queen Victoria's Letters.*

We cannot be blind to that result. We do not wish to be blind to it. We have no prejudice against the proposition. All that we want is to assure ourselves that any measure that we bring forward is one which is required by the public necessities, and will be sanctioned by public approbation and support; and therefore we are perfectly prepared to deal with that question of the borough franchise and the introduction of the working classes by lowering the franchise in boroughs, and by acting in that direction with sincerity; because . . . if you intend to admit the working classes to the franchise by lowering the suffrage in boroughs, you must not keep the promise to the ear and break it to the hope. The lowering of the suffrage must be done in a manner which satisfactorily and completely effects your object, and is at the same time consistent with maintaining the institutions of the country. . . . It is, in our opinion, best for the country that a measure of Parliamentary Reform should be brought forward which is of as conclusive a character as human circumstances will admit of. To obtain that result, it must meet all those fair demands which are now recognised, and which the opinion expressed by the General Election has stamped with public approbation. . . . I claim for Her Majesty's Government the right to deal with the question of Parliamentary Reform, not fettered or hampered by the proposition which they made in the last session, any more than the noble lord has been by his own proposals, but at the same time I assert our intention to deal with it in a large, liberal, and conclusive manner.

The bulk of the Liberal Reformers scoffed at this passage as an instance of rapid and interested conversion in which no confidence could be placed, though for Disraeli, as a student of his speeches on the subject would recognise, it was no conversion at all, but an expression of views long held, but recently subordinated in order to obtain unity in the Cabinet. Bright, forgetful that he had repented his vote to overthrow Derby and Disraeli in 1852, prepared to overthrow them once more, in the fond hope that Russell's presence in the new Government would insure an ampler Reform Bill.

The passage in Disraeli's speech which attracted most attention was an attack on Graham, whose goodwill of the previous year had changed to hostility, and who had

condescended during the election to make use against
the Government of reckless charges of bribery and corruption. Graham was introducing to the electors, as his
colleague, his nephew, Sir Wilfrid Lawson, afterwards well
known as a wit and a temperance reformer, and Disraeli
affected to think that the 'impudent fabrication' must
have been retailed by the nephew rather than by the uncle.

When I saw in the newspapers the name 'City of Carlisle,'
I naturally looked at what was taking place in that quarter.
But reading, I fear a little incorrectly, I confess I did mistake,
at the time, the speech which appears to have been made by
a distinguished member of this House for that of the young
gentleman that he was introducing to his constituents. When
I read that charge upon the Ministry which we were told was
to be the basis of a Parliamentary vote of want of confidence,
when I read statements made without the slightest foundation and with a bitterness which seemed to me to be perfectly
gratuitous, I could not help saying: 'Young men will be
young men.' Youth is, as we all know, somewhat reckless in
assertion, and when we are juvenile and curly one takes a
pride in sarcasm and invective. Nevertheless, one could not
refrain from an interest in a young relative of a distinguished
member of this House, and, although the statements were not
very agreeable to Her Majesty's Ministers, one was glad to
recognise a chip of the old block. I felt — and I am sure my
colleagues shared the sentiment — that when that young
gentleman entered this House, he might, when gazing upon
the venerable form, and listening to the accents of benignant
wisdom that fall from the lips of the right hon. gentleman
the member for Carlisle — he might learn how reckless assertion in time may mature into accuracy of statement, and how
bitterness and invective, however organic, can be controlled
by the vicissitudes of a wise experience.

Lyndhurst wrote to Disraeli next day : 'Is it true that
Graham took prussic acid on his return from the Commons last night?' Graham, however, was quite able to
defend himself, and retorted, later on in the debate, that
Disraeli presented in his own person 'a contradiction to
the Horatian maxim, "Lenit albescens animos capillus,"
because by experience he knows that one may lose one's
curls and still retain one's taste for sarcasm and invective.' He added that he regarded Disraeli 'as the Red

Indian of debate. By the use of the tomahawk he has cut his way to power, and by a recurrence to the scalping process he hopes to prevent the loss of it.' It was a retort quite in the Disraelian vein.

Graham was not the only Opposition leader to receive punishment. Disraeli was satirical over the Liberal meeting at Willis's Rooms which were formerly Almack's.

In the days of our youth Willis's Rooms were managed by patronesses. The distinguished assemblies that met within those walls were controlled by a due admixture of dowagers and youthful beauties, young reputations and worn celebrities, and it was the object of all social ambition to enter there. Now Willis's Rooms are under the direction of patrons, and there are two of those patrons below the gangway. They are the noble lord the member for the City of London [Russell], and the right hon. gentleman the member for North Wiltshire [Sidney Herbert], who have signed the vouchers for the reconciled sections. . . . Well, we have some experience of those great statesmen. We know how the noble lord conducts negotiations. We know how the right hon. gentleman conducts war.[1] You say that we have failed in our negotiations, and that we cannot be trusted in the event of a possible war. Well, then, the noble lord and the right hon. gentleman won't help you much.

Disraeli replied in detail to the various charges brought against the Government, and claimed to have shown that they were 'flimsy and feeble and illusive.' But he made no complaint about the vote of censure. It was of paramount importance to know at once whether Ministers had the confidence of the House. The decision should not be delayed even four-and-twenty hours.

To Mrs. Disraeli.

June 7, 1859. — The grandest speech I ever made : all say so. The Speaker very much. I never heard such cheering.

We have got a majority if they divide to-day ; but that they will try not to do, as they know it. Our fellows don't mean to speak, but to rest on my speech.

I attribute it all to your getting up so often, and especially

---

[1] Sidney Herbert replied that, if the Liberal party formed a Government, they would be ' exposed to the opposition of the Chancellor of the Exchequer, and we all know how he carries on war.'

to the laudanum, for, though I did not sleep, it soothed my head.

There was a very large mob, and I was enthusiastically cheered.

Greville describes the night's debate thus:

On the first night Disraeli made a capital speech, and nobody else on their side would speak at all. This was a sort of manœuvre and attempt to bring about a division that night, for they found out that seventeen of the Opposition had not taken their seats, which would have secured a majority to the Government. The Whigs therefore refused to divide, and put up one man after another to keep the debate open, and eventually obtained an adjournment. Palmerston's speech was in accordance with his declaration at Willis's, and with his ancient practice; it was violently pro-French and anti-Austrian, and it was full of gross falsehoods and misrepresentations, which he well knew to be such. In his seventy-fifth year, and playing the last act of his political life, he is just what he always was.

Disraeli probably had another reason for endeavouring to force the division on the first night. He wished the independent Liberals to vote under the immediate impression of his offers about Reform, before party pressure had had time to work upon them. When the division was taken, on the third night of debate, it was found that very few of the men whose support had been promised followed Lindsay and Roebuck into the Government lobby — not more than half a dozen in all. Others voting with the Government were a few Irish Roman Catholic Liberals; Lord Elcho, afterwards Lord Wemyss, in whom independence was almost a foible; and Gladstone. The vote of censure was carried by thirteen — 323 to 310; and the Government immediately resigned.

To Mrs. Brydges Willyams.

Downing Street, *June* 11, 1859. — The second campaign of the year 1859 ended last night, after an engagement of three days, in the defeat of our cause. The result was evident since the close of the last General Election, and the general engagement could not be avoided, tho' it might perhaps have

been postponed for a few weeks. I preferred, however, quitting office with a numerous and well-organised army, untarnished and undamaged by a succession of struggles and defeats, and full of confidence in their numbers and their future. . . .

Malmesbury insisted at the time, and has maintained in his *Memoirs*, that the Government would not have been defeated had the Blue Book containing his Italian despatches been laid before Parliament. He declared that 'at least twelve or fourteen members of Parliament who voted against us in the fatal division came out of their way at different times and places to assure me that, had they read that correspondence before the debate, they would never have voted for [the] amendment'; and this favourable opinion was shared by Cobden and by Delane of *The Times*. The papers had been promised in the Queen's Speech, and Malmesbury was urgent with Disraeli to have them distributed early enough to affect the division, as the charges of Palmerston, Russell, and their followers, against the Government largely turned on the supposed mismanagement of foreign policy. Disraeli refused, or at any rate neglected, to lay the papers in time, and no satisfactory explanation was offered either then or since. Malmesbury says that Disraeli never gave him any reason, but that he himself was convinced that Disraeli had not read them, and so could not fight them in debate. That does not sound likely when we remember Disraeli's unremitting industry, and especially his omnivorous passion for Blue Books. 'How could I produce them when they were not printed?' was Disraeli's somewhat tart reply to Mr. Kebbel's request for enlightenment. But this suggestion is quite inconsistent with Malmesbury's statements in his appeals to Disraeli during the debate and in his *Memoirs*. The Beaconsfield Papers contain no direct explanation of this puzzle; but Disraeli's correspondence, as we have seen, shows that, while he and Malmesbury were agreed at this crisis in the aims of their foreign policy, he was

The third Earl of Malmesbury.
from the portrait by G. F. Middleton.

frequently dissatisfied with Malmesbury's methods and with his management of the Foreign Office. It may be assumed with some confidence that he doubted whether the papers would produce a favourable impression, and thought it safer to take a vote without them. His judgment in this case was apparently in fault; and, that being so, he characteristically took refuge in silence.

Though the change of Government did not take place till the second week of June, Disraeli never brought in his Budget, but left the financial provision for the year to his successor. The defeat of Ministers on the Reform Bill and the consequent dissolution had postponed the consideration of Ways and Means till the new Parliament. The elaborate preparations which Disraeli made in the autumn and winter for his financial schemes were therefore wasted. But he may have consoled himself by the reflection that the kind of Budget which he originally contemplated, based on a reduction of expenditure, had, principally owing to the demands of the navy, been rendered quite impracticable by the spring of 1859. Few Chancellors of the Exchequer, hardly even Gladstone, have been more profoundly convinced than Disraeli of the necessity of public economy, or more anxious to secure it. He recognised fully, moreover, that economy depends upon policy. We find the Secretary of the Treasury (G. A. Hamilton) writing to him in August, 1858 : ' One of your terse axioms is that expenditure hangs on policy ' — an axiom which hardly originated with Disraeli, but on which he certainly acted.

When the time came in the autumn of 1858 for the framing of the estimates, he directed his private secretary, Earle, to draft a memorandum, for circulation among his colleagues, on the financial condition of the country. In this he pointed out that, as the income tax was generally condemned, and it was the settled policy of the Government that it should be extinguished in 1860, there would be a large prospective deficit in that year, which must be met either by the imposition of taxes or by the reduc-

tion of expenditure.   Parliament could not well be asked
to increase the taxation either on necessaries of life or on
luxuries; the least objectionable suggestion that had been
made was to tax coals.   Fresh taxation seemed therefore
out of the question.   Could not the military establishments, already costing six millions more than in 1853 —
itself a year of increased estimates — be reduced?   He
suggested to his colleagues a serious inquiry into this
expenditure.   If no convincing evidence in its favour
could be adduced, a great reform would be effected; if
the contrary, they would have the opportunity of making
satisfactory provision for the safety of the country.
Political considerations recommended economy to a Conservative Government.   A Reformed Parliament, such as
they would shortly have, if it had to provide for a large
expenditure, would neither practise economy nor tax the
masses; it would increase the taxes on property, the income tax and succession duty — a prophecy abundantly
fulfilled in our subsequent history.

In this Treasury spirit Disraeli waged war against waste
and extravagance and increased estimates in the great
spending departments.

To Lord Derby.

Confidential.   GROSVENOR GATE, *Oct.* 9, 1858. — . . . The
troublesome theme of my daily business, and, I may say,
nightly thoughts, [is] the highly unsatisfactory state of the
War Department as regards its finance. . . .

Although the financial management of the Admiralty, under
the audit of Sir R. Bromley,[1] is of a different character from
that of the War Department, I have reason to believe the
professional management is not one whit superior. . . . I
am sorry to hear you talk of increased expenditure.   There
ought to be reduction, and it is quite compatible with increased
efficiency.   But we have, I know, a thousand difficulties to
contend with.   Still, a good management of the finances is
the only thing which really will get the country with us, and
make us independent of Court and Parliament. . . .

[1] See above, Ch. 2.   Earle in a note of this period writes: ' We want a
Treasury spy — a Bromley — in each department, to warn us of fraudu-
lent demands and to check the expenditure of the various grants.'

I am satisfied with the revenue. . . . If we could only control the military departments in their ignorant waste, I think
I could carry the Government through the session with flying
colors, come what may.

Confidential. Downing Street, *Nov.* 26, 1858. — I enclose
a confidential memorandum, which you can digest before our
meeting to-morrow. This mem. refers to the case of France
only, but the Surveyor-General, in his submission, lays down
a policy — viz., that England should be superior in naval
force to the world *united.* In case of war, we are to assume
that France, Russia, the United States, and the Scandinavian
Powers, are all to be allied against us ! This is the reproduc-
tion, applied to the navy, of the same frenzy which a *reductio
ad absurdum* demolished a year ago with respect to our home
defences on land, when for a time it was maintained that
every part of our coast ought to be fortified or guarded. . . .

Extravagant and wasteful demands Disraeli might be
able to check, but he had to yield to the cumulative evidence, pressed on him steadily by the Queen and the
Prime Minister, as well as by the departments themselves,
of the necessity for considerable establishments. The
state of Europe was restless ; the intentions of France
were ambiguous, but suggestive of adventure. The introduction of steam for the motive power, and iron for the
material, of warships involved complete naval reconstruction ; and the naval activity of France was a challenge that
must be met. 'We must take care that " Rule Britannia "
does not become an old song,' said the King of the Belgians to Disraeli. Hence an increase of a million in the
navy estimates was imperative ; and, defence on land
being needed as well as defence on sea, there could be no
corresponding reduction in the army estimates. Indeed,
the threats of the French Colonels had called into being
a considerable Volunteer movement for additional home
defence ; and the new force thus produced was first
organised by Derby's War Minister, Peel, whose work was
taken up and carried through by his successor. It is to
the credit of the Derby Ministry that they vigorously
forwarded the transformation of the navy, and gave official
recognition to the Volunteers, as they had in 1852 consti-

tuted the Militia ; but the Chancellor of the Exchequer, though he realised that increased estimates could not be avoided, was, as in official duty bound, rather the critic than the inspirer of these valuable measures. Moreover, he pressed economy on the new Government in debate, and urged them to bring it about by a policy of general reduction of armaments.

As in 1852, so in 1858–59, Disraeli, as was inevitable from the awkward situation in the House of Commons, was the animating spirit of the Ministry, though there was a much closer agreement this time between him and Derby on the main issues than there had been over the necessity of abandoning Protection. His ascendancy both in the party and in the House of Commons had become more marked ; but at the same time his steady pursuit of a progressive policy, dictated not merely by his convictions, but by his deficiency in Parliamentary numbers, had alarmed the higher Tories.[1] The difficulties to be faced by a Minister in a minority are well illustrated by a letter which he wrote in the winter to Pakington — a letter which throws, moreover, considerable light on the principles on which Disraeli acted in regard to patronage. It is characteristically free from cant, and outspoken on the claims of party ; but at the same time it shows how party claims can be duly reconciled with the public interest.

To Sir John Pakington.

Confidential. TREASURY, *Dec.* 19, 1858. — A complaining letter to a colleague is not a very pleasant Xmas offering, but I feel confident you will not misinterpret it.

We suffered much last session from the numerical weakness of our staff in the House of Commons. It ought not to be less than 35. The importance of this cannot be overrated.

[1] Greville on Dec. 25, 1859, writes that Disraeli had 'raised himself immensely . . . more perhaps with his opponents and the House of Commons generally than with his own party; but it is universally acknowledged that he led the House with a tact, judgment, and ability, of which he was not before thought capable. While he has thus risen, no rival has sprung up to dispute his pre-eminence.'

Vivian's motion,[1] which was a blow to the Government and the Court, and which may yet lead to serious consequences, was only carried by two votes.

Our staff last session only counted 30, tho' we gained one Cabinet Minister by an accident.[2]   It is now reduced to 29 by the retirement of the late Lord Advocate.   Its deficiency in numbers is occasioned by the absence of 1 Lord in Waiting, 1 Groom in Waiting, 1 Irish Solicitor-General, 1 Lord Advocate, 2 Lords of the Admiralty.   I have given unremitting attention during the recess to attempts to mitigate, at least, this evil.   By providing for George Dundas in the Colonies, I hope to secure a seat for the Lord Advocate.

The generous offer of the Duke of Northumberland to place a seat at the disposal of the Government by the retirement, if necessary, of Josceline Percy, indicated a mode in which one Lord of the Admiralty might be provided for, and it was thought, through the same influence, by a peculiar combination, the Parliamentary representation of the Admiralty might have been otherwise strengthened.

The recent passing over of —— has entirely destroyed these contemplated arrangements, and I cannot refrain from expressing my surprise and great mortification at the course you have taken in this respect.

High as the interests of party rank, I have no wish that they should be supreme.   Efficient service is, without doubt, the superior consideration.   But —— was a much younger man than his favored rival, and was distinguished in his profession, which the present Commander-in-Chief at —— is not.

If there be any individual whom, both from interest and inclination, we ought to consider, it is certainly our former colleague, the Duke of Northumberland;[3] and if there be any member of the present Cabinet who ought to be most careful in showing respect for him, permit me to say it is the present First Lord of the Admiralty.

I cannot but feel that there is a great error on the part of some of my colleagues on the subject of patronage.   They are too apt to deem the preferment at their disposal to be merely a personal privilege.   In my opinion, it partakes of a corporate character.   No doubt the head of a department should exercise a chief and general control over the distribution of its patronage; but there should be habitual communication on this head with his colleagues, and especially with those who are

---

[1] The motion to combine the War Office and the Horse Guards under one responsible Minister.   See above, p. 172.

[2] Lytton, a commoner, filled the seat in Cabinet vacant by Ellenborough's resignation.

[3] First Lord of the Admiralty in the first Derby Ministry.

charged with the management of the House of Commons, never a light task, doubly difficult when the Administration is carried on in the teeth of a majority.

The spirit of the party in the country depends greatly on the distribution of patronage : none can be more aware of this than Lord Derby and myself. The whole patronage of the Treasury is devoted to public purposes — one of its chief Secretaries is known by the title of the Patronage Secretary — but the patronage of the Treasury alone is not enough for the Government to rest upon, and subsidiary aid is required from the other chief departments.

The interests of the party can never require an improper appointment : an improper appointment is a job, and nothing injures a party more than a job. But, at the same time, there is nothing more ruinous to political connection than the fear of justly rewarding your friends, and the promotion of ordinary men of opposite opinions in preference to qualified adherents. It is not becoming in any Minister to decry party who has risen by party. We should always remember that, if we were not partisans, we should not be Ministers. . . .

Pakington in reply vindicated, on professional grounds, the appointment in question, which, he said, had been submitted to and approved by the Prime Minister. He regarded the Admiralty patronage as a most serious responsibility, did not think party motives should be carried into such matters, and believed that the exercise of patronage with strict regard to public interests was the real way to strengthen an Administration — sentiments in which he assumed that Disraeli would concur. The correspondence shows how wise has been the change which made naval lordships purely professional appointments, involving no liability to hunt for a seat in Parliament and, when elected, to vote with the Government.

Disraeli fittingly closed a term of office, in which he had shown, over and over again, in his generous offers to Palmerston, Graham, and Gladstone, his readiness to sink personal claims for the good of the national cause, by a yet more remarkable instance of self-abnegation. In his speech on the Address he had intimated his own and his colleagues' readiness to retire in favour of any other Conservatives 'more willing and more able to advocate the views of their party,' and had continued :

'I have at all times — and what I say is well known to many hon. members — been so anxious to see the efficiency of the public service studied, and the interests of a great political party, the existence of which I believe to be advantageous to the country, preserved, that I have ever been ready to waive my own personal claims.' In this spirit he made a most unexpected proposal to Derby a few hours before the critical division.

To Lord Derby.

Secret.   HOUSE OF COMMONS, *June* 10, 1859.

MY DEAREST LORD, — No one can tell how this will exactly end. Some say a tie, and the Speaker is rather of this opinion, and then he goes with us; but, so far as I can judge, it will be two or three one way or another.

Sending for Palmerston or John Russell is no solution of the difficulty. The result would be a Government without a majority. And for a third man — where is he?

There is only one man who at this moment, with our influence, could combine the whole of the Conservative party, and would immediately obtain a considerable section of those opposite. *It is Stanley.* He could *reconstruct the Cabinet,* which you cannot. My friendship for him is so complete, and his confidence in me so perfect, that if I sate below the gangway he would know I was only there for his interests. Personally, I would have no objection to take office under him, but, for reasons which I will not enter into now, my course is clear. I have long made up my mind never to take office except under yourself, having never had a cloud between us through ten years, always of difficulty, sometimes of mortification. Besides, it is our united withdrawal, under such circumstances, that would give authority and sanction to Stanley. It would entirely sell the Whigs.

I say it with regret, but Malmesbury must go — at least, from his present position — and Clarendon would serve under Stanley. I won't go into detail as to this course. *Depend upon it, it is the solution,* and under such circumstances, greatly influenced by you, and in some degree by myself, Stanley would be able, and would be willing, to take a more Conservative course than any living man.

My personal fortune is slender enough, but if I require it I have a right to a pension,[1] which Sir George Grey and Lord

---

[1] Disraeli obtained a Cabinet pension of £2,000 a year on quitting office at this time.

Glenelg and others have taken.   I mention this that you may not think I am recommending, in the common view of affairs, a too rash course.   I have no *arrière pensée*.   I think it would be a solution advantageous to the country and agreeable to our own feelings.   I am sure it would succeed.— Yours ever, D.

At any rate, it is better than Mr. Addington, for Stanley is a clever fellow, and his Pitt and Dundas would be his father and his friend.

It was a generous, though most fantastic, conception, characteristic of one who retained to the end his romantic belief in youth and its possibilities. But Stanley, who was only thirty-three, was, with all his capacity for public life, as unlike as possible to a Vivian Grey or even a Coningsby, and could never have become a puppet like Endymion. He was much too cautious to take a risk of the kind suggested ; and, though no doubt he was regarded with favour among moderate men of all parties, such a novice could hardly have reconciled a statesman of Clarendon's standing to service under him.   Impracticable, however, as the proposal was, there is no reason to doubt that it was for the moment seriously meant. What Disraeli foresaw and dreaded was that the great historic and national party whose past he idealised, whose present was largely his own work, and in whose future he believed, should be condemned for a long period to support the Conservative Premier of a Liberal Government against his extreme followers, when, by the general prevalence of Conservative opinion in the country, that party was itself entitled to guide the nation. This is the key to all his attempts at combination since the General Election, culminating in this letter to Derby.

Nothing, of course, came of the suggestion, as, after a failure first by Granville — to whom, on Derby's resignation, the Queen had recourse in order to avoid making an invidious choice between Palmerston and Russell — and then by Russell, Palmerston formed a Government. Russell claimed the Foreign Office, where Palmerston would have preferred to have Clarendon ; but the Prime

Minister no doubt consoled himself with the thought that the Foreign Secretary would have his hands too full to prosecute Reform with success. Gladstone, who distrusted Palmerston on almost every subject except the liberation of Italy, then being forwarded by French troops in Lombardy, surprised the world by accepting the Exchequer after voting against a change of Government; and the Peelite leaders in general became absorbed in the Liberal party.

The Conservative Ministry retired from office in good order and in good heart. No definite fault had been found with them, save the undeniable one of not having a majority in the House of Commons. But the party was not altogether happy; and there was considerable discontent with Disraeli on two grounds. Some thought that, in not producing the Italian papers, he had committed a tactical blunder; others were suspicious of his further advances on the question of Reform. He was, however, well received at the party meeting, where Derby discouraged disaffection by the warmth of his acknowledgments to his lieutenant. Mrs. Disraeli wrote to Mrs. Willyams on June 21: 'A great meeting of the Conservatives this morning at Lord Salisbury's. Lord Derby expressed great gratitude to Dis., that he could not get on without him, etc., etc. Dis. much cheered by all.' Derby had already in the House of Lords promised that there should be no factious opposition to the new Ministry; on the contrary, he earnestly hoped he might be able to give them an independent support. Disraeli, in thanking one of his Whips for his services, showed his sense of the difficulty involved in this attitude. 'We shall have,' he wrote, 'to keep together a great party, as Peel had in 1835, whose strength will really increase in proportion to their inaction. But a party does not like to be inert; and to combine repose with a high tone of feeling in the troops is difficult.'

The war in Italy, which the Derby-Disraeli Ministry were condemned for not preventing, was brought, after

the Franco-Sardinian victories of Magenta and Solferino, to a hurried end by Napoleon in the Peace of Villafranca.

To Mrs. Brydges Willyams.

HOUSE OF COMMONS, *Wednesday, July* 13, 1859. — You have heard the great news, I suppose? Peace! I could not write last night, not being able to leave my place. The moment I came into the House, Lord John Russell came over to me, and told me the peace was signed, and that the Government would be obliged to me to ask a question, so that the announcement might be publicly made to the Parliament and the country. Lord John seemed much chagrined, our Government not having been consulted in any way on the matter, and all his fine despatches and new Constitutions for Italy, and all the reputation and historic glory he expected to reap, being as completely gone as if they had been thrown into the Mincio.

These are wonderful times! Wars are as brief as the lightning and as quick as the telegraph!

This was begun in order to put down the Pope, and ends by placing him at the head of all Italy! As for Austria, her power is not sensibly diminished. She has lost a rich and fertile plain, which she can regain whenever the occasion offers and she sallies from her famous fortresses.

The King of Sardinia obtains Lombardy, with its vast debt. He will have to lay heavy taxes on his new subjects, who will seize the first opportunity to pay them in the shape of a rebellion.

In the meantime, Napoleon, mounted on a magnificent charger, which he bought a few days ago for 500 guineas of Mr. Anderson, a fashionable horsedealer in Piccadilly, is to enter Paris in triumph on the 14th! A magnificent spectacle which has only cost 100,000 lives and 50 millions of pounds sterling!

The Peace of Villafranca, and the developments to which it gave rise, were the principal topics with which Disraeli dealt in this short session. He was anxious to limit our European entanglements where British interests were not involved, and accordingly advised Ministers to have nothing to do with a Congress to settle the fate of Italy after the war. He was also alarmed at our rapidly rising expenditure and the vanishing prospect of that

abolition of the income tax to which he was committed,
and urged the advisability of coming to an understanding
with the Emperor of the French for a general reduction
of armaments.   In a speech on the Budget he asked,
What ought to be our course ?

Not to go to Congresses and Conferences in fine dresses and
ribands, to enjoy the petty vanity of settling the fate of petty
Princes.   No ; but to go to your great ally, the Emperor of
the French ; give him credit for the motives which have
animated and influenced him, and say : 'If you are in favour
of peace, if at a great hazard to the mere reputation of the
hour you have terminated this war, join with us in securing
that peace by the only mode in which peace can be secured.
Revive and restore, and even increase, the good feeling which
once existed, which I hope still exists, between the great
countries of England and France ; prove by the diminution of
your armaments that you are sincerely anxious, as we believe
you are, for the peace of Europe and of the world, and we
will join you in a spirit of reciprocal confidence, and, animating alike the industry of both nations, thus achieve conquests
far more valuable than Lombardy, far more valuable than
those wild dreams of a regeneration ever promised, but never
accomplished.' . . .   Instead of going to Congresses and Conferences for petty objects in which England has no interest,
and which may involve England in great disaster, let the noble
lord prove to the world that England is a Power that possesses
and exercises a great influence, especially with France, by
accomplishing that which is much more important than
formal articles of peace ; by bringing about that which will
put an end for ever to the doubts of the sincerity of Princes ;
which will speak to every cabin and cottage in both countries,
as well as to the Houses of Parliament and places of high
resort ; which will prove to the national conviction of the great
countries of Europe that peace is the policy of their rulers.
Let us terminate this disastrous system of rival expenditure,
and mutually agree, with no hypocrisy, but in a manner and
under circumstances which can admit of no doubt — by a
reduction of armaments — that peace is really our policy.
Then, sir, the right hon. gentleman the Chancellor of the
Exchequer may look forward with no apprehension to his
next Budget, and England may then actually witness the
termination of the income tax.

Again and again he protested in the House against
sending a British representative to a Congress to revise

the Treaty of Villafranca.[1] We had nothing to do with
the war, he said, and nothing to do with the peace. It
would be the height of rashness and precipitation to
involve ourselves in the responsibility of a settlement
occasioned by the war. Let France and Austria work
out their sketch, and give the world a finished picture.
Should we ultimately have to put our hand to it, we
should interfere with immensely more effect if we now
exhibited a proper and dignified reserve.

Disraeli had two opportunities this summer and
autumn to hearten his followers and propound his view
of the duties and situation of the Conservative party.
The first was at a dinner given to the late Ministry in
Merchant Taylors' Hall on July 16; the second at a
banquet in October to Derby at Liverpool. At Merchant
Taylors' Hall he pointed to the increasing sympathy and
influence which the party had gained in the country.
It was a great confederation, prepared to assist progress
and to resist revolution, and it had arrived at a commanding position though it had had to abandon power.

I can truly say that, from the earliest moment when I gave
my attention to public affairs, I have ever had it as one of
my main objects to restore the power and repute of the great
party to which we are proud to belong, and which I believe
to be intimately bound up with the welfare and renown of
this country. . . . In attempting, however humbly, to
regulate its fortunes, I have always striven to distinguish
that which was eternal from that which was but accidental
in its opinions. I have always striven to assist in building it
upon a broad and national basis, because I believed it to be a
party peculiarly and essentially national.

Disraeli paid for his unceasing labours of the past year
and a half by prolonged lassitude and weakness in the
autumn. He and his wife remained quietly at Hughenden, with only an occasional visitor like Stanley, who
came for ' Cabinets under the beeches,' until they went to
stay at Knowsley for the Liverpool demonstration.

[1] After some hesitation, the Government determined to send a representative; but the rapid march of events in Italy in 1860 put a European
Congress out of the question.

To Lord Derby.

CARLTON CLUB, *Oct.* 27, 1859. — Affairs have been so ambiguous since the prorogation, and so very critical and perplexing during the week I have been in town, that I have found myself quite unable to offer you any hint as to the course to be adopted in your observations on Saturday ; but this morning I received from the highest authority a communication which throws considerable, not to say complete, light on the general state of affairs abroad — the only topic which in reality interests the country. It is impossible at this moment to enter into details, but I thought it best to write by this post, to express my strong opinion that, with regard to our external relations, you cannot take too high a tone as to the condition, moral and material — *i.e.*, the high spirit and great resources of this country.

Although none know better than the French Government the power and resources of England, it is at this moment the fashion of the Court of France, and the example circulates in all circles, to speak disparagingly of England ; that by not taking part in the Italian war we have sunk into a second-rate Power ; that 'we have no men,' 'our energy exhausted,' the country distracted with factions, and all is a struggle for place.

1. It would be well to dwell on the immense wealth of England (a subject of which they are well aware, and which makes them mad with envy). That wealth not only enormous, but unprecedented. We can raise any sum of money at 3 per cent.; the highest credit of the Continent only at 6 per cent.

2. The extent and soundness of our commerce ; never so vast and never so void of mere speculation.

3. The prosperity and content of the working classes.

4. The high spirit of the community, etc., etc.

At Paris they expect only a fiery criticism of your opponents. Your words will be watched, but when they find that, if England is called upon to put forth her strength, all parties will rally round the Throne, the effect will be considerable.

It may help the present Government out of some difficulties, though I think they will at all events extricate themselves ; but as a matter both of duty and policy I feel confident it is the line you should take.

A most hurried letter.

Derby acted on his lieutenant's advice, so far as to avoid anything like a party attack; but it was left to

Disraeli himself to develop in his peroration the precise line of thought he had suggested to Derby. Supporter as he was of a peaceful policy, he could not, he said, be blind to the signs of the times.

If there be any foreign Government or foreign potentate who, in the supposed distractions and political dissensions of our form of Government, believes that he has found elements on which he may calculate for pursuing with success any scheme of aggression or of violent ambition, then I can assure that Government and that ruler that they mistake the character and the genius of the English people and the English Constitution. And if they count on our dissensions and on the noble rivalries of our public life as the means for the successful prosecution of those designs, they will count on them to their confusion. They will find, if ever the time should come when the independence of this country or the Empire of our Sovereign should indeed be menaced, that the Sovereign of these realms rules over a devoted people and a united Parliament.

The danger of the moment passed away; but Disraeli's prophecy had ample fulfilment in 1914. In the rest of his speech he claimed, as the principal result of his ten years' leadership in the House of Commons, to have put an end to 'the monopoly of Liberalism'—a theory by which 'half the public men of England were held up as individuals incapable and unqualified to attempt any measures which might improve the institutions or administration of the country.' They had brought about a healthy state of political parties: men would now be judged by their policy and their measures, 'not by traditions, which are generally false; not by promises, which are seldom fulfilled.' But they must not suppose that party had no importance because there were no great public questions to settle. The duties of vigilance and criticism perpetually existed. He was prepared, however, to follow the advice which Derby formulated at this banquet, not to compass the early overthrow of Palmerston's Administration, many of whose members and supporters were thoroughly conservative. Derby in his speech formally deprecated a succession of ephemeral

Governments liable to be displaced at any moment by the caprice of half a dozen votes in the House of Commons. It could not be for the advantage of the Conservative party that for the third time it should be prematurely called upon to form a Government without sufficient strength to maintain itself. The party must look to the future and prepare for it.

From Liverpool Disraeli passed to Manchester, where he discoursed in the Free Trade Hall to mechanics' institutes on the benefits of popular education. He did not question that knowledge was its own reward; but he maintained emphatically that, in the England of his day, it also contributed materially to advancement in life. It was an incontrovertible principle, a moral dogma, that every man had his opportunity, and it was his business to prepare himself so as to be ready to seize it. Life was not a lottery, but a science; 'certain qualities and certain talents, properly handled and properly managed, must lead to certain results.' And what a source, he would not say of amusement, but of interest and excitement, was the continual preparation for the inevitable occasion! Like all discourses of the kind worth hearing, this speech of Disraeli's was clearly based on his own life and his own experience. It was as if he had said to the young mechanics of Manchester: 'Use your opportunities as I have done, and you, too, may climb as high.'

To Mrs. Brydges Willyams.

CARLTON CLUB, *Nov.* 7, 1859.— We returned to town on Saturday night, after a week of triumphant progress. The papers have given you some, tho' a faint, impression of the brilliant banquet at Liverpool, and the colossal meeting at Manchester, where there were more than 6,000 persons in the Free Trade Hall — a most beautiful building, and so well proportioned that the voice, without effort, is heard with ease in all parts.

Besides these two great gatherings, we have been guests at three houses — Knowsley, Abney Hall, and Heaton Park, Lord Wilton's — so we have seen and done a great deal. . . .

GROSVENOR GATE, *Nov.* 27, 1859. — We arrived in town on

Friday night, having stayed a day at Pynes with my late
colleague, Sir Stafford Northcote.[1] . . .

We dined at Rothschild's yesterday — a banquet — and met,
among other notabilities, the French Ambassador and the
Austrian Minister, Comte Apponyi. They were on very confidential terms. Who could have supposed this six months
ago?

The year ended sadly for Disraeli, in the death of
his devoted sister. She had been staying at Hughenden
in September, and Mrs. Disraeli had written of her to
Mrs. Willyams: 'She is very delicate. I am sure it is
from not following your system—no doctors, no medi-
cine.' The delicacy was much more serious than Mrs.
Disraeli supposed.

To Frances Anne Lady Londonderry.

GROSVENOR GATE, *Dec.* 12, 1859. — . . . We have returned
to unspeakable sorrow — to the bedside of my only sister, our
nearest and dearest relative, and who is soon, most unexpectedly and suddenly, to be lost to us ! She was a person
of great intelligence and charm — one of those persons who
are the soul of a house and the angelic spirit of a family. . . .

Sarah Disraeli died on December 19. To her brother,
who had experienced to the full what he called in one of
his novels 'a sister's mystical affection,' it was indeed, as
he wrote to his friends Manners and Lennox, a 'great
grief. You know,' he added, 'the blessing of a sister.
Alas ! mine was an only one — my first and ever faithful
friend ! '

---

[1] Northcote had been one of the party at Knowsley, and had written
from there to Lady Northcote: 'Mrs. Disraeli is great fun, and we made
capital friends in the train, though I could not help occasionally pitying
her husband for the startling effect her natural speeches must have upon
the ears of his great friends.   Still, there is something very warm and good
in her manner which makes one forgive a few oddities.   She informed me
she was born in Brampford Speke, and I told her they must come and see
her birthplace some time when they are in Devonshire.   What do you say
to the idea of asking them to Pynes ?   It would complete the astonishment
of our neighbours.'   Lang's *Northcote*, p. 98.

CHAPTER VIII

Disraeli and Gladstonian Finance

1860–1863

John Bright and the majority of the Reformers had preferred to trust Russell's promises in 1859 rather than Disraeli's, and had accordingly taken an active part in upsetting the Conservative Government. A bitter disillusionment was in store for them. The Palmerston Administration only introduced one Reform Bill during the whole duration of a six years' Parliament, and did not prosecute even that solitary effort into the Committee stage. Palmerston's indifference on the subject proved to be a reflection of the public mind; and Russell had to console himself by immersion in foreign affairs — a change of front facilitated by his removal in 1861 from the Commons to the Lords.

But at the beginning of 1860 it looked as if Reform was seriously meant, and as if the Government hoped to pass a Bill by agreement with the Opposition. On January 4 Disraeli wrote to Derby: 'A Cabinet Minister' — it was Charles Villiers, a personal friend of Disraeli's — 'has sounded me, and said communications would be confined, and strictly confined, to P[almerston] and J. R[ussell]. I replied I was ready to listen, of course telling you everything, though engaging that, at present, it should not go further.' Derby was surprised at Villiers's revelations. 'I confess that the signature of your correspondent rather startled me ; for a correspondence with a member of the Cabinet on such a subject has rather a surprising appearance ; but if the correspondence be sanctioned by the Head

of the Government and his chief supporter (and rival), I do not see that it is our duty to remonstrate on the part of the rest of the Cabinet; and we are certainly under no obligation to abstain from such communications.' Eventually Ministers abandoned the idea of coming to an arrangement with the Opposition to pass an agreed Bill; perhaps because neither party was really in earnest about passing any Bill at all.

To Lord Derby.

GROSVENOR GATE, *Jan.* 8, 1860. — . . . As at present advised, it is on the cards — nay, probable — that the following proposition will be submitted to you:

1. £10 county franchise — if the Lords carry £20, to be accepted.
2. £7 value — boroughs.
3. Disfranchisement in a separate Bill, and to take its chance.

I should like to have had your view of this proposition without troubling you with my own; but as we are separated, and time is hurrying on, I will venture to observe, though with great diffidence, that these seem terms which we may substantially obtain without entering into any engagement, and that they are prompted as much by the feelings of their own party as by a desire to conciliate ours. I doubt whether the difference between a £6 and a £7 value is one of Conservative importance: while at the same time it keeps up the mischievous imposture that there is a Conservative party in the Cabinet, on which the Peelites intrigue, as they are doing already, and trying to break up our ranks. A majority of the Committee was in favor of an £8 value, but ultimately yielded to the sense of the ridiculous in turning us out for identity and then proposing £10 and £8. An £8 would have estranged the Radicals: they will grumble about the £7, but take it, I think.

I was asked what we considered a 'temperate measure,' assuming that after what had occurred in Parliament identity was out of the question. I declined to give our opinion on the subject, but said I thought that public opinion would recognise, as a temperate measure equal to the occasion, £20 for county; £8 for boroughs; and the scale of disfranchisement in Lord Derby's Bill. It was said, if that course were taken, the Radicals would take the first opportunity of turning them out. I replied we were sincerely desirous of not disturbing the Government at present, and that, if we

agreed on a Reform Bill, we should, as a matter of course, wish to give them a general support till it had passed, which alone would carry them through the session.

I was pressed as to our conduct in case of a motion on foreign politics. I declined to hold out any expectation of our binding ourselves on that subject. We must always be free to assert our own principles and policy on such a subject, but I did not hesitate to say that we certainly should not encourage any motions on foreign policy brought forward by the Radicals to disturb them; that we should deplore returning to power by their aid. . . .

Confidential. GROSVENOR GATE, *Jan.* 18, 1860. — There was a Cabinet on Monday. . . . Nothing settled. The Committee of the Cabinet, being quite unable to come to any agreement, and it being impossible any longer to delay some general discussion, the question, quite crude, was thrown, like a piece of raw meat, into the assemblage of nineteen last Monday. My correspondent told Palmerston and Lord John that, having commenced the negotiation with me, and after what had passed, it was impossible, he felt, to continue silent, and they agreed that, whatever might occur, they were bound to deal frankly with us. . . .

I gathered that the moderate party is much stronger in tone at this moment, and that Lord John is checked. I suspect he has enough on his hands of another character. . . .

With the beginning of the session on January 24, it became evident that Reform would not occupy the forefront of the Parliamentary stage. Disraeli wrote to Derby on the following day : ' I have frequently observed that, until the Houses meet, it is impossible to hit upon what will be the question of the session, often very different from that anticipated. From all I hear and observe it will be the Commercial Treaty.' This was the treaty with France which Cobden had just negotiated at Paris, and on which was built Gladstone's great Budget of 1860. Popular and Parliamentary interest in the sphere of domestic legislation became concentrated on the financial proposals of the Government, which were revealed in February; and it was to an indifferent and not overfull House that Russell on March 1 expounded his new Reform Bill. It established a £10 occupation franchise in the counties, and reduced the borough franchise to £6. The

redistribution proposed was hardly on a more extensive scale than in the Conservative Bill of the preceding year; twenty-five boroughs were deprived of one member each, fifteen of these seats being allotted to populous counties, nine to populous boroughs, and one to London University. Russell recommended the plan as a simple one, containing as little novelty as possible. Similar Reform Bills were also introduced for Ireland and Scotland.

The proposals were not substantially different from those which Disraeli had expressed his readiness to accept, with a view to a settlement, in his negotiations with Roebuck, Lindsay, and their Radical friends, in the preceding June. But the Parliamentary atmosphere had changed; the apathy steadily manifested by the country about Reform had invaded Parliament; while the bulk, not only of the Conservatives, but of the Whigs and Moderate Liberals, profoundly disliked both the lowering of the borough franchise to £6 and the prospect, if the Bill were passed, of a third dissolution within three years. Disraeli was quick to perceive that, while there was no opportunity for a settlement of the Reform question, there was plenty of opportunity for successful opposition; that dilatory tactics and contemptuous treatment must eventually secure the withdrawal of the Bill and the discredit of the Government. The reception which the Whigs had accorded to his own Bill debarred them from any claim to consideration. On the second reading,[1] Disraeli said it was a bad Bill, which would not even admit so many new electors as his own; it put numbers before fitness; it would only enfranchise a single homogeneous class; it tended to diminish the just and salutary influence of the land. He would not oppose the second reading; but he recommended Russell to withdraw an 'unnecessary, uncalled-for, and mischievous Bill.' The debate was prolonged, in a desultory manner, over six weeks; it was not till May 3 that the Bill, which secured Bright's approval as an instalment, but was openly opposed by many

[1] March 19.

Liberals, was read a second time.　Disraeli wrote to Mrs. Willyams on March 24: ' The new Reform Bill is like the *Great Eastern*, and sticks on its stays.　It will not be launched, and, if ever it do float, I think it will founder; then all will be right.'　The more it was looked at, the less it was liked.　Disraeli had some difficulty in keeping his colleagues on the front bench to the purely passive and waiting tactics which the situation demanded.

To Lord Derby.

HUGHENDEN MANOR, *May* 27, 1860. — . . . The front bench has long been restless — desiring many things, either dangerous or impracticable.　Pakington wants a Royal Commission to inquire into the whole subject of Reform, which is madness : John Manners wants to meet the motion by ' previous question,' which cannot be moved on going into Committee : Estcourt wants ' something to be done,' but has no conception of what it should be.　The fact is our tactics are to watch circumstances, and not to attempt to create them.　The cards will play into our hands if we are quiet. . . .

The Opposition did keep quiet, save to intimate to Palmerston that he could rely on their support in case of a difference with Russell on Reform.　The end came a fortnight later.　On June 4, on the motion to go into Committee, Russell abandoned the Scottish and Irish Bills, and even in regard to the English Bill announced his readiness to accept in Committee a raising of the figure for the borough franchise.　In fact, commented Disraeli, Russell would accept anything, if the House would but agree to something that might shuffle this great impediment to progress out of the course.　Thus the high policy which had destroyed a Ministry and dissolved a Parliament had melted away!　Palmerston gave the Bill perfunctory support in a speech which hardly disguised his willingness to acquiesce in its failure ; and a proposal to adjourn the debate was only defeated by 21 votes.

To Lord Derby.

Private.　Sunday [*June* 10, 1860], 7 *o'clock.* — I have seen the Bear [Ellice].　He says he thinks the Government will

give up the Bill to-morrow: he hopes so. . . . The division was exactly the right thing; the Government expected between 40 and 50 majority, which would have encouraged the violent party; but a small majority indicates the only honorable course — withdrawal. He has seen Johnny, who, he says, is low, but he thinks resigned. By his own account he appears to have said to him everything most disagreeable, having explained to him that he does not understand the question, and that, if Reform is ever treated again, it must be treated on quite different principles. . . .

Disraeli's information was correct. The Government withdrew the Bill on June 11, thus taking, as he said, 'a wise and not an undignified course.' They never introduced another Reform Bill, but contented themselves with passing in the next session a short Act allotting the four vacant seats, two to the West Riding of Yorkshire, one to South Lancashire, and one to Birkenhead — almost exactly the arrangement which the Liberals resisted when proposed by the first Derby-Disraeli Government eight years before.[1] When attention was drawn in 1861, in the debate on the Address, to the absence of Reform from the Government programme, Disraeli expressed his approval of the omission, and Russell sadly confessed that there was not sufficient public support to carry a satisfactory Bill.[2] Bright complained bitterly, and with perfect justice, that the failure to proceed with Reform was a breach of the most explicit pledges, public and private, given by the Government in order to obtain office; but he received scant sympathy, as neither warning nor experience had deterred him from trusting the promises of the Whigs and placing them in power. Even Locke King's motion for identity of suffrage, which had been regularly carried for years, was defeated by 'the previous question' in 1861. Palmerston said that the present was a time for waiting and not for action ; and Disraeli's argument, that Parlia-

[1] See Vol. III., pp. 367, 368.

[2] Stanley wrote to Disraeli from Knowsley on October 13, 1860 : ' I have seen from time to time a good many manufacturers, merchants, and men of the towns ; all agree in their politics ; all were frightened by Lord John's Bill, all praise your tactics, and will discourage a renewal of agitation. The towns are full of money and of Conservative opinion, disguised as Moderate Liberalism.'

ment ought only to deal with a comprehensive measure, had a success which had hitherto been denied it. Russell accepted an earldom at the close of the 1861 session; Reform disappeared finally from all the Queen's Speeches for which Palmerston was responsible, and was hardly advocated seriously even by private members till the Parliament was nearing its term. Disraeli had indeed 'pricked the imposture' of Whig professions to be earnest Reformers.

Reform, therefore, was speedily shelved in the Parliament of 1859–1865; and the principal contentions between parties turned on finance, foreign policy, and the Church. Gladstone was back at the Exchequer, and his dæmonic energy forced finance to the front. 1860 was the year in which his famous Budget of 1853 was to have its full fruition. Terminable annuities to the amount of two millions were due to fall in; and, with that sum in hand, the income tax, which was to have gradually diminished through a period of seven years, was in this year absolutely to cease. Such was the attractive forecast drawn in 1853; the actual fact in 1860 was very different. The Crimean War entirely dislocated the arrangements for the years 1854 to 1856; nevertheless, after it, in 1857 and 1858, not only Gladstone, but Disraeli, anxious to promote both public economy and continuity of policy, impressed upon Parliament the extreme desirability of so ordering finance as to bring about the promised abolition of income tax in 1860. But once again military preparations, due this time to apprehensions of France and to war with China, swelled expenditure; and in his belated Budget of 1859 Gladstone found himself driven to increase income tax instead of diminishing it. This was a bad omen for 1860; and, when that year came, he effected a complete transformation, and built his Budget, not on abolition of income tax, but on a commercial treaty with France, involving a serious loss of Customs dues on wine and brandy and silk, which had to be made good. Entirely regardless of the hopes held out in 1853, and renewed in 1857 and 1858, he once more employed a reimposed and, indeed, largely

augmented income tax, as Peel had done in 1842 and 1845, and he himself in 1853, as the engine by which duties could be abolished on a large scale and the tariff simplified. Though he found a deficit, he did not hesitate to make it larger, trusting that the expansion of trade which might be expected to follow a general relief from tariff shackles would produce an abundant and buoyant revenue. It was a bold policy, and, as regards the public purse, proved in the long run to be a successful one. But it was a repudiation of his own previous arrangements, and a direct challenge to an Opposition which had after some misgiving accepted those arrangements, and had in 1857 and 1858 based their own financial policy upon them.

That challenge Disraeli took up. He did not object to improving our commercial relations with France; on the contrary, he had laboured when in office for the same end. But why had the Government negotiated a treaty on the principle of reciprocity, a principle which had been absolutely rejected in our own commercial system? Why had they engaged us by treaty for what must have been done without any treaty whatever? Apart from this question of principle, he maintained that the actual treaty was not a good one; and confirmation of this view from a very competent source is found in a letter written in 1877, when the wine duties again came under review by a Government of which Beaconsfield was the head:

Sir Louis Mallet to Montagu Corry.

May 10, 1877. — . . . Our present wine duties were, as you know, fixed by Mr. Gladstone with a view to the treaty of 1860.

Mrs. Cobden's recent death has placed in my hands all Mr. Cobden's correspondence with Mr. Gladstone on the subject, and I have for the first time read it. The melancholy result of this perusal is to me that the great objects which I presume both Governments had in view on that occasion have been frustrated by the exorbitant amount of our wine duties, which no one at that time knew.

But, whatever may be the case with France, it is incontestable that both Spain, Portugal, Italy, and our own Colonies, have ever since protested against the scale. . . .

In spite of his disapproval of many of its terms, Disraeli did not directly attack the treaty, though he protested unsuccessfully against the procedure which, in disregard of Pitt's precedent in 1787, asked the House for a sanction of the Budget founded on the treaty before submitting the treaty itself for consideration.   Where he joined issue[1] was on the policy of augmenting an existing deficit by surrendering Customs dues, and then obtaining the necessary revenue by disappointing the legitimate expectations of the country in regard to income tax.   This he considered improvident and profligate finance.[2]   He recalled the failure of the Budget of 1853, owing to 'external circumstances that were not foreseen by one who ought to have been prescient.'   That should teach Ministers not to be too sanguine now, in view of the troubled state of Italy.   But Disraeli disclaimed any idea of wishing to displace the Government.

Neither I nor my colleagues . . . are at all anxious to attempt to reoccupy the places we then[3] filled.   I may, at least, say for myself that, having for more than two years led this House in a minority, I shrink from the unparalleled anxiety and responsibility of such a post; and I would recommend no gentleman ever to adopt that position who has any regard for his nervous system.   The important office which the Chancellor of the Exchequer fills gives ample opportunity to his eager mind and his impetuous rhetoric.   Perhaps in moments of solitary aspiration he has wished to occupy the proud post of leader of the House of Commons, which no one could fill more efficiently.   But from what I have observed

[1] Feb. 21.

[2] The disappearance, without appreciable relief to the taxpayer, of the £2,000,000 derived from the falling in of the terminable annuities, was described by Disraeli with great humour on the hustings in 1865.   The House, he said, was very full on Budget night, as it was known that Gladstone was going to perform a considerable feat.   Gladstone had two millions of taxation which was dying a natural death.   It was a fund to which Englishmen had been looking for relief for half a century.   What did he do with it?   By a feat of legerdemain exceeding that of a professional conjurer 'he took one million and turned it into ducks; then he took another million and turned it into drakes; and for half an hour these ducks and drakes flew cackling about the House of Commons, until at last we got ashamed of one another, and we ordered strangers to withdraw, and determined to keep it a profound secret till Parliament was dissolved.'   [3] In the spring of 1859.

of the right hon. gentleman's temperament, I think I may tell him that it is well for him, however eminent his position, that he reposes at least for a time beneath the *mitis sapientia* of the noble lord the Foreign Secretary and the calm patience of the noble Premier.

Disraeli's attack, which was very indifferently supported by his party, was easily repulsed by a majority of 116. The debates of this month of February, Disraeli told Mrs. Willyams, were 'noisy Parliamentary fights,' but really 'sham battles.' Greville oddly writes of them that Disraeli 'betrays in the House of Commons a sort of consciousness of his inferiority to Gladstone, and of fear of encountering him in debate.' This judgment may be set against the corresponding picture drawn by Lord Houghton, in 1867, of Gladstone 'quite awed by the diabolical cleverness of Dizzy.' Lord Morley declines to accept 'awe' as the right word.[1] In the same way, no one who studies Disraeli's life will accept 'fear' as the right word. Disraeli never hesitated, throughout his career, to encounter any of his eminent adversaries in debate. But he was always generous in his appreciation of an opponent's powers ; and Gladstone, both in opening his financial scheme and in his numerous speeches in this month in defence of the Budget and of the treaty, surpassed himself, and earned Disraeli's tribute.

As the session proceeded, and the details of the Budget came to be examined, the glamour of Gladstone's eloquence wore off. 'Not more than three months ago,' wrote Greville on May 12, 'Gladstone was triumphant and jubilant. . . . There never was a greater reaction in a shorter time. Everybody's voice is now against him, and his famous treaty and his Budget are pronounced enormous and dangerous blunders.' Two days later Disraeli told Mrs. Willyams that Gladstone's reputation had 'collapsed more suddenly and completely than anything since Jonah's gourd.' The demands on the Exchequer for the China War and for national defence increased, and it was felt that the yield from the duties to be repealed was

---

[1] *Gladstone*, Bk. V., ch. 14.

wanted.   The principal of these was the paper duty, the
last of the hindrances to a cheap Press.   Its repeal was
to cost the revenue a million; accordingly, as the financial
pressure increased, the majority for repeal fell from 53
to 9.   Disraeli disliked 'taxes on knowledge,' as he had
frequently shown; but most of the newspaper duties had
already been swept away, and he entered heartily into the
Conservative campaign to retain this particular one at
this moment.   Even the Prime Minister agreed with the
Opposition in resisting his colleague's plan, and wrote to
the Queen that if the Lords threw out the repealing Bill
'they would perform a good public service.'   The Lords
did throw out the Bill, thereby provoking a constitutional
dispute with the Commons as to their rights in regard to
taxation.   Gladstone and the Radicals advocated violent
measures against the Lords; the Conservatives rallied
to the Prime Minister.   Derby sent Malmesbury to Lady
Palmerston to 'assure her of the support of our whole
party against the Radicals, and to give a positive promise
that we will not coalesce with them in or out of office.
Disraeli,' adds Malmesbury, 'is equally determined on this
point.'[1]   Palmerston therefore was able to restrain the
Commons from taking any action beyond the mild protest of comparatively innocuous resolutions; and Disraeli
in the debate had the satisfaction, in Derby's words, of
'knocking J. Russell's and Gladstone's heads together.'
Gladstone had to put up with temporary defeat over the
Excise duty on paper, but he had some consolation at the
close of the session by carrying resolutions for the reduction of the corresponding Customs duty.[2]   Disraeli had
hoped for a further success, though he subsequently protested that he had never really contemplated it; but
Palmerston's representations, that the approval of the
treaty which Parliament had already expressed bound
members to fulfil their engagements under it, prevailed
over the reluctance of many Liberals to continue their
support of Gladstone's proposals.   The numbers were

[1] *Memoirs*, June 1, 1860.   [2] Aug. 6.

266 to 233. 'I hear you have left town not a little disgusted,' wrote Derby to Disraeli. 'It is, however, satisfactory that, if we were defeated on Monday, it was from
no defection of our own people, nor even any miscalcula-
tion on the part of our Whips; but a gross violation of
pledges on the part of the so-called Liberals.'

The long session of 1860 lasted till the end of August.
Besides his action on the Reform Bill and the Budget,
Disraeli intervened with effect both in the discussion of
French and Italian affairs[1] and in defence of Church rates.[2]

To Mrs. Brydges Willyams.

CARLTON CLUB, *June* 20. — It is a long time since I wrote,
but the course of affairs has been very critical, and, indeed,
is so intense at the present moment that I have not been able
to free myself from the absorption of public duties sufficiently
to realise private correspondence.

The withdrawal of the Reform Bill was the culminating
point of three months of masterly manœuvres on the part of
the Opposition, and has shaken the Government to the centre.
They are dispirited and discredited; and have to cope with
numerous difficulties, to meet and manage which requires
both reputation and courage. I myself wish to maintain
them for a season, but I begin to doubt the possibility of
doing so.

Yesterday the King of the Belgians sent for me at Buckingham Palace, and I had a most interesting conference with
him on foreign affairs. He is the wisest Prince in Europe :
natural abilities and great experience; his judgment of men
and things very mature. He proposed that we should in
future maintain together a confidential correspondence.

To-morrow we dine with the Queen. It is unusual to ask
the Leader of Opposition to dine more than once during the
season at the Palace, and I suspect this second invitation will
excite comments. There was a leading article in some of
the Radical journals a few weeks ago, on the enormity of
Lord Derby having dined three times at Court since December.

Friday will be a very hard day for me : for at twelve o'clock
the Committee of the House of Commons meets, which is to
draw up the report on the famous question of the right of the
Lords to throw out the Bill for the repeal of the paper duty;
at six o'clock precisely I am to take the chair for the Prince

---

[1] See Ch. 9.   [2] See Ch. 10.

Consort, at the anniversary dinner of the 'Society of Arts, Manufactures and Commerce'; and as soon as I can get away from St. James's Hall, where the dinner of four hundred of the ablest men in London takes place, I am going, with Mrs. Disraeli, to a ball at the palace. I would, for her sake, gladly escape the latter, as on the following day, Saturday, she gives a great morning fête, in honor of the Queen's review of the Volunteers in Hyde Park, and has invited upwards of seven hundred members of the *beau monde*. I fear the terrible weather will spoil the fête, and that we shall all be drowned. . . .

To Mrs. Disraeli.

July 16, 1860. — No income tax. I could not myself have brought forward a more Conservative Budget;[1] though I would sooner have cut off my right hand than have done so under the same circumstances. Gladstone looked like a beaten hound, and ate no ordinary quantity of dirt.

Bright has not only to pay a paper tax, but it is to be applied to a China War! What a combination of injuries and insults!

To Mrs. Brydges Willyams.

GROSVENOR GATE, *July* 23. — An interesting and exhausting session is drawing to a close. Until the last ten days, the existence of the Government, in its integrity, has been in daily danger — so it beat fox-hunting. The hours very late, sometimes four o'clock in the morning. I have borne it well, as I have contrived to sleep my hours all the same, and with a due quantum of sleep, health and vigor seem to me a mere matter of course. But rising thus at noon, and being obliged to be in your place in the House at four o'clock, your day is necessarily very brief, and all correspondence and general business fall into terrible arrear. . . .

It has been a very gay and brilliant social season; at least Mrs. Disraeli tells me so, for I never go anywhere except Wednesdays off and Saturdays — with rare exceptions. I went, however, to two fêtes on Thursday and Friday last, which amused me. The first was at the Russian Ambassador's, at Chesham House, and was really like a festival in a play, or a masquerade. There were a dozen servants in scarlet liveries, who never left the entrance hall, only bowing to those who arrived, and ushering you to one of the finest and most fantastical staircases in London, reaching to the roof of the

---

[1] This was Gladstone's supplementary financial statement, rendered necessary by the increased expenditure for the China War and by the failure of the repeal of the paper duty.

house, and full of painted and gilded galleries. All the other attendants, who swarmed, were in Court dresses and wore swords.

The other entertainment, which amused me, was a ball, given by the Duchess of Wellington, at Apsley House. I had never been there since the death of the famous old Duke. This magnificent mansion has been entirely redecorated, and with consummate taste and splendor. The gallery, where he used to give his Waterloo banquets, now hung with ruby silk and covered with rare pictures, the spoils of Spain and Portugal, is one of the most effective rooms in this city. The banqueting room, hung with full-length portraits of the sovereigns and notabilities at the Congress of Vienna, most interesting at this moment, when the pact has really become history, and the famous settlement of 1815 is disturbed, and perhaps about to be superseded.

I closed my season last night by making my bow to the wife of my rival, Lady Palmerston, whose crowded saloons at Cambridge House were fuller even than usual, for she had invited all the deputies of the Statistical Congress, a body of men who, for their hideousness, the ladies declare were never equalled: I confess myself to a strange gathering of men with bald heads, and all wearing spectacles. You associate these traits often with learning and profundity, but when one sees 100 bald heads and 100 pairs of spectacles the illusion, or the effect, is impaired.

I hope you are quite well. Summer has set in, as Horace Walpole says, with its usual severity. Lady Ebury said to me the other night that she lived only for climate and the affections. . . .

In his first letter to the King of the Belgians, Disraeli gave his own summary of the results of the session.

To the King of the Belgians.

Aug. 23, 1860. — As the session of Parliament is about to close, it may be convenient to place before your Majesty its results, so far as it has influenced the position of the two great parties.

In the audience which your Majesty was graciously pleased to grant to me in the month of June, I indicated to your Majesty the three causes which had mainly contributed to the consolidation of the Conservative party during this year:

1. The withdrawal by the Government of their Reform Bill.

2. The successful assertion of the authority of the House of Lords.

3. The appearance of a Church party in the House of Commons for the first time since 1840, and the fact of the clergy throughout the country again generally acting with the Conservatives.

Later in the session the discontent with the French treaty, and probably a jealousy of Mr. Gladstone, which a section of the Whig party wished publicly to express, rendered it expedient that a decided opposition should be given to the repeal of the duty on foreign paper. This struggle elicited another important feature in the relative state of parties: viz., the complete alienation of the Roman Catholic party from the present Government, avowedly caused by their Italian policy. On that occasion, while many independent Roman Catholic Irish members voted with the Conservatives, as has been their custom of late, the Whig Roman Catholic members for the first time evinced their disapproval of the Ministry, rose, and in a body left the House, including among many others the leading names of Lord Ed. Howard, Mr. More O'Ferrall, Mr. Monsell, and Sir John Acton.

Had not the very Whig section which had originated the resistance against the repeal of the foreign duty on paper wheeled round in this emergency and supported the Government, Lord Palmerston would have been in a minority, which I was far from desiring and had never contemplated.

Your Majesty will therefore perceive that the course of Italian politics may have a most important influence upon affairs in this country.

What that course may be I will not presume to speculate on, when addressing so wise and well informed a Prince as your Majesty. I should rather be grateful were I to receive on this head an intimation of your Majesty's views.

But assuming I was right in my observations expressed more than two years ago in Parliament, that Lord John Russell was counting without his host in supposing that Italian Liberals would be content merely to take the mild form of English Whiggery, and that he must be prepared to encounter the long-matured machinations of the secret societies in whose existence Lord John then would never believe, events may occur which may render war, and even a general war, a necessity for Louis Napoleon.

The English will enter into a war with France with reluctance, but, once embarked in it, they will never cease until their entire object is attained. If there is to be that war, it is of importance that Lord Palmerston should begin it.

---

[1] Lord E. Howard, W. Monsell, and Sir J. Acton, the historian, were afterwards raised to the peerage, on Gladstone's recommendation, as Lords Howard of Glossop, Emly and Acton.

The consolidation of the Conservative party, of which Disraeli boasted to the King, was certainly greater at the close of the session than at the beginning, thanks largely to his own adroit handling of a delicate situation ; but it was still very imperfect. Indeed, throughout the Palmerston Administration the difficulties of Disraeli's leadership were considerable. Following Derby's advice, the bulk of the party were content to keep Palmerston in office, so long as they could exercise a general control over him. They suspected Disraeli, not without cause, of fretting, now and again, under these tactics, though he professed a general acquiescence in them, and even, at times, actively promoted them ; and many Conservatives were ready to break away from his leadership on any sign of a serious attack on Ministers, especially if there were a likelihood that the attack would be supported by the Radicals. Derby warned him early in January, 1860 : 'I think I ought to tell you that I hear of a cabal getting up among our people, some of whom will have it that you have come to an understanding with the Radicals and mean to throw them over on Reform. . . . I hear that Big Ben [1] (of course) is among the leaders of this *fronde*.' Further details were sent him in the following month by a friendly follower.

From Sir James Fergusson. [2]

Private. 27, CHESHAM STREET, *Feb.* 20, 1860.—. . . I know, from authority I believe to be certain, that lately there was an imminent risk of a defection among those who act with you, so serious that the strong party you had in the House of Commons would not have been at your command : that a considerable number of 'Conservatives' were prepared to impugn supposed acts of yours, and this so recently as on the eve of the meeting of Parliament. . . . This bad feeling, temporarily allayed, I believe, by Lord Derby, was in a great degree dispelled by your speech upon the Bill for the Abolition of Church Rates, as it is said, among other occasions, to have been excited by one upon the Reform Bill last session.

[1] See above, p. 44.   [2] Afterwards Governor of Bombay.

It is represented to me that the loyalty of the party towards you now depends upon your course with regard to the question of the treaty and the Budget: that the general desire of the party is identical with the views which I told Earle had been expressed in conversation with me by Mr. Horsman, viz., that it would be in the last degree distasteful, not only to the great body of the Conservative party, but to most of your late colleagues, were you to attempt to turn out the present Government, with a view to Lord Derby's Administration again taking office; but that you would consolidate and strengthen the party by checking the present dangerous policy of the Government, defeating their measures, while you threw back upon them the language held two years since by Lord Palmerston, and commanded them to keep their places in the face of such defeat. . . .

Though Disraeli's policy during the session was to a large extent such as Fergusson recommended, and though it was remarkably successful, the discontent was only very partially appeased. Greville's diary for 1860 is full of references to the 'disorganisation' of the party and to what he calls 'their undisguised dislike of their leader.' On February 22, in regard to 'Gladstone's triumph' in one of the early Budget debates, he writes that it 'did not seem to be matter of much grief to many of the Conservative party; for I hear that, however they may still act together on a great field-day, the hatred and distrust of Disraeli is greater than ever in the Conservative ranks, and Derby himself, when he heard how his colleague had been demolished, did not seem to care much about it.' On March 18 he repeats a story that 'an eminent Conservative, who had begged not to be quoted, had said that he knew Derby was violently discontented with Disraeli, and prepared to dissolve their political connection.' There is no other evidence of Derby's discontent than the gossip retailed to Greville; and, if it existed, it was only a passing mood. But the disorganisation of the party was undoubted; and in April the most authoritative organ of Conservatism, the *Quarterly Review*, which had ignored Disraeli, both as a novelist and as a politician, till about 1850, and had since then mentioned him only occasionally,

and with obvious dislike, made an attack of calculated
bitterness on his leadership. If the invective lacked
finish, it certainly did not lack gall. Disraeli was described as a 'favourite of misfortune,' who 'went forth
blundering and to blunder,' who had 'unrivalled powers
of conducting his party into the ditch.' The policy of
the late Derby Ministry in adopting Reform was singled
out for special condemnation. There was no difficulty,
the writer held, in divining 'the real parentage' of the
Bill of 1859.

It was of a piece with a policy which had long misguided
and discredited the Conservative party in the House of
Commons. To crush the Whigs by combining with the
Radicals was the first and last maxim of Mr. Disraeli's Parliamentary tactics. He had never led the Conservatives to
victory as Sir Robert Peel had led them to victory. He
had never procured the triumphant assertion of any Conservative principle, or shielded from imminent ruin any
ancient institution. But he had been a successful leader to
this extent, that he had made any Government while he was
in Opposition, next to an impossibility. His tactics were so
various, so flexible, so shameless — the net by which his combinations were gathered in was so wide — he had so admirable
a knack of enticing into the same lobby a happy family of
proud old Tories and foaming Radicals, martial squires jealous for their country's honour, and manufacturers who had
written it off their books as an unmarketable commodity —
that so long as his party backed him no Government was
strong enough to hold out against his attacks. They might
succeed in repelling this sally or that; but sooner or later their
watchful and untiring enemy, perfectly reckless from what
quarter or in what uniform he assaulted, was sure to find out
the weak point at which the fortress could be scaled.

'Opponents,' the writer added, 'were wont to speak of
the laudable discipline of the Tory party. They little
knew the deep and bitter humiliation that was masked
by the outward loyalty of its votes.' Disraeli's speeches
and tactics might well induce the nation to believe that
'Conservatives registered and organised, and lavishly
spent their money and their labour, merely that the ambition of a few, or of one, might be contented.' The party

could only regain the nation's trust 'if with their leaders or without their leaders, they resolutely refuse the fellowship of those who abhor their creed.' But if 'fidelity to a leader who has been tried and has been found wanting is to be preferred to all other considerations,' then 'woe to the blind that lead, woe to the blind that follow!'

It was a wholesale denunciation, hardly qualified by a recognition, in one sentence, of 'some improvement of tone' in Disraeli's conduct in the session of 1860. The effect, indeed, was rather spoilt by the admiration expressed, in contrast to Disraeli's shiftiness, for the consistent Conservatism of Peel — Peel, who took over Roman Catholic Emancipation from the Whigs, and Free Trade from the Radicals! The writer really went behind Peel, and his article was a plea for a return to the Eldonian policy of exclusion and restriction. The great work of Conservatism was apparently to be purely negative — to arrest the march of democracy; the party was envisaged as a territorial and not as a national party. Tories were advised, by one who spoke for many besides himself, to reduce themselves to the state of hopeless inefficiency and narrowness from which Disraeli's genius had rescued them.

Attention was called to this bitter article in the House of Commons by Russell, who naturally inquired who was now the leader of the Tories. *The Times* took the matter up.[1] The leading journal was at that time a strong supporter of Palmerston ; but it was able to do justice to some extent to Disraeli, though it assumed rather a patronising air, and insinuated, quite unjustifiably, that he had never been sincere in his advocacy of Protection. The following passages give, in substance, a true picture of his work :

The Tory party, when Mr. Disraeli first took the lead of them, were in a position of the most marked and violent hostility to the material interests of the whole country, and embarked on a career which seemed to tend to something little short of political annihilation. With untiring patience

[1] June 6.

Mr. Disraeli set himself to bring order out of this chaos. . . . It would be unjust, ungrateful, and ungenerous, in the party which he has redeemed from absolute disorganisation, and made once more a real and effective power in the State, to forget for a single moment its signal obligations to him. . . . He has taught them to profess, at any rate, and probably to feel, a sympathy for the great body of their countrymen, and to recognise the necessity of looking to opinion for support. When he found the Tory party they were armed in impenetrable prejudice; under him they have become no longer an impediment, but competitors with the Liberals in the career of progress. Twice has he led them to office. . . . Having uniformly to fight an uphill battle and to sustain a losing cause, he has acquitted himself in a manner to gain the sympathy of those most keenly opposed to his policy, and to prove that he possesses talents which, under happier circumstances, might have made his Administration eminently creditable to himself and useful to his country.

Russell described the author of the *Quarterly* article as an obscure writer. But there was little secret about the authorship; and the writer was not obscure, but was a rising Conservative politician, Lord Robert Cecil, the member for Stamford; who, as political society found it piquant to reflect, in denouncing the actions of the Ministry of 1858–59 and the conduct of Disraeli, was attacking his own father, the late President of the Council, and that father's personal friend and colleague. Family disagreement, which had made it necessary for him to earn money by his pen, may have sharpened his natural dislike of a policy repugnant to his high Toryism, and a personality which appeared to him, as it had originally to Derby, on the surface uncongenial. As a *Saturday Reviewer*, Robert Cecil had been for some time associated with Disraeli's severest critics; and from this period onwards, in opposition or in office, till foreign politics brought the two men together in the late seventies, he was a leader of the anti-Disraeli section of the Tory party — rather perhaps in the Press than by overt action in Parliament. 'He has written anonymous articles against me before and since I was his colleague; I do not know whether he wrote them when he was my colleague,' said Disraeli in 1868. Happily, the

misunderstandings were finally cleared up, and the reviewer came to appreciate the high qualities of the man whom he had spent his earlier political life in condemning and counterworking.

With this flagrant proof of indiscipline and ill-feeling laid before the world by the oracle of Toryism, it is rather pathetic to find Mrs. Disraeli assuring Mrs. Willyams on May 6 that ' D. was never on better terms with his party,' and on June 6 that ' he never was so popular with his party — all right. The person who wrote against him in the magazine is angry because Dizzy did not give him office — Lord Robert Cecil.' It is true that, except Cecil, no person of real authority in the party lent himself to the attacks. Even Gathorne Hardy, though for some years he distrusted Disraeli, and once in a moment of irritation described him as ' a hateful leader,' was wont to say to complainants: ' I found him your leader; what has he done to deserve deposition? ' [1] But Disraeli himself had no illusions. To such an extent did he resent the ingratitude with which his services to the party had been met, that once again he threatened, and apparently seriously contemplated, resignation in preference to further experience of such unworthy treatment.

To Sir William Miles.

HOUSE OF COMMONS, *June* 11, 1860. — You were speaking to me, the other night, of the state of the party, your regret at its discontented condition, and your hope that, before you left us, those sitting behind me might yet become my supporters. I could not, at the moment, pursue the conversation because our position was then so critical that it required unceasing vigilance, and I could not venture to be frank.

Out of those dangerous waters we have now steered, and the course which I pursued some months ago in great difficulties has succeeded, and, I hope, saved us. I may now, therefore communicate to you without reserve.

I think it is fourteen years ago since yourself, then the leader of the country gentlemen, and another county member — alas! no more — called upon me at my private residence, and appealed to me to assist you at a moment of

[1] Gathorne Hardy's *Cranbrook*, Vol. I., p. 124.

apparently overwhelming disaster. I ultimately agreed to do so, but with great unwillingness, and only because ultimately I found Lord George Bentinck, with whom I had no acquaintance, had undertaken to fulfil the duties of leadership, if I, with others, would support him; and because from my earliest years, my sympathies had been with the landed interest of England.

I need say nothing of the years 1846–7–8. They were not inglorious to the country party.

When the catastrophe occurred at the end of 1848, and we lost Lord George, Lord Derby, with whom I had very slight relations, wrote to me, and asked me to undertake, under certain conditions, the management of our party. I declined to do so, though honoring duly the offer. I saw personal difficulties ahead, and the engagement on my part would have involved the sacrifice of several thousands a year, which I would willingly, having no children, have relinquished, if I possessed the confidence of the gentlemen of England, but which, without that great reward, I was not willing to give up.

After long and earnest representations, principally urged by Lord Derby, the present Duke of Rutland, yourself, and Lord Henry Bentinck, I undertook the office of leading the somewhat shattered remnants of the country party. They had divided on Lord G. Bentinck's great party motion on Irish Railways *120*. This was the condition in which affairs were put in my hands. Before three years had passed, by a series of motions on agricultural burdens made by myself, they had become a moiety of the House of Commons, while I left no stone unturned to reconstruct the Tory party by bringing back the Peelite section to our colors.

This was my unvarying effort, and for this I have always been prepared to make the greatest personal sacrifices. The leadership was offered twice to Lord Palmerston, and once, even so late as 1858, after the Ellenboro' disaster, to Sir James Graham: frequent offers, if not of a precise, of a flattering, nature have been made to Mr. Gladstone — and all at my instance, and, generally, personally.

Nevertheless they failed, and although Lord Derby and myself were unwilling to accept office ever without this reconstruction, we were obliged, in order to save the party from political annihilation, on two occasions to accept the responsibility — always in a great minority; on the last occasion the minority was 120. It was clear that such a state of affairs must always conclude in a dissolution; it was as clear that a dissolution could only restore Tory strength, not establish Tory power.

Of course our measures could not be carried after such dissolutions, great as might be our gain. But the strength of the party was restored. I have, however, to bear the brunt of disaster, and the measures of the Cabinet are called my measures, and I am held as alone to blame for their production.

This from my opponents I could bear, as I have had to bear much; but it is unreasonable that I should endure it from those who ought to be my friends.

The Tory party, as an Opposition, has never stood in a more solid — I would say prouder and more powerful — position than at this moment. The finance of Mr. Gladstone has blown up. The House of Lords exercises a real authority in the State. For the first time since 1841 (say 1839), there has been a real Church party in the House of Commons : the question of Parliamentary Reform has ceased to be a party question, and the Tories are cleared of the taint of opposition to popular franchise : they command half the House, and stand high in the country.

So long as they were in distress, I have borne without a murmur the neglect, the desertion, the personal insults, that I have experienced ; so long even as these were confined to our own ranks, and not the scandal of the world, I would, for party sake, have been silent. But the Tories are no longer in distress — they have abundance of friends ; and, with respect to the privacy of their feelings towards me, they chalk the walls in the market-place with my opprobrium.

I must therefore now take a step, which I wished to have done at the meeting of Parliament, and which nothing but the extreme difficulties and dangers of the party prevented my fulfilling. I must resign a leadership which I unwillingly accepted, and to which it is my opinion that fourteen years of unqualified devotion have not reconciled the party.

I will not communicate this resolve in the first instance to my colleagues, because I do not think that is a fair course to them, or to the party generally.

Your position is independent ; you were originally deputed to solicit my undertaking the office ; and you are in every respect best qualified to take the steps necessary in the present conjuncture. They should be taken with tact, and without unnecessarily exciting attention until all arrangements are completed. . . .

P.S. — I read with pain, but I felt the truth of the statement, in a liberal journal, a day or two ago, that my leadership of the party was one of 'chronic revolt and unceasing conspiracy.'

It was a dignified, if not in every detail historically accurate,[1] letter, setting out a record of great and unimpeachable services. Miles received it with consternation, and immediately consulted with a few of the leading members of the party, such as Walpole, Henley, Trollope, Lord Hotham, and Seymer. They all spoke so highly of Disraeli's conduct of business that he was finally persuaded to take the letter back and treat it as not having been written. Miles reminded him that, 'when the pinch comes, notwithstanding their murmuring and cavil, [the party] come to the scratch like men.' He added: 'I do not think you are sensitive to attacks from our enemies; do not be too susceptible of the follies of our friends. . . . Depend upon it that by advocating well-considered and moderate progress, and the necessity, for the cause of religion, of an Established Church, your lukewarm friends may be converted into ardent supporters, and so thorough a bond of union may be established between yourself and party as may render you irresistible.'

Disraeli's success during the session was so marked that even Cecil was fain, in the *Quarterly* for July, to write of 'Conservative Reaction,' and to temper, in a grudging way, some of his strictures of April, even pretending, in spite of the unambiguous phrases we have quoted, that there had never been any question of change of leadership. At the same time he justified the April article as 'plainly speaking out what everyone was saying of [Disraeli] in private, and no one would say in public.' Now the sinner was treated as repentant. In the session just drawing to a close, 'he has shown no inclination to flinch from the assertion of Conservative principles; he has made no attempts to boil them down to suit the palates of Radical allies. . . . We have a right to assume that the change is permanent, and that Mr. Disraeli has abandoned for ever the "unholy alliances" and the trimming tactics of which events have proved the hollowness and the shame.' It was not a very generous acknowledgment; but it

---

[1] See Vol. III., chs. 4 and 5.

is true that, in the Parliament of 1859–1865, Disraeli, sensitive as ever to the political atmosphere, appeared rather in the character of the defender of the institutions of his country, than in that of their reformer in the social and political spheres; and that, at any rate in the first part of the period, he avoided rather than welcomed Radical co-operation.

The summer and autumn of 1860 were occupied with momentous developments in foreign affairs. Garibaldi landed in Sicily, and produced a revolution both there and subsequently in Naples, with the result of the incorporation in the kingdom of Victor Emmanuel of all Italy except Venetia and a remnant of the Papal States; and in America the first decisive step towards Civil War was taken in the declaration by South Carolina of her secession from the Union. The success of the Italian revolution, which was warmly welcomed in England, strengthened the Government; and Disraeli, recognising that the time was not ripe for adopting the offensive, suggested in the winter that the tender of support which Malmesbury had been authorised to make to Palmerston in the previous session should be renewed in a more formal way for the coming year. 'I should fancy,' he wrote to Derby on December 8, 'that the Ministry have no longer a majority; certainly not, if we show indifference. But however this may be, it is expedient that they should be kept in.'

How Malmesbury carried out his leaders' wishes appears in detail from the Prime Minister's report to the Queen:

Lord Palmerston to Queen Victoria.

Piccadilly, *Jan.* 27, 1861. — . . . Viscount Palmerston saw Lord Malmesbury on Friday before the Cabinet. . . . [Lord Malmesbury] said that he was charged by Lord Derby and Mr. Disraeli with a message similar to that which he had conveyed last year, namely, that if Mr. Gladstone were to propose a democratic Budget making a great transfer of burthens from indirect to direct taxation, and if, the Cabinet refusing its concurrence, Mr. Gladstone were to retire, the Conservative party would give the Government substantial

support except in the case of the Government wishing to take an active part in war against Austria. That this did not, of course, mean an abstinence from usual attacks and criticisms in debate, but that no step would in such case be taken to produce a change of Government. In fact, said Lord Malmesbury, neither the Conservative leaders nor the party wish at present to come into office, and have no intention of taking any step to turn the present Government out. Mr. Bright had, indeed, proposed to Mr. Disraeli to join together with the Radical party the Conservatives, for the purpose of turning out the present Government, and especially to get rid of Viscount Palmerston and Lord John Russell. Mr. Bright said he would in that case give the Conservative Government a two years' existence, and by the end of that time the country, it might be hoped, would be prepared for a good and real Reform Bill, and then a proper Government might be formed.

This proposal, which it must be owned was not very tempting, Lord Malmesbury said had been declined. He also said that Count Persigny, on returning from one of his trips to Paris, had brought a similar proposal from Mr. Cobden for a co-operation of Radicals and Conservatives to overthrow the present Government; but that also had been declined. Viscount Palmerston requested Lord Malmesbury to convey his thanks to Lord Derby and Mr. Disraeli for the handsome communication which they had thus made to him, and to assure them that he fully appreciated the honourable and patriotic motives by which it had been prompted. . . .[1]

The offer of the Opposition to Palmerston was the more handsome and valuable as the by-elections in the country were turning in their favour. 'The Whig candidate won't fight in Aberdeenshire,' wrote Disraeli to Mrs. Willyams on January 19; 'the Whig candidate is beaten in Pembrokeshire; the Whig candidates will be beaten in Wiltshire and Leicester.' The Court, which desired both to keep the Palmerston Administration in office and to strengthen its conservative side, and which always used its influence to mitigate, if not to deprecate, party warfare, was greatly pleased with the arrangement; and the Disraelis received an invitation to stay at Windsor — an attention to the Opposition which gave the quidnuncs occasion for gossip.

[1] *Queen Victoria's Letters.*

To Lord Derby.

GROSVENOR GATE, *Jan.* 28, 1861. — . . . They[1] were very gracious and very communicative. They appeared to me greatly distressed and disgusted with public affairs. I had occasion to mention the state of our own party — its numbers, compactness, general good understanding, its increase of strength ; and I ventured to say that we should probably win every impending election. ' But you have no news-papers,' he exclaimed pettishly, ' the country is governed by newspapers ! and all the liberal journals are in the pay of foreign Powers. So much for the liberty of the Press. How-ever, when Parliament is sitting their influence is less.'

We get from the *Life of the Prince Consort* the Prince's account of Disraeli's conversation. Disraeli said that the Conservative Opposition formed a compact body of 300 members ; but they had no wish for the return of their leaders to office, and, indeed, were anxious to strengthen the hands of the Government in a bold national policy. A movement for the reduction of the expenses of our arma-ments, which had been initiated by Cobden and his friends, and which had taken the shape of a letter to Palmerston, signed by about sixty members of Parliament, had shown the existence of a considerable division in the ranks of the Ministerial supporters. But the Conserva-tive party were in no way inclined to take advantage of this state of things. On the contrary, they were prepared to support the Government, and even to help them out of scrapes, if they get into any ; all they required from them in return being that they should not enter into a line of ' democratic finance.'[2]

To Mrs. Brydges Willyams.

GROSVENOR GATE, *Feb.* 9, 1861. — . . . I think I have got everything now in good order, and have brought the troops into the field in ample numbers and in fine condition.

The difficulty is to keep them in: but forbearance and patience are clearly our game, and though I could, the first night, have destroyed the Government, I was wise enough to refrain. In the meantime, we win every election, and time is big with great events, which will demand a strong, patriotic, and Conservative Government. . . .

---

[1] The Queen and the Prince.   [2] Martin's *Prince Consort*, Vol. V., p. 286.

Gladstone's Budget for 1861 did not propose any great transference of burdens from indirect to direct taxation, and so did not bring into active working the arrangement of the Conservative leaders with Palmerston. But, while taking a penny off the income tax, it selected the paper duty for relief instead of the war taxes on tea and sugar, thus, in the opinion of the Opposition, prosecuting the constitutional quarrel with the Lords at the expense of the real interests of the country. One of the main features of Gladstone's speech was a strong protest against the increasing national expenditure, which amounted this year to nearly 70 millions. Income tax could be dispensed with, he said, if the country was contented to be governed at a cost of 60 millions ; but if 70 millions were wanted income tax was necessary. Disraeli was justifiably severe on this ineffectual outburst.

There is no innovation so gigantic as a Chancellor of the Exchequer denouncing the expenditure as profligate for which he is supplying at the same time the ways and means. If he believes the expenditure to be impolitic, to use the mildest term, on what principle can he vindicate his sitting on that bench ?. . . The right hon. gentleman insinuates that the Government as well as himself are recommending and pursuing an expenditure that is contrary to their conviction of public necessity. It is someone or other, some unknown but irresistible force, that urges them on. Sometimes it appears to be the country, sometimes the House, but never the Ministry.

Under Disraeli's guidance, the Opposition took the line of endeavouring to substitute a reduction of the duty on tea for the repeal of the duty on paper. Such a policy would be at least equally beneficial to the country, would leave the existing sources of revenue undiminished, and would avoid humiliating the Lords. Northcote, who first established this Parliamentary reputation by his speeches in the numerous debates on this Budget, thought the game a good one, but was afraid his leader might spoil it by over-cleverness. 'Disraeli,' he wrote to Lady Northcote on April 19, 'is in the highest spirits because the battle is

to be fought by tactics and not by brute force, and he thinks he is going to display great powers of generalship. I am always a little afraid of his manœuvring, especially when he has a good game, because he always spoils it by overdoing something or other.' [1] Whether Disraeli was to blame or not, Gladstone's vigour overcame both the luke-warmness of his own chief and the attacks of the Opposition. A motion to reduce the tea duty was defeated by 18 votes — it was not a majority, said Disraeli, as it was only in its teens ; and the repeal of the paper duty was carried by 15: 296 to 281.[2] This was not a handsome victory for the Government, but it sufficed ; and the House of Lords made no effort to continue the fight.

In truth, it is always difficult and thankless to organise opposition with a view to dictating to the Executive which of two taxes it shall remit. Moreover, in this case the constitutional question rendered the Conservative position peculiarly embarrassing. Gladstone determined to include all the financial proposals in one Bill, so as to make it impossible for the House of Lords (who had the right to reject, but not to amend, a tax Bill) to pick and choose among the taxes. While this procedure was strongly resented by the Tories, it was felt by many of them to be impossible to declare it to be unconstitutional ; and, as Graham pointed out in debate, 'Up with the Lords and down with the Commons' would not be a good hustings cry for the Opposition at elections. On the constitutional point Walpole and Heathcote declared their support of the Government, and Stanley showed a disposition to take the same view.

From Lord Derby.

St. James's Square, *May 2,* 1861. — Stanley came home with me last night, and I did not like his tone; he was very reserved, but I much fear he is going wrong. He has been talking with Malins [3] (this I heard from M.) and Walpole. Surely there is no fear of the latter? If anybody can keep Stanley right, you can. . . .

[1] Lang's *Northcote,* p. 104.   [2] May 30.
[3] Afterwards Vice-Chancellor Sir Richard Malins.

Disraeli was able to prevail on Stanley to keep silence in debate ; but, with a party thus divided, he naturally discouraged opposition to the second reading of the Finance Bill, and concentrated his efforts on resisting in Committee the clause relating to the paper duty. Even here he had the greatest difficulty to bring Walpole and Heathcote into line.

To Sir William Heathcote.

[*May 27, 1861.*] — I attribute such importance to the unity of the Conservative party that I should, as a general rule, always be ready to waive any course, which I might think it desirable for us to pursue, rather than endanger our complete concord.

Under these circumstances, it is with the utmost pain that I learn the step you and Walpole contemplate taking with reference to the question of the paper duty. The policy of resisting its repeal was adopted after great deliberation, at which Walpole assisted ; and although after that decision I felt it my duty to take every step that I thought likely to effect the desired result, I have been so scrupulous not to move again without materially advancing our object that I have continually refrained from acting, though ever with a distinct reservation of my right to do so, and even an assertion of my future purpose.

It was my opinion that nothing would justify our again trying the issue unless we were assured of the assistance of some of the most eminent members of the Whig party, and even of the course being originated by one of that body. There was a very general and very urgent disposition in our party to support the division of the Budget Bill ; but in deference to your opinions and those of Walpole on that subject I would not sanction the attempt. I inferred, however, from your declaration in your speech that your objection to the financial policy was unchanged.

In the midst of the Whitsun week I received a communication that some of the most influential Whig gentlemen were prepared to speak and vote against the paper clause in Committee, if our party were still prepared to support them. And on this I resolved upon our course.

It was impossible to consult anyone, for everyone was absent ; but with great deference and with no assumption of arrogance, which I hope is foreign from my nature, I would observe that, although the individual entrusted with the conduct of a Parliamentary party would act very unwarrantably in deciding upon a policy without consulting

his principal friends, it is a very different case with respect to the tactics which are to carry that policy into effect. These must necessarily depend upon constantly changing circumstances, and often are the decision of a moment.

If the leader of a Parliamentary party cannot be trusted with deciding on tactics, he really can be entrusted with nothing, and it would be very much like the old Aulic Councils, which, full of prudence and science, always conducted the Austrian armies to discomfiture. . . .

Believing that I was carrying the wishes of the united party entirely into effect by my present course, I view with dismay and the deepest sense of personal vexation your contemplated course.

Upon my representations, some hundreds of gentlemen at great trouble, and even at great expense, have hurried up to the House of Commons. What must be their irritation and their disappointment to find voting against them men like yourself — the principal personages of the party! I entreat you to think of the effect of their mortified feelings on the mustering of our party on subjects of less exciting, but of far more important interest, than a tax or a duty. The labours of two sessions will be destroyed.

Since we have acted together, I have done everything in my power to meet your views, and would without hesitation have prevented the present movement, had I supposed it would have separated us. I write to you with deep emotion, for I know how much is at stake. I entreat you to consider well the course you are taking. I feel persuaded that, if you will view the circumstances in which we are placed deeply and dispassionately, you will not only support me at this moment, but use all your great and just influence with those who are guided by your example. . . .

Besides pleading thus specially with Heathcote and Walpole, who responded to his appeal, Disraeli sent out an urgent letter to others among his followers, warning them that Derby was very anxious that the impending division should prove the unity of the Conservative party. But in spite of all his efforts more than twenty Conservatives absented themselves from the division,[1] a number sufficient to have turned the Government majority of 15 into a minority. Disraeli in consequence, records Raikes in his diary for June 15, ' withdrew himself from the House

[1] May 30.

altogether for three or four days, and declined to return until he had received a satisfactory apology from the malcontents.'[1] But he was anxious not to emphasise the existence of this undercurrent of discontent, and declined a flattering proposal of a demonstration in his favour from his loyal friends.

To Sir Matthew White Ridley.[2]

GROSVENOR GATE, *June* 7, 1861. — I am honored, and deeply gratified, by the invitation which yourself, and others of my friends, have, this morning, brought me from those members of the Carlton Club who are also members of the House of Commons, to meet them at dinner 'as a testimony of the undiminished value they set upon my services to the Conservative party, and of their earnest friendly feeling toward myself.'

My services are at all times amply rewarded by the indulgent belief of my friends, that they contribute, however slightly, to the progress and welfare of the party whose interests with me, I trust, will always be paramount to any personal consideration.

If, therefore, I presume to decline a proposition so flattering as this invitation, it is only because I feel its acceptance at this moment might lead to misconception, and foster a notion as unfounded as it might be mischievous, that there is any material want of concord in the Conservative ranks.

Colleagues as well as followers added to Disraeli's worries at this critical time. When he returned to his seat in the House after his calculated absence, he was met by a long letter of complaint from one who had sat with him in both of Derby's Governments, the essence of the grievance being insufficiency of consultation. Disraeli justified himself in similar terms to those contained in his letter to Heathcote, adding:

After all, politics is like war — roughish work. We should not be over-sensitive. We have enough to do and to bear without imaginary grievances. Somebody must lead — but

[1] Sir Henry Edwards, M.P., wrote to Disraeli in June of the following year: 'Am I at liberty to state in the Carlton and elsewhere that last year — after our defeat — you resigned the leadership of the party, and were pressed into its service again by Trollope, who represented a very influential section of the landed interest in the House of Commons?'

[2] The 4th baronet, M.P. for N. Northumberland 1859–1868.

I wish to live with my colleagues on terms of perfect equality; and after reading your long letter of complaints over again, you will permit me to say that I do not think they are very substantial.

Disraeli had spoken frequently throughout this prolonged fight against a financial policy which created, he said, an artificial surplus in order to perpetrate a financial caprice. The details of dead-and-gone financial debates are wearisome, but a passage may be rescued in which he vindicated the House of Lords. Its power, he said, had no doubt greatly diminished, as that of the Commons had increased.

But the House of Lords still possess a great and growing influence in the conviction of the national mind that an intermediate body between the popular branch of the legislature and absolute legislation is a great security for public liberty and for temperate government. The people of England feel that the existence of a body of that kind is a great blessing; and all the public experience of Europe has assured them that it is a body which cannot be artificially created. They therefore consider it a very fortunate circumstance for this country that such an intermediate body should have risen, supported by property, by tradition, and by experience, ready to act with the critical faculty which is necessary when precipitate legislation is threatened, and at least to obtain time, so that upon all questions of paramount importance the ultimate decision should be founded on the mature opinion of an enlightened nation.

To Mrs. Brydges Willyams.

GROSVENOR GATE, *March* 16, 1861. — It was most kind of you to write after my health. *Between ourselves,* I took advantage of a very slight indisposition to absent myself from some debates, where, had I been present, more serious consequences might have occurred than I care, at this moment, to accomplish.

It is difficult, almost impossible, to keep the present Government in, though the sudden death of the Duchess of Kent,[1] which took place last night, will assist that result. . . .

There was a pitched battle in the Commons last Wednesday, on the county franchise, and the Conservatives gained a great victory in a full House. This has been our second

_____
[1] The Queen's Mother.

great effort before Easter, the first being on the Church rate, when we were only in a minority of 15; and after Easter I think, we shall win on this also. . . .[1]

CARLTON CLUB, *April* 24, 1861. — . . . I have endeavoured to keep the Ministry in, but they tempt their fate, and a critical position has occurred.

On Monday I executed a reconnaissance in force, which will be continued for some days. I hope in the interval to discover the weak part of the enemy's position, and I count in about ten days to give him battle.

This is the real state of affairs. I am quite exhausted in listening to aide-de-camps, instructing generals of division, and writing endless despatches. . . .

HOUSE OF COMMONS, *May* 17, 1861. — . . . I had a very difficult task on Wednesday, in having to propose the health of the Duc d'Aumale, as Chairman of the Literary Fund. I could not allude to the most celebrated of his literary compositions — viz., the pamphlet which he has just published on the present state of affairs in France, and which you have no doubt heard of, perhaps read. It is a masterpiece of composition — of trenchant sarcasm and incisive logic; not unworthy of Junius, or even Pascal. However, I got through my task without blundering, and, I may venture to say to you, with great applause. It was the most brilliant meeting of the kind I ever attended.

The young Princes of France were at different parts of the table, mingling among three hundred distinguished guests. The youths are distinguished in their appearance, with winning manners, and highly educated, bearing wondrous names of historic renown — the Count of Paris, the Duc de Chartres, Gaston of Orleans, Count of Eu, the Prince de Condé, the Duc d'Alençon!

They are exiles, but they are young, and full of hope and dignity — and favored by Nature. . . .

HOUSE OF COMMONS, *June* 3, 1861. — The great battle which commenced this day week, and which, if concluded on that night, would have ended in the defeat of Ministers, terminated on Friday morning at two o'clock, and later, by their escape — by a slight majority. In the very hour of victory, when the signal for the last charge was given, I had the mortification, great for a general indeed, to see a division of my own troops march from the field of contest. One bears this, however, as one bears many things, when the heat of youth is over, and one has experienced, in one's time, what is the surest, perhaps the only, support under discomfiture — the memory of former success.

[1] See below, Ch. 10.

A Government saved by the too prudential forbearance of a section of their foes is not in a proud or a strong position, and I must say I look to the future without dismay. . . .

CARLTON CLUB, *Tuesday, July* 30, 1861.—. . . The end of the session, generally so exhausted and insipid, has been this year of a peculiarly exciting character: reconstructions of Governments, unexpected elevations to the peerage, unexpected death of young Ministers on whose future much depended—and now a great contested election in the City of London, where there has not been such a thing for twenty years—and a Tory in, or nearly in. I don't think the Lord Mayor will quite succeed; for at this hour, three o'clock, he is 100 behind—not much when they had polled 10,000. Such a state of affairs marks a great change in opinion, which has long been occurring. . . .[1]

They say there were never so many marriages as this year, almost all my unappropriated friends are destined in a few days, more or less—the Marquis of Bath, Lord John Manners,[2] Lord Mexborough, etc., etc. Thus the world wags! Strange events every day; the most extraordinary, the retirement of Lord John Russell from the House of Commons!

The retirement and death of Sidney Herbert, recently created Lord Herbert of Lea, coincided with the close of the session; the death of Graham followed in October; Aberdeen and Dalhousie had passed away in the previous year. Of the eminent Peelites with whom Disraeli had so often contended, none were left in the House of Commons at the end of the autumn save the most eminent of all—Gladstone. Even so the tale of deaths was not complete. The Prince Consort passed away in December.

To Lord Derby.

HUGHENDEN MANOR, *Nov.* 15, 1861.—We are engaged to be at Alnwick on the day you so kindly invite us to Knowsley, and having fixed the time ourselves, after much hesitation, I cannot venture to propose a new arrangement. This I much regret, as it would have given me great pleasure to have seen, and conversed with, you.

As for public affairs, no difficulty is solved, or even approaching solution. The recess, hitherto, has advanced

---

[1] The final numbers were—Wood (L.), 5747, Cubitt (C.), 5241. The vacancy was caused by Russell's elevation to the peerage.

[2] This was Lord John's second marriage, to Janetta Hughan. His first wife had died in 1854.

nothing, while the general decomposition proceeds. To be, at the same time, head of the Revolution and head of the Latin race is an inconsistent position, and this is the cause of the perplexities of the Emperor of France; but the Latin race will carry the day, and the compromise with revolution, sooner or later, must be an European war. Our part in it is another question.

Since the days of the House of Atreus, there has never been a tragedy like the Peelites. Incredible that, since the fatal Act of 1846, Peel, Goulburn, Dalhousie, Aberdeen, Graham, Herbert, have all disappeared, and Lincoln getting as blind as Œdipus, while Palmerston, the senior of all, is rollicking! The Mayor of Oxford told me yesterday that Cardwell had been in imminent danger, from dysentery: but this would only have been an affair of the lesser Ajax. Strange that, after all their loves and hates, Graham and Tom Duncombe should die in the same month, and of the same complaint.

To Mrs. Brydges Willyams.

ALNWICK CASTLE, *Nov.* 24, 1861. — Three hundred men, for the last seven years, have been at work daily at this wondrous place, and they are to work for three years more. The result, that the ancient Castle of Hotspur is externally restored in perfect style; while the interior has all the refinement, fancy, and magnificence, of an Italian palace, in the palmiest days of Italian art. . . . The Duke [of Northumberland] has formed a school of carvers in wood, where there are about thirty men, chiefly youths, working like Gibbons or Cellini. . . .

SEAHAM HALL, *Dec.* 8, 1861. — . . . This is a remarkable place, and our hostess [1] is a remarkable woman. Twenty miles hence she has a palace (Wynyard) in a vast park, with forest rides and antlered deer, and all the splendid accessories of feudal life. — But she prefers living in a hall on the shores of the German Ocean, surrounded by her collieries, and her blast-furnaces, and her railroads, and unceasing telegraphs, with a port hewn out of the solid rock, screw steamers and four thousand pitmen under her control. One day she dined the whole 4,000 in one of the factories. In the town of Seaham Harbour, a mile off, she has a regular office, a fine stone building with her name and arms in front, and her flag flying above; and here she transacts, with innumerable agents, immense business — and I remember her five-and-twenty years ago, a mere fine lady; nay, the finest in London! But one must find excitement, if one has brains. . . .

[1] Frances Anne Lady Londonderry. She died Jan. 20, 1865.

The fascination of Gladstone's oratory and the force
of his resolution had procured, though not without serious
setbacks, a general success for his financial policy in 1860
and 1861. But in 1862, partly owing to the American
War, but partly to Ministerial miscalculations, the national
balance-sheet was a gloomy one, and, but for supplemental
grants, the revenue would have shown a serious deficit.
The policy of parting lightly with sources of revenue
received a distinct check, and the Budget only proposed
a few minor changes of taxation. It was, as Disraeli said,
'the sober hour that follows the financial flourishes,' and
he thought the time had come for a critical examination
of Gladstonian finance. He maintained [1] that the policy
of the past two years had resulted in an accumulated
deficiency of £4,000,000, and that during those years
Gladstone had anticipated the resources of the country
to the amount of £3,500,000; so that he had exceeded
the ordinary revenue by the enormous sum of £7,500,000,
at a time when that ordinary revenue was sustained by
war taxation — a war income tax, and war duties on tea
and sugar. 'But is that all? It seems impossible that
there can be any aggravation of such aggravated circumstances. And yet I can show the House that hitherto
they have not measured the amount of the prodigality
of the right hon. gentleman; for not only has he
exceeded during two years the ordinary revenue of the
country by £7,500,000, that revenue being sustained by
war taxation, but he has done this at a period when the
charges for the National Debt had diminished to the extent of £2,000,000 by the lapse of terminable annuities.'

The peroration of Disraeli's speech was a fine specimen
of Parliamentary invective. He maintained that Gladstone should have spoken frankly about the income tax;
that he had no right to 'fritter away the resources of the
country and leave that tax pressing upon us.'

There is something in the speeches of the right hon. gentleman on this subject, and, indeed, on the whole of our financial

[1] April 7, 1862.

system, that fills me with perplexity; which, I think, conveys to the country a sentiment, not merely of perplexity, but of distrust; and it is this, that, while the right hon. gentleman is without parallel or exception the most profuse Finance Minister that ever directed the affairs of this country in time of peace, he is perpetually insinuating — to use the mildest term — both to this House and to the country, that he disapproves of our expenditure, and that he is burning to denounce it. Now, I say that is not a legitimate position for the right hon. gentleman to occupy. If he disapproves of this profuse expenditure, why does he sit on that bench, and lend to its enactment and enforcement all the authority of his character and all the lustre of his reputation? . . . The right hon. gentleman has gained the confidence and support of a party, not very numerous, but still distinguished by talent, perseverance, and, I will add, integrity — I mean the party that calls for a reduction of our expenditure. How is it that that party, which preaches retrenchment and reduction, which believes that all our estimates, and especially the naval and military estimates, are much too extravagant; who are opposed to fortifications, and who do not much like iron ships, always support the Minister who brings forward these excessive estimates, and who provides for this enormous expenditure? This is a great question. This, at least, we know, that while this spendthrift is weeping over pence, while this penurious prodigal is proposing his enormous expenditure, he always contrives to repeal some tax to gratify the interests or feelings of the party of retrenchment. No wonder, then, we no longer hear the same character given of the income tax; no wonder we are no longer reminded of that compact entered into by the House and accepted by the country for its gradual abolition. . . .

I remember some years ago, when the right hon. gentleman was at the head of a small and select party of politicians who were not then absorbed in the gulf of Liberalism, they were accustomed to prattle much about 'political morality.' What then most distinguished the right hon. gentleman and his friends was their monopoly of that admirable quality. They were perpetually thanking God they were not as other men and always pointing their finger at the unfortunate wights who sat opposite to them. Now we see what is the end of political morality. We see the position to which political morality has brought the finances of a great nation. I denounce this system as one which is detrimental to the character of public men, and most injurious to the fortunes of the realm.

Gladstone disputed the accuracy of Disraeli's figures, but he did not deny that the finances of the country demanded grave attention; and Disraeli was justified in the complacency with which he narrated the story of the debate to Mrs. Willyams.

To Mrs. Brydges Willyams.

Private. GROSVENOR GATE, *April* 14, 1862. — The first portion of our Parliamentary campaign has closed, and it ended with a great financial duel. I believe there is no doubt who was the conqueror. In fact the circumstances were so grave and strong that they had only to be put powerfully and clearly before the country to carry conviction.

Nevertheless, it has taken both the House of Commons and the kingdom by surprise. They had heard so much, and so long, of financial skill and prosperity, that, when the balance-sheet was fairly put before them, all were as surprised and startled as if Baring or Rothschild had failed. It was a *coup d'état* — and nobody talks of anything else. It will influence events, though, myself, I trust the tottering government will still totter on. . . .

In truth, Gladstone's position in Palmerston's Cabinet of 1859–1865 was a somewhat false one. On perhaps the most important domestic question throughout its continuance, whether there should be a considerable expenditure on national defence, or a severe policy of national economy, the Chancellor of the Exchequer was in direct and constant conflict with the Prime Minister. In the early years Gladstone was usually worsted in Cabinet on this question, and the fortifications and the iron ships which Palmerston and the services thought necessary were provided. Nevertheless, if Gladstone often tendered his resignation, he as often recalled it; and the country was treated to the undignified spectacle which Disraeli described again and again in biting language. 'We need not maunder in antechambers,' he said, 'to discover differences in the Cabinet, when we have a patriotic Prime Minister appealing to the spirit of the country; and when at the same time we find his Chancellor of the Exchequer, whose duty it is to supply the ways and

means by which those exertions are to be supported, proposing votes with innuendo, and recommending expenditure in a whispered invective.' In 1862, when the necessary defences had been provided, and the financial outlook was grave, that policy of economy, which all Gladstone's exertions in the Cabinet and his hints in public had failed to enforce, was warmly supported and driven home by Disraeli and the Opposition, who resented, in accord with public opinion, the continuance of war taxation in time of peace. Lord Morley has drawn attention to the contrast between the rise of naval and military expenditure during the first half of the Administration, and its decline in the second half to a figure below that at which it stood at the beginning ; but he has omitted to refer to this movement of Disraeli's, which was one of the most conspicuous features of the session of 1862, and nearly brought about the downfall of Palmerston's Government. Derby, who always, and rightly, put defence above economy, was a little doubtful about some of the features of the campaign ; Disraeli's most active supporter and confidant throughout it was Northcote.

To Lord Derby.

Confidential. GROSVENOR GATE, *May* 21, 1862.—. . . There is a Committee on Public Accounts now sitting, of which N[orthcote] is a member. This has greatly assisted him. The revelations before it are frightful, and prove that 'the outlay on stores, during the last two or three years, has been perfectly reckless.' This Committee will of course report. Cobden is on it. Money voted for iron ships has been applied to all kinds of purposes.' The general conclusion is that the ' enormous expenditure has outgrown all control.' The report of this Committee will in all probability greatly affect public opinion, and will prove the wisdom, I think, especially when connected with a falling revenue, of the position which we have assumed, and which Gladstone had his eye on. . . .

From Lord Derby.

ST. JAMES'S SQUARE, *May* 21, 1862.—. . . My only fear has been, and would be, that of holding out expectations

(and especially if they were to lead to an assumption of office) which we could not practically realise without endangering the defences of the country; and especially those connected with the Navy, which we gained so much credit for strengthening, and with which I am sure you would be as unwilling to interfere as I should. I cannot forget that we entered on our examination of the state of the Navy and its expenditure with the hope, and intention, of effecting considerable reductions, and that hope founded also on what seemed very good authority; and that the result was an enormous increase, and the beginning of the 'reconstruction.' . . .

Disraeli used, in a debate on May 8 on expenditure and policy, a phrase which stuck. Instead of acting in cordial alliance with France, he said that we had been trying to govern by a new system of what was called moral power, which meant 'bloated armaments' in time of peace, and produced misconceptions, broils, and distrust, while taxation had found its limit and was sapping the strength of England. The phrase itself at once produced misconception. Disraeli referred to a system which had become general in Europe, and was not confined to, though it was accepted by, this country; and Derby loyally came to his defence in the Lords. Disraeli explained his position in the debate on June 3, in which the movement for retrenchment culminated. Cobden and the Radicals were naturally pressing, side by side with the regular Opposition, for retrenchment; and Stansfeld, then one of their most advanced men, proposed a resolution to the effect that the national expenditure was capable of reduction without compromising the safety, the independence, or the legitimate influence, of the country. This was exactly Disraeli's view, and the Conservative leaders met and determined, while avoiding an alliance with the Radicals, to push their policy in debate and in the division lobby. Palmerston had given notice of an amendment expressing satisfaction at the economy already effected and expectation of more, but insisting rather on the obligation of home defence and of protection of interests abroad. To this it was arranged that Walpole should move a further amendment, pointing more

decidedly to economy, especially to 'diminishing the burden of those taxes which are confessedly of a temporary and exceptional character.'

The contention of the Opposition, which represented indeed the general feeling both of the House and of the country, was so reasonable that Palmerston felt that strong measures must be taken; and before the debate opened he announced that the Government would treat Walpole's amendment as a question of confidence. Walpole, forgetful of the agreement at Derby's house, to which he was a party, and remembering only the Conservative desire to keep Palmerston in office, quailed; and Disraeli had to carry on the debate under the shadow of certain defeat owing to the disaffection of friends. This did not affect the spirit with which he attacked the Government. Further military outlay, he maintained, was not needed, as, owing to the great efforts made by successive Administrations in the last ten years — the creation of the Militia and the Volunteers, and the strengthening of the fleet and the forts — the country was now adequately defended. He declined to believe in the treachery of the French, who were still, as in the time of the Crimean War, our allies. The people of England, though not the most excitable, were the most enthusiastic in the world, especially on the question of national defence. 'In this country, protected by 400,000 men and a commanding fleet in the Channel, to say that freemen are in danger of a midnight invasion from cordial allies is a mystification too monstrous for belief.'

What was the real cause, Disraeli continued, of the permanent influence that this country exercised upon the Continent? It was this:

England is the only country which, when it enters into a quarrel that it believes to be just, never ceases its efforts until it has accomplished its aim; whereas . . . it was always felt in old times and generations that are past — and honourable gentlemen can ascertain whether the present state of Europe makes any difference in this matter — that, with scarcely an exception, there was not a State in Europe, not

even the proudest and most powerful, that could ever enter into a third campaign. Well, what gave us this power of continuing war into which we had entered, and in which we were ready to persevere because we believed it to be just? It was the financial reserve of England. It was the conviction that the reserves of England, when we once chose to engage in a quarrel, were such that it was not a question of one, two, or three campaigns, but that, as we have proved in old days, our determination, supported by our resources, would allow us to prepare for an indefinite struggle when we had an adequate and worthy object in view. If, however, you allow your finances to be sapped and weakened, you are at the same time weakening this prime source of your authority.

It was, therefore, essential to make such reductions as would equalize the charge and the revenue of the country. Palmerston, he added, had proposed an 'awkward and shambling vote of confidence in his own Government,' and had thereby 'appalled' his right honourable friend, Walpole. But the Opposition had not really intended an assault on the Treasury bench, but had merely desired to assert a temperate and practicable policy which they felt sure the House must ultimately adopt and public opinion sanction. 'To-morrow (Derby Day) I believe we shall all be engaged elsewhere. I dare say that many hon. gentlemen who take more interest than I do in that noble pastime will have their favourites. I hope they will not be so unlucky as to find their favourites bolting. If they are placed in that dilemma, they will be better able to understand and sympathise with my feelings on this occasion.' Walpole having withdrawn, Palmerston's resolution was accepted by a great majority.

To Mrs. Brydges Willyams.

Confidential. HOUSE OF COMMONS, *May* 27, 1862. — The newspapers have made you aware of the change that has taken place in public affairs. I have been, as it were, bringing large bodies of troops into the field during the month, and the Government have suddenly found themselves, almost without notice, surrounded, surprised and endangered. The state of the finances gave this opening, and I availed myself

of it. It will ultimately produce their fall, but I wish, myself, rather to discredit than to defeat them. It should go on for eight or ten months more, if possible, when the state of the country, the decline of the revenue, the want of employment in Lancashire, and their profuse and extravagant foreign policy, will combine for their permanent discomfiture. . . .

Confidential. GROSVENOR GATE, *June*, 13, 1862. — When I wrote to you last, I hinted at the financial crisis, that was slowly gathering. The House of Lords followed up the movement of the Commons, and a resolution, then unwisely announced by a Radical member, precipitated affairs. The papers will have told you the result. My second in command lost his head and heart the moment the trumpets sounded for battle. Such an incident never before happened in the House of Commons, and I hope may never happen again. They say you should see everything once. I did what I could to cover the retreat, and mitigate the humiliation of my troops. Between ourselves, as you well know, I had no wish whatever to disturb Lord Palmerston, but you cannot keep a large army in order without letting them, sometimes, smell gunpowder. . . .

The fiasco of the debate left both sections of the Conservatives sore. Disraeli resented the desertion of his colleague, Walpole and his friends the sarcasms of Disraeli. Derby wrote to his lieutenant : ' I will do my best to smooth matters; but I fear it will require time to reunite the party. My own opinion is that you were the person who had the most reason to complain.' Disraeli's admirable temper enabled him after awhile to bring his colleagues together again; so that Earle could report to him on September 13 that Walpole had recently said : ' Several members of the party have been to me to ask me to lead them, but I am under so much obligation to Lord D. and to Disraeli that I could never think of doing anything that could possibly weaken their hands.'

Though Disraeli's immediate Parliamentary success was spoilt by Walpole, the effect of the movement on the Government remained. In the following year, 1863, there was a distinct return to the principles of the ' frugal ' Government of the Duke of Wellington, which Disraeli praised in the debate on the Address. Retrench-

ment was effected in military expenditure. The duty on tea was reduced, and twopence was taken off the income tax; and Disraeli claimed this as a victory for the House of Commons, and inferentially for the Opposition. The Budget in its main features was, he said, the Budget of the House. The arguments used last year had had their effect. It was no longer held to show subserviency to France to obtain by the most legitimate means a reduction of the burdens of the people. It was the House of Commons that had reduced the tea duty and the income tax.

After 1862 the financial debates ceased to be the most crucial issues for the Palmerston Government. Economy was enforced, and the large surpluses which the buoyant trade of the country and the Chancellor of the Exchequer's skilful management provided were mainly utilised, as Disraeli had recommended, in reducing the income tax and the tea and sugar duties. This chapter may, however, be fitly concluded by chronicling two instances in 1863 in which Disraeli took a prominent part in financial discussions. One concerned Gladstone's attempt to subject charities to income tax, on the ground that to exempt them was in effect to make them a contribution from the public funds. Though the Chancellor put forth all his rhetorical powers in the cause, Parliamentary and public feeling was too strong for him, and he had to withdraw. Disraeli pointed out that income tax was a tax on persons, not on property, and that Gladstone's proposals amounted to a confiscation of endowments. Gladstone had bolstered up his argument by denouncing the abuses which had arisen from endowments; but Disraeli had little difficulty in showing that for such evils the application of the income tax was a very inappropriate and inadequate remedy.

The other question was that of a proposed commercial treaty with Italy. Disraeli was all for commercial treaties, such as the great Tory Ministers, Bolingbroke and the younger Pitt, had negotiated with France; but they must

be based on the old Conservative principle of reciprocity. That had been given up : in existing circumstances a commercial treaty was an anachronism.

The age of commercial treaties is past, because you have no means and no materials for negotiation. All you can do is to exercise that moral influence, of which we hear so much, with foreign countries with which you are placed in communication, to lead them by your own example and your own prosperity. . . . From the contemplation of that prosperity, the conviction will grow in those countries that with immense resources they are producing small revenues ; that they are not raising revenues that bear a due relation to their resources, and you may trust to that to lead to reciprocal exchanges and mutual benefits in commercial transactions. But you will gain that as completely, and perhaps sooner, without the embarrassment of commercial treaties than you would with these conventions. I regret that, through the conduct of the Government, and through the extraordinary behaviour of the Free Trade party in patronising artificial agreements of exchange, there has arisen in this country the impression that the best and most politic mode of stimulating commerce is to have recourse to that method. That was a good theory twenty years ago, and not only a good theory, but a good theory which could be put in beneficial practice. . . . You have adopted unrestricted competition as the principle of your commercial code. By accident certain articles were excepted, and two years ago you used them as a means of negotiating a treaty of commerce with a great country, with a large population, and with very rich and valuable resources. You have played all your cards ; and to attempt at the present moment — to pretend that you can assist and support the commerce of this country by commercial treaties is a mere delusion.[1]

[1] Feb. 13, 1863.

CHAPTER IX

1860–1864

While Disraeli demanded public economy at home, he consistently deprecated a policy of adventure abroad. In the debate on the Address in 1860 he laid down what he conceived to be the proper principles of British foreign policy. They are substantially those which he was advocating in the late forties against the intermeddling diplomacy which Palmerston pursued as Russell's Foreign Minister.[1] Russell now, under Palmerston, was carrying on Palmerston's system, but with less dexterity and a rasher enthusiasm. But the House of Commons, Disraeli maintained, was opposed to adventures, and was in favour of what was popularly but incorrectly called a policy of non-interference — non-interference, be it observed, in the domestic affairs of foreign nations.

I do not know any member of this House — either among my colleagues or among those who sit on the other side of the House — who has ever maintained the monstrous proposition that England ought never, under any circumstances, to interfere in the affairs of foreign States. There are conditions under which it may be our imperative duty to interfere. We may clearly interfere in the affairs of foreign countries when the interests or the honour of England are at stake, or when in our opinion the independence of Europe is menaced. But a great responsibility devolves upon that Minister who has to decide when those conditions have arisen. . . . The general principle that we ought not to interfere in the affairs of foreign nations unless there is a clear necessity, and that,

---

[1] See Vol. III., ch. 7, especially pp. 186, 187.

generally speaking, it ought to be held a political dogma that the people of other countries should settle their own affairs without the intervention of foreign influence or foreign power, is one which, I think, the House does not only accept, but, I trust, will cordially agree to.

Special point was given to this passage by the recent efforts of Palmerston and Russell to engage this country during the recess in a policy of active intervention on behalf of the unity of Italy — efforts only checkmated by the determined opposition of the Court. Palmerston professed in the debate that the policy of the Government was that the people of Italy should settle their own affairs; but it is now admitted that the suspicions of Disraeli and the Opposition were well founded.

To Lord Derby.

Grosvenor Gate, *Jan.* 8, 1860. — . . . I hear from Paris that the Emperor has proposed to our Government to enter into a *treaty* for the settlement of Italian affairs, and that Palmerston is highly favorable to the proposition, which was, no doubt, concocted between them without the knowledge of Lord P.'s colleagues. Such a treaty will, I think, be looked upon by the country with very great suspicion, to use the mildest term; and I should think the Cabinet will hesitate before they enter into it. But the Emperor is positive and peremptory. It is the only way by which he can extricate himself, with dash and lustre, from his difficulties, and he offers everything — Suez Canal to be opposed; peace between Spain and Morocco, etc., etc., and government by us to be always impossible. It will be rather ludicrous, after the volunteers and the 10 million loan, should the new session be inaugurated with not only *une entente cordiale*, but an absolute alliance. . . .

Secret. Grosvenor Gate, *Jan.* 14, 1860. — . . . Lord Cowley came over from the Emperor with a distinct proposal for an alliance, ' *offensive and defensive,*' and, strange to say, enforced it, as his own opinion, in the strongest manner. The Emperor had completely got over him. The Court, finding this out, was much disgusted — and countermined. Lord Palmerston and Lord John had held out to the Emperor every hope of success. Gladstone, furiously Italian, was gained to absolute interference, by the mirage of a Commercial Treaty; but when the Cabinet met, the business being opened by Lord John, the strong opinion of Lord Cowley

duly dwelt on, and Lord Palmerston very decisive, they were thoroughly beaten by the Court party!

This is the real state of affairs. You may depend upon its accuracy, and form your own conclusions as to the probable result.

Four foreign questions of great importance successively —and indeed, in some cases, simultaneously — occupied public attention during Palmerston's last Government; and in all of them Disraeli urged, with success, the policy of non-intervention. In regard to three of them, the Italian Risorgimento, with the corollary of the transference of Savoy and Nice from Sardinia to France, the American Civil War, and the Polish insurrection, there were certainly no sufficient British interests involved to warrant armed interference, and Disraeli's action was thoroughly beneficial. There is more doubt about the Schleswig-Holstein dispute between Germany and Denmark; and indeed, in Disraeli's opinion, decided action at an early stage might have averted the catastrophe. But by the time the matter came up for discussion in Parliament, the blunders of Russell's diplomacy had placed serious difficulties in the way of any course of action, and acquiescence in a wrong which England had failed to prevent seemed to be the least unsatisfactory outcome. In regard to all these questions, Russell had at some stage, usually with the active support of the Prime Minister, written strong despatches or taken other steps calculated to lead to armed conflict, only to draw back afterwards, not always without humiliation, under pressure from the Court, or the Cabinet, or the Opposition, or the country. His one great success, accomplished, owing to the prudence of the Court, without fighting, was materially to have advanced by his diplomacy the unity of Italy. But his mismanagement of our relations with America left the country a legacy of bitterness and the *Alabama* claims; and in regard to Poland and Denmark, his well-meant interference, followed as it was by undignified retreat, did nothing but harm to those whom he hoped to befriend. Disraeli may fairly claim to have

helped to diminish the evil consequences of the blunders
of Ministers in foreign policy, and to have done much to
secure the emergence of the country from her troubles
without serious material loss, if with some damage to her
reputation in the world.   His action was the more praise-
worthy as he was generally in opposition to the public
feeling of the moment, counselling moderation when
passions were excited; and on the two most important
questions, the American Civil War and the Schleswig-
Holstein dispute, the prejudices of the great majority of
his own party were strongly arrayed against him.

To Mrs. Brydges Willyams.

GROSVENOR GATE, *Jan.* 16, 1860. — . . . The Emperor of
the French has introduced a new system of governing mankind — by anonymous pamphlets, and by letters from himself
addressed to Mr. Reuter of the Electro-Telegraph !   Wonderful
man !   He delights England with his Protestantism and Free
Trade; and when public opinion is conciliated and regained,
he intends to propose that Savoy shall be surrendered to
France, in order to guard her fertile plains from Sardinia,
who will then be too powerful for him.   And the people of
England, who last month believed he was going to conquer
them, will also believe that.   The fact is, the Emperor is in a
scrape, but he is so clever that his scrapes are preferable to
other persons' success.

G. G., *Jan.* 28, 1860. — . . . Politics most absorbing, and
more mysterious than ever.   The Imperial Free Trader is
now going to seize Savoy and Nice.   The 'natural boundaries' of the Empire are fast developing, and in 1861 he will
be on the Rhine.   It is said that all nations that speak
French belong to France !   Our uncle at Belgium does not
like affairs.

The English people were entirely disinterested in their
strong sympathy with the Italian movement for unity,
but they had no intention of going to war to promote it ;
and they were very indignant when they discovered
that the French Emperor and people, who had actually
fought for the cause, did not propose to imitate their
disinterestedness, but to obtain an accession of territory as
a reward.   Few annexations have been better justified

than those of Savoy and Nice to France; and the violent anger which they aroused in England, and to a less degree on the Continent, would be difficult to understand, if we did not bear in mind the widespread apprehensions in 1860 of a revival by Napoleon III. of the ambitious policy of Napoleon I.   Savoy and Nice were on the French side of the Alpine range which forms the natural boundary of Italy; they were transferred as the result, not of conquest, but of a friendly arrangement between allied States; the transference was subject to a popular vote which proved in each case to be overwhelmingly in its favour; and the two provinces rapidly became thoroughly contented portions of the nation to which they were united.   Bright's exclamation in the House of Commons, 'Perish Savoy!' rather than have a war on the question between England and France, though severely reprobated at the time, contained excellent sense. Disraeli kept his head much better than the Foreign Secretary and other leading politicians on both sides.   He realised that our alliance with France could not be unilateral; and that we were bound to place a favourable construction on her policies, as we expected her to do on ours.   Accordingly, he preferred rather to criticise Ministers who failed to realise the obvious policy of France, than to attack France, who had only acted as might have been expected.   If the doctrine of 'natural boundaries' led to sanguinary wars in Europe, the blame must be laid on the shortsightedness of Ministers.   To Vitzthum, however, who was busily fanning mistrust of Napoleon in England, he talked sympathetically on January 17.

Our course is to keep a sharp watch over Palmerston and Russell, and force them to pursue our foreign policy.   For the present we are more useful and powerful in Opposition than on the Ministerial bench.   If we oppose every territorial aggrandisement on the part of France, we shall in the end paralyse Palmerston and show Napoleon that his alliance with the noble Viscount does not bring him all the tangible advantages he had expected. . . .   The most important thing

for us is to know exactly how far we can depend upon Austria. In spite of all her defeats, we regard her as the centre and nucleus of all Conservative efforts in the field of European politics. If Austria is nowhere, what can we do?[1]

Though he had begun to mistrust Napoleon's policy, Disraeli did not change his mind as to the importance of preserving the French alliance. He was, moreover, constantly fascinated by the personality of the French Emperor, and was flattered by the parallelism between their characters and careers on which the newspapers of the day were insisting. In sending Mrs. Willyams on May 6 a couple of articles of this kind, Mrs. Disraeli wrote: 'I like both, for who would not be delighted to be thought like so great a man as the Emperor? Mr. Gladstone, and many papers, all have made lately the same comparison, "the great similitude."' Earle was encouraged by Disraeli to go to Paris this spring, though not as Disraeli's 'emissary,' to see the Emperor again and sound him on his projects. He found him naturally disgusted with his treatment by England.

From Ralph A. Earle.

Secret and confidential. [PARIS, *April*, 1860.] . . . The Emperor said that nothing could be more ridiculous than the clamour which had been raised about the Swiss annexation, and, taking me to the window, where an elaborate plan of the Swiss cantons and bordering provinces of France was exposed, he showed me in detail that the new frontier would involve Switzerland in no new peril. He then continued:

'The policy which I have always wished to adopt with respect to England is this: I wish to help her where her interests are principally concerned, but in return I claim for France a corresponding consideration from her ally. If you disapprove of these annexations, which are insignificant in themselves, which are made with the consent of the Sovereign who loses them, and with that of the people whose nationality is changed — is not the inference inevitable that you will object to any expansion of France, however unexceptionable its character? These views were accepted by Lord Palmerston and Mr. Disraeli when in opposition, but since they have been Ministers their ideas are changed. . . .'

The Emperor then entered into some general considerations

[1] Vitzthum, Vol. II., pp. 21–23. See above, p. 48.

about the English alliance. . . . The English had lost a great opportunity of consolidating for ever their relations with France. If they had said, 'These annexations do not concern us. We wish well to France, and shall be glad to see her objects attained,' the whole of France would not only have accepted, but would have demanded a close alliance with England. . . .

The Italian Revolution ran a rapid course through the spring, summer, and autumn of 1860, till by winter practically the whole of Italy, with the exception of Rome and Venetia, was united under the House of Savoy.

To Mrs. Brydges Willyams.

May 14, 1860. —. . . Affairs abroad very critical, and great events may be expected every day. Garibaldi's pirate expedition[1] is a spark that will lead to a general conflagration. Who was its promoter ? . . .

HUGHENDEN, *Sept.* 16, 1860. —. . . What an immense event is the Italian Revolution ! Since 1792 we have not had such affairs. This is real history—and what an imbroglio ! A race between the red flag of Mazzini wafted on by the passions of centuries, and the cold diplomatic standard of mere Sardinian ambition. The sovereigns and statesmen of Europe have raised a spirit they will find it difficult to quell. Look out for great events.

Oct. 18, 1860. —. . . Strange news came from Naples last night; more confounding than anything that has happened. Garibaldi is like an eel. Is he playing a cross with Cavour ? Is he a Masaniello ? Is he a Washington ? A great many other questions will be asked before it is all finished.

Dec. 13, 1860. —. . . What is preparing ? A greater revolution, perhaps, in Austria, than ever occurred in France. Then it was 'the rights of *man*' ; now it is 'the rights of *nations.*'

Once I said, in *Coningsby*, there is nothing like Race : it comprises all truths. The world will now comprehend that awful truth.

Dec. 18, 1860. —. . . It is our privilege to live in a wonderful age of rapid and stirring events ; and if time, as the poets say, is not to be counted by calendars, but by incidents and sensation, all our existences will be patriarchal. Lord Mendip, a friend of my father's, used to say that by the parish register and the Peerage he was only 60 ; but, having lived through the French Revolution, he considered he was a hundred at least !

[1] The famous expedition to Sicily.

We have got Italian and Austrian Revolutions, and a great many others coming; and Eastern wars, whether in India, China, or Japan, which beat all the marvels of the Arabian Nights. . . .

The great increase of power which the rise of Italy promised to give to her friend and ally, France, perturbed the King of the Belgians, whose position could only be secure if there were a balance of power on the Continent.

From the King of the Belgians.

Private.   LAEKEN, *Dec.* 19, 1860.

MY DEAR SIR, — You will think me very ungrateful not to have acknowledged sooner your kind communication,[1] but I can plead not guilty to that. The state of Europe is very strange. There is after all a certain sameness in human affairs, but the present time is distinguished by a sort of *leger-de-main*, which is unlike to what history generally shows, and one is constantly tempted to ask: *qui trompe-t-on ici?* Much is owing to the Oriental war; it has brought about, what at all times was justly feared, an understanding between France and Russia, and has given to France a complete supremacy on the Continent.

Happily England has felt the necessity, for its own independence, of being well armed. If that had been neglected, England would have had a sort of existence on sufferance, and would have been exposed to great danger. I trust that the Conservative party will remain faithful to its policy, as it was the first that awakened to the danger. But it is not only in this case that the Conservative party is of the most vital importance; no constitutional Government can be carried on without it, and it is a great misfortune that in the present Parliament there is such a tendency to split into fragments instead of uniting for the public good.

The affairs of Italy are very strangely appreciated in England. Whatever may be the future consequences, the immediate practical result is to give to France allies against Germany, and I don't think that by so doing the real interests of England are wisely consulted. Whatever weakens still more the power of Germany exposes us also here to new dangers, and we can only see this with just apprehension.

I hope that these lines will find you well, and remain, with sentiments of the highest regard and esteem, ever, my dear sir, most faithfully yours, LEOPOLD.

[1] See above, pp. 282, 283.

To the King of the Belgians.

Dec. 23, 1860.

Sir, — Your Majesty's letter reached me only to-day, but, as I am informed that a courier leaves this for Brussels to-morrow, I will not hesitate to have the honor of addressing to you, Sir, a few lines, feeling your Majesty will pardon them for being written *currente calamo*.

The *leger-de-main* which now distinguishes public affairs, and to which your Majesty so graphically refers, appears to me attributable to this circumstance, which the English Government either does not recognise or never sufficiently appreciates.

The French Emperor, to use a homely image, always runs two hares. His first hare was the old traditionary policy of the French Cabinet: a divided Italy and French supremacy. Lord John Russell thought that in bringing about Italian unity he had checkmated Buonaparte; but he only threw the Emperor on his second hare, a much more dangerous animal — *i.e.*, natural headship of the Latin race; Venetia secured by France to Sardinia; and an offensive and defensive alliance between France and Italy, in order that France, in possession of their united resources, may obtain some great object.

Had the Treaty of Villafranca been sedulously supported, instead of systematically decried, by the English Government, there might have been a resting-point, perhaps for some years; and during the interval all our energies might have been applied to what should be the great object of English statesmen, viz., to terminate or at least to counteract the understanding between France and Russia.

At present, if all is dark and perplexing to your Majesty, what must it be to me?

There are no doubt ample materials in Italy, if France chooses to recur to her first policy, to disturb, perhaps destroy, Italian unity in the spring. The coast (Liguria) is republican; the country reactionary; and as for the great towns, each of them not only desires, but *expects*, to be the capital. But these elements to be effective require French manipulation; and it is to be feared that the blind exertions of England will force France to the larger and more dangerous scheme.

Mundy, our Admiral, says the King spoke much against the French, praised the English (though complaining of the brigade), and said that Lord J.'s despatch was 'plus qu'amical c'était magnifique.' When Mundy left the presence, the King shook his hand so violently that he broke his nail. He does

not think favorably of the King's prospects; he says he never witnessed so frigid a reception as that of Victor Emmanuel at the Opera.

One thing is quite clear: Napoleon meditates next year some accession of territory. Otherwise he would not court the English people. One of his principles is always to distinguish between them and their Government, in the hope that, when he makes the great *coup*, public opinion in England may restrain the English Government from resisting him.

Mr. Cobden enforces these views very much on the Emperor, and we must remember that, to the Emperor, Mr Cobden is the Minister of the Queen of Great Britain. This is another of the injurious consequences of that 'untoward affair.'

With respect to the state of the Conservative party in the House of Commons, I can report very favorably of it. It has become very consolidated during the recess, and even increased its numbers by some elections. Our characteristic ignorance respecting foreign politics renders it, however, extremely difficult to direct this immense power to an effective and beneficial end; but the difficulty is only one of time, and opportunities must be taken gradually and skilfully to guide their sentiments.

On the 5th of February, on the Address, such an occasion would naturally offer, when I am expected to speak generally on affairs without contemplating any trial of strength. I trust I do not count entirely without reason on the condescension of your Majesty in assisting me in the interval by your counsel.

The Roman Catholic party, as I anticipated in my last, has made an overture to me for the overthrow of the Government. I discouraged the proposition, though with courtesy.

In his speech on the Address in 1861, Disraeli followed the line of thought suggested in this correspondence, and conjured up a picture of the Emperor of the French coming forward as the head of the Latin race, the emancipator of Italy, with a million bayonets behind him, and in a position to dominate Europe — all through the recklessness of Russell's diplomacy: the 'candid' policy which substituted a speech in the House of Commons for what in old times, in the days of secret diplomacy, would have been the whisper of Downing Street. On the other hand, he called special attention to the French support of the Papal States against the Sardinian Government. 'The contemplated capital of Italy is not in the

possession of the Italians. In this age of jubilant nationality Rome is still garrisoned by the Gauls.'

Regarding the Pope, as he did, as 'an old man on a Semitic throne,' baffling 'the modern Attilas,' Disraeli did not share the general wish of Englishmen for the overthrow of the Temporal Power; and this attitude helped to secure for him not a few Roman Catholic votes which would otherwise have gone to the Liberals. The Pope told Odo Russell in July, 1859: 'Mr. Disraeli was my friend; I regret him.' Earle visited Rome in February, 1861, and reported to Disraeli: 'The Cardinal Minister of the Holy Father sends you a great many messages of compliment, and his Sovereign blessed me on hearing me mentioned as your secretary.' Two months later Earle went to see Cardinal Wiseman, and obtained his good offices towards a working alliance between the Conservative leaders and the Roman Catholic vote in Parliament.

From Ralph A. Earle.

St. Leonards, *April* 26, 1861. — . . . The Cardinal, I am sorry to say, is looking very ill, being here for his health and attending to no business of any kind. He promises to do all in his power, 'as he knows well that, by helping us, he would please those whom it is his highest duty and pleasure to serve.'

In Ireland, he says, there is a very good feeling towards us, and some of those who declined his invitation to help us in 1859 held out hopes of eventual assistance, which is now likely to be realised.

Monsell, Bowyer, and Hennessy, he thinks a very good combination, as they influence three different coteries. The first has great influence with the Irish Bishops and clergy.

The Cardinal . . . concluded by observing that we were quite right in looking to the R.C.'s for our majority, for they could give it us. If there were any prospect of a Government being formed that would carry out a respectable foreign policy, the Catholic constituents and their members would all support it.

Of great exertion he is not capable, and he cannot put himself forward in politics, but quietly he will do whatever may occur to him as likely to serve us. . . .

Instead of putting himself at the head of a militant Franco-Italian alliance, the Emperor of the French, under the influence of the French clergy and of the Empress, resolutely supported the Pope, and Earle reported from Florence towards the close of the year that ' the failure of the Whigs to dislodge the French from Rome is complete.' The cause of Italian unity had another set-back this year in the death of Cavour.

To Mrs. Brydges Willyams.

GROSVENOR GATE, *March* 16, 1861. — . . . An immense suspense in foreign affairs ; but what questions ! The temporal existence of the Pope : the union of the American States : the dissolution of the Ottoman Empire : the unity of Italy : each of them sufficient for a generation ! It is a privilege to live in such an age ; to say nothing of ' Essays and Reviews,' which convulses Christendom, and seems to have shaken down the spire of Chichester Cathedral.

HOUSE OF COMMONS, *April* 11, 1861. — . . . When I was Chancellor of the Exchequer, ten years ago, Cavour was travelling in this country, in order to study the art of taxation, and had letters of introduction to me ; and I knew him well.

CARLTON CLUB, *June* 11, 1861. — The death of Cavour is an immense event ! It is impossible to see the end of the effects it will produce. . . . He was a thorough Italian statesman of the middle ages ; most fertile in device, and utterly unscrupulous ; an almost unrivalled union of subtilty and vigor. . . .

HOUSE OF COMMONS, *Wednesday, June* 19, 1861.— . . . Yesterday, according to royal appointment, I paid my visit to the King of the Belgians at Buckingham Palace, and had a very interesting audience of an hour. The King, who is a statesman, talked to me very freely on the present state of affairs, which remain most critical, and probably will for several years. This is an age of great and rapid events : their quick succession as remarkable as their importance ; and, to a certain extent, mutually mitigating their exciting consequences. The restless and revolutionary spirits, distracted by the choice of materials, pause in the selection ; not from satiety, but from sheer perplexity to decide where most mischief can be accomplished. Garibaldi does not know where to begin — Venice or Hungary — and talks of going to America ! . . .

Disraeli's view of the subsequent treatment of the
Italian question by Palmerston and Russell is shown in an
amusing passage from a speech which he delivered in 1863:

Since the death of Cavour, the programme of the national
party in Italy has been 'movement, development, unity,
Rome'—immense words, *verba sesquipedalia*, used by men
of very little minds and very slight resources. What have
they leant upon? They have leant upon the support of
England. In the English Parliament some gentlemen, if
not with the absolute co-operation of, at least with social encouragement from, the noble lord, constantly brought forward
the subject of the state of Italy. It was let out like a bag-
fox, and followed with a full halloo. Every year we had
the noble lord presented to us as the regenerator of Italy,
the saviour of the country; and the performance ended with
invectives directed against the Pope, and a promise . . .
that Rome should be the capital of a United Italy before the
end of the session. . . . And now, where has all this ended?
Cavour withdrawn from the scene — no commanding mind in
Italy; France naturally jealous of our uncertain and irritating
policy; Rome alarmed; Rome and France leagued against
the unity of Italy; the noble lord conducting a policy of
words, speeches, and despatches; and the Italian Government,
without a leader, still hanging on the accents of English
Ministers, perpetually adopting a line which nothing could
justify except commanding genius and commanding legions,
and holding out to the people the immediate expectation of
Rome being made their capital by the overpowering interference of their English ally.

It may be added that Disraeli, true to his disapproval
of the 'piratical' means by which Italy had been unified,
and anxious to preserve the threatened authority of
the Pope in Rome, absolutely refused to meet Garibaldi
when London went wild over that wonderful Italian's visit
in April, 1864. Derby and other Tory leaders paid their
respects to the visitor at Stafford House or elsewhere;
but when Mrs. Gladstone asked the Disraelis to come to
a party at Carlton House Terrace to meet him, the reply
was a polite but firm 'no'; and the same curt answer
was sent to all similar invitations. Gladstone overlooked
Garibaldi's hostility to religion in view of his services to
liberty; Disraeli regarded him as essentially the foe of

constituted authority in both Church and State, and declined to countenance the orgy of enthusiasm with which
he was welcomed in England both by the populace and
by Society.

As the Italian question became less acute, the American
difficulty increased.   Disraeli wrote to Northcote on
September 12, 1861: 'Our friend Jonathan seems in a
pretty state; it's like the failure of some immense house;
one can hardly realise the enormous results. . . . It is a
privilege to live in such a pantomimic age of glittering
illusions and startling surprises.' Disraeli's view that
the United States were breaking down was the general
opinion among the governing and educated classes in
this country ; but he had the wisdom, denied to other
leading statesmen, to keep his view to himself and his
private friends.   His 'thoughtfulness and statesmanship'
were shown throughout, as John Bright confessed in Parliament, by not saying a word from the front Opposition
bench likely to create difficulty with America.   The
irritation provoked by the sympathy widely expressed in
England for the South bade fair to lead to war this
autumn, when relations were strained over the seizure
by the Federals of Confederate envoys on the British
steamship *Trent*. Happily, the despatch containing the
British demand for their release was so modified in its
language by the dying Prince Consort as to facilitate
the withdrawal of the United States Government from an
untenable position.

In the debate on the Address in 1862, Disraeli, who
had before laid stress on the duty of diplomacy to say
rough things, if they were necessary, kindly, and not
kind things roughly, praised the firm but temperate
course of the Government ; and he added some happy
words of recognition of the honourable manner in which
America had offered reparation. 'When I consider the
great difficulties which the statesmen of North America
have to encounter, when I consider what I may call the
awful emergency which they have been summoned

suddenly to meet, and which, without giving any opinion upon the causes of these transactions, I would venture to say they have met manfully and courageously, I think it becomes England, in dealing with the Government of the United States, to extend to all which they say at least a generous interpretation, and to their acts a liberal construction.' He was determined that Great Britain should preserve neutrality, and should avoid occasions of provocation and irritation ; and in this spirit had protested in the previous session against the precaution which the Government had taken of sending 3,000 men to Canada. This, he held, was not an act of sound policy, as the United States would infer from it that the British Government looked forward with suspicion to the contingency of hostilities. He had another ground for objection, as he explained in a further debate in 1862, that to send troops damped the ardour of the Canadians by indicating a desire to monopolise their defence. The result had been that Canada had refused to pass a Militia Bill. Adderley, the Colonial Reformer, wished to have Canada told that, unless she took measures for self-defence, the British troops would be withdrawn ; but Disraeli, who said he trusted to the sense and spirit of the Canadians, would not go that length.

To Charles E. Adderley.

GROSVENOR GATE, *Jan.* 26, 1862. —. . . You have placed your views before the country in a clear and complete light, but what is taking place convinces me that the theme is beyond the domain of mere reasoning, however just and wise. The passions of the people are very high at the present moment, and if the Ministry chose to send 50,000 men to Canada they would be supported.

When our Colonial System was reconstructed, either the Colonies should have had direct representation, or the military prerogatives of the Crown should have been so secured that the faculty of self-defence in the Colonies should always have been considerable. . . .

Foreign politics and foreign personalities naturally bulked largely in Disraeli's correspondence at this time.

To Mrs. Brydges Willyams.

Private. GROSVENOR GATE, *July* 8, 1862. — If it had not been for the Court being in deep mourning, and the unceasing summer rain, London, this season, would have been a Carnival. There are so many great sights, and such gatherings of innumerable thousands! Of all these, however, I think the most remarkable was the Show of the Royal Agricultural Society. It gave me an idea of one of those great Tartar hordes of which we read — of Genghis Khan and Attila. It was so vast, so busy, and so bovine!

The Pacha of Egypt,[1] who speaks very good French, is the royalty who most exhibits himself. The newspapers have told you of the banquet which the Lord Mayor gave him; and we also met His Highness at a state dinner given to him by the Speaker of the House of Commons and Lady Charlotte Denison, though that was a very small and very select party.

That happened to me which, a year ago, many would have betted 100 to 1 would not have happened to any Englishman in the year of grace 1862. I was asked to dine on the same day by the two rival French Princes — the Duke d'Aumale and the Prince Napoleon! I fulfilled my previous engagement with His *Royal* Highness, but, two days after, I had a long and interesting audience with His *Imperial* Highness, who conversed very frankly and very confidentially on great affairs. The Prince is a true Buonaparte in mind and visage; a very striking likeness of the great Emperor, and all his charlatanry of manner and expression — for he is picturesque and eloquent. On the other hand, the Bourbon Prince is thought to resemble, both in character and physically, his great ancestor, Henri IV.

Private. GROSVENOR GATE, *July* 26, 1862. — The whirl — political and social — begins a little to slacken its fascinating velocity, and the sudden burst of sunshine and blue skies begins to make people remember that there is another and a better world ' out of town.' We have never been home for eight months. . . .

Notwithstanding the Court being in seclusion, London has been full of royal blood this season. The Prince of Carignan, the Prince of Orange, the Princes of Saxony, *cum multis aliis* — all Royal Highnesses; and one *crowned* head, the Grand Duke of Saxe-Weimar. Strange to say, this, though the greatest, was my guest — a great honor. I knew him in early years, when he was Crown Prince only; very literary and accomplished, and proud of the German Athens over which his father ruled, and where Wieland and Herder, Goethe

---

[1] The Khedive Ismail.

HUGHENDEN MANOR-HOUSE.

and Schiller, blazed at the same time. He deigns to be an admirer of my writings, and has often asked me to Weimar, which, unfortunately, I have never visited. So, instead of my being H.R.H.'s guest, he deigned to honor my roof, and met a very choice party — among them Lord and Lady Derby, the Duke of Hamilton, the Russian Ambassador, etc. I shall enclose you the bill of fare, if I can find it. It may amuse a moment. . . .

HUGHENDEN MANOR, *Dec.* 9, 1862. —. . . . They say that the Greeks, resolved to have an English King, in consequence of the refusal of Prince Alfred to be their monarch, intend to elect Lord Stanley. If he accepts the charge, I shall lose a powerful friend and colleague. It is a dazzling adventure for the House of Stanley, but they are not an imaginative race, and, I fancy they will prefer Knowsley to the Parthenon, and Lancashire to the Attic plain.

It is a privilege to live in this age of rapid and brilliant events. What an error to consider it an utilitarian age! It is one of infinite romance. Thrones tumble down and crowns are offered, like a fairy tale, and the most powerful people in the world, male and female, a few years back, were adventurers, exiles, and demireps.

Vive la bagatelle!

GROSVENOR GATE, *Wednesday, Jan.* 21, 1863. — We are now going to Hatfield, where we shall make a rather longer visit than usual, as I have a great deal to do; and Lord and Lady Salisbury, who are real friends, let me do what I like, and not come down to breakfast, and all that sort of thing, so that I can work, and prepare for the coming campaign. A week of quiet mornings is what I now require, in order to digest all I have heard and planned during the last fortnight. I could not well go to Hughenden, as it is full of workmen, and I have this advantage at Hatfield, that it is a palace, full of company, changing every day, and all the most distinguished persons in the country, especially of my own party, in turn appearing. I meet and converse with all these, after the solitude of the morning, every day at dinner, and in the evening, which is very advantageous and suggestive. It allows me to feel the pulse of the ablest on all the questions of the day. God bless you!

Feb. 7, 1863. —. . . . My party was distinguished and brilliant, and I am going to give a series of dinners to my Parliamentary friends of both Houses. The members of the House of Commons like very much to meet members of the House of Lords who have themselves, in their time, sat in the House of Commons. It is like old schoolfellows meeting; the memories of the past are interesting, and from old

experience they understand all the fun of the present. The Duke of Buckingham, the Earl of Shrewsbury, and the Marquis of Normanby, who were all of them a long time in the House of Commons, dine with me on Wednesday, and meet a number of the Lower House.

Lord Derby seems very well, and in good spirits. His conduct during the Lancashire distress appears to have gained him golden opinions from all parties. His subscription of many thousands was munificent, but his administrative talent in managing the vast sums entrusted to the Central Committee by the nation not less admirable. . . .

The Greeks really want to make my friend Lord Stanley their King. This beats any novel. I think he ought to take the crown, but he will not. Had I his youth, I would not hesitate, even with the earldom of Derby in the distance.

The indiscretions of leading statesmen about the American War culminated in a remarkable utterance by Gladstone in the course of a triumphal progress — the first of many such progresses — which he made upon the Tyne in October, 1862. He said: 'There is no doubt that Jefferson Davis and other leaders of the South have made an army; they are making, it appears, a navy; and they have made what is more than either, they have made a nation.' The world naturally jumped to the conclusion that the British Government were about to afford recognition to the Confederate States; and Cornewall Lewis, speaking a week later at Hereford, had specifically to contradict the inference. Disraeli, in his speech on the Address in 1863, after animadverting on Gladstone's apparent departure from the policy of neutrality, said that, for his part, while he had the greatest respect for the Southern States, he felt that there was due from England to the existing authorities in America a large measure of deference in the difficulties which they had to encounter. He had accordingly exerted whatever influence he might possess in endeavouring to dissuade his friends from embarrassing Her Majesty's Government in their position of 'politic and dignified reserve.' He made some unconventional reflections on the general situation.

I have always looked upon the struggle in America in the light of a great revolution. Great revolutions, whatever may be their alleged causes, are not likely to be commenced or to be concluded with precipitation. Before the civil war commenced the United States were colonies; because we should not forget that such communities do not cease to be colonies because they are independent. They were not only colonies, but they were colonising, and they existed under all the conditions of colonial life except that of mere political dependence. But even before the civil war I think that all impartial observers must have been convinced that in that community there were smouldering elements which indicated the possibility of a change, and perhaps of a violent change. The immense increase of population; the still greater increase of wealth; the introduction of foreign races in large numbers as citizens, not brought up under the laws and customs which were adapted to a more limited, and practically a more homogeneous race; the character of the political constitution, consequent perhaps on these circumstances; the absence of any theatre for the ambitious and refined intellects of the country, which deteriorated public spirit and lowered public morality; and, above all, the increasing influence of the United States upon the political fortunes of Europe — these were all circumstances which indicated the more than possibility that the mere colonial character of these communities might suddenly be violently subverted, and those imperial characteristics appear which seem to be the destiny of man. I cannot conceal from myself the conviction that, whoever in this House may be young enough to live to witness the ultimate consequences of this civil war, will see, whenever the waters have subsided, a different America from that which was known to our fathers, and even from that of which this generation has had so much experience. It will be an America of armies, of diplomacy, of rival states and manœuvring Cabinets, of frequent turbulence, and probably of frequent wars.

Two years later, when the Civil War was coming to an end in the victory of the North, Disraeli repeated [1] his warning that America was greatly changing, and acquiring a centralising Government. The balance of power could no longer be confined to Europe, that old Europe to which the United States looked with a want of sympathy. But he held the Americans to be eminently a sagacious people, and he disregarded the violence of their meetings and journals.

[1] March 13, 1865.

I look upon these expressions of opinion as I should look upon those strange and fantastic drinks of which we hear so much, and which are such favourites on the other side of the Atlantic; and I should as soon suppose this rowdy rhetoric was the expression of the real feelings of the American people as that these potations formed the aliment and nutriment of their bodies. . . . The democracy of America must not be confounded with the democracy of the Old World. It is not formed of the scum of turbulent cities, neither is it merely a section of an exhausted middle class, which speculates in stocks, and calls that progress. It is a territorial democracy. Aristotle, who has taught us most of the wise things we know, never said a wiser one than this — that the cultivators of the soil are the least inclined to sedition and to violent courses.

The Civil War has certainly changed America, and produced some of the imperial characteristics, notably a tendency to governmental centralisation, which Disraeli anticipated. But the martial enthusiasm, except in the palmy days of Theodore Roosevelt and the Spanish War, has by no means reached the height which he predicted; though the universal upheaval in Europe since July, 1914, has at last driven the United States to take naval and military preparation seriously in hand.

Palmerston's Government proposed in 1863 to get rid of the perpetual difficulties of the administration of the Ionian Islands by yielding to the wishes of the islanders to be incorporated with Greece; provided that Greece, which had just passed through a revolution, should elect a King who might be expected to adopt a constitutional and peaceful policy. Disraeli, whose action in sending Gladstone as High Commissioner in 1858 had undoubtedly precipitated this solution, became alive, when it was too late, to the military importance of the islands to a Mediterranean Power, and protested vigorously against the sentimental grounds on which cession was advocated. He reminded Parliament that the islands originally came into our possession by the right of conquest.

Professors and rhetoricians find a system for every contingency and a principle for every chance; but you are not going, I hope, to leave the destinies of the British Empire

to prigs and pedants.   The statesmen who construct, and
the warriors who achieve, are only influenced by the instinct
of power, and animated by the love of country.   Those are
the feelings and those the methods which form empires.   There
may be grave questions as to the best mode of obtaining
wealth ; some may be in favour of protection of domestic and
colonial interests, some of unrestricted competition, or some
of what I am quite surprised have now become so modish —
commercial treaties and reciprocal arrangements for the
advantage of commercial exchange, propositions which used
to be scouted in this House ; but there can be no question
either in or out of this House that the best mode of preserving
wealth is power.   A country, and especially a maritime
country, must get possession of the strong places of the world
if it wishes to contribute to its power.

There is sound sense in these general principles, stated
with a refreshing absence of cant ; and undoubtedly Corfu,
and some of the other islands, have a military importance
of the same kind as that of Malta, Gibraltar, and the
Cape of Good Hope, though in different degree.   But
the difficulties of governing the islands, which had been
aggravated by Gladstone's mission and its results, were
extreme ; the possession of Gibraltar and Malta might
well be considered sufficient to secure our Mediterranean
position without Corfu ; and it was good policy, as well
as in accord with liberal and scholarly sentiment, to
encourage the rising Greek kingdom, which had shown
its anxiety to stand well with England by a practically
unanimous offer of the crown to Queen Victoria's second
son, Prince Alfred, Duke of Edinburgh.   The election —
on Prince Alfred's refusal, and the failure of negotiations
with Stanley and others — of Prince George of Denmark,
brother of the Princess of Wales, tended to insure the
friendly interest of both the Court and the people of this
country.

To Mrs. Brydges Willyams.

House of Commons, *Monday, Feb.* 23, 1863. — Nothing
thought of but Poland.   It recalls the days of Thaddeus of
Warsaw, which I dare say you read with a flashing eye and
a flushing cheek.

The cards seem most unexpectedly to throw the Rhine into the grasp of Napoleon. How he must regret the disciplined troops that he has sent, upon a Quixote adventure, to the land of yellow fever and black vomit![1]

Who is to be King of Poland? That's the question now. Poor Greece has not yet been furnished with a crown. Life becomes like a fairy tale, and our intimate acquaintances turn into Sovereign Princes, who the day before were M.P.'s and guardsmen, and fox-hunters.

I am content with being leader of the Opposition — at present an office more of thought than action; but the spring will return.

With the coming to the front in 1863 of the Polish and Danish questions, the defects of Russell's foreign policy could not be concealed. Derby expressed the views of many who generally supported the Government when he wrote to Disraeli in the beginning of the year : 'Denmark, Greece, the Ionian Islands, the Maltese scheme for the Pope, are all points in which Johnny has made more blunders than I had thought it possible to crowd into the space of a few months ; ' and in November: 'Johnny seems to me to have got into such a muddle in every part of the world that I do not see how we are to keep our hands off him. . . . His dealings with Denmark, Poland, and America, have been such as to disgust all parties with whom he has had to do.' A policy of 'meddle and muddle' he afterwards called it in Parliament; while Disraeli was sarcastic over 'the annual harvest of autumnal indiscretions.'

Disraeli entered into the generous feeling of sympathy which pervaded England during this year 1863 on behalf of the Poles, whom the oppression of Russia had goaded into insurrection. But he knew history too well, and was too open-minded, to suppose that the right was all on one side ; and he saw no reason why England should engage in war for a cause that was so little hers. He remembered that similar troubles between Poland and Russia had occurred before, and that the settled policy of England had been not to intervene in arms. He said

[1] The ill-fated expedition to Mexico. See below, p. 348.

in the House of Commons that, if the partition of Poland was a great crime, it was a crime shared by the Polish people, as their national existence could not have been destroyed without some faults on their side. But he strongly eulogised Castlereagh for having striven, though in vain, on behalf of Polish independence at the Congress of Vienna; and he desired that Ministers should make use of their treaty rights to forward a policy favourable to the Poles. That, however, did not necessarily mean war, and he trusted that beneficial changes might be effected without an appeal to 'the last arbiter of human destiny.' Polish 'patriots' abroad, however, came in for his scorn. He said:

I always shrink from any expression of political senti-mentalism. I do not know any people who have suffered so much from political sentimentalism as the Poles. Year after year there have been people living in Paris and London, some of them in a state of comparative luxury, stimulating their unfortunate countrymen in Poland to fruitless insurrection and to useless revolt; and all this time we have been favoured by them with expressions of feeling which, if, expressions of feeling could effect the salvation of nations, have certainly been abundant and profuse.

Russell, ever a friend of human liberty, made drastic demands on the Government of Russia, including a com-plete amnesty for the insurgents, national representation and administration, and recognition of Polish as the offi-cial language. He sought and obtained the co-operation of France and Austria in these demands; but Disraeli sounded in the House a note of caution. The proposals showed no prescience; only a very sanguine politician could believe that Russia would accept them; if accepted, they would raise a phantom of Polish independence, which would lead in due course to a situation similar to the present. But Russell pushed on, and France, which had hitherto shown great reserve, though she was more interested than England in Poland, followed him. Dis-raeli described the fiasco in a speech in 1864:

What must have been the astonishment of the Emperor of the French when he found the English Government embracing the cause of Poland with extraordinary ardour? The noble lord the Secretary of State and the noble lord the First Minister, but especially the former, announced this policy as if it were a policy new to the consideration of statesmen and likely to lead to immense results. He absolutely served a notice to quit on the Emperor of Russia. He sent a copy of this despatch to all the Courts of Europe which were signatories of the Treaty of Vienna, and invited them to follow his example. From the King of Portugal down to the King of Sweden, there was not a signatory of that treaty who was not, as it were, clattering at the palace gates of St. Petersburg, and calling the Tsar to account respecting the affairs of Poland. . . . Is it at all remarkable that the French Government and the French people, cautious as they were before, should have responded to such invitations and such stimulating proposals? We know how the noble lord fooled them to the top of their bent. The House recollects the six propositions to which the attention of the Emperor of Russia was called in the most peremptory manner. . . . An impression pervaded Europe that there was to be a general war, and that England, France, and Austria were united to restore Poland.

The House remembers the end of all this; it remembers the reply of the Russian Minister,[1] couched in a tone of haughty sarcasm and of indignation that deigned to be ironical. There was then but one step to take, according to the French Government, and that was action. They appealed to that England which had herself thus set the example of agitation on the subject; and England, wisely as I think, recurred to her traditionary policy, the Government confessing that it was a momentary indiscretion which had animated her councils for three or four months; that they never meant anything more than words; and a month afterwards, I believe, they sent to St. Petersburg an obscure despatch which may be described as an apology. But this did not alter the position of the French Government and the French Emperor. The Emperor had been induced by us to hold out promises which he could not fulfil. He was placed in a false position towards both the people of Poland and the people of France.[2]

The vicissitudes of the Polish question were reflected in Disraeli's autumn letters.

---

[1] The reply was that Russell was not accurately informed of what was passing in Poland, and that Russia was ready to assume the responsibility before God and man.   [2] July 4, 1864.

To Mrs. Brydges Willyams.

Confidential. GROSVENOR GATE, *July* 21, 1863. — Just when I was anticipating tranquillity and repose, the affairs of the Continent have assumed so serious a character that the worst may be anticipated. For the last fortnight we have received accounts of the most alarming nature, and they have entirely absorbed the attention both of Lord Derby and myself. Lord Napier, our Ambassador at St. Petersburg, says we are again 'drifting into war.'

A war in the centre of Europe, on the pretext of restoring Poland, is a general war, and a long one. The map of Europe will be much changed when it is concluded, but I doubt whether the name of Poland will appear in it.

All the great questions of the day are still unsolved, and the materials for the infernal cauldron are plentiful.

The Rothschilds, who have contracted two loans this year, one to Russia, and the other to Italy — the latter the largest on record, more than thirty millions, and the Russian fifteen — are naturally very nervous.

The state of affairs is enough to shake anyone who has any degree of responsibility. It is the reason I have not written to you, and why my letter now is so little gay.

HUGHENDEN, *Aug.* 7, 1863. — . . . Our Government, frightened, seems to be leaving France in the lurch. There will be no war this year. That's something!

Oct. 17. — . . . The troubles and designs of the French Emperor are aggravated and disturbed by the death of Billault, his only Parliamentary debater, and a first-rate one. With for the first time a real opposition to encounter, and formed of the old trained speakers of Louis Philippe's reign, in addition to the young democracy of oratory, which the last revolution has itself produced, the inconveniences, perhaps the injuries, of this untimely decease, are incalculable. It may even force, by way of distraction, the Emperor into war.

Our own Ministry have managed these affairs very badly, according to their friends. The Polish question is a diplomatic Frankenstein, created, out of cadaverous remnants, by the mystic blundering of Lord Russell.

At present the peace of the world has been preserved, not by statesmen, but by capitalists. For the last three months it has been a struggle between the secret societies and the European millionaires. Rothschild hitherto has won; but the death of Billault may be as fatal for him as the poignard of a Polish patriot: for, I believe, in that part of the world they are called patriots, though in Naples only brigands. . . .

To Lord Derby.

HUGHENDEN MANOR, *Oct.* 30, 1863. — I am very sorry to hear of the gout, but I hope only a light cavalry attack, and that you will be even better, when it has departed. . . .

From what I hear, the Polish affair is virtually extinct — so much for recognising the rights of the insurrectionists as belligerents. The only result of the Polish insurrection has been that Gortchakoff, who, a little more than a year ago, was to have been displaced, in order to secure England and Austria, has become the most popular and powerful Minister of the day. I think John Russell has exposed himself throughout this. Very priggish and pedantic — a policy which was neither flesh, fish, nor fowl, nor etc. . . .

Sir Henry Holland, who has just returned from a visit of six weeks to the Dis-United States, speaks, with wonder, of the splendor and magnificence of life in New York. It is alike glaring and incomprehensible. He has seen nothing like it in any European capital. He was received with equal hospitality. . . .

To Mrs. Brydges Willyams.

HUGHENDEN MANOR, *Nov.* 5, 1863. — . . . The 'great Imperial Sphinx' is at this moment speaking. I shall not know the mysterious utterances until to-morrow, and shall judge of his conduct as much by his silence as his words. The world is very alarmed and very restless. Although England appears to have backed out of the possible war, there are fears that the French ruler has outwitted us, and that by an alliance with Austria, and the aid of the Italian armies, he may cure the partition of Poland by the partition of Prussia!

Austria, in that case, to regain Silesia, which Frederick the Great won, a century ago, from Maria Theresa; France to have the Rhine; and Galicia and Posen to be restored to Poland. If this happen, it will give altogether a new form and color to European politics. The Queen is much alarmed for the future throne of her daughter, the Princess Royal of Prussia; but as the war will be waged for the relief of Poland, of which England has unwisely approved, and to which, in theory, she is pledged, we shall really be checkmated, and scarcely could find an excuse to interfere, even if the nation wished.

So you see there is a good deal on the cards. . . . Adieu! we shall soon meet.[1]

----

[1] Disraeli's last letter to Mrs. Willyams, who died Nov. 11. See Vol. III., ch. 13.

Napoleon was not the danger to Europe that Disraeli, who always exaggerated his power and ability, conceived him to be. But he was able to exercise a decisive influence on the next important question that engaged the attention of our statesmen. By declining to intervene by force on behalf of Denmark against Austria and Prussia, he nullified the diplomatic efforts of Russell and Palmerston, and left to England only the alternatives of fighting alone or an inglorious retreat.

In a letter to Earle in November, Disraeli made the curiously unfortunate remark that 'Prussia, without nationality, the principle of the day, is clearly the subject for partition.' Under the far-seeing guidance of her newly appointed Minister, Bismarck, Prussia was just about to utilize the principle of nationality in so masterly a fashion as to unite all the German peoples, except those who dwelt in Austria, under her own hegemony. Bismarck had himself, with the frankness that was on some occasions one of his diplomatic weapons as much as was duplicity on others, outlined his policy to Disraeli at a party at Brunnow's in 1862. His words were:

I shall soon be compelled to undertake the conduct of the Prussian Government. My first care will be to reorganise the army, with or without the help of the Landtag. . . . As soon as the army shall have been brought into such a condition as to inspire respect, I shall seize the first best pretext to declare war against Austria, dissolve the German Diet, subdue the minor States, and give national unity to Germany under Prussian leadership. I have come here to say this to the Queen's Ministers.

Disraeli had been so impressed at the moment that, after repeating Bismarck's conversation to Vitzthum, he added: 'Take care of that man! He means what he says.'[1] The Schleswig-Holstein question gave Bismarck his opportunity. Both duchies were governed by the King of Denmark, though Holstein was wholly, and Schleswig partially, German in population; and Holstein indeed was part of the German Confederation. This somewhat

[1] Vitzthum, Vol. II., p. 172.

artificial arrangement, which had given rise to popular discontent both in Germany and in Holstein, and had led to a German invasion in 1848,[1] was formally ratified, though not guaranteed, by the Treaty of London in 1852 — a treaty concluded by the first Derby-Disraeli Administration, but founded on a protocol signed in 1850 by Palmerston, as Russell's Foreign Minister. The signatories to the treaty were England, France, Austria, Prussia, Russia, Sweden, and Denmark, but not the German Confederation, the body which had taken the lead in agitating for the annexation of the duchies on the ground of nationality. Austria and Prussia not only signed this treaty, confirming the union of the duchies with Denmark, but had of late pointedly dissociated themselves from the nationalist movement in Germany. Then, in 1863, Bismarck intervened, changed the current of Prussian and Austrian policy, and himself took the lead of the German movement. The death of the Danish King, and a disputed succession in the duchies, greatly forwarded his diplomacy. Russell endeavoured to mediate, but found Denmark as obstinate as the German Powers were determined. The German Powers took up arms, and by February, 1864, both Holstein and Schleswig were in the occupation of their troops.

At the close of the session of 1863 Palmerston had stated in Parliament that, if the rights and independence of Denmark were attacked, those who made the attempt would find that 'it would not be Denmark alone with which they would have to contend'; and Russell's despatches abounded in similar menaces. But Russell's diplomacy, under Palmerston's supervision, was so mismanaged as to insure that it was England who would find herself alone if she endeavoured to vindicate in arms the Treaty of London. The tactless treatment of the Polish question had irritated both Russia and France, her co-signatories, without helping the Poles. It had caused Russia to gravitate to Prussia; it had placed

[1] See Vol. III., pp. 184–186.

France in a false position.   She had been ready to resort
to arms for Poland; England drew back.   There, as in
the case of Italy, France would have been fighting for
the cause of nationality.   England now invited her to
fight against that cause; Napoleon, whose proposal of
a European Congress had been curtly declined by Russell,
not unnaturally refused.   Russell's blunders had reduced
his country to a position of hopeless isolation; and as,
apart from Russell and Palmerston, the prevailing feeling
in the Cabinet was against a rash adventure, an endeavour
was made to settle the matter by compromise at a Conference in London.

Public feeling in England was strongly in favour of
Denmark, as a small State bullied by two of the Great
Powers.   The Manchester School were, of course, against
war; but there was a war party among the Whigs, and
a strong current in favour of forcible intervention
throughout the Conservative party.   Robert Cecil advocated this course in the *Quarterly Review* for January
and April, 1864.   John Manners wrote to Disraeli: 'I
suspect Government will side with Denmark, and, if
Germany persists, enter upon the *most popular*, the
easiest, and the *cheapest* war (for it can be waged by
our navy alone) of the century.   Palmerston will then
become a virtual dictator, and we shall not even have
the poor consolation of having forced upon him the policy
which will have restored his popularity.'   He was anxious
that the party should announce 'a decided Danish
policy.'   Such being the temper of the country and of
the Conservative party, a great responsibility was laid
upon the Tory leaders, whose attitude would turn the
scale.   Disraeli, though he strongly approved of diplomatic action on behalf of Denmark, and was keenly alive
to the disadvantage of having the German power established at the mouth of the Elbe, saw no sufficient occasion
for war.   He wrote to Sir George Sinclair on January 20,
1864: 'An English Government that, in its wisdom, goes
to war with Germany, must make France the mistress

of Europe'; and Mrs. Disraeli declined to associate
herself in February with a committee to help wounded
Danes, on the ground that Disraeli feared the step might
'be embarrassing, and rather tend to inflame heats, than
allay them, at this moment of excitement.' Derby, less
decidedly, took the same line; being influenced in part
by the Queen, whose sympathies were with Germany,
and who invited her late Prime Minister to Osborne to
impress her views upon him.

While the Conference of London was sitting, Derby
feared that Disraeli's anxiety for peace, and for the
confusion of Ministers, might have led him into unguarded communications with German and Austrian
diplomatists.

To Lord Derby.

Confidential. GROSVENOR GATE, *May* 13, 1864. — Conversations with Bernstorff are, in general, so insignificant
that I have difficulty in reproducing to myself the one to
which you refer, though it was so recent.

On Tuesday night at Apponyi's, just as I was going away,
he seized me, himself in much excitement, though more
stupid than usual, if that be possible.

I can only recall the following remarks on my part, which
formed any exception to the platitudes I usually bestow on
him.

He was evidently in a great fright about war. I said:
'Why, an armistice is the first step to peace.' He reminding
me that it was only for a month, I went on to this effect:
'Depend upon it, if you have a long armistice, and nothing
settled at the end of it, you *will* be in danger of war: you
ought not to lose a moment in solving the real difficulty.
What does the Conference understand by the words "integrity
of Denmark"? England is not very disposed to go to war
with Germany about German territory; Denmark no longer
hopes she will, perhaps does not wish her to do so.

'Therefore the future of Holstein ought to be considered
by the Conference as a secondary point: the first thing to
decide is, "What is Denmark?" If you can agree upon
that — and, if you can, you ought to do it quickly — all the
rest will somehow or other find its level, and settle itself.'

Of course, all this was not said continuously or so crudely,
but this, so far as I can recollect, and I really have racked

my brain this morning about it, is the cream of what I said. . . .

The Conference of London broke up without producing any settlement. But it became clear, during its sittings, that public opinion in England, however favourable to Denmark, would not sanction war; and the German Powers proceeded to enforce in arms their own solution, namely, the cession to themselves of all the King of Denmark's rights in the duchies, including the Danish as well as the German portion of Schleswig. The British Cabinet, in which Palmerston and Russell were finally overruled by their colleagues, had to be content with protesting its powerlessness to act without France or Russia, and to explain that, at any rate, neither the independence nor the capital city of Denmark was threatened. No wonder that Disraeli remarked, with sarcasm that was abundantly justified, that, judging from the past, he would have preferred that Cobden and Bright rather than Palmerston had conducted the affairs of the country. The consequences would be almost the same, but our position would have been more consistent and dignified.

At least those honourable gentlemen would threaten nobody; at least they would not tell Denmark that, if she is attacked, she will not find herself alone; at least they would not exasperate Germany by declaiming in the full Parliament of England against the 'aggravated outrages' of her policy; at least they would not lure on Denmark by delusive counsels and fallacious hopes.

Never had an Opposition a clearer case for censuring Ministerial foreign policy; and a motion was made in both Houses regretting that Ministers had failed to uphold the integrity and independence of Denmark, and that their policy had lowered the just influence of England in the councils of Europe, and thereby diminished the securities of peace. Disraeli, in introducing the motion in the Commons,[1] spoke for nearly three hours, quoting the

[1] July 4.

diplomatic correspondence in great detail in order to show
the mismanagement of the Government.   Had Ministers
maintained an understanding with Russia and France,
war would not have broken out, and the independence
and integrity of Denmark would have been maintained.
But they had estranged both Russia and France ; and
after the latter had adopted a definitely neutral attitude,
England should have done the same, and abstained from
all interference, menaces, and promises.   He mocked at
the Conference, which lasted as long as a Carnival, and,
like a Carnival, was 'an affair of masks and mystifica-
tions.'   In the Conference Ministers even proposed the
dismemberment of Denmark — so much for its integrity !
and the placing of the remainder under the guarantee of
the Great Powers, like another Turkey in Europe — so
much for its independence ! His peroration was a
declaration for peace.

   Sir, it is not for any man in this House, on whatever side
he sits, to indicate the policy of this country in our foreign
relations ; it is the duty of no one but the responsible Ministers
of the Crown. The most we can do is to tell the noble lord
what is not our policy. We will not threaten and then refuse
to act. We will not lure on our allies with expectations we
do not fulfil. And, sir, if ever it be the lot of myself, or any
public men with whom I have the honour to act, to carry on
important negotiations on behalf of this country, as the
noble lord and his colleagues have done, I trust that we at
least shall not carry them on in such a manner that it will
be our duty to come to Parliament to announce to the country
that we have no allies, and then declare that England can
never act alone. Sir, those are words which ought never to
have escaped the lips of a British Minister. They are sentiments which ought never to have occurred even to his heart.
I repudiate, I reject them. I remember there was a time
when England, with not a tithe of her present resources,
inspired by a patriotic cause, triumphantly encountered a
world in arms. And, Sir, I believe now, if the occasion were
fitting, if her independence or her honour were assailed, or
her empire endangered — I believe that England would rise
in the magnificence of her might, and struggle triumphantly
for those objects for which men live and nations flourish.
But I, for one, will never consent to go to war to extricate
Ministers from the consequences of their own mistakes. It

is in this spirit that I have drawn up this Address to the Crown. . . . I am ready to vindicate the honour of the country whenever it is necessary, but I have drawn up this Address in the interest of peace.

The debate was felt to involve the fate of the Government ; and it was accordingly prolonged for four nights, during which most of the leading men of all parties spoke. Gladstone was indignant that the House of Commons should be called upon, for the sake of displacing a Government, to record the degradation of its country. Cobden condemned the meddling of diplomatists with the destinies of nations. Horsman said that the Government had made mistakes, but the Opposition had endorsed them, so he could not support a vote of censure. Bernal Osborne riddled Palmerston and Russell with the sarcasm which in old days he reserved for Disraeli. Palmerston appealed for support to the achievements of his Administration, consisting mainly of Gladstone's Budgets, which he himself had thwarted in Cabinet. But, fearing to meet Disraeli's motion with a direct negative, he, the apostle of universal interference and the unsuccessful advocate of interference on this occasion, accepted an amendment moved by Kinglake in favour of noninterference between Germany and Denmark. This was not a frank or straightforward course, said Disraeli in reply ;[1] but it was a successful one. The motion, which had been carried in the Lords by a majority of nine, was defeated in the Commons by eighteen, the numbers being 313 to 295. Thus the House secured what the vast majority desired, the preservation of peace coupled with the maintenance of Palmerston as Minister ; and Disraeli, though his policy prevailed, failed once more to persuade the 1859 Parliament to put him and Derby in office to carry it out.

The following memoranda by Disraeli relating to foreign affairs in 1864 may be added here :

[1] It was in this reply that Disraeli dubbed Horsman a 'superior person.'

August 5, 1864. — Long walk in the park with Brunnow: spoke much of Bismarck. I reminded him he had introduced Bis. to me at a ball at his house two years ago; which he recollected. We agreed a man of great energy. 'An Alberoni,' I added.

Brunnow doubted whether circumstances had favored Alberoni, as they had Bis. Thought there was no person whom circumstances had ever so favored. France holding back because she was offended with England; English Government in a state of *impuissance;* Russia distracted with conflicting interests; Austria for the first time sincere in wishing to act with Prussia; then the weak chivalric character of the King; the enthusiasm of Germany.

'Bismark made a good book,' I said. 'He made a good book, and, what is most strange, he backed the worst horse in the lot. For Prussia is a country without any bottom, and in my opinion could not maintain a real war for 6 months.'

I reminded Brunnow of what he had said about L[ouis] N[apoleon] (the five years). He accepted it: I gave him originally 15 years from 1850, I think. Well, the lease approaches the term.

Gladstone said (1864) that the invasion of Mexico by the Emperor Napoleon was one of the greatest political blunders ever perpetrated — certainly the greatest political blunder of his time. But note: there never was a political move over which the Emperor had so long and so deeply brooded: for many years. In 1857 he mentioned to me his wish and willingness to assist in establishing a European dynasty in Mexico, and said that for his part he would make no opposition to the accession of the Duc d'Aumale to such a throne. He looked upon its establishment as of high European importance.

It was his custom to say that there were two Powers who hated old Europe: Russia and the United States of America.

CHAPTER X

DISRAELI AND THE CHURCH

1860–1865

'There are few great things left in England, and the Church is one.' This was Disraeli's dictum, expressed again and again, with slight variations of phrase, in speech and letter and book; and one of the main objects which he set before himself during the long period of opposition to Palmerston was to strengthen the position of the Church, to secure her from internal disruption and external assault. To a considerable extent, no doubt, he had his eye, as a party leader, on party and political advantage. The tendency of the Church, as a great historic institution, could not fail to be of a conservative character; to establish an active and successful Church party in the House of Commons must benefit the Conservative cause, and help to rally disaffected Conservatives round the leader who raised the ecclesiastical banner.

But it would be a mistake to treat Disraeli's efforts on behalf of the Church, whether in the House of Commons or in the diocesan meetings at which in these years of opposition he frequently appeared and spoke, as mainly adroit electioneering. The Church appealed to him not merely as a great conservative force, not even merely as a majestic historical tradition, but as a conception derived from his own sacred race, and as a living witness on behalf of the spiritual order against the invading materialism of the age.[1] He expounded his view

[1] See Vol. III., ch. 3.

in a draft letter preserved among the Beaconsfield papers
—a letter which was obviously addressed to a clergyman,
but which contains nothing to show definitely to whom
or when it was written, or whether it was actually sent:

 . . . I entirely participated at the time in the feelings that
influenced you in the Oxford Movement, which, I believe,
had it been directed with a discretion equal to its energy and
talents, would have conquered the heart of the nation and
placed the strong religious feeling of the country on a basis
of unassailable authority.

 But on the desolating secession of Newman and his followers, to me so unexpected and still to me so unaccountable,
I withdrew from the disheartening struggle, and only resumed
my weapons, much against the feeling of my political friends,
though accused of party motives, when the enemy seemed
desecrating the hearth.

 I have a certain reverence for the Church of Rome, as I
have for all churches which recognise the divine mission of
the House of Israel; but I confess I was astounded that a
man of the calibre of Newman should have fallen into the
pitfalls of the 17th century, and in his search for a foundation
have stopt short at Rome instead of advancing to Jerusalem.

 For myself, I look upon the Church as the only Jewish
institution that remains, and, irrespective of its being the
depository of divine truth, must ever cling to it as the visible
means which embalms the memory of my race, their deeds
and thoughts, and connects their blood with the origin of
things.

 There are few great things left, and the Church is one.
No doubt its position at this moment is critical, and, indeed,
the whole religious sentiment of the country is in a convulsive
state; but I believe the state of affairs is only one of the
periodical revolts of the Northern races against Semitic
truth, influenced mainly by mortified vanity in never having
been the medium of direct communication with the Almighty;
and that it will end as in previous instances, after much
sorrow and suffering, in their utter discomfiture.

Similarly, in the General Preface to the Novels, 1870,
he deplored the fact that no Churchman equal to the occasion had arisen out of the Oxford Movement, but that
it had fallen into the hands of 'monks and schoolmen.'

The secession of Dr. Newman dealt a blow to the Church
of England under which it still reels. That extraordinary
event has been 'apologised' for, but has never been explained.

It was a mistake and a misfortune. The tradition of the
Anglican Church was powerful. Resting on the Church of
Jerusalem, modified by the divine school of Galilee, it would
have found that rock of truth which Providence, by the
instrumentality of the Semitic race, had promised to St.
Peter. Instead of that, the seceders sought refuge in mediæval
superstitions, which are generally only the embodiments of
pagan ceremonies and creeds.

The vital importance of religion in the constitution of
the State was recognised by Disraeli in his earliest political speculations. 'It is one of the leading principles
of the policy of England,' he wrote in the *Vindication*
in 1835, 'that the religious discipline and future welfare
of our citizens are even of greater importance than their
political or present well-being.' Serious interest, however,
in the Church and Church questions seems to have been
imbibed by him for the first time from the Cambridge
men who formed in the 1841 Parliament his 'Young
England' following, and particularly from Smythe and
Manners. But the Oxford Movement in which they
brought him to sympathise developed in the next few
years a Romeward tendency which alienated his nascent
good-will; and, as we have seen,[1] the part played in
Tancred by the Church, which was to have been its
main theme, is a very poor one. The Protestant outbreak in 1850–51, on the occasion of the Papal Aggression, confirmed Disraeli in his view that Tractarianism had
taken a direction in conflict with the permanent bias of
the British character. For some years, accordingly, he
rather watched, as a critical spectator, the religious
tendencies of the Church and the age, than took any
active part in guiding them. It was the first Derby-
Disraeli Ministry that granted permission to Convocation
to meet for the despatch of business, after an interval of
135 years. But this was done by Derby, the Prime
Minister, and Walpole, the Home Secretary; Disraeli
was certainly not active in the matter, though in later
years he expressed his full approval. Indeed, his first

[1] Vol. III., ch. 3.

public utterance relating to Church affairs, after a long
period of silence, occurs in his electoral campaign, in 1857,
when there was a fear lest the internal quarrels of ecclesiastical parties might be transferred to the political arena
and act disadvantageously to the Tories.   In his address
to his constituents in that year he gave Churchmen the
excellent advice that, instead of quarrelling among themselves, they should evince mutual forbearance, 'unite on
the common ground of ecclesiastical polity,' and oppose
all efforts to impair the integrity of the Church.

Of the parties in the Church, the only one which steadily
supported the Conservatives, a support which had persisted since the days of Dr. Sacheverell, was the old
High Church or Anglican party.   All the other parties,
secure in the belief that the union of Church and State
was regarded as sacred by statesmen of every political
colour, were quite as much, or more, disposed, for one
reason or another, to favour the opposite political connection.   The Evangelicals were attracted to the Whigs
by Russell's aggressive Protestantism and by Palmerston's
Low Church appointments made under Shaftesbury's
influence.   The rising Broad Church School, represented
by Stanley and Jowett, was naturally inclined to enlist
under the banner of Progress.   And, strange to say, even
the Tractarians were being almost insensibly drawn by
the Peelite leaders, Sidney Herbert and Gladstone, who
were Churchmen before they were politicians, into the
ranks of that Liberalism against which Newman's original
movement was in its essence an emphatic protest.   Meanwhile, within the Liberal party, a movement was springing
up hostile to all State establishment of religion.   The
Dissenters, from being a purely religious, were being
organised as a political body ; from defence against
oppression, they passed to attack on what they regarded
as unwarranted privilege ; the Society for the Liberation
of Religion from State control, founded in 1844, began
to exercise serious political influence.   The union of
Church and State was threatened as it had never been

threatened before.   To use the language of a preface to
a collected edition of Disraeli's Church speeches of the
early sixties — a preface which was written by a prominent High Churchman, the sixth Lord Beauchamp, then
Frederick Lygon, but in which we seem to catch the
veritable accents of Lygon's friend and leader : [1]

Measures were astutely devised either to sap some ancient
buttress which supported, or to pull down some stately
pinnacle which adorned, the venerable fabric of the Established
Church.   Distinguished persons in high places, aghast at these
new dangers, counselled surrender ; others advocated a tempo-
rising policy ; but Mr. Disraeli, with rare sagacity, surveyed
the position and comprehended the full consequences of yielding at such a crisis.

The principal measure of the kind before Parliament
at this period was Sir John Trelawny's Bill to abolish
Church rates.   The Church rate was no tyrannical or
hierarchical levy.   It was made by a popular body, the
churchwardens and parishioners in vestry assembled,
and it was devoted to the parochial, if not national,
purposes of defraying the expenses of divine service, repairing the fabric of the parish church, and
paying the salaries of church officials.   It was a
personal charge on the occupier, and the majority in
vestry bound the minority.   If, as happened in many
cases spontaneously, and in others as the result of an
engineered agitation, the rate was not paid, there was
great difficulty in applying compulsion.   The grievance
of the conscientious Dissenter appealed to the Liberal
party, and not to the Liberal party alone ; and Trelawny's
Bill was carried by sufficient majorities through the
Commons in 1855 and 1856, though the Lords opposed
a barrier to further progress.   The keen Churchmen in
the second Derby-Disraeli Ministry, as we have seen,[2]
wished to introduce a measure of compromise in 1858,
but were prevented by Disraeli.   In 1859 they got their

---

[1] Disraeli wrote to Lygon about this republication : 'No one but you
could be the editor, as you know my inmost mind, and there is entire
sympathy between us.'   [2] P. 127.

opportunity, and for the moment Disraeli hoped that their plan, for which Walpole was responsible, would settle the matter. He told the Queen that the Bill had been received with so much favour that he believed it would pass. 'This is very unexpected; and the satisfactory settlement of this long-agitated and agitating question will be a great relief to public life, and tend to restore and augment the good-humour of the country.'[1]

The hope speedily proved delusive : the compromise was rejected, and the majorities in favour of Trelawny's Bill rose to fifty-three in 1858, and even to seventy-four in 1859. Disraeli then began to change the tactics of the party ; to organise a more effective resistance to a Bill which, though plausible enough in itself, was in reality the opening move in a campaign for Disestablishment; to discourage the idea of compromise, and to appeal to the latent conservatism of a Parliament which supported so conservative a statesman as Palmerston. In the session of 1860, while not denying the existence of a grievance, he strongly opposed the second reading of the Bill, which he held would revolutionise the parochial constitution of the country. The real issue to be decided was whether there should be an established Church. The majority dropped to twenty-nine; and on the third reading, in answer to a further appeal by Disraeli on behalf of the Church of England as one of the strongest elements of society, one of the most powerful of our institutions, and the best security of our liberties, what he called Trelawny's rash and ruinous proposition was only carried in the Commons by nine, to perish by an overwhelming majority in the Lords. It is no wonder that, writing to the King of the Belgians on August 23,[2] Disraeli noted, as prominent among the causes which contributed to Conservative consolidation during the session, the appearance of a Church party in the House of Commons for the first time since 1840, and the fact of the clergy throughout the country again generally acting with the Conservatives.

[1] *Queen Victoria's Letters*, Feb. 21, 1859.   [2] See above, pp. 282, 283.

In Disraeli's correspondence with Mrs. Willyams this year, especially during the late autumn, an ecclesiastical flavour may be discerned.

To Mrs. Brydges Willyams.

NEW YEAR'S DAY, 1860.— . . .   Only think of our living to see the Pope on his last legs — and to be betrayed, too, by 'the eldest son of the Church'!   A great Roman Catholic lady told me yesterday that the truth was too obvious; mankind would no longer endure clerical authority.   She pitied them, but was consoled by the conviction of their eventual misery, and that no other authority could long endure.   'As for your Church of England,' she added, 'what are we to think of that?   Four theatres hired, every evening, for "divine" service.   A Bishop preaching at Sadler's Wells, I believe! If theatres will do, what is the use of churches?   And why not one of the usual performers to preach, instead of an ordained priest?'

Do you know, I thought her remarks unanswerable, and did not much care to prove she was wrong, although she thought she was confounding me. . . .

HUGHENDEN, Oct. 18, 1860.— . . .   This year is the triennial visitation of our Diocesan, and I have to receive the Bishop [Wilberforce] at this place.   This is no slight affair, for on these occasions a Bishop is like a Highland chief and moves with a tail.   Besides the descendant of the Apostles, I have to extend hospitality to his Chancellor, his Chaplain, his Secretary, and the Archdeacon of Bucks, and all their servants. . . .

Nov. 11, 1860.— . . .   On Tuesday Lord John Manners and Lord Stanley come down here, to assist me in my great episcopal reception, which commences on Wednesday.   On Thursday Lord Malmesbury and Lord and Lady Salisbury. I hope to clear my house by the end of the week, but I rather doubt it.   Sir William Jolliffe and Colonel Taylor, the chief of my staff, arrive on Friday. . . .

Nov. 18, 1860.— You could not have sent us a more acceptable offering to our banquet, and one, I assure you, more appreciated, than the rosy-colored tribute of Torbay, which quite delighted us for their own merits, and their evidence of the kind thoughts of the donor.   The Bishop was quite delighted.   Prelates love delicacies, and, as he is a wit as well as a priest, he was very playful about Devonian fairies and magic gifts.   It certainly arrived most opportune, and was precious from its history; because no one in Bucks would have tasted a prawn from London, whereas direct from the balmy waters of the West they were a delight.

Our house has been brimful, and is not yet quite emptied. Sir William Jolliffe and Col. Taylor still linger, and leave us to-morrow; all the rest have departed. It has been a week of great and unceasing bustle; but the greatest effort, the Bishop's charge at Wycombe, which I and Lord John Manners thought it but right to attend, and which, irrespective of divine service, was three hours long! It's rightly called a *Visitation*. . . .

The episcopal visitation and charge in November were speedily eclipsed in interest by a speech which Disraeli, as a layman of the diocese, made at a ruridecanal meeting at Amersham on December 4. It was, he told Rose, well considered, and intended as a manifesto. In it he definitely cast aside the idea of compromise on the Church Rate Bill, and urged Church people to stand boldly on their rights. Great issues, he said, were generally tried in this practical country on collateral points; the question of Church rates involved that of a National Church. Churchmen should therefore put internal parties aside and unite and organise; but what should be their policy? There were two opinions. Some were for compromise. He agreed, if compromise meant improvement in detail in regard to method, but not if it meant exemption of Dissenters from the charge. That was not compromise, but surrender — an acknowledgment that the Church of England is no longer a National Church.

This is a public charge of which all the circumstances are of a popular character. It is ancient; it is for a general, not to say a common purpose; it is levied by public votes. If, in a country where the majority decide everything, the minority are, on the ground of conscientious scruple, to be exempted from a public payment, on what principle can society be held together? Landowners might have a conscientious scruple against paying the public creditor; peace societies might have a conscientious scruple against paying war taxes. What the Dissenter demands is, in fact, an oligarchical privilege; and the principle, if conceded and pursued, may lead to general confusion.[1]

[1] A criticism, in advance, of the campaign of 'passive resistance' carried on by some of the Dissenters against the Education Act of 1902.

He felt deeply the responsibility of giving the advice
to refuse to sanction the principle of exemption. He was
opposing the recommendation of the Committee of the
House of Lords in 1859, and what was then the unanimous
opinion of the bench of Bishops. But the Committee
were precipitate : they mistook public humour for public
opinion. What had happened last spring ?

The second reading of Sir John Trelawny's Bill had been
carried by a much reduced majority, and the advocates of
what is fallaciously called compromise were strongly in favour
of what they called seizing the opportunity for a settlement.
I was of a different opinion. I did not think that the advantage the Church had then obtained was only a happy casualty.
I thought it was the break of dawn. I did my utmost to
dissuade my friends from relinquishing the contest, and
ultimately, on my sole responsibility, opposed the third reading
of Sir John Trelawny's Bill. The whole country was agitated
on the occasion by the opponents of the Church to regain
the lost ground. Instead of that, the majority against Church
rates, which had sat like an incubus on the Church for twenty
years, virtually disappeared. We owe to that division our
commanding position.

He recommended the clergy to petition Parliament,
to organise Church Defence associations, and to bring
their influence to bear on their representatives.

'What changes there are in this world!' wrote Rose
on reading the speech. 'Gladstone going to Bradford
with Bright and Cobden and Milner Gibson, and you
leading the Church party throughout the kingdom!'
Derby, good Churchman as he was, was rather aghast at
the pronouncement. 'You will forgive me,' he wrote,
'if I entertain a fear that you have even spoken too
decidedly. . . . The present law is, if not so objectionable
in itself, so difficult of enforcement that, if an amendment could be obtained by some concession, I think it
would be worth the sacrifice.' Disraeli did not reply ;
and Derby, when he next wrote — on January 27, 1861,
just before the session — began : 'I hope you were not
displeased at the frankness with which I expressed my

fears as to the effect of your speech on the Church rate question. I have not heard from you since.'

To Lord Derby.

Private. GROSVENOR GATE, *Jan.* 28, 1861. — I was in hopes that twelve years of trying companionship might have assured you that I was ever grateful for criticism, even from my adversaries, and that it was impossible I could resent the gentle comments of one who, though I have committed so many errors, has never reproached me. The only reason of my silence was that I had nothing to write about. The situation, which I intimated in my last letter, never altered.

As for Church rates, I took the step after great inquiry and reflection ; and I think if I had not taken it our counties would have slipped away. The moment was more than ripe. The enclosed will give you some idea how it worked in Wales, where the clergy, and the Church generally, are weakest. It will work more powerfully in Wiltshire, and, from the numerous communications which reach me, I think I shall have effected my purpose. All that I am afraid of are the Bishops, acted on by a coterie, who hate us, and have flattered themselves they had a monopoly of Church championship. Most of these people are now out of Parliament: Roundell Palmer, B[eresford] Hope and Co. ; but they are unceasingly at work. They can do the Church no good, for they are utterly incapable of managing England, being a finical and fastidious crew, who are more anxious about what they call the Church, than the Church of England. My own Diocesan has left them, and in his triennial charge, this autumn, declared against their projects : the Bishop of Exeter, whom I saw at Torquay, is all right, and will be up for the meeting of Parliament. I have unceasingly worked, since you wrote to me, to counteract any mischief from my movement, and to secure all the good which might accrue from it ; and if the Bishops will only be quiet and not commit themselves any further on the subject, leaving the question to the country and the House of Commons, I have no fear whatever of ultimate success. . . .

Disraeli's determined policy led to a marked Parliamentary success in the session of 1861. He took the precaution, when arranging to give Palmerston general support, to neutralise the Government on this special question. Shaftesbury, who acted as go-between in some of the negotiations, wrote of Palmerston on January 17 :

'Reserving of course his own opinion and freedom of action in respect of Church rates, he distinctly said there was no intention of making it a " Government question." ' Disraeli was also earnest in beating up doubtful Conservative voters. 'It will never do,' he wrote to Malmesbury on February 22, 'to have our own men run riot. The fact is, in internal politics there is only one question now, the maintenance of the Church. There can be no refraining or false Liberalism on such a subject. They are both out of fashion, too!'[1] Accordingly, the second reading of Trelawny's Bill was only carried by a majority of fifteen, and on the third reading, in a very full house, the numbers were equal— 274 each side. The Speaker, interpreting the attitude of the House as one of hesitation, threw his casting vote against the measure. In his speech against the second reading Disraeli gave an interesting insight into his view of the Dissenters' position :

One would almost suppose, from the manner in which the Dissenter was mentioned, that he was some stranger in the country or some wild animal. Why, a Dissenter is our friend, our neighbour, our tenant, our tradesman ; he is an Englishman animated by all the feelings and principles of Englishmen. . . . If he finds himself in a majority in any parish where a rate is proposed, he has a victorious power of self-defence in that majority, and he can by the votes of himself and friends shield himself from these grievances of which you say that he complains. What is the position of a Dissenter in parishes in which he is in a minority ? In that case, if he be animated by the same feelings as any other Englishman — and I know by experience he is so — he yields to the opinion of the majority, for such he knows is the principle upon which our social system is established. If the majority is overwhelming, he yields without a murmur ; if it be slight, he can exercise his influence if he chooses, so that next year the majority may change into a minority.

To Mrs. Brydges Willyams.

CARLTON CLUB, *Thursday, June* 27, 1861. — I wrote to you, about a week ago, on the eve of the Church rate division. I told you how critical it was, and how important success was to me, considering that the resistance of the Bill had been

[1] *Memoirs of an Ex-Minister*, Vol. II., p. 247.

mainly prompted by my counsel. I was not altogether without hope, but not over-sanguine. You have seen in the papers
the strange and wonderful triumph! Such a scene has not
occurred in the House of Commons since the impeachment of
Lord Melville, in the days of Mr. Pitt. . . .

In the autumn of 1861 Disraeli repeated his experiment of addressing a diocesan meeting in Bucks. He
took precautions to be properly reported. 'I will endeavour,' he wrote to Delane, 'to make a *précis* of what
I intend to say, which I will give your envoy if he will
see me before the business. This is rather a difficult
thing for me to do, as it is against my grain, being much
influenced by my audience and the impromptu; but I
must make an effort to entirely control myself, as there
must be no mistake.'

To Mrs. Brydges Willyams.

Most private. HUGHENDEN MANOR, *Nov.* 13, 1861. — The
state of the Church is critical, from dissensions and heresy
among its own children. If it were to fall, philosophy would
not profit: we should only be handed over to a narrow-minded
and ignorant fanaticism. I have been in frequent correspondence of late with the Bishop of Oxford, the Bishop of this
diocese — as you know, a first-rate man; and I have promised
to attend a great diocesan meeting to-morrow at Aylesbury,
and try to give a lead to public opinion in the right direction.
It is a nervous business, for what may be said and done to-
morrow may produce very great effects — like Sacheverell's
sermon, which was nothing till it was preached, and then
nearly set the Thames on fire. After all, it may end to-morrow
in smoke, for a speech is like a play — success seems always a
chance. . . . Think of me to-morrow, a very critical day I
can assure you.

The 'heresy' about which Disraeli was disquieted was
the recent publication of *Essays and Reviews*, a volume of
mildly latitudinarian essays by various Anglican writers.
Disraeli was a rigid maintainer of orthodoxy in belief,
partly, no doubt, from a realisation of the utility of religion
to the civil magistrate, but also, it appears, from intellectual conviction, and from a jealousy on behalf of his
own sacred race, the original recipients and transmitters

of religious truth. He therefore held the speculations of Broad Churchmen in little favour. Five years before, in 1856, we find him writing to Mrs. Willyams about an article in the *Quarterly* [1] on a work by 'a Rev. Mr. Jowett,' which, he tells his correspondent, 'will give you some idea of the rapid and strange advances which German neology, *alias* infidelity, is making in that seat of venerable orthodoxy, the University of Oxford, and especially among clergymen of the Church of England. When the *Quarterly Review* steps forward, it is clear that the plague in the vitals can be no longer concealed.' Accordingly, in his speech at Aylesbury, Disraeli effectively ridiculed the mutually destructive theories put forward by successive schools of German theologians. His criticism has lost none of its point in an age which has witnessed the conservative revolution wrought by Harnack in New Testament criticism. About a century before, he said, German theology, which had been mystical, became critical. A Rationalist school sprang up which explained the supernatural incidents in the sacred narrative by natural causes. After absorbing for half a century the intellect of the country, this school was displaced by one which applied a mythical interpretation to Scripture. But, 'if the mythical theologians triumphantly demonstrated that Rationalism was irrational, so the mythical system itself has become a myth'; and there had been in its place a revival in Germany of pagan pantheism. What had the Church to fear from 'speculations so overreaching, so capricious, and so self-destructive?' He was himself in favour of free inquiry on all subjects, but 'free inquiry should be pursued by free inquirers,' and the authors of *Essays and Reviews* 'have entered into engagements with the people of this country quite inconsistent with the views advanced in those prolusions.'

On the general question of the connection of Church and State, Disraeli deprecated the tendency of some

[1] 'The Neology of the Cloisters,' *Quarterly Review*, Dec. 1855.

High Churchmen to contemplate disestablishment without alarm. It was a fallacy to suppose that the Church after disestablishment would occupy the position which it held in the Middle Ages. The civil power would never 'submit to a superior authority, or even brook a rival.' There would be 'possible struggle, probable spoliation,' and the Church might 'subside into a fastidious, not to say finical congregation.' The connection between Church and State was in unison with the spirit of the age and the soundest principles of political philosophy. 'The most powerful principle which governs man is the religious principle.'

A wise Government, allying itself with religion, would, as it were, consecrate society and sanctify the State. But how is this to be done? It is the problem of modern politics which has always most embarrassed statesmen. No solution of the difficulty can be found in salaried priesthoods and complicated concordats. But by the side of the State in England there has gradually arisen a majestic corporation — wealthy, powerful, independent — with the sanctity of a long tradition, yet sympathising with authority, and full of conciliation, even deference, to the civil power. Broadly and deeply planted in the land, mixed up with all our manners and customs, one of the main guarantees of our local government, and therefore one of the prime securities of our common liberties, the Church of England is part of our history, part of our life, part of England itself.

It is said sometimes that the Church of England is hostile to religious liberty. As well might it be said that the monarchy of England is adverse to political freedom. Both are institutions which insure liberty by securing order.

It was a statesmanlike plea for the union of Church and State; and Disraeli naturally proceeded to urge all Churchmen to come together in its defence. The assault might proceed from a minority, but should not on that account be treated lightly; for 'the history of success is the history of minorities.' 'Clever electioneering speech to clergy and church,' was Bishop Wilberforce's comment in his diary. While not disagreeing, we may add that there was sound sense in Disraeli's advice.

The advice at any rate was taken, and in the following

session of 1862 Trelawny's Bill was actually defeated, on second reading in a full House, by one vote (287 to 286), and a year later by the sufficient majority of ten. 'A House of Commons,' to quote once again Lord Beauchamp's preface, 'which had voted the abolition of Church rates with a tumultuous majority of seventy, negatived the abolition by a majority of ten in a House still more crowded. . . . Churchmen began to appreciate the necessity and power of organisation.'

It was a great Parliamentary success for Disraeli, but was it anything more? That Church rates could not continue indefinitely to be levied compulsorily from Dissenters was as evident to Disraeli as it was to his opponents, or to those of his colleagues who doubted his tactics, and pressed for some form of compromise or arrangement. And as a matter of fact, the struggle ended by the passage, at Gladstone's instance, in 1868, when Disraeli was himself Prime Minister, of a Bill making the Church rate purely voluntary, and thus remedying the grievance. This was indeed a different thing from the crude surrender proposed by Sir John Trelawny. But Disraeli could claim besides that, when he raised the banner of resistance, the friends of the Church were dispirited and disorganised, seeing one outwork falling after another and despairing of saving even the citadel; and that, owing to the spirit and courage which he breathed into their ranks, they realised that, whatever concession might have to be made on this point or on that, there was good hope of securing for the future all for which they seriously cared. It may well be doubted whether the alternative tactics of hastening to give up every doubtful privilege the moment it was called in question would not have resulted in many unnecessary surrenders, and thus fatally impaired the integrity of the stronghold.

In the autumn of 1862, for the third year in succession, Disraeli delivered an important speech[1] on ecclesiastical

---

[1] Wycombe, Oct. 30. 'I am told by great authorities,' wrote Disraeli to Mrs. Willyams, 'that it was the speech of a statesman without cant.'

many of them, on a reluctant Church by one who was
regarded as a fussy Diocesan, and who was suspected,
however unfairly, of disloyalty to the Anglican Communion. The Bishop was himself Disraeli's guest at
Hughenden for the occasion in 1862, and recorded in his
diary that all Disraeli's talk was aimed at Gladstone.
'I and others,' he said, 'kept the Church as [Gladstone's]
nest-egg when he became a Whig, till it was almost
addled.'

To Mrs. Brydges Willyams.

HUGHENDEN, *Nov.* 23, 1862. — . . . The Church is much
agitated by a book disputing the authenticity of the Penta-
teuch, and written by a Bishop, one Dr. Colenso, a Colonial
Bishop. 'Tis a great scandal, and is almost as bad as Kings
becoming Republicans. An indignant clerical critic says it
is a queer name, Colenso — he supposes Italian, probably a
Jesuit. I believe, on the contrary, 'tis good Cornish, and
that you Western people are answerable for the heresy, so
we must leave the Doctor to your friend, the Bishop of
Exeter.

The Palmerston Government, absorbed in foreign
affairs, provided no serious programme of domestic
legislation for the session of 1863, and ecclesiastical
questions occupied much of the attention of Parliament.
The defeat of Trelawny's Church Rate Bill by an appreciable majority, which was at length achieved, was
largely due to the success which had attended Disraeli's
persistent efforts to secure the support of Roman Catholics
by generous treatment of their claims.[1] There was a
conspicuous instance of this policy during the session.
The Government brought in a Bill to provide prisoners,
who did not belong to the Church of England, with the
attendance of ministers of their own religious persuasion.
It was avowedly a Bill mainly for the relief of Roman
Catholic prisoners, and the majority of the Conservative
party took strong exception to it. But Disraeli in the
Commons and Derby in the Lords, with the concurrence

---

[1] Ten Roman Catholic members, who had hitherto supported the Bill,
had on this occasion, Disraeli was told, deliberately abstained from voting.

of most of their late colleagues, supported the measure as one of justice, and secured its passage through Parliament. To a Roman Catholic friend Disraeli explained his views and difficulties:

To Lord Campden.[1]

Private.   HUGHENDEN MANOR, *April* 10, 1863. — I shall certainly support the Prison Ministers Bill, which is conceived in the spirit of the policy of the late Government, and I shall do all I can to induce friends to act with me. I anticipate, however, in that respect, no little difficulty. What neutralises my efforts in these matters is the systematic hostility always shown by the Catholic members of the House of Commons to the Church of England. This is most unwise. We live in times when Churches should act together.

I do not expect Catholic members, generally, to vote, for instance, for Church rates, though were I a Catholic I would do so, but at least they might keep away from such divisions. There would be no difficulty about Prison Ministers Bills, and many other measures of that description, if men of the position of Mr. Monsell would only act in Church affairs as Montalembert recommended. I mention Mr. Monsell; both by position and talents he is a leading man, and might exercise even a more considerable influence. If the Churches drew more together, the following of the Newdegates and the Whalleys would sink into insignificance.

Peto's Bill comes on next Wednesday; most offensive to the English clergy. It would be wise in the Catholic members, and would greatly assist me in my conscientious efforts on their behalf, if they did not mix themselves up with these Pedo or Peto Baptists, or whatever they may be.

Peto's Bill was one to permit Dissenters to be buried by their own ministers and with their own rites in the graveyards of the Established Church. Much as there was to be said in favour of a proposal which in after-years became law, it was felt to be somewhat grasping to demand new and special rights in the graveyards simultaneously with relief from Church rates; and, although the Bill was unexpectedly supported by Gladstone, it was rejected by a large majority — 221 to 96. Disraeli wrote to Mrs. Willyams, April 15: 'A great division in

---

[1] Afterwards second Earl of Gainsborough.

the House of Commons, and a great triumph. I write
to you while the cheers are still ringing in my ears.
Gladstone, to the astonishment of his friends, deserted
the Church, and I replied to him and closed the debate.

With the active or passive assistance of the Roman
Catholic vote, not only were Trelawny's and Peto's Bills
defeated in this session, but a motion to relax the subscription by the clergy to the Thirty-nine Articles was
shelved by means of the previous question. Here once
more Disraeli championed, in common with Robert Cecil
and Walpole, the cause of orthodoxy. It was suggested, he said, that not only should the creed of the
Church be catholic, but that its communion should be
catholic. The professors of all creeds were to belong to
one Church, but were all to retain their own particular
opinions. But that experiment had been tried on the
Continent, particularly in Germany, with the result that
you had 'what without offence may be called an infidel
Church.'

'What do you mean by a Church? I say, No creed,
no Church!'[1] How can you have a Church without a
creed, articles, formularies, and a subscription?' He
agreed that neither Articles nor Prayer-Book were perfect.
'There may be blots in their composition. The Prayer-
Book may be divine, but it is also human.' But, if there
were to be any change, it should not originate in Parliament, which was no longer a lay synod, but should be
initiated by a Royal Commission, and brought under the
consideration of the revived Convocation, before its
ultimate submission to Parliament. It may be observed
in passing that this was the process adopted by the
Government in 1864 and 1865, when the subscription
was made more general, but without any alteration, such
as Disraeli deprecated, of the formularies of the Church.
Here Disraeli threw out a sensible hint that 'something
of a lay element' should be introduced into Convocation.

---

[1] 'Pray remember, Mr. Dean,' said Disraeli one day playfully to Dean
Stanley, 'no dogma, no Dean.'

'Nor do I doubt that there are lay members of the Church at the present moment who, from their learning, their knowledge of men, and their high character, might bring to Convocation such ability and reputation as Selden and Chillingworth might have brought in former days.'   Such a lay representation has now for many years been obtained in the form of 'Houses of Laymen,' to the considerable advantage of the Church.

They had been warned, Disraeli concluded, against a sacerdotal despotism.   But the sacerdotal despotism which he feared was not the re-establishment of the Inquisition or the High Commission Court, but 'that a minister of the Church of England, who is appointed to expound doctrine, should deem that he has a right to invent doctrine.'   The motion was one 'in favour of the priesthood, and not of the laity.'   It was the boast of England that in politics it had reconciled order with liberty.   'What in religious affairs is a greater triumph than this?   It has combined orthodoxy with toleration.'   He preferred to stand on the ancient ground.

A memorandum in the Beaconsfield papers discusses the ecclesiastical situation in 1863:

Bishop of Oxford sent this year to Switzerland; overworked. Certainly no man was ever so busy, preached more sermons, wrote more letters, attended more platform meetings, or infused, generally, such a spirit in his diocese.

I think his present illness, however, is from chagrin. He never recovered the appointment of Dr. Thomson to York.[1] It was a long time vacant, and he was my guest at Hughenden during the interval. I never knew a man more agitated. It was the height of his ambition. I think he would have preferred it to Canterbury. He was a Yorkshireman; the son of a great Yorkshireman, who had represented the undivided county of York; and had fairly won it. It was known that no more Low Church Bishops were to be appointed. That vein had been overworked. Some of the last appointments in that way had been mean and insignificant. The death of the Prince had checked the hopes of the Broad Church, which were once very high. The Prince had managed to push one in, and had intended to have made the Queen insist on Dr.

[1] In the autumn of 1862.

Temple; but the subsequent publication of *Essays and Reviews*, to which he was the leading contributor, would probably have rendered this impossible. . . . [The Prince] had made Stanley and Kingsley already Chaplains.

As Lord Shaftesbury, the great champion of Low Church and maker of Low Church Bishops, was, it was understood, to lie by a little, and as Broad Church was from public feeling impossible, the Bishop of Oxford thought that Gladstone, who was his greatest friend and for whom he had left his natural political allies, would have insisted upon his appointment to York. If Gladstone had threatened to resign as he did about the paper duty, he must have gained his point. But Gladstone made no sign,[1] and a comparatively young Oxonian, at least fifteen years younger, I should think, than the Bishop of Oxford, and, if of any political opinions, a Tory, was appointed. An excellent appointment, in my opinion, but that does not alter the circumstances.

Of all Disraeli's appearances during these years as defender of the Faith, none was so dramatic as that of which the scene was laid in the Sheldonian Theatre at Oxford, on November 25, 1864. He was present on the direct invitation of Bishop Wilberforce, who wrote on September 29: 'Would you come to me with Mrs. Disraeli about November 24, and make us a great speech at Oxford for our society for endowing small livings? I would promise you all the Senior University and the undergraduates and the pick of the county.' Disraeli was very willing, and told Earle on November 2: 'I am meditating a great ecclesiastical function at Oxford this month, which would have been *à propos* for the Dissolution, had it come off.'

The ideas about religion current in the residential and intellectual Oxford which Disraeli came to address were in the main no longer those associated with Newman and Pusey, but those of the rising Broad Church school, whose leaders were Stanley and Jowett, and those of the men of science, rightly clamouring for further recognition in the University, and permeated with the spirit of Darwin's *Origin of Species*, published five years before. Both schools

[1] Gladstone pressed the appointment upon Palmerston, but did not threaten to resign.

gravitated towards the Liberal party; both latitudi-
narianism, in the shape of the Higher Criticism, and
evolution, in its more extravagant claims, impugned the
tradition of the Semitic Scriptures. Whether in a political or in an intellectual and religious aspect, both were
therefore repugnant to Disraeli; and he gladly seized the
opportunity to expose their weaknesses and hold up these
new-fangled lights to scorn and derision.

He turned first to the Broad Church, a party founded,
not like the historical parties of High[1] and Low Church,
on authority, but on the 'singular principle' of criticism.
Criticism being necessarily sceptical, such a party might
very well reject inspiration and miracles, and, as a logical
consequence, the creeds and articles of faith based on
inspiration and miracles. But he could not understand
how, after having arrived at these conscientious conclusions, they should still be 'sworn supporters of ecclesiastical establishments, fervent upholders, or dignitaries, of
the Church.'

If it be true, as I am often told it is, that the age of faith
has passed, then the fact of having an opulent hierarchy,
supported by men of high cultivation, brilliant talents and
eloquence, and perhaps some ambition, with no distinctive
opinions, might be a very harmless state of affairs, and it
would certainly not be a very permanent one. But . . .
when I observe what is passing around us — what is taking
place in this country, and not only in this country, but in
other countries, and even hemispheres — instead of believing
that the age of faith has passed, I hold that the characteristic
of the present age is a craving credulity. Why, my Lord,
man is a being born to believe. And if no Church comes
forward with its title-deeds of truth, sustained by the tradition
of sacred ages and by the conviction of countless generations,
to guide him, he will find altars and idols in his own heart
and his own imagination. But observe this. What must be
the relations of a powerful Church, without distinctive creeds,
with a being of such a nature? Why, of course, the chief
principle of political economy will be observed. Where
there is a great demand there will be a proportionate supply;

---

[1] Throughout his Church speeches of this period Disraeli, much as he
disliked the extreme developments of Ritualism, made no attempt to distinguish between the different schools of High Churchmen.

and commencing, as the new school may, by rejecting the principle of inspiration, it will end by every priest becoming a prophet; and beginning as they do by repudiating the practice of miracles, before long, rest assured, we shall be living in a flitting scene of spiritual phantasmagoria. There are no tenets however extravagant, and no practices however objectionable, which will not in time develop under such a state of affairs; opinions the most absurd and ceremonies the most revolting — 'Qualia demens Ægyptus portenta colat' — perhaps to be followed by the incantations of Canidia and the Corybantian howl.

But consider the country in which all this may take place. Dangerous in all countries, it would be yet more dangerous in England. Our empire is now unrivalled for its extent; but the base — the material base — of that empire is by no means equal to the colossal superstructure. It is not our iron ships; it is not our celebrated regiments; it is not these things which have created, or indeed really maintain, our empire. It is the character of the people. Now, I want to know where that famous character of the English people will be if they are to be influenced and guided by a Church of immense talent, opulence, and power, without any distinctive creed. You have in this country accumulated wealth that never has been equalled, and probably it will still increase. You have a luxury that will some day peradventure rival even your wealth. And the union of such circumstances with a Church without a distinctive creed will lead, I believe, to a dissoluteness of manners and of morals rarely equalled in the history of man, but which prepares the tomb of empires. . . .

Will these opinions succeed? Is there a possibility of their success? My conviction is that they will fail . . . for two reasons. In the first place, having examined all their writings, I believe without any exception, whether they consist of fascinating eloquence, diversified learning, and picturesque sensibility — I speak seriously what I feel — and that too exercised by one honoured in this University, and whom to know is to admire and regard;[1] or whether you find them in the cruder conclusions of prelates[2] who appear to have commenced their theological studies after they had grasped the crosier, and who introduce to society their obsolete discoveries with the startling wonder and frank ingenuousness of their own savages; or whether I read the lucubrations of nebulous professors,[3] who seem in their style to have revived chaos, and who if they could only succeed

[1] Dean Stanley.   [2] Bishop Colenso.
[3] Frederick Denison Maurice.

in obtaining a perpetual study of their writings would go far to realise that eternal punishment to which they object;[1] or, lastly, whether it be the provincial arrogance and the precipitate self-complacency which flash and flare in an essay or review,[2] I find that the common characteristic of their writings in this, that their learning is always second-hand.

The learning was not only second-hand, and therefore not treated with the caution and circumspection natural to those who have prosecuted original research; there was also nothing in it really new. The German scholars from whom it was derived had been anticipated, Disraeli maintained, by the great Hebrew scholars, such as Astruc and Father Simon, who flourished in the eighteenth and the end of the seventeenth century, and whose labours 'formed the mind and inspired the efforts of the two most intellectual bodies of men that have existed certainly since the Greek philosophers . . . the free-thinkers of England and the philosophers of France.'

All that inexorable logic, irresistible rhetoric, bewildering wit, could avail to popularise those views were set in motion to impress the new learning on the minds of the two leading nations of Europe — the people of England and the people of France.   And they produced their effect. . . .   Their promulgation largely contributed to that mighty movement popularly called the French Revolution, which has not yet ended, and which is certainly the greatest event that has happened in the history of man.   Only the fall of the Roman Empire can be compared to it. . . .   Look at the Europe of the present day and the Europe of a century ago.   It is not the same Europe.   Its very form is changed.   Whole nations and great nations, which then flourished, have disappeared. There is not a political constitution in Europe existing at the present time which then existed.   The leading community of the continent of Europe has changed all its landmarks, altered its boundaries, erased its local names.   The whole jurisprudence of Europe has been subverted.   Even the tenure of land, which of all human institutions most affects the character of man, has been altered.   The feudal system has been abolished.   Not merely laws have been changed —

---

[1] In deference to the representations of Bishop Wilberforce and others, Disraeli omitted this clause about eternal punishment when he authorised the republication of the speech.

[2] Jowett and Temple were the most eminent of the authors of *Essays and Reviews*.

not merely manners have been changed — but customs have been changed. And what happened? When the turbulence was over — when the shout of triumph and the wail of agony were alike stilled — when, as it were, the waters had subsided, the sacred heights of Sinai and of Calvary were again revealed, and amid the wreck of thrones and tribunals, of extinct nations and abolished laws, mankind, tried by so many sorrows, purified by so much suffering, and wise with such unprecedented experience, bowed again before the Divine truths that Omnipotence in His ineffable wisdom had entrusted to the custody and the promulgation of a chosen people!

In the latter part of his speech Disraeli turned from the Broad Church to the evolutionists, and attracted the attention of the whole world by a pungent phrase.

The discoveries of science are not, we are told, consistent with the teachings of the Church. . . It is of great importance, when this tattle about science is mentioned, that we should annex to the phrase precise ideas. I hold that the function of science is the interpretation of nature, and the interpretation of the highest nature is the highest science. What is the highest nature? Man is the highest nature. But I must say that when I compare the interpretation of the highest nature by the most advanced, the most fashionable and modish, school of modern science with some other teachings with which we are familiar, I am not prepared to say that the lecture-room is more scientific than the Church.

What is the question now placed before society with a glib assurance the most astounding? The question is this — Is man an ape or an angel? My Lord, I am on the side of the angels.

I repudiate with indignation and abhorrence the contrary view, which is, I believe, foreign to the conscience of humanity: more than that, even in the strictest intellectual point of view, I believe the severest metaphysical analysis is opposed to such a conclusion. But, on the other hand, what does the Church teach us? What is its interpretation of this highest nature? It teaches us that man is made in the image of his Creator — a source of inspiration and of solace — a source from which only can flow every right principle of morals and every Divine truth. . . . It is between these two contending interpretations of the nature of man, and their consequences, that society will have to decide. Their rivalry is at the bottom of all human affairs. Upon our acceptance of that Divine interpretation for which we are indebted to the Church, and of which the Church is the guardian, all sound and salutary legislation depends. That truth is the only security for civilisation, and the only guarantee of real progress.

Froude has drawn for us the picture of the orator who claimed to be on the side of the angels, addressing the University dons and country clergy 'in a black velvet shooting coat and wideawake hat, as if he had been accidentally passing through the town.' How absurd it seemed of this fantastic creature, with his apish tricks, to advance such exalted pretensions on behalf of himself and the human race ! The University wits polished their epigrams. A Fellow of Oriel amused the common-rooms with a set of sapphics, beginning :

> Angelo quis te similem putaret
> Esse, vel divis atavis creatum,
> Cum tuas plane referat dolosus
> Simius artes ?

Both in the University and outside, people asked, What did Disraeli mean? Could he be serious? Was it all mere fireworks intended to dazzle and hoodwink the clergy?

Those who have read and studied *Tancred* and *Lord George Bentinck*, and the speeches and letters on religious and philosophic topics which have been quoted in this biography, know that Disraeli was perfectly serious, and was only concentrating in an unforgettable phrase his most vital convictions. He held that, whatever man may be biologically and physiologically, he is something more ; and that this something more, which transcends biological and physiological science, is the most distinctive and essential thing about him. And even the scientific world is now coming round to this opinion. In order, apparently, to make people understand how entirely in earnest he was in his argument in the Sheldonian Theatre, Disraeli reproduced it in a careful and deliberate form in the General Preface to the Novels, published in 1870. He expressed himself then with less confidence as to the future than he had in 1864 ; but the course of events has largely justified his hope that 'the Teutonic rebellion against the Divine truths entrusted to the Semites' would ultimately meet with the fate of 'the Celtic insurrection' of Voltaire and the Encyclopædists ;

while the incapacity of science to take the place of religion
is now much more widely recognised than it was in the
days when Huxley and Tyndall flourished.   The passage
in which Disraeli ridiculed the claims of modern scientific
men to a monoply of scientific discovery is very typical
of his outlook on the world.

There is no fallacy so flagrant as to suppose that the modern
ages have the peculiar privilege of scientific discovery, or that
they are distinguished as the epochs of the most illustrious
inventions.   On the contrary . . . the greatest discoveries
are not those of modern ages.   No one for a moment can
pretend that printing is so great a discovery as writing, or
algebra as language.   What are the most brilliant of our
chemical discoveries compared with the invention of fire and
the metals ?   It is a vulgar belief that our astronomical
knowledge dates only from the recent century, when it was
rescued from the monks who imprisoned Galileo ; but Hip-
parchus, who lived before our Divine Master, and who among
other sublime achievements discovered the procession of the
equinoxes, ranks with the Newtons and the Keplers ; and
Copernicus, the modern father of our celestial science, avows
himself, in his famous work, as only the champion of Pythag-
oras, whose system he enforces and illustrates.   Even the
most modish schemes of the day on the origin of things, which
captivate as much by their novelty as their truth, may find
their precursors in ancient sages, and after a careful analysis
of the blended elements of imagination and induction which
characterise the new theories, they will be found mainly to rest
on the atom of Epicurus and the monad of Thales. . . .   We may
analyse the sun and penetrate the stars, but man is conscious
that he is made in God's own image, and in his perplexity
he will ever appeal to our Father which art in Heaven.

The speech in the Sheldonian was Disraeli's last great
effort on behalf of the Church before the General Election
of 1865.   He had this and his other main ecclesiastical
speeches of these years collected and republished with a
view to influence public opinion ; and in his address to
his constituents he based the claim of the Conservatives
to the confidence of the country, first and foremost, on
their defence of the Church.   If the response was not
quite what he hoped, it was the popularity of Palmerston
rather than hostility to the Church that was responsible.

It may be interesting to collect here certain scattered memoranda dealing with religion, written by Disraeli during the sixties:

Sir George [Cornewall] Lewis said to me at Bellamy's, 'If there be anything established, it is that the Semitic nations invented the alphabet, and, after all, that may perhaps be considered the greatest achievement of the human race.' . . . 'Of one Semitic nation, the Jews,' I observed, 'it can be said that they invented alike the Ten Commandments and the Lord's Prayer.'

Sir George Lewis thought the merits of the Lord's Prayer exaggerated. There were expressions in it which could not be understood by the million, as, for instance, 'Thy kingdom come' and 'Thine is the kingdom,' which, in fact, referred to the impending 'Kingdom of Heaven,' which was the foundation of the School of Galilee and of real Christianity. I observed that these expressions, though doubtless originally limited in the sense he mentioned, were now of general application, and had always been capable of it. I thought the Lord's Prayer a masterpiece. It was the most perfect exponent of the purest religious feeling, that had yet appeared. And while it soothed the cottage, it was difficult to conceive a society so refined that it would not satisfy.

Assuming that the popular idea of inspiration be abandoned, and the difference between sacred and profane history relinquished, what would be the position of the Hebrew race in universal history, viewed with reference to their influence on man? I thought of advertising, through a medium that would command confidence, £500 or even £1,000 for the best essay on this question — perhaps more precisely expressed. The judges, perhaps, to be Gladstone, Canon Stanley,[1] and myself. Not bound, however, to award the prize unless satisfied with the performance.

Elmley[2] was always saying, 'What did Jesus do before he was thirty? My conviction is that he must have had an eventful youth, and that he had travelled a great deal.' This travelling of Jesus was a great point with Elmley. He frequently recurred to it. I never could agree with him. It seemed such an original mind: so completely formed in seclusion, and, with all its Shakespearian genius, so essentially local. All the illustrations are drawn from inward resources or from surrounding scenery.

[1] Dean Stanley, then Canon of Christ Church, Oxford.

[2] M.P. for Worcestershire W., 1853-1863, then succeeded as fifth Earl Beauchamp; died young in 1866; elder brother of F. Lygon, afterwards sixth Earl. Both brothers were close friends of Disraeli.

After Derby's fiasco in the beginning of 1855, Disraeli had, through his organ the *Press*, endeavoured to cheer his dispirited party by telling them that they might control, if they did not direct, the course of public affairs.[1] A review of this and the two preceding chapters shows that never was that control so brilliantly and so successfully exercised as during the six years of Palmerston's last Administration. Whether we look at Reform, at public economy, at ecclesiastical disputes, or at the great issues of peace and war, the decisive influence, which finally determined the course for policy to pursue, was not that of the Ministry, but of the Opposition, and of Disraeli as its leader in the House of Commons. It was mainly owing to Disraeli's tactics that Russell and Bright were brought to a standstill over Reform; that Palmerston was checked over extravagant expenditure; that the Dissenters and Secularists were stopped in their attacks on the Church; and that Palmerston and Russell were prevented from carrying to the point of military operations their well-meant but ill-managed policy of intervention in the internal affairs of Europe and America. It is, of course, true that in all these matters the Opposition and their leader had, now one, now another, of the strongest men in the Administration secretly favourable to their cause; but that fact detracts very little from the insight and adroitness which seized and utilised the various occasions. The only sphere in which the Opposition met with partial failure was that over which Gladstone's fiery energy presided. In the early years of the Adminstration Gladstone was able, in spite of their protests, to reduce to what they considered a dangerous extent the existing sources of revenue, and to curtail the power and humiliate the pride of the House of Lords. But, on the other hand, in the last half of the period his Budgets largely followed the lines which Disraeli had recommended from the first — a steady reduction of income tax and of the war duties on tea and sugar. It enhances Disraeli's reputation to

[1] See Vol. III., p. 570.

reflect that this successful control of policy was achieved with a party behind him containing an element of active disloyalty, with colleagues seldom in hearty agreement, and in the face of criticism, as often as helpful suggestion, from Derby; and that it was maintained in spite of the fact that, in every pitched battle, faint-heartedness and desertion in his own camp secured for the Government at least a nominal victory.

Throughout the period he was building up his party so as to fit them for office, and keeping constantly before them a national rather than a sectarian or territorial ideal. Take the fine peroration of a speech which he delivered in Parliament at the close of the session of 1862:

Ever since that period of disaster and dismay, when my friends and myself were asked for the first time to sit upon these benches,[1] it has ever been our habit, in counselling the Tory party, to recur gradually but most sincerely to the original elements of that great political connection. To build up a community, not upon Liberal opinions, which anyone may fashion to his fancy, but upon popular principles,[2] which assert equal rights, civil and religious; to uphold the institutions of the country because they are the embodiments of the wants and wishes of the nation, and protect us alike from individual tyranny and popular outrage; equally to resist democracy and oligarchy, and favour that principle of free aristocracy which is the only basis and security for constitutional government; to be vigilant to guard and prompt to vindicate the honour of the country, but to hold aloof from that turbulent diplomacy which only distracts the mind of a people from internal improvement; to lighten taxation; frugally but wisely to administer the public treasure; to favour popular education, because it is the best guarantee for public order; to defend local government, and to be as jealous of the rights of the working man as of the prerogative of the Crown and the privileges of the senate — these were once the principles which regulated Tory statesmen, and I for one have no wish that the Tory party should ever be in power unless they practise them.[3]

Similarly, at a party dinner in 1863, Disraeli summed up the Liberal opinions, to which Conservatives were

[1] 1847.   [2] See Vol. III., p. 22.   [3] Aug. 1, 1862.

opposed, as follows: That the electoral franchise ought
to be democratic, and property deprived of its legitimate
influence; that the union between Church and State
ought to be abolished; that the relations between the
mother-country and the colonies — that national estate
which assured a freehold to Englishmen and an inexhaustible theatre for their energies — should be abrogated;
that the rights of corporations and the privileges of
endowments should be terminated.

The Tory party is only in its proper position when it represents popular principles. Then it is truly irresistible. Then it
can uphold the throne and the altar, the majesty of the empire,
the liberty of the nation, and the rights of the multitude.
There is nothing mean, petty, or exclusive, about the real
character of Toryism. It necessarily depends upon enlarged
sympathies and noble aspirations, because it is essentially
national.

He congratulated the party on their present position
compared with that at the time of Bentinck's death,
when ' we were like a wreck stranded on the beach, and
it was a question who should rifle our stores.'

Contrast that position with our position now! In either
House of Parliament you confront the Ministry with at least
an equal power. You are the advocates of a generous and
a national creed; and as for public men, why, there is not a
subject that can be brought forward in the House of Commons
but I am sure, from every part of the benches on the side on
which I sit, men will come forward who, by the amplitude of
their knowledge, their argumentative power, and their general
ability, will so demean themselves as to command, as they
deserve, the attention of the assembly which they adorn.[1]

Disraeli had a right to be proud of the work which he
had accomplished in resuscitating and nationalising his
party and in imposing their control on the Government.
But office was apparently out of their grasp so long as
Palmerston lived; and on what had been, and must
ultimately be again, the main domestic issue, Parliamentary Reform, there was no fundamental agreement
within the party save to postpone legislation.

[1] June 26, 1863.

CHAPTER XI

DISRAELI AND THE COURT

1861–1863

Queen Victoria, during her long reign, had occasion not infrequently to revise her original opinion of eminent men who rose to be her chief Ministers. In almost every instance, be it said to the credit both of the Sovereign and of the Minister, the change was from distrust to confidence. The only exception was in the case of Gladstone, of whom the Queen and the Prince had thought highly in his middle career, but whose later policies, and perhaps still more the 'pilgrimages of passion'[1] in which he advocated them, caused Her Majesty much disquiet. On the other hand, Peel, as Minister, not only entirely conquered the prejudice caused by the Bedchamber dispute, but even succeeded in inspiring peculiar confidence; and, in a lesser degree, Palmerston, whose conduct as Foreign Secretary had given so much offence, earned her Majesty's respect during his last Administration. But, of course, the most conspicuous change of all was that which took place in regard to Disraeli. In the forties the Court identified itself completely with Peel and his Free Trade policy; and Peel's assailant and destroyer was regarded by the Queen and Prince with especial aversion. This was lessened, but by no means removed, by the experience of the first Derby-Disraeli Ministry, and of the collaboration then initiated with the Prince in the promotion of science and art. The second Derby-Disraeli Ministry resulted in much more

[1] A phrase used by Disraeli of Gladstone's provincial progresses as early as 1866, more than ten years before the first Midlothian campaign.

friendly relations; and in the couple of years between the fall of that Ministry and the death of the Prince, Disraeli, though in opposition, received frequent invitations to the Palace. In January, 1861, he announced with much satisfaction to Mrs. Willyams a forthcoming visit to Windsor in which his wife was included. 'It is Mrs. Disraeli's first visit to Windsor, and it is considered very marked on the part of her Majesty to ask the wife of the leader of the Opposition, when many Cabinet Ministers have been asked there *without* their wives.' This attention caused comment, and Derby asked Disraeli what had passed. 'They were very gracious and very communicative,' was the reply. In fact, a better knowledge of Disraeli's character had overcome the distrust of the Court before the Prince's death; but it was the sympathetic and appreciative manner in which Disraeli treated that tragic event that converted the Queen's somewhat negative feeling towards him into friendly interest, which was ultimately to develop, during his great Ministry, into unbounded and even affectionate confidence.

It was on December 14, 1861, that this heavy blow fell upon the Queen. Already, in the spring of this year, Her Majesty had lost her mother, the Duchess of Kent. In seconding the address of condolence on the Duchess's death, Disraeli had happily emphasised the commanding part which the domestic affections played in the Queen's life. It was generally supposed, he said, that the anguish of affection was scarcely compatible with the pomp of power; 'but she who reigns over us has elected, amid all the splendour of empire, to establish her life on the principle of domestic love.'

To Frances Anne Lady Londonderry.

Confidential. TORQUAY, *Dec.* 19, 1861.—There is a north post from this place, which tempts me to write to you a hurried line, as my news, received this morning from the fountain-head, may not be stale.

It seems that the departed Prince had lectured the Queen severely about giving way so completely on the death of her

The Prince Consort
from an Engraving at Hughenden
presented by H. M. Queen Victoria.

mother, and told her to remember that the blow was dealt by the hand of the All-Wise.   She remembers this now, and keeps saying, ' Now you see I am calm ; I am profiting by his advice, I am doing what he wished.'   The Duchess of Sutherland and Lady Augusta Bruce with her.

On the 17th she saw Lord Granville, who brought Palmerston's [box], and she signed several papers of pressing importance.

The Prince of Wales seems anxious to take his place, and I hear, behaves with great tact and feeling.   The funeral strictly private, which I knew before I left town, or should have remained.   They wish to move the Queen to Osborne, but she puts it off every day, dreading the sight of the glaring daylight, it being impossible for the yacht to bring up under Osborne after dark.   As matters now stand she will go to-day, the Prince of Wales escorting her and returning. . . .

The Prince of Wales wishes not to have the Gren. Guards, and says that they ought to be given to some old General officer.`

He wrote yesterday to Palmerston by desire of his mother, to say that Lord P. would always find her mindful of her duty and of her people, but that her worldly career was at an end. . . .

From the very outset of his personal knowledge of the Prince Consort, at a time when it was the fashion to belittle him, Disraeli conceived a great admiration both for his abilities and for his character.   He told his sister in 1852 that the Prince was the best-educated man he ever met, but not over-educated ; and he told Lord Ponsonby in 1854 that his sentiment towards the Prince was ' one of devotion.' [1]   Further intercourse only strengthened this feeling.   ' With Prince Albert,' he said to Vitzthum just after the death, ' we have buried our Sovereign.   This German Prince has governed England for twenty-one years with a wisdom and energy such as none of our Kings have ever shown. . . .   If he had outlived some of our "old stagers," he would have given us, while retaining all constitutional guarantees, the blessings of absolute government.   Of us younger men who are qualified to enter the Cabinet, there is not one who would not willingly have bowed to his experience.   We are now in the midst of a change of government.' [2]

[1] See Vol. III., pp. 371, 531.   [2] Vitzthum, Vol. II., p. 176.

Disraeli's public tributes to the Prince's memory were particularly felicitous. On the Address in 1862, when the leaders of parties gave formal expression to the general sorrow, Disraeli described him as the 'prime councillor of a realm the political constitution of which did not even recognise his political existence.' He directed special attention to the Prince's services to culture in England. A want of culture had been a great deficiency in the national character. 'He was not satisfied with detecting a want; he resolved to supply it. His plans were deeply laid; they were maturely prepared; and, notwithstanding the obstacles which he inevitably encountered, I am prepared to say they were eminently successful.' Further,

Prince Albert was not a mere patron; he was not one of those who by their gold or by their smiles reward excellence or stimulate exertion. His contributions to the cause of the State were far more powerful and far more precious. He gave to it his thought, his time, his toil; he gave to it his life. On both sides and in all parts of the House I see many gentlemen who occasionally have acted with the Prince at those council boards, where they conferred and consulted upon the great undertakings with which he was connected. I ask them, without fear of a denial, whether he was not the leading spirit, whether his was not the mind which foresaw the difficulty, his not the resources which supplied the remedy; whether his was not the courage which sustained them under apparently overpowering difficulties; whether everyone who worked with him did not feel that he was the real originator of those plans of improvement which they assisted in carrying into effect.

The Queen expressed her thanks.

From Lord Derby.

St. James's Square, *Saturday night* [*Feb.* 8, 1862]. — I have had this afternoon a letter from Charles Phipps, with a complimentary notice from the Queen of my speech of Thursday, ending with the following: 'The Queen would be glad that Mr. Disraeli should also be made aware of H.M.'s grateful sense of his testimony to the worth and character of the Prince — perhaps as discriminating in the characteristics pointed out, and certainly as eloquent in the language employed, as any of those beautiful and glorious orations.' . . .

To Sir Charles Phipps.

GROSVENOR GATE, *Feb.* 9, 1862. — Lord Derby has communicated to me the gracious expressions of Her Majesty, and I should feel obliged to you, if the opportunity offer, to lay before Her Majesty my humble and dutiful acknowledgments.

What I attempted to express on Thursday night I deeply felt. During those conversations with which, of late years, the Prince occasionally honored me, I acquired much, both in knowledge and in feeling, which will ever influence my life.

In further acknowledgment the Queen sent to Disraeli what he termed in reply ' a hallowed gift ' — two engravings of well-known pictures of herself and the Prince.

In 1863, the year of the Prince of Wales's marriage, Disraeli was specially distinguished by Her Majesty, as he has explained in a long and interesting memorandum written at the time :

I heard at the end of the last, and at the beginning of this, year, more than once, from great personages about the Court, that the Queen had said, and repeated, that ' Mr. Disraeli was the only person who appreciated the Prince.'

When Parliament met, too, Her Majesty had occasion to write personally to Lord Derby respecting the Memorial Monument to the Prince, and some necessary steps that might be taken in Parliament thereon ; and she mentioned in the letter that she had no objection to his conferring with Mr. Disraeli, ' towards whom she should always entertain feelings of gratitude for the support which he had always given to the Prince ' in all his undertakings for the refinement of public taste and the improvement of society, or some words to that effect.

Lord Derby was generous enough to read this passage of H.M.'s letter to me.

In March the Royal Wedding took place. The Prince of Wales was married to the Princess of Denmark at Windsor. This alliance made a great sensation and excitement in the country. The long-pent-up feeling of affectionate devotion to the Queen, and of sympathy with her sorrows, came out with that deep and fervid enthusiasm for which the people of England are, I think, remarkable. But the excitement of the nation with their public receptions, and addresses, and processions, and splendid gifts, and the long vista of universal festivity, which was planned, and which lasted the whole

season, was quite equalled among the aristocracy, as to who should, or rather would, be invited to the Royal Wedding.

As the beautiful Chapel of St. George was very limited, and as there were a considerable number of royal guests, and as the principal persons of the Household, the Ambassadors, the Knights of the Garter, and the Cabinet Ministers, were as a matter of course to be invited, it became an interesting question where the line was to be drawn. At last it was whispered about that the limit was to be Duchesses. But as time drew on nobody seemed to be asked, and some great persons received suspicious invitations to a breakfast at Windsor Castle *after* the ceremony. At the same time tickets began to circulate in influential quarters, permitting the bearers to places in the cathedral nave, without the chapel, in order to see the processions pass. At last, however, about a fortnight before the ceremony or less, it was announced that, as there were only —— seats in the chapel, and as Sovereigns and Royal Princes, Knights of the Garter and their wives, Cabinet Ministers and Ambassadors and Great Officers of the Household, and their wives, would nearly fill it, there were necessarily few seats for H.M.'s private friends.

The disappointment and excitement equally increased. I have heard that, when the list was finally submitted to her Majesty, there were only four places not, as it were, officially appropriated. Her Majesty named Lord and Lady de la Warr, her earliest friends, and myself and my wife.

There is no language which can describe the rage, envy, and indignation, of the great world. The Duchess of Marlboro' went into hysterics of mortification at the sight of my wife, who was on terms of considerable intimacy with her, and said it was really shameful, after the reception which the Duke had given the Prince of Wales at Blenheim; and as for the Duchess of Manchester, who had been Mistress of the Robes in Lord Derby's Administration, she positively passed me for the season without recognition.

However, we went, and nothing could be more brilliant and effective than the whole affair[1] was. It is the only pageant which never disappointed me. The beautiful chapel, the glittering dresses, the various processions, first the Knights of the Garter, of the Royal Personages, of the Bridegroom, of the Bride: the heralds, the announcing trumpets, the suspense before the procession appeared, the magnificent music, the Queen in widowed garments in her Gothic cabinet, all deeply interesting or effective.

I had never seen the Queen since the catastrophe, and ventured, being near-sighted, to use my glass. I saw H.M.

[1] March 10.

well, and unfortunately caught her glance: perhaps she was looking to see whether we were there, and triumphing a little in the decided manner in which she had testified 'her gratitude.' I did not venture to use my glass again.

The Prince of Wales, who was habited as a Knight of the Garter, deported himself with great dignity, and conducted himself at the altar, where he was left an unusual time alone, from some accident that occurred in the procession of the bride, with grace and tact: all eyes being upon him.

The way in which the royal personages looked up and bowed to the royal cabinet was singularly graceful and imposing: and in this respect the Princess Mary of Cambridge exceeded them all. Her demeanour was most dignified.

After the ceremony, the festival was very joyous, a great number of guests who had been invited to the breakfast at the Castle then appearing. I should say 500 or 600 persons. The royal personages breakfasted apart: but the mistake was made of not inviting the Ambassadors and their wives to this exclusive repast, who took rank above all the royal guests who were inferior to their Sovereigns whom they personally represented. Comte Apponyi was wroth on this head, and certainly the Hungarian dress of Madame Apponyi, which had only arrived the night before, justified any distinction. It was the most gorgeous and graceful costume ever worn: bright blue velvet, richly embroidered in gold, and astounding sables, but the fancy of the dress exceeded its costly materials.

They had lodgings at Windsor, and the Ambassadress changed her costume before she left Windsor. This was fortunate, for the arrangements for departure were bad; the ladies were mobbed at the station, and, as many of them had tiaras of diamonds, they were in danger of being plundered. Madame Apponyi was separated from the Ambassador; I rescued her, and got her into a railway carriage with my wife and some other grand dames, who had lost their husbands. I think I had to sit on my wife's lap. When we got to Paddington in the rain, there was no ambassadorial carriage: but ours was there, and so we took home safe this brilliant and delightful person.

A great lady of the Court, who was my secret friend, and proved herself on many occasions a real one, told me at the breakfast that the Queen meant to see me. She repeated that the Queen said she was determined to see me. From which, and other things, I inferred that there had been difficulties put in the way. Lord Derby had had an audience of H.M. before the wedding, on the alleged ground of conferring about the Memorial, but understood as a token of

H.M.'s return to public life, and that she would commence
to see her Ministers socially, and exalted persons who had
been near her person. Lord Derby never mentioned any of
the details of this audience to me, but his son did. The
Queen received him in her closet sitting ; the audience was
by no means brief, and Lord Derby stood the whole time,
although recovering from a severe fit of the gout. The Queen
even alluded to this, and said she feared he would suffer by
standing, but offered no seat. So severe was the etiquette.

Notwithstanding my private intimation, time rolled on,
and I never heard anything of my audience. Weeks, even
months, passed.[1] The Queen had received all her principal
Ministers, Lord Clarendon and Lord Derby, and there it
stopped. I saw my friend occasionally in society, and once
she asked me whether I had heard anything ; and when I
replied in the negative, she said, ' Be sure you will, for H.M.
said only the other day she was determined to see Mr. D.'

On —— I received an invitation to Windsor Castle for
April 22, and to stay till the next day.

When I arrived at the Castle, I received a note from Bid-
dulph telling me that the Queen would receive me before
dinner, at a $\frac{1}{4}$ past seven o'clock. He gave me the hint, that
I might make my toilet early, and so be able to leave the
presence chamber for the banquet, which was about an hour
after. After I was dressed, there came another note to
say that Lord John Russell had arrived from town with important despatches, and that the Queen would be engaged,
and would postpone my audience till the morrow after breakfast.

It was the beginning of the Polish Insurrection, and the
Ministry were much perplexed. The despatches were about
Poland. I was struck at dinner by the contrast with the
somewhat subdued tone that prevailed in former days at
the royal dinners. The Prince and Princess of Wales were
our host and hostess. The party large, though consisting
only of courtiers (there were more than two households
blended), the only guests being Earl Russell and myself.
The Prince of Wales gave me the idea of a young man who
had just come into a large estate and was delighted at entertaining his friends. He took out his sister, the Princess
Helena, and sate opposite the Princess of Wales, who was
taken out by Prince Alfred. On the other side of Prince
Alfred was the Countess of Desart (in waiting), and I sate
between her and Lady Augusta Bruce, sister of Lord Elgin,
whom I had met before at Windsor, when she was in attendance on the Duchess of Kent. I was glad to renew my

[1] The delay was just six weeks.

acquaintance with her, for, like all her family, she is clever, and told me in the course of the dinner a great deal.

When the ladies had retired, I was next to Prince Alfred, who invited me to take Lady Desart's vacated seat. I had not seen him since he was a very young and very little midshipman. Though still in his teens, he was much altered, had grown a great deal, a bronzed and manly countenance, with a thoughtful brow; altogether like his father. His brother, the Prince of Wales, was a Guelph, not a Coburg. The Queen said he was exactly like a portrait which they had there of Frederick, Prince of Wales. I thought him very like a portrait also at Windsor of his [great-]grandfather, George the Third, shortly after his accession. Lord Malmesbury said that his general resemblance to his [great-]grandfather was so great that he already was always asking questions and talking loud.

Prince Alfred had just recovered from a severe and dangerous fever, which had prevented (*sic*) being at the wedding. He was detained by it at Malta, and the telegrams, which were constant, were so alarming that one day they feared the wedding could not take place. Alluding to his illness and Malta, we naturally talked of his travels : he had seen a great deal, having been at the Cape, etc. : on all of which he spoke with simplicity and sense. He was glad to be home again. I remember he said, 'What a fine Castle this is! I never saw any one in any country to be compared with it. I love this Castle; I was born in it.'

When we returned to the saloon, the circle was formed as if the Queen were present, but the Prince and Princess did not make the round. She kept apart, and then the Prince came and addressed Lord Russell in the circle, and then led him to the Princess, with whom he conversed for about ten minutes. Then, after a very short space, the Prince came to me, and conversed a little. He asked me whether I thought the Bill for abolishing the City Police would pass? I replied that I had not given any personal attention to the subject, but my impression was not favorable to its success. He said he had heard the same, but it ought to pass : there ought to be only one police for the capital. I perceived from this what I afterwards had proof of, that the passing of the Bill was a capital point with the Court. The opposition to the Bill turned out to be so general throughout the country, that it was eventually withdrawn by the Ministry without a division; not before, however, several courtiers, who had seats in the House of Commons, making (*sic*) speeches against it, which made the discomfiture more flagrant, as well as the particular animus more obvious.

After this, the Prince proposed that he should present me
to H.R.H. and I went up accordingly. I had therefore, at
last, a good opportunity of forming an opinion of her appearance, which was highly favorable. Her face was delicate
and refined; her features regular; her brow well moulded; her
mouth beautiful; her hair good and her ears small. She was
very thin. She had the accomplishment of being gracious
without smiling. She had repose. She spoke English, but
not with the fluency I had expected, and I don't think she
always comprehended what was said. The Prince hovered
about her, and after a few minutes joined the conversation.

I remember nothing very particular about it except that it
fell upon nightingales, and I asked H.R.H. whether she knew
what nightingales fed upon. While she was confessing her
ignorance and her curiosity, the Prince came, and she addressed
the question to him, which he could not answer. I told them
—upon glow-worms; exactly the food which nightingales
should require. The Prince was interested by this, and exclaimed: 'Is that a fact, or is it a myth?'

'Quite a fact, sir; for my woodman is my authority, for
we have a great many nightingales at Hughenden, and a
great many glow-worms.'

'We have got one nightingale at Sandringham,' said the
Prince, smiling.

I remember now that the conversation got to nightingales
in this manner. The Princess told me they were delighted
with their London residence; they awoke in the morning, and
looked into a garden, and heard the birds sing. I said then,
'I fear, not nightingales, madam.'

After this there was the private band, just the same as if
H.M. were present; and at 11 o'clock the Prince and Princess
and attendants retired.

On the morrow I breakfasted with the Lady-in-Waiting and
the Maids of Honor, and Lord John Russell. We had a merry
breakfast, for the ladies wished to make Lord John and
myself talk: and I, who was really somewhat nervous from
my approaching interview, was glad to take refuge in raillery.
Lord John was genial, which, on the whole, he generally has
been with me. For, notwithstanding our fierce public struggles
for long years, and the crusade I have always preached
against High Whiggism, of which he was the incarnate creation, there were really some elements of sympathy between
us, being (sic), with all his hauteur and frigid manner, really
a man of sentiment, and imagination, and culture.

When breakfast was over we were left together, and I
asked him seriously what was the real state of affairs in Poland.
He spoke with great frankness on the matter, and among

other things that the Cabinet had sent a secret agent to Poland in order to obtain some accurate information (I think Oliphant); ' but I can't say,' he added, ' we are much the wiser. The best opinions seem to hold that it will be put down in the summer: but'—and he shrugged his shoulders —' it may not be: and then——' He went to town, and I was left alone with the newspapers. In about a quarter of an hour I was summoned. The attendant led me down part of the great gallery, and then turned off into a familiar corridor; and then, through an antechamber, I was ushered into Prince Albert's special room: a small cabinet, decorated with all the objects of art he loved, and in which I had frequently had the privilege of conferring, and listening at length to his views on public life and politics; when, throwing off his reserve and shyness, he warmed into eloquence, not unmixed with sarcastic humor, but, on all subjects on which he spoke, distinguished by his perfect knowledge and his thought. The room was quite unchanged. It was in every respect as if he had resided in it yesterday: the writing materials, the books, all the indications of habitual occupation. Only one change I observed: a plate on his accustomed chair, with an inscription: ' This was the Prince Consort's chair from 18— to 1861.'

In less than five minutes from my entry, an opposite door opened, and the Queen appeared.

She was still in widow's mourning, and seemed stouter than when I last saw her, but this was perhaps only from her dress. I bowed deeply when she entered, and raised my head with unusual slowness, that I might have a moment for recovery. Her countenance was grave, but serene and kind, and she said, in a most musical voice: ' It is some time since we met.'

Then to some murmuring words of mine H.M. said: ' You have not had a very busy session this year?' In assenting to this, I expressed my wish that politics were in general as serene as the House of Commons. Upon this H.M. entered into the state of public affairs with frankness and some animation, which entirely removed the first embarrassment of the audience. It was then like an audience between a Sovereign and a Minister.

H.M. expressed her conviction that, whatever happened, the American Union could not be restored. She spoke fully about Poland, nor was it difficult to recognise that the insurrection alarmed her from its possible consequences on the state of Germany. H.M., however, it was quite clear, was sanguine that the Russians would suppress it by the summer.

She asked me frankly whether I thought the present Ministry

would get through the session. I said they were weak, but there was no desire to displace them unless a stronger one could be established. She said she hoped no crisis would be brought about wantonly, for, in her forlorn condition, she hardly knew what she could do. I said H.M.'s comfort was an element in all our considerations, and that no action would be taken, I felt sure, unless from commanding necessity.

She said 'Lord Palmerston was grown very old.' I replied, 'But his voice in debate, madam, is as loud as ever.'

'Yes!' she exclaimed with animation. 'And his hand-writing! Did you ever see such a handwriting? So very clear and strong! Nevertheless I see in him a great change, a very great change. His countenance is so changed.'

Then H.M., turning from public affairs, deigned to say that it had given her great pleasure to observe that I had been chosen Trustee of the British Museum in the place of the late Lord Lansdowne: and she spoke for some time on kindred subjects, alluding to what the Prince had done rather than directly referring to him herself.

At last she asked after my wife, and hoped she was well, and then, with a graceful bow, vanished.

On the afternoon of this audience the question of the memorial to the Prince came up in the House of Commons on a resolution for a grant of £50,000, in addition to the £60,000 already collected by voluntary subscriptions. Disraeli pleaded strongly for a monument rather than a work of utility — a monument which 'should, as it were, represent the character of the Prince himself in the harmony of its proportions, in the beauty of its ornament, and in its enduring nature. It should be something direct, significant, and choice, so that those who come after us may say: "This is the type and testimony of a sublime life and a transcendent career, and thus they were recognised by a grateful and admiring people." '[1] A monument was decided on, and London knows it well;

---

[1] Disraeli was dissatisfied with the report of this speech, and apparently sent the Queen a memorandum of his actual words. A draft letter to Her Majesty, preserved among his papers, explains : 'Ld. P. had judiciously arranged that the memorial vote should take precedence of other business, and there were skilled reporters ready who would have faithfully represented what was said on that occasion. But an American debate was irresistibly forced on, and the skilled reporters exhausted their energies on its grey proceedings, so that those who spoke afterwards, on the gentler themes, fell to very rude and uncouth hands.'

whether it entirely carries out Disraeli's aspirations may be doubted.

To Mrs. Willyams, whom he had gratified with an account of his audience in much the same words as in the memorandum, he detailed in a subsequent letter the sequel.

To Mrs. Brydges Willyams.

Confidential. GROSVENOR GATE, *May* 5, 1863. — I must continue, and conclude, my Windsor adventures. When I came up to town on the Thursday, from the Castle, there was a debate in the House of Commons on the vote for a monument to Prince Albert. The Queen, with great delicacy, had not mentioned the subject to me — and of course I did not allude to it.

You probably read the observations which I made on the question in the House of Commons.

That was on Thursday night, and on Saturday morning I received from the Queen her own copy of the speeches of the Prince (the same work which I gave you when first published). The copy was bound in white morocco, and on the fly-leaf, in the Queen's own handwriting, was this inscription : [1]

TO

THE RIGHT HONOURABLE BENJAMIN DISRAELI

IN RECOLLECTION OF THE GREATEST AND BEST OF MEN

FROM THE BELOVED PRINCE'S BROKEN-HEARTED WIDOW

VICTORIA R.

WINDSOR CASTLE,
April 24, 1863.

I think you will agree with me that this is the most remarkable inscription which a Sovereign ever placed in a volume graciously presented to a subject!

But there was also a packet tied with black silk, and that contained a letter! But I must stop, like the Sultana in the Arabian Nights, and I find I cannot conclude as I intended.

This was the Queen's letter :

From Queen Victoria.

WINDSOR CASTLE, *April* 24, 1863. — The Queen cannot resist from expressing, personally, to Mr. Disraeli her deep gratification at the tribute he paid to her adored, beloved,

---

[1] In transcribing the inscription Disraeli made one or two slips, which have been corrected by reference to the original.

and great husband. The perusal of it made her shed many tears, but it was very soothing to her broken heart to see such true appreciation of that spotless and unequalled character.

The Queen asks Mr. Disraeli to accept the accompanying book.

Disraeli, in reply, sent Her Majesty a considered estimate of the Prince's character and career.

To Queen Victoria.

GROSVENOR GATE, *April* 25, 1863. — Mr. Disraeli, with his humble duty to your Majesty, begs permission to express his gratitude to your Majesty, for your Majesty's gracious and affecting condescension, and for the inestimable volume which your Majesty has deigned to present to him.

If, in venturing to touch upon a sacred theme, Mr. Disraeli may have, occasionally, used expressions which your Majesty has been graciously pleased to deem not altogether inadequate to the subject, he has been enabled to do so only because, on that subject, he speaks from the heart, and from long and frequent musing over its ever-living interest.

His acquaintance with the Prince is one of the most satisfactory incidents of his life: full of refined and beautiful memories, and exercising, as he hopes, over his remaining existence, a soothing and exalting influence.

The Prince is the only person, whom Mr. Disraeli has ever known, who realized the Ideal. None with whom he is acquainted have ever approached it. There was in him an union of the manly grace and sublime simplicity, of chivalry with the intellectual splendor of the Attic Academe. The only character in English History that would, in some respects, draw near to him is Sir Philip Sidney: the same high tone, the same universal accomplishment, the same blended tenderness and vigor, the same rare combination of romantic energy and classic repose.

Both left us in their youth. But there is no person in our history who has established such a permanent, and almost mystic, ascendancy over national feeling as Sir Philip Sidney; and the writer of these lines is much mistaken if, as time advances, the thought and sentiment of a progressive age will not cluster round the Prince; his plans will become systems, his suggestions dogmas, and the name of Albert will be accepted as the master-type of a generation of profounder feeling and vaster range than that which he formed and guided with benignant power.

How the Queen was affected by this, it must be confessed, somewhat hyperbolic eulogium may be seen from a letter written to the editor of the Prince's speeches by the lady who afterwards became Dean Stanley's wife.

Lady Augusta Bruce to Arthur Helps.

OSBORNE, *May* 4, 1863. — The Queen knows with what peculiar interest you will read anything from the pen of Mr. Disraeli on the subject which so engrosses Her Majesty; but, independently of this, the Queen has been anxious that you should have an opportunity of perusing the most striking and beautiful letter that Her Majesty has received, and has therefore directed me to send you the enclosed extracts from that in which Mr. Disraeli acknowledges the volume sent to him by the Queen.

I need not tell you how her Majesty has been affected by the depth and delicacy of these touches, or how soothing it is to the Queen to have this inexhaustible theme so treated. . . .

Disraeli failed rather signally this summer in an attempt to help the Court to carry out the Prince Consort's South Kensington schemes. Parliament was asked by the Government, with Disraeli's support, to acquire for the nation both the site and the building of the Exhibition of 1862. There was no difficulty about the site, but the purchase of the building was resented on account of its ugliness and unsuitability. Malmesbury tells us that the scene was extraordinary. 'Disraeli had canvassed his supporters, telling them that he had a letter in his pocket from the Queen. This had a disastrous effect, and when he got up the hooting was so terrific that he could not be heard.' Gladstone had already infuriated the House by using an argument, which was taken as a menace, that the contractors were under no obligation to remove the building. 'So the House,' adds Malmesbury, 'rose *en masse*, and, after a scene of the utmost confusion and excitement, defeated the Government by more than two to one;[1] Gladstone and Disraeli looking equally angry.' Both Disraeli's tact and his knowledge of the House seem to have deserted him,

[1] July 2.

and he was the more chagrined as he had confidently
assured the Court that success was certain in a matter
which the Queen had much at heart.

Disraeli's letters to Mrs. Willyams during the first
half of 1863 are full of Court functions and other festivities incidental to the royal marriage. Celebrations of
the kind, which most British statesmen in the Victorian
era regarded as a necessary bore, whatever pleasure their
wives may have taken in them, were entered into by
Disraeli with a keen zest. The trappings of royal and
noble life appealed to his sense of fitness; and the world
of to-day has largely come round to his view, discarding
the old Benthamite intolerance of everything that could
not prove its economic utility.

To Mrs. Brydges Willyams.

GROSVENOR GATE, *Jan.* 14, 1863. — The Saxon Minister at
this Court, Comte Vitzthum, told me on Sunday that he was
at Dresden in the autumn, on leave of absence from St.
James's, when the Prince of Wales arrived there, and the
King of Saxony consigned His Royal Highness to his care.
He was the Prince's companion for three days, making Dresden (and Saxony, too, for they went several excursions) agreeable to him.

He says the Prince has good talents — not of the high class
of the Princess Royal and Princess Alice, but good. He is
gay, extremely amiable, well informed, and, although simple
and unaffected, quite *grand seigneur.*

The King of Saxony told the Prince not to waste time in
paying state visits of compliment and wearing uniforms,
but to go about in plain clothes and see all that was worth
looking at in Dresden; and 'in the evening we will dine at a
palace in the country where there will be no form, and you
can wear a plain coat.'

After Comte Vitzthum and the Prince had examined the
museums, galleries, etc., the Prince said to him: 'Don't you
think now we might have a little shopping?'

Agreed: and they went to a great jeweller's, and the Prince
bought some bracelets for his future bride; and to some
porcelain shops, where he purchased many objects for his
brothers and sisters; but he never asked the price of anything, which quite delighted the Saxons, who look upon that
as quite *grand seigneur.*

CARLTON CLUB, *Feb.* 25, 1863. — I went to the Prince of Wales's first levée to-day. He received me very cordially, and shook hands with me. I had not seen His Royal Highness for two years. He looked well, and has grown. Sir Henry Holland says that he is 5 ft. 8 in. high, but, then, Sir Henry is not only a physician, but a courtier. However, the Prince certainly looks taller than I ever expected he would turn out to be. . . .

Nobody talks of anything but of the Princess's entrance into London.

GROSVENOR GATE, *March* 4, 1863. — . . . Summer weather, and the world quite mad; all London is encased with tapestried scaffolding and carpeted galleries, and the streets already swarm.

The Lord Mayor has invited us to view the procession from the Mansion House, Baron Rothschild from Piccadilly, and there are many intermediate invitations between these extremes of East and West.

This is for Saturday, the 7th. Tuesday, the 10th, is the bridal day. . . .

March 21, 1863. — I hope you have not had the influenza: if any of your friends have, avoid them; 'tis infectious. It has raged in London — half the House of Commons are absent from their posts: Gladstone ill, Lord Russell *very*. I have escaped comparatively lightly: that is to say, I have not absolutely knocked up, and during the Court festivities have managed to make my appearance, but that was all. Very weak and without energy, and quite unable to write even a letter, which is the reason I have not troubled you.

The wedding was a fine affair — a thing to remember. A perfect pageant, with that sufficient foundation of sentiment which elevates a mere show. The bridal of a young heir to the throne would have been enough in this sense, but the presence of the imperial and widowed mother in her Gothic pavilion, watching everything with intense interest, seeing everything, though herself almost unseen, was deeply dramatic and even affecting. . . .

The Queen was very anxious that an old shoe should be thrown at the royal pair on their departure, and the Lord Chamberlain showed me in confidence the weapon with which he had furnished himself. He took out of his pocket a beautiful white satin slipper, which had been given him, for the occasion, by the Duchess of Brabant; alas! when the hour arrived, his courage failed him, and he hustled the fairy slipper into the carriage. This is a genuine anecdote, which you will not find in the *Illustrated News.*

On the Friday following, the Duchess of Cambridge gave

a grand entertainment to the Danish Royal family at her
rooms at St. James's. The Danish Minister presented me
to the father of the Princess of Wales, the Prince Christian,
still a very young man, or looking so. Five-and-twenty years
ago he came over to Queen Victoria's Coronation as one of
her suitors.

Later in the evening the Duke of Cambridge presented me
to the mother of the bride, the Princess Christian: a woman
of great vivacity and grace, still pretty, and once famously so.

Last evening, the Prince and Princess of Wales, having
returned from Osborne, gave their first evening party at St.
James's Palace, which had not been used for such an occasion
since the reign of George III.

It was a very brilliant affair, limited to 500 guests of the
diplomacy and the *haute noblesse*: all the Dukes and Duchesses
with scarcely an exception. The Prince and Princess looked
like a young couple in a fairy tale. She had on a crown of
diamonds, and walked in procession through the illumined
saloons, while the Queen's private band, of the choicest
musicians, played triumphantly. . . .

June 14, 1863. — This royal honeymoon, of many months,
is perfectly distracting. Nothing but balls and banquets, and
receptions, and inaugurations and processions, so that one
has not a moment to oneself, and lives only in a glittering
bustle. This has been a remarkably busy week. On Monday
a marvellous fête given in the Guildhall by the Corporation
of London — a very great success, and in its splendor and fine
taste quite equalling the similar displays at Paris, which
hitherto we have not approached; for though the Hôtel de
Ville may yield to us in turtle soup, it has always surpassed
our citizens in the elegance and invention of their festivals.
But on Monday Gog and Magog triumphed.

On Tuesday I was taken up with the ' Act of Uniformity '
and the House of Commons, but, though kept up late, I was
in time on Wednesday to take my place in a procession,
when the Prince of Wales inaugurated the uncovering of the
statue of his father at Kensington.

Thursday was a tremendous banquet given to the prince
by the Merchant Taylors' Company, where I had to return
thanks for the House of Commons: a very grand affair with
four Royal Princes and six Dukes present. But everything
yielded in splendor, in brilliancy, in gorgeous magnificence,
to the fête which the Duke and Duchess of Northumberland
gave to the Prince and Princess of Wales on Friday last!

We dined sixty guests of the high nobility in a magnificent
gallery, as fine in dimensions, and far more splendid than the
Galerie de Diane of the Tuileries. Such plate, such diamonds,

so many Duchesses, and Knights of the Garter, were never before assembled together!

To-morrow we go to the glories of Oxford.

June 25, 1863. — Oxford was a Carnival. There was too much crowded into every day. That was the only fault. Every day there were five or six *functions*, as the Spaniards call them. On Wednesday, for example, there was Grand Commemoration; a collation in the Library of All Souls College, which is more than 300 feet long — the noblest of apartments; a bazaar for the Radcliffe infirmary; a garden fête; a boat race, worthy of the Regattas and Ridottos of Venice; a banquet at Exeter College; and a Christ Church Ball — and the Prince and Princess went to all! And all this amid endless cheering, and music, and shouts. Too much even for youth and beauty. We had three days of it, and this holiday made such an arrear of business that I have never been able to get right since my return. As Lord Chesterfield said of the old Duke of Newcastle, who was Minister in his time, I am always running after the three days I have lost. . . .

To-morrow the Conservative Association give me a public dinner; and in the evening the Brigade of Guards are to give the Princess of Wales the most gorgeous ball ever produced in any age or any country. Mrs. Disraeli will be there, and I if possible.

To Lord Derby.

HUGHENDEN MANOR, *Sept.* 2, 1863. — . . . The Queen returns from a not uneventful German campaign, for not only is princess Helena to be married, but Prince Alfred, and that, too, early in the spring: the Princess not inferior to the Princess of Wales! But you know all this.

For my part I think even Princes should sow their wild oats, and not step out paterfamilias from the nursery or the middy's berth. . . .

Mention was made, in Disraeli's account of his audience of the Queen in 1863, of his recent election as a Trustee of the British Museum. Not merely the election itself, but the circumstances in which it took place and the manner in which it was communicated to him, gave Disraeli legitimate satisfaction.

From Lord Palmerston.

94, PICCADILLY, *March* 25, 1863.

MY DEAR MR. DISRAELI, — You will of course receive from the Secretary to the Trustees of the British Museum the

official notification that at a meeting held by them this after-noon you were elected a Trustee in the room of the late Lord Lansdowne; but it may be agreeable to you to know the grounds upon which the choice of the Trustees was made.

The Trustees were of opinion that in making choice of a new colleague they ought to select a person distinguished by literary eminence; that it would be useful to the interests of the Museum that he should be in a prominent position in the House of Commons, so as to be able, when occasions might arise, to explain with authority to the House any matter connected with the Museum which might be brought under discussion; and, lastly, it was felt that, whereas many of the existing Trustees belong more or less to one political party, it was desirable that the choice to be made should show that party politics are not to be permitted to enter within the gates of a building dedicated to Learning and to the Arts. All these considerations seemed to point to you as the proper object of choice, and accordingly you were unanimously elected. — Yours faithfully, PALMERSTON.

To Lord Palmerston.

March, 1863.

MY DEAR LORD, — There are few distinctions I should more highly value than to become a Trustee of the British Museum.

My father was the first man of letters who, much more than half a century ago, began to turn its MS. wealth to account in the illustration of our history, and I have been brought up in a due appreciation of its treasures and a due reverence for its authorities.

But what I most esteem in the present matter are the mode and medium by which my election has been communicated to me.

I hope your Lordship is not quite unaware of the sincere regard which I have always personally entertained for you since our first acquaintance, and, notwithstanding the inevit-able collisions of public life, I can truly say that perhaps no one grudges your greatness less than your obliged and faithful servant, B. DISRAELI.

Disraeli has left a note of his conversation with the Queen about the Museum:

H.M. asked me what I thought of Panizzi,[1] and whether he were equal to the post.

I replied that my official experience was too slight to

---

[1] Principal Librarian, 1856–1866.

permit me to offer a personal opinion, but that he was much esteemed by my colleagues.

H.M. thought it strange that a foreigner should be at the head of an institution so peculiarly national.

I observed that the post had been frequently filled by foreigners; that when I was a boy it was filled by Mr. Planta,[1] a Swiss, and the father of a gentleman who had served Her Majesty's uncles as U.S. of State for Foreign Affairs; that in older days Dr. Maty,[2] who, I believe, was a Frenchman, had been in high office at the Museum. . . . I mentioned also that Mr. Hallam thought very highly of Panizzi, and that my father, a great authority on vernacular literature had been astonished by his intimate acquaintance with English books.

Disraeli attended with assiduity to his duties as Trustee, and when in office never forgot the interests of the Museum. It was mainly due to his clear-sightedness and promptitude that the wonderful Blacas Collection in Paris, which, with its wealth of gems and cameos, the French Emperor was anxious to keep for France, was secured for England and the British Museum at the cost of £48,000. 'This purchase,' wrote Disraeli to the Queen on November 26, 1866, 'will facilitate the plans of the Chancellor of the Exchequer for the separation of the National Collections, and the establishment of the Museum of Natural History at Kensington.' Another matter in which he specially interested himself was the securing for the British Museum, during the 1874 Ministry, of the Castellani Collection, including the fine bronze head of Venus. In fact, his record as Trustee and as Minister is one for which the Museum has reason to be grateful.

[1] Principal Librarian, 1799–1827.
[2] Principal Librarian, 1772–1776.

CHAPTER XII

REFORM REVIVED

1864–1866

'Rest and be thankful'; that was the cold comfort which Russell, the veteran Reformer, offered to his fellow-Reformers in a speech in Scotland in the autumn of 1863. Reform was certainly in a backwater. Not only were the Prime Minister and Parliament indifferent or hostile; but the apparent disruption of the United States, that ideal democratic community which Bright and his friends had constantly held up for imitation, was taken by the ordinary Englishman as evidence that a democratic suffrage was an unstable basis on which to build a State. In Disraeli's words, the collapse of republican institutions must tell immensely in favour of aristocracy. The argument was pressed home repeatedly in Robert Cecil's articles in the *Quarterly Review*. But the Cabinet contained one restless Minister, who was little disposed to accept his colleague Russell's advice. On a Wednesday afternoon[1] in 1864, while a private member's Bill for lowering the borough franchise was occupying the languid attention of the House, Gladstone, who interposed to state the position of the Government, electrified the torpid audience by a momentous declaration: 'I venture to say that every man who is not presumably incapacitated by some consideration of personal unfitness or of political danger is morally entitled to come within the pale of the Constitution.' No

[1] May 11.

public man, outside of the Radical ranks, had hitherto
openly advocated a lowering of the franchise at all com-
parable in extent to that suggested in these words; and
great and widespread was their reverberation.   Curiously
enough, in substance, and indeed in language, the declaration was hardly distinguishable from the pronouncement
of Disraeli's organ, the *Press*, more than ten years before,
in an article written by Stanley,[1] which advocated bringing 'within the pale of the Constitution everyone whose
admission cannot be proved dangerous.' But Disraeli,
who had not seen the article before publication, hastily
dropped this sweeping proposition; and in any case
neither he nor Stanley would have justified it by an appeal to the moral law.

It was this appeal that constituted the most striking
feature of Gladstone's dictum — an appeal which, as
Disraeli said, recalled Rousseau's *Social Contract*, and
Tom Paine's *Rights of Man*. It was an appeal which
was to stand Gladstone in good stead to the end of his
career. He could seldom adopt a policy with enthusiasm
until he had satisfied himself that to carry it out was a
moral, if not a religious, obligation. But, if that were
so, opposition must obviously be inspired by the spirit of
evil; and it was too frequently as the incarnation of
that spirit that Disraeli was regarded by his great rival.
To Disraeli, on the other hand, politics in most of its
phases presented itself as what surely it usually is — a
choice between the more and the less expedient; and he
was naturally disposed to regard as cant an advocacy
which was ostentatiously put on the moral plane. A
toleration, if not an affection, for cant is, however, unless
all our foreign critics are in error, a characteristic of the
British people; and undoubtedly the attitude of moral
superiority which Gladstone constantly assumed was, in
the Britain of the nineteenth century, worth much in
votes.

[1] Nov. 5, 1853. See Vol. III., p. 501.

To Lord Derby.

GROSVENOR GATE, *May* 13, 1864.—. . . Though Gladstone's move was matured, and, indeed, for a considerable time contemplated, I have no doubt the visit and reception of Garibaldi have acted on his impressionable nature, and have betrayed him into a far more extreme position than was at first intended. The consequences must be grave, though I dare say the Cavendishes, Russells, etc., will, in due time, swallow his programme. The smaller Whigs, Beaumonts, Ramsdens, and perhaps Lansdownes and Fitzwilliams, may detach themselves.

Gladstone's declaration, though it disturbed his chief and embarrassed his colleagues, marked him out as the coming Liberal leader, with democratic Reform as a principal feature of his policy; and it was in that capacity that he was welcomed in Lancashire in the following autumn, during an oratorical tour which he made in his native county. But in Parliament, in spite of him, Reform made in 1864 no progress. The ballot was rejected by a majority of 89, and Locke King's County Franchise Bill by 27; while Baines's Borough Franchise Bill was shelved by 56. Finance, foreign affairs, and the Church, were still the topics that occupied men's minds and the attention of Parliament. Disraeli has left a short note describing this session of 1864.

The session a very curious one; I was watching for five months for the proper moment for battle. It was very difficult to restrain our friends. The Government every day more unpopular, and yet it was clear to me that the House would not directly censure them. The tactic was to postpone to the last moment a direct attack, but to defeat them in the interval on some indirect vote, taking advantage of the discontent of the House. Thus, on the Ashantee War[1] we ran them to 6 or 7, and on Stansfeld's affair[2] to 10; on either question they would have resigned. On the direct vote (their Danish policy)[3] their majority was 18, of which

[1] A minor expedition in which there had been excessive loss of life by disease.

[2] Stansfeld, at this time a subordinate member of the Government, had allowed letters for Mazzini, the Italian revolutionist, to be sent to his private address under a false name. It was in this debate that Bright quoted the *Revolutionary Epick* against Disraeli. See Vol. I., pp. 241, 242.

[3] See above, Ch. 9.

they affected to be proud, though in old days it would have been considered a defeat. Sir Robert Peel, on his vote of want of confidence in 1840, moved by Sir John Buller, was beaten by 22, but was Minister next year, 1841.

Lord P., after the division, scrambled up a wearying staircase to the ladies' gallery. My informant, who was behind him, had the good taste and tact to linger. He saw the ladies' gallery open, and Lady Palmerston advance, and they embraced! An interesting scene, and what pluck! To mount those dreadful stairs at three o'clock in the morning, and eighty years of age! My informant would not disturb them. It was a great moment.

Disraeli repeated in the session of 1865 the tactics of reserve which he had practised in 1864, and which seemed to him particularly prudent in view of the forthcoming elections.

To Lord Derby.

Hughenden Manor, *Dec.* 12, 1864. — . . . There is only one point which I wish to submit to you — to consider whether it is necessary that the leaders of Opposition in the two Houses on the first night should make those elaborate and comprehensive surveys of the public situation which, of late years, it has become their habit of doing.

The principle, now conveniently assumed by our opponents, that the Opposition is a body prepared to take office, and therefore bound to give its quasi-official opinion on the conduct of every department, seems to me to have no sound foundation, and is very injurious to us. It forces us to show our cards the first night of the session, and the Government profits accordingly. They see where the breakers are ahead, and what perils they have escaped. . . .

Disraeli could not persuade Derby to silence on the Address; but he was silent himself, and, indeed, did not for many weeks take an active part in debate. In spite of pressure from Derby, he refused to speak on the question of the disestablishment of the Irish Church, which was brought forward by an independent Radical. Derby wrote, March 10, 1865: 'Considering the great stress you have always laid upon Church questions as our main *cheval de bataille*, I hope that you will yourself

consider it not an unfitting occasion for breaking through
(if you should not have done so before) the profound
silence which you have maintained during the present
session.' Disraeli was, as we know, conscious of the
weak points in the position of the Irish Church, and
thought it wiser to take no part in a debate in which
Gladstone expressed at once his dissatisfaction with the
Establishment and his reluctance to take any immediate
step. Disraeli exhibited an ostentatious indifference to
a motion for the repeal of the malt tax, which Fitzroy
Kelly, the principal Law Officer of the last Derby Government, insisted on bringing forward in opposition to his
leader's wishes. In a discussion on the subject in the
previous session, Disraeli had expressed his agreement
as to the objectionable character of the tax, which he
had himself endeavoured to reduce in 1852. But the
question should be dealt with in a large and comprehensive
manner; and, as he had contended over and over again,
the war duty on sugar should first be repealed. In 1864
the motion was rejected by more than two to one; in
1865 it was shelved by a majority of 81.

It was colonial policy which drew Disraeli from his
reserve. The successful Northerners in the United States
appeared to be threatening Canada — Canada, which was
now uniting into a confederation under pressure of events,
and which might, Disraeli thought, become the ' Russia of
the New World.' What was to be the political future of
that and our other colonies? It was the parting of
the ways. Disraeli gave a patriotic lead in a speech on
March 13. How strong the anti-Imperial drift was in
Parliament at the time is shown by the tentative and
hypothetical manner in which he handled the question.

We are on the eve of events of very great importance.
The question we have to ask ourselves is, Is this country
prepared to renounce her American dependencies and
colonies, or are we to retain that tie? Now, if these colonies
expressed a wish to separate the connection, and if they
preferred to be absorbed by the United States, we might

terminate our connection with dignity and without disaster. But if, on the other hand, those views are just which are more generally accepted — if there should be, on the part of Canada and the other North American colonies, a sincere and deep desire to form a considerable State, and develop its resources, and to preserve the patronage and aid of England, until that mature hour when we shall lose our dependency but gain a permanent ally and friend — then it would be the greatest political blunder for us to renounce, relinquish, and avoid, the responsibility of maintaining our interests in Canada at the present moment.

If, from considerations of expense, we were to quit the possessions that we now occupy in North America, it would be ultimately, as regards our resources and wealth, as fatal and disastrous a step as could possibly be taken. Our prosperity would not long remain a consolation to us, and we might then prepare for the invasion of our country and the subjugation of the people. I infer that hon. gentlemen opposite do not express these views, which have, however, found utterance in other quarters; but that they take a truly patriotic and English view of this subject — namely, not to force our connection on any dependency; but if, at a moment of revolution in North America, we find our colonies asserting the principle of their nationality, and if, foreseeing a glorious future, we find them still depending on the faithful and affectionate assistance of England, it would be the most shortsighted and suicidal policy to shrink from the duty that Providence has called upon us to fulfil.

In a subsequent debate on a vote for the defence of Canada, Lowe said that we ought to tell Canada that, if she chose to maintain British connection, it would be at the risk of having to protect herself from American invasion; that it was open to her, if she pleased, to establish herself as an independent republic, or to join the American Republic; and that in any case she should have in England a friend, protector, and ally. Disraeli protested warmly that it was our duty to aid Canada to defend herself in case she were attacked by America. Canada had a great future and all the elements that made a nation. The House ought to cherish the connection with the North American provinces.

The 'mature hour' which Disraeli foresaw has now arrived. From a dependency, Canada — and the state-

ment is true also of Australia, South Africa, and New Zealand — has become 'a permanent ally and friend'; nay more, an integral, self-governing member of the British Empire, only awaiting the formal organisation which cannot long be delayed.

Two deaths in April moved Disraeli to memorable speech. Of his old opponent, Cobden, 'the greatest political character that the pure middle class of this country has yet produced,' he finely said : 'There are some members of Parliament who, though they may not be present, are still members of this House, who are independent of dissolutions, of the caprices of constituencies, and even of the course of time.' When President Lincoln was murdered, he declared that in the character of the victim, and in the accessories of his last moments, there was something so homely and so innocent that it took the subject out of the pomp of history and the ceremonial of diplomacy. It was consolatory to reflect that assassination had never changed the history of the world ; and he expressed a fervent hope that from these awful years of trial the various populations of North America might come out elevated and chastened, rich with that accumulated wisdom, and strong in that disciplined energy, which a young nation could only acquire in a protracted and perilous struggle.

But Disraeli's principal effort in the session of 1865 was on the Reform Question ; and, strangely enough, though but two years were to elapse before he proposed and carried household suffrage, there is no period in the history of his connection with Reform in which he made a more definite stand against a forward movement. The effect of Gladstone's outburst had been rather to frighten Parliament and the politicians than to attract them. The Parliament of 1859 and the Prime Minister who dominated it became more conservative in this respect as they grew older. The discussion took place on Baines's Borough Franchise Bill, which had been the occasion of Gladstone's pronouncement in 1864. Perhaps

the most outstanding feature of the debate was the
definite emergence of an anti-Reform Liberal section,
of which Lowe and Horsman were the leaders. Lowe,
who had recently resigned office in circumstances which
had left him somewhat sore, spoke as a lifelong Liberal,
but one who had no faith in *a priori* rights of man, and
who would not cast in his lot with that particular form
of government called democracy. There could, he
thought, be no greater danger for the country than to
transfer power from the hands of property, industry,
and intelligence, to those of men necessarily occupied
in daily struggles for existence. The Government were
careful to be represented, not by the impulsive Gladstone,
but by an old Whig 'stager' Sir George Grey, who was
ready to read the Bill a second time, but would not
pledge the Government to the £6 franchise which it proposed, or to any large measure of Parliamentary Reform.
Disraeli, ever responsive to the Parliamentary atmosphere in a matter which depended so greatly upon
feeling and opportunity as did Parliamentary Reform,
expressed satisfaction with the general position of the
Government. He proceeded:

All that has occurred, all that I have observed, all the
results of my reflections, lead me to this more and more: that
the principle upon which the constituencies of this country
should be increased is one, not of radical, but, I would say
of lateral reform — the extension of the franchise, not its
degradation. Although — I do not wish in any way to deny
it — being in the most difficult position when the Parliament
of 1859 met, being anxious to assist the Crown and the
Parliament, by proposing some moderate measure which
men on both sides might support, we did, to a certain extent,
agree to some modification of the £10 franchise, yet I confess
that my present opinion is opposed, as it originally was, to
any course of the kind. I think that it would fail in its
object, that it would not secure the introduction of that
particular class which we all desire to introduce, but that it
would introduce many others who are unworthy of the
suffrage. . . . I think it is possible to increase the electoral
body of the country, if the opportunity were favourable and
the necessity urgent, by the introduction of voters upon

principles in unison with the principles of the constitution, so that the suffrage should remain a privilege, and not a right; a privilege to be gained by virtue, by intelligence, by industry, by integrity, and to be exercised for the common good. And I think if you quit that ground, if you once admit that a man has a right to vote whom you cannot prove to be disqualified for it, you would change the character of the Constitution, and you would change it in a manner which will tend to lower the importance of this country.

The question at issue was between an aristocratic government in the proper sense of the term — that is, a government by the best men of all classes — and a democracy. The English were a peculiar people.

You have an ancient, powerful, richly-endowed Church, and perfect religious liberty. You have unbroken order and complete freedom. You have landed estates as large as the Romans, combined with commercial enterprise such as Carthage and Venice united never equalled. And you must remember that this peculiar country, with these strong contrasts, is not governed by force; it is not governed by standing armies; it is governed by a most singular series of traditionary influences, which generation after generation cherishes because it knows that they embalm custom and represent law. And, with this, what have you done? You have created the greatest Empire of modern time. You have amassed a capital of fabulous amount. You have devised and sustained a system of credit still more marvellous. And, above all, you have established and maintained a scheme so vast and complicated of labour and industry, that the history of the world affords no parallel to it. And all these mighty creations are out of all proportion to the essential and indigenous elements and resources of the country. If you destroy that state of society, remember this — England cannot begin again.

The United States and France, with their immense natural resources, could survive great disasters and revolutions; but not England — 'the England we know, the England we live in, the England of which we are proud.' 'I do not mean to say that after great troubles England would become a howling wilderness, or doubt that the good sense of the people would, to some degree, prevail, and some fragments of the national character survive; but it would not be Old England — the England

of power and tradition, of credit and capital, that now exists.' He hoped the House would 'sanction no step that has a tendency to democracy, but that it will maintain the ordered state of free England in which we live.' [1]

The speech was a recantation, in set terms, of the proposals which Disraeli had been ready to accept in June, 1859 ; but at the same time it reiterated his desire to see a decided addition to the working-class element in the constituency. It brought him a letter of gratitude and appreciation from an eminent man with whose social work he had sincere sympathy.

From Lord Shaftesbury.

May 10, 1865. — You will not, I hope, be offended that I presume to thank you for your speech on the Baines Bill. The sentiments and the language were worthy of each other, and a masterly protest against any truckling to democracy. I believe that, in proportion as a man is a deep, sincere, and consistent lover of *social*, civil, and religious liberty, he will be a deep, sincere, and consistent hater of pure democracy, as adverse to all three.

You well showed that America, France, Australia, may endure convulsions, and partially recover from them; but England rests entirely on her institutions.

We have, however, made a great advance towards safety and satisfaction, when so many of all classes and opinions seem to agree that the franchise may be largely extended without being degraded.

The Bill was shelved by the decisive majority of 74, the numbers being 288 against 214 — an unmistakable testimony to the conservative disposition of the expiring Parliament. But interest was rapidly shifting from that Parliament to its successor ; and in his address to his constituents, issued shortly after this debate, Disraeli claimed the confidence of the country for the Conservative party on the twofold ground of its successful defence of the Church and of its attitude towards Reform. On this latter point, he referred to the Conservative Bill of 1859 as a measure which would have greatly extended the Parliamentary suffrage on 'principles in harmony with

[1] May 8.

the Constitution, which wisely recognises the electoral franchise as a privilege, and not a right.' That Bill was defeated by a majority which insisted that the franchise must be lowered in boroughs, and a new Administration was formed pledged to that principle. But only a few nights before, 'the House of Commons, impatient of protracted mystification, reflected the candour of the community, and declared by a vast majority that the franchise in boroughs should not be lowered, and that the principle on which Lord Derby wished to extend it was the just one.' Public opinion might not, perhaps, be yet ripe enough for legislation ; but, when the time for action came, they should legislate 'in the spirit of the English Constitution, which would absorb the best of all classes, and not fall into a democracy, which is the tyranny of one class, and that one the least enlightened.' The Address obviously contemplated that the Conservatives might be called upon to settle the question ; but it certainly led the public to expect that they would favour no solution of which the main feature was an immense lowering of the borough franchise.

Disraeli's attitude in regard to reform brought down upon his head the wrath of his sometime friend, John Bright, who, indeed, saw little to praise, at this election, in the official leaders of either party. 'The treachery of official statesmen' was the keynote of his speeches. Palmerston had treated the subject with 'contemptuous silence,' not even referring to it in a lengthy address to his constituents. As for the Conservatives, 'Lord Derby, speaking through the mouth of his prophet Disraeli,' offered lateral franchise ; in other words, when the working man demanded the vote, he proposed to 'admit — somebody else !' Bright continued : 'Mr. Disraeli is a man of brains, of genius, of a great capacity of action, of a wonderful tenacity of purpose, and of a rare courage. He would have been a statesman if his powers had been directed by any ennobling principle or idea.'

Condemnatory as Bright's speech was, its language showed how greatly Disraeli had advanced in public estimation. When he appealed to the electors of Bucks at the General Election of 1865, he occupied a very different position from that which he had held, eighteen years before, on first seeking their suffrages. Then, indeed, he had accomplished the immense feat of overthrowing Peel, but his future appeared to be uncertain; it was still the fashion, in many circles of distinction, to regard him as a charlatan and to treat him as a pariah. But now he had led his party in the Commons for more than sixteen years — without, however, it must be admitted, entirely securing their allegiance; had twice led the House, as a Minister of the Crown second only in importance to the Prime Minister; and had won further admiration owing to his masterly conduct of the Opposition during the last six difficult years. There were still, no doubt, exclusive regions, mostly of high Whiggery, in which he was looked at askance, and there was a group of aristocratic Tories in Parliament whose grudging attitude was represented by the cricketer among them who said: 'Our team is the Gentlemen of England, with a Player given.' But in Society as a whole, and among his fellow-statesmen, he had obtained remarkable consideration, and he was regarded with favour at Court. In February of this year one of the last of the social barriers gave way before him; and he was elected a member of Grillion's dining club, a select coterie of which it has been customary to make rising politicians of both parties free, but from which the socially objectionable are rigorously excluded. Not only Derby, who, as was natural, had been elected on his first entry into politics in 1825, but most of Disraeli's past and future Cabinet colleagues, even some of comparatively little account, had been chosen several years before the doors opened to him. Gladstone had been a member since 1840. Save for the recognition which it implied, the election gave Disraeli little satisfaction. The dreariness of men's dinners was one of his favourite

themes; and when 'the Club,' at the close of 1868, paid him a similar compliment, he did not conceal from his friend Cairns that, in accepting membership, he followed a social tradition rather than his own inclination.

To Lord Cairns.

Confidential. GROSVENOR GATE, *Dec.* 9, 1868. — *Entre nous,* I greatly dislike our feeble mimicry of 'the feast of reason and the flow of soul' of the eighteenth century.

Lord Stanhope's list of *the* Club seems our friends, the Grillionites, under another name.

I have not dined with those gentry for three years; but my recollection of them is extreme dullness; no genuine and general conversation, but a dozen prigs and bores (generally) whispering to their next-door neighbors over a bad dinner in a dingy room. Not a single thing ever said at Grillion's remains in my memory.

Nevertheless, as you and I are both candidates for the Consulship, we must not run counter to the social traditions of the country any more than against any other traditions; so you can tell Ld. Stanhope, that I shall feel honored in belonging to so classical and renowned a society as the Club.

The recognition of Disraeli's services and statesmanship in his own county at the General Election of 1865 was very marked. Not only was he re-elected without a contest, but he brought in with him, as on no previous occasion, two Conservative colleagues, instead of one Conservative and one Liberal. Gladstone at the same time was discarded, after long forbearance, by the University with the prevailing views of whose graduates he had for some time ceased to be in harmony; and had gone 'unmuzzled' to Lancashire, where he secured with some difficulty a seat for an industrial constituency, to which he appealed in the spirit of his declaration on Baines's Bill and of his popular progresses of the past two years. Gladstone's defeat at Oxford by a Conservative, Gathorne Hardy, with a growing reputation for eloquence and practical ability, was naturally welcome to Disraeli. He congratulated Frederick Lygon, who was a Fellow of All Souls, on 'that historical event,

which I believe to be mainly, if not entirely, owing to your energy and resolution.' He added: 'G. A. Denison [1] will crow till the end of the year. I am glad we helped him to such an euthanasia.'

But Disraeli had few other grounds for satisfaction in the results of the elections. It proved to be hopeless for the Conservatives to contend against the popular and equally conservative Palmerston. The conditions of the last Parliament were just those which the middle-class electorate desired to reproduce — Palmerston as Prime Minister to sustain and guard the national honour and interests, with Gladstone at the Exchequer to promote the national prosperity; but both faced by a strong Conservative opposition, which would prevent Palmerston from involving the country in war, and Gladstone and the Radicals from committing it to democracy. What little chance of a majority the Conservatives might have had was spoilt by a character-istic indiscretion of Derby, who talked in the House of Lords of the necessity of muzzling Roman Catholics [2] — Roman Catholics whom Disraeli had with infinite patience and adroitness brought to realise that, now that they were emancipated, their political affinities were rather with the Conservative than with the Liberal cause. [3] But in his first letter, after the tendency of the elections was clear, Derby attributed the defeat rather to over-confidence and want of exertion. Disraeli demurred.

To Lord Derby.

HUGHENDEN MANOR, *July* 28, 1865.—. . . I have no doubt there were instances on our side of over-confidence.

[1] A combative High Churchman, Archdeacon of Taunton.

[2] On a Bill for modifying the oath required to be taken by Roman Catholic members. Disraeli showed considerable reserve in regard to the Bill in the Commons, but Derby procured its rejection in the Lords.

[3] In a draft letter of 1864 to an anonymous correspondent, preserved among the Beaconsfield papers, Disraeli wrote that he had always looked, from his first entrance into public life, to 'a reconciliation between the Tory party and the Roman Catholic subjects of the Queen. . . . I have never relinquished my purpose, and have now, I hope, accomplished it. If the Tory party is not a national party, it is nothing.'

There always will be. And I feel sure that, if we had succeeded in forcing a dissolution last year, we should have done better; but, on the whole, I cannot conceal from myself that the dissolution took place on fair conditions for the Opposition. The Ministry had no cry, and we had the advantage of six years of unceasing preparation, well employed; for, notwithstanding the result, I think the energy, resource, and general efficiency, of Mr. Spofforth and Lord Nevill,[1] who, after all, were the real managers, were truly admirable — not to say unique.

And on paper affairs looked well enough. After Lord P.'s dissolution in 1857 you had 260 followers in the H. of C. After your own dissolution in 1859, you had 287. At present, with what we consider a great check, you will top 290.

But beneath the surface things are not so fair. The state of Scotland alone is most serious. All influence appears to have slipped away from its proprietors; and if irremediable, if Scotland and the Metropolitan districts are to be entirely, and continuously, arrayed against the Conservative cause, the pull of the table will be too great, and no Conservative Government, unless the basis be extended, will be possible. . . .

In a later letter Derby admitted that his ' unlucky ' reference to the muzzling metaphor might have lost some votes. Disraeli took the opportunity of the correspondence to explain his views as to the party leadership.

To Lord Derby.

Private. HUGHENDEN MANOR, *Aug.* 6, 1865. — . . . You will do me the justice, I hope, to remember that, when some of your followers, ten years ago, suggested, for the common cause, you should condescend to take a subordinate office, I utterly repudiated the scheme. It would then have been most improper, but perhaps not impossible. Now it would be equally improper and quite impossible.

With regard to myself, although I am quite aware that I have had an opportunity in life to which I have not been adequate, still, having led a portion of the House of Commons for seventeen years, I am disinclined, in the decline of life, to serve under anybody in that assembly; and as no one but yourself would offer me its lead, and as we both agree that such a combination would not succeed, I look upon my career in the House of Commons, so far as office is concerned, to have concluded. But I am not at all sure that,

---

[1] Afterwards fifth Earl and first Marquis of Abergavenny, 1826–1915.

at a moment of alarm and embarrassment, an influential body of new adherents might not be disposed to rally round a person who has so considerable a following in the country as yourself. But this can never happen so long as they understand, as a condition precedent of such adhesion, that the leadership in both Houses is to be appropriated by us. And who can blame them? What, therefore, I wish you to do is to take the fitting opportunity to avail yourself of those confidential connections which you have among the Whigs, and let them clearly understand that you are free and prepared to form an anti-revolutionary Government on a broad basis. But this should be done in time, not delayed till the crisis arrives, and when other persons have been hurried into conduct which, had they been aware of the real state of affairs, they would have avoided. This course involves really no sacrifice on my part. The leadership of hopeless opposition is a gloomy affair, and there is little distinction when your course is not associated with the possibility of future power. My retirement from the post would also assist you in another respect. It would be an unanswerable precedent for relieving you from some embarrassing claims, which now weaken you in the country.

From Lord Derby.

KNOWSLEY, *Aug.* 12, 1865.—The suggestion contained in your letter of the 6th inst. is a very generous one on your part; but I felt instinctively, on receiving it, that the course it indicates would not only be entirely repugnant to my own feelings, but that practically it would be found impossible, and, if possible, highly impolitic; and if I did not at once write to say so, it was because, setting all personal considerations aside, I desired fully and impartially to consider whether, under any circumstances, public duty could impose on me the necessity of making such a sacrifice.

The result is the fullest confirmation of the view which I originally took. Though I say 'putting all personal considerations aside,' I cannot forget that you and I have acted together, with perfect cordiality, and, I believe, mutual confidence, for more than seventeen years, I believe that we have been mutually serviceable to each other; my influence with the party has, I hope, served to strengthen your position in the Commons; and I should have looked in vain for anyone in that House, on either side, who would have seconded me with the same ability, faithfulness, and perseverance, which you have exhibited. But my position would be very different if I had a colleague in your place with whom I was politically

associated only by a compromise. Such a state of things would leave me the *nominal* head of a coalition Government, with the lead of the most powerful of the two branches of the legislature in the hands of one entertaining different views, and, not unnaturally, regarding himself less as a colleague than as a rival. Such a position would not be politically tenable, and, personally, it would be intolerable. As I can never hold any office but the first, so neither can I be the head of any but a *bona-fide* Conservative Government.

But even supposing the case which you put, of a sufficient number of moderate Liberals becoming alarmed at the progress of events, and willing to join our ranks, to give us a numerical majority, is there the slightest prospect that among them there could be found one who would be competent to take the lead of the House, or entitled to aspire to it, looking to the proportion between his followers and the party which he joined? Is there, moreover, any prospect that the old Conservative party would submit to such a leadership? . . .

I come, therefore, to the conclusion that neither you nor I, certainly not I, can be members of a Government of which the leaders and the principles should not be distinctly and avowedly Conservative; and as I see little chance of such an accession to our strength as would enable us to conduct a Government on such principles, the conclusion is as obvious with regard to one of us as to the other. . . .

After the General Election, the Disraelis paid a round of visits to great country-houses — two of them Whig, two Tory : Raby, Lowther, Ashridge, Woburn. Country-house visiting, as Disraeli explained in one of his letters in 1863 to Mrs. Willyams,[1] was regarded by him as one of the duties of his position. He met thereby, in undress fashion, all the people of distinction in politics and society, and was enabled 'to feel the pulse of the ablest on all the questions of the day.' But, if he profited, he also suffered. One of his characters in *Lothair* says that life in a country-house is 'a series of meals mitigated by the new dresses of the ladies'; and Mrs. Disraeli confided to Sir William Fraser that ennui and indigestion often cut short her husband's stay. At Raby he saw for the first time a future Prime Minister, Lord Rosebery, then Lord Dalmeny; and also a young man, the son of a

[1] See above, p. 331.

colleague, who was destined to be the most intimate follower and friend of his old age, Montagu Corry. Disraeli has left a note describing these visits.

August 31, Mary Anne and I went to Raby [1] and stayed a week. I believe it was the first reception of the Harry Vanes since their accession.[2] Raby a real castle, and vast, and, though occasionally altered and 'improved,' not substantially changed in character. The general effect feudal and Plantagenet. Though the country in the vicinity not beautiful, the immediate domain well wooded; a herd of 400 deer, and red deer also; but they never blend physically and socially; they live apart.

The Duchess a brilliant woman — sister of Lord Stanhope; she has the quickest, and the finest, perception of humor I know, with extraordinary power of expression, and the Stanhope wit; her conversation unceasing, but never long or wearying; a wondrous flow of drollery, information, social tattle, taste, eloquence; such a ceaseless flow of contemporary anecdote I never heard. And yet she never repeats.

The Duke makes a very good Duke; tall and dignified, but very natural, and, though not exactly good-looking, a good presence and a good expression of countenance, kind eyes. Affectionate to his step-children — hers by her former marriage with Lord Dalmeny, eldest son of Earl of Rosebery. The grandfather yet living.

Her eldest son, Dalmeny, seemed to me very intelligent and formed for his time of life (not yet of age), and not a prig, which might be feared. His younger brother, Everard Primrose, seventeen, very promising. Two sisters; one handsome, and both pleasing.

Of the meeting with Montagu Corry, Disraeli has left no account; but a well-authenticated tradition tells how one wet afternoon the girls of the house-party, on the look-out for amusement, seized on a young man with a reputation for gravity, and insisted on his dancing a breakdown, singing a comic song the while. In the midst of the frolic, Disraeli, who was supposed to be letter-writing in his room, looked in at the door, and, to the confusion of the young man caught playing the fool, remained steadily regarding the scene for some

[1] In the visitors' book at Raby, Disraeli described his profession as 'Patriotism.' Gladstone, a subsequent visitor, called himself 'Apprentice.'

[2] To the dukedom of Cleveland.

minutes. Corry very naturally feared he had forfeited
for ever the good opinion of one with whom he particularly wished to stand well, and who had cordially
welcomed him the previous day for his father's sake.
But Disraeli, though his face had worn its usual mask,
had been greatly attracted by the combination of youth,
ability, good looks, good-nature, and social gifts, and,
after dinner that evening, secured the lifelong devotion
of a prince among private secretaries with the gracious
words, 'I think you must be my impresario.'[1]

The note describing the country house visits proceeds :

Then we went from the ancient to a modern castle, Lowther
—a splendid domain; parks and deer, mountains and lakes.
The house convenient, and handsome in the interior, but the
exterior deplorable, as might be expected from the Gothic
of 1800 and Sir Smirke (*sic*). As my Lord receives no ladies,
but would receive my wife, a female cousin, Lowther, and her
brother, were present, and the rest a silent, but not scanty,
court of retainers.

Then we returned to the south, to Ashridge Castle, Lord
Brownlow's; also a modern erection by Wyatt, but gorgeous,
and in a vast park of wonderfully sylvan beauty.

Lord Brownlow,[2] a good deal beyond six feet high, slender,
rather bent, with one lung already lost, and obliged to pass
the winter at Madeira; intellectual, highly educated, with
a complete sense of duty, and of a soft and amiable disposition; living, as it were, on sufferance, but struggling to
perform his great part. A devoted mother[3] watches every
glance and every wind; shares his annual exile, where she
actually has not a single companion. . . .

Adalbert Cust,[4] B.'s only brother, has both his lungs;
is as tall; well formed, and one of the handsomest young
fellows in England. . . .

Lady Marian a woman of commanding ability. Above
the common height, a fine figure, but a countenance of
animation and intelligence marred by a red and rough
complexion. She always reminded me of Lady Blessington
in face, when Lady B.'s beauty had departed; the eyes were
the same — extremely speaking. Lady Marian had also, like
Lady Blessington, very pretty hands, which tell particularly in
a large woman; well-shaped, and small, and plump, and white.

---

[1] Meynell's *Disraeli*, Vol. I., pp. 164–166.
[2] The 2nd Earl, who died in 1867.   [3] Lady Marian Alford.
[4] The 3rd and present Earl.

Montagu Corry. Lord Rowton,
from a portrait by Von Angeli
at Hughenden.

From Ashridge we went to Woburn Abbey, and paid a visit of several days to Hastings Russell [1] and his wife, Lady Elizabeth, sister of Lady Salisbury. The present Duke of Bedford [2] lives in perfect solitude, and fancies himself unable to encounter the world. . . . He detests the country and country life, especially the provincial magnificence of grand seigneurs. 'Let me live always among chimney-pots,' he says. . . . He must be now nearer sixty than fifty; nor is it probable, he will ever marry. . . . The only person in society he ever sees except Hastings Russell is Poodle Byng, who recommended him to marry and get heirs. 'Why should I?' said the Duke. 'Could I have a better son than Hastings?'

Hastings is his cousin, and will be, in all probability, the future Duke; a young man, at least he looks young, though he has been married twenty years; good-looking, graceful, though hardly the middle size, very intelligent, well-informed and well-meaning. The Duke gave him Oakley and £6,000 a year, and expressed his wish, also, that he would receive every year his friends at Woburn, which is kept up exactly as if His Grace resided there. Hastings has the entire management of the property; it is a principality. . . .

Woburn is fine from its greatness and completeness, everything that the chief seat of a princely English family requires. The house, though not beautiful in its exterior, is vast; the great quadrangle, when lit up at night, with its numerous and flashing windows, reminded Bright, he said when on a visit there, of a factory. Then there are stables not unworthy of Chantilly, a riding-house, a gallery of sculpture, the finest private one, perhaps, in the world. A mass of choice and rare collections of all kinds which have been accumulating for centuries: splendid books, rare MSS.; some fine, many interesting pictures. A park of 3,000 acres, with great variety, and undulation and wild scenes you would not expect in Bedfordshire; splendid oaks, unrivalled cedars; ornate gardens and wilderness drives. And all this only forty miles from town!

The Salisburys, our dear friends, and the Caringtons, were there, and Comte Pahlen, who gives the results of a life experienced in society with taste and terseness, and Odo Russell [3] just arrived from Rome (where he is our Minister), *via* Paris. He brought the new toy, Pharaoh's serpent. Quite a miracle! A most agreeable party, which it could not fail to be with such guests and such a host and hostess, for Lady Elizabeth is quite worthy of her husband.

[1] Afterwards the 9th Duke of Bedford. [2] The 8th Duke.
[3] Afterwards 1st Lord Ampthill.

The predominant feature and organic deficiency of the Russell family is shyness. Even Hastings is not free from it, though he struggles to cover it with an air of uneasy gaiety.

The General Election, though it weakened the Conservative forces, made no serious change in the political situation. So long as Palmerston lived to lead the nation, the Palmerstonian spirit would prevail. Before the new Parliament, elected to support him, could meet, he had passed away. Though in his eighty-first year, he was still actively carrying on the heavy duties of Prime Minister when he died on October 18. There had been few signs to prepare the world, or even his intimates, for the end. Disraeli jotted down some stories which Speaker Denison told him, to illustrate the old statesman's vigour at the beginning of his last session.

At the meeting of the House this year, when I went up to salute the speaker, I asked particularly after his health; he had had a severe attack in the autumn. 'I am all right,' said the Speaker, 'but how is your great man? How is Lord Derby? I dined with the other [1] yesterday, according to custom, as you know. I have had the honor, too, of dining at your right hand. Well, yesterday there was a young man — he is coming into the House now in scarlet uniform (Hanbury Tracy, who was to second the Address) — who sate on my left, and I said to him at the end of the dinner: "Now, you are a very young man, and if I were you, when I went home to-night, I would make a memorandum of what happened to-day; something in this fashion: Mem. — Dined with the Prime Minister, who was upwards of eighty years of age. He ate for dinner too plates of turtle soup; he was then served very amply to a plate of cod and oyster sauce; he then took a paté; afterwards he was helped to two very greasy-looking entrées; he then despatched a plate of roast mutton; there then appeared before him the largest, and to my mind the hardest, slice of ham that ever figured on the table of a nobleman, yet it disappeared, just in time to answer the inquiry of his butler, 'Snipe, my Lord, or pheasant?' He instantly replied 'Pheasant,' thus completing his ninth dish of meat at that meal." I need not tell you what is the state of *his* health.' This is a literal report of an anecdote told by the Speaker with much grave humor.

[1] Palmerston.

A few weeks afterwards — it was after his first levée — he said to me: 'I know you remember a little trait or two I gave you of our friend's health on the Treasury Bench, because I believe you have been pleased to mention what I said on that occasion. Now I will give you another bulletin. He did me the honor of attending my levée last night — which, by the bye, the leader of the Opposition did not do — and was graciously pleased to inquire after my health. "That," I said, "was really of very little importance; but yours, my Lord, is a national affair. I venture to hope you have not entirely disregarded my representations to you on that head, and that you take a little more care of yourself than heretofore." "Oh! I do indeed," he replied; "I very often take a cab at night, and if you have both windows open it is almost as good as walking home." Almost as good!' exclaimed the valetudinarian Speaker with a rueful expression. 'A thorough draught and a northeast wind!' And in a hack cab! What a combination for health!'

Disraeli sincerely regretted his genial opponent's death. As Mrs. Disraeli wrote on October 22 to Lady Cowper: 'Mr. Disraeli had a great regard for Lord Palmerston, and, although circumstances prevented them from acting politically together, there had subsisted between them, for twenty years, a feeling of mutual confidence, which often removed difficulties.' When Parliament met in February, Disraeli found more than one occasion of expressing his appreciation. He spoke of the loss to the authority of the House of Commons by the disappearance 'of so much sagacity, of so much experience, and, I may say, of so much fame'; of the happy disposition of the man, his good temper and good sense; of his geniality and his moderating wisdom. 'He combined in the highest degree two qualities which we seldom find united — energy and experience. . . . I trust that the time may never come when the love of fame shall cease to be the sovereign passion of our public men.[1] But I still think that statesman is peculiarly to be envied who, when he leaves us, leaves not merely the

---

[1] 'We come here for fame,' Disraeli said once at Westminster to Bright, who records the remark in terms which suggest that, in spite of his admiration for Milton, he had scanty tolerance for 'that last infirmity of noble mind.'

memory of great achievements, but also the tender tradition of personal affection and social charm.'

With Palmerston's death the old era passed away. That Russell, who became Prime Minister, and Gladstone, who was to lead the House of Commons, would immediately revive Reform was certain. Disraeli wrote to Lonsdale on October 20 : 'If Johnny is the man, there will be a Reform Bill — very distasteful to the country. The truce of parties is over. I foresee tempestuous times, and great vicissitudes in public life.' Stanley wrote to Disraeli on October 23 : 'The Reform crisis cannot now be delayed. There are at least fifty Conservatives on the Whig side ; the question is, Can we utilise them, and how?' Stanley was for strengthening the hands of the moderate as opposed to the thorough-going Reformers, but Disraeli preferred to maintain his anti-movement attitude of the spring. He talked in this sense to the Whig company whom he met at Wrest in November. He said he thought Russell entirely mistaken in believing a Reform Bill to be necessary for his own position or required by the country. Only the extreme Radicals, some ninety votes, desired it, and they would be counterbalanced by the whole Conservative party, who would resist any demand for Reform.

In fact, Disraeli believed Reform to be still occupying the same position as during the last fifteen or twenty years ; to be merely, or mainly, a game to be played on the Parliamentary stage, useful for the purpose of gaining or retaining office, but not seriously meant either by Whigs or by Tories as a party, however earnest some individual politicians might be in its pursuit. He was probably, for the moment, right. The verdict of the country at the elections had been, unquestionably, in a broad sense, conservative. Though the Reformers had had some successes, particularly in the London boroughs, where John Stuart Mill, the philosopher and economist, and Thomas Hughes, the social reformer, had won seats, yet the great bulk of members had been

returned to support either Palmerston, whose indifference to Reform almost amounted to active hostility,
or the Conservative leaders, who had announced a waiting
game.   The existing electorate was therefore obviously,
on the whole, apathetic on the question ; and Bright's
crusade had down to the General Election failed to
evoke any very clear manifestations on the part of the
unenfranchised working men.

Russell tried, as Palmerston had tried in 1855, and with
the same lack of success, to persuade Stanley to join
his Ministry.   Some thought that Stanley himself might
be able to form a Government on Liberal Conservative
lines ; but Disraeli poured scorn on the idea.

To Ralph A. Earle.

HUGHENDEN, *Nov.* 6, 1865.—Who are the moderate men
of all parties who are to form this new Government?   Opposite to us there is, certainly, Mr. Lowe.   He could not join
us alone, or, if he did, he would be fruitless.

As for the movement in *The Times*, the same organ, and
probably the same pen, agitated as vigorously in favor of
our Reform Bill, yet all the Whigs voted against us, and Mr.
Lowe, then a six-pounder, among them.

So long as the Whig party hold together, nothing can be
done.

The name of Stanley would at first produce some excitement, even an appearance of enthusiasm.   The great towns
would no longer growl; the great employers of labor would
smile; Bass would pay us public compliments, and Peto
embrace us in the lobby.   But when the new Government
were formed, if such a thing were possible, 'the great Liberal
party' would, as usual, reconstruct in Opposition, and
Stanley after a twelvemonth would be kicked out, like his
father, though with a little more respect, and Gladstone
installed as first Minister, with a stronger bench of colleagues,
and some spoil among the Liberal outsiders, who are now
bawling for Stanley.

So long as the Whigs are united, the views you describe
are a fairy tale.

Derby, looking ahead, and noting the appointment
of Chichester Fortescue to be Chief Secretary for Ireland,
scented an attack on the Irish Church.   He hoped

Disraeli would agree that with this the Conservatives must not tamper, and that no member of the English branch would look on the Irish as 'heavy top-hamper, which it is wise to throw overboard to lighten the ship.' Disraeli did not much relish the prospect of fighting on behalf of the Irish Church, but comforted himself with the hope of a speedy break-up of the Ministry.

To Lord Derby.

Private. GROSVENOR GATE, *Nov.* 24, 1865. — . . . If the Government bring forward any specific measure respecting the Irish Church, it is possible that it may be effectually resisted, because it would not be difficult to pick holes in it, and of various kinds and sizes; but I do not think that any general resolution respecting the Irish Church could be successfully withstood in the present Parliament. It is a very unpopular cause, even with many of our best men.

So far as I can learn, the difficulties of the existing Cabinet are so serious that it would at once break up, if there were a successor, but there is none — at least, this is the opinion of Lord Taunton and that class of men. I think, however, myself, that it will not last very long, and for two reasons :

Firstly, because the Prime Minister and the Foreign Secretary are both in the House of Lords, which I hold to be fatal to any Cabinet under any circumstances, and which is really the proximate cause of the present malaise.

Secondly, because all the younger portion of the Liberal party, including those in the Ministry, think that, by getting rid of Lord Russell, they will obtain more, and higher, place under one whom they deem immediately, or at a short interval, must be his successor, viz., the present leader of the House of Commons.

The alternative they contemplate is, that you will decline to take the reins, or that, if you do, with the ancient régime, you must speedily fail. I think they would prefer the latter course, because they could make better terms and arrange and consolidate their resources better in Opposition. In either case Gladstone will declare that he never will take the second post again.

With these views, I cannot refrain from again calling your attention to the suggestions I made respecting the party and its prospects at the end of the summer. Some new combination must be formed, or considerable changes will occur both in Church and State, which neither the necessities of the country require, nor its feelings really sanction.

The conviction that the Government would be short-lived, and would founder on Reform, and that therefore it was imperative to begin at once to make preparations for its successor, grew upon Disraeli as the session approached.

To Lord Stanley.

GROSVENOR GATE, *Jan.* 23, 1866. — . . . I have been here some days, and, pretty well, know everything. The whole affair is utterly rotten; quite ruined; the blow will be struck from the other side. The appointment of Goschen [1] precipitated the revolution. It was the first nail in their coffin, according to Milner Gibson, but the sound of the undertaker in the house has been heard ever since. But what then? The present plan, I hear, is to meet the second reading of the Reform Bill adversely. In that case, I should think, it would be wise to meet it by a resolution; but at present I shall leave them to themselves. The other side will do the business.

That knave, Sir Fitzroy [Kelly], is recommencing his mischievous agitation about the malt tax. He has arranged for a monster meeting in London, and then has the impudence to ask for my counsel. I have given him such a duster in reply that he has gone, I believe for his health, to Torquay. I am taking measures to prevent our men unnecessarily going to his meeting, which many did last year, thinking they were aiding us. Far from sanctioning him, I have told him I shall oppose him actively and personally. He may do immense mischief. . . .

Reform was not the only difficulty the Ministry had to face. A Fenian conspiracy of a serious and wide-spread character had been discovered in Ireland; while in England and Scotland the rinderpest had broken out, and was carrying off thousands of valuable cattle every week. Moreover, public opinion in Great Britain was feverishly excited over the conduct of Governor Eyre, who had suppressed in the autumn, with great prompti-tude and equal severity, a negro rising in Jamaica.

[1] G. J. Goschen, then regarded as a Radical, afterwards the distinguished Liberal Unionist statesman, had just been admitted to the Cabinet as Chancellor of the Duchy of Lancaster, in place of Clarendon, who had succeeded Russell as Foreign Secretary. Goschen was only thirty-four, and had sat in Parliament for the City of London less than three years.

Ministers had instituted an inquiry and suspended the
Governor. Some members of the Tory party, notably
Manners, urged that the Governor's defence should be
taken up as a party question ; but other leading Tories,
such as Northcote and Carnarvon, strongly objected ;
and Disraeli wisely left the question alone and declined
to embarrass the Government. He supported them also
when they proposed to suspend the Habeas Corpus Act
in Ireland, in order to deal with Fenianism. But, in
regard to the cattle disease, he helped to defeat them
on an amendment which Ward Hunt, on behalf of the
agricultural community, proposed in order to make their
Bill more stringent ; and he spoke in favour of compensation to owners whose cattle were slaughtered for
the public good. Derby thought 'affairs most critical,'
and the Government 'at the last extremity,' in the first
fortnight of the session.

Considerable as were the other difficulties before
Ministers, Reform still remained the most serious of
all. The opposition among both Whigs and Liberals,
which had taken definite shape in 1865, manifested itself
at once in both Houses, on the mere mention of the topic
in the Queen's Speech. Lord Grey, the representative
of a great Whig family and the son of the Minister who
carried the first Reform Act, reproached Russell in the
Lords with his desertion of finality ; and Lowe, the leader
of the anti-Reform Liberals in the Commons, told
Adderley that, if the Conservatives would stand firm in
opposing the Ministerial proposals, he would undertake
to bring sufficient Liberals into the same lobby to insure
a majority of fifty against 'any Bill that lowers the
borough franchise by one sixpence.'

Here were, obviously, the elements of that extended
basis, that new combination, for which Disraeli had
vainly urged Derby to arrange. He was ready himself,
as he told Northcote as well as Derby, to resign the lead
and go below the gangway, in order to promote a durable
Administration. But, in spite of some discrepancy in the

language which he used on the subject, he does not appear
to have regarded with much favour the plan that was
most persistently put forward, that Stanley should head
a coalition Government of Conservatives and moderate
Whigs.   It is true that he had proposed an arrangement
of the kind himself when the Government of 1858–59 was
in its death agony; and he seems again to have thrown
out the idea in conversation with Stanley in the autumn
of 1865, much to Stanley's horror.   But the shrinking
from risk and responsibility which Stanley had so
markedly shown had probably by this time convinced
Disraeli that his friend and pupil, with all his great
qualities, had not the making of a leader.   This is the
natural deduction from Disraeli's letter, in November,
to Earle, and from his comment to Northcote, who reported a wild scheme by which Gladstone, with Stanley
as his right-hand man, was to form a Government mainly
Conservative: 'Lady —— wants Stanley to take a leading place.   It won't do.   W. E. G. and S. sound very
well.   One is a man of transcendent ability; the other,
though not of transcendent ability, has considerable
power.   But neither of them can deal with men.   S. is
a mere child in such matters.'   None of the other possibilities which were canvassed among the party — the
leadership of Lord Cranborne,[1] or of General Peel, or
of a Whig like the Duke of Somerset or the Duke of
Devonshire — ever had much promise in them.   One
of the most curious of the developments of this uneasy
period was the temporary conversion of Cranborne and
Carnarvon to the view that it was Derby who was the
difficulty and who must go.   Meanwhile Disraeli kept
his own counsel, showing great reserve in Parliament,
where, once again, he was silent on the Address, but
in private cultivating friendly relations with Lowe, and
even his followers, 'empty fellows' though he thought
them, and promoting Derby's overtures to Whig leaders

---

[1] Lord Robert Cecil had become Lord Cranborne in 1865, on the death
of his elder brother.

such as Lords Westminster and Lansdowne. On one point he was quite emphatic. He had the deepest contempt for the view that it might not be a bad plan to let the Government pass a moderate Reform Bill and so get rid of the question; 'such a course would seat the Whigs for a lifetime.'

It was a comparatively moderate Bill which Gladstone introduced on March 12. It reduced the county franchise to £14 — not so low as the £10 of Derby's and Disraeli's own Bill; and the borough franchise to £7, not so low as the £6 which Disraeli had been ready to accept after the General Election of 1859. It also took the savings bank franchise and the lodger franchise of the Derby-Disraeli proposals. But it abolished the rate-paying clauses in boroughs, and diluted the county constituency by giving copyholders and leaseholders in boroughs the county franchise; moreover it was limited to franchise alone, neither redistribution nor the delimitation of boundaries being dealt with in any way. The Bill had a very unfavourable reception; 'no enthusiasm for it, and sound reason against,' was Gathorne Hardy's entry in his diary. The high Tories, such as Cranborne and Whiteside, denounced it as a democratic measure; but their language was not so forcible as that of Horsman and Lowe. Horsman said the Bill was based on the old stale device of government by numbers; Lowe, that it was of a most dangerous and revolutionary character, leading inevitably to pure democracy. Bright gave it his hearty support, though it did not go nearly so far as he wished. He likened the dissentient Liberals to the discontented who gathered in the Cave of Adullam; and political vocabulary was thereby permanently enriched, 'Cave' and 'Adullamites' becoming rapidly household terms. Disraeli watched the temper of the House narrowly, but did not speak; and the Bill was introduced without a division.

Four days later the Conservative party met to consider their policy, and it fell to Disraeli, in the absence of

Derby from gout, to give them a lead.   Northcote tells
us what passed :

Dis. made a capital speech, reciting the history of the Reform Bills since 1852 ; throwing all the blame of the present
agitation upon W. E. G. ; objecting principally to the county
franchise proposed in this Bill — especially the admission of
copyholders and leaseholders in boroughs to vote for the counties — and still more to the fragmentary character of the
measure. He said it was obviously our duty unanimously to
oppose the Bill on the second reading, but that we must leave
it to our leaders to decide in what form the opposition had
better be made, having reference especially to the feelings and
dispositions of our friends on the other side. The meeting
was most cordial and unanimous.[1]

It was the fragmentary character of the measure which
was seized upon as the point of attack ; and notice of an
amendment declining to proceed with the second reading
till the redistribution scheme was before Parliament was
given by a leading Whig dissentient, Lord Grosvenor,
afterwards first Duke of Westminster, distinguished
alike as a philanthropist and as a sportsman.   That
this was an eminently reasonable proposal is shown by
the fact that the course it recommended of coupling
franchise and redistribution was pursued, in substance,
in all the three great measures of Reform which passed
through Parliament, in 1832, in 1867, and in 1884, though
in the last instance Gladstone fought desperately till the
eleventh hour against this procedure.   The heat which
was engendered in the debates in 1866, and the strenuous-
ness with which the Bill was opposed, were largely due
to the arguments and attitude of its proposer, Gladstone,
which were felt to be such as to justify universal suffrage
and the intimidation of Parliament by popular clamour.
In the House he defended the right of the seven-pounders
to the suffrage on the ground that they were 'our
fellow-Christians, our own flesh and blood' ; but so, of
course, were tramps and paupers and lunatics.   In the
Easter vacation, before the second reading debate, he

[1] Lang's, *Northcote*, p. 154.   Northcote's diary for the session of 1866
throws great light on this period.

went down into Lancashire, and there held up to reprobation Lords Grosvenor and Stanley — who were to propose
and second the amendment, and who were the heirs
of great houses honoured in that part of the country —
as aristocrats who were combining to defeat an act of
justice to the general community. He proceeded to
stake the existence of the Government on the measure;
they had passed the Rubicon, broken the bridge, and
burnt the boats behind them. No wonder that Disraeli
should have remarked about this time to Northcote that
'it was a great advantage to a leader of the House of
Commons that he should be, not unable, but unwilling
to speak.'

The second reading debate began on April 12, and
lasted more than a Parliamentary fortnight. It was a
contest of giants. Stanley, Lytton, Mill, Cairns, Bright,
and Cranborne, all made fine speeches, and Disraeli
summed up the case for the Opposition on the last
night.[1] But by common consent the protagonists were
Lowe and Gladstone. Throughout this session the
struggle tended to become a duel between these two,
Lowe, for one short spell in his career, reaching the
political level of the greatest Parliamentarians. Disraeli
was well content to have it so. He was in constant
communication with Lowe and the Whig dissidents,
mainly through Lord Elcho, and pulled the wires in the
background. He could not have taken, either with
sincerity or with consistency, the whole-hearted anti-
democratic attitude of Lowe. He spoke instead with
caution and circumspection. He pointed out that
Russell and Derby had both in the past battled against
piecemeal Reform; yet here was Russell, under the
influence of Gladstone's theory of the rights of man,
introducing just such a piecemeal Reform himself. He
showed in detail the injustice done to the counties by
the arrangements of the Bill, if passed either without
redistribution or with a redistribution that was un-

[1] April 27.

fairly adjusted. Once more he maintained that the choicest members of the working classes should form a part, and no unimportant part, of the estate of the Commons, but that there should not be an undistinguishing reduction of the franchise. You should represent opinion, not numbers; votes should be weighed, not counted. This was a Bill conceived in the spirit of the American rather than the British Constitution. Gathorne Hardy thought the speech 'too long and not lively'; Gladstone, who followed and wound up the debate, was, in his opinion, 'very fine in parts, but . . . absolutely democratic in argument.' Disraeli had chaffed his rival about a Tory speech made at the Oxford Union in 1831. Gladstone, after administering a solemn rebuke, responded in a classical passage about his generous reception by the Liberals when he came among them as the shipwrecked Æneas came to Dido, *ejectum littore, egentem.* The Bill might fail, he said, but

Exoriare aliquis nostris ex ossibus ultor.

'You cannot fight against the future; time is on our side.' The great social forces were marshalled on behalf of Reform; victory was certain and not far distant.

The prophecy was fulfilled; but, owing in large measure to the faulty temper and mismanagement of the prophet, the victory was achieved by other hands. The division showed that both the Ministry and the Bill were in great peril. The second reading was only carried by a majority of 5. Its opponents mustered 313 against the 318 of its supporters. About 30 Liberals voted against the Government.

After some natural hesitation, the Ministry decided to struggle on and produce their redistribution proposals. Of these the most striking feature was a large extension of the system of grouping two or three small boroughs into one constituency. In his speech on the second reading,[1] Disraeli put in a plea for the small boroughs

[1] May 14.

as a means of representation for varied interests, such as those of the learned professions, and of the Colonial and Indian Empires — a plea which was felt to be weighty and which recalled a somewhat similar line of argument used by Gladstone in 1859. In conclusion, he skilfully diagnosed the unsatisfactory condition into which the Government and House had drifted, and showed a more excellent way.

I am told, as I walk down to the House of Commons, every day by the man in the street ; as I walk down Parliament Street — 'Ibam forte viâ sacrâ' — somebody tells me, 'I hope you are going to settle the question.' Sir, ignorance never settles a question. Questions must be settled by knowledge, and it is not the vexation of an opposition, from whichever side of the House it may come, that prevents this Bill from advancing. It is that we none of us see our way. I say it with a frankness that I trust will be pardoned, I do not believe the question of Parliamentary Reform is thoroughly understood by the country, is thoroughly understood by this House ; and although I dare only utter it in a whisper, I do not believe that it is thoroughly understood by Her Majesty's Government. I often remember with pleasure a passage in Plato, where the great sage descants upon what he calls 'double ignorance' — that is, when a man is ignorant that he is ignorant. But, sir, there is another kind of ignorance that is fatal. There is in the first place an ignorance of principles, and in the second place an ignorance of facts. And that is our position in dealing with this important question. There is not a majority in the House that can decide upon the principles upon which we ought to legislate in regard to this matter ; there is not a man in this House who has at command any reliable facts upon which he can decide those principles. . . . The country, the House of Commons, the Ministry, are — although it may seem an idiomatic, it is a classical phrase, as it was used by Dean Swift — 'in a scrape.' . . . We must help the Government. We must forget the last two months. The right honourable gentleman must recross the Rubicon ; we must rebuild his bridges and supply him with vessels.

Disraeli advised Gladstone to withdraw his present Bills, to obtain carefully prepared statistics about county and borough franchise and about boundaries, and then submit to Parliament in the next session a measure

which might command the sympathies of the country and the sanction of Parliament. Disraeli's sketch of the position was undoubtedly accurate, and his advice thoroughly in harmony with the general feeling of the House. But the Government determined to go forward ; and their foes of both parties drew closer together in their resolve that these Bills, at any rate, which were pressed upon them, as they thought, so unnecessarily and so high-handedly, should by no means become law. Disraeli's was largely the guiding hand, and the Whitsuntide recess was utilized to marshal the forces for a serious fight on the motion to go into Committee. Bouverie, a Whig of considerable standing, had given notice of an instruction to refer both Bills to the same Committee. Captain Hayter,[1] a young Liberal, son of a Liberal Whip, had a motion on the paper objecting to the system of grouping adopted. To these, Knightley, on behalf of the Conservatives, added an instruction to the Committee to make provision against bribery in elections.

From Lord Elcho.

22, St. James's Place, S.W., *May* 15, 1866. — Let me congratulate you on your most excellent and convincing speech — quite unanswerable. It told immensely on both sides of the House, was much cheered by Liberals, and cannot fail to make converts to common-sense and statesmanlike views of a great question. Grosvenor came here last night full of your speech, and I think, when the time comes, we shall find him right in action as he is in opinion. Perhaps it is as well that the debate fell as it did.[2] Your speech thus goes forth unanswered, or, rather, undiluted by other speeches on the same side, for answered it cannot be. . . .

To Ralph A. Earle.

Grosvenor Gate, *May* 19, 1866. — Write immediately to Lord Grosvenor, who lives, I think, at 28, Prince's Gate,

[1] Afterwards Sir Arthur, and now Lord Haversham.

[2] Disraeli did not divide against the second reading of the Redistribution Bill, knowing that he would not secure on that issue a full support of the Adullamites. Derby was restive under these sound, but not showy tactics, and wrote gloomily to the Whip about a ' fiasco.'

and place yourself at his disposal. He expects this, and Lord Elcho requests that you will do it.

You will continue to consult with Lord Grosvenor as to the best means to adopt in the present exigency. . . .

HUGHENDEN, *May* 22, 1866. — Yours just received very satisfactory — as it shows that Grosvenor has not got over his original repugnance to the lowering of the franchise, and that, when a final effort is to be made, the whole of the Adullamites may be counted on.

At present I am clearly of opinion that the young H[ayter] must be utilised; and it may do the business if sanctioned by G[rosvenor].

He must give notice of his resolution on Friday, and Lord D. must pledge the party to support it on Monday. If you can discreetly modify the language, well and good. It will, however, be looked upon as his father's, and so gain confidence.

As to the seconder, that is more serious. . . . It should be a popular man; no harm if from our side, though that is not indispensable. Would Anson do it? . . .

CARLTON CLUB [? *May* 27]. — I shan't be able to see you again to-day. Lord D. says that W. Martin comes on before Knightley and Sandford, and also that if it were the reverse, and either of their motions were negatived, we might altogether be shut out, and find ourselves in the Committee in a jiffy.

This is a result which he, most of all, fears. Then he says that, if the veto be exercised (of which, by the bye, he never heard before), Hayter's amendment could not be moved at all, because it does not refer to the Franchise Bill.

This is serious. What we most fear is a general collapse, and Committee, which would be fatal. If Hayter can be brought on *à propos* to Bouverie's resolution, we must contrive a long debate.

The combined Opposition failed to prevent the Bills from going into Committee; but they achieved further successes which materially damaged the Government. Bouverie's instruction to take the two Bills together was accepted without debate; on Knightley's motion about bribery, Ministers were defeated by 10; Hayter's resolution about grouping was withdrawn after an announcement by Gladstone that the Government did not regard the principle as a vital one. 'We have got them, depend upon it, in a fix,' wrote Elcho to Disraeli on June 2, ' out of which there is no escape with both honour and place.

One or other must be abandoned.' He added, after a
reference to the wavering and trimming of some of the
Adullamites: 'I cannot resist again expressing the real
pleasure it has been, in the midst of so much wavering,
crookedness, and cowardice, to find myself acting with
a man of your frankness, straightforwardness, and resolution.   Forgive my saying this, for I really feel it.'

On getting into Committee the onslaught of the
Opposition was for the moment checked. A motion by
Stanley to postpone the franchise to the redistribution
clauses was defeated by 17, and one by Walpole, to fix
the county franchise at £20 instead of £14, by 16.
Disraeli wrote to his wife on June 8: 'Our troops are a
little dispirited after the two battles of yesterday: but I
think of you, which always sustains me, and I know we
shall find many sources of happiness without politics, if it
comes to that.'

But at this stage the combined forces of Adullamites
and Conservatives advanced a serious principle on which
they could firmly and reasonably take their stand.
The occupation franchises in boroughs and counties
proposed by the Government were based on rental; it
was maintained against them that rating was a much
more satisfactory basis, as it would both associate the
vote with the performance of civic duty, and also
greatly simplify the process of registration. From the
point of view of those who desired to lower the franchise
as little as possible, the rating basis had the additional
advantage of admitting fewer voters, as a house was
rated at from four-fifths to nine-tenths of its rental
value. Ward Hunt, a Tory, moved an amendment to
this effect in regard to the county franchise, and was
only beaten by 7 — 280 to 273. A Whig, Lord Dunkellin,
put on the paper a similar motion affecting the borough
franchise. On June 12 Disraeli wrote hopefully to his
wife: 'Affairs look here pretty well. Lord Clanricarde
has quite joined the Opposition, and his son, Lord
Dunkellin, has given notice of a motion against the

Government.   Grosvenor seems also active, so far as
talking and writing to men.'

Dunkellin's motion proved fatal.   At the close of
a short if warm debate, in which Disraeli took no part,
Gladstone protested that the acceptance of the amendment was incompatible with the progress of the Bill.   It
was nevertheless carried on June 18 against the Government by 11 votes, in a House only slightly less full than
that in which Grosvenor's amendment was rejected.   The
numbers were 315 against 304.   The Opposition hailed
vociferously a result which, after the repeated blows of
the last couple of months, must, they felt, and felt
rightly, involve the downfall of the Government.   The
reluctance of the Queen to change her Ministers while
war was impending between Austria and Prussia postponed the final decision for a week; but then the logic
of the situation prevailed, and Disraeli's opportunity had
come once more.   What could he do with it?   The
attempt of Russell and Gladstone to rush a Palmerstonian Parliament into Reform had failed disastrously.
But they had accomplished a great deal, aided all
unwittingly by their foes.   By the magnificent speeches
and well-sustained debates of the session, and by the
uncertainty of the issue throughout several months,
Liberals and Conservatives had joined in fixing the
attention of the nation upon a subject which it had
been wont to put aside, and they had thus given Reform
the biggest possible advertisement.   Would it be possible,
after all that had happened, even for a Palmerstonian
Parliament to trifle with the question any longer?

CHAPTER XIII

THE REFORM MINISTRY

1866–1867

In the division on Lord Dunkellin's amendment, Taylor, the Conservative Whip, calculated that forty-two Liberals voted with the Opposition. Supposing the Russell Government to resign, the strength and durability of a new Administration must depend to a great extent on the willingness of these seceders to co-operate in forming it. The week that elapsed between the adverse vote and the resignation was largely occupied by meetings of the Adullamite leaders at Elcho's house to decide the terms on which they would join the Conservatives in Government. With characteristic Whig self-sufficiency, they suggested an arrangement which should displace the existing Conservative leaders in both Houses, and give the premiership to a Whig; although the proportion of Adullamites to Conservatives in the House of Commons was as 1 to 7. Ready as Disraeli might be to efface himself, neither he nor Derby could possibly accept such preposterous subordination for their party.

From Lord Derby.

St. James's Square, 7.20 *p.m.* [? *June* 22 *or* 23]. — Grosvenor writes to Wilton:

'After a long conference the opinion expressed was that we could not guarantee Lord Derby the support (in its strict sense) of the Cave; that a Government under a Whig in the House of Lords, such as Lord Clarendon, would be most desirable on all accounts, with Stanley leader in the House of Commons; that, if such an arrangement could be effected

439

there would be every reason for believing that a very strong Government could be formed under those auspices. Present at the meeting: Lord Lansdowne, Lowe, Elcho, Horsman, Gregory, G. Heathcote, A. Anson.'

So much for Adullamite co-operation!

To Lord Derby.

GROSVENOR GATE, *June 23*, 1866. — The terms intimated by Lord Grosvenor, in his letter to Lord Wilton, are not consistent with the honor of the Conservative party, and are framed in ignorance, and misconception, of its elements and character.

I am, and, as you know, ever since the last General Election have been, prepared to withdraw from the leadership of that party in the House of Commons, with the view, and the hope, of seeing it reconstructed on a broader personal basis; but I have only been ready so to act on two conditions:

Firstly, that, whether in or out of office, you should be the chief; and, secondly, that, in the event of your declining the post, you should be succeeded by Lord Stanley.

GROSVENOR GATE, *June 25*, 1866. — The amiable and spirited Elcho[1] has played his unconscious part in a long-matured intrigue.

The question is not Adullamite; it is national. You *must* take the Government; the honor of your house and the necessity of the country alike require it.

What is counted on, and intended (not by the Court), is that you should refuse; that a member of the late Government shall then be sent for, and then that an application should be made to a section of your party to join the Administration; which application will be successful, for all will be broken up.

There is only one course with the Queen: to kiss hands.

And the effect will be this: in four-and-twenty hours, all, Lansdowne, Granville (if you want him), Clanricarde, who thought yesterday you would not have an ' application,' but who will think very differently to-morrow, will be at your feet.

Nothing can prevent your winning, if you grasp the helm. . . .

Derby was entirely of Disraeli's opinion; and the other leading men of the party, with hardly an exception, agreed. The resignation of the Russell Ministry was

---

[1] Elcho had told Derby, in conversation, that ' the only mode of obtaining numerical strength from the moderate Liberals would be a junction with some of their present officials.'

announced on Tuesday, June 26.   The Queen's summons
reached Derby on the following morning; and after consulting Disraeli he called together next day [1] twenty-two
of his political friends, who, in Northcote's words 'were
unanimously of opinion that he ought to attempt the
formation of an Administration on an enlarged basis,
and almost unanimous that, if he failed in that attempt,
he should undertake the Government with his own
friends alone.   Lord Bath alone expressed himself
decidedly against the latter course.'   Disraeli had written
to Earle on the previous day: 'The formation of Lord
Derby's Government is *certain*; but there is a good
chance of its being on a broad basis, with elements that
will command general approbation and support.'   He
spoke in the same optimistic sense at the meeting, adding,
amidst general cheering, that they must be prepared to
make sacrifices for a junction; he himself was prepared
to make the greatest sacrifices.

In spite of Disraeli's optimism and the obvious
necessities of the situation, Derby found it impossible to
secure a Government on a broad basis.   There was,
perhaps, no great reason for surprise that the two
moderate Whigs, Lord Clarendon and the Duke of
Somerset, to whom overtures were made, should have
declined, in spite of their imperfect sympathy with the
Reform policy for which they were responsible.   But
the behaviour of the Adullamites was less explicable and
less defensible.   As Derby put it in conversation with
Lansdowne: 'I looked with more confidence to those
seceders from the Government on the Reform Bill, in
consequence of whose secession the Government were defeated and resigned.   I thought that, as they had mainly
caused the position in which I found myself, I might
fairly look to them for assistance.'   He offered three
seats in the Cabinet, privately intimating that Lansdowne,
Grosvenor, and Gregory,[2] were those on whom he chiefly

---

[1] Thursday, June 28.

[2] M.P. for Co. Galway ; afterwards Governor of Ceylon.

counted. But Lowe, the most powerful Parliamentarian of the party, was strongly opposed to taking office; and eventually, as they could not obtain their Whig Premier, all the leaders declined, though promising an independent support — Horsman, indeed, boggled even at that promise. Derby had to console himself with the reflection, which he had already uttered in conversation with General Grey, that there was not a man among them, except Lowe, who was of the least value as regarded talent.

There was one other quarter in which, at Disraeli's instance, help was sought; but in vain, as Shaftesbury, the great philanthropist, would not quit his social labours for the restraints of office.[1]

To Lord Derby.

Private. GROSVENOR GATE, *June* 27, 1866. — What do you think of utilising Lord Shaftesbury? The suggestion reaches me from Lord Beauchamp — though a keen partisan, a very high Churchman. Lord Shaftesbury would be a representative of Palmerstonian sympathies and influences; powerful with the religious middle class, etc., etc.

He dined with Lord Lansdowne. The latter, whom you may yet gain in a personal interview, could not join you alone;[2] Lord Shaftesbury would remedy that.

It is an adhesion that, I think, would bring strength at elections.

Derby had to fall back on the resources of his own party, but these, largely owing to Disraeli's skilful leadership, were now considerable both in extent and in ability. In the House of Commons alone, the long period of opposition to Palmerston had developed three new men of exceptional capacity, Northcote, Gathorne Hardy, and Cranborne, while Cairns had more than justi-

---

[1] Though Lord Shaftesbury did not accept office, he exerted himself at first to help Ministers. He writes in his diary, August 9, 1866 : 'Have laboured much to put the Government and Derby right with the working classes. . . . Have spoken to Disraeli, whom I found, as I always found him in House of Commons, decided and true to the cause.'

[2] The 4th Marquis of Lansdowne, the son of one distinguished statesman and the father of another, died suddenly on July 5 at the age of fifty, before the new Ministry was completely formed.

fied his early promise.   Disraeli had pondered deeply over
the proper distribution of men and offices ; and there were
three arrangements which he was especially anxious to
effect.   The first, which had been in his mind ever since
1859, was to substitute Stanley for Malmesbury as
Foreign Secretary.   Malmesbury facilitated this change
by a spontaneous withdrawal of his claims ; but neither
the Queen nor Derby quite approved of Stanley for the
post.   'May Lord Stanley not be inclined to go too
far in the line of non-interference?' was the Queen's
warning.   Derby replied that he did not think the office
the most suitable for Stanley, but Stanley the best
choice available for the office.   Stanley's success in the
1866 Ministry justified Disraeli's selection; but the
Queen's warning of that year must have often come back
to his mind between 1876 and 1878.   The second arrangement, in which for the time Disraeli failed, was the
strengthening of Government in the House of Lords
by the appointment of a Lord Chancellor more serviceable
than Chelmsford in council and debate.   The failure was
apparently mainly due to the difficulty of finding a suitable
substitute, as it was desired to keep Cairns in the
Commons; but Derby, in reluctantly reappointing Chelmsford, warned him that he might ask him before long to
give way to another.

The third arrangement which Disraeli had specially
at heart was to secure the assistance in the Cabinet of
his faithful henchman, Northcote.   'I began to say,'
writes Northcote in his diary, narrating a conversation
with Disraeli on June 29, 'that he might naturally
expect me to resume my old place of Financial Secretary,
when he stopped me and said that he had told Lord D.
that under any circumstances, and whether there were
a fusion or not, he must make a point of my having a seat
in the Cabinet . . . ; that he must make my admission
into the Cabinet a condition of his own taking office,
so that the matter was quite settled.'   There is reason
to believe that Disraeli forwarded also the advancement

of Hardy and Cranborne. He was always eager to enlist
talent in Government service; and, though his close
relations with Hardy only began in office, he had marked
his success in the House, and rejoiced in his overthrow
of Gladstone at Oxford. As for Cranborne, Disraeli
was the last man to think permanently worse of a young
politician who attacked his leader, even when that leader
was himself, provided the attack were brilliantly carried
out. The two men had been in amicable relations, as
leader and follower, at least since 1864; and Disraeli
was not likely to forget that Cranborne, whose independent mind and pungent speech had made him a
power in Parliament, was the son, and now the heir
of an old friend and colleague. A further appointment
in which we may trace his hand was that of another
old friend and excellent man of business, Lord Chandos,
who had succeeded in 1861 to the dukedom of Buckingham, to the Presidency of the Council; though it is
probable that the introduction into the Cabinet of Lord
Carnarvon, a man of many gifts and much attraction,
but perhaps of too delicate a fibre for the rough work
of politics, was due rather to Derby.

The one serious difficulty in Derby's path proved to be
the Irish administration, which, with Fenianism rife,
was, as he told the Queen, of paramount importance.
There was, indeed, an excellent and experienced Chief
Secretary to his hand in Lord Naas, soon to become
Lord Mayo, of whom Disraeli wrote at this period:
'I have a high opinion of Naas. I think him eminent
for judgment — a quality rare, in any degree, in an
Irishman; and eminent judgment, with a complete
knowledge of Ireland, is a choice combination for a
Chief Secretary.' But the former Conservative Lord
Lieutenant, Lord Eglinton, was dead, and a successor
was very hard to find. After one or two other un-
successful applications, Disraeli tried in vain to persuade
the modest Manners to take the post. Eventually, after
Derby had almost abandoned his task in despair, what

proved to be an admirable selection was made in the person of Lord Abercorn, a much respected landowner in the North of Ireland. The most important appointment outside the Cabinet was that of Cairns to be Attorney-General, a judicial post being found for Fitzroy Kelly. Lytton received that peerage which Derby would not recommend in 1858–59; and a peerage was also bestowed on Jolliffe, the Whip with whom Disraeli's relations had been particularly close.

Lord Derby's third Cabinet was thus composed :

First Lord of the Treasury . . .	EARL OF DERBY.
Lord Chancellor	LORD CHELMSFORD.
Lord President	DUKE OF BUCKINGHAM.
Lord Privy Seal	EARL OF MALMESBURY.
Home Secretary	S. H. WALPOLE.
Foreign Secretary	LORD STANLEY.
Colonial Secretary	EARL OF CARNARVON.
War Secretary	GENERAL PEEL.
Indian Secretary	VISCOUNT CRANBORNE.
Chancellor of the Exchequer . .	B. DISRAELI.
First Lord of the Admiralty . .	SIR JOHN PAKINGTON.
President of the Board of Trade .	SIR STAFFORD NORTHCOTE.
President of the Poor Law Board	GATHORNE HARDY.
First Commissioner of Works .	LORD JOHN MANNERS.
Chief Secretary for Ireland . .	LORD NAAS.[1]

It was a strong combination with very few weak spots — a proof, in itself alone, of the success with which Disraeli had built up the Conservative party out of the ruins of the late forties, and had attracted to the service of the cause a goodly proportion of the intellect of the country. 'Not a single Scotchman or Irishman among us,' was Northcote's comment after its first meeting;[2] but that defect was speedily remedied by the admission of Naas.

There was one minor appointment which was of more importance to Disraeli, with his temperament and

[1] The Chief Secretary was not taken into the Cabinet until a few weeks after its formation.

[2] Northcote also tells us of an amusing misadventure which befell Disraeli when Ministers went down to Windsor to be sworn in ; how, 'thinking there was a seat at the end of the saloon carriage, he sat down there, and found himself unexpectedly on the floor' (Lang, p. 160).

constitution, than that of most of his Cabinet colleagues.
It is not clear whether he expected that Earle, who had
been in his confidence for nine years, who had taken a
large share in the negotiations with the Adullamites, and
whom he had constantly consulted about the arrangements
for the new Administration, would resume his former
position of Private Secretary. But Earle, who had come
back to Parliament at the General Election of 1865,
desired political office; and Rose told Disraeli that the
party expected that Earle's undeniable services should
be rewarded. Disraeli acknowledged the justice of the
claim, and secured for his young friend the secretaryship
of the Poor Law Board, under Hardy. Earle was completely satisfied.

From Ralph A. Earle.

Friday [? *July* 6]. — I don't know how to thank you
enough. The Secretary of the Poor Law Board does *not*
vacate. I think it would suit me better than the Admiralty,
perhaps, as a contest would be disagreeable. . . .

As to the Secretaryship, I have been thinking much about
it. Would Cameron of Lochiel do? He is intelligent and
devoted to you, but I fear shooting and Scotland might
interfere. If it would be any comfort, I will work for you
at the beginning and put the thing in train.

Disraeli did not require Earle's suggestions as to his
successor. He had already had an application from the
young man who had so greatly attracted him at Raby,
and on July 12 Montagu Corry began his duties in
Downing Street as Private Secretary, with a Treasury
Clerk of a Bucks family, who afterwards became Sir
Charles Fremantle, as his colleague.

From Montagu Corry.

72, Grosvenor Street, *Friday, June* 29, 1866. — It is with
much hesitation that I write to you, and only your kindness
to me when I met you at Raby last autumn induces me to
do so. I have for three years been practising as a barrister,
and am now most anxious to get a start in political life;
and though I can scarcely presume to ask for the honour
of being Private Secretary to yourself, yet I do venture to
hope that, should you know of some member of the Govern-

ment to whom my services might be acceptable, you would be willing to mention me, as one most desirous to serve in that capacity, and to give all my time and energies to the Conservative cause.

In a very few weeks the relation between the Minister and his principal secretary had become of the most intimate and confidential character, and so remained till Disraeli's death, fifteen years later. Corry never quitted the service of his chief, in office or in opposition; and the bonds between them were knit still more closely by Lady Beaconsfield's death in 1872, which left her husband, whom she had carefuly shielded from all domestic worries, peculiarly dependent upon Corry's devotion. On Beaconsfield's final retirement from office in 1880, he shocked the sticklers for precedent by recommending his secretary for a peerage; and by his will he left all his papers, the foundation of the present biography, to that secretary's sole charge, to be dealt with at his absolute discretion. The world, which had always acknowledged Lord Rowton's personal charm, discovered in later years his sterling qualities, when, by starting and directing the system of cheap lodgings for men known as Rowton Houses, he supplied in a practical fashion a serious social need. In *Endymion*,[1] written while Corry was in his service, Disraeli expresses his view of what the relations between Minister and secretary should be, and what in this case they unquestionably were.

The relations between a Minister and his secretary are, or at least should be, among the finest that can subsist between two individuals. Except the married state, there is none in which so great a confidence is involved, in which more forbearance ought to be exercised, or more sympathy ought to exist. There is usually in the relations an identity of interest, and that of the highest kind; and the perpetual difficulties, the alternations of triumph and defeat, develop devotion. A youthful secretary will naturally feel some degree of enthusiasm for his chief, and a wise Minister will never stint his regard for one in whose intelligence and honour he finds he can place confidence.

[1] Chap. 49.

The new Administration was well received; and the
Liberals were for the time so hopelessly broken up
that, in spite of the large majority against it, there was
good hope that it might retain office, provided that
its attitude on Reform was satisfactory to Parliament.
Disraeli grappled with the question in his speech on the
hustings on re-election. He strongly maintained both
the right and the competence of the Government to
effect a settlement, recalling Derby's important share
in carrying the great Reform Bill, and adding with
regard to the only subsequent measure of Reform ever
mentioned with respect, 'Why, I myself brought it
in.' But he declined to give any pledge to introduce
a Reform Bill in the next session, only declaring that,
if Ministers had to legislate, they would not recognise the
rights of man or permit a numerical majority to dictate
to the nation, but would act on the principle that electoral
power should be deposited with the best men of all
classes. This policy, which was echoed in Derby's
subsequent statement in the House of Lords, encountered
no serious resistance in Parliament.

The first duty of a Government coming into office in
July was to wind up the necessary Parliamentary
business ; and Disraeli's official letters to the Queen give
a lively picture of House of Commons life during the
short remainder of the session.

To Queen Victoria.

DOWNING STREET, *Monday night, July* 16, 1886.—The
Chancellor of the Exchequer, with his humble duty to your
Majesty:
The House of Commons met this evening after a month's
abeyance. Nearly the whole evening has been taken up
by an animated and interesting debate on the charter to
the Queen's University (Ireland); brought on by Sir Robert
Peel. It was, with the exception of a clear but technical
speech on the part of Sir Hugh Cairns, confined to the
Opposition.
It was occasionally rather warm, and Mr. Gladstone
concluded with a vindication of passion and fire; but it

was generally felt and observed that he left the House in doubt whether he was in favour of mixed education or not. . . .

Downing Street, *July* 19, 1866. — . . . Lord Cranborne brought forward the Indian Budget, to-night, in a speech which interested the House.

The manner was vigorous, and showed a mastery of his matter which, considering his short experience of office, evidently surprised the House. Persons of weight, in private, of both parties, spoke of the effort with approbation.

The Chancellor of the Exchequer much regrets that, from want of habit, he omitted to send a report on Tuesday night. It was not an eventful one; a discussion on the Ballot, very insipid. The House recoiled from the subject.

Yesterday the Church Rates, a higher tone, but the House wearied.

Downing Street, *July* 20, 1866. — . . . An interesting discussion on foreign affairs opened by Mr. Laing, in a colorless, non-intervention speech. . . .

A considerable oration from Mr. Gladstone, which covered the subject Though glowing and earnest, it was conciliatory, and fair and courteous to the Government.

It produced less sensation than it otherwise would have done, for the House was anxious to hear the new Minister, and Mr. Gladstone was long and too academical.

The new Secretary of State afforded a great contrast to him. Lord Stanley was never more characteristic; at the same time, clear, cautious, and candid. He pleased the House, which evidently gave him, on both sides, its confidence.[1]

House of Commons, *July* 24, 1866. — . . . The discussion in the House to-night on the affairs of the Park was highly and unexpectedly satisfactory.

Though introduced by a speech from Mr. Ayrton, and from some others, in a very full House, which appealed rather to the malevolent passions of a popular assembly, the reply of Mr. Walpole was so dignified, so full of good feeling, and supported by so much adequate knowledge, that a very favourable reaction soon was visible.

This was clenched by an animated speech from Sir George Grey, than which nothing could be more complete, more gentlemanlike and generous.

When Sir George rose, nearly a dozen members of the

---

[1] The discussion turned on the new situation created in Europe by the victory of Prussia over Austria at Sadowa. Stanley said that he could not see that the establishment of a strong, compact Power in North Germany would be either a detriment or a menace to Great Britain, whatever it might be deemed to be by other Powers.

extreme party rose at the same time, but when he sate down the feeling of the House was so decided that none of these gentlemen attempted to follow him. Among these was Mr. Bernal Osborne, who had risen twice.

The Chancellor of the Exchequer hoped that all was over, and over well, but Mr. Cowper would make a speech, chiefly on his flower-beds. This gave breath to the extreme party, and Mr. Mill rose, and delivered a speech hardly worthy of a philosopher, but rather more adapted to Hyde Park.

The Chancellor of the Exchequer ventured to tell him this, and then the matter died off, the general result being that the leading authorities in the House discountenanced entirely the criticism on Mr. Walpole's conduct.

The accounts this evening are that the chief leaders of the mob are now active in their efforts to terminate the disturbances.

HOUSE OF COMMONS, *July* 27, 1866.—. . . The general rumor and understanding, in the House to-night, is that all attempts at tumultuous meetings are now definitively relinquished, and that Monday will be quite tranquil.

It is said that no effort will be made to hold a public meeting in Victoria Park any more than in Hyde Park. The principle that they are Royal Parks is to be fully recognised.

If this be true, as the Chancellor of the Exchequer hopes and believes, he ventures to think that the whole question of the localities of public meetings deserves the serious consideration of your Majesty's servants.

Public meetings are the recognised and indispensable organs of a free constitution. They are safety-valves.

It is desirable, it would seem, that, when the occasion offers, some Act should be passed, recognising and regulating the rights and privileges of your Majesty's Parks, enjoyed, through your Majesty's gracious sanction, by all classes of your Majesty's subjects, and, at the same time, that there should be some public places provided, where the great body of the people, like the Comitia of the Romans, should have the right to assemble, and discuss, and express, their opinion.

Your Majesty will perhaps deign to consider these suggestions.

From Queen Victoria.

OSBORNE, *July* 26, 1866.— The Queen thanks Mr. Disraeli for all his interesting reports, but she is especially anxious to express to him her great satisfaction at the manner in which he carried the vote for the gun-metal for her dear,

great husband's memorial.[1]   She knows how truly he appreciated him !

To Queen Victoria.

DOWNING STREET, *Aug.* 2, 1866.—...   The evening has
been taken up with a dreary debate on the Habeas Corpus
Suspension Act in Ireland.[2]

Mr. Bernal Osborne, at one moment, promised some relief
in a very elaborate speech and evidently, from several
allusions, long matured; but it was old-fashioned and out of
tune and time, and fell very flat. . . .

HOUSE OF COMMONS, *Aug.* 16, 1866.—...   The Extradi-
tion Treaty Act passed, but with a limitation to one year.

We defeated all attempts to exclude 'political offences,'
which would have included everything, but thought it best
to accept the condition of time, as nothing could have prevented the discussion next year; the question must be
reproduced, and, under any circumstances, the opinion of
the House will be taken.   Time brings everything, consolation
and catastrophe; and it is hoped it may help your Majesty's
servants in this matter.

The House meets again to-morrow, but only for a few
minutes.   Its pulse is very low; but extreme unction will not
be administered, I believe, until Friday.

'The affairs of the Park,' referred to in the letters of
July 24 and 27, were the famous Reform riots led by
Beales, when the mob, being forbidden to hold a meeting
in Hyde Park, broke down the railings near the Marble
Arch and worked some havoc in the flower-beds, continu-
ing their demonstrations for three days, July 23, 24, 25.
Grosvenor Gate was close to the centre of disturbance;

---

[1] Palmerston had promised the Queen, in the spring of 1863, that, as
had commonly been done in the case of other public statues, old guns
should be supplied for the statuary of the Albert Memorial. But Gladstone, when application was made to him at the Exchequer, raised the objection that asking for the gun-metal was the same as asking for a fresh
vote, and that it was understood, when £50,000 was voted for the memorial, that the vote was to be final. After much correspondence between
the Court and Ministers, Palmerston finally, in July, 1864, expressed his
concurrence with Gladstone. But contracts had already been entered
into on the faith of the Prime Minister's original promise; and Disraeli,
though Gladstone still considered an application to Parliament 'impolitic,'
easily secured, in July, 1866, the assent of the House of Commons to the
transaction.

[2] The Government renewed the Habeas Corpus Suspension Act, which
had been passed for only a limited period by their predecessors.

and Disraeli, whose duties kept him at the House of
Commons while the riots were in progress, trusted to
his secretary to secure the safety of his wife.

From Montagu Corry.

GROSVENOR GATE, *July* 24 [? 23], 1866, 6.40 *p.m.* — No
mob outside your house now, the Marble Arch being the
centre of attraction ; and even there the police say the
disturbance is lessening.   The Inspector in charge at Grosvenor
Gate tells me that while the crowd was at its worst here
your house was never mentioned as obnoxious — though the
houses of Mr. Walpole and Lord Elcho and others have come
in for some threats.   The soldiers have moved away to the
Marble Arch, and Mrs. Disraeli wishes me to add that the
people in general seem to be thoroughly enjoying themselves ;
and I really believe she sympathises with them.   At any
rate, I am glad to say she is not the least alarmed — nor do
I think you need be at all.

The mob broke down more than the railings of the Park ;
they broke down the nerve of Walpole, the Home Secretary, who was said to have shed tears when a deputation
visited him on the subject.   'This fiasco of Walpole's,'
to use Derby's phrase in a contempory letter to Disraeli,
the constant demonstrations in the streets of London,
and the countenance afforded to the agitators by many
of the Radical leaders, such as J. S. Mill and Bright,
made Disraeli anxious.   He wrote to his wife on July
26 : 'I hope with energy and prudence we may overcome the difficulties, but it is very obvious to me that
the affair is encouraged by our opponents underhand,
with the view of upsetting the Government.   I think
they will fail.'   One happy thought, which he suggested
ineffectually to Derby, might have profoundly modified
the course of political history, if it had been adopted by
the Prime Minister and the Cabinet.

To Lord Derby.

Confidential.   GROSVENOR GATE, *July* 29, 1866. — I would
not trouble you with things when you are dealing with
persons, but things may affect persons.
This is, I think, important ; it is the result of my reflections
this day on what Gladstone said yesterday.
Suppose, instead of discharging the order of the day on

the Reform Bill, you took up the measure where it stops: £6 *rating* for boroughs ; £20 rating for counties, to be brought up on report; the northern boroughs to be enfranchised; no disfranchisement of any kind.

You could carry this in the present House, and rapidly. It would prevent all agitation in the recess; it would cut the ground entirely from under Gladstone; and it would smash the Bath Cabal, for there would be no dangerous question ahead.

Think of this.

The course proposed was too startling, perhaps, for acceptance. The session came to an end without further Parliamentary action about Reform; and the agitation was transferred from London to the country, where large demonstrations were held and violent language was used, in Birmingham, Manchester, Leeds, Glasgow, and Dublin. It is usually assumed that by these proceedings Disraeli was convinced in the early autumn that the demand for Reform had now become a genuinely popular one, and must be treated comprehensively without further delay by a Conservative Ministry. This is an erroneous assumption. Disraeli's suggestion to take up Gladstone's Bill and carry it to the statute-book in a modified form not having been accepted, he thought it more prudent to postpone further action. It was Derby himself who pushed the matter forward. He believed, in his own words, ' that there is a genuine demand *now*, however it may have been excited, but in favour of the acceptance of a moderate and Conservative measure.'

From Lord Derby.

Private. KNOWSLEY, *Sept.* 16, 1866. — . . . I am coming reluctantly to the conclusion that we shall have to deal with the question of Reform. . . . I wish you would consider whether, after all the failures which have taken place, we might not deal with the question in the shape of resolutions, to form the basis of a future Bill. We *need* not make the adoption of any of the resolutions a vital question; while, if we should be beaten on some great leading principle, we should have a definite issue on which to go to the country. This is worth turning in your mind; and I should be glad to hear what you think of it. . . .

Disraeli's reply was not encouraging. 'Observation and reflection,' he wrote on September 24, 'have not yet brought me to your conclusion as to the necessity of bringing in a Bill for Parliamentary Reform; but I hope I say this with becoming diffidence.' Derby, however, immediately received a powerful reinforcement from the highest quarter. He went to Balmoral, where the Queen herself expressed to him her anxiety to have the question settled, and settled by the Conservatives, and her readiness to do anything she could personally to bring opinions together. Accordingly we find him writing to Disraeli on October 9: 'I come myself more and more to the conclusion that in some shape or other we must deal with it, and that immediately'; but he preferred the method of resolutions, which he had previously suggested.

To Lord Derby.

Confidential. HUGHENDEN MANOR, *October* 12, 1866. — I had no idea, when you first wrote to me about 'resolutions,' that you contemplated the possibility of not legislating the session they were passed. If we can succeed in that, we shall indeed be on velvet. This view throws quite a new light on our position, and therefore I will not trouble you now with any remarks on the comparative advantages of Bills or resolutions, in case, as I now conclude, the Cabinet resolves on acting.

It will, I think, be quite unnecessary to have Cabinet Committees of preparation, as of yore; there is so much previous knowledge now, on the main subject, that these preliminary investigations are unnecessary, while they tend to jealousy. The time for meeting will quite suit me.

I shall endeavour to draw up a series of resolutions in your vein. They must, however, be distinct enough for us to fall back upon, as a clear policy, for the country, in case we are forced to appeal to it, which Heaven forfend ! . . .

I think you have decided wisely about Fitzgerald.[1] The morale of a party is injured when any individual who has been encouraged to take a prominent part is neglected in the hour of triumph. He was also personally popular among the rank and file. Our Stanley never thinks anybody in

---

[1] Under-Secretary for Foreign Affairs in 1858–59; appointed Governor of Bombay in 1866.

the House of Commons is equal to anything; and I am not sure he is not right. But the world cannot be governed by this inexorable estimate of human qualities, and the political circle generally will agree that a man who, if in Parliament, would probably have been a Cabinet Minister, is not unfit to be an E.I[ndian] President.

The suggestion which the Queen had tentatively made to Derby she pressed again upon Northcote, who was at Balmoral in October as Minister in attendance. He reported what passed both to Derby and to Disraeli.

From Sir Stafford Northcote.

BALMORAL, *Oct.* 17, 1866. — . . . Nothing can exceed Her Majesty's kindness and friendliness. She is evidently very anxious for our success, but particularly so with regard to the great Reform problems.

A day or two ago General Grey brought me a note in Her Majesty's handwriting, to the effect that she was most anxious for a settlement of the question; that she would gladly render any assistance in her power; that she did not like to speak to me about it, but that her idea was to offer Lord Derby her assistance in communicating with Lord Russell and Gladstone. The General told me she meant to speak to me and consult me on the point, and that this note was a preparatory one. She did accordingly lead up to the subject when I saw her in the evening; but I turned the conversation, and the next morning wrote a note to the General saying that the question was so difficult, any false step so dangerous, and my position as a young and uninfluential member of the Government so delicate, that I had been glad that Her Majesty had not asked for my opinion; that I thought that, if she were to intimate to Lord Derby her willingness to make such a communication as she spoke of, if he thought it desirable, at the same time graciously adding that she did not require any formal answer to the proposal, it might strengthen his hands to be thus made aware of her readiness to support him; but that I thought that a formal offer might be embarrassing, as, if the Cabinet ultimately decided that it was inexpedient that any communication should be made to the Liberal party leaders, it might be awkward to have to decline Her Majesty's gracious proposal. The General told me afterwards that she quite understood my difficulty, that he thought she would probably write to Lord Derby, but would intimate that she did not desire an immediate answer. I told the General that I

thought there would be very little practical use in communicating with Lord Russell or Gladstone; that they would only give vague promises of candid consideration, which would lead to nothing. . . . I reported what had passed to Lord Derby.

Last night the Queen renewed the subject with me, saying that she quite understood my position and could not ask me for an opinion. She was very anxious that something should be done, and discussed the question from what I think an important point of view — the purchasing power of the *nouveaux riches*, 'who buy your Totnes.'

The General has been talking the matter over with me again this morning, and showed me a letter of Lord Grey's, who is very anxious that the question should be settled, and that we should be the men to settle it. (By the bye, the Queen mentioned Lord Grey to me as a person who would be ready to give his assistance to us. I said I had always supposed we should find him friendly. She said, 'Yet you didn't ask him to join the Government.' I said I knew very little of the communications which took place when the Government was forming. She said, 'Well, none was made to him.') Lord Grey thinks it would be equally fatal to us to bring in a Bill, or to abstain from doing anything; and thinks we ought to proceed, as he advised the late Government to do, by way of resolutions; but his idea of resolutions appears to be the affirmation of some general principles, and an Address to the Crown to appoint a Committee of Privy Councillors to draw up a measure.[1] I told the General that I thought the time was passed (if there ever had been a time) for that mode of proceeding; and I discussed with him the idea of resolutions of a more definite character, such as those Lord Derby shadowed out to me at Knowsley. . . . He seemed to think the plan would, or might, answer. . . .

Disraeli was somewhat impatient under the royal suggestion and Grey's scheme, and brushed them both aside in letters, couched in very similar terms, to Derby and to Northcote.

To Sir Stafford Northcote.

HUGHENDEN MANOR, *Oct.* 22, 1866. — I was much obliged to you for your interesting despatch, and appreciate the

[1] In his letter to Derby, Northcote adds that he asked General Grey 'if he proposed that we should make Bright a Privy Councillor, or leave him out altogether.'

The Right Honble Sir Stafford Northcote, Bart.
after the portrait by Edwin Long. R.A.

entire fidelity which I have always experienced from you, and on which I have ever, rightly, counted.   Lord Derby also forwarded to me your letter to him, on Saturday last.

I am much gratified by your successful visit to Balmoral.

I doubt myself whether Lord Grey's scheme, at any time or under any circumstances, would or could have been accepted, but at the present moment, and in the existing state of things, it is the murmuring of children in a dream.

The royal project of gracious interposition with our rivals is a mere phantom.   It pleases the vanity of a Court deprived of substantial power, but we know, from the experience of similar sentimental schemes, that there is nothing practical in it, or, rather, that the only practical result is to convey to our rivals that we are at the same time feeble and perplexed.

Our future, and in some degree the future of our country, depends on the course we shall chalk out for ourselves ; and that must be the result of anxious, grave, and profound deliberation. . . .   The first question for the Cabinet to decide will be, 'Shall we act in the matter of Reform?'   I think the discussion of that question will occupy entirely our first meeting, and will facilitate our subsequent councils, in case we decide on action. . . .

P.S. — I have not room to tell you how entirely I appove and admire the wisdom with which you parried the royal proposition.   It was worthy of Hyde, and you tell it as well.

The Queen was in earnest in her resolve to get the Reform question settled at once, and undoubtedly judged the signs of the times better than her Chancellor of the Exchequer.   Before the month was over, she wrote to the Prime Minister the letter which Northcote had suggested, emphasising the necessity of an early settlement, and offering her services to bring it about.

Queen Victoria to Lord Derby.

Balmoral, *Oct.* 28, 1866. — The Queen has been thinking a great deal, ever since Lord Derby left Balmoral, of the subject on which she had some conversation with him while he was here.   As she then told him, she is convinced that, if the question of Reform be not taken up in earnest by her Ministers, with a view to its settlement, very serious consequences may ensue.

The Queen is well aware of the great difficulties which her Government must be prepared to meet, in any attempt to effect this object, and if she can in any way help in surmounting them, Lord Derby and his colleagues may reckon confidently on her best support and assistance.

It seems evident to the Queen, after the failure of so many successive Administrations, which have all been overthrown in their attempts to settle this question, that it never can be settled unless adverse parties are prepared to concede something, and to meet each other in a spirit of mutual conciliation. Nothing would gratify the Queen more than to be instrumental in bringing about such a disposition; and if Lord Derby thinks there is any chance of its doing good — indeed, she views the matter so seriously that she hardly thinks she would be justified in not making the attempt under any circumstances — she is ready to make a personal appeal to Lord Russell and Mr. Gladstone, and other leading members of both Houses of Parliament, and to urge them, by every consideration of loyalty and patriotism, to meet her present Ministers fairly, in an honest endeavour to find out terms of agreement as might lead to a measure of Reform being proposed which would conciliate the support of all moderate men, and afford at least a chance of setting a question at rest, which, while it continues to be made a subject of agitation, must act injuriously upon the best interests of the country, and may even threaten the disturbance of its peace and tranquillity.

Lord Derby need not answer this letter at once. He is quite at liberty to consult his colleagues upon it previously, and the Queen relies with confidence upon their patriotism not to allow any feelings of a mere party nature to interfere with their candid consideration of her suggestions. . . .

The Cabinet appears to have taken Disraeli's advice and decided both against Grey's scheme and against utilising, at any rate for the present, the Queen's offer to approach the Liberal leaders. But Her Majesty's impulsion and Derby's own conviction sufficed to make Ministers take in hand at once the drafting of Reform Resolutions to be submitted to Parliament next session. The scheme provisionally adopted was quite general in terms; but it followed the principle of the Grosvenor amendment by dealing with redistribution as well as with franchise, and that of the Dunkellin amendment by adopting a rating and not a rental basis. It involved an

increase of the number of electors in both counties and boroughs by a reduction of qualification in the occupation franchise and by the addition of other franchises; more representation for the labouring classes, but without giving any class a preponderating power; no absolute disfranchisement save for corrupt practices; revision of county registration, employment of voting papers, and provision of additional polling-places; and the appointment of a Boundary Commission, which 'should also revise and verify the returns laid before Parliament in its last session, with respect to the possession of the franchise; and obtain such further information as may be the ground for well-considered legislation.' The question of the Commission immediately assumed considerable importance. Derby had written to Disraeli on October 19, with reference to Grey's scheme: 'I think a Commission to frame a measure both inexpedient and impracticable. One for information, following up resolutions of principle, I should think very desirable; but with that object we should not require to appoint Privy Councillors.' Disraeli's main design, at this period, was so to delay matters as to avoid having to introduce actual legislation in the approaching session; and he was quick to see that the only method in which this policy could be combined with effective resolutions was to create a Commission with really important work to do, and not merely to rearrange boundaries. He drew up a memorandum in order to place his point of view clearly before Derby and the Cabinet.

To Lord Derby.

Nov. 18, 1866. — . . . We are entirely unpledged upon the subject [of Parliamentary Reform]. But if no notice is taken of it in the Queen's Speech, or no subsequent announcement of measures is made by the leader of the House of Commons, it is probable that an amendment of a general character may be carried, which will replace the question in the hands of the late Government, and they return to power not more embarrassed by the Radicals than before.

It is not probable that a dissolution, even if granted, would, under these circumstances, help us.

It would seem therefore we must act. How?

1. By the introduction of a Bill?
2. By resolutions leading to a Bill?
3. By resolutions leading to inquiry?

It seems probable that no measure of Parliamentary Reform could be passed by a Conservative Government except in a Parliament where they have essentially a majority.

Resolutions as the basis of a Bill, though not so immediately dangerous as a proposal of direct legislation, would ultimately lead to defeat.

There remains, therefore, to be considered the case of resolutions, which, though laying down a complete scheme, should end in a Royal Commission.

If the difficulty to which in a moment I will advert could be removed, the chances are that this would be a successful course.

It may be assumed that the House of Commons is really opposed to any violent Reform, and to any Reform of any kind which is immediate; and the longer the decision of its opinion can be delayed, the more likely it will be in favor of moderation and postponement.

If the first week of March was fixed for the introduction of the resolutions, the discussion on them need not commence until the first week in April.

If the House then gets involved in the discussion, the Liberal party will probably be broken up.

If, as is more likely, Mr. Gladstone meets the Ministerial motion by a general resolution in favor of immediate legislation, it is not impossible he may be defeated, which will establish the Government. But if he succeed it will probably be by a narrow majority, and the dissolution would then take place on an issue between Bright's policy and our programme.

But to insure the success of such a campaign one condition is necessary: that there should be substantial grounds for a Royal Commission, and this is the difficulty to which I referred.

I myself am at a loss to find these grounds, and this is the point on which the thought of the Cabinet should be concentrated.

If the resolutions at present in your portfolio were adopted, there would be substantial grounds, in a great degree arising from the necessary resettlement of the boundaries of the smaller boroughs; but reflection persuades me that this proposal would not, on the whole, be a wise one; because one of our leading principles should be to enlist, as far as

possible, the sympathies of the small boroughs, and they, perhaps, would deem an alteration of their boundaries only second, as a disaster, to their total disfranchisement.

The settlement of the boundaries of the northern boroughs is not ample enough for a Royal Commission issued under such circumstances. Means to effect such an end might have been adopted in the recess.

It has been suggested that the subject of bribery might be referred to the Royal Commission, and this deserves consideration; but if it were practicable, there is still not a *dignus modus*.

The substantialness of the Royal Commission is the key of the position, and I therefore bring it under your deep consideration.

After further consultation with the Cabinet and the Prime Minister, who was clear that Ministers, in order to extricate themselves from 'the Reform dilemma,' must have a Commission as a 'buffer,' Disraeli redrafted the Resolutions, suggesting that the proposed Commission might be so comprehensive as to embrace inquiries into the extent to which the wage-paid class already had the vote, and why some were excluded and others admitted; how far changes in the value of money had affected the electoral qualification; and how far the franchise might be beneficially extended without the domination of mere numbers; and that the Commission might also investigate and report on bribery and corruption, and revise the boundaries of boroughs.

To Lord Derby.

Confidential. 11, DOWNING STREET, *Dec. 29, 1866.* — . . . I have been most inconveniently summoned to town, in the midst of Christmas, to be sworn in, to-day, a brother of the Trinity House. Those of my brethren who are also country gentlemen must think such a disturbance of a holy festival, on the part of such a body, very strange, and, indeed, scarcely orthodox.

I should like the Cabinet not to be summoned till Thursday, as there are many points of great importance on which consultation is desirable before we meet in formal council. Work thickens. The army question must be grappled with. Then the Portuguese Treaty of Commerce is assuming a practical shape, and a plan of the Post Office for the purchase

of all the private telegraphs of the country demands our decision. These are all heavy affairs, and the latter two fall entirely on the Treasury.

With respect to Reform: I agree with you that it is quite premature to trouble ourselves about the materials [1] of the Royal Commission. . . .

I have not the draft of the Resolutions at hand, but I suspect you will find, on reference to them, that the Resolution pledges the House to 'extension,' not 'reduction,' of the franchise; and 'extension' would include everything.

We must be careful not to commit ourselves both to reduction and 'fancy' franchises, if it be true, as I now hear, that the lodger franchise in the way of extension, and especially among the wage-paid class, would produce incredible results. Indeed, I think that particular franchise should be specifically referred to the Commission, and, indeed, I am rather inclined to refer plurality also, and all the cognate expedients for protecting the minority.

It is quite clear that, throughout the autumn and early winter, Disraeli, far from being stimulated into drastic action by the Reform demonstrations throughout the country, was anxious to postpone legislation as long as possible in order to secure a moderate measure. He was confirmed in this policy by his correspondence with friends and supporters. There was, indeed, one significant exception. Spofforth, who had had a large share in the management of the General Election on the Tory side, told Disraeli that a series of visits in the northern counties had converted him into an advocate of 'a wise and moderate measure next session.' But Cranborne informed him of a strong declaration by Lowe that his valuable support was conditional on no Reform Bill being brought forward in February; Manners saw nothing in what had happened to make such a Bill advisable; and reports from Brooks's Club assured Disraeli that the Liberal party had gone to pieces, and that Bright's greatest friends had been earnestly beseeching him to desist from his mad career.

It must not be forgotten that the circumstances in

---

[1] The context, and Derby's letter, show that Disraeli is referring to the persons to be appointed Royal Commissioners.

which this third Derby-Disraeli Ministry took office
were very different from those which prevailed when the
second Ministry of the kind was formed in 1858. Then
there was an understanding that the Conservatives
should tackle the Reform Question; now they had come
in because Parliament resented having Reform forced
down its throat by Russell and Gladstone. Moreover,
several members of the 1866 Ministry, notably Cranborne,
were very lukewarm Reformers; and Disraeli himself,
in accordance with what he believed to be the opinion
of the country and of Parliament, had taken up in 1865
and in 1866 a much more pronouncedly anti-movement
attitude than had been at all usual with him. Always
an opportunist on Reform, he held during this autumn
that the composition of the Ministry and the temper
of the nation necessitated a policy of moderation and
delay. He was, indeed, for the time, on the question
not of principle, but of tactics, nearer in opinion to his
colleague Cranborne than to his leader Derby.

To Lord Cranborne.

HUGHENDEN MANOR, *Dec.* 26, 1866. — . . . I have throughout been against legislation, and continue so. Lord Derby,
about the time you were here, thought it inevitable, but, as
you know, his views are now modified.

It's a difficult affair, but I think we shall pull through; the
Whigs are very unanimous in wishing the question ' settled ' —
but you and I are not Whigs.

At the same time there must have been lurking at
the back of Disraeli's mind a consciousness that the
Queen might be right in her view, that circumstances
might arise, when Parliament met, to make it desirable,
and indeed necessary, for the Ministry to abandon
the policy of procrastination and deliberation, and to
act — act promptly, thoroughly, and comprehensively.
He published in the winter his collected speeches on
Parliamentary Reform, with a preface asserting that the
views therein expressed were the opinions of the Con-

servative party, and claiming once more for that party the right, if it thought fit, to take up and settle the question. The book was nominally edited, and the preface signed, by his young secretary, Montagu Corry; its exact genesis and history appear from Disraeli's letters.

To Montagu Corry.

HUGHENDEN, *Sept.* 2, 1866. — Longmans want me to publish all my speeches on 'Parliamentary Reform,' in an 8vo vol. They evidently think the subject will revive, and that it may be, in every respect, expedient and advantageous that the collected views of one who has taken an active part in the question should be before the country in a portable form.

I shall not consent, if I do at all, until I have made further observations on the public humor with respect to this question.

But I may eventually have to act with promptitude, and therefore I wish to be prepared for the occasion.

I wish, therefore (not having 'Hansard' at Hughenden), that you would make me a list of my speeches on Parliamentary Reform. . . .

Oct. 4. — . . . Longman is pressing me about the speeches. Have you confidence in the list you sent me? For example, on acceding to office in 1852, I had to speak on a Reform motion — probably one of Hume's — in which I took occasion to observe that, in any future change, the claims of the working class ought to be considered. They had been unwisely dealt with, and neglected, in the measure of 1832. My recollection, faint, is that my observations were brief. They occasioned much discontent, I remember, and particularly at Court. Events have proved they were just, and I felt they were in accordance with true Tory principles. . . .

I think it worth consideration, whether you might not figure in the title-page as editor. It might assist your introduction into public life. We can think about this. . . .

Oct. 16. — I see that Longmans have advertised your volume; in the *Saturday Review*, I think, I saw it. 'Speeches on Parliamentary Reform, by Rt. Hon. B. D., M.P., C. of E., etc.'

A horrid title; it will do for the moment, but when we advance a little, and real advertising begins, there should be something more condensed and simpler. . . . I hate

Rt. Hon.'s and M.P.'s and all that.   C. of E.'s *must* be R.H.'s and M.P.'s and so on, as a matter of course. . . .

Oct. 30. — I send Gladstone's book, which I found on my arrival at Grosvenor Gate, 'With the Publisher's compliments.'

It is a sorry-looking volume; merely a reprint of the speeches of last year, with no evidence of matured and continuous policy.   I hope yours will be much more business-like and impressive, both in matter and in form; but the sooner you get it out the better. . . .

STRATHFIELDSAYE, *Nov.* 29. — My dear Editor — I send you the two proofs, and begin to see daylight.   Herein, also, is a rough sketch of an advertisement, or preface, which you may not only alter in any way you like, but even reconstruct or altogether put aside. . . .

ADVERTISEMENT.

These speeches, commencing at a period even antecedent to the desertion of the principle of finality by Lord John Russell, and ending with the last session, were made by a member of Parliament who, during the whole interval, was either leader of the Opposition or principal Minister of the Queen in the House of Commons.

They represent, therefore, the opinions of a party, and we have the highest authority for stating that, scarcely with an exception, the views, which they represent, were, after due deliberation, adopted by every eminent, man, who has since sate in the councils of Lord Derby, and by every leading country gentleman of the time.

So long as the Whig party were firm in upholding the settlement of 1832, the Tory party, though not insensible to some injustice in that measure, resolved to support its authors against all attempts at further change in the constitution of the House of Commons.   But when the Whigs yielded their position, their political opponents determined to assert the principles which, in their opinion, should guide any future reconstruction, and which from that time have, consequently, been placed before the country in the following speeches with an amplitude of knowledge, and a vigor and versatility of argument and illustration, which have been acknowledged.

These speeches, then, form a complete and consistent record of the main opinions of a great party in the State during the important period in which a further change of the constitution of the House of Commons has been in agitation; and the country, therefore, will now be enabled to see with what justness it has been asserted that the Tory party

are disqualified from dealing with the most difficult of modern
political questions in consequence of their constant and unvarying hostility to any attempt to improve our popular representation. — M. C.

The 'Advertisement' was printed as drafted in the
above letter, with a few slight verbal alterations, and the
volume appeared in January.

Though, in view of the history of the session of 1867,
what went on about Reform behind the scenes in the
autumn of 1866 is of great interest and importance, it
would be a mistake to suppose that Disraeli's energies
were at that time exclusively, or even specially, directed
to the subject. Indeed, Reform did not occupy nearly
so much of his attention as in the autumn of 1858; and
no detailed work whatever was done on it either by him
or by his colleagues. Whereas, in 1858, Disraeli first
elaborated a scheme in conjunction with Stanley, then
hammered out the details in a special Cabinet Committee,
and finally went over all the ground again in full Cabinet;
on the present occasion general resolutions were all with
which Ministers concerned themselves, till the session
of 1867 had begun. The confusion and mishaps of
the early part of that session might well have been
avoided if Disraeli's foresight on this occasion had
been equal to that of the Queen and of the Prime
Minister.

Foreign policy and finance occupied Disraeli at least
as much as Reform. He was anxious to set an example
in office of the unadventurous and economical administration which he had pressed on Parliament in opposition.
Ministers acceded to office while Bismarck was carrying
out that attack upon Austria which, he had frankly confessed to Disraeli some years before, was the immediate
aim of his policy. The division of the spoils of Schleswig-
Holstein was the excuse; and nobody in England wished
to interfere in the internecine quarrels of the German
Powers who had robbed Denmark. In this matter Ministers only carried on the neutral policy of their prede-

cessors.   Disraeli, in his speech on re-election, laid down the broad lines on which any British intervention should rest, giving, after his wont, a philosophical basis to a practical policy.

The abstention of England from any unnecessary interference in the affairs of Europe is the consequence, not of her decline of power, but of her increased strength.   England is no longer a mere European Power; she is the metropolis of a great maritime empire, extending to the boundaries of the farthest ocean.   It is not that England has taken refuge in a state of apathy, that she now almost systematically declines to interfere in the affairs of the Continent of Europe. England is as ready and as willing to interfere as in old days, when the necessity of her position requires it.   There is no Power, indeed, that interferes more than England.   She interferes in Asia, because she is really more an Asiatic Power than a European.   She interferes in Australia, in Africa, and New Zealand, where she carries on war often on a great scale. Therefore, it is not because England does not recognise her duty to interfere in the affairs of the Continent of Europe that persons are justified in declaring that she has relinquished her imperial position, and has taken refuge in the *otium cum dignitate*, which agrees with the decline of life, of power, and of prosperity.   On the contrary, she has a greater sphere of action than any European Power, and she has duties devolving upon her on a much larger scale.   Not that we can ever look with indifference upon what takes place on the Continent.   We are interested in the peace and prosperity of Europe, and I do not say that there may not be occasions in which it may be the duty of England to interfere in European wars.

Though the passage was a plea for non-interference in European affairs, it was far from being an unconditional plea; and the right of England to intervene, and her reserved power to do so with effect, are carefully enforced.   The new Foreign Secretary, Stanley, was indeed a whole-hearted adherent of the policy of non-intervention. But Disraeli himself never lost sight of the difference between meddling with the domestic affairs of European nations, and intervening in their international relations when those relations affected British interests or public law; and the continuous experience of office which he

was now to enjoy for two years and a half, made him
doubt whether the natural reaction from Palmerston's
and Russell's meddlesomeness was not being carried too
far.   It was impossible, he felt, to trust either of the two
principal forces on the Continent, Napoleon III. and
Bismarck.   There was reason to fear that they might
at any moment combine to the disadvantage of British
interests.   Vigilance was all the more necessary, as Disraeli had a poor opinion of British diplomatists.

To Lord Stanley.

GROSVENOR GATE, *Aug.* 17, 1866. — I have read Cowley's
letters with much interest.   Bloomfield's, both handwriting
and matter, are those of a greengrocer; Loftus should be the
foreign editor of the *Morning Herald.*   Morier, as ambassador,
is 'high life below stairs.'   Elliot a partisan.[1]

Mem.: None of your people address you rightly in their
public despatches.   They should be addressed to 'Secretary
the Right Hon. the Lord Stanley, M.P.'

As the Venetians, who were great authorities in their day,
used to say, 'Punctilio is the soul of diplomacy.'

The interests both of the country, and — what Disraeli never neglected — the party, seemed to point to a
more vigorous assertion of British interests.   'Non-
intervention might have been successfully opposed to
Palmerston,' wrote Earle on September 1; 'but it is
impossible for us to gain any popularity in this wise,
which could not be obtained in a greater degree by
Gladstone.'   He feared the Tories might be 'colourless,
neither Cobdenite nor Imperial'; 'a little more expensive than Gladstone and not a whit more glorious and
national.'   The influence of the Queen was strongly
exercised in the same direction, especially in regard to
two questions which the rival intrigues of Napoleon
and Bismarck forced to the front — the independence
of Belgium and of Luxemburg.   The threat to the
first was, for the moment, rather a matter of con-
jecture.

[1] Cowley was at Paris, Bloomfield at Vienna, Loftus at Berlin, Morier
at Frankfort, and Elliot at Florence.

To Lord Stanley.

GROSVENOR GATE, *Dec.* 30, 1866. — I have just heard, from a first-rate quarter, that, at the last Cabinet Council at the Tuileries, a proposition, from Bismarck, suggesting an arrangement by which the Southern States of Germany should blend with Prussia, and that France should take possession of Belgium, was absolutely brought forward, and favored by several of the Ministers, principally by Lavalette. It was opposed by the Minister for Foreign Affairs.

Can this be true? And if so, or if there be any foundation for it, what are Bismarck's relations with us? Have you heard anything from our Goosey Gander at Berlin, a pretty instrument to cope with the Prussian Minister! And Mr. Fane,[1] what does he say? And what shall we say?

The Emperor is like a gambler who has lost half his fortune and restless to recover; likely to make a *coup*, which may be fatally final for himself.

I doubt whether this country would see any further glaring case of public violence and treachery with composure. Reaction is the law of all human affairs; and the reaction from non-intervention must sooner or later set in. I would rather, however, try to prevent mischief — *i.e.*, as long as we can. . . .

The threat to Belgium, the reality of which Bismarck in his own good time revealed to the world, was at the moment treated by Stanley as a *canard*. But the threat to Luxemburg was definitely made in the following spring. The position of Luxemburg largely reproduced the anomalous conditions of Holstein before 1864. It had been a member of the Germanic Confederation, but its ruler, with the title of Grand-Duke, was the King of Holland, from whose Dutch dominions, however, it was separated by many miles. The Germanic Confederation had now been dissolved as a result of Prussia's victory over Austria; but the city and fortress of Luxemburg were still garrisoned by Prussian troops, which, after Prussia's recent aggrandisement, were not unreasonably looked upon by France as a menace on her flank. Napoleon III. opened negotiations with the Dutch Government for the sale of the grand-duchy to France.

---

[1] First Secretary at Paris.

On April 3, 1867, Disraeli wrote to Stanley : ' Rothschilds have received information that the Emperor has definitely informed Bismarck that the arrangement between himself and the King of Holland is concluded, and that he shall act at once on it.'　This transaction was strongly resented in Germany; and for some days war appeared to be imminent, the Emperor telling the Prussian Minister that the possession of Luxemburg involved the question of his own existence.　As the grand-duchy had been guaranteed to the King of Holland by a treaty in 1839, to which Great Britain, with the other Great Powers, was a party, this country was directly interested ; and the Queen's personal intervention, and Stanley's urgent efforts, prevailed to make both sides reasonable.

To Lord Stanley.

WINDSOR CASTLE, *Easter Monday, April* 22, 1867. — My visit here has tumbled me into the midst of the Luxemburg business, and I have had all the despatches, and all the private letters of all the cousins, submitted to me ; and you know all the rest.

I assured our Royal Mistress, and most sincerely, that she was quite under a mistake in supposing that you would not act, if necessary, and that, I knew, you have well considered all the eventualities about Belgium ; that you would never act without determination and constancy ;　and that anything you did or said would have double the effect of the old stagers with their mechanical interference — sometimes bluster and sometimes blundering.

I told Her Majesty, also, that we were not really half a Government until the division of last Friday,[1] and that a hint from you could, and would, do more now than reams of despatches a month ago.

I think she understood all this, and I think I did good.

I pointed out also that, so far as matters went, the question of Belgium was really not on the *tapis*.　This, after reflection, she agreed to : but still thought that, in confidential conversation, our people might let it be known at Berlin and Paris that the violation of Belgian neutrality should not pass with impunity.

At present it seems the pressure should rather be put upon Berlin than on the ancient capital of Julian the Apostate.

[1] On Gladstone's amendment, in Committee, on the Reform Bill, about compound householders.　See below, Ch. 14.

Two things seem to me clear: that France is not prepared, and that Bismarck lies to everyone. His explanations prove his perfidy.

I think, myself, as old Brunnow says, 'it is time for a little reaction,' and that we might begin to dictate a little to Europe. Gladstonism is at a discount.

It's very lucky, however, we didn't take off any taxes, and that by paying off some debt we shall be able to borrow any amount at a very moderate price. That is to say, in case we want it. Nevertheless, as nothing happens which one expects, I begin to believe you will turn out a regular Chatham. . . .

Stanley replied: 'I am ready to go as far as may be necessary in support of Belgium, short of giving an absolute pledge to fight for its independence. Suppose we gave such a pledge, that France and Prussia came to an understanding, Russia and Austria standing aloof, where should we be?' It was a prudent rather than a generous or even a statesmanlike view. According to general belief, we had given such a pledge; in any case it was the traditional policy of England not to permit the Low Countries to be controlled by a dominant military Power. With regard to Luxemburg, Stanley rightly saw that its neutralisation was 'the one indispensable condition of peace'; but he was very reluctant to give the guarantee which would alone make neutralisation effective. The Queen could not understand his hesitation. 'We are already parties to the guarantee of Belgian neutrality and independence,' wrote General Grey on her behalf to Disraeli on May 5, 'and to extend the guarantee of neutrality to Luxemburg does not seem to entail upon us any great additional responsibility.' Her Majesty's arguments, which Disraeli reinforced, prevailed; and at a Conference in London in May a treaty was signed by which the duchy was neutralised under the guarantee of the Powers, and the Prussian garrison withdrawn. Stanley was very insistent in the House of Commons, that the guarantee was a collective and not a separate one ; that the liability was limited, and amounted rather to a moral sanction than to a contingent liability to go

to war.   Derby laboured the same point in the House of
Lords.   Under a collective guarantee, he said, if there
was a difference of opinion among the guarantors, no
one party was called upon to undertake the duty of
enforcing it.   Both statesmen had in view the contingency which Stanley had discussed in writing to
Disraeli, of France and Prussia combining to violate
the treaty.   But their language was unfortunate.   The
real point was : Would England assist either France or
Prussia to support the neutrality of Luxemburg if the
other proceeded to violate it ?   As the Queen and
Disraeli understood the treaty, the answer was Yes.

Throughout this matter the Queen was constantly
appealing to Disraeli for support for a more vigorous
policy than Stanley, with Derby's adherence, was
disposed to pursue.   Disraeli sympathised with Her
Majesty's standpoint, and used his influence to stiffen
Stanley.   The Queen warned Disraeli of the bad effect
produced on the Continent by Derby's and Stanley's
language about Luxemburg, and told him that she had
had to explain that, so long as other Powers, especially
France and Prussia, adhered to the engagements they had
entered into, England would never be found unfaithful
to hers.   Her Majesty anticipated the impending struggle
between France and Prussia, and was not reconciled to
the adoption by this country of a purely fatalistic and
detached attitude.   Was Great Britain to make no
attempt to avert such a calamity ?   If those Powers
were bent on quarrelling with each other, it might be
difficult to prevent them.   Still, if the aggressor were to
know that, in such a quarrel, the moral, and in certain
cases the material, support of England would be given
to the other side — if, for instance, both Powers were
assured that the violation of Belgium and Luxemburg
would certainly bring England into the field — it might
prevent steps being taken on either side that must lead
to war.   To the Queen, as to most contemporary
statesmen, France appeared the most likely violator

of international guarantees, and Disraeli, long as he had
clung to the French alliance, could not contradict her
when she advocated, in adherence to the Prince Consort's
tradition, a good understanding with North Germany;
but the principle remained equally good, whoever might
be the aggressor. Her Majesty struck a chord to which
he responded.

From General the Hon. Charles Grey.

OSBORNE, *July* 29, 1867.— . . . Prussia is not likely to
violate either the neutrality of Luxemburg or the independence of Belgium — indeed, she has no interest to do so —
*unless she sees reason to believe that England means her guarantee
of both these objects to remain a dead letter, in which case she
might think it in her interest to come to an agreement with
France fatal to the independence of the rest of Europe.* . . .
The Queen is confirmed in her opinion of the expediency of
our acting firmly on a well-defined and well-understood
principle of foreign policy, by the result of our intervention
on the Luxemburg question. It is not only that peace was
preserved chiefly by our means, but that our action on that
question went far towards restoring to England the prestige
there can be no doubt she had lost. It is neither for our
national credit nor for the interest of the world that we should
again fall into the state of absolute disregard from which we
have now partly recovered. H.M. would therefore strongly
urge the necessity of your giving your best attention to our
whole system of foreign policy, so as to secure to England the
respect and influence due to her as the Power who, above all
others, can have no ambitious views of her own, nor any
interest but in the preservation of peace. . . .

At the close of the session of 1867 Disraeli assured the
Queen that an impression had been made upon Stanley,
whose opinions, he thought — but apparently was mistaken
in thinking — were undergoing modification.

To Queen Victoria.

DOWNING STREET, *Aug.* 16, 1867.— . . . Lord Stanley
seems to have increased, and increasing, confidence in the
maintenance of European peace; although Lord Stanley is
of a reserved and rather morose temper, and will not go out
of his way to confess that he has been in error, he is really
au fond truthful and impartial; and, if convinced that he has
erred or miscalculated, is never blind to the result, and,

often unavowedly, to a certain degree perhaps unconsciously, will assuredly modify his conduct. So, in the present state of affairs, it is far from improbable that Lord Stanley will, ultimately, be the Minister who will destroy, and shatter to pieces, the decaying theory and system of non-interference.

A consideration of the principal foreign difficulty which had to be dealt with by the new Administration has carried us some way beyond the autumn of 1866. Other questions loomed more largely at first. Portugal proposed a commercial treaty, and there was some hope that Spain also would come in. Disraeli, as Chancellor of the Exchequer, was greatly interested in proposals which might 'increase our markets; and that,' he wrote to Northcote, 'is the main interest of the labouring class.' But the negotiations, after dragging on a long time, proved abortive. The mutterings of trouble with the United States about the *Alabama* Claims, and with Abyssinia over some British prisoners whom King Theodore wrongfully detained, were also beginning at this time to be heard.

Meanwhile Disraeli was urgent in pressing for economy in administration to suit an unaggressive policy; and he made his first attack on the mismanagement of the Admiralty.

To Lord Derby.

Confidential. HUGHENDEN MANOR, *Aug.* 20, 1866. — The maladministration, not to say malversation, of the Admiralty has struck deep into the public mind, and is, at this moment, the predominant feeling of the nation. If dealt with vigorously, it will divert opinion from Parliamentary Reform; if neglected, it may precipitate great political changes.

Some few years ago, when I endeavoured to draw the attention of our party, but not as successfully as I wished, to this subject, I was guided by the information and advice of Mr. Laird, M.P. for Birkenhead.[1] Before I left town, that gentleman requested an interview with me, of which the object was to offer, if I wished it, to resume the reports and counsels that he had previously given me.

Mr. Laird attributes the deplorable administration of the Admiralty, mainly, to two causes:

[1] The shipbuilder and shipowner.

Firstly, the expenditure and waste which are occasioned by the accumulation of stores. . . .

Mr. Laird is of opinion that the surplus stores should be sold, and, consisting mainly of timber, iron, and copper, he believes they may be disposed of at half-price. This would place a large sum at the disposal of the Admiralty.

The second cause of maladministration was pointed out by him to me some years ago, and is now still more enforced, viz., the obstinacy with which the Admiralty has declined building iron ships, and the vast sums which they have vainly expended in cobbling up old wooden vessels.

These are the two principal causes of the present condition of the navy, which, if encountered in a masterly manner, may be a source of strength and reputation to your Government; if neglected, may lead to public disaster.

There increased expenditure will aggravate, not cure, the disease.

I refrain from having any communication with Sir John Pakington on this subject. All extraordinary motion in the great departments should come from you. It confirms your authority and it prevents jealousies. But I earnestly beg you to give your personal attention and energy to this matter. A First Lord is surrounded by the criminals, and it requires intellectual grasp, and a peremptory firmness, to deal with them.

An unexpected military drain was caused by the sudden despatch of troops to Canada to protect the colony against a threatened Fenian raid from the United States. Disraeli was clear that these troops must be recalled directly the danger was past, and that the colony which repudiated any interference from home with her local government should also learn that, in that case, she must provide for her local defence, thus enforcing a doctrine which Adderley had vainly pressed on him a year or two before. The impatience which allowed him to write of the colonies as 'dead-weights' recalls the irritable epithet 'wretched' of fourteen years before ; but, as guardian of the public purse, he did well to protest against the one-sided relation which some colonies seemed then to think fair. The Dominions have long since recognised the obligation on which Disraeli insisted. With regard to the somewhat

sweeping proposal to abandon our West African settlements, it must be remembered that only a year previously a representative Committee of the House of Commons on West African affairs had unanimously reported against any further extension of territory or assumption of government, and that what is now by far the most valuable and prosperous of British possessions in that quarter, Nigeria, was then unappropriated and practically unknown.

To Lord Derby.

HUGHENDEN MANOR, *Sept.* 30, 1866.— . . . Until the American elections have taken place, there will be no chance of anything like sense or moderation in American politics; but there will be a chance then.

Then, also, we must seriously consider our Canadian position, which is most illegitimate. An army maintained in a country which does not permit us even to govern it? What an anomaly!

It never can be our pretence, or our policy, to defend the Canadian frontier against the U. S. If the colonists can't, as a general rule, defend themselves against the Fenians, they can do nothing. They ought to be, and must be, strong enough for that. Power and influence we should exercise in Asia; consequently in Eastern Europe, consequently also in Western Europe; but what is the use of these colonial deadweights which *we do not govern?*

I don't regret what we did the other day about Canada, because the circumstances were very peculiar. A successful raid of the Fenians was not off the cards, which would have upset your untried Ministry, and might have produced an insurrection in Ireland; and it was not fair to the Canadians, when, at the last, they were making some attempts at self-defence, to allow them to be crushed in the bud of their patriotism. But the moment the American elections are over, we should withdraw the great body of our troops, and foster a complete development of self-government.

Leave the Canadians to defend themselves; recall the African squadrons; give up the settlements on the west coast of Africa; and we shall make a saving which will, at the same time, enable us to build ships and have a good Budget.

What is more, we shall have accomplished something definite, tangible, for the good of the country. In these

days, more than ever, the people look to results. What we have done about Canada is perfectly defensible, if it is not looked upon as a permanent increase of our Canadian establishments.

According to my accounts from the Continent, Hartington mentioned at more than one place that our recent despatch of troops is to be made the great point of attack on the part of the Opposition. May they long enjoy that venerable name, which I never yet read, or hear, without thinking there is something personal! . . .

Derby had loyally backed his lieutenant in his demands on Pakington and the Admiralty; but Disraeli had to exercise continual pressure to obtain the results he desired. The circumstances in which Ministers succeeded to office added weight to Disraeli's representations. The City of London was then slowly recovering from the terrible panic caused by the failure in May of the great discount establishment of Overend and Gurney, the most striking incident of a crisis due to the excessive development of speculative companies.

To Sir John Pakington.

HUGHENDEN, *Oct.* 23, 1866. — . . . If your proposition involves a second naval supplemental estimate, and a consequent charge on the balances of the present financial year, I must at once express my inability to provide for it.

Our financial position is not satisfactory. I have been obliged to borrow largely from the bank for the payment of the recent dividends, and though, by the last return, the 20th inst., these advances have been satisfied, still, that result has been accomplished by appropriating the revenue of nearly three weeks of the new quarter, and our balances in the bank are under one million. They ought to be between three and four millions. But that is not all. On these feeble balances the demands are great and unusual. Claims for the advances agreed upon in respect to cattle compensation, Irish railways, and Cheshire distress, are now pouring in.

Although, notwithstanding the financial pressure and the bad harvest, the revenue has wonderfully maintained itself, it, as yet, scarcely realises the estimate of my predecessor, and you may remember in that estimate, virtually, no surplus was provided.

When we acceded to office, the magnificent crop of barley,

then in the fields, gave me reason to believe that the second half of the financial year would have been buoyant from the increased malt tax, then anticipated; but all these hopes have been, since, dashed to the ground.

Under these circumstances, it will be one of my first duties, when the Cabinet reassembles, to call its attention to our financial position, and, discarding every other consideration but that of an inexorable economy, to request its sanction to a proposal that no department of the State shall exceed the amount of the estimates of 1866–67, with a hope that they may not reach them; otherwise we shall get into a scrape.

I ought to observe, with respect to second supplementary estimates — on the ground of good administration alone, so very objectionable — that I have communicated with General Peel on this head; and he has promised me that the increased expenditure for Canadian small arms shall be defrayed out of the supplemental vote of this year. . . .

To Lord Derby.

GROSVENOR GATE, *Feb.* 2, 1867. — The Admiralty is beyond the control of a Chancellor of the Exchequer, or any other subordinate Minister. It is the Prime Minister that can alone deal with that department.

If the Admiralty want more guns, they must proportionately diminish their contract expenditure.

It is useless to attempt to reason with them; you must command. The whole system of administration is palsied by their mutinous spirit. Not another four-and-twenty hours ought to elapse without the estimates being settled. Several acts of great policy — the formation of the army of reserve, and the Portuguese treaty — depend upon the programme on which we agreed, and which, so far as the Admiralty is concerned, gives it more than half a million of excess.

Disraeli's vigorous efforts for economy had their due effect. They gave him an estimated surplus on his 1867 Budget of £1,200,000. This he applied, with general consent, to the reduction of debt, appeasing the indefatigable opponents of the malt tax by the appointment of a Select Committee.

Other subjects of moment which occupied Disraeli's attention during the autumn were the purchase of the telegraphs by the State — 'a great affair, but, though

difficult, it appears to be sound and solid'; and the local government of London, which he pressed upon Hardy, who remarked that it was a 'very puzzling' question, and that 'a number of municipalities would hardly vary from the vestries which are the local governments in many cases justly complained of.' The purchase of the telegraphs Disraeli was to carry through before he quitted office; but the local government of London he left to be reconstituted by Conservative successors after his death. A letter to Northcote tells of other anxieties.

To Sir Stafford Northcote.

HUGHENDEN, *Oct.* 14, 1866. — . . . I am anxious, and rather alarmed about the financial systems of our railway companies. So far as I can judge, from the information that reaches me, nearly the whole of them will collapse; the distress and ruin to many industrial establishments will be great, but the effect on the condition of the working classes, at a moment when there are elements of discontent abroad, would be very serious.

Is it possible for the Government to interfere? It would be a great affair. Between bonds and debentures we should have to deal with more than a hundred million. This is one of the subjects over which we must talk together. . . .

Our great misfortune at present is the acceptance by Cairns of the Lord Justiceship, vacant by the resignation of Knight Bruce. It is an irreparable loss, and falls with peculiar severity on myself, for in debate he was my right arm.

If Cairns had had only a little heart and a little imagination, he would have been by far the first man in the House of Commons; and if he had had only a little heart and a little imagination, he would not have deserted Lord Derby at such a crisis, which may be historic. . . .

We are victims of patronage. Never was such a shower, especially of legal posts.[1]

Cairns was never a strong man physically, and he found the calls of the Attorney-Generalship on his strength to be excessive. He took the opportunity of a vacancy

---

[1] Writing to Lord Barrington on Jan. 29, 1868, Disraeli said : ' I wish, almost, it were an *indoctum parliamentum* again, and that we had no lawyers in it.'

in the Court of Appeal to retire to the bench, without
much consideration for the feelings of his leader in the
House of Commons, who was left to face a critical
session without the aid of his most trusted debater.
Disraeli's letters of this date are full of laments over
this desertion. 'With him I was not afraid to encounter
Gladstone and Roundell Palmer,' he wrote to Corry;
'now I have got them both, without the slightest assistance.' He had not then realized to the full the value
of Gathorne Hardy, who succeeded to Cairns's place as
his 'sword-arm' when the fight was fierce in the House
of Commons.

A pleasant picture of Disraeli's methods in dealing
with business is sketched for us in his notes written
from Hughenden to his secretary during this autumn.

To Montagu Corry.

HUGHENDEN, *Sept.* 2, 1866. —. . . When letters come from
my colleagues marked 'Private,' it is unnecessary to open
them, as no action can be taken on them until they are
forwarded to me. Nothing, therefore, is gained by the
process, which is not necessary, and which my correspondents,
under such circumstances, dislike.

My hand is by no means so bad as my handwriting would
imply; the scrawl is the consequence of the wretched, cheap
huckster's ink, supplied by that miserable department, the
Stationery Office.

Sept. 5. — I enclose you Lord Stanley's letter.

In the first place, obtain immediately for me the answer
of the Board of Trade referred to.[1] Be pleased also to tell
the Board of Trade — I suppose it will be Mr. Cave, as Sir
Stafford is absent — that I wish copies of all correspondence,
etc., that may take place between the Board and the F. O.,
respecting commercial treaties, to be forwarded immediately
to me. The Treasury is the chief, and controlling, department of the State, and it is perfectly absurd that, in matters
which cannot be carried into operation without sensibly
influencing the revenue, we should not have the best information at the earliest date. . . .

Observe what Lord S. says about the 'compares.'[2] As

---

[1] With reference to the proposed commercial treaty with Portugal.

[2] Weekly revenue returns printed for the use of the Treasury.

there is, and has ever been, an entire alliance between us, I wish particularly that his request should be complied with.

But I don't want it to be known in the office. Do this: tell the office that, in future, I wish *two* copies of the 'compare' to be sent to me. It will be your duty to send one immediately to Lord Stanley in a packet marked 'Private' with 'C. of E.' in the corner. . . .

Sept. 9. — . . . I am not surprised B[oard] of T[rade] rather demurs at having to work in September, which is unnatural, but it will give them a lesson, and teach them which department is at the head of the Government.

You, also, have not found the secretariat quite as much of a sinecure as we expected; but you have done your work very well, and it will season you for the impending struggle. . . .

Sept. 11. — . . . Read the enclosed letter from Mr. Wellings, a clergyman of Shropshire. The youth referred to was the godson of the late Mrs. Brydges Willyams, who, about three years ago, made me her heir. She left this lad £3,000, and requested me, if I had the opportunity, of planting him in life. I never saw him, nor wish to see him, but I should like very much to forward his interests — particularly as he does not seem to want much.

The Mr. Lovell referred to is the lawyer to the Brydges Willyams estate, who has communicated with all the legatees, but this matter should not be left to Mr. Lovell any further.

I don't want the boy to be unnecessarily plucked, and therefore I would wish you to write to his uncle, and inquire whether he is prepared to pass the preliminary examination, etc., etc., and generally put things in train. . . .

Sept. 25. — What do you think of the ink they give us? Is it detestable? Or is it this fat, woolly paper, which they think so fine?

The ink is not so bad on my own paper, of which I enclose a specimen; but it soon gets so. I can't think it is the pens. Bad stationery adds much to the labor of life; and whether it be the ink, the pens, or the paper, it seems to me, when in office, I never can write like a gentleman. It's a serious nuisance.

Sept. 26. — We must not make another mistake about our paper. I observe the 'Hughenden' sheet, which I sent you yesterday, is part of a lot which I did not much approve of at the time. I thought it too austere.

Now I write on some 'Grosvenor Gate' paper, which I think perfectly satisfied me in town; but whether it be the office ink or the office pens, my caligraphy has a cheese-mongerish look. . . . The whole subject will employ your

vacant hours till I return to town, as I shall certainly lose
my temper, when real business commences, if my tools are
not first-rate.

You do your business very well, and I am always glad to
hear from you. . . .

Oct. 2. — What you write about Mr. A—— sending the
' compare ' regularly to Mr. Gladstone is distressing.

It appears to me a proceeding highly irregular, and fraught
with injurious consequences, while at the same time I feel
reluctance in interfering, where Mr. Gladstone is concerned.

If Mr. Gladstone, on the ground alleged,[1] as I understand,
by Mr. A——, had asked me for this privilege, considering
his eminence and services, however reluctant to do so, I
should not have hesitated to have accorded it; but there is
a great difference in such a proceeding sanctioned by me,
and a communication, which has the appearance of being
clandestine, between a permanent officer of the Government
and an ex-head of his department.

I do not know of any precedent for such a course, and Mr.
A—— has certainly no right to make one.

Where is the line to be drawn between communications
between Mr. A—— and a late Chancellor of the Exchequer?
Why should they not refer to future Budgets as well as to
past?

Such a proceeding has a tendency to destroy that complete
confidence which ought to exist between me and an officer
in Mr. A——'s position.

I should wish that you should have conferred, on this
matter, with Sir Stafford Northcote, who, from being a
friend of Mr. Gladstone, would have considered the circumstances without prejudice against him, but Sir S. is at
Balmoral.

In the meantime, consult Mr. Hamilton [2] confidentially on
the matter, and report to me. . . .

Oct. 16. —. . . I assume that, after all our experience,
now of many years, of Roman Catholic influences and
interests in Ireland, men like Naas and Taylor, and especially
the former, who is a most able, sensible, and enlightened
man, are taking the right course; and I will not interfere
with them in any way. They know my Irish policy, and
any observations of mine are unnecessary.

[1] That it was fair that an outgoing Chancellor of the Exchequer should
be kept informed of the working of his budget till the end of the financial
year.

[2] The permanent head of the office, who immediately ordered the
practice to be discontinued.

As for Hennessy[1] running with us and Cullen[2] and Co. (Cullen is a mere Whig) at the same time, it is plainly impossible that he can succeed in such an adventure.

The Tipperary election will show whether there be any substance in Monsell's views of a national Roman Catholic party in Ireland. I confess I am not sanguine. . . .

Dec. 21. — . . . I think the time has arrived when the Patronage Secretary of the Treasury (of all men in the world!) should at least learn the office which his master fills, and his due title. Give him at the earliest opportunity a gentle educational hint. Somebody has instructed Hunt long ago — I suppose Hamilton. The manners of D[owning] S[treet] are getting quite American. The tradition of the old etiquette must be gradually revived.

We ought to have made the F. O. Press print all their labels over again, and I think you had better order the circular one. I did insist upon it in the case of 'Earl Derby'! I dare say Colonel Taylor addresses the Lord Chancellor as Lord Chelmsford!

Disraeli, ever an artist on the national stage, was a great upholder of what he sometimes called the etiquette, and sometimes the punctilio, of office. He made it a practice to address a colleague who was a Secretary of State as 'Secretary So-and-So'; his intimate notes to Stanley, when they were in office together, frequently began 'My dear Secretary'; and he expected, when he was responsible for the national Treasury, to be, as a matter of course, himself officially addressed as 'Chancellor of the Exchequer.'

[1] Sir John Pope-Hennessy, appointed Governor of Labuan in 1867, and eventually Governor of Mauritius.

[2] The Cardinal.

CHAPTER XIV

DISRAELI'S PARLIAMENTARY TRIUMPH — I

1867

'Of all possible hares to start, I do not know a better than the extension to household suffrage, coupled with plurality of voting.' In this light-hearted manner was the idea, on which the great measure of 1867 was based, thrown out in a letter from Derby to Disraeli on December 22, 1866. The sentence occurs among a number of suggestions as to the matters which might be submitted for inquiry to the Commission then contemplated by the Government. 'The advantage,' Derby continued, 'of multiplying such questions is that we do not bind ourselves to the adoption of any, but afford an opportunity for feeling the pulse of Parliament and the country on all.' Of this special suggestion Disraeli in reply took no particular notice, save to say that 'extension' of the franchise, the word used in the Resolutions, would include everything.

Household suffrage was no new proposal; but it was one that hitherto both Whigs and Tories had united to oppose. Its Parliamentary sponsor had originally been the Radical, Joseph Hume; but of late years it had been revived by Bright, who, in his Reform campaign in the autumn and winter of 1858–59, definitely committed himself to it as the basis of the borough franchise. Disraeli, on behalf of the Government, as definitely rejected it in his speech moving for leave to bring in the Ministerial Bill of 1859. Arguing against the reduction of the £10 borough franchise, he said: 'It certainly would be most injudicious, not to say intolerable, when we are guarding

484

The Earl of Derby. 1867.

from a portrait at Hughenden.

ourselves against the predominance of a territorial aristocracy and the predominance of a manufacturing and
commercial oligarchy, that we should reform Parliament
by securing the predominance of a household democracy.'
He would have nothing to say to a constituency so monotonous. This was his public language in 1859; but, on
the third reading of the Bill of 1867, he stated that household suffrage was proposed as the principle of the borough
franchise in the Derby-Disraeli Cabinet of 1858–59;
though it was not adopted, on the ground that it would
receive no support from public opinion, which was at that
time against any reduction of the borough franchise whatever. But he added that the Cabinet were unanimous that,
if they attempted to reduce the borough qualification at
all, recourse to household suffrage was inevitable. Henley
at once disputed the statement, so far, at least, as concerned the Cabinet while he remained a member of it —
that is, down to the introduction of the Bill in the House
of Commons. The explanation probably is that what
had become in 1867 the principle was in 1859 the bogey.
That Disraeli and other members of the 1858 Cabinet
were clear-sighted enough to perceive that, when once you
abandoned the £10 limit, there was no logical or substantial basis short of household suffrage, we can well believe;
but, when we remember the attitude of the Government
and of public opinion at the time to Bright's proposal,
we can only read the unanimity of the Cabinet on the
point as meaning that they must adhere without flinching
to the £10 limit, so as to avoid being ultimately driven
to the very unpalatable alternative of household suffrage.
It was a £6 limit, and not household suffrage, that Disraeli
was ready to accept, in May and June, 1859, as a settlement.[1] Indeed, household suffrage does not appear to
have been mentioned in the correspondence about Reform

[1] In his speech on Baines's Bill in 1865, Disraeli said that what the
Government were prepared to propose in June, 1859, was 'not a franchise
of £6, but an arrangement that was to be taken with the rest of the Bill.'
This is vague, and does not affect his readiness to accept Roebuck's terms,
which included a £6 borough franchise. See above, p. 243.

between him and Derby down to the winter of 1866–67. The question is always of £8 or £7 or £6 or £5, even down to July, 1866 ;[1] and of course these were the figures actually proposed or suggested by those Whig and Tory legislators who contemplated the abandonment of the £10 limit. It must be confessed that Disraeli's statement about the Cabinet of 1858 and household suffrage can only be regarded as rather a glaring instance of the besetting sin of Parliamentary statesmen, to make out that there is no inconsistency between the course they may be rightly taking under the exigencies of the moment, and that which they took or recommended in earlier and different circumstances.

It was as a subject for inquiry that Derby first recommended household suffrage. But the Commission to inquire into all the conditions and surroundings of Reform, which was to be of so comprehensive a character as to justify Ministers in postponing legislation for a year, and was accordingly regarded with satisfaction by Derby, Disraeli, and Cranborne, never saw the Parliamentary light. The discussions of January killed it. 'The scheme of an inquiry does not seem to find favour with the public,' wrote that cool observer, Stanley, on January 2. On the same day Corry told Disraeli : 'I have been rather surprised at the unanimity with which all classes, in the provinces where I have been, desire a Reform Bill — from Lord Shaftesbury[2] to the Shropshire rustic.' The next day Disraeli wrote urging on Derby the necessity of coming to an early decision on their 'Reform movements'; 'otherwise I see anarchy ahead. There are many other great matters pressing, but this is paramount.'

The first thing on which Ministers decided was to proceed by resolution, and thereby to associate the House of Commons, as a whole, with the Government in the shaping of Reform. The decision met with the enthusiastic approval of the Queen. 'It is the course,' she

---

[1] See above, p. 452. [2] Corry's uncle.

wrote on January 12, 'dictated by common-sense, and which all who are sincerely desirous of seeing the question settled, and who do not use it as a mere weapon of party warfare, are bound to support.' Her Majesty offered once more to use her good offices with the Opposition, if desired by the Government. Disraeli was equally clear in favour of proceeding by resolution.

To Lord Derby.

Private. GROSVENOR GATE, *Jan.* 13, 1867. — . . . The more I think over it, the more complete seems to me the conclusion, that proceeding by resolution is the Parliamentary, and constitutional, consequence of the conduct of the House of Commons itself upon the question of Parliamentary Reform. The House of Commons first disturbed the settlement of 1832, and the House of Commons has defeated the measures, taken in consequence of that disturbance, of *five* Ministries. . . .

But to decide to proceed by way of resolution was, after all, only to confirm the provisional decision of the autumn. The vital question was : Were the Resolutions to lead up to an inquiry, or to immediate legislation? On this point Disraeli entirely changed his mind within a few weeks or even days. On December 26 he expressed himself as still being opposed to legislation, and not seeing the necessity for the settlement which the Queen desired. But January was not far advanced before he was seeking, in concert with Derby, who had reverted to his original opinion of the autumn, for an enduring basis on which a Reform Bill could be founded. Disraeli's papers throw very little light on this change of attitude. But it was clearly based on a revised estimate of the state of public opinion. He would not admit in the autumn that the success of the agitation which Bright was conducting showed that the country had determined to obtain Reform ; but in January he found the evidence conclusive. It is, of course, obvious that evidence of the kind is cumulative, and that, as it grows, there comes a point when the most reluctant must give way to facts. As soon as Disraeli reached that point

he acted with promptitude and decision.   If the Resolutions were to lead to an immediate Bill, and that Bill was to be a settlement, the Cabinet could not rest in the generalities of the autumn, but, loth as they might be to adventure upon the slippery surface of the details of Reform, must make the attempt at once, so as not to be taken absolutely unawares when Parliament met.

Accordingly Disraeli and Derby both addressed themselves to the question, and before the end of the month had both arrived at the conclusion that rating household suffrage, duly hedged in by securities, was the one safe basis for the borough reduction.   It is not difficult to see how the two leaders, who were Reformers as well as Conservatives, reached this conclusion.   If they were to effect a settlement of the controversy, some logical basis must be found, other than the mere reduction of the limit by a few pounds; and a householder, who was also a ratepayer, had that stake in the prosperity and good government of the country which, from a Conservative point of view, might reasonably be held to qualify him for the franchise.   Besides, 'household suffrage' was, as Gladstone called it, a 'great phrase,' and the creator of Taper and Tadpole knew well the political value of a sonorous cry.   The idea was apparently first broached tentatively in Cabinet by Disraeli in the last week of January.   Cranborne was at once disquieted, perceiving that the safeguards which all the Cabinet were at that time agreed in maintaining might easily be swept away in debate.   Carnarvon, who was shortly to follow Cranborne into retirement on this very question, was quite prepared for household suffrage, provided distinct checks were insisted upon.

From Lord Cranborne.

Confidential.   INDIA OFFICE, *Feb.* 1, 1867. — . . .   What alarmed me in the programme you sketched on Wednesday was the introduction into the resolutions of very specific suffrage — such as household suffrage, which you named. Such a course would make it easy for the other side to frame

an amendment that should drive the waverers into their lobby, and would deprive your concession of all neutralising safeguards. Such a result would be more dangerous in a resolution than in a Bill. I think resolutions are only safe so long as they are general.

From Lord Carnarvon.

Private. GROSVENOR STREET, *Feb.* 2, 1867.—. . . 1. I understand that we are generally agreed upon an attempt at legislation, provided that no unforeseen circumstances arise. In this I quite agree; I see no alternative.

2. My own view is to carry the borough franchise down to a considerable depth in order to get a ledge on which to rest. I believe an arbitrary reduction of £1, £2, or £3 to be of all measures the most fatal. For this reason, I do not — as far as I understand the conditions of the problem to be solved — object to household franchise.

3. But such a reduction needs some very distinct checks. A residential qualification of three years, with the payment of rates and taxes, is excellent: but I feel some fear of depending on one single safeguard. I assume that any plan that we propose will — so far as the leading features of it are concerned — be proposed as a whole: but must we not expect that the moment that the measure is passed agitation against the restrictive portions of it will commence; and, if so, is it not probable that that agitation will have a fairer chance of success if the restrictions upon the freedom of the franchise are narrowed to one single, tangible, very definite point of opposition? . . .

The checks upon which Carnarvon insisted so strongly, and about the maintenance of which Cranborne was so sceptical, were also regarded at this period as indispensable by the Prime Minister.

From Lord Derby.

Confidential. ST. JAMES'S SQUARE, *Feb.* 2, 1867. — I return the papers you left with me. They are conclusive, to my mind, that without plurality of voting we cannot propose household suffrage, which would give the working classes a majority of nearly 2 : 1. Even Gladstone repudiated the idea of giving them *any* majority; and our friends would not, and I think ought not, to listen to it for a moment.

From the first the idea of household suffrage attracted many of the Cabinet, besides Carnarvon. One of the earliest

to entertain it was Malmesbury, who suggested it in conversation to Carnarvon in the previous summer. Pakington wrote to Disraeli on February 1 that he inclined more and more to the belief that the boldest course would be the safest, and that, if they must adopt a novelty, it would be better to take that which was 'simple and effective, rather than one which is complicated, invidious, and incomplete.' Disraeli, moreover, found that a settlement based on rating household suffrage would unite Walpole, who stood for Church and State Conservatism, and Graves, member for Liverpool, a representative of the Tory democracy of that great port, and a man who played a considerable, though unobtrusive, part in determining the event.

To Lord Derby.

Confidential. 11, DOWNING STREET, *Feb.* 4, 1867. — Walpole is very much against 'plural voting.' He says he has only heard but one opinion of it since Horsman's suggestion, ' And is this all the Adullamites have invented ! '

He says there is but only one course, if we legislate ; household suffrage, founded on residence and rating, which he is convinced is most conservative — no compound householders on any account.

So far as he has spoken with our friends, he has heard no difference on the point ; that fighting about £1 or £2 is ridiculous, and probably will give us a worse constituency.

Mr. Graves, the M.P. for Liverpool, has just left me. He was delighted with the Reform par. in the Speech : an immense relief to him : only one opinion out of doors : settlement of the question. But what settlement ?

' Oh ! a moderate settlement.'

' But what do you call moderate ? '

' Oh ! I should say, for myself, household suffrage founded on rating. That's the real thing ; rating is better than any money qualification. There are 10,000 Parliamentary voters now in Liverpool who do not pay their rates — and never will. It is the distribution of seats that is the difficulty ; not the franchise.'

The Reform paragraph of the Queen's Speech, which gave Graves, who was to second the Address, so much satisfaction, ran as follows :

Your attention will be again called to the state of the representation of the people in Parliament; and I trust that your deliberations, conducted in a spirit of moderation and mutual forbearance, may lead to the adoption of measures which, without unduly disturbing the balance of political power, shall freely extend the elective franchise.

This paragraph occupied the forefront of the part of the Speech devoted to projects of domestic legislation; and by it the Cabinet committed themselves to a 'free' extension of the suffrage. In the debate Gladstone insisted, without contradiction, and amid general approval, that the question of Reform stopped the way to all other legislation, and should be promptly dealt with and disposed of. As Derby wrote to Disraeli, Parliament was 'very hot on Reform without delay.'

Ministers showed no lack of promptitude in opening the matter to the House. Parliament met on Tuesday, February 5, and on the following Monday Disraeli introduced the Reform Resolutions. But, in the short interval, the Cabinet had already passed through its first crisis. 'Household suffrage,' which had only been thrown out as a possible idea by Disraeli in the previous week, was, after the Queen's Speech, definitely proposed to the Cabinet by Derby. His suggestion was that the Resolution which referred to borough franchise might recommend that, if plural voting were adopted, it would be safe to introduce household suffrage on a rating basis. Though no details were mentioned, the principle was apparently accepted by the Cabinet. But General Peel at once objected, and threatened resignation if the Resolution were not altered. Disraeli was full of expedients to meet the situation; and for the moment his efforts were successful.

To Lord Derby.

Confidential. 11, DOWNING STREET, *Feb.* 7, 1867. — Besides urging all the considerations, to which you so properly referred, as to the impossibility of carrying on affairs if mutual concessions are not made, and so on, this suggestion might relieve us.

Our great anxiety not to lose his services would make you agree to recast, and modify, the Resolution in question, which

you also might take the occasion of making him understand was your own particular policy, and which you had deeply and carefully considered.

'That the principle of plural voting, if adopted by Parliament, might lead to the adjustment of the borough franchise on a safe and permanent basis.'

The House, and the country (more important) would understand this. If the Resolution be adopted, we could do without Peel. If rejected, we should have to fall back on a moderate reduction of the franchise, coupled with fancy safety valves for the working class. With such a Resolution, Peel could honorably remain until we attempted to carry it into action according to our interpretation of it; and if the House did not sanction our doing so, then, of course, he need not budge.

But you ought to make him understand that it is your personal appreciation of his value, etc., that makes you consent to a change which, in your opinion, enfeebles your policy. It would be a great thing if the resignation could be postponed.

Pardon these crude suggestions of a much-vexed, but faithful, colleague.

HOUSE OF COMMONS, *Thursday* [*Feb.* 7, 1867]. — . . . I have sent you a note to House of Lords, telling you of my interview with Peel, and of its general success. The words I gave you would entirely satisfy him, but I have not committed *you* to them: and if you can devise, with him, more suitable ones for your purpose, you can.

You will find him very placable, except on the phrase 'household suffrage,' when his eye lights up with insanity. He evidently annexes no definite idea to the phrase, but told me that the whole of our back benches would rise and leave us, as one man, if the phrase remained. I believe in three months' time they will unanimously call for it.

But I soothed him, *and it is all right.* You will give the finishing touch.

Though internal dissention had begun, important external support had been already received in the world of journalism. Early in February, Derby wrote to Disraeli: 'It will be a crumb of comfort to you to know that I have had a most satisfactory interview with Delane. He is cordially with us, and will do all in his power to carry us through. He listened most attentively to the whole of our programme, and pronounced oracularly, "I think it will do."' The precedent of the India Bill, introduced in the first instance by Resolutions, and ulti-

mately passed by consent, was quoted to justify the procedure on which Government had resolved.   Accordingly, in
spite of Cabinet troubles, it was with a good heart that
Disraeli rose on Monday, February 11, to move the Reform Resolutions, and to endeavour to persuade the House
of Commons to take the reasonable course of settling this
vexed question by mutual concession and consent.   It
was, no doubt, a convenient doctrine for himself and his
colleagues that, as he began by maintaining, Parliamentary Reform should no longer be a question which
should decide the fate of Ministries.   But his reason was
incontrovertible, that all parties had attempted to deal
with it, in 1852, 1854, 1859, 1860, and 1866, and had
failed.   Ministers therefore proposed to proceed by
resolution, in order to obtain the views of the House
before introducing a Bill.   The main principles of the
Resolutions, as he explained them, were the rating basis ;
a reduction of both county and borough franchise ; a
dealing with redistribution, boundaries, and bribery, as
well as with franchise.   Ministers were not angling
for a policy ; they had distinct principles of their
own ; but they desired the co-operation of the House.
The course of the Government was not one flattering to
themselves, but it was more honourable to assist, however humbly, in effecting a settlement for the public good,
than to bring forward mock measures which the spirit
of party would not allow to pass.   Gladstone made the
obvious comment that everything would depend on
whether the Resolutions were sufficiently precise to form
the basis of a settlement.   He should strongly object
to mere vague preliminary declarations, as the duty of
the House was to extend the franchise and get the question out of the way.

When the Resolutions appeared, their vagueness was
immediately commented on and condemned.   They were
substantially as drafted in the autumn ; but the one about
the borough franchise had been watered down, in order to
retain Peel, to the very general formula, 'that the prin-

ciple of plurality of votes, if adopted by Parliament, would facilitate the settlement of the borough franchise'; and the proposed Royal Commission was only to deal with borough boundaries. The Opposition were at once up in arms, demanding greater precision and definite proposals, and the prospect of Reform by general consent apparently disappeared.

Queen Victoria to Lord Derby.

OSBORNE, *Feb.* 13, 1867. — The Queen cannot help feeling a good deal of fear as to the prospects of a settlement of the Reform question. Mr. Disraeli, in a short account of what passed in the House on Monday, says the Opposition will probably be forced to 'join issue' on the Resolutions.

Thus, then, the party contest, which the Queen had *hoped* and *understood* it was the object of this mode of proceeding to avoid, is to recommence. And though Mr. Disraeli anticipates the defeat of the Opposition, and that the future conduct of the question will then be comparatively easy, this does not by any means reassure the Queen, who had been led to believe (as she is herself firmly convinced) that the question could *only* be settled by mutual concession. . . .

Disraeli refused to give the House any further details as to the Government proposals before he rose on the 25th to move the resolutions; and for the best of all reasons, that the Cabinet were not agreed. When he said that Ministers were not angling for a policy, but had one of their own, he was, no doubt, partly using the brave words which the situation demanded, but mainly thinking of the policy of household suffrage, which the Cabinet, with the exception of Peel, had apparently, in general terms, accepted.[1] But, with a view to retain Peel, he spent the next few days in elaborating a modified scheme emboding a much smaller reduction of the borough franchise. This scheme was explained to the Cabinet on Saturday, the 16th; but entirely failed in its object, as Peel refused to accept even this proposal, and once more

[1] Hardy, when reasoning a few days later with the dissentients, used the argument 'that our personal honour, in allowing our chiefs to state that we were prepared with a Bill, was at stake, and that we must present one in concert' (Gathorne Hardy, Vol. I., p. 199).

tendered his resignation.   Disraeli reported and explained
the whole situation to the Queen at Osborne next day,
and the Beaconsfield papers contain some rough notes
for a letter to Her Majesty recording the conversation.

On February 16, the Cabinet having been summoned to
sanction the definitive propositions to be made on the subject
of P[arliamentary] R[eform] to the House of Commons by
the Chancellor of the Exchequer on Monday, the 25th inst.,
General Peel, after the propositions had been unanimously
adopted by his colleagues, and after they had been modified in
the interval since the preceding Cabinet to meet his views,
announced his inability to sanction any reduction of the franchise, and his intended resignation.

The confusion and embarrassment of such a proceeding at
such a moment were extreme, and as, by a fortunate chance,
the Chancellor of the Exchequer had received Her Majesty's
gracious commands to repair to Osborne on the next day,
Lord Derby was of opinion that it was an occasion to appeal
to Her Majesty for her aid and influence, and authorised the
Chancellor of the Exchequer to confer fully and freely with
Her Majesty on the subject.

The Chancellor of the Exchequer arrived at Osborne on
Sunday, the 17th, and had an audience of Her Majesty on the
same day at 7 o'clock.

Her Majesty, who had been apprised of the resignation,
expressed her regret [at the] loss of Peel : he was a faithful
servant, an able Minister, and one personally very acceptable
to her ; but the Reform Bill, she added, was more important
than General Peel.

Rumours had reached her of the probability of some event
of the kind ; but not confined to one — Lord Cranborne, and
perhaps Mr. Hardy.

[Chancellor of the Exchequer] assured [Her Majesty] that
Lord Cranborne and Mr. Hardy had made the most earnest
appeals in the Cabinet to Peel. Then described General
Peel's conduct during the various phases of the policy of the
Cabinet until the present moment. At the outset, in November, when Lord Derby proposed to proceed by Resolutions,
pledging the House in the first [place] to reduction of franchise, and ending with address to the Crown for inquiry [two
or three illegible words] ; his conduct at the resumption of the
Cabinet after Christmas, when gradually it developed that
the country expected legislation and settlement, not inquiry ;
the final giving up of the plan of inquiry, and proposing
resolutions by way of basis of Bill ; and passage in the

Queen's Speech : throughout all this time Peel's conduct dogged silence. After the Queen's Speech Lord Derby called the attention of the Cabinet to the final revision of the Resolutions, and proposed that, if the principle of plural voting were conceded, we should recommend borough franchise on a rating basis. The Cabinet universally adopted this, but Peel requested that a copy of the Resolutions should be sent to him, which Chancellor of the Exchequer did, and the next morning Peel resigned. The Chancellor of the Exchequer saw him at the House, and, after an interview, proposed a modification of the Resolutions as it now appears, and Peel said he was perfectly satisfied and would remain.

On Saturday, the 16th, Lord Derby requested the Chancellor of the Exchequer to state in detail to the Cabinet the application of the principles which he proposed to make on February 25, and Mr. Disraeli, with regard to the borough franchise, proposed that if the securities were conceded it should rest on a £5 [basis], modifying Lord Derby's original plan in order to conciliate the General.

The Cabinet adopted this view, and when all had spoken, the General, who seemed very sullen, spoke and said that he was not prepared to support any reduction of the franchise. Every argument was used and every appeal was made to him, but in vain. Lord Derby reminded the General that for many months he had repeatedly sanctioned their first Resolution, which pledged them to reduction.

After the Cabinet the Chancellor of the Exchequer received Lord Derby's instructions to lay the matter before Her Majesty, and, as a last resource, to invite Her Majesty's aid.

Her Majesty seemed to intimate that the retirement of General Peel alone might not, perhaps, be injurious to the Cabinet on this particular question of Reform (and that after that was settled), but graciously invited the Chancellor of the Exchequer to enter into discussion as to the best course.

The Chancellor of the Exchequer, encouraged by Her Majesty's kindness, put the opposite views before Her Majesty : on one side the greater chance of success with the Reform Bill ; on the other that of a homogeneous Cabinet, and the weakness and injury which, generally speaking, secessions at critical moments occasion ; and he humbly offered his opinion that, on the whole, it was more prudent, if possible, to retain him.

Her Majesty then most graciously said she was willing and prepared to do anything in her power to support the Administration, as she desired above all things that the Reform question should be settled, and added, if Lord Derby wished it, she would certainly write to Peel.

Chancellor of the Exchequer said that he might presume

to answer for Lord Derby's wishes, as there was entire confidence between them, and at the time of the first resignation Chancellor of the Exchequer had suggested to Lord Derby to appeal to Her Majesty; but Lord Derby said he was reluctant to press too much upon the Queen, whose personal interference should be reserved for other questions, and he thought he ought to keep his colleagues in order.

Her Majesty then entered into the inquiry as to the sort of letter she should write, and encouraged the Chancellor of the Exchequer to give his views.

Chancellor of the Exchequer said it was not a case for argument or reference to details of measures; it should rather be an expression of Her Majesty's deep interest in the question, a declaration of Her Majesty's personal desire that a measure should be passed, but mainly an appeal to the personal devotion of the General, which was, no doubt, very great to Her Majesty.

Her Majesty deigned to listen to these suggestions, and mused as they were made.

Her Majesty then with great frankness opened the delicate question as to what was to be done in case of his persistence. What would Lord Derby do?

The Chancellor of the Exchequer said that he probably might try to gain some additional strength, and, as he was in communication with Lord Grosvenor, might perhaps appeal to —— [The rest is missing].

This draft seems to prove that Disraeli, however he may have decided in his own mind in favour of household suffrage, was still drifting as to the best immediate policy for the Cabinet to adopt. One of the points that comes out most strongly from a study of his papers is his constant anxiety to keep colleagues from resigning, even at the cost of modifying his own cherished policies. As in the winter of 1858–59, and during the anxious times of 1876–78, far from assuming an uncompromising attitude, he showed himself ready to go even to extreme lengths in order to preserve the harmony of the Cabinet unbroken. Peel, as he was the only dissentient, gave way for the moment to the representations of the Queen and of his colleagues; but as his hostility was rather to the general principle than to the extent of borough franchise reduction, there was no object in proceeding with the modified scheme.

From this time, therefore, Disraeli, and Derby, too, must have taken a definite resolve to press forward with a Bill on the basis of household suffrage, with residence, personal payment of rates, and perhaps dual voting, as checks. Disraeli brought the scheme in detail before the Cabinet on Tuesday, February 19. 'All was smooth,' recorded Hardy in his diary; and even Cranborne, doubtful as he was about what he regarded as a 'very dangerous experiment,' which demanded all the securities that could be got, was still prepared to go forward. Only he urged, in a letter to Derby on Friday, February 22, in anticipation of the final Cabinet discussion on the Saturday, that the limit of the direct taxation franchise, which was to give a second vote, should be ten instead of twenty shillings. That would bring in, he calculated, the great bulk of the payers both of house tax and of income tax. 'You propose to take in every ratepayer. It will only be making your system complete and avoiding needless anomalies to take in every direct taxpayer.'

All remained smooth on the surface during the week, and on the Saturday, February 23, the comprehensive scheme was adopted, apparently by general consent, with the understanding that Disraeli should explain it to the House of Commons on the following Monday. 'The Cabinet unanimous for the great plan. Baxter [who was acting as draftsman] must stop to see me,' scribbled Disraeli to his private secretary. But Sunday, as all politicians know, is, or was, till the week-end habit greatly diminished its critical importance, often a day of political heart-searching and caballing; and never with more fatal effect than on this occasion. On the Monday morning Disraeli was greeted, before he rose, by a hurried note from Derby, written at 8.45 a.m., saying: 'The enclosed, just received, is utter ruin. What on earth are we to do?' The enclosure was Cranborne's threat of resignation, endorsed by Carnarvon.

Lord Cranborne to Lord Derby.

INDIA OFFICE, *Sunday evening* [*Feb.* 24, 1867].— I trust you will believe that it gives me great pain to have to say what I am going to say.

I find, on closely examining the scheme which Mr. Disraeli brought to the notice of the Cabinet five days ago, that its effect will be to throw the small boroughs almost, and many of them entirely, into the hands of the voter whose qualification is lower than £10. I do not think such a proceeding is for the interest of the country. I am sure it is not in accordance with the hopes which those of us who took an active part in resisting Mr. Gladstone's Bill last year raised in those whom we induced to vote with us. I find that, in almost every case, those of our friends who sit for boroughs with less than 25,000 inhabitants (a majority of the boroughs) will be in a much worse condition in consequence of our Bill than they would have been in consequence of Mr. Gladstone's.

Under ordinary circumstances I should apologise to you for not having discovered this difficulty before. But in the present case I cannot blame myself on this account. This proposition was made on Tuesday last — to my extreme surprise; and though, since that day, I have devoted every spare moment to the study of the statistics, it was not till to-day that I could obtain the leisure, from heavy departmental work, in order to go through them, borough by borough. Mr. Baxter's error has been that he has made the calculation *in a lump*, and has assumed that the effect would be distributed equally over all boroughs. This assumption is unfounded : for while in small boroughs the addition is large and the counterpoise small, in the large boroughs, where we are hopelessly overmatched, the counterpoise is large and the addition small. I hope by to-morrow morning to have a statement ready which will show this fact in detail.

Unable, therefore, to concur in this scheme, I have to ask you to be good enough to summon a meeting of the Cabinet before the meeting of the party to-morrow. Lord Carnarvon, to whom this evening I showed the figures, concurs with me in this request.

At the same time I am bound in candour to say that I do not see my way to an alternative proposal. The error of attempting to frame a Reform Bill during the week previous to its production is one that, in my opinion, cannot be redeemed.

I need not say how deeply grieved I am by any act of mine to cause inconvenience to you. Though I think the abandonment of the policy under which the Queen's Speech was framed

was a disastrous step. I would gladly have gone as far as I could possibly do to prevent any embarrassment to the Cabinet. But if I assented to this scheme, now that I know what its effect will be, I could not look in the face those whom last year I urged to resist Mr. Gladstone. I am convinced that it will, if passed, be the ruin of the Conservative party. . . .

Disraeli's comment to Derby was : ' This is stabbing in the back ! I will come to you as soon as possible, but I am not up, being indisposed ; but I shall rally immediately in such dangers. It seems like treachery.' Hardy, whom Cranborne and Carnarvon had vainly endeavoured to seduce from his allegiance on the Sunday night, bears witness that Derby and Disraeli, though much mortified, ' took the sudden and trying emergency well.' How sudden and trying the emergency was, was made clear by an indiscreet speech which Pakington delivered on the hustings when he sought re-election on change of office. Ministers had thought that everything was settled on the Saturday, and so were all dispersed and could not be collected till half-past one. They were then informed that Cranborne and Carnarvon had seceded, objecting to the details of the Bill which they all believed had been unanimously adopted. Here was a pretty business ! It was now two o'clock ; at half-past two Derby had to address the party in Downing Street, and at half-past four Disraeli had to explain the Reform scheme in the House. Literally, the Cabinet had not more than *ten minutes*, said Pakington, to make up their minds on their course. In order to retain their colleagues, they hurriedly determined, apparently on Stanley's suggestion, to recur, in substance, to the milder scheme of the previous Saturday week, which had been drawn up in the hope of placating Peel. This, therefore, was the scheme, known to history by the nickname of the ' Ten Minutes' Bill, that Derby explained to the party meeting, and Disraeli to the House of Commons.

' I am going down to the House. The ship floats ; that is all,' was the note Disraeli sent to his wife. It was a strange scene in Parliament that afternoon : a House packed in every corner, with members even sitting on

the floor, the galleries and the bar crowded with peers, ambassadors, and other distinguished strangers, headed by the Prince of Wales; and a calm, passionless orator recommending, in a very unenthusiastic fashion, to the attention of members, proposals for which he had no particular affection, and which were very similar in kind to those which Gladstone had unsuccessfully offered a year before, save that the borough franchise was to be £6 rating instead of £7 rental, and the county franchise £20 rating instead of £14 rental. Various fancy franchises were mentioned; but, on the other hand, the principle of plurality, adopted in the Resolutions, was given up. The redistribution proposed was to apply to thirty seats. Such were the main features of the Bill which the Government would introduce on the passing of the Resolutions; but Disraeli asked the House to pass the Resolutions first.

When Disraeli sat down, a storm of indignation burst on his head. Lowe, who had never really shared the friendliness generally felt by the Adullamites for the Government, poured scorn on the attitude of Ministers, whom he described as coming to the House with the cry, 'Say what you like to us, only, for God's sake, leave us our places.' Why were Ministers to have the mark of Cain set upon them, that nobody might kill them? Let the two parties give up this Dutch auction in which the country was to be knocked down to the one who proposed the swiftest element for its destruction. Government should withdraw the Resolutions and bring in a Bill. 'Touch the nettle timidly, and it will sting you; but grasp it firmly, you are unhurt, and can tear it at your leisure.' Bright also urged the withdrawal of the Resolutions, and derided the detailed proposals made that afternoon. He demanded, and promised not factiously to oppose, 'a substantial and satisfactory Bill,' which should settle the question. The support that Ministers got from their own friends was slight, and cries of 'Withdraw!' and 'Bring in a Bill!' assailed the Chancellor during his reply to critics.

Montagu Corry to Mrs. Disraeli.

HOUSE OF COMMONS, *Monday, Feb.* 25, 1867, 9.20. — Clouds always pass away at last, and that terrible one of to-day already looks less dense. In spite of the unexampled trial he has gone through, the Ch. of the Exch. made an admirably clear and forcible statement, which on the whole was well received. . . .

I have seen him since the debate, decidedly in better spirits, while at this moment he is at dinner with Lord Stanley, and by the time you see him, depend upon it, he will be himself again. Only one person in the world sympathises with him to-day as you do, and I can only say that even *my* veneration has been increased by the noble way in which he has borne himself.

If Disraeli was in better spirits after the debate, it was probably for quite another reason than that assumed by his admiring young secretary. He certainly was under no illusion as to the popularity of the scheme he had perforce introduced. If not that evening, then undoubtedly the next day, he realised that events were working in favour of the bolder course which he and Derby desired, and that the only safety of the Government would lie in a reversion to it. Lowe had a premonition of what was coming. It was said at one time, he remarked, on the question of Reform, that they were within twenty-four hours of a revolution. He believed that they had been within much fewer hours than that of household suffrage, which he himself held in great dread. The arguments in favour of household suffrage were winning converts rapidly, not only within the Cabinet, but in the party outside. The veteran Henley, who stood out from the Cabinet, was known to hold this view. The smaller Bill, which was to preserve the harmony of the Cabinet, had no special attraction for its followers. They perceived at once that it contained no hope of a final settlement. Accordingly that Monday evening, in the inner sanctum of Toryism, the smoking-room of the Carlton Club, Graves, who had already expounded his views to Disraeli, strongly urged on his fellow-members, who had met there after the debate, that the municipal suffrage

was the only basis on which a successful Reform Bill
could rest.   He found a willing audience and immediate
support.

The movement thus started in the club gained fresh
impetus next morning, not merely among county members, who would not be affected by a great lowering of
the borough franchise, but among the borough members
themselves, who would suffer if the lowering proved, from
a Conservative point of view, to be a mistake.   Four of
these — Laird, the shipbuilder, who sat for Birkenhead;
Goldney, M.P. for Chippenham; Jervis, M.P. for Har-
wich; and Graves himself, who represented Liverpool —
were deputed to convey to Disraeli the intensity of the
feeling.   Graves, in a statement drawn up a year and a half
later for Montagu Corry, thus describes what happened:

I met the Chancellor [of the Exchequer] in the lobby of the
House and explained the object of the desired interview.   He
said it was too late.   I inquired if it was too late for a
friendly amendment.   He replied it was, adding we should
certainly upset the Government; to which I ventured to
reply that our anxiety was rather for the country and our
party, and assured him the feeling was so strong it would find
vent in some embarrassing way.   Once more I urged the
reception of the deputation, when the Chancellor, throwing off
the reserve which had thus far marked our interview, said
it was no use to discuss the matter with any deputation, as
he was free to admit he had long been of the opinion that
rating and residence were the true principles for a Reform
Bill, and added: 'Lord Derby was also of this opinion.'   I
simply replied: 'In that case I would undertake to give him
proof of the strength of the feeling amongst the borough
members on the subject.'   That night I obtained two-and-
twenty signatures in favour of the principle of municipal
suffrage. . . .   A greater instance of loyalty to colleagues has
rarely been met with than Mr. Disraeli displayed in his interview with me.

This talk with Graves was not the only important
political development of the day.   The Liberals met to
the number of 289 under Gladstone's leadership, and determined to demand the setting aside of the Resolutions
and the production of a Bill; but Disraeli anticipated them

by an announcement to that effect when the House met.
' What must be done is best done without the appearance
of compulsion,' wrote Stanley, and the Cabinet agreed.
Disraeli gracefully covered his retreat by acknowledging
a disposition on the part of the House to afford the Ministerial proposals a fair and candid consideration, to secure
which was the main object of proceeding by resolution.

To Lord Derby.

Confidential. HOUSE OF COMMONS, *Feb.* 26, 1867. — I have
requested Taylor to furnish you, without loss of time, with
two reports :
    1. The general result of the effect, on the small boroughs,
of your plan.
    2. A special report, from every member of a small borough,
on our side, of his individual feelings and wishes.
    Sir Henry Edwards and Mr. Waterhouse, for example, who
have just been with me, are members for small boroughs.
They are absolutely for the great plan. Is that feeling general
or universal ?
    I dined alone with Walpole, who thinks that our fall now is
only an affair of a little time, assuming that, in our present
feeble position, all the sections will reunite for a vote against
which it would be absurd to appeal to the country. *That,* he
thinks, is Gladstone's tactic : to play with us until we are con-
temptible. As Sir Lawrence Palk says, ' Till he comes in with
household suffrage, which is getting riper every moment.' At
present the House expects ' compensation.'
    I tried Walpole hard as to regaining our position. He
thought if certain persons left, and you reorganised your
Ministry, that it would not be looked upon as changing our
front, but that, with a frank and obvious explanation, it would
do us good and strengthen us in the country. It was evident
that he was contemplating the old story of a reconstruction
with the Adullamites. I don't think that can be brought
about : what we must think of is the country, not the House
of Commons. But it would never have done, as Pakington
proposed, to have thrown ourselves on the House of Commons
with three Secretaries of State in abeyance. A policy must be
supported by a *complete* Cabinet.
    Rather than die in a ditch, think of this, if the worst comes
— The Duke of Buckingham *vice* Carnarvon ; the Duke of
Richmond *vice* Buckingham ; Pakington *vice* Peel ; Corry *vice*
Pakington ; Northcote *vice* Cranborne ; Cave without Cabinet
vice Northcote.

At the same time, I must tell you that I have since heard from Noel that a meeting at the Carlton will probably take place, and some memorial will be signed by the party to Cranborne, Peel, etc., to show them they have completely misapprehended the feeling and spirit of the party. This, of course, would be good.

Next day, Wednesday, February 27, Disraeli, following Derby, had an audience of the Queen. The nature of the conversation that then passed is apparent from the following letters:

To Lord Derby.

[*Feb.* 27.] — I had my audience, which was long and animated. She said she did not like to see you dispirited. I replied you were, naturally, chagrined at such incidents, but I saw a marked improvement in your countenance since your audience to-day. She said, and repeated, she would do anything.

Still more important was my interview with Stanley, who exhausted the subject in the most logical manner, and concluded there was only one thing to be done, and that was to recur to our original position; but how was that to be done? He added, 'Only by the pressure of the party. . . .'

From General the Hon. Charles Grey.

WINDSOR CASTLE, *Feb.* 28, 1867. — Immediately on my return to Windsor yesterday evening, I wrote you a very hasty line, by the Queen's command;[1] for Her Majesty was anxious to give you every support in the opinion you had yourself expressed in your interview with her, that nothing should be done in a hurry, and that it would be far better not to summon any Cabinet before the usual day of its meeting.

Her Majesty was sorry to see that both you and Lord Derby seemed to take a gloomy view of the prospects of the Government in its endeavours to settle this question; for which, as far as Her Majesty can judge from the accounts of what passed on Monday night in the House of Commons, and from the tone of the Press, she can see no sufficient reason.

It is true that the numbers who attended Mr. Gladstone's meeting are formidable, if they could be united in opposition to the Government. But it is reasonable to suppose that a large proportion of those who attended went there sincerely anxious for a settlement of the question, and only desirous

---

[1] Grey had written, on Her Majesty's instructions: 'A bold front, and cheery language, will go a great way in securing victory.'

of hearing what course Mr. Gladstone would recommend, with that view. . . . The pinching point, as Mr. Bright says, is the amount of the franchise, and you stand upon firm and intelligible ground when you take the sense of the House upon a £6 rating as the lowest point to which a Conservative Government can go. But there is nothing, as you say, to prevent your stating an alternative plan of a simple rating franchise, with the provision against the undue preponderance of mere numbers afforded by your proposed second vote, and, if beat upon the first proposal, taking the sense of the House on the second. But there seems every advantage in your adhering in the first instance to the £6 rating. In the first place, it will probably avert further unpleasant discussions in the Cabinet; and in the next it will avoid the appearance of weakness, to which I have already alluded, inseparable from frequent changes of plan. Nor does it seem at all certain that you will be beat on the £6 franchise. . . . Her Majesty wishes me to add to this that, if Lord Derby should think it more advisable to take the bolder course, which, on the first impulse of the moment, the Queen recommended to him, he may depend, as she then assured him, on her best support. But, on further consideration, Her Majesty is inclined to think, unless the disposition shown in the Cabinet should make the more decided line necessary, that it would be better to avoid the appearance of disunion, and consequent weakness, which would be occasioned by the retirement of the three Ministers. . . .

Meanwhile Disraeli kept up a steady pressure on Derby to accept the resignations, reconstruct the Cabinet, and revert to the large scheme.

To Lord Derby.

GROSVENOR GATE, *Feb.* 27, 1867. — I think Gladstone's position, and even tone, seemed changed since the declaration of our definite policy. Although there may not be, probably is not, any compact alliance yet, he has nevertheless succeeded in getting the party together, and even in combining them in an united action: the assault on the Resolutions. Lord Russell, Bright, Grosvenor, all under the same roof!

He will proceed slowly, and feel his way: but I little doubt that, by the time we get into Committee on our Bill, he will be prepared to try five against six, and probably succeed. What shall we do then? He will count on our giving up the Bill, with nothing to go to the country on. I will not, however, trouble you now with all these various considerations, but, if you wish it, will call upon you anywhere after the Court. If

Gladstone have these views, it would hardly seem that the
Queen could interpose with my advantage. The most he
would offer would be that you should go on with the Bill as
amended by the House; but even if, from a sense of duty, you
might be inclined to do this, the malcontents in the Cabinet
would leave you, and therefore you would be forced to resign, or reconstruct. If there is to be reconstruction, I think
it should be at once.

I could not see Northcote yesterday — a wise head: and
Stanley was away. . . .

Confidential [Feb. 27]. — I had not read The Times when
I wrote early this morning. If you follow the course there
indicated, they will censure your Government immediately
the Bill is passed, and you will not be able to appeal to the
country, as the new constituency will not be registered.

It appears to me that Gladstone has committed himself in
a manner which may extricate you. He is for £5 rating;
you can truly say that is no better settlement than £6 — worse;
and therefore you can revert to your original scheme in preference. If they throw out the Bill on the second reading,
or defeat your boro' qualification, you could dissolve with
honor, and a prospect of success, and meet Parliament, at
any rate, with a powerful party.

I conceive that Gladstone has weakened and embarrassed
his position by his programme. But, no doubt, with this
prospect, you must reconstruct at once if the malcontent colleagues will not, on reflection, see they are only cutting the
throat of the party by not supporting you.

The pressure from the party which Stanley, and no
doubt Disraeli too, was hoping for, was duly applied.
The ardour of Graves and his friends who sat for boroughs
was naturally stimulated by Disraeli's avowal, and
Wednesday saw a great extention of the Carlton movement. The county members joined hands with the
borough members, and on the Thursday a meeting,
at which some 150 were present, was held in the
club, under Sir Matthew White Ridley's presidency.
Laird and Graves had drafted resolutions, but, as
the meeting was not unanimous, they were not pressed.
A decided majority, however, proved to be in favour
of household suffrage in boroughs with three years'
residence and personal payment of rates. There was
a minority who protested; but Derby and Disraeli

were told that if the leaders were willing to go that
length — as the best means of resisting further changes
and obtaining a lasting settlement — they would be supported by a majority of the Conservatives, and by sufficient Liberals to carry the Bill. Ridley, Banks Stanhope,
Laird, Graves, H. Baillie, and Barttelot, were the principal speakers for the majority ; and Beresford Hope, James
Lowther, and George Bentinck, for the minority. Fraser,
in *Disraeli and his Day*, calls the meeting a 'county
caucus,' selfishly prepared to sacrifice the interests of
borough members. But this is a serious misrepresenta-
tion. The movement began with the borough members,
though influential county members subsequently adhered
to it ; and the meeting was generally representative of
the party in the House of Commons. The feeling that a
thorough settlement should be made, and made by the
Tory party, was rapidly growing ; and it must never be
forgotten that Tories had no special reason for wishing
to preserve a constituency which, like that created in 1832,
had, with few exceptions, steadily supported the Whigs
who created it. A generous extension to a new and
respectable class, the rate-paying householders, might
well inure to the benefit of a party which claimed to be
national, and dethrone one which was still largely
oligarchical. Feelings of this kind, which were powerful
with Disraeli, were widely shared in influential quarters
among the party.

Disraeli's spirits steadily rose as this critical week wore
on. The Adullamites also met on the Thursday, eighty in
number, Disraeli was told, and declared for household
suffrage and plurality. 'All I hear and observe,' he wrote
to Derby on that evening, 'more and more convinces me
that the bold line is the safer one, and, moreover, that
it will be successful.' The Queen, indeed, still expressed
a preference for the Ten Minutes Bill, but, with that
loyalty to her servants which always distinguished Her
Majesty, was quite ready to yield her view and hearten
her Ministers, in order that a settlement might be effected.

To Lord Derby.

Confidential. *Mar.* 1, 1867. — General Grey, *au fond,* is try-ing to carry Gladstone's Franchise Bill of last year. He thinks it the best way to settle the question : it will settle you and your party. He has unceasingly impressed the Queen, since Wednesday, with the expediency of your not receding from your £6 position, and, therefore, you will find a change in the Queen's mind, for which it is well that you should be prepared. She will not, however, recede a jot from her engagements to you if she finds you firm and confident. . . .

From Lord Derby.

Friday morning [*Mar.* 1]. — There is no doubt that Grey has been working on the Queen in favour of the £6; but the en-closed, received last night, will show you how fully we may rely on her support.

[Enclosure.]

Queen Victoria to Lord Derby.

Windsor Castle, *Feb.* 28, 1867. — Though General Grey has written fully in *her* name to Mr. Disraeli, she wishes to add a few lines herself to express her earnest hope that Lord Derby will *not* be too much discouraged, and that, *on reflection,* she is inclined to think that it might be wisest and best, *if possible,* to *adhere* to the measure as announced by Mr. Dis-raeli to the House. He may, however, be sure of her support in whatever course he will, after *due consideration,* propose to her to pursue. The Queen feels *sure* a *bold* front must be shown, and the country will then see that the Government is sincere in trying to settle this *vexed* and *vital* question of Reform. She hopes to find Lord Derby in better spirits and less worried when she sees him to-morrow.

The support of the bulk of the Tories, of the main body of the Adullamites, and of the Queen, was secured for Derby's and Disraeli's policy. What about the keen Reformers, led by Disraeli's friendly foe, John Bright? A conversation in the lobby on Friday, March 1, which Bright has recorded in his journal, and which is quoted in Trevelyan's *Life,* gave him assurance of their disposi-tion. Disraeli told Bright that he meant to do this thing, if it could possibly be done, and then extracted from him the information and advice which he desired. Bright writes :

I told him of a conversation with three of his party in the smoking-room, how far they were willing to go, and that at the pace they were moving I should soon have to hold them back. He thought they were fair specimens of a considerable section of the party. I advised him to advance his offers so far in regard to the suffrage that he would not be driven to accept defeat on every proposition; that £5 rating franchise or household suffrage would save him in the boroughs, and that £10 or £12 would do for the counties.[1] He said he did not care much for the counties. The working-class question was the real question, and that was the thing that demanded to be settled. He had once proposed a £10 franchise for the counties. He said: 'You will attack me whatever I propose.' I said: 'No, I will not. I will do all I can fairly to help a Bill through, if you will do the right thing. I am against faction, and if our leaders do as you did last year I shall openly denounce them. . . .'

As we were talking, Mr. Brand, the Opposition 'Whip,' went by, and Disraeli said: 'He will think it is a Coalition,' that he and I should be seen in conversation at such a crisis as this. At parting he pressed my hand with an apparent earnestness of feeling, saying: 'Well, whatever happens, you and I will always be friends.'

It was necessary for the Cabinet to come at once to a fateful decision. Everything pointed to a bold policy. The ill reception of the Ten Minutes Bill, the Carlton meeting, the Adullamite meeting, Bright's advice and support, that spirit of the age which rarely found Disraeli unresponsive — all urged advance. What public feeling was at the moment is depicted for us by an acute and impartial onlooker, Matthew Arnold, who wrote to his mother on the day of the Cabinet Council: 'I am in hopes that Lord Derby and Disraeli will take heart of grace, bring in a good measure of Reform, and let Cranborne and others leave them if they like. . . . Quite a passionate desire to get the question done with is springing up, and is gaining all the better Conservatives themselves.'[2]

Even colleagues supposed to be least affected by Disraeli's progressive ideas, such as Walpole and Hardy,

[1] Bright sent Disraeli a few days later a confidential memorandum, making this proposal, which corresponded with the Bill as finally passed, in more detail. See Trevelyan's *Bright*, pp. 381, 382.

[2] M. Arnold's *Letters*, Vol. I., p. 353.

pointedly dissociated themselves from the Cranborne group; and Malmesbury, who was detained at Heron Court by Lady Malmesbury's serious illness, wrote decisively to the same effect.

Lord Malmesbury to Lord Derby.

Private. HERON COURT, *Mar.* 1, 1867. — . . . Perhaps away from the scene of our distracted councils I may see a little more clearly than others what our position is.

I do not hesitate to say that the only course that can save our credit before the country is for your master mind to determine what is the best Bill, and, in spite of secession, of a menacing Press, and of all plausible intrigues whatever, to adhere to that Bill. Nor have I any doubt as to which is the best. I always preferred household suffrage (properly counterpoised) to any halfway resting-place, and I believe the whole country is of that opinion. If it is yours also, as it seemed to be when I last met you in Cabinet, I would urge you to act upon it. The loss of three able and honourable men is a great one, but far greater would be the loss of reputation which a vacillating and subservient policy would inevitably bring upon us personally, and upon our party. No colleagues can be worth that sacrifice.

Accordingly on Saturday, March 2, the Cabinet decided to revert to their original plan, and Cranborne, Carnarvon, and Peel resigned. Peel, who had been the first to feel alarm, was the most reluctant to take the final step, and called out, we are told, after the others as they were leaving the room : 'I will waive my objections if you will.' The conduct of the three seceders has been variously judged. What is and what is not a principle in a matter so essentially of detail as Parliamentary Reform is very difficult to determine. But, undoubtedly, continuance in the Cabinet at this period involved consent to two main propositions : first, that the suffrage, in the language of the Queen's Speech, should be 'freely' extended; secondly, that in the provisions of the Bill the co-operation of the House, in which the Government were in a minority, should be willingly accepted, so that the settlement might be of a permanent and agreed character. The seceders were not prepared to make such large additions

to the electorate as these propositions involved; and in those circumstances they were right to withdraw.

Of the manner of the withdrawal, and of the *animus* shown by the principal seceder, Cranborne, there is more to be said. Hardy, a witness friendly to both sides, wrote in his diary on February 26: 'Clearly Cranborne will not long act with Disraeli; that is at the bottom of it.' As we have seen, Cranborne, through all the early years of his Parliamentary life, profoundly distrusted Disraeli, and attacked him violently in the Press. He did not put off his suspicions when he joined him as a colleague; nor did Disraeli's friendly behaviour to him, and frequent consultation with him since they took office together,[1] remove his prejudice. His treatment of Derby and Disraeli and the rest of his colleagues in this matter was very inconsiderate. He had had warning that household suffrage was in his leaders' minds before the Queen's Speech, and had assented to it in general terms just after the session had opened. Reform was a subject with which he had been familiar at least ever since he wrote a philosophical essay on it in 1858; and, therefore, what was notice sufficient to make Peel resign ought to have been sufficient to make Cranborne begin those upsetting calculations which he delayed until after the Cabinet had accepted the larger measure, and had notified the Queen of their decision.

The postponement of action to the eleventh hour, the endeavour to embarrass his colleagues by inducing others to accompany him, and the virulence with which, after resignation, he attacked and denounced his leaders, require a good deal of justification. His plea is understood to have been that those leaders, Derby and Disraeli, had made, behind the backs of their colleagues, a secret agreement, certainly at the time of the formation of the 1866 Government, prob-

---

[1] The late Sir Charles Freemantle, who was Disraeli's secretary at the time, told me that Disraeli's desire to keep in touch with, and consult, Cranborne between July, 1866, and February, 1867, was very marked. See above, p. 463.

ably ever since 1859, that household suffrage should be adopted by the Conservatives as their principle of Reform. The facts which have been brought out in this biography show how ill-founded and unworthy was this suspicion, though some unguarded remarks of Derby's, and Disraeli's attempt on the third reading to connect his present policy with his policy in 1859, gave a colourable pretext for entertaining it. The Reform Bill of 1867 was an improvisation by Derby and Disraeli, and its inception dates back no farther than the January of 1867. The guiding principle, which led to such surprising results, was the willing acceptance of the co-operation of the House of Commons. The truth is that Cranborne, having adopted, from his first entry into Parliament, a jaundiced view of his leaders, and especially of Disraeli, refused to open his mind to the plain evidences, under his eyes as a Minister, of Disraeli's loyalty to colleagues, to the interests of the Conservative party, and to the great institutions of the country.

On the Monday, Derby gave a full account in the Lords of the Cabinet crisis and of the resignations, but in the Commons Disraeli merely said that the Government had determined 'to revert to their original policy' in regard to the franchise, and in consequence three Cabinet Ministers had resigned. The House was naturally very restive under this treatment.

To Lord Derby.

GROSVENOR GATE, *Monday, Mar. 4.* — We have had a bad night in the House of Commons. They would let Peel do nothing. He has put off his business[1] till Thursday; they will let him do nothing then. Nothing can be more insolent, bullying, and defiant, than they are. I am confident they will not let Pakington move the estimates, and he himself says it is not of the slightest importance.

The sooner we get out of this mess, the better. If we had moved the writs, they would have been daunted.

The House, too, is sulky now, because there has been an explanation in the Lords, and not in the Commons.

[1] The Army Estimates.

The proposal for the introduction of the Bill for the 18th passed without comment, but I shall be surprised if, to-morrow, some adverse move is not hatched by them.   The fear of a dissolution may check them, but that is all. . . .

The explanations to the Commons were tendered on the following night, when Disraeli pointed out that the Ten Minutes Bill, which had been introduced in order to preserve the integrity of the Cabinet, had given satisfaction to no party.   'It seemed to us, therefore, that we were fast sinking into that unsatisfactory state which distinguished last session, when one proposition was met by another not materially differing from it, and that the attempt to bring this great question to a solution would have been fruitless in the present, as it had been in preceding sessions.   But, sir, we are conscious that there is some difference between this and the preceding session ; and we did believe and hold that, if the question were not seriously and earnestly and vigorously grappled with, it would not be for the honour of Parliament or the advantage of the country.'   Lord Derby had therefore advised reversion to the original course in order to provide a solution of the problem.   Disraeli deplored the resulting loss of three colleagues.   'If my resignation of office could have prevented that unfortunate result, that resignation was at the command of my noble friend.   It was at his command, then, as it has always been. . . .   But the state of affairs would not have been bettered by my retiring from office.'   He paid a special tribute to Cranborne, 'whose commanding talents, clear intelligence, capacity for labour, and power of expression, will always, I am sure, qualify him for taking a leading part in the affairs of this country.'   He had already written him a graceful letter about his forthcoming explanation — an explanation which followed the lines of the letter of February 24 to Derby.   It is impossible to avoid the reflection that Disraeli's treatment of Cranborne contracts very favourably with Cranborne's treatment of Disraeli.

To Lord Cranborne.

DOWNING STREET, *Mar.* 5, 1867. — Lord Derby has written to me what has taken place between you. I shall say something when the House meets. It will not displease you, tho' it will only feebly express my sense of your services and loss, and I hope it will disembarrass us all of the difficulties inseparable from our position.

Lord Derby says you are to consult with me what you are to say, I mean as to Cabinet secrets, but I have such confidence in you, in every respect, that such previous communication is quite unnecessary.

Disraeli's vague language and Cranborne's criticisms suggested that household suffrage was to be the basis of the Bill; and Lowe and Horsman denounced, while Bright welcomed, the prospect. Both Cranborne and Peel treated the proposed checks and securities as worthless. Stanley, in reply, indignantly repudiated the notion that the Conservatives would outbid any party, or adopt Bright's policy in their Bill.

The whole discussion was, of course, in advance of detailed knowledge, and Ministers immediately set to work, under Disraeli's guidance, to reduce the measure into shape. The offices vacated by the resignations had been filled up very much in the way suggested by Disraeli. Northcote succeeded Cranborne, Pakington Peel, and the Duke of Buckingham Carnarvon. The resulting vacancies at the Board of Trade, the Admiralty, and the Council, were made good by the appointment of the Duke of Richmond,[1] Henry Corry (Montagu Corry's father), and the Duke of Marlborough. That the Cabinet difficulties should have been solved by the promotion of three Dukes provoked many a smile, and the reflection that the arrangement was characteristic of Disraeli.

The place of authority in the Cabinet which was vacant by Cranborne's resignation was occupied by Hardy. The wreckers had failed to inveigle him; and Disraeli and Derby immediately took him into their special confidence on Reform, and he became Disraeli's lieutenant in

---

[1] The sixth Duke. See Vol. III., p. 203.

carrying the Bill through the Commons. His diary contains the following: '*March* 5. — Disraeli had a long talk with me, going through the heads of our proposed Reform, and said he and I must do it, but there must be full and early explanation with the Cabinet, and no putting off. *March* 7. — I had more talk with Disraeli, whose fault is that he is always looking for what will suit others, rather than what is sound in itself. . . . I am to go to Lord Derby to-day on the same subject.'[1] The main troubles of the reconstructed Cabinet naturally occurred about the checks and securities. The principal checks under discussion were residence for a substantial period, personal payment of rates, and dual voting — that is, giving property a second vote so as to balance numbers. For dual voting Disraeli never had any particular affection; and he felt sure the House of Commons would not accept it. He therefore tried to persuade the Cabinet not to commit themselves to it at all; and Derby, on the whole, took the same view. The Beaconsfield papers contain a note in Derby's handwriting: 'If we do not take care, we shall have another break-up. Duality will defeat us; abandonment of it will destroy us.' This note is endorsed: 'Written by Ld. D. in Cabinet Sat. March 9, 1867, to the C. of E., who was pressing Mr. H[ardy] and Mr. W[alpole] to give up the dual vote.' The Duke of Buckingham declared that he could not support the Bill if the dual vote was withdrawn, and Malmesbury kept writing from Heron Court: 'I hope one of the conditions is that we stick through thick and thin and in full to our counterpoises or to some certainly equivalent;' 'we ought to resign rather than carry or suffer to be carried household suffrage *pur et simple.*' 'We must watch and hope,' wrote Disraeli on March 11 to Northcote; 'things are not so dark as they seemed.' Dual voting, in consequence of the obstinacy of some Ministers, made its appearance in the Bill, but in a very half-hearted fashion. The Queen, to whom the

[1] Gathorne Hardy, Vol. I., p. 203.

Bill was sent as soon as the Cabinet had passed it, fixed
on this point at once, and was greatly reassured when
Disraeli told her confidently in reply that Derby did
not intend to make the second vote a vital question.
'H.M. wishes me,' Grey added, 'again to repeat the
expression of her sincere and anxious hope that this Bill
may pass the ordeal of the two Houses in a shape that
the Government will accept, and that it may settle this
important question for many years to come.'

How the new situation was regarded in the enemy's
camp was explained to Disraeli in an interesting letter on
March 8 from a friend in their midst, relating the conversation at a Liberal dinner-party. Milner Gibson thought
that Government could not pass any Bill, and that Russell
would be back in office in a few weeks. Horsman dilated
on the profligacy of the Ministry — they were like Peel in
1846. 'To which Ayrton and others replied that there
was this difference, that you are strictly consistent; that
you are carrying out your leading political idea of restoring the Tory party to popularity, and vindicating
their claims to be the champions of real popular rights.'
Seely said he and many other Liberals would support
the Government on the ground that it was better to have
the question settled by Derby rather than by Beales
and Potter. 'They all admitted that no Minister was
placed in a more difficult position, in our times, than you
were put into by the conduct of the three deserters in not
having deserted earlier.'

The Bill had been drafted by Dudley Baxter, a partner
of Philip Rose in the firm of Baxter, Rose and Norton.
But it was obviously desirable to have the first expert
assistance before submitting it to the scrutiny of a critical
House of Commons. There was no regular Treasury
draftsman at that date, the tradition, largely created
by Gladstone, that the Treasury was the proper source
of legislation, not having yet grown up. But there was a
notable expert at the Home Office, who afterwards became Lord Thring, and he was consulted, and reported

unfavourably on the amateur draft. Baxter resented this criticism, and refused to communicate with Thring. What was to be done? It was now Thursday afternoon, March 14. The Bill was to be finally revised by the Cabinet on the Saturday, introduced by Disraeli on the Monday, and circulated in print to members of Parliament on the Tuesday morning. 'What have you done *re* Thring *v.* Baxter?' wrote Derby on this Thursday. 'The defendant has done all the work, and the plaintiff has all the real knowledge and experience on his side.'

To Lord Derby.

HOUSE OF COMMONS, *Thursday, Mar.* 14, 1867.—It was painful, but decision was absolutely necessary. I decided for Thring. He will sit up all night,[1] and, I believe, we shall have the Bill printed for the Cabinet on Saturday. I have written myself to Baxter.

Much depends on to-morrow.

Grosvenor has established a newspaper — the *Day* — and has engaged Kebbel, an Oxford man, well acquainted with the Press, but a fine writer, and a scholar, for editor. Grosvenor and Elcho were with Kebbel to-day, giving him his final instructions: he asked them, for his general government, to let him know what they really thought would be the result. Grosvenor said that if our policy was what he understood it to be, household suffrage, absolute rate-paying, and compensatory arrangement against compound householders, they had ascertained they could pull the Government through, *provided our men went straight*.

That is the question. Banks Stanhope has written to Taylor that real rating will unite the party to a man, or something like it. But there is Hotham, Cecil, and Co. Gladstone's great fight is against real rating — that is ascertained.

At dinner Stanley said he thought we had a good chance, at any rate a policy, and no Minister was ever more justified in going to the country.

'Much depends on to-morrow.' The Government took the unprecedented, but, in the circumstances, honest and straightforward, course of calling their followers together in Downing Street, explaining the terms of their Bill to them three days before its production in Parlia-

---

[1] Thring worked on the Friday with two shorthand writers from ten to six, and completed the draft, which was printed during the night.

ment, and asking for their confidence and support. It was a large meeting, 195 members of Parliament attending, and 43, who were unable to be present, sending letters of adhesion to the Government. Derby was perfectly candid. Household rating suffrage was to be the basis of the borough franchise, and the only conditions which he pronounced to be essential were payment of rates and two years' residence; he explained that compound house-holders, or those whose landlords at present paid a composition for the rates and charged the amount in the rent, would be permitted to obtain the vote by assuming personal payment themselves. The dual vote would be proposed, but he admitted that the Government were not strongly wedded to it. If necessary, they would be prepared to recommend dissolution. This frank treatment of the party, which contrasted, as was pointed out at the meeting, so favourably with Peel's behaviour over Roman Catholic Emancipation and Free Trade, had an admirable effect. Henley, the most respected Conservative leader outside the Government, expressed his full adhesion. He held that household suffrage, with payment of rates, was the true basis of the right to vote according to the principles of the Constitution. These sentiments were echoed by others. The seceders kept quiet, the only expression of dissent coming from Heathcote, the senior member for Oxford University, who believed that the measure would destroy the influence of rank, property, and education, by the force of numbers.

Once again there was a crowded House, on Monday, March 18, to hear Disraeli introduce the Government Reform Bill — this time no makeshift, but the Bill which, after emendation by the co-operation of the House, Ministers hoped to pass into law. But the interest had, to a large extent, been discounted by Derby's speech to his party on the Friday. Everyone knew that the basis of the new borough franchise was to be household suffrage, qualified by personal rating and by two years' residence; that the payment of twenty shillings in direct taxes

would also give a vote over and above the vote already obtained as a householder ; that there would be an educational franchise, and that £50 in the funds or in the savings bank would give a vote. It was known, moreover, that the county franchise would be reduced from £50 to £15 rating, and that the redistribution would be on the same scale as in the previous Bill. No surprises as to the provisions were, therefore, to be looked for; interest would lie in the manner in which Disraeli would present the scheme to the House, and in the reception which the different sections would accord to it.

At the outset Disraeli claimed that the object of the Bill was to establish the character and functions of the House 'on a broad, popular basis'; to concede a liberal measure of popular privileges, but by no means to confer democratic rights. Hitherto the proposals which had been made to alter the borough franchise, right down to the Bill of 1866, had all been in the nature of a diminution in the £10 value fixed by the great Reform Act. But last year a most important principle was asserted, the principle of rating; it was carried against the then Government, and caused their retirement. 'A great decision was arrived at by the unerring instinct of the House.' It meant that 'the being rated to the poor, and the paying of the rates, constituted a fair assurance that the man who fulfilled those conditions was one likely to be characterised by regularity of life and general trustworthiness of conduct.' It was found to be unsatisfactory to connect this principle of rating with value. So the Government considered the principle without reference to value, and found that it would admit 237,000. There were 486,000 compound householders. These, not having the qualification of personal rating, should not have the vote ; but every facility would be given to them to enter their names on the rate-book, and thus acquire the qualification. Household rating was the only solid foundation for the borough franchise: the only possible settlement. The alternative was a £5 rating ; but that

would be a Serbonian bog, and would inevitably lead to manhood suffrage.

It was said that this new basis of household rating suffrage was an assault on the power of the middle classes. But the twenty shillings direct taxation franchise would largely give the middle classes a second vote. This would probably add 200,000 votes. The fancy franchises altogether would add 100,000. The £15 rating county franchise would add 171,000; and, taking the other franchises, there would be a general addition to the county franchise of 300,000. Disraeli defended the moderate nature of the redistribution scheme, which was based on the principle of no absolute disfranchisement of boroughs, by saying that, unless you were prepared to reconstruct the electoral map of England, you must be prudent and practical.

He referred shortly to the very great difficulties and sacrifices which had been involved in the preparation of the Bill, and his own chagrin and mortification. But he had done his duty. 'In attempting to bring the question to this point we have lost those whose absence from our councils we more than regret; we have had to appeal to a high-spirited party to make what, no doubt, to some was, to a certain extent, a sacrifice of principle, much sacrifice of sentiment, and much sacrifice of interest. But we have not appealed in vain.' The party, he declared, felt the time had come for an extensive and complete settlement. If there were checks or counterpoises in this scheme, so there were in the British Constitution. They wished to prevent a preponderance of any class, and to give a representation to the nation.

No sooner had the Chancellor sat down than Gladstone rose, and fell tooth and nail upon the Bill. It was both too wide and too full of checks. It would only admit 140,000 new voters. He opposed the reduction to household suffrage; but he opposed equally the restrictions on household suffrage — personal rating and the dual vote. He demanded a lodger franchise. He foreshadowed a

vehement opposition. The general reception was uncertain, but Henley for the Conservatives, and Roebuck and Bernal Osborne for the Independent Liberals, urged that the Bill should go to Committee for amendment. Almost all the speakers, whether Conservative or Liberal, showed hostility to the dual vote. The small knot of Conservative malcontents, Cranborne, Heathcote, Beresford Hope, and Sandford, sounded at once a note of bitter antagonism; Cranborne predicting that the checks would all be swept away, and household suffrage pure and simple be the result. Disraeli, in reply, declared with much emphasis that the Government would never introduce household suffrage pure and simple. He was as yet insufficiently acquainted with those intricacies of compound householding, which ultimately drove him, in pursuit of a settlement, into something hardly distinguishable from the solution which he deprecated.

The reception was not good enough to augur favourably for the future of the Bill. The principal Ministers, such as Hardy, were despondent; the Liberal leaders thought the enemy who had overthrown them was delivered into their hands. Gladstone gathered his followers together, anxious to dispose of both Bill and Ministers on the second reading; but he found, to his discomfiture, that wrecking tactics would not be supported, and that at least a second reading must be accorded to his rival's Bill. His recalcitrant following might not be prepared to beard him to his face; but they made it sufficiently clear that they would not all follow him into the ' No ' division lobby.

To Lord Derby.

Confidential. GROSVENOR GATE, *Mar.* 24, 1867. — It is very trying, and no doubt we shall, both of us, always remember the year 1867.

But there is more than hope. . . . I must tell you that there are 100 men on the other side against Gladstone, but they are *moutons ;* there is nobody who can speak against him.

At the meeting, there was no one, though the feeling was so strong, that by murmuring, round robins, and scuffling of feet, they controlled ' iracundus Achilles.' . . .

In truth, Gladstone made the astounding mistake of supposing that, after a definite and final basis, such as household rating, had been proposed by the Government for borough franchise, it would be possible to get the Liberal party to follow him in restricting extension to a £5 value. Though he was no longer in a position to divide, he yet took up this attitude with great keenness in his speech on the second reading, a week later, Monday, March 25, laying down dogmatically what was and what was not to be done. But several Liberals who were enthusiasts for Reform, among whom Fawcett, the blind economist, was conspicuous, saw that they were getting a great and sufficient principle established, and refused to support their leader. Bright, indeed, backed Gladstone up, because he fixed his eyes rather upon the limitations than the main principle, and so regarded the Bill as a deception. Hardy made a vigorous speech in which he insisted that it was a rating franchise Bill, rather than a household suffrage Bill, but at the same time expressed the readiness of the Government for mutual concession and forbearance. Several independent Liberals came to the help of Ministers; and it was felt that the general upshot of the debate would be mainly determined by the character of the Chancellor's speech in reply at the close of the second night.

Derby, who was deeply involved in the policy of the Bill, wrote to Disraeli as the debate drew to an end:

From Lord Derby.

St. James's Square, 9.30 [*Mar.* 26]. — I am anxious for reports from your House. . . .

Last night was excellent. Hardy has quite vindicated our selection of him, and has placed himself in the front rank as a debater. The Sol.-Gen. seems to have done very well also, and Roebuck's was a most useful speech, and full of sound sense. P. Talbot sat by Delane all through the debate, and the latter said: 'Gladstone has done you more good than all your Cabinet put together.'

Shall you close to-night? If so, excuse me for saying that I hope you will be as short and pithy as possible, striking the

keynote which I understand to have been agreed upon between us, of willingness to consult the opinion of *the House*, but refusal to submit to the dictation of *one assumed* leader of a party. If you are going to speak, don't trouble yourself to answer, but depute somebody to write or to come up.

Disraeli received this note just as he was about to rise to deliver one of his most memorable and successful speeches; and brilliantly did he carry out the policy of Derby's last sentences — refusal to submit to Gladstone's dictation, coupled with ready deference to the general feeling of the House. He had to defend, he said, what was called one night a revolutionary measure, and then, on the next, a measure of extreme restriction. He strongly maintained, on the contrary, that it was a Bill founded on a popular and a rational principle. Yet it was attacked with violent excitement by Gladstone.

The right hon. gentleman gets up and addresses me in a tone which, I must say, is very unusual in this House. Not that I at all care for the heat he displays, although really his manner is sometimes so very excited and so alarming that one might almost feel thankful that gentlemen in this House, who sit on opposite sides of this table, are divided by a good broad piece of furniture.

Gladstone had peremptorily demanded a lodger franchise. Well, as Disraeli had proposed it in 1859, he could hardly be supposed to have a prejudice against it; but his colleagues, when he suggested it in Cabinet, had naturally said that it was inconsistent with the principle of rating. Moreover, last year Gladstone had spoken of lodger franchise as a very insignificant affair. It was a question for Committee.

Disraeli went in detail through Gladstone's demands and menaces, showing the inconsistencies in which the Opposition leader had involved himself in his resolve at all hazards to destroy the Government and the Bill. He scoffed at his exaggerated fears of the corruption of the new voters; apparently he thought the great body of the people were not to be trusted. Gladstone had fulminated against a two years' residence — the very provision which

he had himself laid down in 1866 for his lodger franchise. Rating and residence, said Disraeli, were essential, and the House would make a great error if it reduced the term of residence. A franchise based on direct taxation, which Gladstone had condemned, had been proposed by Russell in 1852 and 1854. He twitted Gladstone with his demand in general terms that redistribution must be enlarged, without specifying which of his friends' seats he meant to disfranchise. As to the county franchise, Ministers had made a very large reduction from £50 to £15, but the exact figure was of secondary importance, and should be left to Committee. In deference to the general opinion of all parties, the dual vote, which had been introduced as a protection to the middle classes, would be abandoned.

Disraeli dilated on the governing inconsistency of Gladstone's opposition, which wished at one and the same time to have a more restricted suffrage and to do away with the checks proposed for household suffrage. That was blowing hot and cold at once. One of the most pregnant passages in the speech was that in which he dealt with the calculations as to the number of persons to be enfranchised under the Bill.

Our Bill is not framed, as was the one of last session, to enfranchise a specific number of persons. We do not attempt that. We lay down a principle, and let that principle work; but if you ask us what will be the result of its working, we say — although we do not wish to found our policy upon it — that we do not apprehend the number that will be admitted to the enjoyment of the franchise will exceed the number contemplated by the Bill of last session. But there is this difference between our proposition and the proposition made by the right hon. gentleman. The proposition of the right hon. gentleman was founded upon a state of things which was liable to be changed the next year, when the question might possibly have to be raised again, while the proposition that we make is founded upon a principle that is not liable to alteration.

In his final sentences, Disraeli laid down broadly, and in the most unmistakable terms, the desire of the Govern-

ment for the co-operation of the House, and their readiness to defer to it.

One word before I conclude. I hear much of the struggle of parties in this House, and I hear much of combinations that may occur, and courses that may be taken, which may affect the fate of this Bill. All I can say on the part of my colleagues and myself is that we have no other wish at the present moment than, with the co-operation of this House, to bring the question of Parliamentary Reform to a settlement. I know the Parliamentary incredulity with which many will receive avowals that we are only influenced in the course we are taking by a sense of duty; but I do assure the House — if they need such assurances after what they have gone through, after the sacrifices we have made, after having surrendered our political connection with men whom we more than regarded — I can assure them no other principle animates us but a conviction that we ought not to desert our posts until this question has been settled. Rest assured that it is not for the weal of England that this settlement should be delayed. You may think that the horizon is not disturbed at the present juncture. You may think that surrounding circumstances may be favourable to dilatory action. Some of you may think, in the excitement of the moment, that ambition may be gratified, and that the country may look favourably upon those who prevent the passing of this Bill. Do not believe it. There is a deep responsibility with regard to this question, resting, not on the Government merely, but upon the whole House of Commons. We are prepared, as I think I have shown, to act in all sincerity in this matter. Act with us cordially and candidly: assist us to carry this measure. We will not shrink from deferring to your suggestions so long as they are consistent with the main object of this Bill, which we have never concealed from you, and which is to preserve the representative character of the House of Commons. Act with us, I say, cordially and candidly; you will find on our side complete reciprocity of feeling. Pass the Bill, and then change the Ministry if you like.

With this reasonable and attractive appeal ringing in their ears, the House passed the second reading without a division. There is an almost universal consensus of opinion that the speech was the turning-point of the session; that it practically secured the carrying of a Reform Bill under the conduct of the Government. A young journalist, then on the threshold of a distinguished

career, who was no friend to Disraeli, wrote of it at
the time: 'Its exuberance caught the House. Its bold
caricature of Mr. Gladstone's cloud-compelling manner
placed an obstacle such as ridicule can rarely raise in the
path of the official Opposition. The whole House seemed
tickled too much ever seriously to fall out with Mr. Disraeli on this subject again. . . . Men who have heard
Mr. Disraeli throughout his career agree that never did
he show such mastery over his audience, such boundless
histrionic resource.'[1] Liberals such as Lord Enfield and
Hastings Russell, Manners reported, were as loud in praise
of the speech as Conservatives; and Disraeli's colleagues
were unanimous. 'Masterly' is Malmesbury's epithet,
'brilliant' Hardy's. Manners heard on all sides nothing
but admiration and satisfaction. Even the unenthusiastic
Stanley wrote: 'The speech of last night has pleased
all our friends. I think it one of the best you have
ever made ; and, after our troubles, it has come like the
warm weather after frost and snow.' Derby was entirely
satisfied.

From Lord Derby.

St. James's Square, *Mar.* 27, 1867. — I cannot let the day
pass over without offering you my cordial congratulations on
your splendid achievement of last night. I hear from all
quarters that it was the finest speech you ever made ; and you
seem to have carried the House bodily away with you. In
fact, you have won our game for us ; and in writing to the
Queen this morning to announce your 'triumphant success,' I
told H.M. that I now, for the first time, entertained a sanguine
hope of carrying a Bill through in the course of the present
session. . . .

There was one episode connected with the reversion of
the Cabinet to the larger Bill which caused a small public
scandal, and much personal pain to Disraeli. When
Earle, at his own wish, exchanged his private secretaryship to Disraeli for public office in the new Ministry, he
did not realise that he necessarily cut himself off from the
intimate intercourse and admission to the arcana of politics

[1] Article by Sir Edward Russell in *Belgravia*, Sept., 1867.

which he had previously enjoyed. But it would be very imprudent of a Minister to admit more than his actual secretaries to the privilege of confidential information; and, when Earle manifested a tendency to frequent the secretaries' room and expect to be treated as if he were still one of them, Disraeli gave Corry and Fremantle distinct instructions that matters of confidence should not be imparted to him. Earle marked Corry's rapid advance to a degree of intimacy to which he had never himself attained; his feelings were deeply wounded; he brooded over what he regarded as slights and humiliations; and in February poured out his heart to Rose, accusing Disraeli of altered demeanour, of snubbing him before subordinates, and of excluding him, in spite of ten years of devotion, from his confidence. Finally, when the Household Suffrage Bill was introduced, he determined to follow the three seceding Ministers, resigned his office, and from his place in Parliament attacked the Bill and the Minister who introduced it. 'A more painful exhibition,' says Fraser, 'never was witnessed.' It appeared to be an act of unprovoked ingratitude, and Earle had no power of speaking which could render his criticism of his late chief palatable to the House. A letter to a friend gives a glimpse into Disraeli's feelings on this outburst.

To Lord Beauchamp.

HUGHENDEN, *April* 18, 1867. — . . . There are, no doubt, breakers yet ahead, but I feel great hope of overcoming them, and of realising the dream of my life and re-establishing Toryism on a national foundation.

The only black spot in this great business, and which I would not notice to anyone but yourself, is the treason of Earle! I have known him for ten years, and, tho' warned from the first by the Cowleys, whom he had treated as he has treated me, I utterly disregarded their intimations, and ascribed them all to prejudice and misapprehension.

I have worked for his welfare more earnestly than for my own, and do not believe that I ever, even in the most trying times, gave him a hasty or unkind word. I loaded him with favors, and among them introduced him to you. I am ashamed of my want of discrimination. . . .

We may sympathise with Disraeli's grief at Earle's ingratitude; but it is impossible not to remember, when he refers to Earle's misbehaviour to Cowley, the British Ambassador in Paris, that Disraeli himself had profited by it.[1] Earle not only quitted office, but, in a short time, Parliament and English politics; and, for the rest of what was not destined to be a long life, engaged in a successful financial career in the Near East.

In spite of Disraeli's appeal for general co-operation, and the large amount of response which it elicited, Gladstone obstinately persisted in his attempt to substitute a £5 value in the place of rating household suffrage as the basis of the borough franchise. He called his followers together on Friday, April 5, and his ardour and insistence obtained a general assent to the proposal that, on the following Monday, an instruction to that effect should be moved by Coleridge, afterwards Lord Chief Justice. But, though cowed, the household suffrage Liberals were not convinced. They met subsequently in the tea-room of the House of Commons, and determined not to support the official policy of the Opposition. Disraeli wrote what he heard to Derby, who at this crisis in his party's fate was once more absent from Cabinet councils owing to gout.

To Lord Derby.

Confidential.   GROSVENOR GATE, *Sunday* [?*April* 7].— Gladstone is more violent than ever, and the Independents who baffled him the other day have had a council, at which it was discussed whether some communication should not be opened with Mr. Henley and Colonel Wilson Patten, in order to assist the Government and pass the Bill: the names even were mentioned of managers of the conference on the part of the Independent Liberals — Mr. Whitbread and Mr. Clay. It is said that, whatever statement is made by us, Gladstone means to propose to his party an abstract resolution on the Speaker leaving the chair, to the effect that no settlement, etc., can be satisfactory which recognises in electoral rights a distinction between rich and poor. . . .

[1] See above, p. 68.

The tea-room revolt spiked Gladstone's guns. 'The House met,' wrote Hardy on April 8; 'rumours rife that a large meeting of Liberals had thrown over Gladstone, and that his instruction, so far as it was hostile, was to be withdrawn. Locke asked Disraeli if he would accept the change. His answer was admirable. Gladstone lowering and gloomy, full of mortification, no doubt. A desultory talk, and we were in Committee, but reported progress at once. . . . The disunion on the other side seems complete.' 'Disraeli's insolent triumph' was the entry of a fervent Gladstonite in his diary.

From General the Hon. Charles Grey.

WINDSOR CASTLE, *April* 9, 1867. — The Queen desires me to write in her name to say how much pleased she is by the result of last night's proceedings in the House of Commons. . . . It was, in all probability, the suspicion that Gladstone was seeking the means of destroying the measure altogether that caused the defection from him, and any want of conciliation on the part of the Government might operate equally injuriously against them. . . .

But Gladstone had not yet learnt his lesson. There was a real and serious difficulty in the compound householders, which was not met by Disraeli's plan of facilitating direct payment of rates by this class. Gladstone determined to make this question the ground for one more attempt to oust Disraeli and the Government from the control of the Reform question, and to retransfer it to his own hands. He accordingly gave notice of drastic amendments dispensing with personal rating and recurring to the £5 value; and before the debate came on there were negotiations between the tea-room Liberals and the Government, at which an attempt was made to find some compromise which should eliminate the compound householder. A 'secret' Cabinet was held, on Malmesbury's suggestion, at Lord Barrington's house, but Hardy and Walpole appear to have resisted concessions which Disraeli was prepared to make, and no

arrangement was effected.   The upshot of the division was
therefore very doubtful, as Cranborne and his friends
proposed to vote with Gladstone.   Beresford Hope,
who was of Dutch extraction, enlivened the debate
with a vehement attack upon the ' Asian mystery.'   He
was a speaker who affected airs and postures ; so Disraeli
lightly retorted that there was a 'Batavian grace' in
his invectives which took the sting out of what he said.
A vigorous speech by Hardy had a great effect.   Disraeli
had given him sagacious advice which he had followed.
' Permit me to intimate that, without in the slightest
degree compromising your convictions, it is expedient
not to make an unnecessarily uncompromising speech
to-night ; and with regard to the question on which the
Cabinet was so divided this morning, it seems to me
unnecessary to touch on it.'   Bright once more rallied
to Gladstone's side, supporting the £5, or it might be
£4 or £3, value against his own policy of household
suffrage.   Disraeli, when he came to wind up the debate,
went straight to the point.   It was really a question
between Gladstone's hard-and-fast line and his own
logical position.   Gladstone's amendment was merely
one more attempt to overthrow Disraeli and reseat
himself in power.

The right hon. gentleman opposite is a candidate for power,
and no man has a greater right to be a candidate for power.
The right hon. gentleman is an opponent with whom any
man may be proud to have to contend.   I know nothing more
legitimate than the ambition of such a man, and I am sure I
bear the right hon. gentleman no ill-will, or as little ill-will as
a man can bear, for the efforts which he may make to change
his position and to cross from one side of the House to the
other.   But I am sure the right hon. gentleman will not be
offended if I, without passion, but, I am sure, clearly, express
to the House what I believe to be his position with regard to
the Government, and this question.   I can quite understand
how the right hon. gentleman should be so very emulous to deal
with this important question with which Her Majesty's Government have felt it their duty to grapple ; but the right hon.
gentleman seems to forget what he ought to remember.   The
right hon. gentleman has had his innings.   He has dealt with

the subject of Parliamentary Reform very recently, and in
this House — in this House elected under the auspices of a
Government of which he was a member; and he introduced
a measure with the advantage, which we have never had, of
being supported by a large majority. I do not begrudge the
right hon. gentleman those advantages, but I may still remind
him of them; and I say, under these circumstances, we have a
right that there should be no great eagerness to make party
attacks. I cannot but view the amendments proposed by the
right hon. gentleman in this light. They are not amendments
to our Bill. They are counter-propositions. . . . I acknowledge the right hon. gentleman's position and talents — that he
is perfectly justified in attacking the Government; but do not
let us misunderstand the motion or the conduct of the right
hon. gentleman. Nothing can be more legitimate. It is a
party attack; and the endeavour to parry it as a party attack
is in accordance with the tactics which were understood to
be adopted in the House on this subject.

But as regards the House of Commons, generally speaking,
I wish, on the part of Her Majesty's Government, whatever
may be the decision to-night, whatever may be the consequences of this division, to say that in dealing with this question Her Majesty's Government have never for a moment
swerved from those sentiments which, with the full concurrence and desire of my colleagues, I have often expressed in
this House — namely, that we are most anxious to co-operate
with the House in bringing this question of Parliamentary
Reform to a satisfactory settlement; and although we could
not swerve with respect to the borough franchise from those
principles which we regarded as vital — namely, personal payment of rates and residence — still, with regard to almost
every other point which has been mentioned in our discussion,
we are most anxious, in Committee, after a fair deliberation,
and after an interchange of opinion, to adopt that course
which the House in its wisdom may think most expedient and
desirable.

Gladstone, in reply, affected to be unable to understand
how Disraeli could be ready to consult the House, and
yet unwilling to accept amendments from the Opposition
leader. But the House realised that Gladstone's was a
wrecking amendment, and the first division on the
Reform Bill of 1867, taken on the night of Friday, April
12, gave a majority of twenty-one for the Government.
The result had been throughout uncertain, and Gladstone

had to the last expected a victory.   He felt it to be 'a
smash, perhaps, without example.'   The Conservative
cheering was loud and long, and, as Mr. Kebbel writes,
'none rushed to shake hands with the Chancellor of the
Exchequer more enthusiastically than those Tory country
gentlemen whom he was absurdly said to have betrayed.'
The enthusiasm was not all expended at Westminster.
A quarter of an hour or so later, there was a number of
excited Conservative members collected for supper at
the Carlton Club.   Disraeli looked in at the club on his
way home, and as he entered the large, crowded dining-
room the cheers rang out again and again, and Sir Matthew
Ridley interpreted the feeling of the party by proposing a
toast : 'Here's the man who rode the race, who took the
time, who kept the time, and who did the trick!'   They
crowded round their leader, and pressed him to stay and
sup with them.   Mr. Kebbel gives us the sequel.

As Lady Beaconsfield told me afterwards, with manifest
pride and joy, 'Dizzy came home to me.'   And she then proceeded to describe the supper : 'I had got him a raised pie
from Fortnum and Mason's, and a bottle of champagne, and he
ate half the pie and drank all the champagne, and then he
said : "Why, my dear, you are more like a mistress than a
wife."'   And I could see that she took it as a very high compliment indeed.[1]

Gladstone and Bright were as much cast down as the
Conservatives were elated.   The story ran that Bright
said that night at the Reform Club to Bernal Osborne :
'You may do what you like, Osborne, but you will never
manage to put salt on Dizzy's tail.'   Gladstone was so
chagrined at his desertion by the tea-room party that
he appeared for a while to contemplate retirement to a
back bench.   But the House adjourned after the division
for the Easter recess, and there was a quiet opportunity
for the reconsideration of rash impulses.

[1] *Lord Beaconsfield and Other Tory Memories*, p. 40.

CHAPTER XV

DISRAELI'S PARLIAMENTARY TRIUMPH — II

1867

Disraeli retired to Hughenden for the Easter recess in high spirits after the unexpectedly satisfactory campaign of the early spring. Corry wrote to tell him the vivid impression which had been made in the depths of the English countryside; his old friend Vitzthum — now no longer Saxon Minister in London, owing to Prussia's victory over the German Confederation — forwarded from Dresden a thoughtful appreciation of the situation as it looked to a well-informed foreigner who knew England.

From Montagu Corry.

ROWTON CASTLE, SHREWSBURY, *Easter Sunday, April* 21, 1867. — . . . Your name is in the mouth of every labourer, who, without knowing what 'Reform' means, or caring, hears that Mr. —— has won a great victory. I leave the blank, as it is impossible to express the Protean variety which a name, revered and cherished by me, here assumes. My private opinion is that my aunt's carpenter, who 'heard say that Mr. Disraeli had laid Mr. Gladstone on his back,' thinks that you really knocked that godly man down. I have too much jealousy for your fair fame to undeceive him.

From Count Vitzthum.

HÔTEL DE SAXE, DRESDEN, *April* 21, 1867. — . . . I never regretted my absence from England so much. I need not to tell you the joy I felt at your victory. I was sure of it. May I tell you frankly why? Looking on, without party bias, during fourteen years, I could not help being struck by the fact that you appeared the only man in England working for posterity. Your genius bore, to my eyes, always the historical stamp, and I never listened to a speech of yours without thinking, this word, this sentence, will be remembered a hundred years hence. . . .

If I understand right your present position, you are the Œdipus who solved the Sphinx's riddle; you have thrown in the chasm worn-out prejudices, and you put the good ship in order before the great storm which may blow over for a moment, but which soon will shake Europe from one end to the other. At the eve of such a crisis, what are ten-pounders and lodgers? The great point was to settle and to subdue this internal agitation, and I think you paved the way for a settlement which will last until the resettlement of Europe. . . .

But, though the Bill was well begun, the thorny questions ahead pressed upon Disraeli at Hughenden, and followed him to Windsor, where he was asked to spend Easter. 'I am sorry to say,' he writes to Corry on Good Friday, 'the Compound Householder has found his way to Hughenden, introduced by Lord Cairns.'[1] At Windsor it was the Lodger who was troubling him.

To Lord Stanley.

WINDSOR CASTLE, *Easter Monday, April* 22, 1867. —. . . As for domestic affairs, we ought to carry our Reform now in a canter, if all I hear be true.

We can't take Torrens's lodger, and I doubt whether the House will take him at any rate or rent.

I wish, in the interval of settling the affairs of Europe, you would get up an anti-lodger speech, or a speech on the subject either way; as I think our debates want a little variety, and the House will get tired of the eternal partridge of your affectionate colleague, THE CHANCELLOR OF THE EXCHEQUER.[2]

'Or a speech on the subject either way!' How the old Disraeli comes out in a flash! Detail, even important detail, was almost as nothing; lodger franchise had been one of his own proposals in former years, and he regarded it now as a pure question of tactics; but the Bill, with or without lodger franchise, was to pass in a canter! That was what mattered. Stanley was in favour of lodger franchise, and may have decided Disraeli's course. 'I am so deeply pledged to the principle,' he replied, 'that I cannot speak against it; but we may fix the limit where we please.

[1] Cairns, who was now a Lord Justice of Appeal, had been made a peer, and was resuming his political activity.

[2] This is the latter part of the letter printed above on pp. 470, 471.

I think £15 would do no harm. It would swamp only constituencies which are already as radical as they well can be. I think our Bill, or at least a Bill, is safe.' Stanley, it will be seen, entered with grim humour into the situation. 'Or at least a Bill' is the apt retort to Disraeli's fling.

Before Easter Disraeli had resisted, and successfully resisted, Gladstone's repeated attempts to take the Reform question out of his hands and substitute a £5 value with all its logical consequences. After Easter he showed the readiness which he had frequently proclaimed to co-operate with the House and to accept the amendments which the general sense of Parliament desired. Gladstone and the official Liberals, and Bright, who acted generally with them, did not even yet desist from occasional attempts to impose their own scheme, but these efforts signally failed. During the Easter recess they had countenanced or instigated great popular gatherings which, strangely enough, treated a Bill establishing rating household suffrage as a virtual denial of working men's rights. Gladstone received and encouraged a deputation from a society engaged in promoting this movement, and was amusingly chaffed in the House of Commons by Disraeli.

I regret very much that these spouters of stale sedition, these obsolete incendiaries, should have come forward to pay their homage to one who, wherever he may sit, must always be the pride and ornament of the House:

> Who but must laugh if such a man there be,
> Who would not weep if Atticus were he?

Nothing has surprised me more in the ebullitions which have recently occurred than their extremely intolerant character. Everybody who does not agree with somebody is looked upon as a fool, or as being merely influenced by a total want of principle in conducting public affairs. But, sir, I cannot bring myself to believe that that is the temper of the House of Commons or the temper of the country.

On the whole, however, Gladstone was content, after Easter, to take a less conspicuous part in debate ; and

amendments, which came from private members in all
quarters of the House, were frequently offered, and accepted, modified, or rejected, without his intervention at
all.   No doubt the general nature of these amendments was
to widen the proposed enfranchisement, as was inevitable,
seeing that the Liberals had a majority of sixty or seventy
in the House, and the tea-room party and many of the
Adullamites were some of the most convinced supporters
of the principle of the Bill.   But many of the enfranchis-
ing amendments had strong Conservative support, from
Henley and others; the forward section of the Conservative
party being as resolved as the Government that the outcome of this legislation should be a real settlement that
would stand for many years.   Malmesbury's diary bears
witness to this tendency.   For May he writes : ' Cabinets
all May on Reform Bill.   The *laissez-aller* system followed
by the Government trying to make the best they could
of it, but constantly yielding something.   The Conservative members seem disposed to adopt anything, and
to think that it is "in for a penny, in for a pound."'

The first important amendment which was discussed
after Easter was one by Ayrton, an Independent Radical,
reducing the two years' residence proposed for the new
voter to the one year which was all that was required of
the ten-pounder.   The Government resisted, but were
badly beaten by eighty-one votes ; and they promptly
put in practice the readiness to defer to the opinion of
the House which they had repeatedly announced.

From General the Hon. Charles Grey.

Osborne, *May* 4, 1867. — The Queen desires me to thank
you for your letter of the night before last.   She was very
sorry to hear of the defeat of the Government by so large a
majority, though rejoiced to find that you did not consider
the points on which you were beat vital.

Her Majesty now desires me to express her earnest hope
that you will avoid, as far as possible, the mistake made by
the late Government, and should further amendments be
carried against you, in a way to show that they are in accordance with the feeling of the House and of the country, that

you will not refuse to accept them, and thus again postpone
the settlement of this question, as Lord Russell did, the Queen
thinks, so unnecessarily last year.

The Queen was thus entirely at one with the course
which Disraeli had marked out and was steadfastly
following. The question of lodgers was the next to which
it was applied. It was found that there was a general
feeling in the House that it would be unfair to exclude
lodgers, who were really in exactly similar circumstances
to the householders who were to be admitted, save in the
nature of their occupation. Two or three families of
precisely the same status often lived in one house ; while
the head of one only would rank as a householder. Disraeli could have no insuperable objection to a franchise
which he had once proposed himself ; and it was agreed
to admit lodgers down to a £10 limit.

The troublesome question of the compound householder
had now to be faced. The difficulty was that the new
system would apply so irregularly. The Small Tenements
Act and local Acts with the same object affected some
boroughs only; others were entirely innocent of the compound householder. Half a million votes were in question. To the timid Whig or Tory it seemed most important not to swamp the constituencies with this swarm of
what he fancied to be barbarian invaders ; to the Radical
the Bill was hopelessly incomplete without their inclusion. For Disraeli and the bulk of the Conservative for-
wards who believed in the efficacy of personal rating,
the principle of the Bill was involved. 'We lay down a
principle,' he had said on the second reading, 'and let
that principle work.' If these half-million could be rated
personally, they ought to have the vote as they would
have the responsibility; otherwise they had no claim to
it. This view is the clue to Disraeli's attitude on the
various attempts to solve the question. His own
plan had been to grant special facilities for placing the
compound householder's name on the rate-book. But
that offered many difficulties ; and as General Grey wrote

on the Queen's behalf: 'She fears that you are preparing
for yourself a probable, if not a certain, defeat.' But he
could not well accept Hibbert's amendment, which gave
the householder a vote on paying his composition, without being directly rated. That would be to surrender
the principle on which the Bill was founded. Gladstone
came vehemently to Hibbert's aid, and accused the
Government of 'fraud and dissimulation,' or at least of
taking care that the apparent extension of the franchise
should not be realised. 'I prefer the invective of Tor-
quemada to the insinuation of Loyola,' replied Disraeli.
The amendment was defeated by sixty-six votes.

In asking the House to reject Hibbert's amendment,
Disraeli expressed a strong desire to find a solution of
the difficulty, commended the matter to the consideration of the Committee, and trusted that with their aid
the Government might still conduct it to a happy termination. An amendment was immediately proposed by
Hodgkinson, M.P. for Newark, which was open to none
of the previous objections, but which would enfranchise
at one blow the whole of the half-million whose advent
moderate Reformers dreaded. This amendment swept
away the Small Tenements Act and other local Acts, and
made the occupier alone the person responsible for local
rates. Bright, his biographer tells us,[1] was the author of
the proposal, and Gladstone spoke in its favour, though
treating it as a forlorn hope. But here was Disraeli's
principle of personal rating conceded. What was he to
do? His leading colleague in the Commons, Hardy,
was not by his side, but seeking re-election on change
of office. Hardy had been, with general approval, appointed to take over the Home Secretaryship from
Walpole, who had once again had to deal with Reform
meetings in the parks, and, having once again failed to
do so with success, had resigned his office, though remaining in the Cabinet without portfolio. Disraeli, left
alone, acted up to the principle of personal rating, and,

[1] Trevelyan's *Bright*, p. 376.

to the astonishment of a thin House, announced at the dinner-hour his acceptance of the amendment. He was naturally eager to get his principal lieutenant's approval.

To Gathorne Hardy.

GROSVENOR GATE, *May* 18, 1867. — I have had great difficulties about the Reform Bill since we parted, and have terribly missed your aid and counsel.

On Thursday night, Dalgleish gave notice of a motion for Committee on Compound Householders, which, if carried, would have 'hung up' the Bill, and which, as it was to be supported by all the Independent Liberals and many of our own men, would certainly have been carried. I prevailed on him, yesterday morning, to give this intention up, but he informed us at the same time that he, and all his friends, and many of ours, as we knew, must support Hodgkinson's amendment for repeal of Small Tenements Act.

I sent off to you, but you had gone to Osborne: Lord Barrington told me, however, that you had mentioned to him that you were not unfavorable to the repeal in itself. I sent for Lambert, who, after long consultation with myself and Thring, said, if required, he could effect the repeal of the Rating Bill in five clauses, and was in favor of it. Two months ago such a repeal was impossible: but a very great change had occurred in the public mind on this matter. Two months ago Gladstone would have placed himself at the head of the Vestries and 'Civilisation': now we were secretly informed, he intended to reorganise on the principle of repeal of Local Acts.

In this state of doubt and difficulty I went down to the House; and about nine o'clock, being quite alone on our bench, and only forty-five men on our side, some of whom were going to vote for Hodgkinson, the amendment was moved, and, as I had been led somewhat to believe, Gladstone got up (his benches with about a hundred men) and made his meditated *coup*, which you will read.

I tried to get up some debate, or, rather, I waited for it, for I could do no more, but it was impossible. His 'appeal' to me prevented anyone but Bass and Co. speaking, and they were for Hodgkinson. I waited until the question was put, when, having revolved everything in my mind, I felt that the critical moment had arrived, and when, without in the slightest degree receding from our principle and position of a rating and residential franchise, we might take a step which would destroy the present agitation and extinguish Gladstone and Co. I therefore accepted the spirit of H.'s amendment.

It was most painful, truly grievous and annoying, to act in

such a matter without your personal and immediate countenance; and I can't conceal from myself, tho' I felt the pulse
of many in the course of the morning, feeling that some crisis
which required decision might arrive — I say I cannot conceal
from myself that this course may excite some discontent;
but if you stand by me all will go right.

I have no reason to doubt the adhesion of the Cabinet, with
the exception of the Duke of Bucks, whom I have not seen.
If the Cabinet is united to-day, all will go right, and no further
opposition to the Reform Bill will take place.

I had always, from our frequent conversations on the subject, inferred that, in theory, you were opposed to the Rating
Bills, but were of opinion, as I was myself, that it was unwise,
not to say impossible, for us to touch them. But if the Opposition originated the move, that was a great difference. I
inferred also, from what Barrington impressed on me, that
you were not insensible to the change of public opinion on
this subject.

I have written all this off to you, *curr. cal.*, that you might
fully understand all I feel at this moment. It is a critical one
which requires alike courage and conciliation for all. I hope
you may, on the whole, not disapprove of my course; but I
feel confident that, if you do not entirely, you will for the sake
of the party, and perhaps a little for mine, support a colleague
who has endeavoured to do his best in great difficulties.

Hardy, on consideration, agreed. In retrospect he
wrote: ' We had so far stepped in that we could not, on
such a point, draw back ; but it was a new proof that a
great measure ought not to be in the hand of a minority,
but with those who can mould and resist the moulding
of others.' To Disraeli, at the time, he wrote that the
course taken was logical and consistent. ' We have never
treated compounding as a check which we insisted on, but,
finding it so prevalent, did our best to open a way out of
it, to those who desired to be voters. . . . Though the
change may now be more rapid than we anticipated, I do
not see upon what principle we can object to enabling all
who pay their rates to come upon the register.' [1]

Disraeli put a bold face on the change in the House.
The amendment, he said, would carry out the principle
of the Bill; the Government had originally introduced a

---

[1] Gathorne Hardy, Vol. I., pp. 207–211.

similar provision, and had only withdrawn it to avoid overloading the ship. But the word flew round from the half-empty House to the lobbies and the clubs that Disraeli had now conceded what amounted to pure household suffrage,[1] in spite of the previous protestations made by his colleagues and by himself ; and Cranborne and Lowe, looking merely at the great numbers added to the constituency, both poured forth copious jeremiads, which from their strongly anti-democratic point of view were well justified. On the other hand, that unimpeachable old Tory, Henley, entirely backed up the Government. They were carrying out, he said, their fundamental principle ; it was the most Conservative thing in the Bill. Disraeli fully realised the enormous numerical addition that would be made to the constituency, and, till he had received Hardy's consent, was most anxious. The morning after the concession, he sent an early note to his wife: ' Dearest, come to me when you are up and breakfasted, as it is necessary to confer on affairs before you go into the world ' ; and he was greatly relieved to receive the reply: 'All right; Mr. Hardy highly approves.'

The concession of the lodger franchise and the abolition of compounding opened the borough franchise so widely that the *raison d'être* of the direct tax franchise and the ' fancy franchises ' was taken away. Practically everyone who would be enfranchised under those clauses must be either a rate-paying householder or a lodger ; and Disraeli, naturally, made no serious opposition to their elimination. With regard to the county franchise, the original proposal of the Government was to fix it at £15 rating. Locke King, in pursuance of his constant policy, to which Disraeli and his colleagues had been temporarily converted in 1859, moved to substitute £10. There was a meeting of county members, which urged the Government to fix

---

[1] Gladstone's Government, in 1869, on the plea of administrative convenience, restored compounding for local rates without electoral disqualification, thus eliminating the rating principle and establishing in boroughs household suffrage, pure and simple.

a lower rate than £15; and, when a moderate Liberal suggested £12 as a compromise, Disraeli adopted it as such.

To Queen Victoria.

House of Commons, *May* 27, 1867. — The Chancellor of the Exchequer, with his humble duty to your Majesty.

The Reform Bill makes good, and even great, progress. We have had a most important and successful night, and the feeling of the house is excellent.

We meet again to-morrow morning, and shall, at the least, have four sittings per week.

The Chancellor of the Exchequer takes even a sanguine view of affairs, and counts on sending the Bill up to the Lords in the earlier part of July.

The House received the announcement of the remission of the capital punishments of the traitor-convicts with dignified satisfaction.

As the proposed measure of enfranchisement had been enlarged, enormously in the boroughs, slightly in the counties, so the Government scheme of redistribution, which was originally of a somewhat limited character, was considerably extended in Committee; though the extension was on the same lines, and did not involve any absolute disfranchishment of boroughs, save for electoral corruption. The Government had proposed to take away one member from boroughs below 7,000 population, and, of the thirty seats obtained in this manner and by disfranchisement of corrupt places, to give fourteen to new boroughs, fifteen to counties, and one to London University. On the ground that this scheme did not go far enough to give reasonable hope of a permanent settlement, Laing, an independent Liberal member, proposed that the limit below which the second member should be taken away from boroughs should be 10,000 instead of 7,000 population. He had an elaborate scheme for disposing of the extra seats thus obtained, which involved giving a second member to towns over 50,000 population, and a third member to both towns and counties over 150,000. Disraeli resisted the enlargement on behalf of the Government; but seventy-two Conservatives voted

against their leaders, and the amendment was carried by
the great majority of 127.   Once again the party had
forced the hands of the Government.   Whether on this
occasion Disraeli wished to have pressure put upon him,
as he had over the Ten Minutes Bill, it is difficult to
say; but there is a curious letter from Lennox on the
circumstances of the division :

From Lord Henry Lennox.

June 2. — While you, as organ of the Government, were
speaking against Mr. Laing's amendment, W. Spofforth, the
paid agent of the party, was diligently whipping in favour of
it, and, with considerable audacity, asserting that the Government wished to be beaten on the point.

For the truth of this, incredible as it seems, I am ready to
vouch ; and even more, that his whipping was enforced upon
our men by a list which he held in his hand, and which professed to give the statistics why Laing's amendment ought to
be carried, and why the Government wished to be beaten. . . .

Laing's motion was, at most, merely an extension of the
principle on which redistribution was dealt with in the
Bill.   When another Liberal endeavoured to introduce
the principle of total disfranchisement with regard to
all boroughs under 5,000 population, Disraeli successfully
resisted the change by the considerable majority of fifty-
two.   But he was ready to remodel and enlarge his
scheme in accordance with the vote on Laing's amendment.   'Several Cabinets during this month on the Reform Bill, which each time become more radical,' wrote
Malmesbury in June.   On the 13th, Disraeli explained
the new plan of redistribution of the forty-five seats
given by the adoption of the 10,000 population limit.
Nineteen were to go to towns, mostly new boroughs, and
twenty-five to counties, and there was one University
seat.   As the small boroughs represented the rural population, it was fair that the extra seats taken from them
should go mainly to the counties.   But a strenuous attempt was made to get a third member for the largest
towns.   One such amendment by Laing was beaten by
eight votes ; but subsequently Disraeli consented to a

compromise by which Liverpool, Manchester, Birmingham, and Leeds, were each given a third member, the seats being obtained by withdrawing proposed new boroughs from the schedule. This compromise, which in no way altered the balance as between county and town, and which was therefore eminently reasonable, gave Disraeli a bad quarter of an hour, both in Cabinet and in the House. Hardy wrote in his diary: 'Our course about the large boroughs is, to my mind, unsatisfactory, and again and again I long to be out of the bother. General Peel attacked us vehemently, and the House sneered at Disraeli's surrender. Odious work!' Peel's attack, on this occasion particularly undeserved, was indeed bitter; he seemed to be avenging Disraeli's treatment of his brother. The proceedings on the Bill, he said, had taught him three things — first, that nothing had so little vitality as a 'vital point'; secondly, that nothing was so insecure as a 'security'; and, thirdly, that nothing was so elastic as the conscience of a Cabinet Minister.

Thus Disraeli had consented to allow the House to enlarge both the enfranchisement and the redistribution proposed in the Bill; but he had preserved the principles on which he had based each, rating and residence in one case, no disfranchisement and no entire reconstruction in the other. It remains to notice how he dealt with a few incidental questions. On voting papers, he was beaten on a division by thirty-eight; it was a mere matter of machinery, and the Government accepted the decision of the House. To all proposals of minority voting and minority representation, he showed a determined hostility. J. S. Mill brought forward Hare's plan, which has in later days received so much favour. The House generally thought the scheme was impracticable, and Disraeli was merely its mouthpiece in recommending withdrawal. A motion by Lowe in favour of cumulative voting, that is, permission to the voter in all cases of two- or three-member seats to cast all his votes for one of the candidates, met with much more support, not only

J. S. Mill, but Fawcett, one of the tea-room party, as
well as Cranborne, speaking for it. Though rejected at
first on Bright's and Disraeli's advice, the scheme was
revived in another form by the Lords. On a proposal
by Mill to enable women to vote, which was defeated by
196 to 73, Disraeli took no part ; he did not even vote.

The carrying of the Reform Bill through Committee in
the House of Commons was the work of Disraeli, and of
Disraeli alone. He was always in his place, never
at a loss, but always armed with facts and arguments ;
full of tact and conciliation where these were required,
or of retort and sarcasm when a wrecking amendment
was persisted in ; but on indifferent points of detail,
no one in the House so indifferent as he. It was
estimated that he spoke on the Bill more than 300
times. It was what in modern slang is called a ' one-
man show,' as was pointed out in quaint, but forcible,
language by Bernal Osborne. He bade the House rely
on the Chancellor of the Exchequer, who had ' lugged up
that great omnibus-full of stupid, heavy country gentlemen,' and converted them into Radical Reformers. ' In
fact, the Chancellor of the Exchequer is the Ministry by
himself, for it could not exist a day without him, and all
the rest who sit near him are the most respectable pawns
on the board, their opinion being not worth a pin.'

One shrewd observer insisted that Disraeli's capacity
for silence, even more than his power of speech, was the
principal agent in carrying the Bill.

But for this power to hold his tongue, Mr. Disraeli would
never have got this Bill through the House. Moreover, he
seems to be able to silence his colleagues' tongues, either by
positive and inexorable command or by the mesmeric power
of example. In reviewing the course of this Bill, it is astonishing to find how little speaking came from the Treasury Bench.
. . . The Chancellor of the Exchequer has ruled his Ministry
with despotic power. ' You must speak,' he seemed to say
to one, and he spoke. To others he issued no commands,
and they were silent. . . . Further, it has been remarked
that, whatever may have been done in the Cabinet, in the
House the leader appeared to consult none of his colleagues.

. . . In short, Disraeli has steered this Bill through himself; alone he did it; and with what wonderful skill none but those who watched him from night to night can know.[1]

This observer adds that there was generally no one present with Disraeli in his private room during the progress of the Bill except his secretary Corry, and Lambert, of the Poor Law Board, who was greatly consulted as a statistician. There was also, no doubt, almost always Thring, the draftsman, who has recorded that Disraeli 'seemed to have an intuitive perception of what would pass the House of Commons; but he cared nothing for the details of a Bill, and, once satisfied with the principle, he troubled comparatively little about its arrangements and construction.' Thring added:

It was in course of preparing this Reform Bill of 1867, and watching every night its passage through Parliament, that I had ample means, for the first and last time, of judging of Mr. D.'s characteristics. I was constantly struck by his great skill in overcoming difficulties as they arose in Parliament, and his tact in meeting, by judicious compromises, the objections of his opponents. His courtesy to me never failed, even under the most trying circumstances.

By the middle of July the long labour of Committee and Report was over, and the Bill was set down for third reading on the 15th. The debate resolved itself into a violent attack on Disraeli and the Government, conducted by Cranborne and Lowe. Cranborne said that when the Bill was read a second time it bristled with securities which had all now disappeared. He attributed the parentage of the measure, in the shape in which it emerged from Committee, to Gladstone, whose demands, he said, had all been conceded. He omitted, by the way, to mention that Gladstone's principal demand had been for a £5 value for the borough franchise, and that this had been successfully resisted. If the concession of Gladstone's demands and the adoption of Bright's principles were a triumph, then the Conservative Party had never won so signal a triumph as this. The party had been misled by

[1] W. White's *Inner Life of the House of Commons*, Vol. II., pp. 76, 77.

the mystery and reticence of its leaders.   There had been
a political betrayal without a parallel in our annals.
Lowe said they were entering upon an epoch of revolution.
We must educate our new masters in order to avert the
consequences of a measure which every honest and educated Englishman regarded with shame, scorn, and indignation.   Bright hailed the Bill as giving the best permanent foundation for the suffrage, though he would
have agreed to a more limited measure ; and Elcho, as a
leading Adullamite, accepted the Bill as a satisfactory
settlement, and said the course of events had justified
the action his party had taken last year.   He especially
selected for praise Disraeli's management of the question
as contrasted with Gladstone's.

   Disraeli's speech was naturally, in form, an answer to
the diatribes of Cranborne and Lowe.   He was easily
able to show that he himself for the last twenty years
had steadily spoken in favour of increasing the representation of the working classes; and he added that statement
about the discussion of household suffrage in the Cabinet
of 1858–59 on which we have already commented.   The
Government did not believe in the enfranchisement of
a favoured portion of the working classes, a sort of Pretorian Guard.   That would have been the result of setting
up a limit of an £8, £7, £6, or £5 value, such as Gladstone's
proposal of the present year.   It was better to appeal to the
sympathies of the great body of the people.   He gave the
following interesting account of the evolution of the Bill.

   We acceded to power last year, and we found it was absolutely necessary to deal with this question ; we came into power
unpledged, and I have heard, with some astonishment, reproaches in regard to our change of opinion.   I am not here to
defend, to vindicate, or even to mitigate, every expression I may
have used on this subject during the course of many years, but I
can appeal to the general tenor of the policy we have recommended.   I have always said that the question of Parliamentary Reform was one which it was quite open to the Conservative party to deal with.   I have said so in this House, and
on the hustings, in the presence of my countrymen, a hundred
times.   I have always said, and I say so now, that, when you

come to a settlement of this question, you cannot be bound
to any particular scheme, as if you were settling the duties on
sugar; but dealing with the question on great constitutional
principles, and which I hope to show have not been deviated
from, you must deal with it also with a due regard to the spirit
of the time and the requirements of the country. . . . Believing that another failure would be fatal, not merely to the
Conservative party, but most dangerous to the country, we resolved to settle it if we could. . . . Knowing the majority was
against us, and knowing the difficulties we had to deal with, being in a minority — and even with a majority our predecessors
had not succeeded — after due deliberation we were of opinion
that the only mode of arriving at a settlement was to take the
House into council with us, and by our united efforts, and the
frank communication of ideas, to attain a satisfactory solution.
. . . It was in harmony with these views that I placed resolutions on the table. It is very true that at that time — in the
month of March or February, it may be — you derided those
resolutions and ridiculed the appeal; but reflection proved the
policy was just, and you have adopted it. . . . You have all
co-operated with us, and it is by that frank and cordial co-
operation that we have arrived at a third reading.

Disraeli had no difficulty in exposing the inaccuracy
of Cranborne's statement that the securities in the original Bill had been 'obsequiously' yielded to Gladstone's
'imperious dictation.' The preceding narrative has
shown in how many cases it was the feeling, sometimes
the almost unanimous feeling, of the Conservative party
itself which determined the action of the Government, so
that Disraeli could plead that 'the party on this question
has always been in advance of the Government. There
is not a security that we have proposed that has not been
objected to by the Conservative party.' If the policy of
the Bill of 1859, retaining the £10 limit, could no longer
be upheld, then there was no safe resting-place till rating
household suffrage. In regard to redistribution, there
had been no disfranchisement, but there had been a very
considerable attempt to do justice to the inadequately
represented millions of dwellers in the counties. He ridiculed Lowe's speech, with its classical tags, as that of
'some inspired schoolboy,' and poured contempt upon its
'doleful vaticinations.'

For my part, I do not believe that the country is in danger.
I think England is safe in the race of men who inhabit her;
that she is safe in something much more precious than her
accumulated capital — her accumulated experience; she is safe
in her national character, in her fame, in the traditions of a
thousand years, and in that glorious future which I believe
awaits her.

The Bill passed the third reading in the Commons
without a division; it had yet to run the gauntlet of the
House of Lords.   Undoubtedly the vast extension which
it had received in Committee had alarmed even some of
the most convinced friends of a real settlement; and it
was thought that the Lords might reasonably reduce its
proportions.   The Queen wrote to Derby that she did
not wish to say anything that could embarrass the Government, and that she felt it would be impossible to
recede from the concessions already made to popular
feeling; but that she hoped Ministers would give a fair
consideration to any amendments which might be proposed in the House of Lords 'with a view to avert the
danger which many people apprehend from the great
increase of democratic power.'   Derby, however, as well
as Disraeli, realised that it was essential there should be
no narrowing of the scope of the Bill; and the thorough
fashion in which, after its transmogrification in the Commons, it was adopted by the most powerful man in
the Lords, made its acceptance there fairly safe, unless
the great Whig peers could bring themselves to play over
again, in concert with the Tory seceders, the game in
which Gladstone had, not without humiliation, failed.
Derby called his followers in the Upper House together,
and urgently requested their support for a Bill which,
he said, notwithstanding Gladstone's factiousness, the
Government had, by making fair concessions and owing
to the inimitable tact and temper of the Chancellor of
the Exchequer, passed with the practically unanimous
consent of the House of Commons.   The high Tory peers
grumbled, but came to heel.   The threatened Whig opposition collapsed; as Disraeli wrote to Derby, 'the younger

generation, Granville, Argyll, and Co., shrank from the too ridiculous climax — of a Reform Bill in 1867 opposed by Lord Grey and the Whigs.' Accordingly, in spite of an inopportune fit of gout which compelled Derby for a while to hand over the conduct of the measure to Malmesbury, the Bill passed through all its stages with comparatively small amendment.

The most notable incidents of the passage of the Bill through the Lords were a speech of dark foreboding by Shaftesbury, the emergence of Cairns as a strong defender of the scheme, and two characteristic sayings by Derby, one related by Granville, but not denied, the other uttered on the third reading by Derby himself. Granville's story was that Derby's answer to a Conservative friend, who reproached him with his revolutionary proposals, was merely, 'Don't you see how we have dished the Whigs?' The third reading speech admitted and defended the experimental character of the Bill: 'No doubt we are making a great experiment and taking a leap in the dark, but I have the greatest confidence in the sound sense of my fellow-countrymen, and I entertain a strong hope that the extended franchise which we are now conferring upon them will be the means of placing the institutions of this country on a firmer basis.'

The amendments of the Lords caused very little difficulty. The contentious ones were all rejected, though perfunctorily supported by Disraeli, with the exception of one proposed and carried by Cairns, giving a certain representation to minorities, by enacting that in the three-member constituencies, which were about a dozen in number, each elector should have only two votes. Disraeli did not himself approve this system any more than Gladstone and Bright, who strongly opposed it; but, in spite of having helped to defeat a somewhat similar amendment by Lowe, he was not sorry to try an experiment which proceeded from his friend Cairns, and to secure the acceptance of at least one of the Lords' contentious amendments. His sense of humour was, no

doubt, tickled by the fact that it would certainly give the third seat in his own constituency of Bucks to the Liberals — that third seat which, in the present Parliament, for the first time since his own first return in 1847, was filled by a Conservative. With this and a few other minor alterations, the Bill, which only dealt with England, became law on August 15, progress with the corresponding Bills for Scotland and Ireland being perforce postponed till the following session.

Ministers were, naturally, in the highest spirits at the Greenwich whitebait dinner. Stanley is said to have been the only Minister present who wore evening dress; so he was dubbed 'the Reverend Mr. Stanley,' called to the chair, and asked to say grace. Gordon, the Lord Advocate, sang a jovial Scotch song written for the occasion by Lord Neaves, the Judge, called 'The Ministerial Cogie' — 'cogie' meaning literally a small wooden drinking vessel, and metaphorically any pleasant mixture. 'The Bill is safe, the Bill is passed,' it began, and went on to celebrate the 'dishing' of the Whigs and the triumph of the Tories.

> Now from this day the country's sway
>   Belongs to no Whig fogie;
> And none can now of Tories say
>   They scrimped the people's cogie.

Gordon's demeanour was usually grave and austere, and it was noticed that the incongruity of the man and the song moved Disraeli to one of his very rare bursts of hearty laughter.

In a speech at the usual Mansion House banquet to Ministers just before the close of the session, Disraeli reviewed his great achievement, and related it to what had been his life-work in politics, the restoration of the Tory party to its due place in the government of the country. The claim to have terminated the monopoly of Liberalism is a repetition of the sentiments of his speech at Liverpool in the autumn of 1859; the vindication of Toryism as the national and popular party pervades all his political writings and speeches from first to last.

I have seen in my time several monopolies terminated, and recently I have seen the termination of the monopoly of Liberalism. Nor are we to be surprised when we see that certain persons who believed that they had an hereditary right, whenever it was necessary, to renovate the institutions of their country, should be somewhat displeased that any other persons should presume to interfere with those changes which, I hope in the spirit of true patriotism, they believed the requirements of the State rendered necessary. But I am sure that when the hubbub has subsided, when the shrieks and screams which were heard some time ago, and which have already subsided into sobs and sighs, shall be thoroughly appeased, nothing more terrible will be discovered to have occurred than that the Tory party has resumed its natural functions in the government of the country. For what is the Tory party unless it represents national feeling? If it do not represent national feeling, Toryism is nothing. It does not depend upon hereditary coteries of exclusive nobles. It does not attempt power by attracting to itself the spurious force which may accidentally arise from advocating cosmopolitan principles or talking cosmopolitan jargon. The Tory party is nothing unless it represent and uphold the institutions of the country. . . . I cannot help believing that, because my Lord Derby and his colleagues have taken a happy opportunity to enlarge the privileges of the people of England, we have not done anything but strengthen the institutions of the country, the essence of whose force is that they represent the interests and guard the rights of the people.

The party as a whole, though some were vindictive and many more bewildered over the great transformation scene of the year, were not unappreciative of the magnitude of their leaders' performance; and several demonstrations, especially in the great urban centres, were arranged in their honour, and in celebration of the passing of the Bill. The chief of these were in Lancashire, where Derby was naturally the principal figure, and in Edinburgh, where Disraeli was invited by his Scottish admirers to a banquet such as Edinburgh in former days had offered to statesmen of the calibre of Grey and Peel.

To Lord Derby.

CHANCELLOR OF THE EXCHEQUER, *Oct.* 18, 1867. — I congratulate you on the Manchester demonstration. It will do great good, especially at this moment. . . .

And I thank you for the kind manner in which you spoke of myself, and which you invariably do.[1]

I came up to town for change of air, for when the leaf falls I fall. I never can escape : luckily my attack is as regular as the trade winds, and occurs at a time when it little signifies, and can be kept secret. Unfortunately, this year I have something to do — the Edinburgh banquet. How I am to get there I know not, but I feel I shall. I think of troops that have marched thirty miles, and then, on empty stomachs, too, have to fight. They do fight, and often conquer.

Unfortunately, the Queen, I am sure entirely from kindness, and to do me honor at this particular moment, has asked me to pay a visit to Balmoral before the dinner, and to fix my time. This, I feel sure, would quite finish me, and I have written to General Grey, and have a hope his friendliness may extricate me from this overwhelming honor.[2] . . .

Disraeli's visit to Scotland was a memorable one. He had apparently never been in that country since the autumn of 1825, when, as a boy of twenty, he went north on two occasions to see Scott and Lockhart on Murray's behalf in connection with the founding of the *Representative*.[3] The miscarriage of that undertaking had probably given him rather a distaste for Scotland, which the ingrained Liberalism of the Scotch, especially of the working classes among them, did nothing to remove ; and he was, moreover, throughout his life, wont to jar upon the feelings of ultra-patriotic Scotsmen by almost invariably using 'England' as a short term to express the United Kingdom of Great Britain and Ireland, in that respect erring — if it be an error — in company, it is only fair to say, with most of the leading statesmen of the time. But his democratic Toryism had met with a ready response from the younger generation of Scottish Conservatives, represented by men like Bannerman-Robertson and Stormonth-Darling, both eventually law officers and Judges ; and, despite the ridicule of the leading Scottish journal, the *Scotsman*, and the lukewarmness or opposi-

---

[1] Derby said that it was mainly due to Disraeli's tact, temper, and judgment, that the arduous undertaking in which they were engaged had not resulted, instead of a triumphant success, in disastrous failure.

[2] The Queen excused Disraeli from attendance at Balmoral.

[3] See Vol. I., ch. 5.

tion of certain influential Conservatives, such as the Duke of Buccleuch and Disraeli's old friend Sir George Sinclair, the banquet, which was presided over by Sir William Stirling Maxwell, was an enormous success.

Disraeli, in his speech, vindicated the historical title of the Tories to deal with Reform, from the first efforts of Bolingbroke and Wyndham, through the policy of the younger Pitt, down to his own and Derby's action. Dealing with the most recent history, he said :

I had to prepare the mind of the country, and to educate — if it be not arrogant to use such a phrase — to educate our party. It is a large party, and requires its attention to be called to questions of this kind with some pressure. I had to prepare the mind of Parliament and the country on this question of Reform. This was not only with the concurrence of Lord Derby, but of my colleagues.

The points on which Disraeli claimed to have educated his party were certain principles of Reform, including the necessity of comprehensiveness, of increased county representation, and of the rating basis ; not, however, of household suffrage, as has often been wrongly asserted. But he doubtless meant to hint, and the world at once acknowledged, that the educating process had not been confined to Reform. The phrase aptly described the whole course of his leadership of the party out of the narrow policies of the late forties into the broad and national programme of the 1866 Administration.

Two striking passages followed, the first on the principle of the Bill :

When you try to settle any great question, there are two considerations which statesmen ought not to forget. First of all, let your plan be founded upon some principle. But that is not enough. Let it also be a principle that is in harmony with the manners and customs of the people you are attempting to legislate for. Now I say, when you come to this question of the suffrage for boroughs, there is a principle in saying a man shall have a vote who has, by his residence and his contribution to local taxation, proved that he is interested in the welfare of his community. That man is a man whom you may trust in preference to a migratory pauper. That is a prin-

ciple; and then, if you can apply that principle in harmony
with the manners and customs of your country, then I say
that you have the chance of a solution — a happy solution —
of a great question.   When you find it was an old custom of
the country that the householder should possess this suffrage
— that the man who, by his residence and his rate, proved he
was one who, on an average, might fairly be looked upon as a
responsible and trustworthy individual — you had your principle, and you had your traditionary practice to consecrate
your principle.   A rating and residential borough franchise
was not new even in modern times.   It had been tried in
the Municipal Act.

The acceptance of the Hodgkinson amendment, he
maintained, was the logical consequence of this principle:

We had insisted that no man should vote who did not pay
rates.   We had sympathised with the compound householder
by having prepared clauses by which his vote might be facilitated, and if he chose to come forward and commit suicide,
and say, 'I will no longer be a compound householder, but I
will give up these privileges and pay rates,' what was our
duty?   It would have been most inconsistent in us to resist
such a proposal.   I say that the compound householder bowing down, and giving up his peculiar position, and saying,
'In order to exercise the suffrage I will pay the rate,' was the
very triumph of the principle of our Bill.

These plain statements, Disraeli proceeded, disposed
of the 'enormous nonsense' which had been circulated
through the country by Liberals and by Conservative
seceders.   If the principle of the Bill was thus maintained,
what became of the talk of the unprincipled withdrawal
of checks and securities, 'the betrayal of our friends, who
insisted upon being betrayed'?   The two great quarter-
lies, Whig and Tory, had just published articles, both
harping on this same string, the article in the *Quarterly
Review* being Cranborne's famous philippic, 'The Conservative Surrender.'   The nature of the argument is sufficiently indicated by the title; the pungency of the writing
rivalled the writer's first attack on Disraeli in the same
review seven years before.   Disraeli's comment was conceived in his happiest vein.

He who has written the summary of the session in the
Edinburgh is not mounted on the fiery barb of Francis Jeffrey;

he is rather placed upon a prancing hearse horse, with which
he consummates the entombment of Whig principles.   The
'Conservative Surrender' . . . is what one would call a *replica*.
You have had the subject treated in speeches, in articles, in
reviews, and sometimes in manifestoes.   The colouring is not
without charm, but the drawing is inaccurate, the perspective
is false, the subject is monotonous. . . .   I should say that
article was written by a very clever man who has made a very
great mistake.   The leaders of the Conservative party are
false; the Conservative party are false.   They do not know
that they have been abused; they have not recognised that
their confidence has been betrayed and outraged.   I see many
gentlemen here who have been, no doubt, inspectors, like myself, as magistrates, of peculiar asylums, who meet there some
cases which I have always thought at the same time the most
absurd and the most distressing; it is when the lunatic believes
all the world is mad, and that he himself is sane.

But to pass from such gloomy imagery: really these *Edinburgh* and *Quarterly Reviews,* no man admires them more than
myself.   But I admire them as I do first-rate, first-class post-
houses, which in old days, for half a century or so — to use a
Manchester phrase — carried on a roaring trade.   Then there
comes some revolution or progress which no person can ever
have contemplated.   They find things are altered.   They do
not understand them, and, instead of that intense competition
and mutual vindictiveness which before distinguished them,
they suddenly quite agree.   The boots of the 'Blue Boar' and
the chambermaid of the 'Red Lion' embrace, and are quite
in accord in this — in denouncing the infamy of railroads.

Towards the close of his speech Disraeli looked to the
future:

In a progressive country change is constant; and the great
question is, not whether you should resist change which is inevitable, but whether that change should be carried out in
deference to the manners, the customs, the laws, the traditions of the people, or in deference to abstract principles and
arbitrary and general doctrines.   The one is a national system;
the other, to give it an epithet, a noble epithet which perhaps
it may deserve, is a philosophic system.   Both have great
advantages; the national party is supported by the fervour
of patriotism; the philosophical party has a singular exemption from the force of prejudice.

Disraeli concluded by recalling the 'three master influences which have at all times guided and controlled
all other powers and passions.'   These were, as he had

said in a speech[1] in Bucks in 1863, Industry, Liberty, and Religion. 'So long as this sacred combination influences the destiny of this country, it will not die.'

The Edinburgh functions included the conferment of the freedom of the city by the Corporation, and of the honorary degree of LL.D. by the University, and also an evening meeting of working men in the Music Hall. A Conservative open meeting in Scotland was at that time an entirely new experiment, but Disraeli fairly captivated his audience.

From Mrs. Dundas of Arniston.

ARNISTON, GOREBRIDGE, N.B., *Nov.* 7, 1867. — . . . Mr. Dundas . . . returned from the meeting of working men, much pleased with the enthusiastic reception you met with.

I was much amused a few days afterwards at hearing a very Radical servant in Edinburgh say he had gone to the meeting, and he said he knew plenty of fellows went there to make a row. ' But,' quoth my friend, 'I came back *almost* a Tory. I was prejudeeced against the Chancellor; but you know he jist showed sich tack (? tact) that he made us all think like him. I never saw sich tack before in my life.' . . .

The Dundases of Arniston had entertained the Disraelis for the first few days of the Scottish expedition; for the remainder the visitors were the guests of Lord Advocate Gordon at his house in Edinburgh. There they met the young Lord Bute, whose story suggested the novel of *Lothair*, on which Disraeli was engaged less than two years later; and there he and his wife came under the friendly but critical inspection of a leading Scottish literary man of the day, Sir John Skelton, who, in the *Table Talk of Shirley*,[2] has given us a vivid and penetrating sketch of the Disraeli of 1867, 'clari giganteo triumpho.'

Old Lady Ruthven was there — a miraculous old woman. She and Mrs. Disraeli, sitting over the fire with their feet on the fender, making between them the funniest pair — the witches in *Macbeth*, or what you will. And the potent wizard himself, with his olive complexion and coal-black eyes, and the mighty dome of his forehead (no Christian temple, be sure), is unlike any living creature one has met. I had never

---

[1] See above, p. 364.   [2] P. 247.

seen him in the daylight before, and the daylight accentuates
his strangeness. The face is more like a mask than ever, and
the division between him and mere mortals more marked. I
would as soon have thought of sitting down at table with
Hamlet, or Lear, or the Wandering Jew. He was indeed more
than cordial; especially appreciative of the Scottish allies—'rari
nantes in gurgite vasto'—who had stood by him through thick
and thin. 'I fancied, indeed, till last night, that north of the
border I was not loved; but last night made amends for much.
We were so delighted with our reception, Mrs. Disraeli and I,
that after we got home we actually danced a jig (or was it a
hornpipe?) in our bedroom.'

They say, and say truly enough, What an actor the man is!
and yet the ultimate impression is of absolute sincerity and
unreserve. Grant Duff will have it that he is an alien.
What's England to him, or he to England? There is just
where they are wrong. Whig or Radical or Tory don't matter
much, perhaps; but this mightier Venice—this Imperial
Republic on which the sun never sets—that vision fascinates
him, or I am much mistaken. England is the Israel of his
imagination, and he will be the Imperial Minister before he
dies—if he gets the chance.

Skelton had a real insight into Disraeli's character and
policy; but greater literary men showed less discernment.
Carlyle prophesied woe in his 'Shooting Niagara.' A
Conservative English poet, Coventry Patmore, was horrified. He dubbed 1867

> The year of the great crime,
> When the false English nobles, and their Jew,
> By God demented, slew
> The trust they stood twice pledged to keep from wrong.

Patmore, at any rate, realised that 'the Jew' could not
have carried the Reform Bill without the ' English nobles.'
Speaking broadly, the party went with Disraeli ; and
Derby's own class followed the leader whom they trusted.
The landed aristocracy, no doubt, regarded with considerable misgiving the policy which they nevertheless accepted ; by the urban Tories of the rank and file, the back-
bone of the Tory democracy, it was welcomed, in many
quarters with enthusiasm. The active dissentients were
very few in number ; but they included the most incisive
writer of the party, and were supported by its most

weighty organ.. Posterity has been asked to look at the
conduct of the Conservative leaders through the spectacles
either of Lord Salisbury and the *Quarterly*, or of the
Whigs and Liberals who were 'dished,' or of idolaters of
the middle class, like Lowe. What Disraeli did in 1867
has been treated, accordingly, with the same unfairness
as what he did in 1846 and 1852.

What is the trust the leaders are charged with betray-
ing? The Conservatives certainly had no trust to resist
Reform. Disraeli had preached the doctrine that Reform
was no Whig preserve for twenty years, and the party
had definitely accepted it in 1859. Where the leaders are
vulnerable is on the score of surrendering the government of the country to the control of mere numbers. They
had protested against any policy which should entrust
power to a single class; they had advocated admitting
freely the more educated and skilled members of the
working classes, but not the working classes in bulk.
Disraeli's speeches and addresses, especially during
the Palmerston régime, at the General Election of 1865,
and when the 1866 Bill was before the House, abounded,
as we have seen, in this sense. Reform should be
lateral; there should be extension, not degradation;
the choicest members of the working class should be
freely admitted, but there should be no undistinguishing
reduction of the franchise; opinion, not numbers, should
be represented; votes should be weighed, not counted.
In fact, the policy of the Pretorian guard of working men,
which Disraeli deprecated and ridiculed in his speech on
the third reading in 1867, was apparently his own policy,
from the days when he first suggested fancy franchises in
1848 down to the debates on the Bill of 1866; fancy franchises were even introduced into the Bill of 1867 as originally explained to the House of Commons. It was a
policy for which there was much to be said; so thorough
and consistent a friend of the working men as Shaftesbury
held to it throughout, and denounced the Bill of 1867 for
its departure from it.

But no policy of the kind could be a permanent settlement; and in all his previous efforts at Reform, particularly in the Bill of 1859, Disraeli, did not aim at a permanent settlement, but at a temporary expedient, which should merely satisfy the immediate demand. The aim of all Russell's various Bills since 1852 had been the same; there was no pretence of laying down a final principle. But this time the question was to be settled. The great debates of 1866 and the continued agitation in the country had prepared men's minds to expect a definite solution. The Republicans of the Northern States, whose apparent failure had so long discredited democratic government, had at length emerged triumphant, and thereby re-established the reputation of their institutions. The British artisan, with manhood suffrage prevalent in the two countries, America and France, which most influenced him, would insist before long upon a like enfranchisement, unless a broad and satisfactory basis were conceded. There is a passage in 'The Conservative Surrender,' where the writer is contrasting the general opposition to household suffrage in 1866 with its general acceptance in 1867, which has a significance hardly perceived by himself. When household suffrage was openly proposed by the Ministry, he writes, 'it was received with much murmuring indeed in private, but externally with almost universal acceptance. Only a few scattered men here and there in Parliament ventured to oppose it.' He rejects the simple and obvious explanation that it was generally recognised to be the settlement which the situation required.

The credit for first recognising that the hour had come for a real settlement is due, as we have seen, primarily to the Queen, and next to Derby. Disraeli was reluctant to admit the weight of the accumulating evidence. His attitude in the autumn of 1866 makes indeed a serious deduction from his reputation for foresight; and many of his difficulties in the session of 1867, and of the inconsistencies into which he and his colleagues were betrayed

in debate, sprang from what Cranborne deservedly called
'the error of attempting to frame a Reform Bill during
the week previous to its production.' But, when Disraeli did finally acknowledge that decisive action was
necessary, he was prompt, in conjunction with Derby,
in sweeping aside temporary expedients, and founding himself upon an abiding principle. There is no
evidence to show whether the definite acceptance of
rating household suffrage is due rather to Disraeli or
to Derby; both based themselves upon it in January,
1867. Both, too, cordially accepted the only method by
which a settlement could be affected—the policy of wel-
coming, and deferring to, the co-operation of the House
of Commons in the application of the principle adopted.
But Derby was not so quick as Disraeli to see that the
frank acceptance of this method could hardly fail to involve the disappearance of checks and securities to which
he originally attached importance. The actual determination of what amendments should be accepted and
what resisted necessarily devolved mainly on the leader
of the House of Commons; and for the shape in which the
Bill emerged from Committee—for the fact, indeed, that
it emerged with safety at all — Disraeli was almost solely
responsible. But that he had Derby's support throughout is clear from the whole-hearted fashion in which the
Prime Minister urged his followers in the Lords to pass
the Bill substantially as it stood.

When it was a question of a permanent settlement,
numbers necessarily became a secondary consideration.
A principle had to be found that would not be disturbed:
if possible, a principle that would work automatically by
admitting gradually all desirable citizens. Rating household suffrage, in the actual state of the community, admirably fulfilled the conditions. The extensive use of the
system of compound householding would apparently prevent the immediate swamping of the ten-pounders by the
swarm of new voters; while the provisions for enabling
the compound householder to get upon the rate-book

would, it was hoped, prevent a feeling of grievance and enable all the more responsible among them to acquire the franchise sooner or later. Unfortunately neither Derby nor Disraeli, owing to the hurry in which their Bill was improvised, realised at first how very local and capricious the distribution of the compound householding system was; how the application of their principle would enfranchise practically the whole of one community and leave another, whose circumstances were in every other respect similar, as completely unenfranchised as before. As the discussion proceeded, it became clear that the facilities provided in the Bill would not meet the grievance; and Disraeli was faced with the alternative of accepting the domination of numbers, which he deprecated, or abandoning the idea of a permanent settlement. When the first alternative was presented in such a form as to preserve the principle of the Bill, and subject the compound householder to the steadying and conservative influence of personal payment of rates, he could not hesitate; and his prompt action, taken on his own responsibility, carried not only Derby's assent, but that of the whole Cabinet.

Undoubtedly the upshot of the Act was, roughly speaking, to double the constituency by adding about a million new voters, mostly of one class — a result which neither Derby nor Disraeli had originally contemplated, but which they had reached by a perfectly open and honourable road. Disraeli, at any rate, was confident of the ultimate benefit both to the country and to the party. He wrote to a working men's club about this time: 'None are so interested in maintaining the institutions of the country as the working classes. The rich and the powerful will not find much difficulty under any circumstances in maintaining their rights, but the privileges of the people can only be defended and secured by popular institutions.' He kept ever before his eyes the establishment of the Conservative party on a national and popular basis. Some weeks before the acceptance of the

Hodgkinson amendment he told his friend Beauchamp that he now began to see his way to realize the dream of his life. Ever since the reactionary proceedings of the Liverpool Administration, the Tory party had been associated in the popular mind with a policy of exclusion and restriction. Peel had endeavoured to remove the reproach, but he had gone too fast and too far for his party; and the Whigs regained and held the allegiance of the middle-class electorate. Since 1846 all Disraeli's efforts and combinations had been unavailing to obtain a majority at the polls. Now was the supreme moment to show that, however much Conservatism revered our institutions, it did not distrust the people. Events have largely justified Disraeli's policy. The constituency which the Reform Act of 1867 created, and which was logically completed by the extension of household franchise to the counties in 1884, gave the Conservative party, either alone or in alliance with the Unionist Liberals, majorities at four General Elections — 1874, 1886, 1895, and 1900; insuring a fair spell of power to Disraeli himself, and a much longer tenure, by one of the caprices of fortune, to the statesman who worked his hardest against Disraeli to prevent that constituency from coming into being — Lord Salisbury. The existence, in considerable numbers, of the Conservative working man, whom it was the fashion of the Liberals of the sixties to treat as a myth, has been shown over and over again by the immense polls cast for the party in the largest urban constituencies. If the association of aristocracy and democracy which Disraeli brought about has given Conservative, as well as national, policy a strong bias in the direction of social reform, that is a result which would have been thoroughly acceptable to the author of *Sybil*.

Whatever might be thought of the Bill, there was no doubt or question of the personal triumph of Disraeli. In a cartoon labelled 'D'Israel-i in Triumph,' *Punch* depicted him as the Egyptian Sphinx being dragged to

D'ISRAEL-I IN TRIUMPH;

Reproduced, by kind permission of the Proprietors, from 'Punch,' June 15, 1867.

THE MODERN SPHYNX.

(*Suggested by* MR. POYNTER'S *admirable Picture of* "*Israel in Egypt.*")

the Temple of Reform by a straining team of eminent
politicians of all parties, some pulling willingly, some
under fear of Derby's whip. What were the facts ? Every
Government of the last fifteen years had taken the Reform question in hand ; and every Government had failed
with more or less of discredit.   Disraeli, with a majority of
seventy against him, had carried his Bill ; a Bill, moreover,
that was no temporary makeshift, but established the
borough franchise on a basis which has not in essentials
been altered through a generation and a half, and which
seems likely to be permanent.   Disraeli and Gladstone
had definitely measured their strength against each
other over this issue ;   and victory had rested unmis-
takably with Disraeli.   'Why is Gladstone like a tele-
scope ? ' was a riddle which had a great vogue in Tory
circles.   'Because Disraeli draws him out, looks through
him and shuts him up.'   Gladstone's miscarriage in
1866 served brilliantly to set off Disraeli's achievement in 1867.   If any contemporary was a good judge of
success, it was Bishop Wilberforce.   Writing in August
at the end of the session, he declared : ' The most wonderful thing is the rise of Disraeli.   It is not the mere
assertion of talent, as you hear so many say.   It seems
to me quite beside that.   He has been able to teach
the House of Commons almost to ignore Gladstone ;
and at present lords it over him.'   Gladstone talked to
his own friends of 'the diabolical cleverness of Dizzy.'
But, as the Bishop saw, there was more than cleverness.
There was even more than wit, humour, sarcasm, and
irony.   There were good temper, patience, tact, resource,
judgment, resolution, courage, and loyalty ; in fact — in
spite of the violent and unfounded reproaches of tricki-
ness and of (in Gladstone's phrase) 'revolting cynicism' —
there was what is summed up in one word, character.

Gigantic as was the task of carrying a comprehensive
Reform Bill through a Parliament in which Ministers
had a large majority against them, it by no means represented their sole achievement for the session.   As in 1852

and in 1858, Disraeli's judicious management of the House and the energy of his colleagues succeeded in putting on the statute-book several useful measures besides.   The social reform which Disraeli's preaching and practice had made an integral part of Conservative policy was forwarded by legislation materially extending the operation of the Factory Acts, and by establishing proper provision in London for the sick and insane poor ; and a Trades Union Commission was appointed.   But by far the most important measure, after the Reform Bill, was a Bill which Carnarvon prepared and introduced in the House of Lords, though he had ceased to be Minister when it became law, to federate the North American Colonies into one Dominion.   In connection with the federation, Parliament also guaranteed a loan for a railway from Quebec to Halifax.   The policy of these Canadian measures was one in which both front benches concurred ;   Carnarvon was carrying through what Cardwell had initiated.   But Radicals and economists, Bright and Lowe, sniffed at the proposals, and suggested that these Colonies should rather be encouraged either to join the United States, or to set up for themselves.   Disraeli and the Government, on the other hand, were patriotically carrying to a further stage the policy which, after the establishment of British Columbia, they had announced in the Queen's Speech in the summer of 1858 — that British North America should be occupied 'in an unbroken chain, from the Atlantic to the Pacific, by a loyal and industrious population of subjects of the British Crown.' [1]

There was, however, at least one important measure which Government failed to pass, in circumstances explained by Disraeli to the Queen :

To Queen Victoria.

DOWNING STREET, *Aug.* 16, 1867. — The Chancellor of the Exchequer, with his humble duty to your Majesty.

He has now virtually brought the business of the House of

----

[1] See above, p. 170.

Commons to a conclusion, and it will only meet on Monday to complete the business of the House of Lords.

He regrets that H.M.'s Government were obliged to relinquish the Parks Bill yesterday, after a division which showed that the House was desirous of legislation on the subject, but it was impossible to proceed with the Bill without considerably lengthening the session.

The truth is that the whole dealing with this subject, from the commencement, has been a series of errors, originating in a fundamental one. The matter was originally treated by your Majesty's Government without sufficient knowledge and sufficient thought. . . . It will require great tact and temper to bring all this right, but it will be done. . . .

Disraeli found time, in this busy session, to explain to his peer colleagues the constitutionality of the use of proxies in the Upper House; but the common-sense view prevailed that lords who wished to record their votes ought to come and hear the arguments, and the practice was discontinued.

To Lord Malmesbury.

July 10, 1867. — The Constitution of this country is a monarchy, modified in its action by the co-ordinate authority of the Estates of the Realm. An Estate is a political order invested with privilege for a public purpose.

There are three Estates: the Lords Spiritual, the Lords Temporal, and the Commons. The Estates of the Lords Spiritual and Temporal being very limited in number, their members can easily meet in their own chamber. The Estate of the Commons, being, on the contrary, very numerous, choose, for convenience, representatives instead of holding general meetings, like the Polish Diets.

The House of Commons is not an Estate of the Realm; its members are only the proxies of an Estate. The Lords, in using proxies, possess and exercise the same privilege as the Commons, no more; and if it is not convenient for them to attend the meetings of their orders, they have the right to choose their representatives.[1] . . .

To Sir Stafford Northcote.

July 20, 1867. — I can't refrain from congratulating you on the brilliant success of your fête,[2] one of the most striking

---

[1] *Memoirs of an Ex-Minister*, under date.

[2] A ball at the India Office in honour of the Sultan of Turkey, who paid a visit this summer to England.

festivals of the century—if, indeed, ever exceeded at any
time.   The space, the proportion, beauty of form and color,
and the glittering guests, produced a *coup d'œil* unrivalled ;
heightened by the occasion so strange and picturesque.

The admirable arrangements, so perfect and so unusual,
and which put everyone at their ease, were worthy of the historic scene.

The long session did not close till August 21, and after
his Herculean exertions Disraeli was glad indeed to escape
to the repose of Hughenden.   But the repose was rudely
broken before many days had passed.   The Queen's
Speech had contained an ominous paragraph about the
British captives detained by King Theodore of Abyssinia.
Her Majesty was advised to express regret that her efforts
to obtain their release had, so far, proved ineffectual,
and to add that she had found it necessary to address
to Theodore 'a peremptory demand for their immediate
liberation, and to take measures for supporting that
demand, should it ultimately be found necessary to resort
to force.'   By the beginning of September it became clear
that Theodore would not yield, and preparations were in
progress for an expedition from India.

To Lord Derby.

Confidential.   HUGHENDEN, *Sept.* 8, 1867.— So long as there
was a wild chance of the captives being released, I would not
trouble you ; but now, when that hope seems over, I must call
your consideration to the difficult and dangerous position to
which, it seems to me, your Government is drifting.

We are carrying on a war, and an expensive war, without
the sanction of Parliament.

I feel persuaded that this is exactly a condition of affairs
which, in February next, the whole 'Liberal' party will
resent; and they will do it under the leadership of Gladstone,
who, from the line which he pursued in the instance of the
Persian War, will advance, in this case, with additional
authority.

I see only one mode of extricating ourselves from this impending peril, and that is a very disagreeable one.   Parliament ought, in my opinion, to be called together as soon as
practicable.

The refusal of the ultimatum, and the act of war consequent
thereon, would be the logical occasion.

The earlier the Houses are summoned, the more anxious they will be to get away again.

At present the contemplated expedition is popular with the country, and the expenditure already incurred would not only be condoned, but might, under the peculiar circumstances, be justified.

From Lord Derby.

Confidential. KNOWSLEY, *Sept.* 10, 1867. — . . . One of the severest and most painful attacks of gout that I have had for years. In point of fact, it has been long due, and my London doctor only succeeded in patching me up for the exigencies of the session, in which, however, he was happily successful. But if the increasing frequency of these attacks is to continue, I feel that the time cannot be far distant when I must seek for restoration to health in absolute withdrawal from the public service. In the meantime, while I remain in it, I will not shrink from any possible performance of its duties.

To Lord Derby.

HUGHENDEN, *Sept.* 14, 1867. — . . . I am selfish in hoping you will not quit public life, as my career will terminate with yours : but it is not for that reason that I beg you will let me know how you are getting on, by the 'ready and confidential pen' to which I offer my sympathies and kindest regards.

Unfortunately the next news which the 'ready and confidential pen' of Lady Derby had to send Disraeli, on September 26, was that Derby had been once again attacked by 'the worst fit of gout he has had for a very long time,' and had no hope of leaving his bed for many days. Most of the arrangements for the November session had to be made, therefore, by Disraeli. As it was clear that Parliament could not have its attention confined to the single question of Abyssinia, it was decided that the form the sitting should assume should be that of the commencement of the session of 1868, and therefore a regular Queen's Speech would be necessary, with a programme of legislation. 'You cannot introduce great changes,' as Stanley wrote on September 24, 'dependent on the decision of the legislature, because that legislature is itself about to be superseded ; ' 'measures of practical utility and second-rate importance are those which seem

most likely to succeed, and most suitable to the circumstances.'

The session was to open on Tuesday, November 19;
and, the week before, Mrs. Disraeli, who was now
seventy-five, and who had just been through all the
excitements of the Scottish expedition, was struck
down by serious illness. Her condition grew worse,
and Disraeli appealed to Stanley 'as a comrade in arms,
and the friend of my public life,' to take his place at
the official dinner of the leader of the House on the eve
of the session. 'This has been,' he added, 'a critical
day in my wife's life, but not a bad one. There seems
a favorable turn, and I count almost on being in my
place to-morrow.' His hopes were justified, and he was
able to attend the debate on the Address, and to hear
and respond, with tears (it was noted) in his eyes, to
the sympathetic allusion which Gladstone made to Mrs.
Disraeli's condition. There was a strong mutual regard
between Mrs. Disraeli and Gladstone, which often exercised a mollifying influence at a crisis. She told Mr.
Kebbel that, after a sharp encounter in the House of
Commons, Gladstone would frequently come round to
Grosvenor Gate just to show he bore no malice. Mindful of this, Disraeli feared that his words in the House
had been an insufficient expression of gratitude for sympathy, and he wrote to amplify them, adding: 'My wife
had always a strong personal regard for you, and being
of a vivid and original character, she could comprehend
and value your great gifts and qualities.'[1] Gladstone
replied with grace and feeling: 'I have always been grateful for, and have sincerely reciprocated, Mrs. Disraeli's
regard, and during the recent crisis I was naturally mindful of it; but, even if I had not had the honour and pleasure of knowing her, it would have been impossible not to
sympathise with you at a moment when the fortitude
necessary to bear the labours and trials of your station
was subjected to a new burden of a character so crushing
and peculiar.'

[1] *Gladstone*, Book VII., ch. 3.

To Queen Victoria.

DOWNING STREET, *Nov.* 19, 1867. — The Chancellor of the Exchequer, with his humble duty to your Majesty.

The address to your Majesty's Speech was moved this evening by Mr. Hart Dyke, with grace and great ability : a young man, good-looking and very popular.   He gained the whole House.   M.P. for W. Kent.

Mr. Gladstone rose immediately, and made a very fair and just speech, and very kind and considerate to the Chancellor of the Exchequer, who was much touched by it.

And he begs leave to offer to your Majesty his very grateful thanks for all your Majesty's sympathy and gracious kindness in his great sorrow.

Your Majesty is too good.   This morning all seemed dark, and he was told to hope no more ; but within three hours of this there was a change, and everything became hopeful : a state of complete composure, but accompanied by increased strength.

Mrs. Disraeli got slowly better, but the anxiety, coupled with the pressure of public business, was too much for her husband, and after moving and carrying, in spite of Lowe's acrid opposition, the vote of credit of £2,000,000 for the Abyssinian Expedition, he collapsed himself. 'When I got home on Wednesday morning,' he wrote on November 30 to Stanley, 'in the cab in which you kindly tumbled me, I could not get out, and the driver, I fancy, thought I was drunk.'   He had to get his Secretary to the Treasury, Ward Hunt, to move the supplementary Budget.

To Sir Stafford Northcote.

(*In pencil.*) GROSVENOR GATE.   I am obliged to write to you on my back, and can't move, though I am otherwise well enough.   I am clear that nothing should be postponed.

Hunt will find no difficulty.   If he do, which is impossible, the House, I am sure, will take the division on a subsequent stage.

With regard to India, you are quite sufficient to fight the battle.   You know the case thoroughly, can speak as often as you like, and will win.

Sooner than have the business postponed, I will come down and be carried into the House.   I am serious in this, and beg, therefore, that you will let me know, that I may prepare.

Disraeli's illness was first diagnosed as sciatica, 'which frightens me,' he wrote humorously in pencil to Corry. 'James, my man, says his mother has the *sciatics*, and they last a year at least. But, though depressed, I have still faith in my star. I think it would be a ridiculous conclusion of my career; and, after all, ridicule settles nothing and nobody.' It was, however, not sciatica, but the statesman's foe, gout, which had attacked Disraeli. He and his wife were ill simultaneously in the Grosvenor Gate house, and she preserved the pencilled notes she received from him in a bundle labelled, 'Notes from dear Dizzy during our illness, when we could not leave our rooms. At the end of the month (Dec. 1867), we were both quite well.' Here are some specimens :

To Mrs. Disraeli.

Being on my back, pardon the pencil.

You have sent me the most amusing and charming letter I ever had. It beats Horace Walpole and Mme. de Sévigné.

Grosvenor Gate has become a hospital, but a hospital with you is worth a palace with anybody else. — Your own D.

I have had a sleepless night, and in agony the whole time. This morning the pain in the foot became greatly mitigated, and I dozed a little from 6 to 8. I have been nearly a week in bed, and am much worse than when I took to it. . . . My only consolation is that you are better and stronger. I never felt worse or more desponding. I am so irritated at the blundering manner in which I have been treated.

We have been separated four days, and under the same roof! How very strange!

To Sir Stafford Northcote.

(*In pencil.*) GROSVENOR GATE, *Dec* 7, 1867. — My dinner, consisting, I am sorry to say, of a tapioca pudding, need not have prevented us meeting yesterday; but my butler is a pompous booby. . . .

We shall remain in town at present. Mrs. Disraeli must not leave her room, tho' getting on well.

Disraeli had hardly recovered from his somewhat serious attack when he was called upon to deal with an

acute stage of the Fenian Conspiracy. The policy of outrage was transferred this autumn from Ireland to England, and culminated in two grave crimes — the murder of Police-Sergeant Brett at Manchester on September 18, and the blowing up of Clerkenwell Prison on December 13. Hitherto the measures for meeting the conspiracy had been left, in the main, to the very efficient Home Secretary, Gathorne Hardy. When the Clerkenwell explosion occurred, Derby was at Knowsley, and Disraeli, who was still in London, took the lead.

To Lord Derby.

Confidential. Dec. 14, 1867. Affairs here are very serious. I have contrived to get Colonel Fielding [1] over, though after inexpressible difficulties, and even now doubt whether I shall be able to set him to work, so great are the obstacles at every step; but it must be done. I have not been able to see Hardy until to-day, and, unfortunately, he has gone out of town again, but will be here on Monday.

It is my opinion that nothing effective can be done, in any way, in these dangers, if we don't get rid of Mayne.[2] I have spoken to Hardy, who says he 'wishes to God he would resign'; but surely, when even the safety of the State is at stake, there ought to be no false delicacy on such a point? I am too harassed to go into detail, which would require a volume on these matters. I think you ought to interfere.

I took upon myself to send Government aid to the Clerkenwell sufferers.

Confidential. Dec. 16, 1867. I will not trouble you with all the schemes, conferences, hopes, and disappointments, of this busy day. The result is that Colonel Fielding, who has just left my room, has undertaken to ascertain, if possible, the relation between the Fenians in England and the revolutionary societies abroad. . . .

There is no doubt that there is a system of organised incendiarism afloat, and we credibly hear of men coming from America, who are to take empty houses in various parts of London, and set them on fire, probably simultaneously. Colonel Fielding would have wished to have grappled with these impending calamities.

[1] He was brought from Ireland and put in charge of a special detective department to cope with Fenianism in England.

[2] Sir Richard Mayne, Commissioner of Police. He was seventy-one years old.

Many of the miscreants who are to perpetrate these crimes are now here, and are known — and we can't touch them. I think the Habeas Corpus ought to be suspended. However, the Colonel undertakes the original purpose. . . .

Most secret.   Dec. 16, 1867. — . . . You remember Mrs. Montgomery and her strange, but now not improbable, information a year ago.

She now informs me that, on Saturday morning last, a dying Irishman in one of the London hospitals confessed that, early in the session, there was a plot, quite matured, to blow up the Houses of Parliament by gunpowder introduced through the gas-pipes; but it failed through the House being two well watched. They are going, however, to blow up another prison, but which, though pressed, he refrained from declaring.

I have sent this information to Hardy, though silent as to the source. Gunpowder through gas-pipes is a new idea, and worth attention. . . .

Confidential.   Dec. 17, 1867. — Affairs appear to be so serious that last night the Cabinet in town (seven strong) agreed to meet and confer, mainly on the critical condition of the Metropolis. Four Secretaries of State (Northcote away), myself, the Lord Chancellor, and Corry.

Hardy's bulletins, some received this morning, were of a most anxious and menacing character: but the chief feature was a telegram from Lord Monck, informing the Duke of Bucks that, some eight days past, a Danish brigantine left New York with a band of thirty men sworn to assassinate H.M. and her Ministers. Lord Monck is not an alarmist, and particularly deprecates the expense of Trans-Atlantic telegrams; but in this instance he requests a telegram of receipt.

We have no powers to cope with such circumstances as these, and others which are taking place under our nose.

The Duke of Bucks has ascertained that on the day named such a vessel did leave New York, and, with the prevailing westerly wind, may be expected to arrive in four or five days. Ostensibly chartered for Dieppe, it is to land its passengers in the Bristol Channel. What are we to do? If they land, and are seized, Habeas Corpus will immediately release them. If stopped on the high seas, we may be involved in a war with America.

For my part, I should not hesitate advising seizure, and trusting to a Parliamentary indemnity; but it seems that Habeas Corpus is too strong even for such daring, and that we should violate the law without gaining our purpose. If we call Parliament together, the object will be apprehended by these miscreants and their like, and, during the interval that

must elapse before the meeting of Parliament, every crime and plot will be stimulated and encouraged to avail themselves of the vanishing opportunity. . . .

The Canadian story turned out to be a hoax, and the Queen chaffed the Cabinet and Hardy for paying any attention to it.   The Government aid to the Clerkenwell sufferers was distributed by Disraeli through Montagu Corry, who thus probably obtained his first initiation into the work of practical philanthropy.   Henry Matthews, afterwards Lord Llandaff, wrote to Corry on December 18 that his beneficent exertions in Clerkenwell did the utmost honour to his chief and himself. 'It reads quite like an oriental story; as though you were secretary to a Vizier of Haroun-al-Raschid, rather than to a Minister of Queen Victoria.'

The Clerkenwell outrage was a turning-point in Irish politics.   Six days after the explosion Gladstone announced at Southport that the time had come for an Irish policy on Irish lines which should deal with Church, land, and college in turn.   The first effect, even on some who were to be his colleagues within a year, of this acceptance of crime as a legitimate ground for concession, was hardly what he wished.   Lowe, wrote Lennox, who met him at dinner at Christmas-time, 'denounced Gladstone's speech as disgraceful'; and added, 'Several of our party want to bid for Fenian support, and, if they do, the country will administer them a sound chastisement.'   But Gladstone had better gauged the temper of the new voters; and was preparing to trump Disraeli's Irish policy of firm administration, patience, and conciliation with more spectacular and drastic methods.

CHAPTER XVI

PRIME MINISTER

1868

The great Parliamentary triumph which Disraeli enjoyed in 1867 was appropriately followed by his succession, early in 1868, to the first place among the servants of the Crown. But, when the year opened, no immediate change was anticipated.

To Lord Derby.

DOWNING STREET, *New Year's Day,* 1868. — I send you the compliments of the season. It is the first time that you have been Premier for three continuous years — 1866, 1867, and 1868. I hope a good omen.

You have done also very well for your friends : 3 Garters, 4 Bishoprics, 8 Lord Lieutenancies, and almost the whole Bench in the three kingdoms.

European affairs are not satisfactory. The Emperor of the French has to choose between what are called Liberal institutions and war — and does not like either. But a war will be a war of Louis Quinze, and such slow and balanced successes will soon weary the great nation. I think he feels this.

Stanley seems a little nervous about the *Alabama* claims. The Americans are reckless partisans, and will do much for the Irish vote, though, except the Irish, nobody in America wants to go to war with us. Nevertheless, I doubt whether the Irish vote is yet strong enough to insure such a catastrophe. At present all that the Fenians have done is to strengthen your Government. . . .

While Derby remained at Knowsley, Disraeli was busily occupied in London with preparations for the session, but in constant correspondence with his chief. Though this Parliament had received sentence of death through the Reform Act, and was therefore hardly com-

petent to cope with new party issues, there was a large
programme before the Government, partly consisting of
supplementary Reform measures — Irish and Scottish Reform Bills and a Corrupt Practices Bill; and partly of
important administrative and departmental measures,
affecting bankruptcy, railways, and the transfer of the
telegraphs to the State. To these there was added
the thorny Education problem, which Russell had
again raised in the Lords before Christmas; and Disraeli's special attention was claimed by Admiralty administration — a constant preoccupation of his during his
periods of rule at the Exchequer. Moreover, Ireland,
which Stanley called this January in a speech at Bristol
'the question of the hour,' and which certainly proved to
be the question of the session, was always in the background. Besides the Irish Reform Bill, a further suspension of habeas corpus in the island was inevitable, and
Roman Catholic University Education was also under
consideration. When the time came in mid-January for
the Cabinet to resume its meetings and get its programme
into shape, Derby had once more succumbed to gout, and
Disraeli was in despair.

To Lord Stanley.

Confidential. Downing Street, ½ past 4 o'clock, Jan. 17,
1868. — Your box just come in. I'm in despair about the gout.
The Cabinet ought to have met after Epiphany. There is
work enough now for *de die in diem.*

This is the urgency. Lord Derby entirely disapproved of
my suggestion as to the treatment of the Education question
by the establishment of an Education Minister, and legislation for 1869. I won't give you his reasons here, being pressed
for time, and wishing you to see him at once. Enough that I
don't contest his decision, and believe that we must deal with
the question at once.

To deal with the question in a moonshiny way won't do.
The D. of Marlboro' has been with me all this afternoon, and
has unfolded the project of the Council Office. I think it excellent: large, I would almost say complete, and yet moderate and prudent. But it is a scheme which would require frequent Cabinets and minute discussion.

Question is, Shall the Cabinet, under these circumstances,

meet on Tuesday, and again on Thursday, when you will all
have returned from Bristol, and so on? I think it best.
We can rough-hew and prepare the way, like Merewether and
Phayre, and, when your father takes the field, can proceed to
action.

But I can't advise such a course without the chief's sanction,
and even wish. Obtain his sentiments upon this head.

I confess, if the Cabinet is postponed till Tuesday week,
and perhaps even later, I should tremble for consequences.

I hope you will be able to make this out, but my hand is
palsied with pencraft all day.

A small selection from Disraeli's frequent and copious
letters during the next two or three weeks to the Prime
Minister and to the Queen will give some idea of the difficulties he had to surmount, and of his energy and versatility in dealing with them.

To Lord Derby.

Confidential. Downing Street, *Jan.* 28, 1868. — . . . The
state of our finances will not permit any increase in our expenditure; but if the state of our finances would do so, the
requisitions of the Admiralty are unwise and unnecessary.
Last year there was the same pressure, on the ground of the
great increase of the American navy. We successfully resisted the appeal, and it now turns out that the Americans
have no navy, and not an ironclad except for coast defence.
Now it is the old bugbear of the French navy. The American
panic is now a French panic. The Admiralty wants a large
increase of our ironclad fleet; but it offers no plan how this
increase is to be effected, except by the vulgar expedient of a
large increase of the navy estimates. Let them spend less
money annually on small unarmored wooden ships. Why do
they maintain up to their present strength the numerous
squadron of small unarmored ships that we have scattered
over the world? This is the keystone of the position. We
spend an enormous sum annually for building and repairing
these vessels for their three-yearly reliefs. Why? First, for
old-fashioned notions, that we should not otherwise have employment for our officers and men. Second, for our colonists
and merchants, etc. There is no answer to the first reason,
except the question, Why should we keep up more men and
officers than we have employment for? As to the second
reason, suppose an insult were offered, or an injury inflicted,
on some of our merchants in Peru, or the Brazils, or the River
Plate. Would any naval officer in this age of telegraphs,

take upon himself to redress these insults and injuries?   He
would send home for orders.   But this commodore of sloops
could not exact reparation, even if he would.   The smallest
South American State has an ironclad at command that could
destroy his whole force.   The Americans have flying squadrons, and we must imitate them.

I have not seen the second paper of the Admiralty, which,
very improperly, has not been sent to me (as the first was);
but if it be full of the battle of Lissa, I can only say that, in
that instance, the Italian guns and gunnery were notoriously
deficient, and that Tegethoff secured his wooden walls by
covering them over with chain cables.   A naval administration that wants to increase our ironclads, and at the same time
wants to keep up a large reserve of wooden ships as well,
and the old-fashioned distribution of that force, wants what is
impossible with the present navy estimates, which were largely
increased last year.

As for the Admiralty view of the present condition of the
French navy, I believe it is marked by the usual exaggeration and false coloring which always accompanies these estimates.   Five of the French ironclads mentioned only mount
the old weak armament, while we have only one labouring
under that grave disability.

Let the Admiralty build ironclads, but they must adapt
their naval policy to the changed circumstances which the
introduction of naval armor has introduced.   Two wooden
line-of-battle ships could be built for the cost of one ironclad,
and the armament of the present day costs 50 per cent. more
than in the days of ' the wooden walls of old England.'

Irrespective of all I have said, the management of the Admiralty, with regard to ship-building, is at this moment so decried and distrusted that, if the House of Commons wished
to increase its naval expenditure, it would not entrust the office
to a department constituted as at present.

But what is the state of our finances — and that with a
costly war?   I have directed the heads of the financial departments to prepare provisional estimates of the revenue of next
year.   I received them last night, and result is most unsatisfactory.   We must prepare for an increase of taxation, which
can no longer be limited to an additional twopence to the income tax.   When a Chancellor of the Exchequer has to contemplate increasing the duties on tea and malt, the wild
suggestions of these ignorant and narrow-minded Admirals
are doubly distressing. . . .

Confidential.   DOWNING STREET, *Jan.* 30, 1868. — I am in
receipt of your letter on the Education measure. . . .   Any
forced decisions, at this moment, on conscience clauses and

rating, and boards of managers, would break up the Cabinet.

What the Cabinet decided on, I may say unanimously, was that legislation was necessary; that it should be preliminary, not definitive; that, to be preliminary and not insignificant, the institution of an Education Minister was necessary, whose duties should be very large — no longer confined to the application of the Revised Code, but harmonising the system of lower class with pauper education; dealing with the distribution of endowments, which the forthcoming Report on Middle Class Education will render necessary; supervising all the departments of art and science, and, as proposed by Lord Stanley, and much approved, controlling generally Irish education. It was felt that, if our Bill were limited to census and incorporation, the Opposition would successfully start Mr. Bruce's[1] Bill, and the question of the day would be taken out of our hands. It was felt that, if our action was limited to extending aid to the poor schools, a minute to be laid on the table would be sufficient, and that in the present temper of Parliament and the country that would not suffice.

I have seen to-day several of our most influential colleagues, and *separately*, on this matter. I have no hesitation in saying that the project of a measure preliminary, but of magnitude, is the only scheme by which unanimity in counsel can be obtained. I think myself that success in Parliament might thus also be secured.

If we gain a year, the public mind, now in a state of effervescent inquiry on these matters, will ripen on such subjects as conscience clauses and rating, and especially on the non-interference of the State with the religious element in schools, which might render conscience clauses unnecessary. But time is required.

It is sad work to have to write on such matters, and not confer together. But I am sure you will pardon every uncouth and imperfect phrase. I only wish to be a faithful steward to you in your troubles, to give you the best information I can, and counsel to which the advantage of being on the scene of action may give some value. . . .

To Queen Victoria.

DOWNING STREET, *Feb.* 4, 1868. *Six o'clock.* — . . . The Cabinet concluded the discussion of all the principles (not many) involved in the new Education Bill, and appointed a Committee — Lord President, Duke of Bucks, Mr. Walpole, and Lord John Manners — to finish some details.

[1] Home Secretary, Dec., 1868; afterwards 1st Lord Aberdare.

The Cabinet is unanimous on all points of principle, but the Duke of Marlboro' wishes the Lord President to be the *ex-officio* Education Minister on a great scale, which is not an arrangement which would be popular in the House of Commons, as it would seem to close the House of Commons to the Minister for Education : for the precedent of Lord John Russell sitting in the Lower House is not a very strong one. He sate so only a few months, and was no ordinary man : had led the House of Commons twelve years, six of which he was Prime Minister, and was himself of ducal birth. . . .

To Lord Derby.

DOWNING STREET, ½ *past six, Feb.* 6, 1868. — A very busy, but tranquil, Cabinet. Scotch Bill gone through, and waiting, for finish, the Lord Advocate on Tuesday — our last Cabinet.
Irish Bill discussed.
Letter from the Lord Chief Justice of England in the name, and with the unanimous authority, of all the Judges, protesting against the Parliamentary Elections Bill as 'an impossibility.' [1] In short, the Judges have struck ! As I am to bring in the Bill the first night, this was awkward. However, we set to work like men. We must fall back on our original proposition, which the S[elect] Committee of the House of Commons very conceitedly altered.
All going on very right with the Duke of Marlboro'. Duke of Richmond of great assistance to me in this matter. I have gained time and mollified him. He will do whatever you decide on.
But, so far as I can judge, the Education flame is more bright than lasting, and in a month's time I am not sure the Lord President may not bring in a strictly preparatory measure in the House of Lords, and keep the great question for the next Parliament. But it must be in the Lords now ; at any rate, we want education discussed by Dukes and Bishops. It will have a beneficial effect on all. . . .

To Queen Victoria.

DOWNING STREET, *Feb.* 15, 1868. — The Chancellor of the Exchequer, with his humble duty to your Majesty.
In the Cabinet to-day he brought forward the condition of your Majesty's navy, with reference to the navy estimates, and in consequence of some observations of your Majesty on the subject, when he was last at Osborne.
He has, since that period, been unceasingly working to effect some change in our system of naval expenditure, and to adapt

---

[1] The Bill put upon the Judges the trial of election petitions.

it more to modern requirements; and he has the utmost gratification in informing your Majesty that he has induced the
Cabinet, this day, unanimously to adopt his views; that the
naval estimates have been reconstructed; and, without any
material increase of expenditure, your Majesty will now have
a real and, he hopes, rapidly increasing naval reserve.

The Cabinet determined to-day to lay down immediately
three more ironclads.

He calculates that your Majesty will have at the end of this
year a reserve of seven ironclads, irrespective of these three,
which will take two years to finish. . . .

It was only by correspondence that Derby had been
able to participate in these decisions and arrangements.
The gout had this time obtained a complete mastery over
him, and the resumption of the session on February 13
found him still incapacitated, with no prospect of early
return to health and work. An article in *The Times* of
February 11 urged the necessity, in view of Derby's condition, for reconstruction of the Government, and two
days later Derby told Disraeli that he contemplated
resignation.

From Lord Derby.

Confidential. KNOWSLEY, *Feb.* 13, 1868. — Parliament sitting, and I still lying here, like a useless log! You may
imagine how much this annoys me, and the more so as,
although I hope that I have turned the corner within the last
day or two, after a slight relapse of three or four days, my
doctors (for I have two in attendance) will not venture to name
any time for my probable removal. . . .

I have for some time been aware that the increased frequency
of my attacks of illness would, at no distant period, incapa-
citate me for the discharge of my public duties. During the
past year I have hardly ever been really well, and the steps
which I have been obliged to take for patching myself up for
particular occasions have not been without their effect on my
general health; and I am warned that there are symptoms
which will require constant vigilance, probably for the remainder
of my life, if I wish to guard against a sudden and complete
break-up. To no one except the Queen have I communicated
upon this subject, on which it is due to you that you should
receive the earliest intelligence. What I have said, however,
to H.M. is simply this: that while, on the one hand, my increasing infirmities hold out little expectation of my being

able for any long period to serve Her Majesty, I hoped she would do me the justice to believe that I would not willingly desert her service during a period of difficulty: but that, if the appearance of political affairs should be smooth, I hoped that H.M. would bear in mind my anxious desire to be relieved from duties to which I should shortly find myself unequal. I added that I thought it was right that H.M. should be the first person to receive an intimation of my views, in order that she might have full time to consider the course which it might be necessary for her to pursue.

Nothing could be kinder and more considerate than the answer which I received, in which, after some gratifying expressions of her personal feeling, and the assurance that she shrank from the idea of being deprived of my services, she added that she had no right to place her own wishes in opposition to the considerations of health, and even of life, which I brought before her. She hoped, however, at all events, that my resignation would not be tendered during the course of the present session; and to this I have no hesitation in agreeing, so long as my colleagues are willing to overlook the probably inefficient manner in which I shall be able to discharge my duties. To no other member of the Cabinet, not even to Stanley, have I made my intentions known. But what particularly pleased me in the Queen's answer was that she by no means contemplated the break-up of the present Government as the result of my retirement. And I am sure that, so far as she is concerned, you, with the aid of the majority of our present colleagues, will receive the same cordial support which I have enjoyed.

I am very much annoyed that the Chancellor should not have been ready with his Bankruptcy Bill. Not only was it distinctly understood in November that that measure should be brought forward in the House of Lords, but I wrote some weeks since to press it upon his particular attention. . . .

To Lord Derby.

Confidential. DOWNING STREET, *Feb.* 14, 1868. — I received your letter this morning, and learn, with deep regret, that there is no immediate prospect of the Cabinet having the advantage of your guidance and authority.

I cannot shut my eyes to the danger of the present state of affairs, but, after twenty years of confidential co-operation, scarcely with a cloud, I need not, I feel convinced, assure you, at this critical moment, that all shall be done on my part which perfect devotion can accomplish, to maintain, unimpaired and unsullied, your interests and influence.

The plan of delaying the resignation till the close of the session proved quite impracticable. There was so serious a relapse on February 16 that Stanley was telegraphed for to Knowsley.

From Lord Derby.

Confidential. KNOWSLEY, *Feb.* 19, 1868. — Stanley will have given you a full account of the state in which he found me, and will have prepared you for the communication which I should not be justified in delaying, of the absolute necessity of my resigning my present office. I am certainly better, and I hope in a fair way towards recovery ; but that recovery must be very slow, and my doctors not only do not encourage me to hope to move from hence much under a month, but are unanimous in their opinion that, if I hope to regain a moderate degree of health, absolute repose of mind and body for some months to come is indispensable. I had hoped that I might have been enabled to struggle through the present session ; but, as matters stand, my attempt to do so would not only be a certain failure, but would involve a risk of life which I am not justified in incurring.

I have not yet written positively to the Queen, nor will I do so until I hear from you ; but I ought not to delay making this announcement to H.M. longer than is absolutely necessary. I am not insensible of the public inconvenience which may be caused by my resignation at this moment, nor of the increased difficulties in which it will place you. I trust, however, that, if H.M. should send for you, which, under the circumstances, I should think most probable, you will not shrink from the heavy additional responsibility. You may be assured of receiving from me all the support which, out of office, it is in my power to give ; and, so far as I can, I shall urge upon our friends to extend to you, separately, the same generous confidence which, for twenty years, they have reposed in us jointly. And I cannot make this communication without gratefully acknowledging your cordial and loyal co-operation with me, in good times and bad, throughout that long period : nor, above all, the courage, skill, and judgment, with which you triumphantly carried the Government through all the difficulties and dangers of the last year.

I think I ought not to resign without asking the Queen, if she desires to mark her approval of my services, to allow me to recommend some five or six names for the honour of the peerage. . . . My intention of resigning has been already surmised, and will, no doubt, be very generally anticipated : but I should be obliged by your not announcing it as an

irrevocable decision, even to our colleagues, until I shall have had an opportunity of submitting it to, and having it accepted by, the Queen.

Derby, it will be seen, had no doubt as to who ought to be, and would be, his successor; and it is pleasant to read the cordial and thoroughly merited tribute which the retiring chief pays to his tried lieutenant.

To Lord Derby.

Confidential.   DOWNING STREET, *Feb.* 20, 1868.

MY DEAREST LORD, — I have not sufficient command of myself at this moment to express what I feel about what has happened, and, after all, has happened so rapidly and so unexpectedly!

All I will say is that I never contemplated nor desired it. I was entirely content with my position, and all that I aspired to was that, after a Government of tolerable length, and, at least, fair repute, my retirement from public affairs should have accompanied your own; satisfied that I had enjoyed my opportunity in life, and proud that I had been long confidentially connected with one of the most eminent men of my time, and for whom I entertain profound respect and affection.

I will not shrink from the situation, but I do not underrate its gravity, and mainly count, when you are convalescent, on your guidance and support.

I have talked over affairs with Stanley. Our difficulty will be our more than debating weakness in the House of Lords. If, when you were present there, you felt the necessity of some support, what must be the state of things now, with Lord Chelmsford and Lord Malmesbury for the managers? Such a condition is impossible; and it appears to me most desirable, as you once contemplated, and once formally mentioned to Lord Chelmsford, that Lord Cairns should be induced to take the Great Seal.

After him, I think the Duke of Marlborough the most competent man in our ranks to address a senate. He has culture, intellectual grasp, and moral energy — great qualities, though in him they may have been developed, perhaps, in too contracted a sphere. . . .

I hope Lady Derby has not suffered from all her anxieties and labors. I am, hers and yours ever, — D.

Derby, on receipt of this letter, at once forwarded his resignation to the Queen, who was at Osborne. An

extract from his letter will show the exact terms of his resignation, and what he wrote about his successor.

Lord Derby to Queen Victoria.

Feb. 21, 1868. — . . . Lord Derby greatly regrets the inconvenience to which he knows that his retirement must subject the public service, and the additional trouble which it must entail upon your Majesty. But he has reason to believe that, the fact of his retirement being once understood, there would be no pressure from any quarter for the immediate and formal resignation of his office — perhaps not until he should be enabled to surrender it to your Majesty in person. In the meantime, if he may be permitted to offer any suggestion to your Majesty as to his successor, he would venture to submit that, as there is no question of any political change, your Majesty should apply to the Chancellor of the Exchequer, who has held the most important and, next to his own, the most prominent post in the present Government. Lord Derby believes that, although with a deep sense of the responsibility attaching to it, he would not shrink from undertaking the duty; and that he, and he only, could command the cordial support, *en masse*, of his present colleagues. . . .

Disraeli already knew that, on Derby's resignation, the Queen would entrust the fortunes of the Ministry to his hands. Just a month earlier he had been specially invited for a couple of days to Osborne. His letters to his wife were discreet, but they suggested that what had passed was momentous and gratifying. In the first letter he said that Her Majesty was 'most gracious and agreeable'; the second ran as follows:

To Mrs. Disraeli.

[*Jan.* 25, 1868]. — The most successful visit I ever had: all that I could wish and hope. I was with the Queen an hour yesterday. She spoke of everything without reserve or formality.

A brilliant day here.

The Queen ordered a vessel at Portsmouth to be at my disposal, as there was some difficulty about going.

M. Corry a lucky fellow. He had to come down here yesterday on some business, and Her Majesty, hearing of it, invited him to dine with the household and sleep here!

'All that I could wish and hope.' The words are strong, but they were justified. A note by Corry, himself at

Osborne at the time, explains that before Disraeli's audience 'General Grey came to his room to inform Mr. D. that the Queen intended to make him her First Minister on Lord D.'s resignation. Mr. D. was much struck by the fact that his old rival at Wycombe should become the bearer of such a message.' [1] The Queen had already been warned by Derby that his resignation could not be long deferred, and thus graciously herself intimated to Disraeli his approaching elevation and her own satisfaction at the prospect.

The hour had now come, and Grey arrived in London with the expected message from the Queen, and with instructions to place himself at Disraeli's disposal in case of any difficulty with his colleagues. But Grey brought also Derby's letter of resignation, and on reading it Disraeli, in view of the ambiguity of its terms, and the suggestion that the formal but necessary steps might be indefinitely postponed, hesitated to proceed with his task. He consulted Stanley, and Stanley both wrote and telegraphed to his father.

Lord Stanley to Lord Derby.

Feb. 24, 1868. — Disraeli sent for me, very anxious and agitated, about 12 o'clock to-day ; explained that all was going well, the Queen had been most gracious, would give him every support, and, if any of his colleagues objected to the new arrangement, she would see what her personal influence could effect in securing their adhesion. . . . She wished him to go down to Osborne to-morrow to kiss hands.

But . . . a letter of yours to the Queen, shown him by Grey, seemed to imply that you did not contemplate the immediate formation of a new Ministry under him. Under these circumstances he thought it would be indelicate, and might hurt your feelings, if he were to consider the matter as settled.

I combated these scruples. . . . The end of it was, we agreed to telegraph down for your sanction.

Derby's telegram in reply was as mysterious as his letter. 'Glad there are no difficulties,' it ran. 'Will write by post. Do nothing formal till you hear. A few days indispensable to me.' This, as Disraeli wrote to

[1] See Vol. I., pp. 211–222.

Lord Barrington, made things more confused than ever; and the result of letter and telegram was entirely to paralyse action on this Monday, February 24, which should have seen the arrangements for the reconstituted Ministry well on the road to completion. Happily, the next morning brought another letter from Derby, making it clear that he had no desire to delay the formation of a new Administration, but merely wished to settle the peerages and a few minor matters before taking the formal final step.

From Lord Derby.

Confidential. KNOWSLEY, *Feb.* 24, 1868. — I was about to write to you, when I received Stanley's telegram, from which I am glad to find that you have no serious difficulties in the way of forming a Government.

I hope that neither you nor he will have misunderstood the purport of my telegraphic answer. You will not for a moment suppose that I wish to retain nominal office for an hour longer than is absolutely necessary ; on the contrary, the sooner the new arrangements can be made, the better it would be for all parties, and the more agreeable to me, nor can there be the slightest objection to its being publicly known that my resignation has been tendered and accepted, and that you have been charged with the duty of forming a new Administration. But I have only this morning heard, by a few lines from the Queen, Her Majesty's acceptance of my resignation, and I am promised a fuller answer, probably by to-morrow's post.

Her Majesty has said nothing as yet upon the subject of the peerages, and I have consequently been unable to write to any of those to whom I propose to offer them. I require, therefore a few days for the disposal of this subject, and of other minor matters which I shall have to wind up, and which I shall have no power of doing after you have once formally kissed hands as Minister. This final and formal step is the only one for which I think it necessary to ask for a short delay.

You have my best wishes for the success of your endeavour to form your Government, and if I can be in any way of service to you, you may entirely command me. I will not trouble you with speculations as to your probable arrangements. Your main difficulties, as it seems to me, will be the Exchequer and the lead in the Lords. Could you not, to avoid extensive changes, continue for the present session to hold the former in conjunction with the office of First Lord of the Treasury ?

I know the work will be tremendous, but such a combination in former times was not unusual. As to the Lords, Cairns would undoubtedly be a great acquisition to your Government; but Stanley, who suggested him as a possible leader, forgot that it would be impossible for a Lord Chancellor to hold that office. I shall be most anxious to hear your contemplated arrangements, and that you have every prospect of success in the arduous task which you have undertaken.

By the receipt of this letter on the Tuesday morning Disraeli's scruples were removed, and in the course of the day he was able to make most of his arrangements; but before going down to Osborne to kiss hands he waited Derby's pleasure.

To General the Hon. Charles Grey.

2, GROSVENOR GATE, *Feb.* 25, 1868. — I have not written to the Queen, because I thought you could keep Her Majesty *au fait*, and that it would be better for me to be silent till I could give H.M. a digested account.

Lord Cairns has accepted the Great Seal, and all my colleagues have placed themselves at my disposal, except Walpole, who, I fear, is still at Ealing.

I am deeply considering the question of the Chancellor of Exchequer, but have done nothing: the more so, as about two hours ago I received a mysterious intimation not to precipitate affairs in this direction, as ' a most important and influential adhesion' was possible. I conclude it can't be Gladstone ! . . .

To Lord Derby.

GROSVENOR GATE, *Feb.* 25, 1868. — I remain in London, though supposed to be at Osborne : if I be forced to go down, I shall not kiss hands, nor shall I until I have your sanction. . . .

From Lord Derby.

(*Telegram.*) *Feb.* 25, 5 p.m. — I have heard from H.M. My formal resignation is sent in.

Confidential. *Feb.* 26, 1868. — I feel very sensibly your kindness in postponing, to suit my convenience, your formal acceptance of office. My chief object in asking for a short delay was that I might be enabled as Minister to communicate to a few of our friends H.M.'s consent to my recommendation of their promotion to the peerage. This I have now received, and if there should be any trifling matter which I ought to wind up before leaving office, I am sure I may rely upon you to afford every facility for having it done. . . .

To Lord Derby.

GROSVENOR GATE, *Feb.* 27, 1868. — I duly received your telegram of yesterday and your letter this morning. I have, therefore, arranged to go down to-day by 3 o'clock train, and therefore, I suppose, in four-and-twenty hours the thing will be done. . . . I think Hunt must be the Chancellor of the Exchequer, and I have prepared the Queen for it. . . .

With respect to some intimation in your letter of your wishes being attended to in some slight matters, permit me to say very distinctly, once and for ever, that, in the position in which I am so unexpectedly placed, I consider myself, and shall always consider myself, only your deputy. Your wishes will always be commands to me, and commands that will be heartily obeyed. I shall never take any step of importance in public life without apprising you of it before it is decided on, and without at least seeking the counsel which, I trust, will never be refused.

And I do, even solemnly, entreat you never to permit any sentiment of estrangement to arise between us, but to extend to me for ever that complete confidence which has subsisted so long between us; which has been the pride and honor of my life, and which it will ever be my constant effort to cherish and deserve.

From Lord Derby.

Private. *Feb.* 28, 1868. — One line to thank you for your very kind letter of yesterday, and to assure you that, so far as I am concerned, there is no danger of any sentiment of estrangement arising between us, who for more than twenty years have worked together with unreserved and unbroken confidence. But I cannot accept for you the position which you are willing to accept for yourself, of being considered as my deputy. You have fairly and most honourably won your way to the highest round of the political ladder, and long may you continue to retain your position! At the same time, whenever you are inclined to consult me or ask for my opinion, I shall be most happy to give it you frankly and unreservedly. But I shall not be so unreasonable as to expect that it shall always be adopted, or be surprised, still less affronted, if upon any ground you find yourself unable to act upon it. . . .

Before concluding, let me beg of you to offer my congratulations to Mrs. Disraeli upon your having attained a post your pre-eminent fitness for which she will not be inclined to dispute.

Disraeli's behaviour to Derby throughout this crisis was a model of delicacy and good feeling, and, if Derby

may have seemed a little inconsiderate and dilatory, the serious state of his health is a sufficient excuse.

Disraeli had now become the Queen's First Minister, and was necessarily about to enter into a much more intimate relation with Her Majesty than he had ever enjoyed before. At the outset he struck, both in letter and audience, the note of chivalrous devotion, as of one who, while he reverenced his Sovereign, never forgot that she was a woman — a note which was to characterise all his intercourse with Her Majesty, and was to help to win for him a unique place in her esteem and confidence.

To Queen Victoria.

DOWNING STREET, 12 *o'clock*, *Feb.* 26, 1868. — Mr. Disraeli with his humble duty to your Majesty.

He ventures to express his sense of your Majesty's most gracious kindness to him, and of the high honor which your Majesty has been graciously pleased to confer on him.

He can only offer devotion.

It will be his delight and duty to render the transaction of affairs as easy to your Majesty as possible : and in smaller matters he hopes he may succeed in this ; but he ventures to trust that, in the great affairs of state, your Majesty will deign not to withhold from him the benefit of your Majesty's guidance.

Your Majesty's life has been passed in constant communion with great men, and the knowledge and management of important transactions. Even if your Majesty were not gifted with those great abilities, which all now acknowledge, this rare and choice experience must give your Majesty an advantage in judgment which few living persons, and probably no living prince, can rival.

He whom your Majesty has so highly preferred presumes to trust to your Majesty's condescension in this behalf.

Mr. Disraeli proposes to have the honor of waiting on your Majesty to-morrow (Thursday) afternoon. . . .

From Queen Victoria.

OSBORNE, *Feb.* 27, 1868. — The Queen thanks Mr. Disraeli very much for his kind letter received to-day, and can assure him of her cordial support in the arduous task which he has undertaken.

It must be a proud moment for him to feel that his own

talent and successful labours in the service of his Sovereign and country have earned for him the high and influential position in which he is now placed.

The Queen has ever found Mr. Disraeli most zealous in her service, and most ready to meet her wishes, and she only wishes her beloved husband were here now to assist him with his guidance !

The Queen rejoices to see how much unanimity he has found amongst his colleagues. She will be glad to see Mr. Disraeli to-morrow, but does not ask him to stay overnight, as she knows how precious every moment must be to him. . . .

To Mrs. Disraeli.

Osborne, *Feb.* 28, 1868. — I arrived here yesterday at seven o'clock, and had an audience about half an hour afterwards. The Queen came into her closet with a very radiant face, holding out her hand, and saying, 'You must kiss hands,' which I did immediately, and very heartily, falling on my knee. Then she sate down, which she never used to do, and only does to her First Minister, and talked over affairs for half an hour (I standing), so that I had scarcely time to dress for dinner. . . .

Disraeli, in writing to Corry, added that he said to the Queen that he 'kissed her hand in faith and loving loyalty.' He was frankly and unaffectedly happy. 'All is sunshine here,' he wrote to more than one correspondent, 'moral and material.'

All the old colleagues to whom he applied rallied round Disraeli, with the exception of Walpole, who had remained reluctantly in the Cabinet for some months without any office, and who now, in spite of remonstrances from the Queen, took the opportunity of retiring. One colleague, we have seen, Disraeli felt bound to leave out. The Government, with Derby gone, was peculiarly weak in the House of Lords, and one of its weakest members was the Lord Chancellor, Chelmsford. He had been a distinguished and successful advocate, but he was neither a great lawyer nor a very skilful debater ; and a complaint of his dilatoriness appears in Derby's first letter to Disraeli about resignation. Disraeli had always thought him an inefficient Chancellor, and had been opposed to his re-

The Rt. Hon. Earl Cairns.
from a portrait by Dickinson
at Hughenden.

appointment in 1866;[1] nor had he ever been at all sympathetic with one who was among the bitterest and most
persistent opponents of the Jewish cause.   Chelmsford's
dislike and distrust of Disraeli had been markedly shown
in a short correspondence in this very month of February.
On a vacancy occurring among the Judges, Disraeli, as
leader of the Commons, expressed a hope that the Chancellor would not treat with indifference the claims of the
Conservative lawyers in Parliament[2]—a not unreasonable
request, which has been made by many leaders of the
House, and complied with, perhaps too often, by many
Chancellors.   Chelmsford immediately suspected a job,
and mounted the high horse ; his trust was a sacred one,
his choice would be governed by fitness, not politics,
and he would not suffer the smallest interference with his
judicial appointments.[3]

Disraeli applied the test of fitness to the Chancellor himself, and found him wanting.   Derby had expressly intimated, more than once, to Chelmsford that he contemplated
asking him, after a time, to make way upon the Woolsack
for Cairns, who was not only a lawyer of the highest class,
but a statesman excelling in debate.   That arrangement
Disraeli considered it to be imperative now to carry out.[4]
He has been accused by Chelmsford and Chelmsford's
friends of a want of tact and delicacy in his manner of
opening the subject to him ; but the letter which he
actually wrote seems hardly to warrant this reproach.   It
should be remembered that, with the resignation of its
head, the Derby Cabinet became *ipso facto* dissolved, and
that no Minister had a right to his post save on the direct
invitation of the new Prime Minister.

[1] See above, p. 443.

[2] In a note to Derby during 1867, Disraeli had written : ' I can't speak to
the Lord Chancellor, for I lose my temper with him.   With prodigious
patronage, he does nothing for the party, and is so insensible of his great
obligations to you and his own demerits.'

[3] Atlay's *Victorian Chancellors*, Vol. II., pp. 121–125, where Chelmsford's own version of the controversy is given at length.

[4] It was a ' painful but necessary ' change, wrote Hardy in his diary.

To Lord Chelmsford.

11, DOWNING STREET [? *Feb.* 26].

DEAR LORD CHANCELLOR, — The announcement in Parliament has informed you of the accepted resignation of Lord Derby, and of the office which the Queen has graciously confided to me of forming a new Government.

My first wish is to recall to the management of affairs my former colleagues, but there are some obstacles to this course, and the principal one is found in the House over which you preside. If Lord Derby in his time was so sensible of the weakness of our party in debate in the House of Lords that he was constrained to submit to yourself an arrangement which, though delayed, he still contemplated, I am sure you will feel that, without Lord Derby, I have no option but in having recourse to his plan, among others, of strengthening Her Majesty's Government in the Upper House of Parliament. If, therefore, for this reason, and for no other, it is not in my power to submit your name for the custody of the Great Seal to the Queen in the list of the new Government, I can assure you it would afford me sincere gratification if you could suggest to me some other mode by which Her Majesty might testify her sense of your services.

Chelmsford answered hotly and angrily, expressing his disbelief in Derby's still contemplating a change on the Woolsack, and declining to suggest any other mode in which his own services might be recognised. He appealed from Disraeli to Derby; he took the Press into his confidence over his grievance. Two days later he had to confess that Derby confirmed Disraeli's statement; but he complained that Disraeli had not recalled to his recollection the particulars of the arrangement; and he talked of his ' dismissal,' and of the slur upon his reputation which only some mark of Her Majesty's gracious approval could remove. Disraeli's reply was justifiably short.

To Lord Chelmsford.

OSBORNE, *Feb.* 29, 1868. — I received your letter this morning. I only alluded to your understanding with Lord Derby because I thought it must be impressed on your memory, and did not wish to dwell in detail on circumstances necessarily of a character not agreeable.

After the allusion to that understanding, and the necessity

of my acting on it, the rest of my letter invited communication. You could have arranged with me any cause for your retirement most to your liking, and you could have responded to my inquiry. Instead of that, from a total misapprehension of my communication, which was really influenced by delicacy, the public have been invited to our confidential communications, with the usual consequences under such circumstances.

I shall do nothing to add to the controversy, but shall be always ready to show the great respect I entertain for you.

It was not found possible to come to an understanding as to the distinction to be conferred by Her Majesty on the outgoing Chancellor. The Grand Cross of the Bath, which Disraeli offered, Chelmsford declined, suggesting in his turn that he might be advanced to the dignity of an earldom, as were Loughborough, Eldon, and Cottenham, a suggestion which it is not surprising that Disraeli could not accept. Accordingly, Chelmsford retired in dudgeon; and society and the clubs were entertained by stories of his bitter jokes and of Disraeli's pungent retort. It was said that the ex-Chancellor talked of premature elevation making some people *dizzy*, and that he distinguished the old and new Administrations as the 'Derby' and the 'Hoax'; while the new Prime Minister was declared to have curtly summed up his former colleague in the biting words, 'Useless in council, feeble in debate, and — a jester!'

Disraeli's wise resolve not to inflict too heavy a strain on his own strength created a vacancy at the Exchequer, which he quitted to become First Lord of the Treasury. The natural successor would have been Northcote, who had been his lieutenant in all his financial combats with Gladstone in the past decade. But Northcote could not very well be spared from the India Office during the Abyssinian War, and Disraeli determined, somewhat to the public surprise, to promote Ward Hunt, the Secretary to the Treasury, whose good work he had often noticed and commended.[1] The appointment was well received. 'It

[1] The changes consequent on this promotion enabled Disraeli to offer subordinate office to the distinguished man who is now Lord St. Aldwyn.

was, of course, my own suggestion,' Disraeli wrote to
Delane, whose approval had been ascertained at the
dinner-table ; 'but it was carped at by commonplace
minds, who seemed shocked at the sudden elevation,
and talked of other people as being "looked up to" in
the city.   Your clear and sagacious judgment came to
my aid opportunely, which should teach both of us the
advantage of dining out.'[1]

The Whips and the party managers urged that overtures
should be made to Cranborne and to Peel.   One of them
thought he discerned a change of tone on Cranborne's
part ; another wrote, 'He would not accept, but it would
please the party.'   In deference to these representations
Disraeli, always placable, sounded Cranborne through
Northcote.   The refusal was immediate and uncompromising.   The time for reconciliation in office had not
come, though the rank and file of the recalcitrants were
reported to be less disaffected than before.   At any rate,
Corry wrote, February 27 : 'Taylor, Noel, and Barrington, are well pleased with the feeling at the Carlton.
Even Sandford tells me that he feels less hostility to a
Government with you at the head, than to one led by
Lord D.   What you did last session might have been
expected of you from your known opinions, but Lord
Derby's conduct was unpardonable.'

Cairns, though the most powerful member of the Ministry in the House of Lords, could not, as Derby pointed
out, lead that House from the Woolsack; and Disraeli
had therefore to appoint a leader from among his other
peer colleagues.   He turned first to the Duke of Marlborough, who was himself a friend of some years' standing,
and who had married the daughter of one of his most
intimate friends, Frances Anne Lady Londonderry.   In
him he discerned 'culture, intellectual grasp, and moral
energy.'   But the Duke told Disraeli that Malmesbury,
who had filled the place in Derby's frequent absences,
had a prior claim, and Disraeli accepted the suggestion.

[1] Dasent's *Delane*, Vol. II., pp. 222, 223.

Malmesbury was, naturally, anxious that his utterances in the Lords should be kept duly in accord with those of his new chief. 'When I lived at Whitehall Gardens during Peel's Government,' he wrote, 'I used to see the Duke [of Wellington] ride into [Peel's] garden every morning at eleven and stay a quarter of an hour. This was to go over the minutes of the day together for the House of Lords. God forbid we should follow exactly this military routine, but whenever I think your direction desirable I want a general *lascia passare* to you about that hour.'

'A great triumph of intellect and courage and patience and unscrupulousness employed in the service of a party full of prejudices and selfishness and wanting in brains. The Tories have hired Disraeli, and he has his reward from them.' That was the grudging tribute paid to Disraeli by Bright in his diary. Intellect, courage, and patience, were undoubtedly leading elements in Disraeli's composition. A certain lack of scruple on some occasions may be laid to his charge, as to that of almost all vigorous personalities in the field of politics ; but the persistent faithfulness of his career as Conservative leader sufficiently rebuts the accusation that unscrupulousness was in any sense a note of his political character. The suggestion that his relation to his party was that of a hired bravo is ridiculous. There was a revolutionary side to his character, which was, of course, most conspicuous in youth ; but there was a much stronger vein in him of historic and aristocratic sentiment, which naturally inclined him, as it had his father before him, to espouse the Tory cause.

Intellect, courage, and patience, carried to a high pitch, constitute genius ; and it was the due recognition and just elevation of genius which Lord Houghton rightly hailed in Disraeli's accession to the Premiership.

From Lord Houghton.

Rome, *Mar.* 12, 1868. — The days of our familiar intercourse lie so far away that I hardly know whether personal interest would justify me in writing to you on the event which, after

all, is only the natural sequence of your political work, did I not feel such earnest satisfaction in the recognition of your intellectual worth and in the fair reward of industrious mental power.

When one looks back on many years of political life, one is, no doubt, more conscious of the unjust elevation of poor abilities and common characters than of the depression of any remarkable faculties or real desert. But there is assuredly a tendency in the English mind to dislike and distrust original individuality as such, and to do its worst to limit the scope and effect of the talents it does not entirely comprehend. When, therefore, genius makes its own way in public life, there is a good beyond the momentary gain and a true national advantage. . . .

From Odilon Barrot.

Paris, 1 *mars,* 1868. — Laissez-moi vous offrir toutes mes félicitations pour votre avènement à un rang qui, on peut le dire, est le plus élevé auquel un homme, qui n'est pas assis sur un grand trône, puisse aspirer — Premier Ministre d'Angleterre !

Though there had been an anticipation in some quarters that the Tories might look once again to the great houses for a successor to Derby, and the names both of Stanley and of Richmond were mentioned, the public at large and the Press recognised that Disraeli was the rightful heir, and his promotion was favourably received. The party, as a whole, knowing well that the choice was Derby's as well as the Queen's, tendered Disraeli loyal adherence; and the dissentients over the Reform Bill made no protest. The House of Commons, as might be expected, gave a generous welcome to its foremost gladiator. Westminster Hall and the lobbies were packed to see him pass and to cheer him, while his reception in the Chamber itself, writes Lord Ronald Gower, was 'all but enthusiastic. When he entered . . . J. S. Mill was on his legs, but he had to interrupt his speech for several minutes on account of the ringing cheers that Disraeli's appearance evoked.' His statement was brief, as its keynote was that he would continue Lord Derby's policy. In foreign affairs the Government would pursue peace, without selfish isolation; in domestic affairs, 'a

liberal policy.'   Disraeli paused to give effect to the
unexpected phrase, and then continued, 'a truly liberal
policy — a policy that will not shrink from any changes
which are required by the wants of the age that we live in,
but will never forget that it is our happy lot to dwell
in an ancient and historic country.'   Critics naturally
interpreted this oracular sentence as meaning that the
Government would resist where resistance was possible,
but consent to all such changes as Parliamentary exigencies
made inevitable.   There was no debate, and little comment, in the House.   Bouverie admitted that Disraeli
had fairly earned his promotion, but added that the position of the Government in the House was weak ; as for
the Liberals, they had leaders who could not lead and
followers who would not follow.

Mrs. Disraeli to Lady de Rothschild.

Feb. 25, 1868.

MY VERY DEAR LADY DE ROTHSCHILD, — By the time this
reaches you, Dizzy will be Prime Minister of England !   Lord
Stanley is to annouce this at the House of Commons to-day.
Yours affectionately, — M. A. DISRAELI.

It is pleasant to think of the pride and happiness of
Mrs. Disraeli in the elevation of the husband whose coming greatness she had prophesied from the first, and whose
ambitions her own self-sacrificing affection had so eminently forwarded.   An occasion for the display of her
triumph and for the congratulations of the world was
speedily provided.   'Will you lend your reception-rooms
to my wife for a couple of nights or so ?' wrote Disraeli
to Stanley early in March.   'According to the Whips,
there must be some high festivals on a very extensive
scale ; and she can do nothing with D[owning] S[treet],
it is so dingy and decaying.'   So the fine rooms of the
still unfinished Foreign Office were thrown open on Wednesday, March 26, in order that Mrs. Disraeli, as the
Prime Minister's wife, might hold a grand reception.   It
was a miserable night, with a storm of wind and sleet

sweeping over the town; but nevertheless there was an immense gathering both of society and of the Conservative party, with a sprinkling of Liberal friends such as the Gladstones, Bishop Wilberforce, one of the guests, wrote in his diary: 'Dizzy in his glory, leading about the Princess of Wales; the Prince of Wales, Mrs. Dizzy — she looking very ill and haggard. The impenetrable man low.' It was such a party as the author of *Coningsby* and *Lothair* loved to describe, with half enthusiasm and half satire; and this time the author himself and his wife were the leading figures in the show.

'Yes, I have climbed to the top of the greasy pole,' was the Prime Minister's jaunty reply to congratulations. No one realized better than he how difficult it would be to maintain himself in that precarious elevation. With the shield of Derby gone, he would have to justify himself afresh to his own party; and his opponents, and more particularly their discomfited chief, would be all the more eager to pull him down. Even assuming that he could command the ungrudging support of the whole of the Conservatives, he would still, if the other sections of the House of Commons could effectively combine, be in a minority of sixty or seventy. If, however, a strict party fight could be avoided, he might hope to keep his power and place comparatively undisturbed down to the impending General Election, and to appeal, with a fair possibility of success, to the new electors as the man who had enfranchised them. But Gladstone was as capable of a bold, dramatic stroke as was Disraeli; and the new Prime Minister, who had so recently dominated the scene, was to find, in the moment of his elevation, that authority over the expiring House of Commons had largely passed once again to his rival, and that the election was to be fought on a novel and most embarrassing issue of that rival's choice.

INDEX

THE following pages contain advertisements of Macmillan
books by the same author and on kindred subjects.

The Life of Benjamin Disraeli, Earl of Beaconsfield — *Continued*

PRESS COMMENT

" Benjamin Disraeli was doubtless one of the most picturesque, brilliant, astute politicians that England ever produced. There are few of the older men of this generation, familiar with the political events of the Victorian period of British history, who have not formed firm convictions of this man's character and influence. He was in all probability the most aggressive statesman, and the most highly praised and severely criticised man that ever rose to fame and influence in the British Parliament. Although for a generation, men have not ceased to wonder at the enormous success he was able to achieve against odds which, to ordinary mortals, would have seemed impossible barriers."

— *The Boston Herald.*

" It is on the whole a very human, though egotistical Disraeli that the biographer gives us, brilliant, witty, ambitious, but by no means the unscrupulous adventurer that the late Goldwin Smith and other enemies have depicted. His best defence is his own personal letters, which the author has wisely allowed to constitute the bulk of the book." — *Chicago Record-Herald.*

" Disraeli had extraordinary powers, infinite ambition, audacious genius and industry, and in tracing thirty-three years of this extraordinary career Mr. Monypenny has made a book vitally interesting in its revelation of character."

— *Des Moines Capitol.*

" The volume leaves Disraeli just as he entered upon his parliamentary career, and if the material for the succeeding volumes is handled frankly as that used in the present, the biography shall be one of the most interesting of recent years. Disraeli had a far more picturesque personality than Gladstone, and the biographies of the two great rivals furnish interesting comparisons." — *The World To-day.*

THE MACMILLAN COMPANY

Publishers   **64-66 Fifth Avenue**   **New York**

A NEW LIGHT ON VICTORIAN POLITICS

A COMPANION VOLUME TO MONYPENNY'S
LIFE OF THE EARL OF BEACONSFIELD

BENJAMIN DISRAELI

ON

WHIGS AND WHIGGISM

EDITED WITH AN INTRODUCTION BY WILLIAM HUTCHEON

Cloth, 8vo, $3.00

In this interesting book Mr. Hutcheon brings together many valuable writings contributed to the Press by Disraeli during his struggle in the thirties to obtain a foothold in politics. Some of them are familiar to close students of the life and work of Disraeli and by reputation to a wider circle. The rest are here republished for the first time. These will be welcomed by those — and the number is steadily growing — who follow with interest the various phases of the career of that marvelously diversified personality. Mr. Hutcheon has thought it well to go outside the period so far covered by Mr. Monypenny's authoritative " Life " now in process of publication and to open for a moment the pages of a later chapter when, after a lapse of over ten years, Disraeli renewed his connection with journalism. Two extracts are given from his anonymous contribution to his own periodical, *The Press*, which was founded in 1853. To facilitate comparison and research, and to complete the record of Disraeli's political writings of the period, there are included the " Vindication," the Runnymede Letters, and other known works. Readers will thus be enabled to trace for themselves at first-hand, in a setting deliberately kept free from party bias, the gradual evolution of a career that in its opening stages offered so many enigmas to the historian, and has been so diversely interpreted.

THE MACMILLAN COMPANY

Publishers   **64–66 Fifth Avenue**   **New York**

The Life of Andrew Jackson

By JOHN SPENCER BASSETT, Ph.D.

WITH ILLUSTRATIONS. NEW EDITION. TWO VOLUMES IN ONE

Cloth, 8vo, $2.50

This is a one-volume edition of a biography that has, since its first publication several years ago, come to be regarded as one of the most faithful stories of Jackson's life and of its effect on the nation that has ever been written. Professor Bassett has not slighted Jackson's failings or his virtues; he has tried to refrain from commenting upon his actions; he has sought to present a true picture of the political manipulations which surrounded Jackson and in which he was an important factor. The volume contributes largely to a clearer realization not only of the character of a great man but also of the complex period in which he lived.

The Writings of John Quincy Adams

VOLUME VI. EDITED BY

WORTHINGTON C. FORD

Cloth, 8vo, $3.50

This volume brings Mr. Ford's remarkable series up to the year 1821. Mr. Adams's last dispatches from London, while minister there, deal with the matters left undetermined by the Treaty of Ghent and with his association with the English reformers of the day.

THE MACMILLAN COMPANY

Publishers   64–66 Fifth Avenue   New York